W9-BGS-437

Soviet Foreign Policy in Perspective

THE DORSEY SERIES IN POLITICAL SCIENCE

EDITOR NORTON E. LONG *University of Illinois*

AKE *A Theory of Political Integration*

BROWN & WAHLKE (eds.) *The American Political System: Notes and Readings*

DRAGNICH *Major European Governments* rev. ed.

EDELMANN *Latin American Government and Politics: The Dynamics of a Revolutionary Society* rev. ed.

FROHOCK *The Nature of Political Inquiry*

GRIPP *Patterns of Soviet Politics* rev. ed.

ISAAK *Scope and Methods of Political Science: An Introduction to the Methodology of Political Inquiry*

JACOB & ATHERTON *The Dynamics of International Organization: The Making of World Order*

JACOBINI *International Law: A Text* rev. ed.

LUTTBEG (ed.) *Public Opinion and Public Policy: Models of Political Linkage*

MACRIDIS & BROWN *The De Gaulle Republic*

MACRIDIS & BROWN (eds.) *Comparative Politics: Notes and Readings* 3d ed.

MANGONE *The Elements of International Law* rev. ed.

MEEHAN *Contemporary Political Thought: A Critical Study*

MEEHAN *Explanation in Social Science: A System Paradigm*

MEEHAN *The Theory and Method of Political Analysis*

MINAR *Ideas and Politics: The American Experience*

MURPHY *Political Theory: A Conceptual Analysis*

NAGEL *The Legal Process from a Behavioral Perspective*

ROBINSON *Congress and Foreign Policy-Making: A Study in Legislative Influence and Initiative* rev. ed.

ROELOFS *The Language of Modern Politics: An Introduction to the Study of Government*

SARGENT *Contemporary Political Ideologies: A Comparative Analysis*

SIGLER *An Introduction to the Legal System*

SPIRO *World Politics: The Global System*

WESSON *Soviet Foreign Policy in Perspective*

Soviet Foreign Policy in Perspective

ROBERT G. WESSON
Associate Professor of Political Science
University of California, Santa Barbara

1969
THE
DORSEY
PRESS Homewood, Illinois
Irwin-Dorsey Limited, Georgetown, Ontario

First Printing, August, 1969

Library of Congress Catalog Card No. 71-86861

Printed in the United States of America

Preface

It is more than ever essential that we understand Soviet foreign policy, yet we are no nearer than ever to doing so. Perhaps it is not really possible. Our understanding of the political system which makes Soviet foreign policy is at best tentative and superficial, and the West has often misread its trends. But analysis of the ways in which the Soviet Union has responded to the challenges, dangers, and opportunities of the outside world, the ways in which it has set itself apart from other states, should give some ideas of the mainsprings of its behavior. The present book attempts to show something of how Soviet foreign policy has evolved in response to internal as well as external needs, how it has matured with the Soviet state, how and why ideology has affected perception and motivation, and ways in which the problems of management of the Soviet state merge into the problems of control of the Soviet sphere and of relations to the world without.

A book is the work of many persons besides the one whose name appears on the title page. Among those who have been helpful in the preparation of this book I should like to mention particularly Professor Wolfram F. Hanrieder, Professor Robert A. Rupen, and Mr. Peter Haslund, who read the entire manuscript and offered many valuable comments and needed suggestions. Credit for careful and intelligent editing goes to Mr. Harry H. Bingham. And the task would have been about twice as long without the faithful and devoted assistance of Deborah Wesson at every stage.

Santa Barbara,
July, 1969

ROBERT G. WESSON

Table of Contents

Introduction: The Problem of Soviet Foreign Policy

In the brutality of power, this world has been bipolar for a generation, and it promises to remain so. The temper of international relations, and indeed the future of civilization, rest with the United States and the Soviet Union. These superpowers represent not only overwhelming force but contrasting models of political and economic development. Nothing is more important than to understand the mainsprings of their behavior.

Yet, if American policy is often unclear, Soviet foreign policy seems far more so. Repeatedly, the world has been puzzled or surprised by Soviet actions. The German generals at Brest Litovsk were nonplussed when their Bolshevik counterparts, instead of trying to bargain over peace terms, unloosed a flood of revolutionary oratory. In August, 1939, not only Westerners but many Russians were shocked when the supposedly mortal enemies, the Nazis and the Communists, embraced. In August, 1968, the Czech leaders themselves were taken completely by surprise when Soviet armies invaded their country only a few weeks after agreement had apparently been reached. The Russians have fervently advocated the most contradictory goals, fomenting revolutionary change and at the same time promoting peace and good-neighborly relations. Russia has tried to represent both a threatening worldwide political movement and a national state. The West correspondingly has never been quite sure how far to oppose the U.S.S.R. or to hope for conciliation and accommodation.

It can hardly be said that the foreign policy of any great power is always unambiguous, logical, and purposeful. Everywhere and at nearly all times there have been miscalculations and follies. For example, the urge of British and French leaders in the spring of 1940 to go to war with Russia to save Finland, when they were making no progress in their war against Hitler, was as miscalculated as the Soviet attack on Finland. The Western powers in the years prior to the outbreak of World War II committed a series of blunders in regard to the Rhineland crisis, the invasion of Austria, the Spanish civil war, Munich, the guarantee given to Poland, and negotiations for an alliance with Russia. But Soviet policy, perhaps more than that of most powers, has been shadowed by ineptness and futility. One may recall, for example, in a few postwar years, such Russian miscalculations as the attempt to secure a slice of Iran, the break with Tito's Yugoslavia, the Berlin blockade, and the Korean war. At least, to Western observers Soviet behavior has always been exceptionally difficult to understand.

One reason is the secrecy which surrounds Soviet foreign policy, which is made by a very few men behind barred gates. Soviet writers claim that their state acts uniquely for the benefit of the people, unlike capitalistic or "bourgeois" states, which they hold to be guided by selfish and antipopular interests of the possessors. But the political springs of the huge and extremely complex Soviet governmental structure are entirely hidden. We can only guess how much influence the military leadership—the Soviet equivalent of the American military-industrial complex—or the Soviet commercial interests, party ideologists, and so on, exercise on decision making. For example, we cannot assess the importance of East German and Czechoslovak production of uranium and heavy machinery in the determination to retain control of these areas. In the Soviet interest in Iran, we can only guess the relative weights of strategic considerations, desire for petroleum resources, the nationality affiliations of peoples of Iran and Soviet Azerbaidzhan, the traditional Russian interest in the area, and the vanity of a Stalin or a Khrushchev. It can hardly be contended that because an economic interest is incorporated in the governmental structure, it ceases to carry weight politically. Certainly, Soviet foreign policy is no more based on a single consideration than is that of the United States, as personalities, political, economic, and strategic needs jostle for attention.

Secrecy has always been a deliberate policy. There has been little effort even to explain and analyze ex post facto political situations and Soviet responses in factural terms, either to the outside world or to the Soviet people, who are neither consulted nor allowed to judge. The ouster of Khrushchev was at first attributed to his physical condition and then vaguely and never explicitly justified by reference to his "harebrained schemes" and the like. The Soviet people were given only the most nebulous idea of what was going on in Czechoslovakia prior to the intervention of August, 1968. Such secretiveness permits sudden and surprising shifts of policy, as in the Nazi-Soviet rapprochement in 1939. It also permits much to go on out of sight; for example, Chinese and Soviet leaders were feuding for four or five years before there was any public admission of disagreement between the two ostensibly brotherly Communist powers.

Decision making in the inner recesses has not produced rationality but the contrary. Soviet leaders have lacked sources of information common in opener cultures. They have not had the advantages of the probings and comments of free journalism; and they have been under little compulsion to explain and justify policies adopted. Criticism has been lacking where it is most needed; if in the best-ordered states, bureaucrats limit their reports to what their superiors want to hear, authoritarian rulers are seldom able to get honest and unbiased information. Moreover, it is not to be expected that foreign policy decisions would generally reflect great sophistication in a semibackward country which has undergone violent change of social structure. Although the Soviet foreign ministers (or "commissars") until 1939, Chicherin and Litvinov, were men of considerable culture, they had little real authority; and the few political leaders with experience in international affairs were wiped out by Stalin's purges. Khrushchev, a man of scanty formal education, at least learned from his extensive travels, which brought more realism into his outlook by the end of his career. Today, few members of the Brezhnev-Kosygin politburo would seem to have much background for judgment of foreign policy. The leadership of no other great power, except mainland China, has so little direct contact with independent powers. If the Soviet Union has not made more egregious mistakes, this has been due to the native shrewdness of men like Stalin, Molotov, and Khrushchev, who have pulled themselves to the top by their wits in a ruthless political competition.

If one attempts to make theoretical sense of everything the Soviet Union has done, he will find himself weaving a web of fantasy; sheer bungling and ignorance have had much to do with the making and execution of Soviet foreign policy. Tourists to the Soviet Union regularly become familiarized with the inability of the authorities to cope with deviations from routine. The highest leadership of the Soviet Union for decades placed in control of a large part of Soviet science a charlatan geneticist, Lysenko, who was perennially propounding simpleminded panaceas for agriculture, such as feeding heifers cream to make them grow up to be producers of richer milk. Khrushchev, like Stalin, believed what he anxiously wished to believe, that there were easy shortcuts to agricultural prosperity. A major shortcoming of Soviet foreign policy has been the propensity to make wishful assessments of difficult situations. An extreme case was Stalin's belief in 1939 that the Finnish masses would welcome the Soviet army. The overestimation of prospects has been a recurrent factor in Soviet foreign policy and an essential consideration in its understanding.

Illusions of the devilish cleverness of the Soviet leadership have been fostered primarily to influence Western policy makers. Actually, subtlety and cunning have been conspicuously lacking in Soviet behavior in world affairs, which has been more marked by clumsiness and self-righteous disregard of the reactions of others. Thus, leaders of the Comintern in the 1920's did not mind letting it be known that Chinese Communists were to cooperate with Nationalist leaders only for the ultimate purpose of destroying them. Again and again noncommunist countries have been given notice of Soviet intentions, or at least hopes, of presiding over their ruin, as Khrushchev challenged American opinion with his boast, "We will bury you." Likewise, at a time when the Soviet leadership wished above all to avoid war, from the latter part of 1940 until the attack came in June, 1941, Soviet policy toward Nazi Germany was maladroit in the extreme. Provocative and meddling actions, at least as seen by the triumphant Nazis, were mixed with attempts at appeasement that only demonstrated weakness. Soviet policy has often seemed worse in language than in substance, as its presentation has usually suffered from wooden dullness, unimaginative repetitiveness, lack of sophistication, and failure to understand opposing positions. Stubborn dogmatism and offensive language, together with a certain haughtiness toward foreigners, have often made the Soviet case appear less convincing to Westerners than it may have merited.

Nonetheless, the Soviet leaders have always placed great emphasis on propaganda. As masters of a state for which indoctrination is of the essence, they regard words as weapons. Their articles of faith encourage them to believe that they can gain acceptance for their views if they can only convey them to the masses in the Western world, who are by definition opposed to their own bourgeois governments. Thus, from the call for peace of the first proclamation of the Revolution to many utopian disarmament proposals and postwar ban-the-bomb campaigns, the Soviet government has sought to speak over the heads of unfriendly alien regimes. In the mass of immoderate denunciation and praise couched in stereotyped phraseology, it is usually difficult to guess what Soviet leaders themselves really believe or take seriously, as persuasion mingles with self-persuasion. When the Soviet press hammers continually at the dangers of West German revanchism, it is not clear to what extent this represents a real fear of Germany or a use of the German issue to justify Soviet domination of Eastern Europe, for which German pacifism would be entirely inconvenient. One is entitled to greater skepticism because Soviet propaganda is capable of playing very discordant tunes, as (in 1968) that capitalism was losing ground everywhere and that capitalist influences were a mortal danger for a long-established communist regime. On the other hand, when the Russians proclaimed in the summer of 1968 that they would not tolerate further Czech deviation, they were more serious than most observers in the West, or in Czechoslovakia, imagined.

Inseparable from propaganda is the ideology[1] which complicates and,

[1] By "ideology" is here meant the sum of beliefs taught for political utility. In the Soviet case, this includes the following: the universal validity of the Soviet way as model for the future in the terms of Marxism; the monopoly of power of the

as seen by nonbelievers, distorts the presentation and substance of Soviet foreign policy. In the most mundane way, this impedes understanding as the student gropes for grains of solid information in haystacks of prolixity produced not to inform but to convince, if not actually to confuse. Soviet discourse has often required a good deal of translation. Actions of the most ordinary power politics, such as exploiting differences among antagonists, are treated in universalistic terms, as questions of high ideals involving the contest of socialism against capitalism-imperialism. It cannot be admitted that politics involves conflicts of power, prestige, and interest (other than capitalistic); all must be placed in a framework of semi-Marxist logic. Even in doing something so obvious and acceptable as working for the security and strength of the Soviet state, the Soviet leaders have been constrained to rationalize it as a matter of principle, the state representing not an entity of itself but the fortress of the world proletariat, the vanguard of the movement.

More basically, ideology clouds purposes. If American diplomacy has been somewhat befogged by contradictions between moral and material purposes,[2] it has been far more difficult for outsiders to judge how far the Russians have been and are motivated by a universalist mission, *ipso facto* threatening to other states. It can be argued that Soviet foreign policy has always, whatever the messianic pretenses, served Soviet national interests, but the lens of ideology has caused the national interest to be seen as different from what has ordinarily been regarded as national interest in the West. Bolshevik leaders at first thought of themselves, as they were regarded abroad, not as rulers of a traditional state but as bearers of a grand mission of revolutionary change; their "national interest," then, was world proletarian revolution. To the disappointment of some, they found themselves riding not a revolutionary wave but a great state, *de facto* successor of the tsarist empire; overwhelming problems at hand demanded most, sometimes practically all, of their energies, and the overriding objective became to preserve and strengthen this state and their own position in it. This required normal diplomatic and commercial relations, but for years the Comintern loudly proclaimed the overthrow of the governments which the foreign commissariat was trying to conciliate.

Communist party as agent of the proletariat, the virtuous and progressive sector of society; socialization of the economy in the hands of the single unifying party; the deification of Lenin, the father figure of the Soviet world; proletarian internationalism, which has been hardly separable from devotion to the Soviet Union; and a pervasive distrust and hostility for an evil outside world. The canon of Marxism is included insofar as it is suitable as an intellectual base. Many lesser doctrines have been woven in, such as the priority of heavy industry and collectivization of agriculture. Various dogmas of international relations, such as the evil nature of the Federal German Republic and Israel, have also been propagated so insistently as to take on an ideological flavor.

[2] Cf. George F. Kennan's classics statement in *American Diplomacy, 1900–1950* (Chicago: University of Chicago Press, 1951).

Dreams of world revolution faded, and it became evident that the interests of the Soviet state as such had an absolute priority over any needs of foreign communism, but the language and rationale of Soviet foreign policy have remained remarkably close to its ideal basis. The Khrushchev policy of seeking to influence the Third World was remarkably similar in theory to that of Lenin. "Socialism" (definable simply as the Soviet system), the "working class," and so on, remain sacred if not operative concepts; in August, 1968, the right to override national sovereignty was claimed not on grounds of strategic necessity but of "proletarian internationalism."

It is a remarkable continuity that a modernizing state should hold, at least nominally, to the basic ideology with which it made a revolution more than half a century ago. This is certainly no mere inertia. A political philosophy must always answer ongoing needs, and the continuity of Marxism-Leninism in Soviet policy is the continuity of Lenin's state and its fundamental political needs. The Soviet Union with its dependent states is an inward-looking empire, for which external trade is relatively unimportant and uninteresting. It has no real alliances. Perhaps the leaders, bearing responsibility for the progress of the economy and culture as well as more conventional burdens of government, have little energy to concern themselves with external affairs. Their primary problems are internal, the maintenance of the integrity and strength of their vast realm. According to one report, only about 7 percent of the instruction hours in higher party schools is given to foreign affairs.[3] It should not be surprising that internal political needs should dominate style and outlook of foreign policy.

Questions of the relation of internal, domestic political, to external, systemic determinants of international relations have received a good deal of attention in theory of international relations.[4] Theoretical discussion is unnecessary here, but the Soviet Union is the prime example of a state the foreign policy of which can be understood only by taking fully into account the requirements of the political system. The Soviet leaders, like those of any state, have reacted to external situations. When faced with danger, they have been quite realistic. But their fundamental attitudes are dictated by their own condition more than by actions or attitudes of outside powers, and for them foreign policy is basically an extension of domestic.

Soviet foreign policy may thus be regarded as a complicated mingling of contradictory elements, internal and external, the one or the other

---

[3] Wolfgang Leonhard, *The Kremlin since Stalin* (London: Oxford University Press, 1962), p. 2.

[4] For a bibliography on this subject, see Wolfram F. Hanrieder, *West German Foreign Policy, 1949–1953* (Stanford, Calif.: Stanford University Press, 1967), pp. 249–51.

becoming more prominent according to the circumstances. As an authoritarian state claiming a more or less messianic rationale, the Soviet Union dislikes the advanced, libertarian states of the West and wants their hostility; it has preferred to take truculent positions and blatantly to reject Western values, morality, and institutions. On the other hand, it wishes peace and has usually been more interested in keeping its gains than in reaching out for new; war represents a risk of terrible loss while promising no great improvement. Soviet leaders have always, and probably sincerely, spoken of their desire for peace and have seldom, despite ordinary overconfidence, been tempted into adventures.

At the same time, from its earliest days the Soviet state has been well aware of the desirability, perhaps the absolute necessity, of trade and borrowing from the West, securing benefits within the existent world order. Hence Soviet foreign policy has had from its beginnings a dual aspect: the overthrow of alien institutions and the establishment of normal relations, the drive to indirect or direct territorial expansion along with peaceful coexistence. In this way, Khrushchev aspired to a duopoly with the United States even while making clear his conviction that the Soviet Union and its form of society should prevail over the United States and everything this country stands for. Not many countries would be capable of so violently denouncing supposed enemies as the Soviet Union has denounced the Bonn regime and yet dealing with them in a perfectly businesslike manner.

So far as this book has a theme, it is the dichotomous character of Soviet foreign policy and its dependence on basic domestic political imperatives. This has been in evidence for many decades; it is to some extent inherent in the Russian state as it existed before as well as after the Revolution. It was most acute in the first years; it took on somewhat different aspects under Stalin and Khrushchev; it persists, with changes of tone but much continuity of substance, down to the present. Soviet foreign policy appears especially difficult or puzzling to outside observers because its ways are those of the Soviet state: secrecy, reliance on propaganda, justification and formulation of objectives in ideal terms; and it is as ambiguous as the Soviet political system.

I

Tsarist Foundations

Expansion

The Soviet Union is between two and three times as large as the United States, China, or Brazil, forty times larger than France, second in size in Europe. The Soviet Union is also the home of many nationalities, officially 169, among whom the Russians proper constitute about half the population. The Soviet Union comprises a federation of fifteen sovereign republics, legally equal in rights and free, according to the constitution, to withdraw from the Union.

The Russia of the tsars, by contrast, called itself an empire and was proud of it. Its ruler, whose designation came through the Byzantine world state and was derived from *Caesar*, held scores of titles as though he truly possessed the earth; he rejoiced in the allegiance of peoples nearly as diverse as those who once composed the maritime empire of Britain—43 percent of his subjects, according to somewhat doubtful statistics, were Russians. Finns, Poles, Little Russians, Caucasians of a score of nations, Turks, and other Central Asiatics, Mongols, and others paraded colorfully at his military reviews. The tsar was not the head of a nation like a European prince but the autocrat and symbol of the peoples of a universe.

This destiny came to the Russians despite the fact that unlike Romans, Incas, Mongols, and other great conquerors of history, they were never a militaristic people. Russia never had an Alexander or even the equivalent of a Julius Caesar, and its history celebrates few really impressive victories. The ruler of modern times most successful in expanding the empire was a woman, Catherine, who ruled from the palaces of St. Petersburg. Like Stalin she was a foreigner, and perhaps like him was partly motivated by a desire to legitimatize herself as a Russian ruler. Much of the expansion of Russia was nonviolent or accomplished with minimal force; many territories, such as the Ukraine, much of the Caucasus and Central Asia, and vast reaches of northern Asia have fallen to Russia without a major campaign.

Since the time of Peter, the Russians have never attacked a major power. Instead they have expanded into areas of weakness, halting on encountering strong opposition. They have acted purposefully, securing frontiers by controlling lands from which threats might come, occupying lands with unsettled government, liberating coreligionists or fellow Slavs, or seeking outlets to warm seas. In its inception, the Muscovite state, coming out from under decaying Tatar rule, undertook a mission both religious and national: to liberate the Orthodox from a heathen servitude and to gather together the fractured Russian lands. This was achieved by inheritance, diplomacy, and force where necessary; and when it was completed, Russia was already a very large state lacking in definite frontiers and imbued with a sense, which has never been lost, of the rightness of expansion. Almost inevitably it flowed outward wherever resistance was feeble, especially to the south and east.

Not long after the reunion of Great Russian lands, in the middle of the sixteenth century, Ivan the Terrible, heeding the call of a dissident faction, took the Tatar stronghold of Kazan on the Volga; thereafter Russia was a multinational state. The drive against the crumbling Tatar and other Moslem powers went forward with encouraging ease. It was motivated by nationalist spirit, mixed with a religious crusading mentality akin to that of the Castilian reconquest of Spain from the Moors, joined to a sense of bearing superior civilization to backward peoples. The push across Siberia against scattered, disunited, and rather primitive people was rapid, reaching the Pacific in the seventeenth century. In east Asia, practically the present boundaries were reached by 1860. Further inroads into Chinese territories led to war with Japan and were turned back; however, a protectorate was established over Outer Mongolia, which after the Revolution was converted into the first Soviet satellite.

Expansion in Central Asia, against better organized and more populous states than in Siberia, lasted through the nineteenth century. Acquisitions required further acquisitions to protect them, and dissensions among the natives facilitated many advances. Generals often proceeded with the offensive-defense on their own, and the government supported their efforts if they were successful; as Nicholas I once said, "Where the Russian flag has once been hoisted it must not be lowered."[1] Large areas, however, were kept as vassal states, to be incorporated in the Union only after the advent of bolshevism. This vast empire building went on at the same time that Britain, France, and Germany were carving out large sections of the less developed world for their own, but there was a

---

[1] R. Tucker in Ivo J. Lederer (ed.), *Russian Foreign Policy* (New Haven, Conn.: Yale University Press, 1962), p. 176.

profound difference: the aggrandizement of Russia, economically backward but politically strong, was carried through for political and ideological, not commercial, reasons.

Religion was at once a motivating force and a weapon of southward expansion against the Turkish Empire, as Russia pressed around either side of the Black Sea, then toward Constantinople and Persia. In the middle of the seventeenth century, the Orthodox Ukraine, pressed by Catholic Poland and with its back to Moslem Turkey, asked for protection. Somewhat similarly, Christian Georgia and part of Armenia accepted Russian overlordship for fear of Persia and Turkey.

A major aspiration during the nineteenth century was to advance toward the Balkans, Constantinople, and the Straits. This was an impractical objective, but in it were mingled themes of naval strategy, desire for an outlet for the growing grain exports of south Russia, liberation of Slavic and Orthodox subjects of the sultan and, perhaps most powerful of all, the urge to crown tsardom with possession of the ancient Byzantine capital, the second Rome and symbol of universal rule. But Britain was determined to keep Russia from control of the Straits, much as Truman resolved in 1947 to protect Greece and Turkey. Consequently, Russia made little progress in this direction; and the principal gain, a protectorate over Bulgaria as a result of the Russo-Turkish War of 1878, was temporary.

The push westward was usually still more difficult, as Russia encountered nations technically not more backward but more advanced than itself. The drive to the Baltic litoral was costly, but it brought direct contact with the West. Fortunately for Russia, Poland, which was a very large multinational state, weakened under an immobile constitution and loose government. Under a pretext of assisting the Ukrainian and Orthodox peasantry of eastern Poland against Polish Catholic overlords and of restoring Polish liberties, Catherine the Great was able to send in Russian forces in 1767, disrupt the state, and bring a large stretch of formerly Polish Ukraine and Lithuania into the empire. Additional gains came from the victory of the allied forces over Napoleon: Finland and most of ethnic Poland, both of which were joined only by personal union under the tsar. On national or racial grounds, Russian aspirations in World War I included, as well as the Straits, Austrian Galicia to round out the Ukraine, the remainder of Polish lands held by Germany, and a protectorate over Czechoslovakia.

Acquisition was followed by incorporation. Because of desire for uniformity, the urge of the bureaucracy (the most powerful class) to rule, and the apparent need to tighten bonds in order to pacify restive peoples, territories gradually progressed toward full incorporation in the centralized tsarist state. The Ukrainian leaders who opted for Russia expected to keep autonomy, but after Ukrainian loyalty appeared dubious, Ukrainian rights were gradually whittled down until the Ukraine was divided into Russian provinces in 1775, and even the name disappeared; in 1863, the Ukrainian language was proclaimed to be nonexistent.

Where there was less national feeling, absorption was apt to be rapid; where there was more, it was slow and hesitant. Some areas, in the Caucasus and Central Asia, retained autonomy under the native aristocracy. Poland came in as a separate kingdom, with its own army, constitution, administration, and representative although powerless assembly. After an insurrection in 1830, the constitution was abolished, but Poland retained substantial rights and liberties. After another and more hopeless uprising in 1863, which again received sympathy and no more from the West, the remaining Polish rights and liberties were abolished and russification began; after 1872 education could be only in the Russian language. Finland never rebelled, but there too autonomy was under pressure in the last decades of tsarist rule. Despite the solemn promise of the tsars to observe its rights, bureaucratic-centralist encroachments caused much resentment in the latter part of the nineteenth century. In 1901 the Finnish armed forces were amalgamated into the Russian, and the diet was stripped of almost all powers. The liberal half-revolution of 1905 restored Finnish autonomy, but the tsarist government soon resumed the erosion of Finnish rights.

This acquisition of nations was neither a failure nor an overwhelming success. The empire was not usually seething with unrest, but Russians as well as minorities rebelled occasionally against the tsars. On the other hand, various areas, such as the Ukraine, larger than France and with a comparable population, were chronically discontented. The nationalities were not like immigrants to the United States, readily absorbed into the national melt, but were historic peoples occupying homelands more or less forcibly taken and held by a foreign government. It would be remarkable if they, unlike peoples similarly held by such empires as the Austrian or Turkish, should accept their condition quite happily.

However, the Russians, having been subjected to Tatar rule, had little feeling of racial superiority. The regime was ready to treat subject peoples as equals, provided only that they accept the empire and its religion. Natives who turned Orthodox were freely admitted into Russian society and political life; and for generations prior to the mid-nineteenth century, various minorities received at least equal favor with Russians. Baltic Germans were prominent, if not dominant, in the bureaucracy. Early in the nineteenth century, the Russian empire was much less Russian than the contemporary Soviet Union and decidedly international, with a French-speaking aristocracy and nobles and bureaucrats of many nationalities; only a small minority of the advisors of Alexander I were Russians. Rulership was for the benefit of no one ethnic group, but it helped or hurt all alike and benefited mostly the apparatus itself.

But the traditional answers to the basic problem of unity were becoming less adequate in the latter decades of the nineteenth century. Modernization, Western-influenced nationalistic sentiments, and the growth of independent educated classes raised popular awareness and separatist feelings. As minorities became more restive, the Russians asserted more strongly their own national sentiments. They began to regard the tsar as a Russian ruler, not the imperial father of many nations. Russification became official policy; it was no longer enough to be loyal—good subjects should be Russian. It came to seem that the empire had to be russified or dissolved, and dissolution was unthinkable. By World War I, the problem was acute, as shown by the readiness of many, especially Poles and Ukrainians, to fight for the Central Powers.

Ideology and Messianism

The monarch of a universe is high priest of a universal mission. Having grown to be so much more than a self-coherent nation, the Russian empire badly needed, as all such empires do, abstract principles of order and unity;[2] and much of the world outlook of the tsarist as of the Soviet state was shaped by the search for a basis of unity for its many peoples. It fashioned a set of principles, roundly called ideology, out of various ideas current in the political atmosphere of the times, although it never achieved a coherent and thorough system.

Even before Ivan III had finished putting together the Russian principalities in the fifteenth century, he set himself up as heir of the Byzantine tradition and took the title of Caesar or emperor, superior to kings. His successor was addressed as "Sole autocrat of the universe, the only Caesar of the Christians," and Ivan IV (the Terrible) was pleased to regard himself as descendant of Augustus and monarch of the Third Rome, destined to succeed Rome and Byzantium as master of the earth. As Ivan's Russia acquired parts of the former Tatar empire, it also took over, along with ceremonials and political ways, some of the universalist tradition of that expansive empire.

Medieval notions of the universal heritage of Rome faded in the seventeenth and eighteenth centuries, as Russia became more like a part of the European state system. Legitimacy was still served, however, by the monarchic-autocratic ideal. Loyalty to a person or a royal lineage is a natural bond for multinational states; as Alexander I said, "The least weakening of autocracy would lead to the separation of many provinces."[3] The church also served; Orthodoxy stressed obedience and com-

---

[2] R. G. Wesson, *The Imperial Order* (Berkeley: University of California Press, 1967), pp. 167–90.

[3] H. Seton-Watson, *The Russian Empire, 1801–1917* (Oxford: Clarendon Press, 1967), p. 75.

munity, and belonging to it was practically equivalent to acceptance of the tsar. Faith was usually at issue in expansion, as Russia marched against Moslem Tatars and Turks, Catholic Poles, or Lutheran Swedes, or carried the church to heathens of Siberia; religious affinities abetted the acquisition of the Ukraine, Georgia, Armenia, and Polish and Lithuanian lands. From the days of Peter, the tsarist government sought to extend its protection to Orthodox peoples of the Turkish Empire. It was long the Russian mission to spread the truths of faith to a fallen world.

In the 1890's, the Russian court held it very important that rulers of Bulgaria should subscribe to the Orthodox creed, and Orthodoxy was sometimes regarded as the saving spirit of the age. But by that time religious faith, like reverence for a ruling house, was losing force and political utility. Compelled to communicate with the West, to become partially integrated into its structure and ways in order to defend itself, Russia could not admit only the ideas it needed and exclude those poisonous to its political system and imperial integrity. Modernization also meant the growth of classes as teachers, jurists, engineers, and artists, who were highly susceptible to the contagion of constitutionalism and nationalism. The latter was a principle of legitimacy for nations, but it was as evil a threat for tsardom as for the Hapsburg empire; and policies of russianization probably caused more resentment than assimilation, especially in the western and more advanced areas.

A compromise between nationalism and imperial universalism was the idea of Slavic brotherhood, a compromise suitable because about three quarters of the population of the empire spoke one or another Slavic language. Pan-Slavism was an adaptation of Western ideas, especially the romantic nationalism of Herder, to Russian conditions and anti-Western purposes, somewhat as bolshevism represented an adaptation of Marxism to the needs of the Russian realm. It never became an official ideology, although it sometimes received indirect official encouragement. Indeed, idealizing freedom and justice for all Slavs, it was in some respects embarrassing to the government. Nor did it even convert the bulk of intellectuals, then as now inclined to liberal views. But its appeal was deep; as a leading exponent, Danilevski, put it, "For every Slav: Russian, Czech, Serb (etc) . . . the ideal of Slavdom must be the highest ideal, higher than any earthly good. . . ."[4]

Exalting the special qualities of the Slavs, Pan-Slavism made a virtue of the primitiveness which mortified educated Russians in their relations with the West, somewhat as the Bolsheviks were to exalt the virtues of the proletariat. Close to the spirit of Orthodoxy (which embraced the bulk of Slavs), Pan-Slavism fitted expansion into Slavic Europe, particu-

---

[4] Hans Kohn, *Panslavism, Its History and Ideology* (Notre Dame, Ind.: University of Notre Dame Press, 1953), pp. 179, 195.

larly the Balkans, where it looked to Russian brotherhood over Serbia, Montenegro, and Bulgaria. In some confusion, Danilevski called for a reunion of all Slavs, with Constantinople for its capital. Enthusiasm came to its height in the Russo-Turkish War of 1877–78 and subsided as this failed to achieve any brilliant success. Disappointed patriots were inclined to turn elsewhere; Dostoevski, for example, turned his attention from the Balkans to Asia. But diffuse Slavic feeling remained important and exerted a permanent pressure on the government. Emphasizing the fundamental antagonism of Germans and Slavs, it made more difficult the continuation of the beneficial alliance with Germany and Austria, which lasted through most of the nineteenth century. Eventually it helped to propel Russia into a ruinous war to save Serbia. Stalin revived it, like Pan-Orthodoxy, during and after World War II.

In the aftermath of victory over Napoleon, Alexander I had been able to see himself as "the depository of a sacred holy mission" and arbiter of peace for the world, but Russia declined in strength through the nineteenth century. The government, after the Crimean War, took a fairly sober view of its capabilities; the more or less mediocre tsars of the nineteenth century lacked the vast vision of their predecessors. Seeking to maintain a universal autocratic empire in the face of currents of nationalism and liberalism, compelled to learn from and respect a more advanced West, Russia became as never before uncertain of its fundamental role.

Yet the sense of mission was by no means lost. The limitless horizons of Russia seemed to suggest universality, and things Russian kept on a mystic quality; Moscow, the Kremlin, and the Russian soul had and still have a significance beyond the equivalents of mere nations. The outlook of no other country was so suffused with messianic ideas, equating political dreams with the realization of divine command, combining traditions of holy empire, responsibility to God for the redemption of mankind, and imperial pride in the service of peace and justice. Ordinary Russians still thought their race was due fairly soon to conquer the world.[5] In the face of Russia's weakness, various intellectuals, such as Tiutchev, proclaimed the universal empire with its universal faith as a principle of order and union against the division and disorder of the capitalist West.[6] Russia was to be, after Isreal, the Chosen People. Such themes became almost an obsession with Dostoevski in the latter part of his life: Russia, land of true freedom under the paternal tsar, was to save a Europe on the point of violent collapse and become the protectress of all mankind in the new era.

The Russian mission was felt as unselfish, nonimperialist, and unaggressive, "a covenant of universal human fellowship," as Dostoevski put it. Yet brotherhood was to be spread by the sword; as in bolshevism, the

---

[5] Thomas A. Bailey, *America Faces Russia* (Ithaca, N.Y.: Cornell University Press, 1950), p. 55.

[6] Kohn, *Panslavism, Its History and Ideology*, p. 151.

vision of peace was mingled with a war cry. Mixed with admiration for the West was fear and hatred. A long experience of necessary borrowing made Russia exceptionally receptive to Western ideas; intellectuals admired, often uncritically, the culture and especially the science of the West. They saw Russia as humiliatingly inferior in material things. Yet Russia, even in backwardness and apparent weakness, could only be overwhelmingly great; Western material superiority was compensated for, overcompensated for, in the view of some ideologues, by the moral superiority of Russia and the nobility of its mission contrasted to the meanness of the West. For such writers as Danilevski and Dostoevski, the West was doomed, despite its achievements, because of its injustices, alienation, and bourgeois greed, while Russia represented a fresh and renovating force. Like essayists in *Pravda,* many intellectuals, radicals and conservatives alike, saw misery, hypocrisy, and oppression in the West, but not in Russia, where these qualities were actually much more in evidence. In Russia they saw true democracy under the autocrat or in native communal institutions. They believed that Russian faith and moral unity would somehow overcome the West, just as Western liberals thought that individualism and nationalism were on the way to overcoming Russia.

Russia and the West

Westerners, like Russians, have usually seen that vast empire as more potent than it really was. In actual fact, Russia was seldom aggressive where it faced strength. It fought well only when attacked, and it exerted appreciable influence only on adjacent lands. Tsarist foreign policy, which the West regarded as peculiarly cunning and purposeful because of its slightly enigmatic character, was in reality inconsistent and ineffective. The West has usually been a graver problem for Russia than vice versa. The thrust of invasion has mostly been from west to east; the Poles early in the seventeenth century, the Swedes early in the eighteenth, the French early in the nineteenth, the Germans twice in the twentieth have raised a mortal threat to the existence of the empire.

Whether political influence flowed from west to east or the reverse depended on the strength and firmness of the Russian state. A series of weak sovereigns and palace cliques after Peter the Great opened the land to an unprecedented inflow of alien ways, including at one time the suggestion of a constitution. On the contrary, when Russian armies followed the retreating legions of Napoleon from Moscow to Paris, Russia exerted a political influence more extensive than that of the Soviet Union after World War II. It was the turn of the West to be apprehensive; the most difficult part of the peace negotiations revolved around containing the victorious Russians.

Alexander I presented his foreign policy in the ideological garb of legitimacy and Christianity; these were fused in the visionary Holy Alliance, which became the symbol of political reaction. The theme of Russian policy in Europe became the support of absolutism in alliance with the absolutist rulers of Austria and Germany for the purpose of suppressing independence movements, particularly that of the Poles. So far as he could, the tsar supported traditional rulers everywhere, even in distant South America—moves to this end evoked the Monroe Doctrine. Nicholas I wanted military action to restore the kings ousted from France in 1830 and in 1848. The best he could manage was to save the Austrian monarchy by smashing rebellion in Hungary. Marx and Engels saw Russia as the chief bastion of reaction and, in contrast to the later Soviet position, made readiness to combat Russia the test of socialist sincerity.[7]

The tsarist empire was much less effective as a bulwark of authoritarianism than Marx and Engels supposed. Its principles were inconsistent, and even in victory Russia was ideologically infirm. It is said that troops returning home from France after 1815 were segregated for fear of the political infection to which they had been exposed; and officers affected by that contagion attempted to give Russia a constitution in the Decembrist rising of 1825. In its complacency and attempted isolation after 1815, Russia decayed until its power was only a facade.

This facade was smashed in the Crimean War, which turned into a remarkable demonstration of the superiority of Western over Russian arms. Internally, it brought awareness of dangerous weakness and an era of reform, highlighted by the emancipation of the serfs. Externally, it put an end to ideas of military intervention abroad in favor of monarchy, much reduced the importance of autocracy and ideology, and increased the influence of nationalism in foreign policy. Instead of standing behind the moral barricade of an entente with the politically sympathetic Germanic powers, Russia in 1891 yielded to the dictates of frank power politics and entered a counterideological alliance with republican France. This was nearly as distasteful for tsarist Russia as alliance with a bourgeois power would be for Soviet Russia, but pro-Slavic and anti-German feeling had become more important than antirepublicanism. Another new departure was a partial shift of mission from universal peace by hegemony to peace by disarmament. Lacking funds for modernization of the artillery, the tsar called a disarmament conference, indulged his fondness for grand causes, and reaped a harvest of favorable publicity, like that which later rewarded dramatic Soviet proposals of arms reduction.

Barred from further expansion in Europe, Russia turned east, took much of Central Asia, and thrust farther into east Asia. This led to a

---

[7] Karl Marx and Friedrich Engels, *The Russian Menace to Europe* (Glencoe, Ill.: Free Press, 1964).

foolish conflict with Japan and another frustrating defeat, which meant another blow to autocracy as the guiding principle of the empire. Russia underwent an abortive revolution of Western inspiration and acquired a semiconstitution. In foreign policy there was further retrenchment and settlement of long-standing differences with England along the southern frontier.

In the decade of weakness between the Japanese defeat and World War I, Russia still longed for Constantinople and the Straits but made no progress in this or any other direction. Rather, subject peoples were stirring, in the Russian empire as in the Austro-Hungarian monarchy. Austria sought to crush Serbia in 1914 in a desperate hope of stabilizing its South Slavic minority; Russia felt it necessary to come to the aid of Serbia to maintain its moral authority over its Slavic minorities. Entry into the war was contrary to the interests of the autocracy; many around Nicholas realized that it might well prove fatal to the dynasty. But foreign defeats and Western influences had so far eroded the position of the tsar that he had to yield to feelings of nationality.

Tsars and Commissars

Weakness culminated in defeat in World War I, revolution, and loss of large parts of the empire. In a few years the new regime recovered the losses in Asia, but on the western frontier Russia was cut back to roughly what it had held two centuries earlier, under Peter the Great. It was also enfeebled and impoverished as hardly any major state has been in modern times, and it was excluded from the councils of the powers as never before.

Russia was excluded from Europe because of both its weakness and revulsion against its doctrines. The new, Bolshevik Russia proclaimed itself in all ways opposite to the regime which it had replaced, and its foreign policies were loudly advertised as the opposite of those of its hated predecessors. It stood not for dominion but for equality, not for traditional rulers but for the new power of the proletariat, not for established order but for universal social revolution. It spoke not of imperial unity but of the sovereignty of minority nationalities and their equal rights. It derided the old dream of gaining control of Constantinople and grandly renounced concessions and privileges the tsars had struggled to obtain in Persia and Manchuria. It carried on foreign relations more through Communist parties than a regular diplomatic service, preferring to treat with representatives of the workers rather than their exploiters.

The new rulers of Russia claimed to erect a new, peoples' state on the ruins of tsardom. But much of the flamboyant trimmings on the new Bolshevik Russia soon began to peel off. It became apparent that the new construction was built not on the ruins but on the foundations of the old, and as time went on, more and more elements of continuity emerged. The similarities between Soviet and tsarist foreign policy (with due allowance for changes in the world environment) became more striking than their disparities.

Certainly by the 1930's and high Stalinism, it was evident that old Muscovy had quite as much to do with the Soviet system as did dialectical materialism. Before as after the Revolution, Russian government was essentially coercive and elitist, despite appearances of equality which were emphatic under the Soviets but not slight under the imperial regime. Strong tsars treated everyone practically as slaves, as did Stalin; and the Bolsheviks inherited much of the mentality of the authoritarian empire, including anti-Semitism, which crept back after a few years of revolutionary idealism. After as before the Revolution, the bureaucracy was the dominant caste, seconded by the military, the most obvious differences of the Soviet system being more discipline and less corruption. The new Russia tried, like the old but much more effectively, to control the economy and to industrialize by state action. Tsarist governments used police controls, indoctrination, and censorship freely, although less systematically and thoroughly. In the nineteenth as in the twentieth century, the Russian government was at odds with large parts of its population, especially the liberal intellectuals who wanted to move much farther and faster than the government was prepared to concede.

The basic problem of needing to learn from the West while fearing its subversive ideas has hung over Russia for centuries. Ivan IV was enraged that his boyars were seduced by Polish liberties. The old Russia surrounded itself with an iron curtain, leakier than that of the Soviets but solid at times under strong monarchs. Foreign envoys were regarded as at least potential spies, kept under surveillance and isolated from the people. Francis Dana, the earliest American representative to St. Petersburg, complained of police harassment, opening of mail, procrastinating, dissimulating and evasive officials, and the futility of reasoned argument; of his troubles only bribery has ceased to be important.[8]

In the old Russia as in the new, foreign policy was decided by a very few persons without much consideration for popular opinion. This has often made for capriciousness, and foreign policy has frequently depended on the character of the ruler. The nominal exponent of foreign policy, the foreign minister, has usually had a minor place in decision making in tsarist as in Soviet times. Tsarist diplomacy left behind the crudity, haughtiness, and very bad manners of Muscovite times and came to fair acceptance of international modes, much as the Soviet regime has followed a similar course more rapidly. But Russian diplomacy never

---

[8] Bailey, *America Faces Russia*, p. 7.

quite laid aside its deep-rooted suspicions of the West, its feeling of apartness, and its extraordinary blending of high moral purpose and higher moral statement with ruthless self-seeking.

The mission which the old Russia assumed was stated very differently from that of the new, but beneath the surface there was much in common. It held itself up as bearer of peace and harmony to a troubled and fractious world, and true freedom was written on its, as on Soviet, banners. Dostoevski, like Lenin, viewed opposition to Russia as a malevolent conspiracy. He believed in a climactic struggle against the evil forces of the West and in the role of the poor and humble folk of Russia as makers of a new era of history. Official like revolutionary circles in tsarist Russia saw liberal capitalism as a great moral and political evil, while they admired the supposed collectivist virtues of the less privileged classes.

The West responded in the nineteenth century somewhat as it has in our day. Some saw in Russia a workshop of new historic forces or were attracted by the idea of a great unifying authority, despotic as it might be. Others feared that the weakness and division of Europe might enable the tsars to achieve world dominion—fears based more on their exclusivism and repressive domestic policies and maltreatment of Jews and other minorities than on their actions abroad. The French historian Michelet, in the middle of the nineteenth century, saw Russia as a revolutionary power under absolutist forms. Its propaganda yesterday, he wrote, "told us: I am Christianity; tomorrow it will tell us: I am socialism."[9] In the latter part of the century, Pan-Slavism became the name of the "Russian danger." Karl Marx, one of those who most energetically warned against Russian expansion, said the Russians covered aggression with talk of peace and help for small nations, and he denounced Pan-Slavism as a "vast conspiracy" forwarded by innumerable agents. Engels similarly argued that Russian foreign policy had long been directed toward world domination by a "gang of adventurers."[10]

The Soviet Union came out of a profound and searing revolution, fraught with the passionate drives and hatreds of deep social change. Slogans, attitudes and doctrines of the Revolution became embedded in Soviet mentality; its heroism and glorious traditions and the impressive figure of Lenin are an essential part of its past and its legitimation. But for half a century the Soviet Union has been, so to speak, convalescing from the traumatic experience and getting back toward the fundamentals of a nonrevolutionary time, or getting closer to where one might suppose Russia would be now if there had been no violent revolution. This is practically inevitable. The Soviet Union occupies nearly the same area, is

---

[9] Kohn, *Panslavism, Its History and Ideology*, p. 109.

[10] R. Tucker in Lederer (ed.), *Russian Foreign Policy*, p. 171.

inhabited by the same peoples, and has the same neighbors as prerevolutionary Russia. The drive to maritime outlets and the pursuit of strategic positions remain, despite the Bolshevik belief at one time that all such questions were overridden by the issue of social revolution. Thus, there was as much interest in Manchuria, Persia, the Balkans, and so on, after as before the Revolution.

There has been continuity of strategy, too; when Russia was weak in Siberia after 1905 as after the Revolution, there were proposals for interesting the United States in Sakhalin to block the threat of Japan.[11] Along with conspiratorial traditions of antitsarist revolutionaries, much of the state apparatus and bureaucracy went over into the service of the new regime. Lenin in 1922 saw the Soviet apparatus as a carry-over from the tsarist, "barely anointed with the Soviet chrism." There is also continuity because Soviet leaders are aware of history. At least since Stalin undertook the rehabilitation of the tsarist past in the 1930's, the trials and glories of Russia, from battles against the Mongols through Alexander Nevsky, Napoleon, the Crimean War, and beyond, have been restored as part of the Soviet heritage, like the civil war of 1918–21 and the "Great Fatherland War" against Hitler. Soviet history textbooks give much space to the period before 1917, and there is not much in their coverage of this period to offend a loyal subject of Nicholas II. How strongly history may have influenced Soviet policy one can only guess; seldom have there been such revealing statements as Stalin's exultation over recovery from Japan of all the losses of 1905. Stalin on many occasions gave the impression that he was preoccupied in proving himself a worthy ruler by recovering the territorial losses of World War I, and he sought repeatedly to achieve the control of the Straits for which they had longed.

More basically, Soviet foreign policy has to be a continuation of the tsarist because both are subject to the same basic compulsions. Both, forming vast worlds to themselves, face primary problems very different from those of ordinary European states: how to borrow from the West without incurring dangerous infection, how to maintain centralized control of the huge multinational imperial realm. The Bolshevik Revolution swept away the incrustations of the tsarist empire, replaced its creaky organization, and gave it a revived and modernized rationale to replace the vague and contradictory ideals of the nineteenth century. But it is still "Holy Russia," something between a universal empire and a nation among nations.

---

[11] William A. Williams, *American-Russian Relations, 1781–1947* (New York: Rinehart & Co., 1952), pp. 52–53.

II

Lenin and Revolutionism

1. LENIN'S WORK

The Revolution with its attendant disorders cost an unparalleled economic setback, many years of hardship, the loss of most of the educated classes, and tens of millions of lives. In compensation, it gave the Russian realm an ideology and a ruling political party. These two were and are conmingled, as the ideology justified and moralized the party which was the support, guardian, and exponent of the ideology; they were the ideal and political aspects of a new kind of government. They gave cohesion, firm leadership, and purpose, to form a strong state in place of the ramshackle tsarist regime. Ideology and political party alike were Western ideas so well adapted to Russian needs as to be changed in their essence. Adaptation and application to the Russian empire were the tour de force of Lenin, who thereby became founder of the Soviet state.

Marxism came to Russia in the 1870's—the Russian was the first translation of *Das Kapital*, passed by censors as too dull to be harmful. Despite the fact that it was intended for the most advanced countries, it had the same instant appeal for discontented intellectuals of Russia that it has had since for many persons of underdeveloped countries, especially students, journalists, teachers, and the educated but unappreciated. New myths were needed, as ideas of autocracy and Orthodoxy came to seem threadbare, the monarchy had lost allure, and the church was decadent. Pan-Slavism lost promise after the war with Turkey (1877–78), and Russian power and hopes were declining, while westernization was tearing apart the fabric of Russian society. More than ever, it seemed necessary to learn from the West. For some, this meant taking over Western ways of capitalism, liberalism, and constitutional government, although these were alien to the Russian tradition and menacing to all that the Russian state had become, and adopting them meant a painful turning away from the pride and values of the empire. Those who could not accept outright westernization found a more appealing answer in Marxism. It was a Western ideology more advanced (it claimed) than the bourgeois, perverted West was prepared to accept; through it, Russia could overleap its teachers.

Marxism appealed to a country obviously great yet humiliated by inferiority, because its ideology was both Western and anti-Western. Promising the destruction of the Western social order, it neatly fit the ambivalence of much of Russian thought toward the alien and deeply hostile West and gave a certitude of moral superiority. It appealed to the anticapitalism which ran deep and was the common coin of revolutionaries and reactionaries, Populists, agrarian socialists, and monarchists as well as Marxists. Marxism at the same time realistically accepted the necessity of the industrialization which was going forward rapidly in the last decades before the war and held it a necessary step toward a better age. Socialization of the economy was agreeable because most large-scale capitalism was foreign, and a great deal of state ownership or control was already customary. The collectivist strain in Marxism fitted a land which had long proclaimed the primacy of social over individual goals and idealized community as seen in the communal institutions of the peasantry or the togetherness (*sobornost*) of the empire.

The universalism of Marxism, for which clashes of nations were insignificant compared to the conflicts of classes, was pleasing for a society with a weakly developed sense of nationality. A transnational philosophy was equally suitable for uniting the members of unhappy minorities in Russia in a single revolutionary organization and for holding together and governing the empire. For a suffering Russia, Marxism promised a utopia of peace, harmony, and brotherhood. To those who hated the inequities which mocked tsarist claims to equality, it said that differences were based on force and fraud, and promised a classless society. For intellectuals, its critique of the Western order was based on impressive scholarship, a claim of science and modernism, and a grand and orderly philosophic system. Making history a struggle of contraries, looking to ultimate progress through dispossession of the possessors and hence calling on militancy, Marxism also harmonized with the extremism and violence characteristic of Russian thought and politics, which saw the world not in shades of compromise but in vivid colors of absolute good and evil.

On the other hand, Marxism taken straight was entirely unsuited to Russia for several fundamental reasons. It saw progress as a straight road, each stage to come after the other. The Revolution and the building of socialism should have come atop the most advanced capitalism of the West, not the backwardness and feeble capitalistic development of a country such as Russia. The only way strict Marxists in Russia could bring utopia closer was by helping capitalism to achieve its normal growth. Possibly it was their task, as the more moderate Russian Social

Democrats or Marxists contended, to endeavor to make this development as liberal and democratic as possible, although it is not clear how much this could contribute to the ultimate goal. Marxism was inapplicable to Russia also because it was not a land of an industrial proletariat but of a preindustrial peasantry, and traditional Marxism regarded the peasants as a wholly negative and backward force.

Finally, Marxism was basically democratic; this was excellent in theory but unsuited for Russian political conditions. Political parties were not legal before 1905; organizations designed to change the character of the state had to be more or less conspiratorial and secret, hence almost necessarily elitist. In the West, a Marxist movement could base itself directly on the proletariat, for the sake of which it supposedly existed; in Russia, trade unions were illegal or at best extremely limited. For the same reason, labor leaders in the West easily emerged from the proletariat, whereas Russian intellectuals became self-appointed leaders and inspirers of such proletariat as they could find. Moreover, Marxism in the last decades of the Old Regime was evolving away from its extremist-utopian outlook and toward compromises with bourgeois society, reducing its attractiveness for discontented Russians. The revolution which Marx and Engels believed just around the corner in 1847 failed to arrive.[1] European workers, tiring of waiting for the apocalyptic overthrow of the old order, formed effective trade unions, found themselves beneficiaries as well as victims of capitalism, and became interested in reform and loyal to their own nations.

Lenin in each of these respects refashioned Marxism to make it suitable for political agitation in Russia and ultimately for the conquest of power; and these alterations became of great importance for the world outlook of Lenin's state. In part, Lenin perceived differently. Was Russia too backward in industrial development for Marxist agitation? Not so, replied Lenin; if the Russian proletariat was numerically small compared to the mass of peasants, it was concentrated in a few large cities and plants; this gave it disproportionate potentialities. In addition, Lenin found in the countryside a lot of small-scale capitalism, as a minority (the kulaks) built up their holdings, squeezed the majority, and reduced them to a landless proletariat. This sort of "proletariat" had little to do with Marxist ideas, according to which factory labor was prepared by discipline and union to become the ruling class of the future, but Lenin saw better than more dogmatic Marxists that the peasantry represented a great, perhaps the greatest, revolutionary force in Russia, and only with its support could there be a revolution.

In all respects Lenin stressed whatever he perceived as conducive to revolution. According to one of his early associates, he thought of noth-

---

[1] Alfred G. Meyer, *Communism* (New York: Random House, Inc., 1962), p. 22.

ing else in the day and dreamed of nothing else at night,[2] while for most Marxists in the West revolution was ceasing to be much more than an occasional slogan and for most Marxists in Russia it was only a distant vision. He had the utmost scorn for those who would lead the workers in demands for wage increases instead of concentrating on the overthrow of the government, and he always set himself against compromise and compromisers, even if this meant splitting the small band of his adherents. Western social democracy was always deeply unsympathetic to him; he never formed a personal relation with any Western socialist leader through fifteen years of residence in the West.[3]

Lenin drew apart from social democracy most violently over the issue of war and nationalism. Firmly convinced that the nation-state was outdated, he was with rare consistency unfriendly to nationalist causes. He rejoiced over the defeat of his country by the Japanese in 1904, and after the Revolution he signed away large areas of Russia fairly lightheartedly. Above all, he was one of a small minority who indignantly opposed the World War from the beginning. Lenin at first simply could not believe that the German Social Democrats, who for years had proclaimed their principled opposition to war, supported their government and voted war credits (a disbelief which showed how isolated he was from Western reality). He concluded that they were labor aristocrats and traitors to the socialist movement. His reaction was to call for a new, Third International. But when Lenin managed to get together a handful of leftist socialists at the Zimmerwald conference, only a few of the delegates stood with him. Russian Social Democrats, not only Lenin's followers but Mensheviks as well, were almost the only European socialists to abstain from supporting the war; among them, Lenin was almost alone in wishing the defeat of tsarist Russia.

The doctrinal basis of Lenin's position was his theory of imperialism. As explained in his *Imperialism, the Last Stage of Capitalism*, monopoly and finance capital needs to reach out for fields of investment, that is, colonial empire, from which are drawn profits to placate or bribe the proletariat, or at least the labor leaders, of the exploiting countries. But the anarchy and contradictions of capitalism are not overcome, only transferred to the international arena as nations quarrel over the distribution of colonies and markets. Hence under capitalism war is inevitable, but war (as indicated by the title of Lenin's book) should break the hold of capitalism and permit revolution to triumph. This interpretation, which Lenin formulated in the first years of World War I on the basis of ideas he had long held, was by no means original; Lenin borrowed

---

[2] Julius Braunthal, *History of the International* (New York: Frederick A. Praeger, Inc., 1967), Vol. II, 1914–1943, p. 43.

[3] Franz Borkenau, *European Communism* (London: Faber & Faber, Ltd., 1953), p. 27.

liberally (without acknowledgment) from such students as Hobson and Hilferding. Although Marx was inclined to regard imperialism as a civilizing force, and capitalism as an influence for peace, much of the world liked and likes to believe that some nations are rich because they make others poor, that surplus capital requires expansion, and that capitalist-imperialist conflicts cause war.

There were serious logical weaknesses in Lenin's argument, as he failed to investigate the relation of colonial empire to wages and took very partial causes of imperialism and war as the whole answer. But it attractively laid the blame for the cataclysm not on human weakness and folly but on the social-political enemy, capitalism, and promised that if this enemy could only be overcome there would be no more wars. Giving a new assurance of the millennium, it also had the merit of explaining the failure of revolution to come visibly nearer in the nearly seventy years since the Communist Manifesto.

Best of all from Lenin's viewpoint, it added to the opposition of oppressed and oppressing classes that of exploited and exploiting nations; and the exploited, to which Russia belonged, were held to be the vehicle of revolution and of the forward march of history. At one time, Lenin included Russia, which had done a great deal of expanding, in his scheme of imperialism, but this was not very satisfactory, as Russia was troubled by no surplus of capital; as an important field for investment of West European countries, Russia could be treated as semicolonial. As Lenin put it, then, capitalism could be overthrown not where it was most advanced, but where it was weakest. Hence, world revolution could start in Russia; indeed, Lenin convinced himself that it could only start with the overthrow of tsardom, the world bastion of reaction as perceived long ago by Marx. The honor of inaugurating the new era of history would then fall not to the perverted social democrats of the West but to the Russian proletariat and its leaders.

If backwardness became superiority and the poorer and less industrialized nation could become the bearer of class conflict and historical destiny, this implied a different kind of political leadership from that envisaged by Marx, a revolutionary party unlike the Marxist parties of the West. It could be contended in an autocratic and police-ridden country that the political organization should be tightly structured, limited in membership, more or less secret, and firmly guided by the leadership. Where the proletariat was relatively backward, it was not unreasonable to argue, as Lenin did, that it could not generate revolutionary purpose and ideals spontaneously but these must be injected into it by nonproletarian revolutionaries (like Lenin, whose father was raised to the nobility); the party, not the workers, incorporated the purpose of the proletariat. Essential, then, was not economic development but tactics, organization, and especially the quality of leadership; and the great attention which

Lenin devoted to this was perhaps the greatest key to his success. This meant also that the dictatorship of the proletariat could only be dictatorial, unrepresentative of the proletariat, not to speak of the majority of the population. Lenin considered democracy a hypocritical pretense.

This was much more Russian than Marxist, and the Bolsheviks were much more Russian revolutionaries who found Marxist approaches useful than Marxists who happened to be working in Russia. Russian radicals had long been fonder of causes than welfare and rather divorced from the people and popular aspirations, and Lenin's organizational scheme was somewhat suggestive of the tsarist state with its aristocracy of service. The idea of an elitist, conspiratorial socialist party was entirely un-Marxist. If elitist leadership is accepted, the leadership, not the membership, is important, and the latter can be drawn from any source, as has in fact occurred in the Communist movement; the party ceased to have any real class basis. It was a long way from Marx's idea of revolution as the bursting of overripe capitalism to Lenin's idea of revolution by political action of a party organized for this end. The thesis that the Western working classes were deactivated because of imperialism also elevated political over economic determination and raised all manner of questions about the nature of conflict. National drives came into play, and the anticipated crushing crisis was not economic but primarily political.

In brief, Lenin politicized Marxism for use in an empire where oppression was (as he virtually admitted[4]) primarily political. He equated Marxism with revolution and was correspondingly flexible; at the same time, he was a stickler for the letter of Marx and polemicized preferably by quotation. Hence he was involved in contradictions and never evolved clearly and systematically his theories, which were shaped for the needs of revolution in Russia and nowhere else. Perhaps Marx, or at least the young Marx, would have done the same; he was ready to welcome a good revolution whether or not it jibed with abstract propositions. Whatever the scientific or logical weakness of Leninism, it served as a basis for a powerful political movement. The result in the West was failure, the splitting and frustration of a formerly promising labor movement. Where conditions were basically more like those in Russia, especially in China,

---

[4] "What, may I ask, is the sense of explaining to the workers the form of value, the nature of the bourgeois order, and the revolutionary role of the proletariat, if here in Russia the exploitation of the working people is generally and universally explained, not at all by the bourgeois organization of the social economy, but, for example, by the lack of land, by the redemption of payments, or by the tyranny of the administration? What sense lies in explaining to the workers the theory of class warfare if that theory cannot explain even their relations to the factory owner (our capitalism being artificially planted by the government), not to mention the masses of 'the people' who do not belong to the class of factory workers which has formed." (V. I. Lenin, *Sobbranie Sochinenii* [Moscow, 1920–23], Vol. I, pp. 274–75; quoted by Alfred G. Meyer, *Leninism* [Cambridge, Mass.: Harvard University Press, 1957], p. 236.)

the Leninist model led to nationalistic political power unrelated to a proletariat.

Lenin's Opportunity

All this doctrine, despite its political virtuosity, would have meant little if Russia had not fallen into the maelstrom of an unbearable war, just as communism in the decades since Lenin has fought its way to power only where grave political disturbances—as in China and Eastern Europe—have paved the way for it. Russian society before 1914 had its ailments—corruption and inefficiency of the government, deep social and national divisions, philosophical malaise, and uncertainty under the strains of modernization and uneven economic development. But before the war, Russia was basically rather conservative; there were only a few indications of revolution, beside some rumblings of labor troubles. If the ineffective monarchy had somehow been overthrown, the movement would certainly have stopped far short of Bolshevik radicalism. The success of the latter was part of the breakdown of the Russian economy, political fabric, and morale, which began with the first defeats suffered in 1914; it was part of the price of the senseless and senselessly prolonged agony of World War I, which shook European civilization to its foundations.

The most obvious effect of the war was to profoundly discredit the entire tsarist political system, as masses of bravely fighting men suffered defeat after defeat because of the glaring incompetence of the regime, and losses mounted in a cause of which the people had little understanding. Bitterness and war weariness merged into growing antiwesternism. Disillusioned in the Western alliance and isolated from the West for some years by German blockade, Russia tended to revert to older authoritarian patterns. Reactionaries at court and leftist extremists joined in rejection of the Western orientation, the former desiring to return to old patterns and alliance with autocratic Germany, the latter to strike out on new roads.

The liberals who came to power when the tsarist regime collapsed in March, 1914, wished to remain faithful to their Western inspiration and commitments and at first contemplated no change in the war policy; the Allies somewhat fatuously hoped that the change of government implied a reinvigoration of Russia's war effort. For a time, there was some improvement, as the new, democratically inclined government seemed more worth defending than the old, but as defeats continued and misery increased, antiwar sentiment grew. In May the reluctance of the Provisional Government to renounce the annexations promised by the Allies (particularly the Straits) brought the first crisis of the regime and forced the resignation of the pro-Western foreign minister. Much of the press began accusing Britain and France of waging a selfish imperialist war. The Petrograd Soviet, dominated by non-Bolshevik socialists, stated the aspirations of a large part of the people in terms much like those used then and later by the Bolsheviks: "The speediest possible attainment of a general peace on the principle of the self-determination of nationalities without annexations or indemnities. . . ." It appealed to world socialist unity, denounced the secret treaties, and called the war a "monstrous crime on the part of the imperialists."[5]

Other leftist parties, the Mensheviks and the Socialist-Revolutionaries, were for peace, but peace at almost any price was the main plank of the Bolskevik platform. Lenin again showed his indifference to nationalistic sentiments by returning to Russia from exile in Switzerland through Germany and by agreement with the German government—an action which exposed him to persistent accusations of being a German agent. The day after his arrival in April, 1917, Lenin proclaimed that the struggle was of no interest to workers and peasants and had to be ended the only way it could be, by the overthrow of capitalism. Bolshevist defeatism and antipatriotism were at first unpopular, but in the months up to November the growing longing for peace drew ever larger numbers into the Bolshevik cause. To be for peace practically meant to be a Bolshevik. Lenin was not consistent, as he admitted that peace could be achieved only through a general movement, but concentration on the injustice not of ownership but of war brought him the support which enabled him to take power—especially the support of the soldiers who had no more stomach for fighting.

Ideological extremism under ordinary conditions kept the Bolsheviks a tiny sect—there were only three Bolsheviks active in Petrograd two weeks after the overthrow of the tsar[6]—but it helped to carry them to power in the turbulence of 1917. The organization which Lenin had so striven for many years to build became an effective political instrument in the general muddle and confusion. In the drive for power, Lenin had with his usual elasticity given up his principle of limiting party membership to thoroughgoing revolutionaries and had built up a mass party of hundreds of thousands. But control was carefully kept in the inner circle. Emphasizing unity, leadership, and ruthlessness against class enemies—all enemies, then as subsequently, could be treated as class enemies and thus wholly evil—the Bolsheviks were the strongest power seekers in the revolutionary situation, while the Provisional Government, like the tsarist government, lacked unifying principles. A new integration seemed necessary to hold the state together in its adversity, and none could supply this so well as Lenin and his party.

Lenin was a cautious realist who several times, as in the rioting of July,

---

[5] Robert D. Warth, *Soviet Russia in World Politics* (New York: Twayne Publishers, Inc., 1963), p. 31.

[6] M. Florinsky, *World Revolution and the USSR* (New York: Macmillan Co., 1933), p. 31.

1917, acted to restrain the wilder anarchistic elements of his following. But he did not shrink from violence he felt was necessary for the cause. The moderate Marxists were convinced that an attempt to implant socialism by force in a backward country could bring only dictatorship, but Lenin believed a violent coup was necessary to smash the old order and provide a fitting debut for the new. By the first days of November, 1917, the Bolsheviks had won over most of the garrison of Petrograd and controlled most of the soviets, the only representative organs in Russia, and the Provisional Government was rent by division; the Minister of War even felt impelled to subscribe to the Bolshevik slogan of immediate peace. A peaceful campaign to replace the Kerensky ministry with a Bolshevik-dominated one should have succeeded easily.

But to make Lenin's armed rising, the Red Guards of armed factory workers were called out; there was a good deal of shouting and some shooting, and they entered the Winter Palace through an open door to expel the bourgeois ministers. The Bolsheviks have spent much time subsequently in glamorizing this episode as heroic and scientific, planned by the genius of Lenin and carried out by the elemental force of the proletariat. It became part of the Russian claim to the leadership of world communism, and it has been held up as a model that all subsequent socialist revolutions should follow. Yet it was made much less by a proletarian rising than by subverting the army; and the government it toppled was nearly as ready to fall as that of the tsars eight months earlier, which had been pulled down with no help at all from the party which had been working for fifteen years and more to overthrow it. The Bolshevik success was less in leading a wave of history than in being best prepared to seize power in a fluid situation, and this has been no less true of subsequent successes of the movement calling itself "Communist."

2. FIRST STEPS

When Lenin's party ousted the Provisional Government and proclaimed Soviet power on November 7, 1917, they thought of themselves not as assuming the government of a traditional state but as beginning a movement of world social revolution. In the years following, they learned exactly the contrary; the universal movement failed entirely while, contrary to the expectations of their enemies and of the Bolsheviks, including Lenin, they affirmed their rule of the Russian domain.

The very idea of state foreign policy was alien to them. Marxism hardly dealt with international relations, and Leninism recognized them only as bandits' quarrels. Apart from the fact that traditional diplomacy, with its protocol and aristocratic background, was the antithesis of the proletarian regime, the notion of a socialist state having foreign relations was anomalous. It was taken for granted that a socialist revolution was an international movement without national boundaries; the Soviet regime at first claimed no definite territorial extension. Minorities of the tsarist empire might wish to separate, while other peoples would surely join; revolution in Russia and Europe and the ending of the imperialist war should come together as part of one apocalyptic breakup of the outworn order. Loyalty was not to the state but to the movement; and the universal revolutionary movement, representing the future, freedom and justice, was not to bargain with the evil and the doomed past but simply to uphold its right. Russia in its travail turned away from the community of states, of which it had since Peter become increasingly a member, removed itself from international society, and reaffirmed its universal-imperial destiny.

It was easier for the Bolsheviks to regard their polity as supranational because much of the leadership was non-Russian, many being of minority nationalities, as Poles (Dzerzhinski), Georgians (Stalin), or Jews (Trotsky, Radek, Zinoviev), and others. Nearly all of them had spent many years in exile, where they associated themselves with West European radicalism, and their passion was not for a national but, as they saw it, a universal cause, and their claim to legitimate power rested on their representing this world movement. When they got around to organizing a state, they opened its citizenship to foreigners, much as the French Revolution in 1792 had naturalized all foreigners who joined in "the defense of liberty." Western statesmen regarded the new Soviet regime as it regarded itself, not as the government of Russia but as a group of international revolutionists who happened to gain control in Russia.

Probably most Bolsheviks in their first months of power would have been glad to trade a German revolution for the Russian one. Lenin theorized that Russia could provide the spark to set the conflagration, but it was inconceivable that the spark could burn unless it mingled in a world upheaval; and world revolution meant, in Bolshevik eyes, revolution in Germany, land of the strongest Marxist party and the most modern industry. In arguing for an early coup in October, 1917, Lenin pointed to reports of a ripening revolutionary situation in Germany, which made it the duty of the Russian proletariat to strike. Expecting momentarily to be overthrown unless stronger socialist movements came to their assistance, either because of the backwardness of Russia or because imperialist powers would throttle the revolution in its cradle, Lenin envisioned leadership passing to a more developed country. Berlin should be the new capital of the socialist state, and he would have the glory of the pathbreaker. As Stalin stated in 1924, "Leninism is not merely a Russian but an international phenomenon."[7]

---

[7] J. Stalin, *Works* (Moscow, 1953), Vol. VI, p. 72.

At first, interstate relations were hardly considered even an adjunct to agitation. To emphasize their break with the past, the Bolsheviks named not "ministers" but "commissars"; and Lenin doubted that a foreign commissar was necessary. Trotsky, a strategist only of revolution, accepted the post to have plenty of free time for party business. "I will issue a few revolutionary pamphlets and then close up shop," he exulted.[8] He is said to have appeared, in fact, only once at the ministry, in order to arrange publication of the secret treaties between Russia and its allies and to dismiss employees unwilling to perpetrate what to them was sacrilege. Very few employees of the tsarist foreign ministry, a much lower proportion than in other ministries, were willing to cooperate; and the previous diplomats and experts were replaced by Bolshevik agitators, workers, sailors, and Red Guards. Russian representatives abroad were also summarily discharged. Instead of traditional departments, a Press Bureau and a Bureau of International Revolutionary Propaganda were set up.

Trotsky proceeded to announce abolition of the old diplomacy of lies and intrigues; the Soviets would deal with peoples directly. Decrying secret negotiation (which Stalin was one day to carry to unprecedented extremes), the Bolsheviks spoke as loudly as they could to the whole world, hoping to influence not governments but peoples, who would compel their governments to adopt the right policies. By publication of the secret treaties, Lenin wished to show up the imperialist aims of the war in which millions died. There was nothing extremely scandalous in these promises of territorial compensation for wartime cooperation, the most important of which was the reluctant allocation of the Straits to Russia by the Western powers. Such deals had been widely mooted, and their disclosure stirred up no great waves of revulsion. It was, however, a strong slap at diplomatic convention.

The repudiation (February, 1918) of debts was a more powerful blow against the sanctities of the old order. This move was recommended not only by revolutionary but material considerations, as the Russian was by far the largest external debt in the world. Violently protested at the time, this abrogation of engagements was to form the meat of years of acrimony between Soviet Russia and the West. Another departure from accepted international practices was the establishment of a state monopoly of foreign trade. The basis of Soviet foreign economic policy, this state monopoly complicated dealings for many years, until the world learned to cope with the Soviet mixture of commerce and diplomacy and the Soviets learned to separate commerce and revolutionary agitation.

At first the Bolsheviks neither sought nor gave diplomatic recognition. When they were compelled to have diplomatic representation, first with Germany after the peace of Brest Litovsk, they tossed niceties to the winds. Adolf Joffe arrived in Berlin scattering inflammatory pamphlets

---

[8] L. Trotsky, *My Life* (New York: Charles Scribner's Sons, 1930), p. 341.

against the government to which he was accredited. Early Bolshevik diplomats, if they could be so called, thought it quite proper to insult their foreign counterparts; indeed, a fondness for vituperative language has frequently made relations with the Soviet Union, and the tasks of those dealing with it, less pleasant down to the present. A more idealistic innovation of Bolshevik diplomacy proved less permanent. It was decreed that all emissaries in the new Soviet foreign service should have the same rank ("Plenipotentiary") and that all foreign representatives should be treated alike. But this was soon eroded by practical necessities of rank and the desire that Soviet diplomats should enjoy whatever status and prestige they could claim, until in Stalin's time the Soviet foreign service became nearly as formal and protocol-conscious as that of the tsars.

Search for Peace

The new Soviet state proclaimed equality of nations and races, anti-imperialism and freedom of the world's enslaved. But the theme on which the Bolsheviks had ridden to power was simply peace, and this was the first need of the new government, the more imperative as the army was demoralized. Its first official act, a "Decree on Peace," which called for an end to the war without annexations or indemnities, was broadcast to the world with no effort to communicate formally with the governments concerned. A few days later, notes were sent to the belligerents proposing a general conference. These communications, while propagandistic, were more moderate in tone than usual in subsequent declarations, perhaps reflecting a real hope that the Allies would see the wisdom of sitting down to negotiate an end to the war. Lenin, in complete misconception of wartime politics, had long felt that an appeal for peace would receive such massive support from all peoples that governments would be compelled to bow to it.

It was not surprising that the Allies, who had rejected more appealing peace moves when the war was deadlocked in 1916, should decline to heed the call of a band dedicated to the overthrow of all governments when the entry of the United States into the contest made their victory practically sure. The only reaction from the Allies was the issuance by President Wilson of his Fourteen Points, which took the principal points of the Leninist program and added assurances to Russia; issued in January, 1918, when the Bolsheviks were already negotiating with the Germans at Brest Litovsk, this was designed not to make peace but to encourage the Russians to continue fighting.

The only positive response was given by the Germans, whose armies stood deep within Russia but who badly needed more strength on the western front if they were to hope for victory. When the Russian commander, supported by Allied representatives, refused to enter armistice talks, he was summarily replaced; an armistice was quickly arranged, and the Bolsheviks' first experience in interstate dealings got underway at Brest Litovsk, a town near the front between the two armies, on December 22, 1917.

The negotiations were unique. The Central Powers were represented by generals and foreign ministers; Bolshevik Russia by Adolf Joffe, an ascetic revolutionary intellectual, seconded by a worker, a sailor, a woman who had earned fame as an assassin, and a peasant picked up off the street at the last minute when someone noted the lack of a representative of his class. The latter were brought along only for show, and their chief contribution to the discussions was the amusement caused by their naïvete. Purposes were equally contrasting. The Germanic powers wanted to work rapidly for the conclusion of a peace which would free them from the burdens of the eastern front and permit the obtaining of much needed goods, especially foodstuffs. The Bolshevik side, on the other hand, was hardly serious about negotiation but wanted to use the peace talks as a forum for propaganda against the war and the warring powers, particularly Germany. They also wished to kill as much time as possible until inevitable revolution in Germany should come to their rescue. This is a fairly common tactic, but it has been rather a Soviet specialty.

Endless incendiary oratory to serve both purposes was encouraged from time to time by reports of strikes and disorders in Germany; as ever since, the Leninists have hailed any rash of strikes as a harbinger of the approaching revolutionary storm. The Germans agreed, to their subsequent regret, to hold public meetings; and the Soviet delegates used them to speak not to the negotiators but to the German proletariat and people, and also to the Allied peoples, in hopes that they would force their governments to join in and support the Bolsheviks against the Germans. The German Army they tried to reach directly, both by unauthorized dissemination of literature and by fraternization with Russian soldiers, permitted on a limited basis by the armistice agreement—a demand which the German authorities found childish but which the Bolsheviks thought practically guaranteed their revolutionary success.

As usual, Lenin and Trotsky wildly overestimated both the influence of the proletariat and its receptivity to propaganda from abroad. It was ingenuous to suppose that a victorious German Army could be subverted while it was winning just because the Bolsheviks had been able to subvert a defeated Russian army. Although the German commanders were sufficiently worried to take countermeasures, there was not much evidence of success. However, the Soviet authorities were so confident in the power of their words that they continued the demobilization of the old Russian army, thus deliberately weakening themselves in the face of the enemy. Trotsky and many like him were so self-deluded that they were sure the German people would not allow resumption of hostilities or that the soldiers would refuse to obey orders to attack.

The Bolshevik delegates were not interested in territory and conditions but in the only thing they knew well, propaganda and social struggle. But by crude and tactless behavior they heightened, as often afterwards, ill will against themselves. They were always ready to bring up irrelevant matters intended to irritate their negotiating partners, as when the Germans wished to discuss the evacuation of Persia they denounced the violation of Belgian neutrality.[9] To German generals they expounded the necessity of world revolution and attacked German militarism and the Kaiser in the most offensive language. The Germans, who with naïvete of their own failed to use the occasion to propagandize themselves as saviors of Europe from the horrors of Bolshevism, were exasperated; in particular, General Hoffmann, German chief of staff, became a fierce anti-Bolshevik and subsequent organizer of intervention.

Not seeking the best terms, the Bolsheviks got the worst. Accepting the principle of self-determination proclaimed by the Soviets, the Germans interpreted this to mean separation of large territories inhabited by non-Russians, especially the Baltic lands and the Ukraine; the Soviet delegation saw self-determination as requiring first of all the withdrawal of the German forces. The Germans proceeded to recognize the independence of a Ukrainian government dependent on themselves and to demand Soviet renunciation of Polish and Baltic lands. Lenin, for whom hopes in Germany weighed less than realities in Russia, wished to accept this but was outvoted. After a break in negotiations, Trotsky went back as head of the delegation to Brest Litovsk, this time leaving out the sons of the people. After more palaver, he declared with a flourish that the Soviets refused to accept German terms but ceased hostilities, his famous, "No war, no peace," and withdrew congratulating himself on the brilliant gesture. Puzzled at first, the Germans were glad to be relieved of the necessity of breaking off talks or denouncing the armistice; and they resumed an unhindered advance toward the Russian heartland, where nothing at all had been done to prepare resistance. Verbal pyrotechnics had failed against military realities.

The Soviet government, scurrying from threatened Petrograd to lodge itself in the medieval fortress of Moscow's Kremlin, found itself confronted with perhaps the hardest decision it has ever taken. Faced with the prospect of surrender to German demands and extensive territorial losses, a large number, perhaps a large majority[10] of Bolshevik leaders (and nearly all of other leftist parties) favored rejection and revolutionary, if necessary guerrilla, warfare against the Germans. Extreme revolutionists who would, if necessary, sacrifice the Soviet state to the international movement, joined the nationalists who could not admit such territorial

---

[9] Louis F. Fischer, *The Soviets in World Affairs, 1917–1929* (Princeton, N.J.: Princeton University Press, 1951), Vol. I, p. 43.

[10] Ruth Fischer, *Stalin and German Communism* (Cambridge, Mass.: Harvard University Press, 1948), p. 35; Trotsky, *My Life*, p. 383.

sacrifices. Lenin stated his case in practical terms: revolution might be slow to triumph in Germany; meanwhile it was necessary to preserve the existing nucleus of the world socialist movement, to give the new and still infirm Soviet state a "breathing space" to get on its feet.

Lenin, who had been in 1914 and April, 1917, almost alone in his complete opposition to the war, had great difficulty in swinging his party and the Soviet government; he finally won acceptance, after Trotsky changed sides, by a vote of 7 to 6. Nearly half the party Central Committee resigned in protest, and the doctrinaire Communists for a time carried on a campaign of opposition. A Soviet delegation then went back to Brest Litovsk and signed without discussion a peace considerably more severe (the German armies having advanced far in the meanwhile) than the one they had rejected. It was, nonetheless, hardly draconian. It separated most of the non-Russian peoples in the West from the rule of Moscow—Central Asia and the Caucasus had fallen away in any case—but otherwise imposed no hardships. One can only guess what might have been the course of history if it had been maintained in effect and three centuries of Russian empire building thus undone.

Acceptance of the peace of Brest Litovsk was a decisive rejection of universal revolutionary internationalism before this really got started. Russia acted not like the embodiment of a messianic movement but like a state interested above all in self-preservation, and this has been the mainspring of Soviet behavior ever since. The international proletariat was of no help; Lenin admitted that the course of events could not be foreseen; world revolution was delayed and could be delayed again and indefinitely. Hence, for some unforeseeable time it was necessary to face and deal with capitalist powers otherwise than by agitation for their overthrow; it followed, as leftist Communists sadly predicted, that the Soviets would turn from socialist idealism to something like bourgeois nationalism. It also followed that the Bolsheviks had to build up a functioning state. Before Brest Litovsk, they had done little but issue proclamations; after it, they got down to the business of defending and governing a country.[11] Moreover, to maintain power in the face of general opposition, they had to impose a one-party dictatorship.

Making peace also meant the conversion of the Foreign Commissariat from a makeshift propaganda center to a conventional foreign office under an official, Chicherin, who was more interested in diplomacy than revolution.

The Soviet government found itself for the first time engaged in state relations; a German ambassador was received in Moscow and a Soviet

---

[11] Adam B. Ulam, *Expansion anl Coexistence* (New York: Frederick A. Praeger, Inc., 1968), p. 82.

ambassador went to Berlin. Relations were not entirely normal. The first appearance of the German diplomat was at a May Day parade, at which German marchers carried banners calling for the overthrow of his government. Not long afterwards, he was assassinated by Socialist-Revolutionaries who wanted resumption of the war, and Lenin had to hasten to express nonproletarian sorrow. The Soviet ambassador in Berlin regarded himself as an uninhibited revolutionist and proceeded, in a country at war, to establish a directorate of the German revolution, subsidizing opposition papers, delivering incendiary literature, and advising German socialists, until he and his staff were expelled on the eve of the Armistice. By the peace treaty, the Soviet government had pledged to refrain from anti-German propaganda, but this meant at most that responsibility was disclaimed or shifted to the party.

The Germans, on the other hand, ranged rather cavalierly through the Ukraine and beyond in their desperate quest of raw materials; and they supported anti-Bolshevik regimes in the Caucasus and Finland. Very ordinary and secret negotiations in August, 1918, led to a new agreement by which Russia had to pay a large indemnity and make other concessions; Lenin must have had no inkling that the German ship was sinking. The Soviets greeted with joy, however, the annulment of the treaty of Brest Litovsk in November, as a result, as they put it, not of Allied arms but of "simultaneous blows dealt by the German and Russian revolutionary proletariat."[12]

In foreign policy, Brest Litovsk left a tradition of flexibility, of yielding if necessary to the superior force of the moment to save the essential basis of power. Lenin's decision has been much praised by Soviet writers, and Khrushchev cited the wisdom of this precedent after the Cuban withdrawal of 1962. But whether Lenin was wise to force acceptance of the peace is moot. His principal reason was that the Russian army had virtually ceased to exist, thanks in large measure to Bolshevik policy. There was no force to prevent German occupation of at least the main centers of Russia, and it was precisely in these centers that the Bolsheviks had their bases of support. They were city folk, talkers much more than fighters, and they could hardly conceive of carrying on the struggle from the countryside.

But the surrender did amount to something of a betrayal of revolutionary hopes in the West, as German socialists complained. It gave a real boost to the Kaiser's government and set back the German revolution which the Bolsheviks hoped would save them. Germany did not have forces available to occupy very much of Russia; the difficulties caused to the occupying forces by an unorganized popular resistance in the smaller area of the Ukraine showed that revolutionary war would not have been

[12] Warth, *Soviet Russia in World Politics,* p. 66.

impossible. It would not have been necessary to struggle long; the opposition was correct in expectation of an early Allied victory in the West. On the other hand, a German victory, or an Allied deal with Germany leaving it free in the East, would have been fatal for the Soviets. There is little doubt that a Mao or a Tito would have chosen to fight, and the kind of warfare Lenin declined to undertake has become a Communist specialty—harrying lines of communication, hit-and-run attacks, the effort to deprive the enemy of victory and make occupation too costly until he can be driven from one point after another. But Lenin turned down the opportunity to ally communism with nationalism, which has so often been the key to Communist success.

Lenin clearly did not feel capable of leading such a combat, which might have made him into a great leader of the whole nation. What was gained, in any event, was not much. The Bolshevik party was deeply divided; although the dissident Left Communists soon returned to the fold, morale was hurt. The basis of the Soviet regime was much narrowed, as the Left Socialist-Revolutionaries, who had been valuable junior partners in the government and who had much more peasant support than the Bolsheviks, went over to the opposition. Moderates were outraged, and the old accusation that Lenin, or the Bolsheviks in general, were in the service of Germany seemed to be corroborated. The "breathing space" to which Lenin attributed such importance was only a few uneasy months, during which German depredations continued and Lenin had reason enough to fear that they might attack again. The war with Germany was traded for an even more destructive civil war, which very nearly brought the Soviet experiment to an inglorious end and which left the country utterly exhausted and impoverished. Brest Litovsk also gave a bad start to Soviet relations with the West. Until then, it had been uncertain how they would evolve; after what the Allies regarded as a treasonous breach of the Russian undertaking to make no separate peace came the intervention, blockade, and only slow and hesitant resumption of relations.

The Allies and Intervention

It has often been asked when the cold war between the Soviet Union and the West began. Perhaps the best answer is 1917. Relations between the Soviets and the Western powers, especially Britain and the United States, have never been (as the Russians like to put it) "frank and comradely"; there has been at all times, even when circumstances and political necessities brought them together, a barrier of distrust. This historical fact is ascribable to the gulf between political philosophies and systems, but it cannot be ignored that relations began under a heavy cloud.

Bad feeling was apparent even before the Bolshevik Revolution. The Allies wishfully regarded the February overthrow of the tsar as a sort of anti-German patriotic outburst; rid of an unpopular and oppressive regime infected by pro-German sentiments, Russia would make a more effective contribution to the cause upon which all their attention was concentrated. The main interest of the Allies was in keeping Russia fighting as actively as possible; the Russian people and government, on the contrary, had increasingly to be driven or urged to battle. The Russians seemed to be failing in their duty, while the Allies lacked knowledge and sympathy for the problems they faced. Recriminations and friction grew, as did Allied disappointment and annoyance, until by August many leaders of the United States and other powers were looking for a strong man to restore order, crush the Bolsheviks, and replace the ineffectual Kerensky.

The Allied governments considered Lenin a German agent, as the Provisional Government charged. He had, of course, returned to Russia by courtesy of the German government, and there were many rumors that the Germans secretly financed the Bolshevik party, an action which would be more than understandable in view of its utility to them. At times it seemed difficult to understand the extremism of Lenin's position, as he held British, French, and American capitalism responsible for the war; and Western observers did not hesitate to call it treason. Before the Revolution, the British ambassador in Petrograd was urging the Kerensky government to arrest Lenin as a dangerous subversive, a qualification which was hardly extreme in the light of his public pronouncements.[13] Earlier, Trotsky had been detained in Halifax by British authorities and released only at the instance of the euphoric Provisional Government. Chicherin, who became Soviet foreign minister after Trotsky's four months' tenure, and with whom the Western powers had to deal for a decade, was released from British imprisonment only after the Revolution, when Trotsky held Britishers as hostages.

After the Bolsheviks assumed power, there was no question of diplomatic recognition. Not only was the Bolshevik program extremely repugnant, in its attack at once on the war and private property; their government, established by an armed coup, represented a forcible imposition without, so far as the Allies knew, popular consent or a shred of legitimacy. Being contrary to the nature of things, it could have no permanency—a judgment which Lenin fairly well shared, as he expressed joyous surprise when the Soviet regime lasted more than the seventy days of its chosen predecessor, the Paris Commune. Hence the immediate reaction—and one which in the case of the United States lasted until recognition in

---

[13] Sir George Buchanan, *My Mission to Russia* (Boston: Little, Brown & Co., 1923), p. 119.

1933—was simply to wait for the freak to go away. Again and again, dozens of times in the first two years, it seemed, or was reported, that the Soviet government was, as it should be, on the point of collapse—and only good fortune, able leadership, and the divisions of its enemies somewhat miraculously saved it. There was no point in establishing formal relations with a government due soon to be replaced.

But minds were not entirely closed to possibilities of dealings with the Soviet government. While official Allied representatives in the first months held aloof, they maintained unofficial contacts, notably through the representative of the American Red Cross and a British ex-consular official, with the Soviet leadership; and a number of those who dealt with Lenin and Trotsky were impressed with their ability and dedication. The principal subject of discussion was Soviet continuance in the war. During the months of Bolshevik negotiations at Brest Litovsk, several positive proposals were made, only to fall by the wayside in a muddle caused by distrust heightened by ignorance, as communications were bad and home governments poorly informed. While the Soviets were debating acceptance of the German conditions, no one could decide to give a concrete promise of help.

The Bolsheviks for their part were sufficiently sensitive to their obligations to insist, in the armistice negotiations, that German troops not be transferred to the western front. Whatever their incriminations of the imperialistic capitalists they, or at least the more practical minded among them, were fully prepared to accept Allied assistance. Many held it a great moral lapse, but Lenin was ready to welcome "potatoes and arms from the bandits of Anglo-French imperialism," covering his elasticity with hard language. He was even willing to contemplate American participation in the industrial development of Russia. In March and April, 1918, Bolshevik leaders, especially Trotsky and the foreign commissar, Chicherin, were at their most correct and cooperative. There were moves toward getting Allied officers to train a revived Russian army, and it seemed possible for a few weeks that Allied forces might enter Russia by invitation of the Soviet government.[14] American and British representatives were encouraged to believe that the Soviet government would refuse to ratify the Treaty of Brest Litovsk and remain in the war if the Allies came to its assistance. Under military pressure, the Bolsheviks signed, and the course was set toward bad relations for a long time to come. The Bolsheviks, finding their way in the new world of international relations, saw confirmation of the hostility of the West. The Western powers, on the other hand, saw no more reason for consideration for a regime which seemed wholly bad.

---

[14] George F. Kennan, *The Decision to Intervene* (Princeton, N.J.: Princeton University Press, 1958), pp. 108, 126.

It was fortunate for the Soviet government that the Allies were caught up in the emotions of the war and so failed to adopt the obvious policy of a settlement with Germany at their expense—a policy which Lenin feared and which would logically follow if hostility to socialism were the overriding urge of the capitalists. They were far from being so consistent, but after the Soviet withdrawal from the war and the departure in February, 1918, of the Allied ambassadors from Petrograd, they felt free to intervene against the Bolshevik regime, an operation which was undertaken for various conflicting motives, with very little coordination and without real determination. Not surprisingly, it was a dismal failure.

At first it was anti-German. The Western powers had been involved in the Russian military effort, and they were not disposed to pull out simply because the Soviet regime made peace; thus, British forces landed at Murmansk in March, with Soviet consent, to protect munitions stores there. The fact that the Germans had been ranging over much of south Russia and the Caucasus suggested the advisability of sending Allied forces into these areas, and there were various impractical ideas of reestablishing with Western forces the second front which the Russians had abandoned. This meant ignoring or overriding the Soviet government, which was not taken very seriously in any case. A second front seemed possible at one time because of the presence in eastern Russia of about 50,000 Czech troops, deserters from the Austro-Hungarian armies. These men were to have been evacuated through Siberia for use on the Western front, but they found themselves at war with the Bolsheviks, at least partly because Trotsky treated them with colossal arrogance. In the disorganized situation of June, 1918, they were in control of the railroad from the Volga to Vladivostok; and the Allies, equating Bolshevik with German power, could feel that a second front had indeed been established, a thousand or so miles from Germany.

Action against Germany could be a motive or in part an excuse for intervention only for a few months until November. Mixed with it were some imperialistic motives, particularly in the case of Japanese occupation of East Siberia and support for anti-Bolsheviks there. In April Japanese troops landed at Vladivostok, ostensibly to hold Siberia from a fantastic threat of German occupation and to protect Japanese nationals. To check the Japanese, who put in some 70,000 men, by far the largest Allied force sent onto Russian territory, President Wilson sent an American contingent of 7,000. The United States had no interest in any Russian territory nor in the dismemberment of the empire; it was even slow to recognize the independence of the Baltic republics despite their strong ethnic claim to nationhood. The other principal Allies, however, stimulated by the Japanese example, may have had some ideas of profiting from Russian weakness. Southern Russia and the Ukraine were made a zone of French responsibility, and there may have been thoughts of a sphere of influence. The British were naturally interested in the oil of the Caucasus and to some extent were carrying on the old rivalry of empires in the region of Persia and the Caspian, where small detachments roamed for a year or two. Unlike the United States, Britain recognized and supported the new republics of Georgia and Azerbaidzhan.

More important was the desire, as Churchill put it, to strangle the Bolshevik monstrosity in its cradle. This desire was not unanimous; some neighbors of Russia, as Japan and Poland, guessed that a more conventionally governed Russia might be more aggressive and stronger, and so had little desire to remove the Bolsheviks except from territories of interest to themselves. There was a little of this feeling in England, too, that a White Russia would be a more difficult neighbor for the empire in Asia than a Red Russia which promised freedom for minorities. But dominant sectors, especially in Britain and most of all in France, where bitterness at the Soviets for leaving the war and repudiating their debts was highest, felt that bolshevism was a menace to decent order and traditional civilization (a judgment in which the Bolsheviks, with a change of values, thoroughly concurred). Hence, on a larger scale as resources were freed by the end of the war against Germany, they undertook to support anti-Bolshevik forces in Russia in the confidence that a slight effort would suffice to restore Russia to the company of civilized nations.

Of anti-Bolshevik movements there was an embarrassing abundance, and a confused intervention was overlaid on a more confused civil conflict. It had its beginnings in the unsettledness of the empire following the overthrow of the monarchy, as controls lapsed in outlying areas on the one hand and as the central government proved unable to provide any firm basis of unity. In September, 1917, General Kornilov, with the support of conservatives and many moderates, made his effort to replace the Kerensky regime. He succeeded only in so weakening it as to make it unable to resist the Leninists, but many of his followers found their way to south Russia, where they set up an anti-Bolshevik force even before the Bolsheviks took power.

In January, 1918, Lenin dispersed the elected, largely anti-Bolshevik Constituent Assembly; a good many of its members drifted to the Volga region and formed another and more democratic anti-Bolshevik nucleus. In July the peasant leftist party, the Socialist-Revolutionaries, wishing to renew the war against Germany, assassinated the German ambassador and started an uprising which for a few days came near toppling the Soviet state. The Czechs took over most of the thread of civilization running across Siberia and joined the fray, although with quickly declining enthusiasm. In the Far East, adventurers of various stripes raised their banners.

All around the borders, minority groups proclaimed new statehood. By August, 1918, dozens of political authorities of all complexions claimed sovereignty on the territory of the former Russian empire.

Of these, the most promising seemed to be the movement of Admiral Kolchak, which in the spring of 1919 controlled most of Siberia and was threatening Moscow from the east. The Allies, long looking in vain for a potential Russian government, offered him support in return for a statement of democratic constitutional intentions. This was easily given, although Kolchak was sufficiently authoritarian to regard the American army as pro-Bolshevik. But by this time the political field had become polarized between monarchists and Bolsheviks, and whatever liberal-democratic elements there had been had found themselves crushed between the extremes. Allied help to the contrary, Kolchak was repulsed and destroyed, as was a few months later a still more serious threat by another conservative officer, Denikin, to the south. The war-weary Allies, disillusioned in the anti-Bolshevik cause, their forces plagued by bad morale, abandoned the operation as futile. By the end of 1919, the civil war was practically over and the continued existence of the Bolshevik regime was fairly well assured.

The principal reason for the Allied failure was the lack of precisely what the Bolsheviks saw in the intervention, a concerted purpose of overthrowing them. Some fairly large armies were sent, but they did little actual fighting, and it is doubtful that they did the White cause more good than harm. The Allies gave substantial military supplies, mostly leftovers from the war just concluded, to the value of about a billion dollars. They also gave a great deal of advice. But they had no agreed plan, and there was friction among them, as between Japanese and Americans in Siberia. The moderate socialists and democratic forces in Russia withdrew from the fight or went over to the Soviet side as leadership of the opposition passed to uncompromising adherents of the Old Regime. These repelled the peasants by insisting on the rights of landholders, and the Western powers were not inspired to do much simply to bring back a government like the tsarist, with which they had had unhappy experiences. Most strongly, however, the White leaders were unbending upholders of the Russian empire as they had known it. Largely operating from the periphery, that is, minority areas, they made "Great Russia, One and Indivisible," their motto[15] and tried to restore Russian rule without even the legitimacy of a tsar. Hence they were often fighting not only the Reds but the national movements.

The Soviet state, on the other hand, survived this testing for basically the same reason that had enabled Lenin to gain power in 1917, the ability

---

[15] Richard Pipes, *The Formation of the Soviet Union* (2d. ed.; Cambridge, Mass.: Harvard University Press, 1964), p. 215.

to combine a broad doctrinal appeal with effective organization. The firmness of party structure meant that Lenin had a network of authority reaching into every corner of the territory controlled by the Soviets, into factories and squadrons. It was typical of the civil war that wherever the need was great, a Communist or little group of Communists would enter to take charge, restore morale, and put things in order. Unlike their mostly muddled opponents, the Bolsheviks had a fairly clear, although often unrealistic, idea of what they were fighting for. The belief that they had a scientific and universally valid, modern theory of history, which promised ultimate victory, stiffened the morale of their forces in defeat. The Whites, to the contrary, when defeated tended to disintegrate for lack of a conception of the future.

The Bolsheviks most remarkably managed, with Marxist cement, to combine nationalism and internationalism. Pointing to the foreign intervention, they called on Russian patriotism as well as antiaristocratic feeling and were able to get some support from former tsarist officers as well as workers and peasants fearful the old owners would return. Bone-tired people who had thrown over the war against Germany still volunteered, sometimes in large numbers, to fight the civil war. At the same time, the Leninists, offering the Russian people leadership in the redemption of the world, promised equality and freedom to the minorities; the Bolshevik cause knew no limits of nationality. The contest was, withal, very close. Several times the Soviet state tottered near defeat. The Bolsheviks retained control at all times of only a small fraction of European Russia around and between the two main cities, Moscow and Petrograd; Soviet Russia was like a besieged fortress in a contest where defeat meant death.

Russia was to a rare degree cut off from the West, encircled by enemies on all sides. Its only port, Petrograd, was blockaded by the Allies until the beginning of 1920. Foreign trade was reduced to a trivial amount of smuggling; even Soviet gold was embargoed in the West. Allied representatives mostly departed in the spring of 1918; even the neutral Scandinavian nations not only did not establish diplomatic relations but withdrew their missions and expelled Soviet representatives. In 1919 the only foreign official in Soviet Russia was a representative of the Danish Red Cross.[16]

It was in this isolation, strain, and danger that the Soviet system and Soviet mentality took shape. Lenin and his followers had had clear ideas of what they opposed and fine dreams of what they were going to achieve but very little notion of what socialism meant, how it should be organized, and how the state should protect itself. In the exigencies of securing

---

[16] Edward H. Carr, *The Bolshevik Revolution,* Vol. III: *Soviet Russia and the World* (London: Macmillan & Co., Ltd., 1953), p. 114.

their own survival and that of their system, they came to answers which became a permanent part of the Soviet way.

The Bolsheviks before the Revolution were debaters and speechmakers, frequently political hairsplitters. Their attack on problems was primarily verbal, and Lenin's insistence on forceful revolutionary action even at the climax was distasteful to many or most of the leaders. Words were the weapons they knew and used best. When Kornilov tried to overthrow the Provisional Government, they successfully foiled him by sending agitators who persuaded the railway workers to sabotage and the troops to desert. Their way to power was antimilitary; it lay primarily in persuading the army of the wrongness of the war. In seeking to make peace at Brest Litovsk, they mustered pamphlets and fiery speeches against military force in the delusion that they could sway the German proletariat or German soldiers to save them. They were still continuing the dissolution of the old armed forces, not even trying to hold together as much as they could.

Marxism had no place for an army except as an instrument of the ruling classes; only a workers' militia could be countenanced. But before the peace was signed, the Bolsheviks began to turn the Red Guard into a new military force, and as dangers grew, they, especially Trotsky (who left Foreign Affairs for Defense) desperately whipped up a new Red Army. In the course of the next two years, this became a force of several millions, with many tsarist officers to give expertise, poorly equipped but effective, at least on the defensive. The Bolshevik mentality absorbed a good deal of military vocabulary, and there was talk of shock troops, frontal assaults, and brigadiers of labor taking objectives by storm. The civil war, far more than the seizure of power, furnished the heroic themes of Soviet literature and art for many years. The state founded by a coterie of sloppy theoreticians of social progress became almost as imbued with military lore as Prussia.

Concurrently, the state was centralized and hardened. The Bolsheviks took power with no very definite program even for nationalization of industry; this was introduced step by step partly because private owners fled in the civil strife, partly because of the exigencies of war. In the extreme shortage of practically everything, all important goods were rationed, and the economy became in theory entirely subject to bureaucratic control. The whole population was subject, from April, 1918, to mobilization for military or labor service. As to be against the Bolsheviks was to be against the Soviet state, other political parties were step by step reduced to impotence and eliminated entirely. The secret police and frank terror were introduced, whether in response to White terror or to maintain a minority in power; and they became a permanent feature of the Soviet landscape. Within the Bolshevik party itself, freedom of discussion and political action were reduced. All these developments might have come with no civil war, and the narrowing of authority within the party continued in peacetime down to the extreme of Stalin's autocracy; but in the long and dire emergency of the civil war, the Soviet system was forged.

The struggle of 1918–21 also hardened the Soviet mentality. In the high degree of isolation, which was fortified by the destruction or emigration of most of the educated classes, it was easy for the Bolsheviks to exaggerate the very real attack on themselves, which was the more impressive as it fitted their preconceptions. They came to view their war, not as a chaotic jumble of currents and motives begun by Russians whom the Western powers supported without enthusiasm, but as a grand machination of imperialism, as though the major concern of all the powerful capitalistic states was to destroy the homeland of socialism in the cataclysmic struggle of the ages. Although the participation of foreign armies was trivial, Soviet histories treat the civil war as a series of campaigns of the Entente. Isolation, fear, and suspicion bred ethnocentrism and ideological antagonism toward the outside world far exceeding that of prerevolutionary Russia. It was a useful justification of strong authority to see the Soviets as a threatened fortress. They naturally continued to view the world in this frame of struggle and foreign hostility, even while congratulating themselves on the inability of the capitalists effectively to unite. The continuation of this mentality was easier, as the civil war had no sharp termination but tapered off; not until 1922 or 1923 was there fair tranquillity through that part of the Russian empire governed by the Soviets. It was easy for them to go on expecting a renewed attack; and they did so, or talked in such terms, practically until the violent assault of the Nazis. They have never ceased reminding themselves, and occasionally the world, how they were subjected to and repulsed the assault of world capitalism.

3. FIXING THE BORDERS

Reconquest of the Empire

The Soviet state began as an international movement without definite territorial limits. Most of its leaders took for granted that it would spark and merge into a world socialist polity or be extinguished. Not merely in 1919, when it was pressed into a small area of central European Russia, but even when the civil war was won in 1920, few imagined that it could regain control of the many areas of eastern Siberia, Central Asia, the Caucasus, and the Baltic, which had escaped the rule of Moscow. Yet all of these except the last were recovered as Russian power spread out again in its historical pattern and restored the empire everywhere separatism was not reinforced by external power.

This was possible, despite the extreme material weakness of the Soviet state, because the only broadly unifying political party was armed with an ideology which at once consecrated freedom and unity. There was obvious need for something like this long before the Revolution. The tsarist approach, in effect to deny the importance or the existence of national differences in a spirit of autocratic universalism, was no longer sustainable. It was particularly necessary for a socialist party to come to terms with the problem, as the minorities were the best recruiting grounds for radicalism and a major factor in the breakdown of the old order. Many, not only of the Bolsheviks but of Mensheviks and other leftist groups, were Balts, Poles, Jews, Georgians, Armenians, or others. Hence national self-determination was an inextricable and important part of the fight against the tsarist regime, the "prison-house of nationalities" (in Lenin's phrase). At the same time, nationalism threatened the unity of the revolutionary movement, which tended to divide on national lines after it acquired more freedom of expression with the semirevolution of 1905. Thus, before as after the Revolution there was needed an approach which would appeal to or at least appease national sentiments while preserving the integrity of the movement.

It was Lenin's merit and a key to his ultimate success that he, more than any other Russian leader, conservative, liberal, or radical, saw this necessity and answered it effectively. His first point was simply to seek the trust and adherence of exploited nations by recognizing their nationhood and denouncing imperialism, in the Russian as in the British empire. By his theory, the exploitation of subject territories was the essence of imperialism, a prime evil of capitalism. *Ipso facto*, it could not exist under socialism, which Lenin seems to have believed would mean true freedom. As he quoted Engels in 1916, "The victorious proletariat cannot impose happiness on any nation whatever without thereby undermining its own victory."[17]

Nonetheless, the proletariat must remain together in freedom as, in Lenin's view, its interests dictated. As Marx before him, Lenin thought the socialist state should be large and centralized, while national separatism was essentially bourgeois, a product of capitalism. The historical process and the building of socialism required the amalgamation of small nations, which could be achieved as "national superstitions" were discarded. Giving self-determination and overthrowing capitalism should end the reasons for the irrational and unprogressive division of peoples. Independence should be countenanced in the assurance that it would cease to be desired as the peoples saw themselves no longer threatened by

---

[17] V. I. Lenin, *Collected Works* (Moscow, 1964), Vol. XXII, p. 86.

oppression; in the dialectic, independence should yield to a higher unity. Lenin's position here was not unlike but stronger than that of the moderate socialists who assumed that the minorities would be content to remain part of a democratic Russian federation.

The national principle was also subordinated to the class principle. Stalin, who was concerned more with control and less with freedom than Lenin, stated firmly in his 1913 essay on the nationality question (an assignment which Lenin gave him as a representative Georgian) that self-determination should be exercised only by the proletarian party in the light of the broad interests of the class struggle. Similarly, shortly after the Revolution he wrote, "The principle of self-determination must be a means of fighting for socialism and must be subordinated to the principles of socialism."[18] This went much beyond the Leninist idea that minorities might be brought to see their own higher interest in foregoing their rights for the sake of proletarian internationalism. But it was entirely in keeping with the central doctrine of Lenin's socialism, the "dictatorship of the proletariat," within which there is little room for self-determination. And Lenin made sure of the instrument for applying proletarian internationalism. Setting himself firmly against the demands for separate organizations, he insisted that the Bolshevik party should be a unitary organization. The party incorporating the will of the proletariat, the ruling part of the people, could not be divided; so far as the party could rule, self-determination was stripped of political reality.

In pursuit of this policy, a decree of November 15, 1917, signed by Lenin and Stalin, commissar of nationalities, promised full freedom, including the right of secession, to the nations of Russia. With or without cognizance of this authorization, the minorities asserted themselves in the breakdown of the authority which tied them together. In defeat and revolution, and especially with the coming to power in Petrograd of the Bolshevik party, which lacked a strong following in many parts and aroused passionate opposition in other parties everywhere, the exodus was general. Not only peoples with a strong historic tradition, such as Finland, Poland, Georgia, Armenia, the three Baltic states, and the Ukraine, but many others, including Azerbaidzhan, White Russia, the North Caucasus, Cossacks of the Don, the Kuban and Siberia, Tatars and Turkestan declared independence.

The Ukraine was already reaching for self-rule under the Provisional Government. Full independence was declared, with German encouragement, while negotiations were being carried on at Brest Litovsk. To the amazement of the Germans, the Soviet government accepted with alacrity the idea of Ukrainian independence. But Lenin, in his message recognizing Ukrainian sovereignty, at the same time demanded the establishment of a

---

[18] J. Stalin, *Works* (Moscow, 1953), Vol. IV, p. 32.

Bolshevik regime; if the Ukrainian leaders found this illogical, they did not understand Leninist political logic. After the withdrawal of the Germans, the land was torn by civil war, in which the Bolshviks were helped by the presence, especially in the eastern Ukraine, of a good many Russians, while Ukrainian nationalism was discredited by association with the occupying power. Its fate was decided by the outcome of the civil war, but there were substantial concessions to Ukrainian sentiments for several years. Until 1923 the country remained bound to Soviet Russia only by treaties of alliance and cooperation. The Ukraine even carried on, formally, its own foreign relations; it was represented along with Soviet Russia at the Lausanne Conference in 1922. The russification policy of the tsars was reversed; in fact, Russians resident there had some grounds for complaint of being "Ukrainianized."

The Caucasus, with non-Slavic peoples and fewer Russians, presented different problems. In the spring of 1920, when the Bolsheviks undertook the conquest of the region, an internal communist movement gained control of Azerbaidzhan. Armenia was sovietized without serious resistance in the face of a Turkish threat, much as it had previously accepted protection of the tsars. Georgia, a region with a large population and better capabilities of independence, held out longer. A republic was set up in 1918 under Menshevik leadership. Having redistributed large landholdings and nationalized principal industries, it was the world's only democratic socialist republic. The Soviet government recognized its independence by treaty in March, 1920; but the Soviet ambassador set about forthwith undermining the republic. In February, 1921, the Soviet army was sent in to support local Communists; and, after a month of fighting, a Bolshevik government was set up.[19] Like the Ukraine, the Transcaucasian states remained formally independent for a few years and were not fully incorporated until 1924. Since then they have, in their cultural particularity, managed to maintain a good deal of distinctiveness.

The course of events in Central Asia was again rather different. Much of the area had not been formally annexed by the tsarist state but formed the emirates of Khiva and Bukhara. These had a will for independence, although in the complete lack of natives with administrative or military experience and technical training there was little practical basis for it. There were large numbers of Russian colonists who looked to any government in Russia which would support them, and sovietization was a fairly straight fight between Russian and native forces, like extension of Russian power in tsarist times. Autonomous Soviet governments, set up in 1919–20, were called "Peoples' Republics" like governments of Eastern Europe thirty years later. For a few years they enjoyed some latitude, and

---

[19] Pipes, *Formation of the Soviet Union,* p. 215.

tsarist russification was left behind.[20] But they became officially "socialist" on admission to the Soviet Union in 1924, when, with the inclusion of areas carved out of Soviet Russia, there were formed five somewhat artificially divided Soviet republics.

The reassertion of Moscow's authority over East Siberia and the Maritime Provinces was complicated by the intervention of Japan, which desired to keep a sphere of influence there or at least to prevent its control by a strong central Russian authority. The Soviet government, with characteristic elasticity, set up a nominally independent Far Eastern Republic to facilitate Japanese evacuation. The puppet Republic also had some diplomatic utility, as it could enter doors locked against the frankly Bolshevik government of Moscow; it successfully represented the Soviet position at the Washington Conference of November, 1921. After the Japanese withdrawal, largely under American pressure, it was promptly dissolved. Further prolonged negotiations were required to secure Japanese departure from north Sakhalin, and this had to be bought with coal and oil concessions, which caused constant friction for the next two decades.

The Bolsheviks also restored Russian power in Mongolia. Nominally under Chinese sovereignty until 1945, Outer Mongolia was under Russian influence after 1911, as fear of Chinese encroachment caused Mongols to look to Russia for protection. Russian influence was shattered by the Revolution; but after defeating the Whites in Siberia, in 1921 the Bolsheviks pursued the forces of a wild anti-Communist, Baron Ungern-Sternberg, into Mongolia. There they cooperated in the establishment of an anti-Chinese and pro-Russian but otherwise mixed government. There was some setting of the poor against the rich and the merchants, and lands were redivided, but the social revolution at first was largely pretense.[21] Intensive sovietization was begun in 1924, as many advisers, including Mongols from Siberia, were placed in important positions. In 1925 the Soviet army was pulled out except for training and advisory personnel, and the Mongolian People's Republic settled down to the apparently permanent status of satellite, a status less resented because Mongolia had so long been subordinate to China.

Tsarist holdings were thus restored around most of the periphery. But in the West, the weak Soviet state met much stronger opposition, and the most westernized areas were lost. In the disorders of 1918, the Rumanians seized Bessarabia, which had been under Russia since 1812 but whose population was ethnically largely Rumanian. The Soviet government

---

[20] Serge A. Zenkovsky, *Pan-Turkism and Islam in Russia* (Cambridge, Mass.: Harvard University Press, 1960), p. 268.

[21] George G. S. Murphy, *Soviet Mongolia* (Berkeley: University of California Press, 1966), p. 2; Louis Fischer, *Soviets in World Affairs,* Vol. II, p. 538.

never recognized the loss, and it remained a serious point of friction and impediment to normal relations with Rumania. In the Baltic area, there was in each of the three countries a struggle between pro- and anti-Soviet elements. German or British help for the nationalist forces enabled them to triumph and establish independent republics, which were duly recognized and lasted until World War II permitted Soviet power to overwhelm them. Civil war was still fiercer in Finland, where there was a substantial Communist movement. When the Bolsheviks made their Revolution in Petrograd, they confidently expected next-door Finland to follow. When it did not, however, they promptly recognized Finnish independence; and German assistance gave victory to the Whites. In the case of the Poles, Russia's largest minority in the West, among whom bolshevism had no strength, the Bolsheviks welcomed independence, perhaps partly because Karl Marx was so exercised in the Polish cause.

After a few years' grace, the ostensibly autonomous republics, except for Mongolia, which had not been a part of the tsarist empire and sovereignty over which was claimed by China, were drawn into the formally federated but actually very centralized Soviet Union. Yet concessions to appearances and nonpolitical particularity were successful in reconciling many nationalists. The simple adoption of the colorless designation of "Soviet" instead of "Russian" for the union was a major stroke. Soviet policy has been more concerned with unity than exploitation, and it has done everything possible to convince minorities that union with Russia is economically advantageous. In the first Soviet years, native languages and culture were encouraged—a policy which hardly interfered with political control and in some ways facilitated it, as peoples, especially in Central Asia, were artificially divided into partly synthetic nationalities, while unifying movements, as among the Turkic or Mongol peoples, were firmly opposed. The liberal Soviet nationality policy was also an asset against Western imperialism, especially British, as it was earlier used against the power of the tsar. For a time, contacts were encouraged between Soviet Central Asia and peoples across the borders; and the Soviet constitution, which consecrated (and still consecrates) a right of free secession, was held up as a model for the world socialist state.

Lenin seems to have wished to make Soviet nationality policy a fair compromise between independence and union. Late in 1922, he suggested that the Soviet republics should be really independent except for foreign affairs and defense.[22] As a true internationalist, he berated Russian chauvinism and deplored the maltreatment of Central Asians by Russian colonial bosses garbed as Bolsheviks. Most strongly, at the end of his

---

[22] Pipes, *Formation of the Soviet Union*, p. 287.

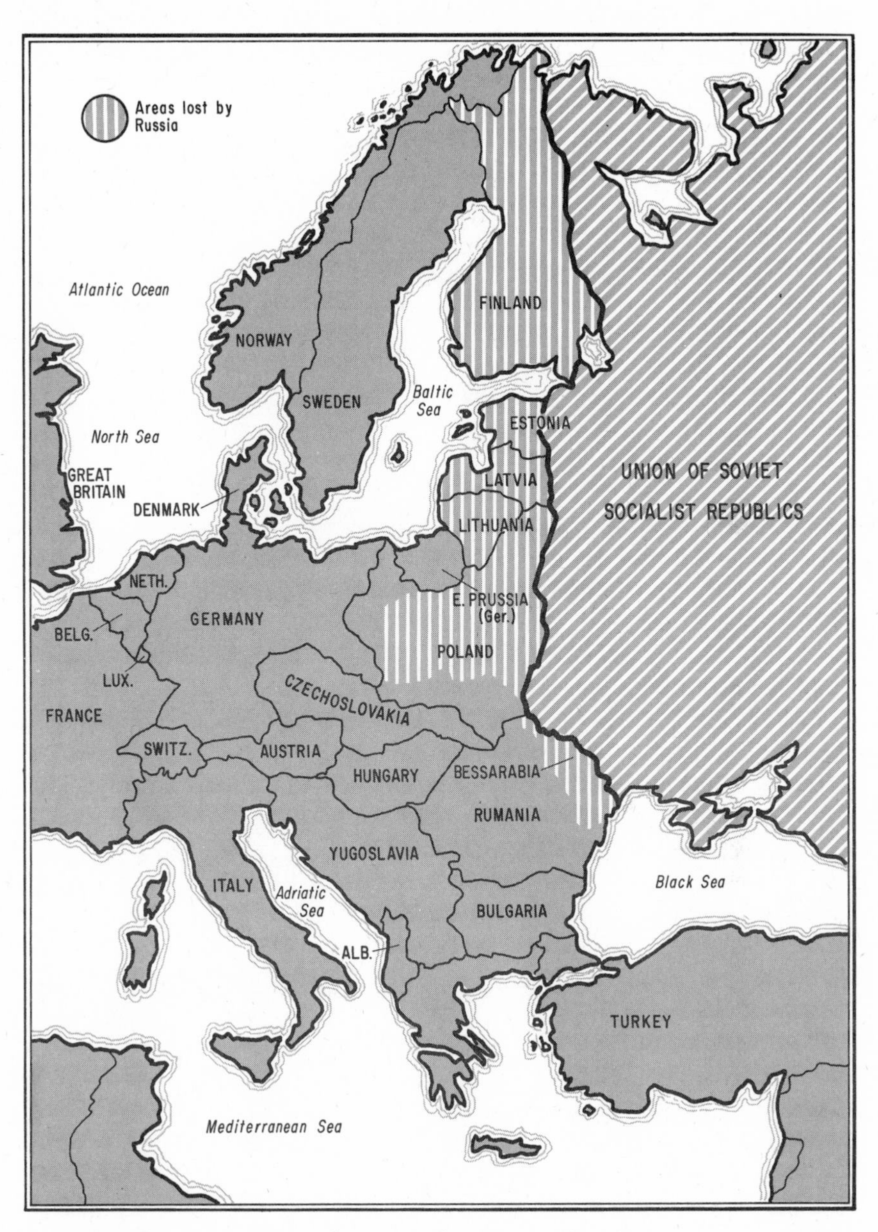

Central and eastern Europe between the wars. The shaded areas were lost for to the Russian empire in the extreme weakness of 1917–1919. Except for Finland and central Poland, they were recovered by Stalin under his agreement with Hitler in 1939–1940.

active political life, he broke with Stalin over the latter's brutality in Georgia; he insisted, in his illness, on an investigation of the invasion and its aftermath and was depressed over the evidence of Soviet oppression.

The basic problem, however, remained unsolved. Russian dominion, in view of the numerical superiority of the Russians, was almost unavoidable. Russians of all political shades, monarchist, liberal, moderate socialist, or Bolshevik, almost unanimously favored unity (as they still do); tsarist officers served gladly in the Soviet army regathering the pieces of the empire. Lenin's successors, moreover, frequently lacked his tact and the political sensitivity which made Russian predominance less irritating. At the same time, the sense of world mission, without which it was hard to expect historically and culturally disparate communities to be primarily loyal to Moscow, faded as the world failed to follow the Russian example. Lenin expected the minorities, freed from bourgeois influences, to be grateful for Russian generosity and to place the supranational above the national welfare. He failed to consider that they might have their own ideas.

War with Poland

The uncertainty of the border between Russia and Poland led to Soviet Russia's first foreign war and an exciting but traumatically unsuccessful effort to spread bolshevism by force.

The extreme weakness of Russia in the civil war was an invitation to the Polish state, revived with the blessing of the Western Allies after a century's submergence, to recover the huge territories it had once possessed from the Baltic to the Black Sea and including much of the Ukraine. Very likely Poland, if it had struck when the Soviet republic was sorely pressed, could have pushed it over the edge to destruction. But the Poles knew that a White Russia would be more chauvinistic and assertive of territorial claims and believed that it would be stronger and more dangerous to them than a Red Russia. Hence when General Denikin seemed to be winning in 1919, the Poles held back, only to strike rapidly into the Ukraine in the spring of 1920. By so doing, however, they galvanized the Red Army into unexpected effectiveness, and the Poles were thrown back as swiftly as they had advanced.

When the Red Army reached the limits of ethnic Poland, the Curzon lines which the Allies had earlier drawn, the leadership faced a crucial decision: to end the war there or to carry communism on bayonets into Poland and perhaps Germany. Lenin, who had previously opposed Trotsky's wish to invade Estonia, believed that Polish workers would rise to welcome communist invaders, and the Red army plunged ahead. As it advanced, it organized soviets, and a Polish Communist Revolutionary committee was established to administer occupied territories until they could be turned over to a Polish communist government. Faith in world revolution, which had fallen dispiritedly, soared anew, as the Soviets awaited the Polish revolution. The Second Congress of the Comintern (which was not consulted, although it was supposed to be the general staff of world communism) was happily meeting in Moscow; the delegates watched the progress of the army on a large map and cheered as red pins were moved westward. Revolutionism was blended with Russian nationalism and Soviet state interest. Former tsarist commanders, eager to recover a tsarist possession, were rallied to an army which welcomed foreign communist volunteers and which regarded itself as an arm not of a state but of the world proletariat.

The Red Army pressed on to the gates of Warsaw, and the West, always disposed to exaggerate either the weakness or the danger of Russia, trembled. But Western, mostly French, assistance arrived; and workers came to the aid not of the invaders but of their own government. The overextended Bolshevik forces, which always fought better on the defensive than the offensive, faltered and fell back. Many Soviet leaders wished to continue to fight for better peace terms; but Lenin, with the indifference to territorial losses he showed at Brest Litovsk and on other occasions, agreed to the cession to Poland of a large strip of the Ukraine and White Russia. He apparently believed that this liberality would make for friendship with the new Poland. But the holding of over two and a half million non-Poles in the eastern marches made Poland perennially fearful of Russia and consequently hostile. With lands the loss of which was regretted by Germany on one side and by Russia on the other, Poland was a perpetual temptation for a German-Soviet entente and a new partition, as came in 1939. For the Soviets, on the contrary, the bursting of the revolutionary bubble seems to have been salutary. Lenin said that Soviet troops should never again be used to give direct aid to revolution abroad. Only in 1939 did Stalin deviate from this wisdom and use the Soviet army for the extension of communism.

4. FOR WORLD REVOLUTION

The Leninists seized power in November, 1917, claiming not to assume power in a state but to usher in a new era of history in which separate states would cease to matter. Many Bolsheviks, internationalists and idealists, were genuinely attached to the cause beyond considerations of political benefit; but the passion for world revolution was at least equaled by the need for it. In months prior to November, 1917, Lenin was looking eagerly for signs of the uprising in Germany which should bring him to power in Russia. After he achieved power with no help from the German proletariat, it still seemed that maintenance of Communist power required its extension. The only way they reasonably saw to end the war and at the same time maintain their independence was through a broader, especially German revolutionary movement. Marxist-Leninist theory also required this. It was at first inconceivable that Soviet Russia by itself could make the socialist revolution it aspired to make; and unless it spread, this conflagration would burn out or be extinguished, as the Paris Commune was brought to a speedy end when the rest of France failed to join it. And the expectation of great upheaval was not a wild one in the troubled world of 1917 and 1918.

Eagerness for world revolution might have slackened rather rapidly if the Soviets had been able to relax and turn to the formidable problems of restructuring Russia, but civil war and Allied intervention raised it to a new heat. Belief that Russia was the forge of history, where the future was being hammered out for the benefit of all mankind, was an essential part of the utopianism and ideological orientation of the day and was vital to the morale of the usually rather desperate Bolshevik cause. Without faith in the inevitable world revolution, the storm always just over the horizon and about to confound their enemies of the capitalist camp, they must have succumbed to despair in the dark days. But defeats at home could be balanced by victories of proletarian brothers abroad; in 1919 Lenin again and again referred to the world socialist state in the making.

Defense of the state seemed to coincide with the anticapitalist struggle everywhere, as the interventionist powers were the leaders of world capitalism; and Marxist science promised victory to the progressive movement. Even if there were few signs of revolution in England or France, leftist protests, strikes, and efforts to halt shipments of munitions and the like gave substance to the vision of foreign workers rallying to the cause. An outsider might contend that the Soviet effort—in reality feeble but in appearance menacing—to export their revolution hurt far more than it helped, as it was the principal reason for the Allies' interest in their overthrow; but this reasoning, like such reasoning through subsequent decades, is academic. The Bolsheviks reacted to the world situation as they perceived it in ideological light. Lenin believed the Allies were inevitably hostile regardless of what Soviet Russia did, if only from a desire to return it to semicolonial subjection, while the loyalty of the working classes was its shield.

As the civil war came to a close, world revolution was no longer so urgently necessary. There was less and less point, also, to counting on something which was visibly receding from the horizon. But it was still in order. Having won the civil war, the Bolsheviks had a feeling that they should go forward; there was no reason in their philosophy for halting at any borders, while the defeat of the main capitalist powers by the infant Soviet republic suggested that they were ripe for demolition. Moreover, if in the Marxist view it had seemed impossible for the relatively poor and backward Russia of 1917 to attain socialism by itself, the Russia of 1920 was far poorer and more backward, virtually thrust back to the preindustrial age by the immense disorder and destruction. How to build socialism without help was a quandary, and the Soviet leadership could imagine no better promise than that a relatively advanced industrial country—Germany again was chiefly in view—should join it; political action should furnish a quick cure for almost hopeless economic backwardness. Consequently, for years the Soviet state pursued the will-of-the-wisp of world revolution in the illusion that the Russian Revolution, a Russian affair arising from weaknesses of Russian society and the strains of defeat, was fulfillment of a universal Marxist apocalypse.

Revolutionary Stirrings

In December, 1917, the Soviet government announced, with a candor that was soon dissipated, an appropriation of 2 million rubles for the "revolutionary international movement." But in fact the Bolsheviks had neither the material nor organizational means for taking any consequential part in the turbulence of Europe in the wake of the war. They were not even able to inform themselves, in their extreme and hard-pressed isolation, about details of European events.

Lack of information gave free rein to optimism. Scanning the news of a disturbed world, Soviet leaders saw every strike as a portent, every riot as a beginning of revolution, now in Poland, now in Italy, and mostly in Germany (a habit of mind which has been retained to this day, as the Soviet press has countless times reported the gathering and irrepressible discontent of the working classes or the mounting crises of capitalism). On November 1, 1918, *Pravda* saw so keenly as to headline, "World Revolution Has Begun." The disturbances of postwar Europe were ascribed to the ripening economic and class conflict of Marxism-Leninism and the example of the Russian Revolution. The influence of the latter was grossly exaggerated by both its friends and its enemies and may have been negative, as it repelled the powerful more than it inspired the oppressed.

What revolutionary impetus there was in Europe, 1918–20, was largely a reaction to defeat and its discrediting of the old order, in the same way that defeat had brought revolution to Russia. Indeed, the Paris Commune, Lenin's prototype of the Soviet state, had been born of military defeat, not economic overripeness. Although the masses were receptive as never since to a message of redemption after the years of torment, there were real suggestions of revolution only in the defeated powers, Germany and Hungary. Yet these gave soaring hopes. As Zinoviev, in charge of the international project, wrote in the spring of 1919:

Now as we write these lines, the Third International has as its foundation-stones three Soviet republics—those in Russia, in Hungary, and in Bavaria. But no one will be surprised if at the moment when these lines appear in print we shall have not three but six or more Soviet republics. . . . Perhaps we shall see—for a few years and side by side with communist Europe—American capitalism will continue to exist. Perhaps even in England capitalism will continue to exist for a year or two, side by side with communism in the whole of continental Europe.[23]

The dream came nearest to realization in Hungary. The Soviet republic of Bela Kun was not the result, however, of a proletarian insurrection or even a coup but of a desperate situation and an Allied ultimatum. This drove a moderate government to resign in favor of a socialist-communist coalition. Its reasons were nationalistic, hope that the leftists might be able better to mobilize the people for resistance and to secure aid from Russia, the only potential ally in sight; the Communist role was seen as more military than revolutionary, as it came to be in the rise to power of Mao and Tito. But the parallel of Hungary in 1919 to Russia in 1917 was fairly close, as the proletariat was small, the social order anachronistic, and social democracy and democratic traditions were weak. The Bolsheviks welcomed the Hungarian Soviet state the more joyously as their own outlook was parlous at the time; they hoped and sought to come to its aid to join the two revolutions. But the military situation did not permit; and a Rumanian invasion, supported by the Allies, brought Hungarian communism to a quick end for a generation.

Much greater hopes were laid on Germany, perhaps the most advanced of industrial nations and prime focus of Marxist attention since the 1880's. The effort to demobilize the German army by propaganda during the Brest Litovsk negotiations showed little results, but this did not discourage the indefatigable revolutionizers. The posting of a Soviet ambassador to Berlin in pursuance of the peace treaty (which forbad hostile propaganda) seemed a heaven-sent opportunity; and Joffe, who refused to present credentials to the Kaiser, quickly and with ample funds set up veritable headquarters of subversion. The German government was remarkably tolerant but finally expelled him a few days before the armistice and its own fall.

With the overthrow of the Kaiser and the installation of a Social Democratic government, hopes skyrocketed. There was an obvious parallel to the overthrow of the tsar and the installation of the Provisional Government, and the sequel could only be the same or better, German Marxism being so much stronger and the German proletariat so much more numerous and politically conscious. The differences, which the Bolsheviks did not see, were more decisive than the resemblances. The German revolution of November 1918 was not a call for the destruction

[23] Florinsky, *World Revolution and the USSR,* p. 42.

of an unsatisfactory social order but a change at the top evoked by defeat and the necessity of dealing with the Western powers with reasonably democratic credentials. The German army, far from dissolved in defeat, was largely intact, and it was not pro-Bolshevik. The working class, by virtue of its strength, had become "bourgeoisified" and had acquired some stake in the prevailing order. The German Social Democratic party, being old, well-organized and powerful, had become accustomed despite its Marxist inspiration to working in the framework of constituted society and had developed its own vested interests. Moreover, the German Social Democratic leadership shared the antipathy of most Germans for semibarbarous Russia; having justified support for the war in 1914 by hostility to the tsarist regime, these leaders were of no mind to take lessons from Russian Bolsheviks in 1918 and risk making Germany a Russian dependency.

The Soviet ambassador, who expected the new German government to invite him back to Berlin, was disappointed, as the Social Democrats completed the breaking of relations. The German president, Ebert, faced the problem not of an unbearable war, as Kerensky had, but of keeping of order to make as favorable a peace as possible. Whereas Kerensky had rejected Kornilov, Ebert leaned on generals of the Reichswehr, who supported a Social Democratic government in return for the freedom which it allowed them—a harmony impossible in the more deeply divided Russian society. When the Soviet government, itself suffering food shortage, offered a small shipment of grain, the Germans humiliatingly rejected it in the realistic expectation that much more could be obtained from America. It remained only for the Russians to cry treason at the Social Democrats. But they had been denouncing the "social patriots" as traitors for years, and it was naïve to expect the latter to embrace those who could consign them, like other socialist parties in Russia, to the dustbin of history. The Social Democrats were also aware of historical parallels.

Faith in the German revolution had to look to the radical left, but this was fragmented, and the nearest thing to a Lenin-style party was small and rather academically oriented. Street fighting in Berlin, in January, 1919, was easily suppressed; and the two outstanding leaders, Karl Liebknecht and Rosa Luxemburg, were killed. Thereafter, the prospects of revolution in Germany were slight, although Lenin's hopes continued to be inflated with news of strikes and riots in Germany, to sink again until the next rosy report. A German Communist party was built up, in due course, to important size, mostly through the splitting of the Independent (antiwar) Social Democrats. But better prospects for Soviet dealing with Germany were offered by the German rightists, who toyed with bolshevism for political support while the moderates looked to America for bread and loans. When Karl Radek was imprisoned as an illegal Russian agent in

Germany during most of 1919, his comfortable prison cell became something of a mecca for German generals and extreme conservatives hopeful of an understanding with their eastern neighbor to offset pressures from the west.

German communism had one moment of glory, however, somewhat apart from the main currents of agitation and intrigue. In April, 1919, a Soviet republic was proclaimed in Bavaria. It was a piece of utopian adventurism, led by Russians who were affiliated not with Lenin's party but with his Socialist-Revolutionary opponents and who acted independently of the German Communist party.[24] Nonetheless, it gave the Bolsheviks a brief fillip, and they adopted it gladly, as Marx had adopted the non-Marxist Paris Commune. Having no resonance elsewhere, it was suppressed after a few weeks by force. The result was to leave Bavaria a stronghold of reaction during the lifetime of Weimar Germany.

Organizing Revolution

If Europe failed to follow the revolutionary road, this could only be due to the failure of the leadership. To enable Germany and other countries to emulate Russia, it was necessary to guide them to the type of political organization which had succeeded in Russia. Lenin had wished to establish a new International ever since the lapse of the socialist parties in 1914, but the first real step in this direction was taken at a low point in the civil war. In January, 1919, the Russian party issued a call to the workers of the world to unite in a Third International. After some preliminary gatherings, the founding First Congress of the Communist International was hastily convened (in fear that the Social Democrats might reunite after their wartime divisions) in Moscow in March. Because of the isolation of Russia, only five of thirty-five "delegates" claiming to represent the world's proletariat were actually from abroad, the rest being either Russians or foreign communists happening to be in Moscow. The only foreign movements represented, the German, Austrian, and Hungarian, were mere splinters, and the German delegate was at first opposed to the principal purpose, the founding of the new International. The Congress planned a permanent residence in Berlin, but the Comintern never met except in Moscow. It was a Russian show, an extraordinary meeting that debated universal revolution while practically without followers except in Russia, almost without news of the world which they proposed to transform, and almost entirely ignored by it.

The Second, and real founding, Congress of the Comintern took place under very different conditions in July–August, 1920. The blockade had been lifted and communication with the West was tolerably easy. The

---

[24] Borkenau, *European Communism*, p. 41.

Soviets had surprised everyone by practically winning the civil war, and they seemed to be defeating Poland. Although the postwar ferment had subsided, hopes were still strong that it would surge again or that the civil war victory might carry into a sweep into the West. It was about the highest tide of international communism until after World War II. Russian and foreign communists resident or exiled in Russia were again a majority, but now some two hundred delegates stood for a considerable radical following in the principal countries of Europe. German was its lingua franca, and it had some claim to be a genuine international body.

Its principal business was to adopt the set of rules drawn up by Lenin to press the Third International strictly into the Bolshevik mold. Far from opening the doors to all who wished to associate themselves with the noble endeavor of the workers, it laid down the rigorous Twenty-One Conditions for affiliation designed to restrict membership to unconditional adherents of Leninism. In order to be acceptable a party was obliged to cleanse itself of all reformists, to have an illegal organization as well as a legal one if permitted, to carry on subversive propaganda in the armed forces of its country, to assist Soviet Republics in all possible ways, and to obey all resolutions of Congresses or the Executive Committee. It had to set itself against the legality of its state and to subordinate itself to a theoretically international but increasingly Russian-dominated organization. Other obligatory provisions were that all member parties should call themselves "Communist," that the Executive Committee should have the right to demand the exclusion of disobedient elements, and that parties should carry on no relations among themselves except through the central authority. Individual parties should submit their programs to the Executive Committee for approval. The avowed aim was the establishment of the "dictatorship of the proletariat and of the International Soviet Republic." For this goal, Communist parties were enjoined to "utilize bourgeois state institutions in order to destroy them," inviting repression by a remarkable frankness that arose from self-righteousness and carelessness of others' views.[25]

In the euphoria of the hour, these rules and conditions were adopted with little real debate, although quite free discussion was still permitted; but they represented a fateful departure. No previous International had tried so to control its components or indeed to govern them at all except by persuasion. That the Third International should have been so insistent on central authority resulted on the one hand from the authoritarian disposition of Lenin and Russian politics, on the other from the situation in which the Comintern found itself. Long before, Lenin in his factional contest had strongly emphasized the purity of the party as a dedicated revolutionary core; it was on this point that he split from the more mod-

---

[25] Carr, *Bolshevik Revolution,* Vol. III, p. 200.

erate socialists in 1903. He regarded the backsliding of the Social Democrats in World War I as the fault of nonrevolutionary leadership, as was their shameful failure to make a revolution after the more firmly led Bolshevik party had shown the way.

Confident that they were the absolute center of history and correspondingly worthy of emulation, the Russians felt entitled to give lessons to socialists of other countries. Lenin in his last major work, *The Infantile Disease of "Leftism" in Communism*, written in April–May, 1920, took the position that the Russian Revolution should serve as a model of universal significance if not applicability. If the Russians succeeded while others failed, it was obviously necessary to learn better from the methods of the former, while the myth that Lenin had scientifically planned the Russian Revolution encouraged planning other revolutions similarly. Lenin and his fellows in the Russian party began forthwith to give suggestions, which increasingly became orders, in matters of leadership, organization, and tactics. The Communist movement became in consequence organizationally oriented, requiring not primarily right belief but willingness to follow faithfully the dictates of the center, which possessed or defined political truth.

The result was to impose on parties in Western Europe tactics suitable for a disciplined and obedient Russian party in the exceptional circumstances of 1917. They were confused and divided, enthusiastic for the great victory of a socialist party in Russia, less prepared to follow closely its leadership and example in a very different setting. The insistence on complete conformity and submission meant that everywhere the socialist movement was split into opposing camps. The revolution-bent, usually a minority of the membership and everywhere in the West a fraction of the leadership, formed new Communist parties. The remaining socialist parties, stripped of their more radical elements, became increasingly moderate and reformist.

The Communist parties in these circumstances lost a great deal in compensation for whatever they gained by association with a successful revolution and a major state. The requirement that, even in democratic countries, they must organize illegally and work to undermine the armed forces involved them, along with Soviet policy, in subversion. Uninclined to be squeamish about means to power and cynically scornful of bourgeois-democratic institutions, Lenin expected his followers abroad to be the same. Subjection to a distant and increasingly bureaucratic authority, which was unfamiliar with local needs and conditions, deprived the Communist parties of flexibility. Although Lenin had tacked to gain power, as in adopting the non-Marxist agrarian program of the Socialist-Revolutionaries, the foreign Communist parties were to follow strict orthodoxy. Capable and forceful leaders often came into conflict with the central direction and were replaced by docile party hacks. The Russians, moreover, did not hesitate to make demands of foreign comrades; it was typical that they scoffed at Italian and other Communists who, in the difficult years after the end of the war, were afraid that revolution might bring economic breakdown and hunger; such considerations were held to be a betrayal of the ideal.[26] But subservience to and identification with the Russian cause meant that communists were everywhere antinational. This was no enormous burden in the immediate aftermath of the war, when nationalism was much discredited; but as national feeling revived, it became the greatest barrier to their popularity and chances of gaining power. It was not easy for the Russians to see that their efforts to bind foreign parties to their forms and discipline hurt the cause for which they supposedly existed. But the organization of the Comintern, far from mobilizing revolutionary energies, stifled them.

Split Movement

The antagonism of Soviet communism for moderate socialism has been an essential part of the Leninist approach from the years before the Revolution when Lenin's principal energies were dedicated to factional wrestling against those more prone to compromise. It has continued, despite efforts at various times to come to tactical understandings with socialists, more or less to the present; the invasion of Czechoslovakia may be attributed in part to fear that its communism might be edging toward social democracy. It has seemed a part of the fundamental set of Soviet political thinking or ideology, corresponding to basic political needs.

Lenin saw in the "social patriots" the main obstacle to revolutionary action, at least as bad as outright capitalist opponents; and both of the first two Congresses of the Comintern devoted their main attention to combating not the class enemy but the rivals for leadership of the working classes. Large socialist parties, impressed with the only Marxist group to have come into political power, were eager, for the most part, to affiliate with the Russian Revolution; but the effort of the Comintern was not to draw adherents but to exclude all those inadequately dedicated. Sometimes the Russian leadership seemed actually to prefer narrow parties and to take pleasure in splits, which supposedly meant revolutionary purity.

It is not easy to understand why the Communists should be so determined to oppose those who fairly well shared their overriding proclaimed goals of ending capitalism and constructing a socialist society. One obvious reason was that Lenin had come to power after years of splitting and opposition to moderates; and it was easy to believe, despite the fact that the nearest successes, as in Soviet Hungary, had come through cooperation with other socialist groups, that this strategy should succeed

---

[26] Braunthal, *History of the International,* Vol. II, p. 204.

elsewhere. Unlike bourgeois parties, Social Democrats were immediate competitors, especially for control of labor unions; it is psychologically understandable that animosity should be directed first against those who seemed to be the immediate obstacle to Communist progress.

Lenin and his fellows could never understand why Western workers, who had more than their chains to lose, could be so passive and appreciative of advantages to be won by legal and moderate action. The answer, and the reason for the otherwise unaccountable failure of revolution in the West, had to be treason, which was accounted for in Lenin's theories about imperialism and the bribing of the "labor aristocrats." At first Lenin was even willing to believe that Western radical parties, unlike his own, could be democratic if they could only be rid of their perverted leadership.[27]

Lenin also believed, or wanted to believe, that the revolutionary movement would be more effective if coordinated from a single center. The practice of the Comintern presumed that knowledge and leadership resided only at the center, which was expert in a theory which was in fact very thin and gave few definitive answers. There was no conception that local men could know local realities better than the successful practitioners of Marxism in Moscow. The latter consequently stressed unconditional obedience and orthodoxy, supposedly desired as means to revolutionary change but actually goals in themselves, and felt, in their authoritarian mentality, more hatred for the heretic or deviant than for the outsider and frank enemy.

For socialists of Western Europe, to accept the Comintern's conditions meant breaking with traditions and usually leadership. They were expected to renounce a developed tradition of legality and constitutionalism and to give up a strong and useful adherence to democracy and civil liberties in favor of an unpromising sectarian struggle. They were called upon to purge as traitors men who, unlike the large majority of Bolshevik leaders, were sons of the working class and who had been dedicated socialists all their lives. It is not surprising that most, usually after some vacillation, held back; and the new Communist parties which emerged from the splits were everywhere weaker than the socialists had been.

In France, the majority of the socialist membership accepted affiliation with the Comintern, partly because of French revolutionary traditions; but most of the leadership rejected it; and the trade unions were divided. The British Labour party, although prepared to help Soviet Russia by opposing the shipment of munitions to Poland, was overwhelmingly opposed. To this day, the Communist party has remained insignificant or minor in England and in the countries of firmest democratic tradition, as

---

[27] Richard Lowenthal, *World Communism* (New York: Oxford University Press, Inc., 1966), p. 237.

Scandinavia and the Low Countries. In countries of Eastern Europe, with political and social background more like that of Russia, communist parties were more popular but were usually repressed in short order. In Italy, because of Comintern narrowness, a promising socialist movement was sundered with much ill feeling; and a smallish minority finally formed a conformist Italian Communist party. The division opened the way for Mussolini; the Communists declined to join in opposition to fascism until he had attained power and began repressing them.

The opposition of Communists and socialists was perhaps strongest and most momentous in Germany. There, in the advanced industrial country nearest to Russia, which showed most signs of eruption in defeat and which the Bolsheviks considered an oppressed country because it had lost its colonies and had been burdened with capitalist reparations, Moscow was most eager to see revolution and most convinced that it should come. But there the majority socialists were most attached to the constitutional order. Indeed, they were the most pro-Western of the German parties, looking to betterment of relations with England and France while strong nationalists were often inclined to look to Russia, Bolshevik or not, for help against the strictures of Versailles.

The German Communist party, which came out of a split of the minority antiwar Independent Social Democrats, was a legion of bitter outs. Set apart from the main currents of German life, opposed by the majority of the workers, facing an efficient, conservative army, this group of self-appointed transformers of society was prodded again and again by the Russians to make a revolution, since according to the book Germany had to have a revolution; but most of their energy went into opposing not the German power structure but the Social Democrats.

Ebbing Revolutionism

In the failure of the world proletariat to cast off its chains, the organization dedicated to that purpose changed from an assemblage of mostly idealistic and independent-minded social radicals to the mindless arm of Soviet dictatorship. Failure increased dependency and dependency made revolutionary success inconceivable. Such was the decadence of the Communist movement that even the near-collapse of capitalism in the economic depression of the 1930's brought no important victories to it, only to reactionary movements nourished on anticommunism.

When Lenin saw revolution in the West inexplicably lagging, he and his party could readily believe the remedy was to reshape the Western parties in the image of the successful Russian party. Each failure, weakening and discrediting the foreign party, delivered it more fully into the control of the Russian leadership of the Comintern and made the Bolshevik model more obligatory. No one could admit a fundamental mistake;

lack of success had to be ascribed to failures of leadership and tactics, while it was assumed as a matter of principle that the strategy of the class struggle should be everywhere the same. This could only mean direction from the center or by the Russian party. Practically, the definition of a Communist came to be one who accepted this discipline, and the essence of the Communist ideology became uncritical adherence to the Soviet pattern. To justify their continued existence in times of no revolutionary prospects, Communist parties in the West rested on Soviet mythology and moral support and the image of a Soviet Russia carrying forward the banner of the era of revolutionary socialism. They could be sustained usually only by Soviet subsidies, which introduced elements of corruption and rotted the last shreds of independence. As they obediently stressed subversive activities, they were further driven to accept tight discipline and complete dependence on the Russian center.

The basis of Comintern control was laid by the Second Congress, 1920, and Comintern statutes remained essentially unchanged thereafter. But the growing strength of the Soviet state, with final victory in civil war, political stabilization, and beginnings of reconstruction raised the Russian party still farther over Western parties struggling in the political wilderness. The Russians, who from the first thought of the Comintern more as a single party than as a league of parties, soon began giving orders directly to its bureaucracy. By 1922 the Comintern was given a structure closely resembling the Russian party and like it suited for central control with some appearances of consultation. Despite the statutory requirement of yearly congresses, these still somewhat representative gatherings were not entirely convenient. None was called for 1923, and only three more ever met.

This tightening and subjection of the Communist movement was accompanied by emphasis on service to the Soviet state. The excuse was that it was essential to guard and strengthen the precious headquarters of world revolutionary socialism; the Bolsheviks believed that their interests were those of the world cause, as the interests of the workers everywhere were by definition the same. As the new order was settled in Russia and failed elsewhere, only Russia was the strength of communism and only on Russia could utopian hopes be based. Within a year of the Revolution, the power of Russia was taken as almost equivalent to the health of the world movement, and it was difficult to know whether "proletarian revolution" was really much more than a slogan useful for morale and self-assurance.

The Russians also began mixing conventional patriotism with revolutionary-socialist emotions. As early as March, 1918, *Pravda* called for greater exertions for the "defense of the socialist fatherland."[28] The civil

---

[28] Frederick C. Barghoorn, *Soviet Russian Nationalism* (New York: Oxford University Press, Inc., 1956), p. 13.

war was in part an antiforeign struggle, because White armies were sponsored, supplied, and seconded by foreign forces. Russian nationalism, which saw the Bolsheviks as the only force capable of holding the domain together, merged with a sort of newly emerging Soviet patriotism, a pride in the Soviet state as a new kind of organization, promising a better life and an example for mankind. As these feelings were fused, it did not much matter whether one thought world revolution indispensable for the Soviet state or the preservation of the Soviet state as necessary for world revolution, or indeed both. In the Polish War, patriotic and revolutionary drives harmonized entirely; the road to Warsaw equally represented restoration of Russian power and extension of the Revolution. While tsarist officers were joining the Red Army, Lenin spoke of the need for the nation, victorious over the bourgeoisie at home, to sacrifice for the international cause. Emotions of Russian greatness revived in step with enthusiastic visions of carrying the torch of revolution to the inflammable West.

When the wars were over, the fusion of interests of the world and national cause disappeared. There was still some expectation that Western revolution would bring economic succor to battered Russia, but this was a fading hope. Trade, perhaps credit from the capitalistic powers hungry for markets, was much more of an immediate possibility than the cooperation of a Communist Germany. Moreover, there entered a contradiction that trying for one hurt chances of getting the other. Failure to carry revolution through Poland with bayonets and the coolness of Polish workers to the call were sobering. The doctrinal retreat of Lenin's New Economic Policy, whereby the dreams of rapid establishment of a communist economy were given up in favor of the advantages of private trading, made it a little ridiculous to daydream of remaking the world and dealt Communist militance a blow from which it never recovered. It began to seem that the millennium might be indefinitely postponed. At the Third Congress of the Comintern, in June–July, 1921, Lenin spoke not as previously of the world movement but of the situation in Russia. The main task, as seen at the Congress, was no longer turning the world upside down but keeping the focus of socialism alive in Russia amid grave difficulties for which the theorists were entirely unprepared.

Eyes turned away from distant ideological involvements to the home front, to the vast needs of rebuilding the fearfully devastated country. In 1922 the May Day slogans for the first time made no mention of World Revolution. Lenin discovered that one Soviet tractor was worth more than ten foreign communists, and that communism, once a social order to be achieved by political action, equaled "Soviet power plus electrification." This was practically equivalent to Stalin's slightly later formulation, "Socialism in One Country."

Since then, the Soviet government has usually been far more concerned with domestic than foreign affairs, and the propagation of world communism has seldom been more than a marginal interest, ordinarily a very minor one. Correspondingly, the importance of Soviet Russia was spelled out more explicitly for the Comintern. The Fourth Congress, in November, 1922, stated plainly that the duty of foreign communist parties was to support the power and greatness of the Soviet state; and the sluggish world proletariat, in a bit of theoretical inconsistency, was blamed for its troubles. Soviet Russia, with the recovery of nearly all the Russian empire, had now returned to the international stage; and its foreign policy was no longer to be attuned to the needs of the Communist movement, but vice versa. Right became not an abstract or international cause but the need of the Soviet state. Such terms as Marxism, proletarian revolution, class struggle, communism, socialism, and the like became words without definite content.

The policies of the Comintern, bound to a revolutionary ideology and wholly subject to Soviet demands, became more ambiguous and troubled as these visibly diverged. The Communists kept telling themselves that a new wave of revolution was sure to come along; and they clung to this myth to justify their existence. Yet there had plainly to be a new strategy after the Comintern Congress in 1921 acknowledged the stabilization of capitalism. The answer was that the parties should turn from the making of revolution, for which they had supposedly been forced into the Leninist mold and subjected to Comintern discipline, to the winning of the masses, for which they had been largely incapacitated. They should work for economic objectives much like the Social Democrats, previously castigated for this sin.

Having divided the left, the Communists were now given the task of an equivocal reunification, the "United Front," directed partly at cooperation with the Social Democrats, more at undercutting them by winning away their membership, first to embrace and then destroy. Real collaboration was impossible, because the Communists were too closely harnessed to the Soviet wagon, and their potential partners had every reason to fear their embrace. The Communists regarded Social Democrats, in the authoritarian mentality, not as misguided but as basically traitorous. They wished to retain full freedom, especially freedom to criticize, never surrendered the claim to sole power, and made no secret of their ultimate objective. Lenin said with Bolshevik frankness that the Communists should support the British Labour party "as the rope supports the man being hanged." Yet the Communists seemed resentful if not surprised when their advances were rebuffed.

The United Front made little headway. A related move was slightly more successful, the establishment of "Front" organizations to bring in people not prepared for active and disciplined work as Communists. Relief societies for the succor of starving Russians were set up to forward

Communist objectives without the organizational demands of the Comintern. A new labor international, the Profintern, was established in 1921 to draw strength away from the Amsterdam International of trade unions affiliated with or sympathetic to the socialist parties. In parallel with the Communist parties, the Profintern tried to arrange a united front with the International which it sought to annihilate. The potential of front organizations was much reduced by the demand for tight control over them, and they amounted to little or nothing until many years later the Fascists provided them, and a better United (or "Popular") Front, with a better cause.

The area where Communist hopes were highest was Germany. Endowed with a large proletariat and advanced industry and held to be a victim of capitalist imperialism, this country was triply suited for revolution. It was also by far the most important country to the Russians, as they fondly nourished visions of coupling German organization and planned production to Russian manpower and resources. In March, 1921, the German Communist party, under Soviet prodding, called the workers again to general strike and insurrection. In the amoralism inherent in the Leninist approach, it was proposed that the party should blow up its own headquarters to shake the workers from the apathy[29] which, being contrary to theory and pretenses, could not be admitted. There was desultory fighting for nearly a week, much of it between Communist and noncommunist workers. Total failure cast gloom over the Comintern Congress a few months later and contributed to its changes of front. The official response, however, was to claim success in the inevitability of history, to shift blame from the Comintern, which had given the instructions, to the Germans who had obeyed, and to begin cleansing the party of dissidents.

After a setback which might have been expected to liquidate it as a political force, the German Communist party recovered strength, as after its other disasters, with remarkable rapidity. This suggests a deep appeal of its authoritarianism to the German milieu, as does the relative success of hard-line communism in the German Democratic Republic in recent years, or the strength and dynamism of the authoritarian Nazis. The Communist appeal was, in fact, perceptibly related to that of the rightists. Radek and others, noting the willingness of many defeated German militarists and industrialists to look eastward, held that German nationalism, like that of the semicolonial Asian countries was not evil, as it was directed against the principal capitalistic powers; communism appeared in their eyes as national bolshevism, true bearer of German national feeling. At the time of the French occupation of the Ruhr, the German Communist party espoused as a hero a young martyr of the resistance who had previously been an anticommunist fighter. For a time Communist and

[29] Braunthal, *History of the International,* Vol. II, p. 237.

Nazi leaders met, and on a few occasions they addressed joint meetings, a practice ended by the Nazis. The Soviet government saw a Rightist Germany as preferable to a Social Democratic one, while the holders of force in Germany were surprisingly indifferent to the blatant and outrageous, although really ineffectual meddling of the Comintern in German politics.

It was in the crisis brought by political troubles, the occupation of the Ruhr in 1923, and accompanying inflation that the German Communist party made its last fling at seizing power. This effort, still more synthetic than the previous one, was planned in detail by the Soviet Politburo. Trotsky, devotee of "Permanent Revolution," was especially eager to stake everything on the German uprising, while Stalin was dubious and in one of his rare pronouncements on Comintern affairs tried to discourage it.[30] Experts and agitators, money and munitions were supplied generously; to assist historical parallels, the date was fixed for November 7. Failing to perceive that radical revolution is impossible unless the armed forces are broken or immobilized, the loyal German Communists went ahead with their schemes. The government forestalled them by dissolving a part-Communist government in Saxony, and the rising was called off except by error, in Hamburg, where disorders were bloodily suppressed. The Reichswehr, despite its favor for a Russian connection for practical purposes, was merciless against a threat of communism at home.

After this, workers' revolution was never again taken seriously, and no real attempt was made to export revolution except by Soviet armies. The Comintern ceased to figure importantly in Soviet calculations, and Lenin's vision of history retained a limited credibility only because a great state theoretically supported it. There were still some hopes for radical movements under Soviet inspiration. Prospects for peasant discontent seemed bright in the Balkans, and a Peasant International was founded in Moscow. Peasant revolutions in Rumania, Yugoslavia, or Bulgaria (where a promising Communist party was crushed by rightist reaction in 1923) were vaguely supposed to lead to "worker-peasant" governments and spill over to more industrialized countries. But the Peasant International was practically stillborn and lapsed in a year.[31] The shattering of hopes for the German revolution to rescue the Russian threw the latter onto its own moral resources and required dealing with a world supposed to be irremediably hostile.

Probing in Asia

Situated between East and West, the Soviet regime, like the tsarist regime before it, shifted its attention whichever way promise was brighter.

[30] Edward H. Carr, *The Interregnum, 1923–1924* (New York: Macmillan Co., 1954), p. 202.

[31] Carr, *The Interregnum, 1923–1924*, pp. 195–96.

At first the gaze of Lenin and other Soviet leaders was entirely riveted on the West, whence should come news of revolution and salvation. As this news failed to arrive and successive flarings of disorder were less and less bright, eyes turned more to the oppressed masses of Asia. But while Soviet policy in Germany was peculiarly befogged by ideological preconceptions, Marxism-Leninism gave few answers about the less developed countries of Asia and their relations with the new socialist Russia. Consequently, dealings with countries on the Asiatic frontiers of Russia were more pragmatic and a little more successful.

That economically backward countries could have anything like a socialist revolution was hardly conceivable in Marxist economic determinism, and the idea that they should contribute importantly to the overthrow of capitalism was alien to European socialism before the Russian Revolution. Even Lenin, in arguing for the socialist possibilities of Russia, was at pains to stress the capitalistic development of that country and the concentration of industry which compensated in part for its overall feebleness. But Lenin was not fussy about economic causation, and he was early impressed by the revolutionary stirrings around Russia's Asian borders, as new forces overthrew or tried to overthrow outworn dynasties in Persia in 1906, in Turkey in 1908, and in China in 1912. In his eclecticism, Lenin saw in these a potential contribution to the world socialist movement, as though any break in the world order meant progress. His politicizing revision of economic determinism gave a theoretical foundation for this interest. If nations, as well as classes, are oppressed, it is in order that they should revolt in wars of liberation. If Russia was suitable for revolution because capitalism was weak there, in Asia capitalism was weaker and the masses were more miserable under harsher imperialist exploitation.

There was some talk of supporting the oppressed peoples of the East from the morrow of the Revolution, but it was not taken seriously until 1920, when Lenin suggested that the basic slogan be amended to "Proletarians of all nations, and oppressed nations, unite," thus fully equating national with class oppression. A dramatic call went out from the "First Congress of the Peoples of the East" held in Baku in September, 1920. This colorful gathering was organized in Bolshevik style, and Zinoviev, president of the Comintern, spoke of the revolutionary destiny of the Asiatic masses; but the delegates, mostly nationalists of Moslem Asia, were interested not in Marxism or socialism but in Holy War against Britain, the chief imperial power of the area.[32]

In that far-off world, in which the British Empire seemed the dominant force on earth, the call for holy revolutionary war against Britain coincided with the needs of Soviet and Russian foreign policy. In the latter

---

[32] George Lenczowski, *Russia and the West in Iran* (Ithaca, N.Y.: Cornell University Press, 1949), p. 8.

decades of the nineteenth century, Russia was perennially in conflict with British power along the Asian frontier. The civil war saw English and Russian forces again contesting the Middle East. Lenin was updating an old rivalry when he reasoned that revolution in Europe might require undercutting capitalism by depriving it of colonial nourishment. Perhaps the millions of India and China would join those of Russia to swing the destiny of mankind, and the road to Paris and Berlin might lie through Delhi and Peking, an attractive fantasy for a hard-pressed state and one which has been revived by Maoist China. Ideology and power politics, Comintern policy and Soviet state interests, often at odds in Europe, coincided neatly in Asia.

How the policy of stirring the Asian periphery of Russia should be understood in doctrinal terms was less clear. When the call went out for revolution, questions had to be decided in Marxist terms—what kind of revolution was to be made for what result, and by whom. In the ordinary understanding of the sequence of stages of history, it was inconceivable that a backward country, in the "feudal" state ("feudal" having acquired a Marxist meaning much broader than that usual in Western historiography) should leap over the stage of capitalism and bourgeois development. Lenin answered the first question much as he had answered it for Russia: colonial countries could indeed make a socialist revolution, that is, go directly to socialism, if assisted by the enlightened proletariat of advanced countries concurrently inaugurating socialism. By extension, they could do so if assisted by the Soviet proletariat, although this was supposedly dependent in turn upon revolution in the West.

This was of somewhat academic significance, as most Bolsheviks, like Lenin, were fairly well satisfied to act as seemed desirable and let the dogma take care of itself. But the question of who was to carry out the revolution was of extreme practical and political importance: What classes should communist parties in Asia recruit for membership, and with whom, if anyone, should they cooperate? A closely related problem, and one which has troubled Soviet foreign policy to this day, was how far to cooperate with governments which were opposed to major capitalist powers but which were noncommunist or anticommunist.

Lenin's answers were as usual practical and politic. Having successfully advocated alliance with the peasantry to make revolution in Russia, he wanted to see peasants stirred by the call for land division in Asia and was prepared, somewhat in the way of Mao, to look to them to power a revolution. This would be nationalistic in spirit, but the party, which in Russia had to inject revolutionary theory into the working class, could guide the peasantry also. Lenin hoped in 1920 that peasant soviets could replace workers' soviets, and the Marxist party could lead the peasant or nationalist revolution toward socialism. Without such elasticity, there would have been practically nothing for communism to do in Asia. The only country with a considerable proletariat, Japan, had no need for nationalistic revolution and was embarrassingly unreceptive to Marxism; the Japanese Communist party through the 1920's was only large enough to arouse the annoyance and hatred of ruling circles and hinder Soviet efforts to improve relations.

The related question of relations with bourgeois elements was more complicated, aroused controversy, and received no satisfactory answer. The First Congress of the Comintern equated liberation of colonies with the overthrow of capitalism, but Lenin advocated translating communism "into the language of each nation," suggesting a good deal of flexibility.[33] Sometimes he spoke as though the Soviet struggle was not so much against capitalism as against imperialism. In his view, any uprising in colonies or semicolonies could be regarded as a blow to capitalism and was hence to be encouraged; anyone in Asia who was anti-British was a potential ally, a position far broader than that assumed in Europe. Communists, then, should support bourgeois nationalists in their own countries for the sake of the world cause, or in practice to harm the opponents of Soviet Russia. As noncommunist nationalist movements were everywhere far stronger than the Asian Communist parties, this meant that revolution should be made by nationalism, not Marxism, led by the bourgeoisie, not the proletariat.

This policy of revolution led by the bourgeoisie and powered by the peasantry suited Soviet state interests fairly well. It also fitted, and was in part a continuation of, nationality policy in the civil war, which required Soviet Russia, standing forth as champion of national liberation, to cooperate with any elements of the minority peoples who would join against the Whites. But it involved contradictions. While for sensible practical reasons the Comintern was favoring working with nonrevolutionary, even bourgeois, groups in Asia, it was for less sensible reasons anathematizing those who would cooperate with moderate socialists in Europe. Lenin admitted "progressive capitalism" in underdeveloped countries, where capitalism was apt to be least progressive; it could not be admitted in Europe, even in small and entirely nonimperialistic nations. Lenin insisted that the party, an organization for which he always had a special fondness, should always firmly maintain its separate organization and freedom of action. But there was some question of the role of a Communist party if the goal was not a communist revolution. The answer was that a Communist party should first cooperate with the bourgeoisie in the national liberation struggle and then turn on the exploiters and destroy them.

It was excessively naïve to expect nationalist leaders to open the doors to an organization dedicated to their undoing; they, possessing the means of

[33] Carr, *Bolshevik Revolution*, Vol. III, p. 236.

force, could be counted on to smash the communist parties instead of waiting to be thrown aside themselves. This is exactly what nationalist recipients of Soviet support did when they perceived a Communist threat, as in China and Turkey. The Communists wanted to use and discard their allies; the outcome was, in Lenin's as in Khrushchev's day, usually the reverse. Nor was cooperation with middle-class nationalists pleasing to the few Communists who could be mustered in Asian countries. Their hatred was first of all against the upper classes in their native land; such hatred was the chief, perhaps only, reason for their being Communists, and to tell them that they should for an indefinite time lay aside their social causes and work with those whom they hated was to condemn them to frustration. The policy was at best a semifailure, as was the Popular Front policy of the latter 1930's for the same reason, the lack of a basis of trust.

These principles were in theory universal but in fact limited to the immediate periphery of the Soviet Union. Southern Asia, Africa, and Latin America were too far from Soviet power and immediate Soviet interest to be seriously considered until after World War II. In its outset, Soviet policy toward the underdeveloped world amounted to policy toward China, Persia (Iran), Afghanistan, and Turkey, each of which presented somewhat different problems and was treated in its own way.

Russian influence in China was destroyed by the Revolution and civil war, and the Soviet government found itself quite cut off from politics in that area for several years. Making the best of this situation, the Soviet government in 1919 grandly renounced Russian special rights and privileges in China. This declaration, issued as Kolchak was pressing hard against the Soviets from the east, was intended to prompt the Chinese to give what help they could to the struggling Soviets and so included the gift of ownership of the Chinese Eastern Railway, which the Russians had built across Manchuria to shorten the journey to Vladivostok.

When the military situation improved in a few months, the manifesto was amended to exclude renunciation of this valuable property, and this imperialistic interest was an important factor in Soviet Far Eastern policy until sold to Japan in 1935.[34] Nor did the Soviet relinquishment of commercial concessions have much importance for the state trading monopoly. Nonetheless, Soviet generosity, at a time when Western powers were disinclined to surrender their special rights in China and the Japanese were making new demands, made a powerful impression on Chinese opinion and much increased willingness on the part of nationalists and intellectuals to look to the Soviet example of anti-imperialism. When no other great power was prepared to deal with China on a basis of formal

---

[34] Allen S. Whiting, *Soviet Policies in China, 1917–1924* (New York: Columbia University Press, 1954), p. 33.

equality, Soviet Russia was for a number of years decidedly successful in influencing events in China.

The outstanding nationalistic intellectual who was much influenced in favor of the Soviet way was Sun Yat-sen, leader of the Nationalist (Kuomintang) party in revolt in southern China. Like most Western-educated Chinese, he was convinced that the country must both westernize and radically reform in order to save itself. Turning from the Western powers, which seemed largely discredited by their selfish actions in China and which raised no shining promise of political redemption, he saw in the Russian Revolution a potential model. In 1923 he met Joffe, who had earlier made his mark as first Soviet ambassador to Berlin; together they issued a statement stressing Soviet support for the "national revolution" in China and agreement that China should strive for unity and independence, not socialism or communism.[35] Sun also requested Comintern assistance in the reorganization of his party. This was given; Michael Borodin, the Comintern emissary, proved an effective party organizer. Leninist methods were better suited for the Chinese than for the Western milieu. For a few years, Soviet relations with the Nationalist movement were close and advantageous to both sides.

To continue and strengthen this relation, helping to build a friendly nationalistic China as a counterweight to both Japan and Britain in the Far East, would seem an obvious and promising Soviet policy. But there was also a Communist party, started in 1920 with the help of Comintern representatives. Like Sun's movement, it was as much nationalist as revolutionary in inception, having grown out of the anti-Japanese movement. The Russians had high hopes for it because, with their penchant for historical parallels, they thought China had had its 1905 revolution in 1912, and so should have its 1917 in the early 1920's. Lenin hence wanted a proletarian nucleus to guide and control the bourgeois-nationalist movement. The solution adopted was for the Communists to join the Nationalist KMT party as individuals, while retaining their own party organization. The Communists, who did not have much mass following, accepted this in hopes of working more effectively through KMT channels if not, with luck, converting it. Sun and his Nationalists were unwilling to enter an alliance with the Communist party but could use the activists in its ranks. The marriage of convenience could function, however, only so long as victory and power were distant; it ended tragically for the Communists after the revolutionary armies pushed victorious to central China and captured Shanghai in 1927.

While Soviet policy was trying to ride the two horses of communism and nationalism, the Foreign Commissariat was also seeking to work with

---

[35] For text see Alvin Z. Rubinstein (ed.), *The Foreign Policy of the Soviet Union* (New York: Random House, Inc., 1966), pp. 100–105.

the ineffectual but internationally recognized government in Peking, dealing not only in revolution but also in ordinary state relations. In 1924, after much haggling, diplomatic recognition was formalized by a treaty confirming the return to China of the tsarist concessions (except the Chinese Eastern Railway). By this and by its propaganda, the Soviet government sought to encourage nationalism among the conservatives or reactionaries of Peking as well as in the bourgeois-based, mildly socialistic Nationalist party and the radicals of the Communist party. But the Peking government was mortally afraid of communism, and relations with Moscow were agitated and unrewarding for both sides. Soviet policy had still another horse to ride in China, the semi-independent warlords of the border regions, with whom Bolshevik commissars dealt in a spirit of pure power politics in Oriental style. Soviet policy in China during the early 1920's showed a good dose of realism, shaded and confused by ideological preoccupations which ultimately wrecked the good start.

With Persia, problems and opportunities were different. There was no nationalist revolution going on, as one had already succeeded in 1909; and communists were still fewer than in China. On the other hand, there was much turmoil, giving rise to dreams of revolution in Persia opening the door of the Orient.[36] As the Red Army pressed to completion of the conquest of the Caucasus, it came to the aid of an uprising in the former tsarist sphere of influence in Persia; and in 1920 the so-called Ghilan Republic was formed. Its leaders were Iranian nationalists, Caucasian dissidents, and Russian Bolsheviks, using the language of the Comintern but lacking any coherent policies. The situation was remarkably parallel to Stalin's attempt to carve out an Azerbaidzhan republic in 1946; and in 1920 as in 1946 the Russians were unable to establish a solid regime. Lenin decided, against Stalin's wishes but in agreement with Chicherin and the Foreign Commissariat, that improvement of relations with Persia and Britain was more important than maintaining the puppet regime. Soviet troops were withdrawn in September, 1921, after a stay of a year and a half, and the Persian army stamped out the revolt without difficulty. Despite their universalism, the Bolsheviks had a good deal of respect for the boundaries of the empire which they had inherited.

While Soviet troops were in Ghilan, a treaty formalizing diplomatic relations and the annulment of tsarist concessions had been signed; and after Soviet forces were withdrawn, an ambassador was allowed to take up residence in Teheran. It was officially declared that socialist revolution in Persia would have to await the consolidation of bourgeois development; reassured, the shah, Reza Khan, for a time had rather cordial relations with the Soviet government. This regarded him as a man of the

---

[36] Lenczowski, *Russia and the West*, p. 10.

people and a promising progressive and lent no support to antigovernment movements in the northern part of the country. However, the Soviet government was not troubled by the contradiction of dealing with the shah and calling on his "working class" to struggle for communism, and the Soviet ambassador busied himself assisting the leftist press and movements. Although relations cooled somewhat, as the shah harassed Persian communists, they remained fairly good for many years.

For centuries Turkey had been much more a hereditary foe of Russia than Persia, and the border was less well defined. In the Russian weakness of the Revolution, Turkey was able to recover two provinces, Kars and Ardahan, taken by Russia in the previous century and inhabited by neither Turks nor Russians. The two provinces remained a Soviet irredenta and were claimed by Stalin after World War II. Thus, there was ample reason for friction between the two states. However, Turkey like Russia was an empire on the edge of Europe and subject (although much less than Russia) to Western influence and westernizing drives prior to World War I. Like Russia it was defeated, and the shattered old order was replaced by a radical revolutionary regime led by Kemal Atatürk. Differing from the Bolshevik revolution particularly in lacking universalism, which the relatively modest size of the Turkish domain did not inspire, Kemal's revolution was fundamentally akin to it. In fighting the Western powers, it adopted Western and modern, partly socialistic patterns, including secular education, reduction of the established religion, emancipation of women, much control of the economy and industrialization by the state, and a monopoly of foreign trade. Kemal was a natural ally for the Bolsheviks.

For a time, relations were close. Radek in 1919 proposed that Turkish nationalism and Bolshevik proletarianism should join against British imperialism;[37] and in 1920 Kemal, still fighting in the windup of the war, urged such an alliance. The Soviet leadership, getting over initial uncertainty as to whether principles allowed cooperation with a nonsocialist state, came to an entente. Under it, the Bolsheviks were free to recover nearly all the Caucasus which the tsars had held, but they were to refrain from agitation in Anatolia. They also sent arms and military advisers to help the Turks against the Greeks. Kemal adopted the Leninist terminology of the "oppressed peoples" against "international capital" to end the "rule of the bourgeoisie." He also for a time was affiliated with the Comintern through a fake Turkish Communist party, although he firmly repressed Turkish Communists and had some of them tossed into the sea.

As the Turks came toward victory and saw less need for Soviet aid, the

---

[37] Edward H. Carr, *German-Soviet Relations between the Two World Wars* (Baltimore, Md.: Johns Hopkins Press, 1951), p. 18.

friendship cooled. At the Lausanne Conference in November, 1922, the Soviet delegation, proposing full Turkish control and closure of the Straits, took a position more favorable to the Turks than did the Turkish delegation, now more desirous of pleasing the British. But in 1923, Bukharin saw Turkey as playing an objectively revolutionary role by virtue of opposition to imperialism. Turkish suppression of procommunist tendencies became more severe, but Moscow was inclined only to raise an occasional cry of pain while doing nothing to disturb continued good relations.

Soviet relations with Afghanistan were simpler. There was no Communist movement, as Afghanistan, unlike Persia, had seen no consequential Western penetration; and politics, although complicated, was quite feudal. The contest between Soviet and British influence in Afghanistan, despite some revolutionary phraseology, seemed little more than an updating of the long-standing rivalry. The king was more anti-British than anti-Bolshevik, and a treaty of friendship signed in February, 1921, provided that the Soviet government would render him economic assistance. For several years, the desperately impoverished Soviet regime paid a subsidy of half a million dollars yearly (mostly in goods) to an oriental monarch. Since then, in the absence of native communism and of apparent Soviet desires to export or promote it artificially, the Soviet state has enjoyed more tranquil and generally friendly relations with Afghanistan than with any other neighbor.

In its revolutionary-internationalist impulse, Soviet power spread out to the limits of the Russian empire, even encompassing the tsarist protectorate of Mongolia. But the revolutionary wave halted there, and dreams of inflaming Asia proved as empty as those of raising Poland and Germany. This is a little strange, as the ideas and ways of bolshevism were (and are) more applicable to poor countries than rich, to authoritarian countries of backward social order than to relatively democratic ones. A key element of bolshevism is a protest against the penetration and disruption of Western capitalism, and for this reason Leninism has always had an emotional appeal to peoples ready to blame capitalistic imperialism for their poverty and backwardness. Yet prior to Khrushchev, the Soviet Union had only slight or ephemeral success in the underdeveloped world.

One reason was a limitedness of Russian horizons, broad as these were. In the civil war, the Soviet forces were mostly Russians and operated to some degree in the Russian tradition; what had belonged to the tsars was theirs to recover, so far as this could be done with available strength. Revolutionary internationalism was vital to consolidation of Soviet control of the borderlands; once these had been secured, it could be allowed to flag. Beyond the old frontiers, the Russians had no great urge to press. The Soviet government for several decades afterwards paid very little attention, even in propaganda, to the great needy world beyond. Poverty was a potent restraint. It was futile indeed for the Russian government, sunk in economic breakdown on top of backwardness, to be devoting much effort and attention to Asian lands which, unlike Western countries, could not give anything if they should become socialist but would demand aid from Russia.

The situation slowly improved after 1922, when famine brought the Soviet regime to its economic nadir and even Chinese delegates to a Congress of Toilers of the Far East in Moscow were disconcerted by the bad food.[38] But the Soviet economy could supply neither the goods furnished by the Western exploiters of less advanced countries nor the means of power which would help procommunist or pro-Soviet parties to prevail. And the Soviet state itself was constrained by economic need. The First Congress of the Peoples of the East remained the last, and its journal soon ceased to appear, probably because trade with England (a trade agreement was signed in March, 1921) was more important than propagation of the revolutionary message.

After 1921 consolidation rather than advance was the keynote of Soviet policy in the neighboring Asian countries. Lenin was prepared to deal with potentates as long as they were prepared to deal with the Soviet government and preferably took a fairly anti-Western or anti-British stance. In a concession to practicality, the sacred principle of the state monopoly of foreign trade was sacrificed, and private merchants were allowed to travel and trade across the borders to China, Afghanistan, and Persia—a measure doctrinally rationalized on the grounds that these countries had "trade capitalism," in contrast to the "finance capitalism" of the West.[39] This dispensation lasted until near the end of the 1920's and the great tightening of incipient Stalinism.

Soviet policy in Asia, facing situations quite alien to Marxist schemes of history, showed fair adaptability, although unable to free itself entirely from ideological preconceptions and always inclined to lay hopes on any group which was prepared to subscribe to Bolshevik doctrines. The remarkable fact, however, is not change but continuity, as more ambitious and better supported efforts of post-Stalin leaders to advance Soviet influence in the underdeveloped world met the same dilemmas—to theorize nationalistic and peasant movements into a Marxist scheme or to hold to doctrinal consistency, to support native leaders who were determined to remain independent or to earn their enmity by helping subversive movements, to cultivate antiwesternism for its own sake or to esteem the goodwill of Western powers.

---

[38] Robert C. North, *Moscow and the Chinese Communists* (Stanford, Calif.: Stanford University Press, 1953), p. 62.

[39] Louis Fischer, *Soviets in World Affairs, 1917–1929*, Vol. II, p. 588.

5. NORMAL STATE RELATIONS

Antipathies and Practicalities

For an age hardened to political extremism, it is hard to imagine how shocking the Bolshevik seizure of power was to civilized Western society. Until World War I brought its senseless destruction, the world had progressed steadily, both economically and politically. The way of the enlightened future was that of improved freedom and order through constitutional, representative government, as proved in the most advanced countries. It was taken for granted that the means to increased wealth was the one which had served to elevate the free nations to modernity—maximum respect for the rights of private property. Russia had been following, although at some distance, the general trend to improvement both in the growth of a Western-style economy and toward a moderate and unoppressive political system. In the forward way of the world, Russia, and other nations farther from the Western pattern, such as Turkey and China, could only be expected to continue on this road. If a country wished to share the blessings of civilization, it had to adopt the ways of civilization.

The Bolsheviks seemed to assault almost everything taken for granted in a country like England or the United States. If the reaction of shocked amazement was not tremendous, it was due only to engrossment in the struggle against Germany, paucity of information, and a belief that Bolshevism could not be quite real, could not be so radical in practice, and certainly, in the tumultuous Russian scene, could not last. Openly contemptuous of legality, contract, and all accepted codes, the Bolsheviks were viewed as wild agitators who had gained power by shameless demagoguery and by stirring up the lowest classes against their betters. They therefore were not be considered a government. It seemed out of reason to recognize them as such—the more so as they did not pretend to be an ordinary government but spoke madly of doing away with all governments as they had been known. Not only did the Bolsheviks proclaim their purpose of destroying the basic principle of society, private property, but they scorned all accepted political systems, liberal-democratic as well as traditional-monarchic; and they sought to replace by some new creed the fundamental principle of the Western state system, national loyalty.

Further acquaintance with bolshevism, as it developed in practice, deepened the horror. Perfidious abandonment of the war strengthened the conviction that Lenin and his henchmen were not representative of the nation but a sorry accident. The Leninists insolently claimed a superior morality, which degraded all morality. They taunted the respectable world with bad manners and barbaric arrogance. They repudiated treaties and debts. They had utmost contempt for individualism, thrift, and the respected virtues of hardworking middle-class society. They scorned legal and judicial process. They persecuted not just a particular religion but all religions, both by propaganda and violence, destroying churches and murdering priests; and who could come to a decent understanding with the offensively godless? They undermined the family, millennial pillar of social order; reports persistently had it that the women of Russia, like its industry, had been nationalized.

The feelings of the West are exemplified by the comments of a sober, factual publication, *Whitaker's Almanac*, which for 1919 stated, "Under Bolshevik rule the country has been given over to anarchy and promiscuous assassination." For 1920 the comment was, "Bolshevik rule has proved to be anarchy accompanied by indiscriminate slaughter and outrage," and for 1921, "Soviet rule has hitherto been accompanied by indiscriminate slaughter and outrage." To accept such a regime was to condone its crimes, social, national, and international. Until at length it became apparent that the Bolsheviks were not going to be replaced by some more respectable authority, it was difficult indeed for the Western powers to contemplate receiving them into the community of civilized nations.

There is no need to inquire as to how much of this attitude was justified. There were certainly elements of haughtiness and smugness, of selfish conceit on the part of elites which did not perceive that their benignly progressing world lacked justice for many, both of the less affluent classes and of colonial peoples. The Bolsheviks felt that their cause was entirely right, and they were not much more inclined at first to see the need for normal state relations with the imperialist-capitalist powers than these were with them. For the Bolsheviks, too, the other side lacked legitimacy, and there was little point in trying to deal seriously with them as they could not be expected to last long. Lenin looked upon the diplomatic deals of traditional states as mere robbers' quarrels, and to this day Soviet writers maintain that socialist international relations are entirely dissimilar to those of the power-minded, aggressive, and inherently imperialistic capitalist states. The drives of socialist nations, that is, are held to be essentially peaceful, while war is an outcome of capitalism. Believing the Western powers unprincipled, the Bolsheviks felt free to act without principle toward them. Economic and class relations, moreover, were essential, while political relations were secondary. The duty of the Soviet state was not to traffic with the capitalist governments but to assist, or at least cheer, their overthrow.

Even when it became desirable or unavoidable to have dealings with

Western powers, the Soviet government failed to perceive or chose to ignore the contradiction between carrying on normal relations with a state and working to subvert it. The leaders kept the habits of revolutionary agitators. As revolutionaries, they had no patience with niceties and legalities and held it natural that Soviet embassies should be centers of propaganda against the governments to which they were accredited. As former conspirators, they had few inhibitions regarding tactics. Intolerant and rigid in dogmatic positions at home, they were intolerant and dogmatically rigid in treating with foreigners. Accustomed to exaggeration and violent language, they subjected foreign leaders to violent propagandistic barrages, abuse, and insults. Moralistically oriented, accustomed to a world of black and white, they had little idea of realistic bargaining and compromise but felt satisfied in a stance of righteous principle; it was enough (and the habit has not been lost to this day) to answer an opponent by denigration of his motives.

Worst was the expectation of hostility. Russia had long viewed the West with distrust, and this feeling was reinforced by the isolation and trauma of World War I. The Marxist-Leninist world view multiplied xenophobia by postulating irreconciliable class conflict between socialist Russia and reactionary capitalist Western countries. It gave a theoretical reason for Western aggression; capitalist states could have only evil intentions toward the Soviet state which mortally threatened them by daring to exist. This idea owed much to the reality of the civil war and intervention, as well as to Marxist teachings. In the war, it became a summons for mobilization and a plea for support, uniting patriotic defense with the revolutionary cause. After the war, it was easily retained, as Lenin said in 1920 that the countries which had failed in the intervention could not permanently accept the existence of a socialist state; and it continued to be useful as a call for dedication and a justification for discipline.

Soviet Russia and the leading Western states thus seemed practically doomed to bad relations and endless misunderstandings. But Lenin, ever more disposed than most of his associates to acknowledge reality, changed his ideas about the possibility of a socialist state getting along with capitalist ones; and Western statesmen began to think of the Bolshevik regime not as a bunch of irresponsible adventurers unaccountably possessed of authority but as political leaders to reckon with even if they were evil. As it became obvious that both sides were likely to be around indefinitely, it became equally obvious that they had to do business and could profit by doing so. The revolution was over; normalization was on the way.

Much of the change of attitude was on the part of the Western powers. They discovered to their amazement that the Bolsheviks actually could manage a government; military victory vindicated the Soviet regime as victory usually does. As the war with Germany was left behind, anger over the separate peace abated. With the end of the civil war and the Allies' involvement in it, passions cooled. Far from chafing for a new conflict, the Western powers desired nothing so much as tranquillity. The strident voices of Russian émigrés, who had much to do with policies of Western states while these had little direct information from Russia, were less heard. It appeared that many of the worst reports were not true; Russian women had not been nationalized. Lenin in fact was rather straitlaced, and much of Russian life and government seemed to proceed in fairly conventional channels. As the world settled down, Russia could not be ignored as a power factor, albeit at first a feeble one. By no means least, a Europe in considerable economic trouble could not help looking with exaggerated hopes to the largest country of the world, partly for inexpensive raw materials customarily drawn from Russia, more for a market for manufactures. The Western need for trade was much less than the Russians in their self-inflation imagined, but it was enough to overcome a good deal of ideological distaste. Consequently, as soon as the effort to displace the Bolshevik regime was given up, the Western powers were receptive to any indications of return of sanity and normalcy and ready to renew some kind of relations even with a self-styled socialist and revolutionary Russia.

Bolshevik Russia did not fail to show signs of what the West regarded as sanity. The needs of universalist revolution diverged immediately from those of the state as a state. The failure of the semirevolutionary call for peace trumpeted on the morrow of the seizure of power compelled the Soviet government to begin deciding like a nation to carry on or wind up the war with Germany. They tried in vain to evade the issue; Trotsky's "No war, no peace" was a revolutionary bleat. The decision taken was unpleasant for the Allies, but it meant that, as an idealistic Bolshevik, Uritsky, lamented, "Having seized power, we have forgotten about world revolution."[40]

As revolution hung fire, diplomatic relations could be useful for the security of the world socialist center, the Soviet state. The theme of inevitable conflict with capitalist states because of their very nature, however useful for requiring sacrifice at home, was not necessarily operative in foreign policy. To the contrary, Lenin was prepared to collaborate (although without much trust or intimacy, just as Communists in the underdeveloped countries were instructed to collaborate with bourgeois nationalists without merging or surrendering freedom of action) with some foreign countries against others, to exploit divisions in the capitalist

---

[40] Carr, *Bolshevik Revolution,* Vol. III, p. 46.

world and to divide potentially hostile governments. This was rationalized, of course, in terms of revolutionary strategy, but it amounted to perfectly understandable *Realpolitik* and balance-of-power politics.

The effort to profit by divisions among capitalist powers was contrary to Marxist spirit and emphasis on the primacy of class conflict, but it agreed well with Lenin's philosophy and ideas of the selfish and shortsighted drives of the bourgeois state. Russia, the semicolonial exploitation of which Lenin held of great importance for the imperialist states, could divide them not only by diplomacy but by offering concessions for the development of Russian resources. Lenin called this a form of war against capitalism in an exemplary demonstration of the ability to rationalize almost anything. The Soviet government, desperately eager for foreign capital and credits and for trade on any terms possible, was convinced that Western powers must be driven by their thirst for profits to respond. There was consequently very soon an effort to separate party and government dealings. While the former went on its agitational career, the latter tried to do business; the less prospects for the former, the more interest in the latter. In dealing, one becomes habituated to compromise and neglect of principle, and there was good reason to hope that the Soviet state and the Western powers could learn to get along at least fairly well.

Hiatus of Civil War

The way of Russia back into the community of nations would have been much easier and quicker if no civil conflict had jeopardized the existence of the Bolshevik regime and ranged it and the Western powers on opposite sides of a confused war. A long and fearsome chain of troubles might have been lessened if not avoided. During several years of fighting, the Bolshevik state was hardened in its militance and authoritarianism, and attitudes of hostility became ingrained on both sides. Promoting the overthrow of capitalism took on new urgency, to save the Soviet system as well as to bring a happier world order. The Western powers, having committed men, money, and prestige to the overthrow of the Bolsheviks, found it harder and more humiliating to swallow the necessity of dealing with them as equals. Relations were in complete abeyance for a long time; the respective sides became accustomed to lack of diplomatic contact and adjusted to it, much as the United States became completely adjusted to lack of diplomatic and commercial relations with Communist China. Whereas ending relations meant breaking a habit, their reopening meant breaking another habit.

Efforts at negotiation were made at various times between the peace of Brest Litovsk and the end of the civil war. Already in 1918 the Soviet government was trying to interest capitalists, especially American, who seemed less dangerous than others, in concessions. A note on this subject sent to the American government in October was, however, so insulting as to have a contrary effect. By December, the Bolsheviks changed their tune and approached Wilson more tactfully in an appeal to his humanity and sense of justice. The attempt to get American support against Britain and France was not entirely unsuccessful, and Wilson wanted to invite the Soviets to the Paris Peace Conference. The French vetoed this, perhaps misguidedly, as the Russians felt excluded from the Versailles system and permanently hostile to it until the Nazi threat overtook them. The French and minor Allies were generally inclined to a hard anti-Bolshevik line, while Wilson and Lloyd George were more moderate; all, however, were decidedly ignorant of events in Russia.

In 1919 there was an effort to get Bolsheviks and their White opponents to discuss peace at a meeting on the Turkish island of Prinkipo. The Bolsheviks with customary elasticity accepted and, with some imputation that the Allies could be bought, hinted extensive territorial or economic concessions in hopes of buying time. The French sabotaged the meeting and the anti-Bolsheviks rejected it. In April the Bolsheviks agreed to a peace proposal amounting to partitioning the empire, as there should be an armistice with each authority retaining the territory it controlled.[41] As usually occurs in contests of bitter enemies, while the side feeling itself losing might be amenable to compromise, the confident side insisted on its principles. In the civil war, the Whites were usually overconfident. The Bolsheviks, in their distress, were more desirous of negotiations and diplomatic relations; but they were rebuffed. Anti-Bolshevism became a major theme of the Paris Peace Conference, as weaker powers used it as their best argument. Thus, Poland had to have a loan to ward off the danger, and Germany needed food for the same purpose. Until the civil war was decided, doors did not open but only closed tighter.

Emergence, 1919–22

As the civil war dragged toward a close, the Russians began looking toward a peaceful order and some sort of normalization. In late 1919, Chicherin, the Soviet foreign commissar, was speaking of the need of economic cooperation with England, and the British, drawing away from the French stand of unyielding opposition to Bolshevism, began thinking of prospects of trade. About the same time, negotiations were begun in Copenhagen between British and Soviet representatives regarding prisoners, the first formal contact made by any Allied government with the Soviets in more than a year. An agreement for exchange of prisoners in February, 1920, was followed by such agreements with other countries.

[41] A. A. Akhtamzian (ed.), *Istoriia mezhdunarodnykh otnoshenii i vneshnei politiki SSSR*, Vol. I: 1917–1939 (Moscow: Izdatelstvo Mezdunarodnye Otnosheniia, 1967), p. 105

The Allied blockade had been officially lifted in January, and Lloyd George expressed the fairly well-justified hope, often cherished since then, that commerce would civilize the Bolsheviks.

On lifting the blockade, the Allies advised the new Baltic states to establish normal relations with the new Soviet Russia. Exhausted Russia was willing to undertake what Chicherin called the first "experiment in peaceful coexistence," although Lenin, forgetting that peace is the enemy of revolution, justified the peace on the dubious logic that Estonia was about to have its revolution anyway. In February, 1920, peace was signed with Estonia on liberal terms designed to impress world opinion, including an indemnity in gold (the noncommercially inclined Bolsheviks of the first years were rather free with the metal inherited from their predecessors). Diplomatic relations were established, and Estonia soon became a funnel for Soviet trade, what there was of it, with the West. The other Baltic states followed quickly, as did Finland. In another turn toward conventional behavior, the Soviet government formally asserted itself as successor to the rights of the tsarist government, specifically in regard to Spitzbergen.[42]

Although the blockade was ended, trade was minimal, as the Bolsheviks had hardly anything to sell and no means of payment, except gold, of which they had obtained about $500 million. This was boycotted in the West as stolen property, but it was sold through Estonia and Scandinavia until reluctance to touch it was broken by love of gain. In hopes of swelling the trickle of trade, the British opened unofficial talks in May, 1920, not with the Soviet government, which was still inadmissible, but with Russian cooperatives, which were in fact agents of the government. An unofficial trade agreement was negotiated at this time with Sweden.

The trend toward normalization was interrupted by the resumption of armed conflict in the summer of 1920, the war with Poland and then the last major flareup of civil war, the Wrangel campaign in south Russia. In the latter part of the year, however, the idea of concessions to capitalist interests, mooted in 1918, reappeared. An American concern negotiated for rights in Kamchatka, a Soviet tactic to secure American protection against Japan. Trotsky hopefully said, with reference to the United States, "Not only can we live with bourgeois governments, we can work with them within very broad limits." *De facto* diplomatic relations were established with Germany in July. Lenin said in November, 1920, that the continued existence of the Soviet state depended on division in the ranks of the capitalist powers, a significant change from the position that it depended on their succumbing to a revolutionary storm; and playing capitalist powers against each other required normal if not friendly relations with at least some of them.

---

[42] Carr, *Bolshevik Revolution,* Vol. III, p. 158.

The real turn came in the spring of 1921. The end of the civil war saw a psychological reaction and yielding to lassitude. The drive to world revolution had come to nothing, the German Communists having floundered in their second major effort. The effort to introduce a socialist economic order at home had also come to grief and given way to Lenin's New Economic Policy. Utopia was not a near prospect, and there was a new awareness of mundane material values. The acceptance of private trade and small-scale capitalism to rescue the Soviet economy in the face of hunger and discontent implied compromise abroad for the sake of trade. Reconstruction was the order of the day and the way to advance the cause; Lenin, much as Khrushchev nearly forty years later, said Russian economic success should be the key to the world victory of socialism. If concessions to native bourgeois elements were useful, equally might foreign capital and capitalists be invited to cooperate; and Soviet Russia, not much troubled by the incongruity of continuing to proclaim absolute abhorrence of capitalism, began seriously to look for credit and investors.

The Anglo-Russian trade agreements which had been under dilatory discussion for ten months were wound up in March. They got over the question of claims by ignoring them, implied *de facto* recognition, and cost the Soviet side a promise to refrain from propaganda—which was indeed somewhat abated. Commercial agreements with various other countries followed, but there was no rush to closer relations; and in the atmosphere of distrust, offers of concessions found few takers, the most successful being some Scandinavian concerns. Those who had intervened in Russia against the Bolsheviks for supposedly powerful reasons did not soon change attitudes, although fear of bolshevism declined as the West returned to stability and the Bolsheviks seemed safely confined within their borders.

The atmosphere was also improved by the famine relief given by the United States without conditions or return, a lesson to Bolshevik leaders, although they dismissed it as selfishly motivated. But large areas of friction remained. Even while seeking commercial concessions, the Bolsheviks could not bring themselves to give up their duality of policy, and they were in the curious position of trying most energetically to undermine and cultivate the self-same states. Most revolutionary activity was directed against Britain (especially in Persia and India) and Germany, the states whose goodwill was most important, the one as market and potential source of credit, the other as the only potential friend among the Western powers. The pretense that the Comintern was separate from the Soviet government only made it a little easier to ignore antipropaganda clauses regularly inserted in commercial conventions.

Outwardly, most controversy was over the tsarist debts, which the Soviet government had immediately and scornfully repudiated, and the claims of owners of confiscated private property. Concerning them, in the early 1920's, there were endless pourparlers and conferences, all resulting only in irritation. The debts of the tsarist and provisional governments, amounting to the equivalent of some tens of billions of dollars, were large enough to be worth repudiating; and the Bolsheviks, more on practical than principled grounds, were of no mind to assume responsibility for them. To offset Allied claims, Chicherin presented a huge bill for losses due to the Allied intervention, but the Soviet side was willing to pay something if at the same time it could get large credits. It might have been possible to reach an accommodation here, but the question of private debts was stickier; the Western powers were more insistent and the Russians less yielding in regard to private than public interests. Agreement was impossible in the long run, although it several times seemed near. In time, the Western powers softened their position, but the Bolsheviks hardened theirs as they became less desperate for economic assistance as recovery proceeded. Fairly soon, benefiting from capitalist competition, they were getting credits from eager sellers, Germany and Italy in the lead, on a purely commercial basis.

Debt negotiations, however, led to another major step in the slow return of Russia to the international company. A great diplomatic conclave at Genoa in April–May, 1922, met to settle the relations of Soviet Russia to the capitalist world and to outline projects for international cooperation in the Russian economy. It was the first appearance of Soviet diplomats on the world stage; the West, which a few years earlier would have been rather horrified, awaited their appearance with much curiosity. Coming frankly as merchants, they had studied protocol; and to the pleasurable surprise of the West they showed up in top hats, cutaways, and silk gloves.[43] Their behavior was not much less conventional. Lenin had instructed the delegation to seek agreement in hopes of forwarding the peaceful evolution of capitalism to socialism, the possibility of which he doubted but was willing to try. The Soviet government had already acknowledged tsarist obligations in principle; and Chicherin, recognizing the permanence of the old order along with the new, called for collaboration in reconstruction, disarmament, and internationalization of waterways. There was bickering about concessions, properties in Russia, and oil fields; agreement could not be reached because the West demanded protective guarantees which the Russians, ever extremely sensitive on the issue of sovereignty, would not consider. The Genoa Conference meant recognition of Soviet Russia as a formal equal of the great powers, although none of them had yet granted *de jure* recognition. Its only important concrete result was a great deal different from what its sponsors intended, the Rapallo agreement between Russia and Germany, the Soviet

[43] Louis Fischer, *Soviets in World Affairs, 1917–1929,* Vol. I, p. 321.

regime's first diplomatic success as well as one of its most brilliant.

German Breakthrough

For some years, relations between defeated Germany and ostracized Russia had been relatively warm. The Leninist view of imperialism regarded all nations as equally guilty for the war; the Russians, excluded from the postwar system, saw Germany as a fellow defeated nation and sufferer at the hands of the Allied powers and potential ally against Poland. Germany, on the other hand, was ready to receive a crumb of support from anywhere, particularly as friction continued over such issues as Upper Silesia. Various German circles, such as generals bitter in defeat and industrialists mindful that Germany had supplied nearly half the imports of tsarist Russia, were extremely eager, despite the antithesis of political philosophies, to join hands with the Russians. Of practical necessity, the German government looked west, but it sought to strengthen its position by leaning east. The first independent act of German foreign policy after defeat was refusal, in 1919, to participate in the blockade of Russia. In 1920 there was an agreement for mutual repatriation of prisoners; and many Germans looked with glee to the prospective defeat of Poland, with hopes of possibly recovering eastern territories in *de facto* cooperation with the Bolsheviks.

Having learned something from the failure of Joffe's scandalous conduct, new Soviet envoys to Germany behaved rather cautiously and kept fairly well out of Comintern affairs, which were conducted directly between Moscow and the Communist party. Even before diplomatic relations were resumed, the German Reichswehr, independently of the civilian government, began working out arrangements for evading restrictions of the Treaty of Versailles by making and practicing with prohibited equipment, planes, tanks, and submarines in Russia, in return cooperating in the training of the Red Army. The German military were no more troubled by accepting arms from the state which was working for the overthrow of their government than the Bolsheviks were by simultaneously arming the German communists and the Reichswehr which was to suppress them.

The groundwork was thus prepared for a political entente. Not long before the Genoa meeting, an advantageous commercial agreement had been signed between the two powers, in the Soviet style of treating trade as a token of political attitudes, much as a trade agreement preceded the Nazi-Soviet pact of 1939. At Genoa, the Germans found themselves ostracized and fearful of complete isolation if the Russians came to agreement with the Entente powers, a possibility which the Russians allowed them to believe might well occur. The Treaty of Versailles, moreover, had unintentionally placed a trump in the hands of the Russians: for the sake of an expected anti-Bolshevik government, Russia was given title to reparations from Germany. The Germans feared that they might thus be called upon to pay the defaulted French-held Russian bonds; the Russians could trade renunciation of this claim for German renunciation of its claims, which were slight, against Soviet Russia.

This rather innocuous mutual renunciation, along with the resumption of *de jure* diplomatic and consular relations, was the principal provision of the Rapallo agreement, as it was named after the spa near Genoa where the German and Soviet negotiators privately met. However, it created a great stir in the West and has been held up ever since as the symbol of German-Russian understanding. Its importance was mostly psychological. Germany and Russia ended their isolation, acting together in defiance of Allied opinion. It practically wrote finis to the whole question of debts and claims, as Russia obligated itself to give Germany benefits equal to any settlement made with any other power. It gave the Soviet leaders confidence in their ability to divide the Western powers, that is, to play power politics like other nations, and so increased the preference for dealing with bourgeois governments rather than revolutionary workers. The German Communist party took some time to digest the fact that Soviet attitude toward a bourgeois government depended much less on the needs of the world movement than on its relations to Soviet state policy.

In the next year or so, Soviet-German relations moved to their maximum cordiality. Russia turned to strong denunciation of Versailles, as colonizing Germany for the benefit of "the imperialist robbers." The struggle against Versailles was regarded as a struggle against capitalism, as though a continuation of the civil war; and the German fight for liberation was seen as parallel with nationalist movements of Asia. Chicherin even suggested German-Soviet cooperation in Turkey, Persia, and Afghanistan;[44] the Germans declined lest England be antagonized.

Communist policies in Germany also suffered the contradictions between national and revolutionary goals which plagued them in underdeveloped countries. Comintern plotting was tolerated to a remarkable degree, but it prevented the development of any real confidence; without it, one might suppose the two states would have naturally drifted into true alliance. There was more muddle than method in the Soviet dual policy: the Foreign Commissariat, headed by Chicherin and supported by Lenin so far as he was not incapacitated, wanted to do business with the government; the Comintern, with Trotsky, Zinoviev, and Kamenev, wanted energetic fomenting of insurrection. In 1923 the Soviet government took up the German national cause against the French occupation of the Ruhr, while the German Communist party continued to exert itself

[44] Louis Fischer, *Soviets in World Affairs, 1917–1929,* Vol. II, p. 591.

for revolution. In the fall of 1923, after Germany had disappointed the Russians by coming to terms with France, the Comintern had its way in planning a "German October." Its failure led to a crisis of German-Soviet governmental and trade relations, as Soviet offices were raided and citizens were arrested. Although this was patched up, improved relations of Germany with the West decreased the urge to look to the unattractive eastern partner, and German-Soviet relations never recovered their earlier warmth. Withal, it was Germany which helped Russia out of isolation after the Revolution, as Lenin and his fellows had confidently expected. But it was the German Right which brought assistance; dealings with German Marxism brought the Soviets only frustration.

Return to the Community, 1922–25

After the Genoa Conference, there was further progress along the road to accommodation and normalization of relations between Russia and the capitalist world. The Japanese finally withdrew their forces from Siberia, and fairly normal relations had been established with nearly all the countries on the Soviet borders. Chronic Anglo-French friction precluded any united anti-Soviet front. It had become fairly well accepted in the West that Russia would have its strange economic and political system; many, like the Poles, felt it was as well to have a weak Red Russia as a presumably stronger and more nationally aggressive White Russia. In the economic retreat of the New Economic Policy it was coming to seem more and more likely that Russia would revert, under compulsions of reality, to something like capitalism. *Whitaker's Almanac*, which had written of the Bolsheviks in terms of anarchy and massacre, in its 1922 and 1923 editions retreated to merely emphasizing the mercenary armed forces on which the regime allegedly rested, and for 1924 expressed approval of its economic reforms.

At this time, there entered what became a recurrent theme of Soviet diplomacy, disarmament. Lenin, who earlier had rejected the idea as a delusion distracting the masses from revolution, came to believe that disarmament negotiations could be useful to strengthen pacific inclinations in the West.[45] In December, 1922, a disarmament conference in Moscow was attended by Poland, Finland, and the three Baltic republics. Concrete results were nil, but it seemed politically advantageous to Russia; and it was followed by many moves in this direction, whereby Russia had nothing to lose and something to gain in terms of world opinion. Soviet propaganda also began giving more attention to the preservation of peace and less to the stirring of agitated situations. Somewhat inconsistently, Russia was and long remained resolutely opposed to the League of

[45] Lincoln P. Bloomfield *et al.*, *Krushchev and the Arms Race* (Cambridge, Mass.: MIT Press, 1966), p. 8.

Nations, which it regarded as largely directed against itself, in the conviction that the Soviet experiment was the center of world affairs. However, the Soviet government began attending specialized agencies of the League.

Much of the road was uphill, as basic attitudes remained. Soviet oil was sold with difficulty in 1922–23, since it was treated as stolen property. Prepared to pay less for recognition as the need became less urgent after the good harvest of 1922, the Russians felt their markets were indispensable for European prosperity and tried to bargain accordingly. Business remained much behind hopes, as almost nothing came of the touted policy of concessions in Russia, while the Soviet state trading policy was already trying to reduce import needs by buying machines to produce the goods otherwise to be imported. The Russians admitted no retreat from revolutionary principles: the constitution of the Soviet Union, drawn up as a formal union of Russia and the affiliated Soviet republics, proclaimed not a national but a potentially universal state open to new adherents; and it was assumed that any new communist state would automatically adhere. If Soviet diplomats reverted to less equalitarian and more conventional titles and wore top hats, Soviet manners were still (and in some ways continued until after Stalin to be) immature; for example, the Russians ranted violently at Switzerland for alleged responsibility for the assassination of a Soviet delegate by an anti-Bolshevik Russian. A hard jolt was the 1923 crisis of the Curzon Ultimatum, provoked by the anti-British propaganda in the Near and Middle East. The Conservative British government threatened denunciation of the trade agreement. The Soviet government, regarding Britain as the citadel of world capitalism and the main potential enemy, appeared fearful lest this should herald a new intervention, perhaps in conjunction with Poland. Having shortly before spoken in truculent terms, it sent a humble reply, promising not to "spread discontent or support rebellion in any part of the British Empire." [46]

By 1924 the situation had ripened so that regular and full relations could hardly be delayed much longer. Soviet economic recovery was impressive, the currency had been stabilized after years of inflation, and the economic system looked increasingly respectable. In England, the Conservative government was followed by a Labour government headed by Ramsay MacDonald, who, although regarded by the Bolsheviks as a traitor to the working class, was more hospitably disposed toward them than were the empire-minded Conservatives. Recognition was given soon after MacDonald took office in January, 1924, although exchange of ambassadors was postponed pending settlement of the debt question. Fascist Italy had granted recognition a few days earlier, with expectations of trade benefits. French recognition also came after protracted conversations and a change to a less conservative government.

---

[46] Carr, *Interregnum, 1923–1924,* p. 172.

Smaller powers of Western Europe generally saw no reason to hold back, although Spain, for one, declined. In Eastern Europe, fear of communism was stronger and Soviet success was much less. Hungary, Bulgaria, and Yugoslavia, having repressed local leftists, remained hostile, rejecting not only diplomatic but also, for the most part, commercial relations. Czechoslovakia recognized *de facto* in 1922 but withheld *de jure* recognition until the Nazi era. As the Soviet Union refused to acknowledge Rumanian possession of Bessarabia, there were no contacts at all between the two countries. Latin America, likewise fearful of the Communist threat to its generally stiff social order, kept doors closed. Only Mexico and Uruguay recognized the Soviet Union in the 1920's, and Mexico broke relations again after a few years on grounds of Communist subversion.

The United States also rebuffed Soviet overtures but for its own reasons. American claims were much smaller than those of the principal European creditors of Russia, and Bolshevik hostility to America, a highly respected but distant power and one only marginally involved in the intervention, was much less than toward Britain and France. But while Americans were free to deal with the Bolsheviks if they wished without encouragement or hindrance, the United States felt little need to seek Soviet trade. This country indulged its ideological preconceptions. The American Secretary of State announced that since production rests on sanctity of contract and private property, there could be no basis for trade or need for relations with a government which denied these principles. Some American business interests disagreed, but this remained the American position, fully supported by organized labor, even more anticommunist than labor moderates and Social Democrats in Europe, until 1933, when economic difficulties, a menacing world situation, and a new administration in Washington brought change.

Soviet Russia thus emerged, some seven years after its Revolution, from the phenomenal isolation of the Leninist period, obtaining full recognition of the major powers of Europe without paying the price it would have been willing to pay earlier. But there remained much distrust, and Russia under its Soviet government was not accepted as a diplomatic partner by many of the smaller countries. To this day, the Soviet Union has never had an effective peacetime alliance with a noncommunist power, and it is (with Communist China) the only great power whose ambassadors are excluded from a large number of countries, especially but not only in Latin America. The land of the Soviets remained a world half apart, a member yet not fully a member of the community of states.

Soviet diplomacy adapted itself to international conventions more fully in form than in substance, and the defense of state interests was mixed with and compromised by ideological urges. Chicherin, who headed the Foreign Commissariat through the Leninist and into the Stalinist period, was a onetime tsarist diplomat of aristocratic birth and education. An idealistic socialist who had fluctuated between Mensheviks and Bolsheviks and rejoined the Bolsheviks only in 1917, he was a man of the Western tradition. He was fairly frank and accessible and wanted his diplomatic service to follow the accepted rules. He had no love for the Comintern, which undercut his work, and he made public jokes about it. But Chicherin, the only holdover from the tsarist Foreign Office, was valued mostly for his technical competence. He had no standing in higher party circles, which were in the first years preoccupied with the more important business of revolution making; and he received the honor of membership in the Central Committee only in 1925. He had some power of decision only while the Politburo was divided after Lenin was partly or entirely incapacitated after the fall of 1921 and until Stalin became supreme, from 1922 to about 1927.

It is not surprising that Soviet diplomacy was a mixture of correct and propagandistic language and gestures. Soviet treaties of the early years, made for practical ends, often included violent denunciation of evils of capitalism or imperialism, along with exaltation of Soviet goals. Soviet foreign missions did not entirely shed functions of forwarding revolution. Even mundane exchange of goods was not a straightforward matter. Russian trade was handled politically as well as commercially, not merely by state agencies but for the most part through offices abroad, for which extraterritoriality was demanded; foreign salesmen were permitted little or no contact with consumers in Russia.[47] It was never quite clear how far Soviet state interests were understandable in the traditional terms of state interests of the Western world. The Russians themselves claimed they were as different, in their virtue, as white from black.

Fundamentally, Soviet purposes may be regarded as defensive. Bolshevik leaders thought of the capitalist states as being innately hostile and feared or claimed to fear that they would return to the attack. The evil day was to be postponed as long as possible to permit maximum consolidation of Soviet power, by the means to hand—disarmament negotiations, emphasis on peace and peaceful Soviet intentions, which would lead the masses to put pressure on their governments, and especially by taking maximum advantage of the contradictions of the world without: between imperialist nations and their colonies or semicolonies, between rival capitalist nations, and between classes within them.

To the nations of Western Europe, this defensive seemed rather offensive, especially in its effort to mobilize the proletariat against the possessors. The threat of Bolshevik-inspired revolution, however, was about as unreal as the danger of a new concerted intervention against the Soviet system, as the radical movement only lost strength when split and partly

[47] Louis Fischer, *Soviets in World Affairs, 1917–1929*, Vol. II, p. 589.

straitjacketed from Moscow. Probably because they found the Comintern more irritating than menacing, there was no genuine organized effort, which a gravely weakened Russia might resist with difficulty, to choke Soviet Russia.

The only European power which had any purpose of attacking the self-declared enemy of existing states during the entire interwar period was Germany, the one most favored by the Bolsheviks. Relations between Russia and Fascist Italy were cordial enough through the 1920's, a fact which encouraged Stalin later to believe he could profitably do business with Hitler. France tried to build a *cordon sanitaire*, a security system of East European states, especially Poland, against both Russia and Germany, and remained cold through the decade; but France wanted only security for itself. In England, where Marxist influence was especially weak, currents of sympathy were especially strong, perhaps for that reason. But before relations could be settled in 1924, Communist activities in England and relations with Russia became a political issue. Into the electoral campaign there was cast a letter allegedly from Zinoviev but almost certainly faked, ordering subversion; the Labour government fell, and relations remained frozen. Most countries, like the United States, although willing to do business with the Soviet regime if there were business to be done, regarded its purposes with hostility and distrust and hoped it would in time evolve toward sanity.

The main themes of relations between Soviet Russia and the outside world thus came to the fore as postrevolutionary violence was left behind. Despite the enormous changes which have come over the world and Russia, particularly its growth to gigantic physical power, much has remained constant for decades thereafter and in the 1960's. After unadulterated revolutionism had given way to eagerness for trade and talk of peaceful coexistence, Soviet foreign relations ceased to change very much because the Soviet state itself continued fundamentally the same.

III

Stalin and Nationalist Reversion

1. SOCIALISM IN ONE COUNTRY

The one-man rule of Stalin capped the antiautocratic Russian Revolution, much as Napoleon followed the libertarian French Revolution. In both cases, the new autocrat, half foreign to the society he ruled, came to full power about a decade after the revolution. Both leaders saw a reversion from revolutionary idealism to more traditional authoritarian patterns; as the rule of Napoleon blended ways of Bourbon and Jacobin France, Stalinism was a hybrid of communism and tsarism.

As revolutionary drives with a partly imported and Western-oriented ideology wore out, the primitive elements of Russian political life came back to the fore. In the thinking of Lenin, there was a good deal of progressive internationalism; hardfisted authoritarian politics was alloyed with democratic-revolutionary ideals. Stalin's was a simpler form of autocracy, with more self-centered reactionary nationalism covered by less idealistic veneer. If Lenin sought to rule by conviction and respect, Stalin ruled by maneuver, force, and fear. For Lenin, communism involved a faith plus the discipline of the party and his leadership; for Stalin, it was little more than blind loyalty to his person. From political bossism, Stalin step by step raised himself to something like classical despotism of the most exaggerated type, with total power over the lives of everyone, including his closest associates. Stalin was given incredible personal adulation. His seclusion was such that he saw very little of the country (Stalin was accused by Khrushchev of never having visited a village from 1928 until his death). Obscure palace politics prevailed, wherein the secret police and the personal secretariat of the dictator were leading *de facto* powers over the government and the party. The drives of Stalinism were the needs of unlimited personal power, with small regard for niceties, doctrines, or public or world opinion.

This reversion to political aspects of the tsarist past, indeed, not to the

The Granger Collection

Lenin and Stalin in 1923. Lenin at this time was partly incapacitated; and Stalin, as party secretary, had acquired great influence in the party apparatus, which he was in a few years to translate into dictatorship.

late nineteenth but to the sixteenth century, is understandable in a country of primitive peasantry which had lost the greater part of its westernized educated classes, had seen education practically suspended for years, and had been torn and bled by prolonged misfortune such as has hardly even befallen a civilized land. How much was attributable to the personal character of Stalin no one can determine. Certainly, the period of his rule was marked by his personality. It is an indication of this that under Khrushchev there was some return to motifs and ways of Lenin's day. Stalin was suspicious beyond political necessity, and the irrational scope of the purges, damaging his own state and political apparatus by removal of many faithful servants and so weakening the armed forces as to risk defeat, is unaccountable without reference to his idiosyncracies. His irascible temper, testified to by his daughter and Khrushchev, also must have had a great deal to do with Soviet foreign policy, as it did in the 1948 dispute with Tito (of whom Stalin said, "I will shake my little finger and there will be no more Tito," as quoted by Khrushchev in his 1956 "Secret Speech.") On the other hand, the caution of Soviet behavior and the effort to avoid war unless easy victory was assured were probably related to Stalin's pattern of political action—avoiding direct confrontations, dividing and weakening opposition until he had secured maximum advantages.

Such an interpretation of Soviet actions could be carried far, as may become apparent in pages following. But Stalin's character cannot be taken as a large answer to the whys of Soviet policy. Stalin came to the helm because his character fitted the political needs of the time, and he used power as circumstances permitted. He could be very reasonable and moderate, and part of his strength before he made himself absolute was precisely in his reputation for practicality and moderation. But he represented the postrevolutionary type of leadership, the shift from rule by agitator-politicians and revolutionary intellectuals to the rule of bureaucrats and bosses, from men who overturned an old society in the name of Marxist ideals to men who came to the top because they were best able to grasp power in the political struggle and to exert authority through the new apparatus. When the task of radical political change was done and the idealistic and messianic feelings faded, a different kind of leader was called upon to take over.

The prerevolutionary Bolshevik party had two parts, the émigré, intellectual, internationalist-socialist, and the uneducated, native, antisocial (at times bandit) elements. Stalin took little part in exile politics, spoke no foreign language, disliked superior intellectuals, had little interest in world revolution, had few claims either as orator or as theorist, and did not even figure prominently in the making of the Revolution. After Lenin passed from the scene, he and his kind of Bolshevik took over and gave Russia and Russian policy a new cast.

This did not mean shedding the mantle of universalism and the posture of promoters of a new world order. Neither an idealistic revolutionary nor an intellectual, Stalin perforce bowed to ideology, swore by the memory of Lenin never to abandon world revolution, and claimed legitimacy as interpreter, after Lenin, of Marxism. It served as justification for party leadership of the masses, which became equivalent to Stalin's authority, that the party had a universal mission overriding any petty cavils at its actions and requiring the cooperation and sacrifices of every citizen. If the proletariat, whose will was incorporated in the party, had to come everywhere to victory, opposition was pointless. The headship of Russia in the cause of world regeneration was pleasing to Russians and to the Stalinists who ran the state and vaguely hoped to come into leadership over a larger chunk of the earth; it was taken for granted through the 1920's and even after that any communized state would become part of the Soviet Union.[1]

Moreover, it was desirable to set Russia apart from the West, distrust for which was a theme of Russian thought, of Leninism, and still more of post-Leninist Russia. Thus, the Soviet constitution spoke of the division of the world into the camps of good and evil, of socialism and capitalism. Marxism-Leninism gave reasons to reject Western ideas and influences subversive of the whole Soviet structure and party-ruled state. In due time, the idea of revolutionary change and the needs of a socialist state surrounded by class enemies were used to support the Stalinist programs of collectivization and industrialization and the imposition of terror, ostensibly directed primarily against agents of capitalist powers.

In reality, however, Stalin had no great interest in the victory of Communism abroad, unless it could be made subject to his control. He could not overtly stand in the way of foreign Communist parties striking for power and had to lend some support to their activities, but his equation of the Communist movement with Soviet power made their victory doubtfully desirable. Stalin's essential policy was not the spread of a principle but personal power; he was concerned not that other states be Communist but that they be weak and divided. So little fondness did he have for the Comintern that, almost alone among the top leadership, he never bothered to address its Congress. He even called it a "grocers' shop,"[2] and a little later spoke of its purpose, world revolution, as an "idiotic slogan."[3]

The doctrinal assertion of this position was "Socialism in One Coun-

---

[1] Louis Fischer, *The Soviets in World Affairs, 1917–1929* (Princeton, N.J.: Princeton University Press, 1951), Vol. I, p. 457.

[2] Günther Nollau, *International Communism and World Revolution* (New York: Frederick A. Praeger, Inc., 1961), p. 89.

[3] Thomas A. Bailey, *America Faces Russia* (Ithaca, N.Y.: Cornell University Press, 1950), p. 157.

try," Stalin's chief addition to Leninist theory. The Bolshevik party had made its Revolution in the conviction that it was only part of a world movement; from the Marxist point of view, only on this basis were they possibly justified in attempting a socialist revolution in a relatively backward country. This outlook served well during the civil war. Afterwards, the feeling remained strong among Bolsheviks, especially those of the émigré-intellectual breed, that the support of more advanced states was indispensable for the progress of socialism in Russia, where the proletariat was much smaller than it had been before the Revolution and the party's "Dictatorship of the Proletariat" was a thin lid over the basically peasant country. Trotsky in particular adhered to his idea of "Permanent Revolution," that the Russian Revolution could only degenerate unless it spread —an idea which he later found confirmed in the Stalinist dictatorship. Even Stalin admitted the duty of the land of victorious revolution to support revolution abroad and insisted that socialism was in danger as long as encircled by capitalism.

The potential for proletarian revolution in the West had, however, vanished in 1923. The domestic concerns of rebuilding the economy, with the complications of trying to manage all aspects of life, engrossed the attention of the Soviet leadership; and foreign affairs, conventional or revolutionary, played a small and decreasing part in their lives. In 1923–24, only about one fifth of about four thousand questions studied by the Politburo pertained to external affairs.[4] "Peaceful coexistence" had already been accepted as a necessity. The unavoidable deduction was that socialism had to be built in Russia if it was to be built at all.

The only politically admissible conclusion, that the Revolution had not really failed and socialism could be built in Russia by itself (although it could not be brought to completion without a broader victory), was stated by Stalin in the latter part of 1924. He tossed out the thesis of "Socialism in One Country" rather casually but soon perceived its great usefulness as a stick with which to beat his more internationalist opponents, led by Trotsky. There ensued a battle of quotations as each side sought to prove its correctness by citing Lenin. Lenin's writings became scripture after his death, as his successors sought to hold his heritage without possessing his personal authority. It was fortunate for flexibility that Lenin lived into and wrote for a time of peace and rebuilding, and supporters of Socialism in One Country could find some support in his voluminous pronouncements. But if Stalin's revolution-minded opponents had the better of the citations, their position was defeatist and unpopular. Workers and party members alike were weary of being told that their future depended on a world movement which inexplicably failed to

---

[4] Sidney I. Ploss, "Studying the Domestic Determinants of Soviet Foreign Policy," *Canadian Slavic Studies*, Vol. I, No. 1 (Spring, 1967), p. 48.

materialize and that they must support foreign workers who seemed unwilling to help themselves. Stalin absolved Russia of the duty, by now wearisome, of aiding international communism. Trotsky and others of his character and outlook were politically bound to the world ideal, and its failure made theirs.

Socialism in One Country was the translation into political doctrine of the concurrent acknowledgment that capitalism had come into a period of "relative stabilization." As Stalin said at the end of 1925: "The seizure of power [by the proletariat] is not on the order of the day, neither today nor tomorrow. . . . We have to find new forms of the proletarian movement. . . ." There was not too much socialism even in Russia at the time, when economic liberalization was at its height with many concessions to the peasants, free trade, and much small-scale private enterprise. The "new form of the proletarian movement," as Stalin then saw it, was simply the economic modernization of Russia, for which foreign trade was more essential than foreign revolution.

It may be argued on practical grounds that the better way to advance the cause of socialism was to strengthen the power of the homeland of socialism, but this deprived the foreign Communist parties of their *raison d'être* and consigned the Comintern to isolation and frustration. Their function could then be little more than to serve as adjuncts of Soviet power. It became their prime duty not to forward a cause in their own nations but to defend the existing socialist state, and the true Communist was the obedient follower of the Soviet Union, in due course, of Stalin. The less progress the foreign parties made, the more obvious that all hopes rested with the mighty fatherland of the workers.

In the ideological form in which this was presented, most communists were unaware of the reality of Soviet control.[5] The foreign parties understood that Moscow spoke with superior wisdom, and subservience became self-perpetuating as the independent-minded drifted away and were replaced by more docile cadres. The Comintern hastened this flux when it moved after 1923 from spasmodic interference to direct control of foreign parties. Always taking the un-Marxian attitude that failure was due not to objective economic and class conditions but to tactics or leadership, it was ready to disavow and punish anyone who was unsuccessful in carrying out its instructions. The German party in particular was repeatedly purged. In it, and to some extent in other parties, the often brilliant, if sometimes unbalanced, revolutionary leaders in the tradition of Rosa Luxemburg and Karl Liebknecht were replaced, in 1924 and after, by good proletarian types lacking ideas or education, such as Ernst Thaelmann, who were content to act as figureheads for the Stalinist

---

[5] Gabriel Almond, *Appeals of Communism* (Princeton, N.J.: Princeton University Press, 1954), p. 382.

apparatus.[6] At the same time, the weakness of the foreign parties meant dependence on subsidies from Moscow to keep in existence through lean years.

The Comintern was transformed from a gathering of world radicals to an offshoot of the Soviet state. Members of the Comintern Presidium acquired the right to attend conventions of member parties, but these virtually lost representation in the central apparatus. The open, often violent, clash of opinions of Leninist times was silenced. By the Fifth Congress (1924), there was synthetic unanimity, and subsequently there was no more room for dissent in the Comintern than in Stalin's party Congresses. After 1924, only twice again did the theoretically supreme body of the Comintern meet, in 1928 and 1935. After 1925, the Comintern was infiltrated by the Soviet secret police and was largely administered by Soviet-paid functionaries.

Hardly troubled by what policies the Comintern might follow, Stalin was much concerned to subject it. The Comintern had a high place in the ideological, although not the practical, structure of Soviet politics as long as world revolution was taken seriously in theory. As late as 1923, when the contest for Lenin's succession was taking shape, the support of the German party was important for prestige within the Soviet Politburo, and dissident factions could think of appealing to the Comintern as though to a higher court. It was, of course, the stronghold of the internationalist-revolutionary Communists, those least likely to be faithful Stalinists. Stalin was always suspicious that foreign Communists, whose superiority in Marxist dialectics he resented, were conspiring with his domestic opponents. Independent foreign Communist parties would encourage the independence of men who had been formed in international socialism. So far as Soviet-led socialism had pretenses to being a single movement, it was imperative that no part of it remain uncontrolled and so a potential menace. It was also essential for Stalin's claim to Lenin's succession that he have the support of the world movement.

Without much more than a facade of internationalism, lacking the fairly imaginative leadership of Lenin, moulded to the ways and purposes of Stalinism, the world Communist movement entered bleaker years. Hopes laid on Germany quite evaporated. Coups which the Comintern tried to manufacture in Estonia and Bulgaria fell very flat and led only to more repressions. There were some attempts to form United Fronts, although this policy was principally an exercise in its antithesis, the undercutting of socialist parties. An effort to work with Pilsudski came to grief; the Polish Communist party broke up in defeat. Instead of growing firmer, the attachment of Western working classes to the Soviet Union

---

[6] Franz Borkenau, *European Communism* (London: Faber & Faber, Ltd., 1953), p. 60.

weakened as the glory of the Revolution receded, nothing resembling utopia appeared, and this state became much like a power among powers. As always, the Soviet leadership took comfort from, and made the most of, any strike as a token of class war and sign of an approaching storm. But the chief hope, through the prosperous 1920's, was that perhaps a new war would bring a new revolutionary outburst.

There was a glimmer of exciting near-success in England. In 1926 a miners' strike flared up to a general strike. It was not at all Marxist or Communist in leadership or inspiration; the tiny British Communist party had been bitterly opposed to the Labour party as communist parties regularly opposed more moderate socialists. But Soviet leaders hung on the wires for the nine days it lasted and sent over a million dollars of "private contributions."[7] The results were wholly negative, contrary to the ordinary Bolshevik assumption that any such episode represents training and ripening of revolutionary forces. The British labor movement, which previously had been turning leftwards sufficiently to form an Anglo-Russian Trade Union Council, repudiated this body and became more hostile to the Bolsheviks. Much of British public opinion, regarding the whole affair as Moscow organized or at least Moscow inspired, was indignant. The following year, the government, alleging subversion and hostile propaganda, raided the premises of the Soviet trade mission and broke off the diplomatic relations which had never been fully established, causing a serious setback to the whole Soviet diplomatic position.

Failure in China

The outlook being so dismal in Europe, the Comintern looked with some optimism in the mid-20's to China, and high hopes were placed there until the bloody rout of 1927. The old regime was broken and discredited, and near-anarchy prevailed. Like Russia, China was attracted by and yet resented the West, and the answer of a westernizing anti-Western movement fitted both. Perhaps never have Soviet influence and advice been more welcome than in the seething China of 1920–26, and this is the only area in which the Comintern was successful in transferring its patterns to a strong political drive. Sun Yat-sen, like many discontented intellectuals of his China and of less advanced countries down to the times of Castro, was strongly drawn toward the Bolshevik model; and he saw less difference between his outlook and that of Soviet Russia as the latter became more nationalistic. Consequently, the Comintern adviser, Michael Borodin, was given broad authority to reorganize the KMT, or Nationalist party, which he did his best to convert into a copy of the Soviet Communist party, with a broad base under democratic centralism and

---

[7] Fischer, *Soviets in World Affairs,* Vol. II, p. 626.

effective central control. Borodin also became practically policy director and drew up a leftist economic program, with proposals for mild land reform and protection of workers' rights, which helped it to become a political instead of a merely military group like many others in China.

This policy would seem straightforward and promising. The chief complication arose from the presence on the scene of a small Communist party professing Leninism and adhering to Comintern discipline. As long as the Nationalists were far from power, the Communists and the KMT could work together fairly well under a coalition agreement whereby Communists entered the KMT as individuals but kept their own party. But after Sun's death, when the Nationalist armies marched north from their Canton base and gained control of central China, this ceased to be workable. In 1926 the leading Nationalist general, Chiang Kai-shek, who had learned much from study in Russia, showed his temper by turning against his Communist allies. The Soviet Politburo then became sharply divided. The waning Trotskyites, who had disliked collaboration with "bourgeois nationalists" from the first, wanted the Chinese party to push straight for socialist revolution. This was a slightly incongruous position for those who had strongly argued that Russia was unprepared to build socialism without external support, but political urges override logic. Stalin insisted on the policy of alliance, and the Comintern ordered the Chinese party to continue with the KMT and Chiang despite his anticommunist actions. Probably Stalin felt that he could not change because that would amount to conceding the correctness of his opponents.

Disaster was the outcome. Chiang massacred as many Communists as he could and expelled his Soviet advisers. As though to complete the destruction of communism in China, the Comintern ordered uprisings in the cities. The Chinese comrades argued and protested but obeyed. The bloody repression of the Canton insurrection, in December, 1927, left little more than small rural bands, which eventually became, under Mao-Tse-tung, a virtually new Chinese Communist party which owed nothing to the Comintern.

Such a dramatic reversal where expectations had been highest caused recriminations. It would have been a serious embarrassment for Stalin but for the fact that he was by that time strong enough to stifle discussion within the Soviet Union. The Comintern naturally blamed the Chinese Communist leaders as insufficiently orthodox and obedient. The Leftists or Trotskyites blamed Stalin's policy of postponing revolutionary action and exposing the Communist party by requiring its partial merger with the Nationalists, sacrificing, as they saw it, the revolutionary ideal to a foreign policy interest.

But it can also be argued that there was, in Marxist terms, no prospect at all for socialist revolution in China, and encouraging the Chinese comrades to proceed on their own, without even a narrow proletariat like that of tsarist Russia behind them, was pure adventurism inviting only trouble.

In fact, neither Stalin nor Trotsky had any understanding of the Chinese puzzle, and it was grotesque for them, Bukharin, and other Comintern bigwigs with no background in Chinese affairs and only scanty and partial information, to sit in Moscow and plot the course of revolution in China. The error of the Comintern was not so much in any particular course of action as in the whole approach of outsiders' attempting to guide from a distance the Chinese political battle. It is hardly imaginable that the Bolsheviks would have come to power in Russia in 1917 if a foreign body had been pulling the strings.

Aside from this question of competence, the entire Comintern policy in backward nations was inconsistent. When Soviet advisors taught the KMT organizational strength, there was no reason why it would not be used for the benefit of the KMT. Soviet patterns of organization for power were stronger than Soviet social philosophy; leaders around the world have been happy to imitate the Soviet party without adopting its goals, often to turn Communist methods against Communists. The Chinese Communists for their part wished to use the KMT and then discard it; Stalin, with crude frankness, stated that Chiang was to be "squeezed like a lemon and then thrown away."[8]

The policy of working with the KMT while seeking to replace it was possible only as long as external danger to both parties was great, as prior to the Nationalist victories of 1926; it became qualifiedly possible again in the Japanese invasion of the 1930's. This was the underlying difficulty of ambiguous support for social revolutionary and/or nationalist anti-Western forces in the colonial or semicolonial countries. The two could never really be hitched as a team; unable really to decide between them, the Russians failed with both. The Communists by themselves were usually impotent and served mostly to alarm conservative (and powerful) elements in the nationalist ranks. Unable to find real common ground with the Soviets, the nationalists preferred to come to terms with Western powers, who had much more to offer.

The whole attempt to deal with China in Marxist and dogmatic terms was highly unrealistic. It was repeatedly sought to derive explanations in terms of economic classes which hardly existed and to categorize leaders by class affiliations which did not fit reality. Generals would be switched from one class to another according to changes of their or Comintern policies. When the KMT failed to behave as a party should in the Marxist book, the Comintern resorted to terminological evasion, with designations such as "revolutionary parliament," although it had been closely modeled after Lenin's own party.[9] The Comintern could not free itself from the idea that the only true revolutionary force must be the proletariat; hence,

---

[8] Robert C. North, *Moscow and the Chinese Communists* (Stanford, Calif.: Stanford University Press, 1953), p. 96.

[9] Conrad Brandt, *Stalin's Failure in China* (Cambridge, Mass.: Harvard University Press, 1958), p. 9.

although the urban population was not working-class in the Marxian sense, it insisted on utterly futile attempts to seize power in the large cities. It is hard to avoid the conclusion that not only Soviet interests but social radicalism in China would have prospered far better if the Russians had been content to support China as an anti-imperialist power and keep hands off internal politics; but this could have required renunciation of claims to superior wisdom and virtue.

The KMT went on to control of China and bitter enmity to the Soviet Union until Japanese aggression forced the Chinese to look anywhere for friends. The Peking regime had meanwhile broken relations over the perennial issue of Soviet propaganda. Soviet diplomacy in China, riding very high in 1924, was a wreck in 1928; having tried to play all lines, the recognized government in Peking, the Nationalists, and the Communists, it came to grief with all. The Chinese Communist party, driven out of the cities, turned into a peasant revolutionary band under Mao. It continued to pay lip service to the Comintern but was never again a satellite to the body which had led it to grief. As a final debit, the Russians' unsuccessful effort to mobilize Chinese nationalism against the West contributed to the British break of relations and the setback to Soviet diplomacy in Europe.

Left Turn

By the end of 1927, Communist parties were decadent; eight years after the founding of the Comintern, they had less than one tenth as many members as socialist parties. In many countries they were repressed or nonexistent. Practically nothing had been achieved through the colonial world to which Lenin had looked eagerly. The most promising venture, in China, had the most dismal outcome. Feebler attempts at United Fronts, in Poland and Britain, were equally unfruitful, and in the latter case had led to a break of relations and widespread chilling of the atmosphere for Soviet diplomats.

The British break of relations led Stalin to speak of the danger of attack by the leading capitalist powers, Britain and France, probably not directly but with and through Poland. In December, 1927, he asserted that the era of capitalist stabilization with its "peaceful coexistence" was ending, to be followed by "a period of new revolutionary upheaval" which would be accompanied by "imperialist assaults and preparation for aggression against the USSR," headed by Britain.[10] Stalin often pointed to the insecurity of the Soviet Union encircled by capitalism and the inevitability of conflict, but now the menace was pointed up as immediate. A few months later, when the break of relations had receded without any

[10] X. J. Eudin and H. H. Fischer, *Soviet Russia and the West, 1920–1927* (Stanford, Calif.: Stanford University Press, 1957), p. 407.

further threat, the Soviet Party Congress underlined the same message of imminent danger.

Domestic politics had as much to do with it as external reality. Capitalism was, and continued to be for a year or two, exceptionally stable and flourishing; the world was as tranquil as at any time since 1914. That the Soviet leadership did not take danger of war seriously then or for years thereafter is shown by the fact that no military measures were taken, and the Red Army hardly increased in size from 1923 until 1937, when there was a real storm cloud on the horizon. But a war scare and call to close ranks in defense of socialism were very useful against the Trotskyite opposition, then engaged in its last serious attempt to shake Stalin's hold.

The change of direction in the late 1920's, however, went much further. It amounted to a remaking of the Revolution on the national stage, with foreign aspirations and fears only part of the scenery. In part it may have been from economic imperatives that a new course was dictated. Recovery had gone about as far as it could on the basis of restoring idled and damaged industrial capacity. The rate of growth of production, very high for several years after 1922, had slowed down markedly. To resume rapid progress it was imperative to mobilize large amounts of capital, and this could not be done without radical change of the economy. It seemed also that growth potential was much limited by the failure of the peasantry to increase grain deliveries, a failure attributable in part to the failure of industry to offer much in return. It was Stalin's answer to the economic dilemmas—less a reasoned or planned answer than a course of action in which one move and the response to it led to another in a sort of political chain reaction—to collectivize the peasantry so that grain could be secured with minimal compensation and to give top priority to forced-draft industrialization in the First Five-Year Plan.

This amounted to Stalin's taking over and exaggerating the policies of the Left within the Soviet party. The Left, which in the Communist context means those who favor strong action, consisted in 1923–26 roughly of the Comintern leaders, who wanted radical transformation and movement toward socialism at home as well as the making of socialist revolutions abroad. Stalin was able to deprive them of authority by allying himself with the Right, or moderate wing of the party, now led by the one-time leftist Bukharin. In 1927–28 Stalin, well on the way to monarchic power, took up the program of the Left and used it against the doubters of the Right. When the economic situation called for new action, Stalin had reached a political position enabling him to take strong actions, which, in turn, gave him and the Communist party immensely stronger control over the nation and all aspects of its life.

The storm, which undoubtedly far exceeded Stalin's original expectations, was in its way a more radical revolution than that of 1917, far more deeply changing the way of life of nearly everyone in the land. The

Soviet system, as it has continued until today, was as much made in 1928–34 as in 1917–18. The collectivization of the peasantry, then still the large majority of the population, was placed on the agenda in 1928, gathered speed in 1929, and became a tempest in 1930, so violent as to endanger stability of the regime. After a brief retreat, it was resumed more carefully and made nearly complete in 1934. The Five-Year Plan was announced with great fanfare in October, 1928, for the building of heavy industry as it had never been built before. It grew into a frenzy of repeatedly raised goals, a storming of utopia by the concentration of all resources on basic economic building by an all-powerful state. Stalin looked to advance not from international communism, which seemed more and more useless, but from Soviet industrial and military power securely in his hands. The Plan was a logical deduction from Socialism in One Country.

To generate the enthusiasm or consent necessary to the transformation of the Soviet Union, a doctrinal rationale was necessary. This meant a threat of attack from a world seen in Marxist categories. While Marxism lost relevance for the workers of the most advanced countries, those for whom it was intended, as they found ways to benefit from the capitalist system, it remained useful for pushing modernization, rationalizing and making more bearable crash industrialization. Sacrifices were required; the Russian standard of living, which by 1928 had hardly passed the 1913 level, sank deeply through 1934. Marxism also furnished the chief political justification for the socialization or collectivization of means of production in agriculture.

These years thus saw a sharp rise of ideological temperature in the Soviet Union, but in practice it was entirely internal, even isolationist. More than ever, a Soviet tractor or factory was worth a host of foreign Communists. *Izvestiia* had two or three lead articles on foreign affairs weekly between 1924 and 1927; in following years, about one every two weeks. So far as the world outside was seen at all, it was viewed in terms of Soviet problems and passions. The struggle between the socialist-Soviet world and the capitalist outside was stressed as not since the civil war. Foreign contacts were reduced, and the economy was built toward autarky, to reduce dependence on capitalist markets and suppliers, to secure independence of armament production, and to reduce contagions from abroad. If trade for a while increased, it was to procure machines to make imports unnecessary.

In the affirmation of personal power and the upheaval of society, police controls and repression were enormously strengthened; typically, the internal passport, a tsarist abomination to Lenin, was reintroduced. Opposition of any kind became, in and beyond tsarist tradition, equivalent to rebellion or treason. Departing from any Marxist ideas of the dismantling of the coercive apparatus of the state under socialism, Stalin held that it must be raised and sharpened. This sharpening, which was to culminate in the massive and destructive purges of 1936–38, already in the latter 1920's meant expulsions, deportations, removal of those less than unconditionally loyal. With the growing xenophobia, opposition was increasingly blamed on imperialist machinations, bent on sabotage and disruption of socialism; from 1928, trials stressed foreign connections of the accused. Foreign engineers and technicians, German, British, and French, were also put on the docket in spy trials, which caused loud cries of outrage in the West and made a lamentable contribution to already very bad state of Soviet foreign relations.

This hardening extended to relations with minority nationalities. The middle 1920's had been a time of relative autonomy; Ukrainian Communists were even able to advocate a "national communism" foreshadowing Titoism and the effect of East Europeans to combine national feelings with Communist party rule.[11] But from 1929, cultural and political autonomy were under strong and growing pressure, as all were subjected to the central drives. Ukrainian peasants and Central Asian nomads were alike collectivized, and any hint of a separate destiny became high treason to socialism. Mongolia, the only satellite, was also forced, after some relaxed years, into the mold. Trade and external contacts were practically limited to the Soviet Union; collectivization and antireligious campaigns echoed those going on in Russia.

Communism, Social Democracy, and Nazism

International communism, having become largely a Soviet creature, reflected these changes and tensions. The Sixth (and next-last) Congress of the Comintern proclaimed the danger of war in 1928, when the world was at its most placid in the wake of the Kellogg-Briand Pact outlawing war, and accused the League of Nations of preparing an assault on the Soviet Union when the latter was profitably participating in its special organizations.[12] The "General staff of world proletariat" asseverated the unqualified necessity of violent revolution when prospects for such violence were at their lowest. This was little more than sanction for the Stalinist domestic program; as Trotsky accused, leftist talk covered factual abandonment of international aims. More than ever, Marxism-Leninism became simply equivalent to state interest; it became the first duty of Communists to protect the Soviet Union, and internationalism was loyalty to it and Stalin. It was not important that membership be numerous, as loyalty was more essential. Communist parties fell into deeper isolation as

[11] M. Pap in Waldemar Gurian (ed.), *Soviet Imperialism, Its Origins and Tactics* (Notre Dame, Ind.: University of Notre Dame Press, 1953), p. 52.

[12] Alexander Dallin, *The Soviet Union at the United Nations* (New York: Frederick A. Praeger, Inc., 1962), p. 16.

the Soviet Union drew away from the world. If Communist parties were illegal, it was all the better in Stalin's view, as that increased their dependence; Moscow has usually seemed indifferent to the sufferings of adherents abroad. Not much was left of doctrine, but the Comintern could not reappraise the world and take account of the real situation because this would have deprived it of reasons for existence. The party had to have a utopian mission, if only verbally; kept pure by purge, it was the sole repository of truth, which consisted of little more than its attitude of loyalty to the leadership and enmity to the world outside.

With little mission of seizing power, the parties were useful to Stalin as a claque to uphold his prestige as leader of the world movement and as an agency of division and disruption abroad. It became their purpose to fight not so much capitalists as those who might be Stalin's rivals or who corresponded to his antagonists in Russia, non-Stalinist leftists or Social Democrats. These had been courted off and on for United Fronts in previous years; now they were promoted from "social patriots" to "social fascists," betrayers if not murderers of the working class. To all the old Leninist reasons for hating the Second International—rivalry for leadership of the workers, the belief that moderate socialists more than outright close opponents stood in the way of victory, etc.—were added new Stalinist ones—dislike for equalitarianism, democracy, and proletarianism, and paranoid hatred for any suggestion of a challenge to Stalinist authority.

The truculent line adopted in 1928 was of most importance in Germany, and there it had the most disastrous outcome. The German Communist party readily accepted it, purged the doubters, and pursued it uncritically, through great changes of economic and political conditions, as long as Hitler left them freedom to do anything. Perhaps not all blame for the quarrel rests with the Communists; the Social Democrats for their part seemed more interested in conserving their positions than in advancing a revolutionary cause, and they tried to win more respectability by dissociating themselves from the partisans of a Stalinism notorious for crudity and cruelty. But Stalin failed to realize or did not wish to realize that the Social Democrats were the natural allies of the Soviet Union in its striving for peace and security. For his political purposes, they could only be enemies.

While the legalistic and pacific socialists were treated as a menace, the rising tribe of Nazis perhaps represented an opportunity. There was no explanation in the communist book for the phenomenon of fascism. The Comintern had learned little from experience with Mussolini and with lesser dictatorships of the Right in Eastern Europe, and the lesson of Bolshevik success in standing with the Kerensky government against the rightist Kornilov coup in 1917 was forgotten. It could not be perceived that nazism could be more or less revolutionary, as Marxism gave the proletariat sole title to revolution. The Nazis, being a bourgeois party, could not be really worse than other parties of the same class basis, such as the liberal democrats. If they should come to power, they could not last long; rather, their rise was seen as a hopeful indication of the terror of the bourgeoisie before the oncoming proletarian storm, the signs of which were multiplying. Moreover, if some of the older-style Bolsheviks (purged or soon to be) saw nazism as a barbaric menace, Stalin saw potential utility in its capacity to destroy the Social Democrats, "freeing the workers of illusions" and opening the way to inevitable Communist power. The Communists, with their preparations for underground activity and greater revolutionary talents, felt they could better survive. At least this was the argument; we cannot be sure whether Stalin believed it or found it useful. It is not surprising that he should have been prepared to see some good in nazism, as there was a certain spiritual kinship. Hitler before 1933 took lessons from Stalin, whose character he always grudgingly admired, and National Socialism might well be regarded as an exaggerated Socialism in One Country.

It was less illogical to see potential virtue in nazism from the point of view of Soviet state policy. Rightists and nationalists in Germany had long favored a more pro-Russian orientation and less cordiality toward England and France than liberals and socialists, and it was hard to suppose that a more violently nationalistic Germany would be different. Germany and Soviet Russia stood together against Versailles. The Soviet nightmare was a European coalition, and it was easy to guess that a Hitler would be less capable of leading one than a more conventional leader. If he was vociferously anti-Bolshevik, this was no reason to expect his foreign policy to stick to ideological goals any more than that of the Soviet Union did.

Intentionally or not, the Communists were of great assistance to the Nazis in their march to rule over Germany. The Left, badly split with its more aggressive minority in the Communist party, expended much of its energies in internecine struggle, with loss of prestige and political capacity. By opposition on principle to anything the more moderate or constitutional parties might propose, the Communists made it much easier for the anticonstitutional nationalists and right-wing parties to come forward. As early as 1925, the insistence of the Communists on keeping their presidential candidate in the field gave victory to the aging military hero, Hindenburg, over the center candidate. From 1930, when the Communists had fairly large representation in the Reichstag, their obstruction contributed to the failure of parliamentary government—a failure which wishful thinking viewed as preparatory to Communist power. In the summer of 1931, the German Communists on Stalin's orders joined the Nazis against the Social Democratic government of Prussia. There were street brawls between Nazis and Communists, but when the Nazis moved against Social Democrats, the Communists would at least stand aside.

The greater contribution of the Communists to Hitler's power was unintentional and indirect. The Stalinization of the German party increased repugnance for it and Hitler's ability to use the cry of antibolshevism. Like Mussolini before him, Hitler was able to make far more effective use of anticommunism than the Communists made of their ideology. Communist street fighting, rioting, and sundry disorder, even active preparation for an armed uprising in 1932,[13] were the best excuse for Nazi violence and repressions. Hitler rode forward on the increase of Communist strength after 1929. As Communist votes rose in a series of elections through 1932, the Communists saw this as evidence of the correctness of their policies and imminence of victory, although Nazi votes rose much more. (In the July, 1932, elections, the Nazis won 235 seats in the Reichstag to 133 for the Social Democrats and 89 for the Communists.) Although the Communist party had no real strategy for revolution, it came to seem, or was made to seem, that Germany was faced with a choice between communism and nazism, and even Germans who wanted close relations with Russia were afraid that victory of the former would mean subordination to Stalin.

For a long time after the Nazis took power and destroyed the German Communist party, Stalin continued to hope for good relations with them. In May, 1933, the protocol of renewal of the German-Soviet treaty of 1926, which had been considerably delayed, was ratified; the Soviet Union was the first state to have a treaty with the new Germany. In December, 1933, the Comintern was still speaking of Social Democracy as the main enemy.[14] Only as Nazi policy evolved, especially with the January, 1934, treaty with Poland and the implied threat of German-Polish cooperation at Russian expense, did the Soviet government conclude that it must take countermeasures.

State Relations

While the Comintern was on a course of frustration, Soviet foreign relations were about as healthy as permitted by ideological-political complications. Under Chicherin, whom Stalin disliked but did not purge, Soviet diplomacy had more flexibility than it usually had later. His deputy and successor Litvinov was also fairly reasonable and approachable. Like Chicherin he had no standing in high party circles and was only late admitted to the Central Committee. In Stalin's disinterest in foreign affairs, he often had a fairly free hand to negotiate and put a respectable face on Soviet reality. A sincere Bolshevik, Litvinov apparently saw the Revolution as the means to a better life, but he considered that prospects for the overthrow of capitalism had disappeared with the end of the war;

[13] Nollau, *International Communism*, p. 111.

[14] Julius Braunthal, *History of the International* (New York: Frederick A. Praeger, Inc., 1967), Vol. II, p. 395.

and when he differed from official policy, it was always on the side of accommodation. He wished to settle the Bessarabian issue with Rumania, which Stalin preferred to keep as an irredenta; he opposed such hard-line steps as making trouble for Britain in Asia, the repudiation of debts, and the closing of foreign consulates in Russia.[15] It was possible for such differences to exist only because Stalin was still busy consolidating control at home; in the 1920's the Foreign Commissariat could indulge its dislike for Comintern politicians.

The main business of Soviet diplomacy at this time and in years following was the respectable one of security. There was no visible threat and not much real fear; the Soviet army, somewhat over half a million men, was smaller than that of France. But memories of the intervention were kept and exaggerated, and the basic hostility of capitalism was ideologically assumed. The Foreign Commissariat had the task of countering this hostility, which in reality meant countering the effects of the Comintern. The Soviet government wished to prevent any hostile combination and tended to feel that almost any combination in which it did not participate was directed against it. But its behavior often antagonized all and sundry and by equivocalness caused distrust on both sides of controversies.

The Soviet Union wished in practice to support the balance of power, which meant security for it as for other weak nations. As Chicherin said, "Our policy is to support the feebler."[16] But ideology inhibited the formation of political ententes which might have made this support of balance of power more effective. A fixation that the League of Nations was a creature of the capitalist powers, and so automatically evil, prevented entry into the League. There was also fear that League commissions and observers might nose into Soviet affairs. From 1925 efforts were made to induce Russia to join, for the supposed civilizing effects of membership, but it was willing to participate only in some subsidiary agencies. In theory, the Soviets remained unalterably opposed to bourgeois diplomacy. Soviet disarmament policy was also rendered less effective, even as propaganda, by Soviet attitudes. Dramatic proposals, partaking of communist utopianism, were made confessedly with the idea that they could only unmask capitalist hypocrisy, as only socialism could bring an end to war, and the imperialist powers could never agree to any disarmament.[17] The most dramatic scene occurred when Litvinov appeared before a League of Nations conference in 1927 to demand the destruction of all weapons, much as Khrushchev was to do before the

---

[15] H. Roberts in Gordon A. Craig and Felix Gilbert, *The Diplomats* (New York: Atheneum Publishers, 1965), p. 365.

[16] Fischer, *Soviets in World Affairs*, Vol. II, p. 827.

[17] Alexander Dallin *et al.*, *The Soviet Union and Disarmament* (New York: Frederick A. Praeger, Inc., 1964), p. 17.

United Nations. Supported only by the powers disarmed by treaty, Germany and Turkey, he reaped a public relations triumph which would have been greater if he had not mixed a large dose of propaganda in his speech.

Unlike the civilized world in general, the Soviet Union was not invited to be an original signatory of the Kellogg-Briand Pact; and it at first branded that innocuous instrument as preparation for an attack on itself. However, the Soviet Union was invited to adhere, and it hastened to do so, reaping some advantage by negotiating its immediate taking effect in the Baltic region. Somewhat ironically, Russia was the first of many countries to ignore the Kellogg-Briand Pact. In 1929 Chinese authorities seized control of the Chinese Eastern Railway, which the Soviets had inherited from the tsars. After protests, charges, and countercharges, the Soviet Union sent in troops, there was a little fighting, and the Chinese capitulated. This action was possibly justified in the disordered condition of Manchuria at the time, but it seemed a little abnormal for the Marxist state to use force in defense of an imperialist position. It hurt the relations the Russians were trying to cultivate with the United States, whose protest was rudely rebutted; and it may have provided some precedent for the Japanese intervention in Manchuria two years later, which was justified on similar grounds.

A secondary objective of Soviet diplomacy was the promotion of trade, as equipment was vitally needed for rebuilding and industrialization. Such efforts as were made to settle the old questions of debts and claims came to nothing because of frictions and misunderstandings, but other nations' defaults on reparations and war debts made it easier and easier for the Soviet government simply to brush aside the matter. Perhaps to offset their repudiation of tsarist obligations, the Russians made a point, as they have done to this day, of correctness in meeting their bills. They consequently began to receive some credits from abroad, chiefly from Germany; but they were still charged very high interest rates. Insignificant in 1922, Soviet trade rose steadily in volume, especially as the Five-Year Plan demanded unprecedented quantities of machinery, reaching a peak in 1930–32, when the volume of Soviet exchanges was comparable to that of Switzerland or Sweden, 2.44 percent of world trade in 1931 against 3.8 percent for Russia in 1913.[18] Trade with Russia was important for a few major suppliers, especially Germany, formerly leading trading partner of tsarist Russia, which in 1932 provided nearly half of Soviet imports. German liberality in credits was a principal reason for the large German share of Soviet trade, an important reason for the Russians to cultivate good relations.

The Russians, convinced that the capitalists would do anything for a

---

[18] Max Beloff, *The Foreign Policy of Soviet Russia* (London: Oxford University Press, 1947), Vol. I, p. 32.

profit, tried to use trade as a political weapon, sometimes overtly. Soviet purchases from England dropped by four fifths after the break of relations, creating pressure for their renewal, which a new Labour government agreed to in 1929. The effectiveness of this political arm was, however, much less than it might have been. Soviet business methods were cumbersome, erratic, and discouraging to foreigners, who consequently charged high prices and commissions. The unpleasantness occasionally visited on Westerners working in the Soviet Union caused bad feeling and sometimes embargoes. The activities, and still more the words, of the Comintern were a continuing burden for the foreign-trade organizations. State management of Soviet exports was regarded as unfair competition and gave rise to cries of dumping; in 1931 France tried to organize a united front against it. There was not really much cause for concern, as Stalin's agricultural policies drastically reduced supplies available for export about the time the French were becoming exercised over them. Imports declined in tandem, and foreign engineers were gradually phased out after 1930, as the Soviets made a virtue of self-sufficiency.

Friendliest states to the Soviet Union at this time were Turkey, Italy, and Germany. To Turkey, the Soviet Union extended economic aid in the form of interest-free loans repayable in Turkish products, although Turkish Communists were handled very roughly. As always until 1945, Soviet attention was concentrated on Germany, regarded as an oppressed nation in Leninist terms. German-Soviet military collaboration, to which only the Social Democrats were opposed, was very valuable for the still poorly weaponed and trained Red Army. With the stabilization of Germany, the Comintern ceased to be a serious disturbance. But the intimacy of the two pariahs diminished as Germany, and to a lesser degree Russia, regained respectability. The Soviets were much opposed to the Locarno Pact, a treaty of nonaggression and friendship between Germany, Britain, France, and Italy, regarding it as an anti-Soviet front. The Germans proceeded over Russian objections and blandishments but afterwards mollified them with a favorable trade agreement and by a neutrality pact, the Berlin Treaty of 1926, which was continued into the Hitler era. Thereafter, the principal bond between Germany and Russia was common antagonism to Poland, composed of territories of the former German and Russian empires, while the warmth of German-Russian relations rose and fell inversely with the warmth of relations between Germany and the former Entente.

The Red Army manual of 1929, which found Germany the best disposed of capitalist powers, singled out Britain as the most hostile.[19] Stalin also thought the strongest contradiction in world politics was the capitalist rivalry of Britain and the United States. Relations with the

---

[19] Beloff, *Foreign Policy of Soviet Russia*, Vol. I, p. 32.

United States continued in a curious ambivalence. A large part of the industrial plant of the Five-Year Plan was built with American technical assistance, and of Western powers the Russians most respected the United States. They continually hoped that large contracts would bring favor in the State Department.[20] But the very existence of Soviet society was a reflection on the perfection of American success, and as long as Republicans remained in power and the prosperity rode high, there was no evident need for compromise of American principles.

Altogether, in the years from the end of the civil war until 1930, the Soviet Union made very slow progress toward resuming the position corresponding to its stature. When Britain and the Soviet Union finally got around to exchanging ambassadors in 1929, King George refused to receive the representative of the government which he regarded as murderer of his cousin. Many small powers continued, like the United States, to decline diplomatic relations. In Eastern Europe in particular, Soviet influence was humiliatingly slight; despite a series of nonaggression treaties, most of the western neighbors of Russia were decidedly hostile and none was really friendly. The Soviet Union was still something of a pariah, barely tolerated by the international community.

While becoming less revolutionary, Stalinist Russia did little to erase the conservatives' (and liberals') horror of bolshevism. Stalin was even less prepared than Lenin to deal with the Western powers, to whose culture he was a stranger. He also interfered directly; from 1923 he was sending his opponents, such as Rakovsky, Kamenev, and Krassin, into still honorable exile as ambassadors in leading countries, where they were not always able to separate their new diplomatic from their old conspiratorial careers. Rakovsky in Paris, for example, signed a declaration calling on French soldiers to desert in case of war. Embassies were also becoming permeated by Soviet secret services, as espionage became a larger scale and more regular activity than peacetime usage had allowed.[21] Stalinist diplomacy was cynical without being clever; the relative flexibility of Lenin's latter years was gone. Soviet indifference to what may be called respectable world opinion was exhibited in show trials wherein foreigners working in Russia were accused, along with Soviet citizens considered subversive, of counterrevolutionary deeds. The major trouble of Soviet foreign policy was no longer revolutionary idealism but authoritarian crudity and political myth kept for domestic purposes.

After 1929 Soviet standing in the world improved somewhat, thanks to world economic crisis and the new aggressiveness of Germany and Japan. As France felt the pressure of rising German nationalism, it became inclined to mend relations with its historic ally. The first Soviet nonag-

---

[20] William A. Williams, *American-Russian Relations, 1781–1947* (New York: Rinehart & Co., 1952), p. 212.

[21] David J. Dallin, *Soviet Espionage* (New Haven, Conn.: Yale University Press, 1955), pp. 4–8.

gression pact with one of the former Allied powers was signed with France in 1932. As Japan began its career of conquest on the mainland with the invasion of Manchuria in 1930, relations with Nationalist China, broken since 1927, were restored; their cordiality thereafter corresponded to the threat to both parties from Japan. Japanese advances also facilitated diplomatic recognition of Soviet Russia by the United States in 1933, although this owed more to the change of administrations and to the new desirability of Soviet trade in the depression. Soviet purchases had dropped sharply, and it was indicated that they could not be expected to recover without recognition.

Economic troubles should logically have been even more promising for the spread of communism than helpful for Soviet diplomacy. As trade and production shrank in 1929–34, the masses of unemployed swelled and misery became despair. The expanding Soviet economy with its labor shortage contrasted dramatically with the Western failure, and large numbers of intellectuals began looking to Russia for visions of a better future. Yet the Soviet Union and the Communist movement profited strangely little. The ability to pay for imports shrank, and the tendency after 1931 was not to take advantage of Western eagerness to trade but to rebuff it. Although the Soviet industrial plant was built up, the Russian standard of living declined quite as much as that of hard-hit Western countries. When Western intellectuals were becoming more charitable toward the exciting Soviet experiment, Stalinism was clamping down on intellectual freedom, turning far narrower and more repulsive to the West than in the looser years of the 1920's, rather anti-intellectual except for the needs of practical construction. The conversion of the intellectuals hardly progressed beyond disillusionment with their own societies. The re-radicalization of Russia, new antireligious drives, and the brutalities of collectivization rekindled old antipathies. When millions of workers in the West found themselves so reduced that they had little to lose but their chains, and Europe was swarming with potential recruits for social revolution, the degradation of the Comintern prevented its attaining even as much success as it had harvested in 1919–23. Its existence probably served to inhibit renovatory changes which should reasonably have come from the travails of the depression. The result was not utopian change but rightist reaction, the first victims of which were the Communists.

2. SEARCH FOR SECURITY

New Outlook

With the Japanese progress in Manchuria in the early 1930's and the consolidation of Nazi rule in Germany, Soviet Russia for the first time since 1921 faced a real danger of attack. This was no ideological bogey of assault by the leading but decidedly pacific capitalist powers, but the reality of a menace by militaristic states bent on glory and expansion by force. It was not a vision of a new intervention by powers which had withdrawn wearily from a halfhearted effort to turn back the Revolution, but a threat from the powers which had made the greatest effort to secure Russian lands in 1918–21. Japan had then clung to a large part of Siberia until eased out; now it seemed to regret that weakness. Germany, which in 1918 carved out a sphere in the east, now proclaimed a new and stronger need for *Lebensraum* and the will to destroy Bolshevism.

Stalin and his advisors may not have weighed the danger so heavily as seems justified in retrospect; they were so often guilty of overconfidence that one may doubt that they were as much afraid in the 1930's as reality warranted. However, they had cause enough for concern in the public pronouncements of powerful leaders, especially Hitler, who seemed bent on making antibolshevism the cornerstone not only of his furious propaganda but of his foreign policy. At least, the atmosphere of the 1930's was very different from that of the latter 1920's, with war and military adventures the order of the day. Militarism, chauvinism, and braggadocio thrust aside the idea of a legal and progressive international order.

Soviet policies changed to match this new environment. Communist parties received a new assignment in the service of the Soviet Union, no longer to fight the Social Democratic rivals but to join with them and other willing forces to oppose the fascist threat. Soviet diplomacy took on a new seriousness and purpose, and for the first time Soviet diplomats undertook negotiations for joint political and potentially military action with capitalist states. The line of the Communist parties and of Soviet diplomacy became, in other words, more realistic and purposeful in the face of danger. At the same time, the Soviet Union became much less Marxist and more nationalistic.

It may have been mostly from imitation of the successful example of Hitler that Stalin turned in 1934 to nationalism as a force to mobilize and drive people and brought back much of the Old Russia which had been partly submerged by revolutionary mission. Patriotism had been held a reactionary ideology to deaden proletarian class consciousness; the workers should have no fatherland. Since 1918 the workers had had a "socialist fatherland," but Stalin made this a Russian reality. "Russia," previously not a proper word, became semisacred. After 1934 there was a swelling stream of books on Russian folklore, literature, and technological and military achievements.[22] Up to 1933, the accepted treatment of history was strictly Marxist with no patriotic-Russian bias and no apologies for tsarist imperialism. Afterwards, the leading exponents of this school hav-

---

[22] Frederick C. Barghoorn, *Soviet Russian Nationalism* (New York: Oxford University Press, Inc., 1956), p. 151.

ing been purged, Russianism came back in full force. The "Motherland" recovered a mystic aura, and feudal princes and conquering tsars, such as Alexander Nevsky, Ivan the Terrible, Peter the Great, and Catherine, were glorified. Tsarist generals who had won spurs in repression of revolutionary movements, such as Suvorov and Kutuzov, became Soviet heroes.

Stalin, who in 1930 had proclaimed the cultural superiority of the Great Russians, became increasingly a Russian patriot. There was a sort of fusion between the mission of communism and the spread of Russian culture, as the Stalinist regime consciously identified itself with historic Russia and its foreign policy goals. After 1937 the Russian language was compulsory for schools in the minority areas beginning with the third grade, as russification came again to the fore. The Russian language acquired a world mission, becoming a mighty weapon in the struggle for communism. Internationalism became nationalism, and the Soviet Union became a supernation in which Russian culture and traditions were dominant and somehow representative of the broader mission of the whole.

There were related changes in all aspects of Soviet life. The industrialization drive increased its emphasis on strength and military capability. The Red Army, relieved of its ostensible role of coming to the aid of foreign proletariats and pledged to fight for country and victory, was made increasingly professional. Ranks, which had been nearly abolished in the equalitarianism of the Revolution, were restored in 1935, with large differences of pay between men and officers and between junior and senior officers.[23] Soviet diplomats acquired uniforms modeled after those of tsarist days. Art and literature, forced into the mould of "socialist realism," gave less attention to social or class questions and much more to heroic individuals, from shock workers to Stalin. Discipline returned to Soviet education after years of experimentation. Fairly loose attitudes toward marriage and family were replaced by strict, neo-Puritan canons of morality. The cherished equalitarianism of the Revolution was buried under a mass of distinctions and gross differences of pay and standing. In the party, the ordinary workers were swamped by the new upper class of specialists and technicians. As the world mission was laid aside, the remaining internationalists were purged from the party, which was little more than Stalin's tool or rubber stamp with a minimum of Marxist doctrine. The Stalinist constitution of 1936 left out the overt internationalism of its predecessors, aside from the right to admit new republics.

Popular Front

The new purpose of fighting fascism reinvigorated the decaying international movement. Its first reason for existence, to promote general

[23] Raymond L. Garthoff, *Soviet Military Policy* (New York: Frederick A. Praeger, Inc., 1963), pp. 34–35.

proletarian revolution, had been practically reduced by the latter 1920's to empty slogans. Its secondary purpose, to protect and serve, if possible to extend, Soviet state power, had limited relevance for the people whom it professed to serve, as did its utility as ideological window dressing for the needs of the Soviet system. But the cause of defense of the Soviet Union against Hitlerite Germany merged into the defense of human rights, dignity, and freedoms against fascist inhumanity. Placing their organizational capacity at the service of a popular cause, Communist parties achieved considerable success for the first time since the immediate aftermath of World War I and found new life. They might have achieved much more but for their fundamental rigidities and fetters holding them tight to a Stalinism which was entering its most nightmarish period.

The turnaround was slow to come. The Soviet press was at first remarkably patient in the face of Nazi abuse. Although Hitler's rapprochement with Poland in January, 1934, implied a deal at the expense of the Soviet Union, in February, 1934, the Comintern boss, Manuilsky, held to the old story that the rise of fascism had weakened Germany and strengthened the Communist party by disillusioning the workers. England was still viewed as the capital of world reaction, although Germany and Japan were seen as the potential spearheads of capitalist attack on the Soviet Union. In March, the Comintern executive declared that a United Front could be formed only by fighting the socialists.[24] The blood purge in June, 1934, of the Nazi Left made still more remote the likelihood of improved relations with the Soviet Union, but as late as January, 1935, Molotov was stressing the possibility of getting along well with fascist states.

But in May, 1935, the Soviet Union signed with France an alliance which, although feeble, was a monumental step away from the old abhorrence of all capitalist governments. In August the Seventh (and last) Congress of the Comintern heard the famed Bulgarian Communist, Dimitrov, proclaim the new policy: no longer were all capitalist states held to be imperialistic, but they were divided into the aggressive and peace loving; Communist parties should cherish bourgeois democracy until it could be replaced by proletarian democracy. They should defend the international cause by sinking deep roots in the native land and building on national radical and patriotic traditions. The threat of imperialist war was no longer to be countered in the Leninist way by revolution and civil war but by the formation of a broad popular antifascist movement; communists should join not only socialists but middle-class parties in Popular Fronts. The bourgeois state, by corollary, was not so much to be smashed as transformed, while the dictatorship of the proletariat was half forgotten. By this metamorphosis, the Comintern fairly well reversed its spots,

---

[24] Braunthal, *History of the International,* Vol. II, p. 423.

becoming the defender of traditional democracy, moderate change, and the interests of the whole people.

This was all very sensible and appropriate for security in a world of mounting tensions and dangers, the logical outcome of Moscow's disillusionment with Hitler and the belated realization that strife between Communists and Socialists had opened him the way to power. It not only served Soviet interests but raised the prestige of the Communist parties and swelled their membership—fascists were by far the best recruiters the pro-Soviet parties ever had. The "new Democracy" to come between bourgeois democracy and socialism was suitable strategy in countries where "dictatorship of the proletariat" caused shudders. It was likewise prudent to call for replacement of fascist regimes not by communism but by the leftist democracy of the Popular Front. In deference to the needs of Soviet security, the Communist parties made a salutary shift from an unrealizable to a fairly rational political goal.

This turn rapidly brought international communism, in 1936, to its highest point of the period between the aftermath of World War I and the entry of Russia into World War II, in numbers, intellectual and political acceptability, and influence. For the first time, Communist parties became much like other parties and could hope to share their prospects, with advantages of a devoted directive nucleus and good organizational discipline. But newfound respectability had some cost, as moderation in doctrine and close contact with more easygoing socialists and middle-of-the-road groups tended to erode militancy. Some zealots and those of near-anarchist mentality (a deviation regarded in old-time Communist circles as less dangerous than social democracy) tended to splinter off; some leftist-socialists, such as the Independent Labour party in England, split with the Communists over the heresy of sacrificing the supposed interests of the proletariat to the needs of Soviet defense.

Much worse, the Communist movement in compacting with those it was sworn to destroy—the destruction of whom was its *raison d'être* and sole claim to leadership of the Left—suffered the irremediable contradictions which it suffered in the less advanced nations in trying to join with nationalistic groups against Western imperialism. It was impossible to reconcile the aim of combating fascism with that of destroying the capitalist basis of society. The Communists' embrace of the socialists had something of the spirit of a boa constrictor embracing a deer; they were to keep at all times not only their own organization but freedom to criticize and support their own philosophy. This they insisted on doing in violent language which spoiled many projected agreements. They could not cease trying to undermine the organizations with whom they entered or wished to enter into alliance, just as the Chinese Communist party menaced the KMT even while supporting it. They particularly stepped up efforts to capture the trade unions, youth groups, and the like, from socialist leadership. It appeared that the principal beneficiaries of cooperation were to be the Communists.

The control of the Communist parties by a Soviet organization, tending to become tighter through the 1930's, was an almost unsurmountable bar to any real understanding, whatever the effort to give the parties a national garb. It is typical that the 1935 Comintern Congress, while laying the foundations for the sharpest turn to moderation international communism has ever taken, by its oratory and vocabulary revived all the old fears; and the United States and Britain protested as though by reflex this derevolutionizing meeting. Stalinism was inseparable from dogmatic authority, narrowness, and violence. It was some help after 1934 that Stalinist policy turned a bit more temperate in the Second than it had been in the First Five-Year Plan, and the worst of collectivization was past. In 1936 the new Stalinist constitution of the Soviet Union was unveiled as the "most democratic in the world," and this helped the claim of Communist parties to be sincere democrats. But the great purges followed, massacres of a barbarity unknown in the Western world since the Roman Empire. An incidental result of the purges was the decimation of the Comintern. Foreign Communists in Moscow were fortunate if they remained alive (those who did mostly came later into positions of power in Eastern Europe), while nearly all the old Leninist leaders of international communism, from Zinoviev and Bukharin down, were shot.

The most critical contradiction of the Popular Front was in the question of defense, and here the Communist movement showed the limits of its flexibility. The 1935 Congress was confused; while calling for opposition to fascism it pointed to Anglo-American antagonism as the main imperialist contradiction and reiterated, with qualifications, the traditional opposition to military expenditures and military service. An exception was made only for the French Communists, whom Stalin had instructed in view of the Franco-Soviet treaty to cease opposing conscription. There was subsequently more equivocation, but it was impossible for a Communist party wholeheartedly to support the military effort of a capitalist state (unless, as later, allied with the Soviet Union) and remain a Communist party. This was utterly anti-Leninist and cost the loyalty of those who could not bring themselves so easily to surrender the traditional leftist stance. Yet it was absurd to speak of standing united against fascism while making political capital of opposition to armaments and military service designed to oppose fascist aggression.

Because of this basic incompatibility, distrust, and conflict of purpose, the Popular Front could nowhere realize its potentialities. The Communist party had full political rights, lending attractions to a bargain with them, in only a few countries in the middle 1930's; and there was not much interest in a Popular Front except in countries which felt threatened by fascism. There was some cooperation between leftist parties in the Balkans. In war conditions in Spain and feebly in China, there were analogous arrangements for cooperation in the antifascist cause. The classic *Front populaire* was in France, where conditions were the most favorable: important Socialist and Communist parties, free parliamentary system, native radical tradition, and nationalistic fear of German expansion.

With the annihilation of the old mainstay of the Comintern, the German Communist party, the French party became the leading Soviet bridgehead in the West. In the spring of 1934, long before the new line was made general doctrine, the French Communists were given instructions for resistance to fascism, defense of democracy, and joint action with the socialists. In July, they came to an agreement with the socialists; and within a few months they were taking on a garb of patriotism, dropping the anticlericalism obligatory not only for Communists but for the Left in France, and appealing to all classes. With the signing of the (defective) alliance with the Soviet Union, they switched to support of national defense—a change of line which the Communists could carry through much more readily than the Socialists, for whom loyalty to principles was more, loyalty to the organization less, important.

The formal Popular Front was an electoral alliance on the basis of support for the Soviet alliance among Communists, Socialists, and the moderate middle-class Radical-Socialists, formed in July, 1935. The parties subscribed to a common program but conducted separate campaigns for the general election of the following spring. It gave a glorious victory to the leftist parties; the Communists particularly benefited, raising their parliamentary delegation from 10 to 72, somewhat to the alarm of their partners. A Popular Front government was formed with great expectations under the premiership of the mild Socialist, Leon Blum. The Communists refused on ideological grounds to join it—a preference for freedom to criticize over a share of power and responsibility, sharply contrasting with the eagerness of the French party to remain in the government after World War II. They were still, in 1936, thinking to some extent in the wornout analogies of the Russian Revolution. Blum was their Kerensky, to be discarded in due course.

Communist policies not unnaturally were confused; on the one hand, they opposed some socialistic measures, such as nationalizing the Bank of France, on the ground that they would be detrimental to antifascist cooperation with the middle classes. On the other hand, they carried on agitation and led strikes in an effort to gain authority with the workers. Frictions grew and hopes shrank, particularly as the Spanish Civil War divided the Front between those who were eager to fight fascism in Spain and those who felt France must move cautiously and beware of offending the British determination to keep uninvolved and hopefully to isolate the Spanish conflagration. The decaying Popular Front came to an end in 1938, succeeded by a government prepared for Munich.

The new line of the Comintern was applicable only where a fascist menace was evident; in most of Asia the anti-German stance was not appropriate, as the chief Western imperialist in view continued to be England, and the idea of Germany opposing the British Empire was rather pleasing. However, Popular Front policies made it easier to drop the social radicalism of proletarian revolution, unpromising where there was practically no proletariat, and to make cooperation with other parties at least faintly possible.

The only important such cooperation was in China, where Japanese armies were actually fighting on ever larger areas of historic China. Mao's Communists, having built up a peasant state in southern China after the 1927 fiasco, incorporated it as a Soviet republic; under pressure from Nationalist armies, they had in 1935 taken the famous Long March around the interior to the northern part of China. This brought them face to face with Japanese expansion when Popular Front was the Communist word; it was by taking the leadership in the national struggle that the Chinese Communists, in a manner diametrically opposite to that of the Leninists in 1917, built up the position which gave them ultimate victory.

A strong point of their propaganda was the demand that the Chiang government cease persecuting patriotic Chinese and join with them in the national cause. Not much came of this until the curious episode of December, 1936, when Chiang was arrested by a dissident general who sympathized with the Communists. The Russians, disinclined as usual to see the Chinese Communists take revolutionary action, pressed for his release, a condition of which was his pledge to cooperate with the Communists in fighting the Japanese. In the arrangements made, the Communists, in accordance with their accepted style, kept their own organization and freedom of action, making concessions mostly of form, as acknowledging the sovereignty of the KMT government. When the Japanese attacked central China in July, 1937, the two parties were driven closer together. The best period of cooperation was from then until Nazi-Soviet collaboration and later the Soviet-Japanese nonaggression treaty of April, 1941, reduced Communist enthusiasm for the anti-Japanese campaign.

Intervention in Spain

Spain saw a different species of Popular Front with an active task of fighting fascism militarily. This faced Soviet foreign policy with complicated and delicate problems, and its responses were highly revealing of Soviet ways and purposes.

The Spanish civil war was not begun by the Communist party, although it was soon made the chief issue and might have been the chief gainer from the revolutionary situation, which was created as usual not by economic dialectics but by political violence. In the Popular Front established for the elections of 1936, the Communist was the smallest of four parties; its membership was only 6 percent of the total.[25] But the generals' insurrection against the leftist Republic, representing intransigent conservative forces, raised the banner of anticommunism and appealed to Italy and Germany for military assistance. The Soviet inclination was not to meddle but to avoid complications. Although fascist assistance to the Spanish rebels was prompt and massive, for some months the Russians only sent messages of sympathy, published indignant articles, held solidarity meetings, and took collections of food and clothing. Fighting began late in July, but not until September was the decision taken to send military aid—a decision taken in Stalin's absence from Moscow, and perhaps contrary to his wishes, by those whose internationalist idealism was stronger than his.

The decision to intervene was, however, carried through with energy, and within two months the Soviet Union was a major factor in the conflict. But its contribution remained very much smaller than that of Germany and Italy to the forces of General Francisco Franco, and direct Soviet involvement was kept as slight as possible. Spain was never used as a military training or testing ground. Soviet personnel was minimal and never acknowledged, a few tank drivers, pilots, technicians, and advisers, never more than some two thousand Russians and usually many less. Arms sent were not given but sold, prepaid in gold. So far as possible, aid for the Spanish Republic was made an international rather than a Soviet cause, with campaigns and committees working on and arousing sympathies throughout the Western world. The International Brigade, whose help was more moral than military, enlisted sundry leftists and men of democratic and liberal views, not revolutionaries. No Russians were allowed to volunteer, and Soviet advisors kept clear of it.

There may have been some Soviet purpose of engaging fascist forces at a distance, or hopes that Britain and France would see their own interests in preventing a German-Italian victory in Spain. It did not have that effect. While the Soviet regime was prevented by geography from entering effectively without the concurrence of the Western powers, Soviet participation made the struggle what the fascist powers wished to make it, part of their anticommunist crusade. For Britain, France, and the West in general, it was easier to view the conflict as one of fascism versus communism, of which they could agreeably wash their hands; the only country other than the Soviet Union willing to sell arms to the Spanish Republic was revolutionary Mexico.

Probably the Soviet Union was entangled against its will, at least against Stalin's, into standing by its verbal ideological commitment to a world movement. By dependence on Soviet munitions and Communist-recruited and organized volunteers and because of the extraordinary growth

[25] David T. Cattell, *Communism and the Spanish Civil War* (Berkeley: University of California Press, 1955), p. 21.

of the Communist party, the Spanish Republic came largely under Communist domination, although Soviet influence waxed and waned as supplies came or lagged. But it was apparently not Stalin's purpose to acquire a faraway and probably unmanageable satellite. It was certainly not his intention to reorder Spanish society. In December, 1936, for the sake of good relations with the Western powers, Stalin urged the Spanish government to avoid radicalism, and the Communist party was instructed not to try to take governmental power.

The party, faithful to the United Front ideal of putting defense ahead of social aims, actually became the right wing of the governing coalition. It drew not manual workers but peasants, shopkeepers, and even many small businessmen. Laying aside the dictatorship of the proletariat, it opposed revolutionary committees, workmen's militia, and peasant land seizure, while the essence of its program was Stalinist order, discipline, and state control over trade unions and essential industry alike, a "people's democracy" which was to be copied in Eastern Europe a decade later. The Communists were most attentive to the security forces and vigilance against enemy elements, or anticommunists. The anarchists, whose party before the civil war had been much larger than the Communist, behaved much more in the Leninist pattern, as they formed local revolutionary committees, confiscated and collectivized land and industries, and violently attacked the church. Consequently, the Communists, who got along well enough with leftist bourgeois parties, were continually at odds with revolutionary parties, who were equated with enemy agents.

The Spanish Communist party made its major purpose, along with combatting the fascist-supported rebels, the struggle against non-Stalinist revolutionaries, especially those of a Trotskyite orientation. A heavy price of Soviet aid was war on dissidents, which was sometimes given precedence over the needs of the war and which contributed to the defeat. Soviet penetration was especially strong in the police and censorship of the Spanish Republic, and it was used to satisfy through purges Stalin's deep and unvarying fear of a leftist alternative to Stalinism.[26] So intense was this fear that the Russians who went to Spain to carry out Stalin's will, party and military advisors and diplomats, were nearly to the last man purged as infected after their return to the Soviet Union.

The Soviet program in Spain put the Soviet Union on the right side of the developing world struggle, as seen by many liberals and republicans in the West as well as communists, even while Spanish communism was behaving practically as an apparatus of totalitarian power without ideals except total power. But its broader diplomatic purpose was defeated by contradictions like those which have usually plagued and complicated

---

[26] David T. Cattell, *Soviet Diplomacy and the Spanish Civil War* (Berkeley: University of California Press, 1957), p. 118.

Soviet foreign policy. European conservatives naturally assumed that Stalin, in line with what the Comintern had been saying for many years, wanted to institute communism wherever possible. The growth of Soviet and Communist influence in Spain seemed to prove them right, as the Spanish Communist party, more helped by its advantages of organization and Soviet support than hurt by lack of other principles than obedience to Soviet demands, managed to multiply its membership many fold and grasp more and more positions of influence in the outwardly bourgeois state.

It did not help that the Anglo-French nonintervention policy made the Spanish Republic dependent on Soviet aid and unable to resist the Communists. If Stalin wished for French rather than Soviet help for the antifascist cause (or British if that had been possible) this was seen as an effort to embroil the Western powers against Germany and Italy in the undeniable Soviet interest of causing trouble for potential enemies. The British wished to avoid antagonizing the fascist powers in hopes of a West European settlement, or at least to avoid driving Italy, which was more committed in Spain with large forces on the ground, closer to Germany. The means adopted was an arms embargo, to which the Soviet government felt that it had to subscribe, as did the fascist powers. The embargo was fatal for the republican cause, as Germany and Italy could violate it on a large scale while Russia because of distance and lack of naval power, as well as fear of antagonizing the governments of Britain and France, could not; it amounted to appeasement rather less justifiable than that of Munich.

Never disposed to sacrifice itself for quixotic causes, the Soviet Union took the prudent course and began to reduce its aid to the Spanish Republic in 1937; it lasted, in force, only a single season. Attention was turned toward domestic affairs; the purges were at their height and struck the military forces with incapacitating violence. In 1938 there were rising dangers from Japan in the Far East, and crises were brewing in Central Europe. The home front came first; Soviet aid was halted, and Spanish leftism was left to its agonies.

From the Soviet point of view, the broad policy of collective antifascism had shown its bankruptcy, just as the only promising Popular Front, that in France, was wrecked on the issue of Spain. Distrust between Britain and France on one side and the Soviet Union on the other was much heightened, opening the way to the Anglo-French deal with Germany at Munich, excluding Russia, and to the German-Soviet deal, excluding the Western powers, a year later.

Facing Japan

Although farther from the vitals of Russia and secondary to the danger from Germany, Japanese expansion presented a delicate set of problems for Soviet diplomacy; and over the years from 1934 to 1939, it tried to meet them in a variety of ways. The first tendency was appeasement in hopes of satisfying Japan and keeping it from alliance with Germany. This was exemplified principally in the sale in 1935 on unfavorable terms of the Chinese Eastern Railway, the tsarist property which a few years earlier had been considered worth a little war with the Chinese. This meant Soviet withdrawal from the old sphere of influence in northern Manchuria, which had been more or less recovered by 1930, and consequent exposure of the strategic position of Vladivostok. Subsequently, the Soviet government suggested arbitration of the frontier between Siberia and Manchukuo by a neutral third party, an important ideological concession, as previously it had held that no neutrality between socialism and capitalism was possible. Japan, however, proceeded to enter a semialliance with Italy and Germany, the Anti-Comintern Pact; and Japan, facing more real Communist opposition in its empire-building than its European partners, took the anticommunist commitment seriously.

As in Europe, the Soviets looked for support of other status quo powers in vain. The League of Nations temporized and did nothing. Britain was reluctant to antagonize the former ally, Japan, the more so as the situation nearer home was cloudy. The Russians strongly suspected that the British would like to turn Japan against Siberia instead of British positions to the south. The United States took a more forward position against aggression in Asia than in Europe, but American relations with the Soviet Union continued cool, still troubled by the old questions of tsarist debts and communist propaganda.

It was consequently a relief for the Russians when the Japanese instead of heading north struck into China proper in July, 1937, thus becoming entangled in an unwinnable war. The Soviets entered a nonaggression treaty with China and began supplying arms, at first on a modest scale but in growing volume until the German attack of June, 1941. In these years, Soviet aid, amounting to several hundred million dollars and delivered largely across Sinkiang (which was under Soviet influence through most of the 1930's and until German invasion brought withdrawal in 1941) was almost the only outside assistance which China received. Including munitions, military instructors, and loans, it was given to the Chiang government, not the Chinese Communists. The Chinese Communist party was able, however, by morale, discipline and militant effectiveness to lay the foundations of power during these disturbed years.

The Japanese were not prepared to take on the Soviet Union while ever more deeply engaged in China, but they kept up unremitting and occasionally violent pressure. Friction over Japanese fisheries in Siberian waters, over border quarrels, over Japanese concessions in Sakhalin, questions of travelers, espionage, and the consulates of the respective countries supplemented the antagonism arising from Soviet support for the Chinese struggle. Each summer, 1937 through 1939, clashes grew into a little war, mostly along the border of Mongolia, whither Soviet troops had returned in 1935. Here, with no prospect of assistance from any other power, the Soviets stood and fought, with heavy artillery, tanks, and planes. Many thousands were killed on both sides. The Red Army gave an excellent account of itself, a fact little noticed in the West. But fears for the eastern territories made the Russians think better of seeking a deal with Hitler in the West. Soviet-Japanese relations were calmer after the Nazi-Soviet pact, as the Japanese ceased to count on German help. But until 1940 they thought of attacking Russia to end its support for Chinese resistance, and only when the Japanese committed themselves to war against the West at Pearl Harbor could the Soviet Union feel secure on its eastern flank.

Failure of Collective Security

In the face of danger, the Soviet Union discarded or let fall into second place the old dichotomy of socialism versus capitalism and began to discriminate between peaceful and aggressive powers. Just as the new danger required that Communist parties give up revolutionary aims, cooperate with whoever was amenable in the interests of antifascist defense, and behave less like revolutionary conspiracies and more like conventional political parties, it led the Soviet state to participate in organizations dominated by capitalist states, to deal with such states as friendly equals, and to behave more like an ordinary security-minded power. Probably there was little expectation that any Western powers would come to the aid of the Soviet Union, but it was important to encourage the West to resist Germany, somewhat as Germany earlier had been encouraged against the West, to prevent the old nightmare of a general anti-Soviet coalition.

The formal world body dedicated to collective security was the Versailles-born League of Nations. Having regarded this body as something close to the incarnation of evil and a potential anti-Soviet conspiracy (Lenin once called it the "alliance of world bandits"), the Soviet leadership changed its view in 1933–34, especially as Germany and Japan haughtily withdrew, to the reverse. Despite some opposition and complications, the Soviet Union joined in September, 1934, with a permanent seat on the Council. This was a blow to the Comintern, a competitive international organization, and was another retreat from Leninism. But it meant an increase of Soviet prestige, the practical completion of formal readmission to international society, and it gave a useful forum, like the United Nations in later days, from which Soviet views could be broadcast to the world. Having reversed policy, the Soviet Union made the most of it. From a detractor of the Versailles settlement, it became one of the strongest defenders of the sanctity of treaties; attempts at revision became imperialist plots. Finding the League no longer capitalist, the Soviet Union became perhaps its most consistent, certainly its most articulate, supporter down to the eve of World War II.

League membership facilitated pacts with individual states, most importantly France. Pre-Hitler revival of German nationalism led to some rapprochement of France, previously perhaps most consistently unfriendly of the great powers, with the Soviet Union. A nonaggression pact was signed in 1932, although ratified only after Hitler assumed office. The French army, like the Reichswehr disposed to overlook ideological differences, pushed for a closer relation; as the menace of German invasion seemed to loom again, thoughts went back to the old bond with Russia and the invasion of East Prussia which may have saved Paris in 1914. A security pact, albeit in weak terms, was negotiated in 1935, but it met considerable resistance; ratification was brought nine months later by German reoccupation of the demilitarized Rhineland.

The Franco-Soviet treaty was supplemented by one between the Soviet Union and Czechoslovakia. This would seem a beginning of a formidable security network, but it never, despite steadily rising fears of Germany, acquired practical importance. The Soviet-Czech treaty was to come into effect only if the French took action under their agreement. The Franco-Soviet pact was never taken seriously enough to be fleshed out by a military convention. Both were little more than an ineffective show of antifascist solidarity, papering over deep distrust and a background of ill will, indicated by the failure of Czechoslovakia to extend *de jure* recognition until 1934. Their utility to the Soviet Union, in any case, was indirect. Germany could hardly attack without crossing Poland, already a French ally. But the alliance barred any entente of France with Germany, secondarily of Poland with Germany, at Soviet expense. This contingency was much feared since Germany in 1934–35 was suggesting joint ventures with Poland while raising the key of anti-Soviet propaganda.

In 1936 the dangers became much more acute. Hitler's antibolshevism reached new stridency, and he allowed himself to dream aloud of the riches of the Ukraine and Urals. German rearmament got into full swing. An incidental result was that German industrialists, long prone to seek markets in the east, lost much of their interest in a Russian orientation; German-Soviet trade declined markedly after 1936. Germany and Italy formed a partnership for aggression, and Germany increasingly made anticommunism an international cause. In November, 1936, most sinister of all for the Russians, Japan joined Germany and Italy in the Anti-Comintern Pact, an instrument which was ostensibly ideological but which covered a military agreement which did not bother to mention communism.

In these circumstances, the Soviet Union wished to draw lines and confront the revisionist or aggressor nations with a solid counteralliance of the nonrevisionist or peace-loving nations. The Western powers, however, were considerably less clear in their approach, which was at this time and until the spring of 1939 primarily to settle disputes, find common ground, and hopefully to come to a generally acceptable settlement. The Italian invasion of Ethiopia brought a great outcry but little action to save the principle of collective security and the position of the League of Nations as guarantor of world order. While the British government felt that strong measures would be unwise, probably making Mussolini dependent on Hitler, the Soviet Union called for effective sanctions. Again, in the crisis of the militarization of the Rhineland, British coolness precluded any action, whether or not the French might have determined to use force.

The government whose position was critical in these questions and in all collective security negotiations up to their end in August, 1939, was the British. Its relations with the Soviets had improved somewhat after diplomatic relations were fully established in 1929, and irritants diminished as the Soviets withdrew from their old anti-British campaign in Asia, and in the Far East the formerly opposed countries were now both apprehensive of Japan. But there was no developing warmth as between Russia and France. A large or at least influential sector of British opinion continued very anti-Bolshevik, and many conservatives preferred Nazi Germany over Soviet Russia. In dickering over the revision of the Straits convention, at Montreux in 1936, Britain was pushing the old theme of barring the Mediterranean to Russia. A naval agreement with Germany gave British assent to naval rebuilding in defiance of the peace treaties. When League sanctions seemed to have failed in 1936, the British reaction was rather to dilute the League and make it noncoercive in hopes that all nations might be persuaded to participate. They suspected that the efforts to strengthen the League and make it an effective opponent of aggression were designed to set the capitalist world at odds for the benefit of communism.

The outcome, as of many efforts at Soviet-Western collaboration, was in all ways poor. The Western powers neither treated Germany well, conceding frankly the rearmament they were in no position to deny, nor did they erect firm barriers to the expansion of German power, and in effect encouraged the Nazis to gain their ends by force and bluster, to the discredit of their opponents. The Soviet Union, on the other hand, was rebuffed and given to understand that it must look to its own security in its own way. It did; after 1936, Soviet support for collective security cooled and a note of isolationism and self-reliance entered Soviet statements. This may have had to do not only with disillusionment with the Western powers but with confidence in growing Soviet might. The industrialization program was going forward soundly, and rearmament was progressing. Never bothered by pacifism, vocal in the West in the 1930's, the Soviet Union steadily increased military spending from 1934 onwards; expenditures further grew fourfold in the two years after 1936, and the army began a rapid growth that carried it from 590,000 in 1937 to 4,200,000 in June, 1941.

Divergent Roads

How little spirit of cooperation there was between the Western powers and the Soviet Union was shown in March, 1938, when Hitler carried through the absorption of Austria. There was no idea of consultation with Russia, nominal ally of France, although the acquisition enormously raised Hitler's standing and gave him a base for further advances in central Europe. Russia seemed to be quite excluded from the field of vision of the democratic Western powers, especially England. When Litvinov proposed discussions regarding collective security, he was quite ignored. Probably the Russians began taking a more serious view of the world; hardly by coincidence, the last of the great purge trials was concluded on the day Hitler took Austria.

Next in line stood Czechoslovakia, whose defenses had been outflanked and whose large German minority was beguiled by dreams of sharing the grandeur of the Third Reich. Promising to liberate oppressed Germans and denouncing Czechoslovakia as an outpost of Bolshevism in Central Europe, Hitler built up tremendous tension through the summer and early fall, facing Europe with an apparent choice between destructive war and yielding to his demands. There was again no consultation between East and West. The Russians were highly skeptical of Western intentions and were thinking of relying only on their own capabilities. Britain and France for their part were very dubious whether the Soviet Union could and would do anything effective to help Czechoslovakia or would be pleased to see them go to war with Germany.

The Soviet government encouraged the Czechs to resist, repeatedly promising help if the French fulfilled their engagement. There was no common boundary between Czechoslovakia and the Soviet Union, so military assistance would have had to cross Poland or Rumania, and both of these were more afraid of Bolshevik Russia than of Nazi Germany and adamantly opposed to seeing the Red Army on their soil. Some contended that these French allies could have been persuaded to consent by League of Nations pressure, but no effort was made. The Poles even joined shortsightedly in Hitler's enterprise for the sake of a few square miles of territory. The Czechs, because of British and French opposition, could not request Soviet help alone, if this had been forthcoming. Hence, when Britain and France yielded to Hitler and signed the Munich agreement, the Czechs could only bow and the Russians could only protest from the distant sidelines.

In recriminations after the Munich settlement had soured, the Soviets pointed virtuously to their willingness to stand against fascism and fight for collective security and the independence of Czechoslovakia, while British and French appeasers betrayed honor, their (the French) pledged word, and their own security. The Soviet government's professions of willingness to do its duty made a powerful impression and created much pressure on Western governments to secure Soviet adherence to new security arrangements in 1939. It may be, however, that the Soviet leadership saw the unlikelihood that it would be called upon to meet its commitments and gave itself the luxury of taking a noble position with small risk. Little was done to prepare the Soviet people for the idea of fighting over Czechoslovakia; the relative calm and silence of the press contrasted with the campaign of denunciation and indignation which swept across the land a few months earlier in protest against Japanese probings of the Mongolian border. Nothing was done on either the Czech or the Russian side to prepare for military cooperation.

At the height of the Munich crisis the Soviet Union, snubbed and scorned, began pointing to the imperialist nature of the British and French governments, erasing the distinction between peace-loving and aggressive states. They failed to act against aggression, the Soviets said, because of fear of their working classes. As relations deteriorated, the Soviets played up the fear that France and especially Britain wanted to direct the thrust of Hitlerism against themselves. Certainly it was the inclination of the Western powers in the aftermath of Munich to deal as best they might with Hitler and exclude Soviet Russia from Europe. The Russians correspondingly, with no friend among major powers, retired to diplomatic isolation, from which they would emerge on their own terms.

Last Efforts

With the opening of 1939, there was some sense of relaxation in the Soviet Union, as the worst of the purges was left behind and the chastened country settled down to a stable dictatorship. There was much emphasis on military preparedness, mixed with confident talk of smashing any aggressor. The ideas of the Popular Front were dead, and relations with the Western democracies were frigid; in France the Communist party continued to campaign against military preparations. But suddenly the search for agreement for collective security became again and more urgently than before the order of the day.

The event which shocked the West into courting Soviet cooperation against Hitler was the occupation of the rump of Czechoslovakia by

German forces in March. In a sense, this changed little, as what was left of that nation had become practically a German satellite. If full German rule had been gradually and quietly imposed, the world would perhaps hardly have noticed. But the brutal treatment of the Czechs and the brusque and frank incorporation of Bohemia into the Reich as a protectorate put the West on notice that Hitler's aim was not merely the unification of ethnic Germans but indefinite conquest. It also seemed significant that the Carpatho-Ukraine, the Ukrainian-speaking tail of former Czechoslovakia, which had been set up as a center for Ukrainian nationalist agitation after Munich, was turned over to Hungary—a message, it appeared, that Hitler's designs were not against Russia and bolshevism but nearer the West.

It was consequently easy for the West to resolve that it could not afford to permit the aggressor to become stronger. Then Hitler, without giving the world a decent moment to digest the occupation of Bohemia, turned to Poland with demands for Danzig and more or less of the former German territories awarded Poland at Versailles, at the same time proposing military cooperation. The Poles, proud and more confident than their strength justified, rejected both concessions and cooperation. Chamberlain, seeking to make up in firmness for earlier softness, on behalf of the British government gave Poland, and a short time later Rumania, a firm and unconditional guarantee of support. But by guaranteeing Poland he practically guaranteed Russia against German attack. Thus, when he set about seeking the cooperation of the Soviet Union, the only power in a position to give the Poles much direct help, he had given away his most important card.

There followed from the end of March, 1939, until August 23, an unhappy and unpleasant series of negotiations, during which neither party was eager for agreement and both sides were paralyzed by distrust. It was a British dread that war against Germany might be won in alliance with Soviet Russia, placing all of Eastern Europe under the presumably permanent control of the Red Army and the Soviet system—as in fact ultimately happened. This was even more of a nightmare for smaller countries of Europe which had to be included in a workable security system, such as Rumania and Poland; all of Eastern and much of Central Europe were more deeply afraid of Russia than Germany.

At the same time, the British Conservatives could not bring themselves to surrender entirely their hopes of detaching Italy from the Rome-Berlin Axis, which seemed precluded by any arrangement with Russia. It did not seem reasonable to alienate much of Europe for the adherence of a power which was rated, perhaps by wishful thinking, inferior to Poland. Russia, on the other hand, cherished an older and deeper distrust for England than for Germany. The Soviets well remembered the hostile position of the Western powers in regard to the Spanish Civil war and Munich and realized that they would prefer an accord with Germany to one with the Soviet Union. There was equivocation on both sides, as the actions of the Western powers sometimes did not seem to correspond to their professed anxiety to come to an agreement, while most of the time the Soviet government was dickering simultaneously with the Western democracies and Nazi Germany to see which would offer most.

When the Russians called for a hard military alliance, the British, who preferred a demonstration of unity which hopefully might suffice to deter aggression, made weaker counterproposals. Immediately thereafter, the pro-Western Litvinov was replaced, on May 3, by Molotov as foreign commissar. This was even more significant than was realized at the time. Litvinov, a Jew who had made himself practically the symbol of collective security, stood in the way of any deal with Hitler. He was also symbolic of the era when the Foreign Commissariat, regarded as of secondary importance, was allowed some latitude and freedom to offset Stalinist crudity and brutality. A minor figure in the Soviet party, Litvinov was something of an anachronism by the time of his dismissal; it was slightly miraculous that he survived when all four of his assistants and almost all heads of departments and leading Soviet diplomats were shot. The voice of Molotov, who stood next to the boss, was the authentic voice of Stalinism. Taciturn, impenetrable, dour, coldly logical, he was a pillar of the cold war whom Western diplomats respected even as they felt baffled and frustrated by him. Molotov also completed the renewal of personnel begun in 1938, as experienced diplomats and men familiar with the outside world were replaced by homegrown and party-bred apparatus men.

After Molotov took the foreign post, there was no immediate evidence of change of line, aside from what might be inferred from the announcement of a large increase of defense spending. Negotiations dragged over who would promise to protect whom under precisely what circumstances, and there was much discussion of how to meet indirect aggression. Neither side was willing to give the other authority to decide on war. The Soviets step by step raised their price; and behind them the British, with the French in tow, raised their offers, until by summer the Russians were rejecting more than they had asked in the spring. Finally, the sticking question was whether the Soviet government would be given a virtual protectorate over the Baltic states. These justifiably saw Russia as more of a threat to their fragile independence than Germany, with which Latvia and Estonia had in June concluded friendship pacts. The British and French found it hard to compromise to this extent the principle for which they were supposedly standing, the right of small nations to independence. Hitler, with no such scruples, offered Stalin a sphere on the Baltic and a share of Poland as well. While a British-French military mission with restricted authority was talking in Moscow (Chamberlain readily flew to consult Hitler but sent second-rate officials to Stalin), and some effort was finally being made to work out military arrangements between Russia and the Western powers, the world was dumbfounded, despite abundant warnings, by the news that the Nazi foreign minister, von Ribbentrop, was expected in Moscow to sign a treaty on August 23.

Incompatibilities

Much has been written concerning the failure of Britain and France during the crucial years of rising German power, 1936–39, to come to an understanding with the Soviet Union, which shared their interest in stopping aggression. If the peace-loving powers had only stood together, Nazi Germany would hardly have dared embark upon military adventure, and the world might have been spared the unspeakable calamity of World War II. In this failure, much guilt is laid on the shoulders of the Western democracies, particularly Britain, in whose lead France felt constrained to follow. In Spain, they declined to support a constitutional, republican, and at first quite non-Communist (although socially radical) government against insurgents armed and assisted by Germany and Italy. They did nothing at all to support Austrian independence, and they abandoned Czechoslovakia which France had promised to defend. Chamberlain, coming home from Munich confident that he had served peace, became a symbol of political myopia if not cowardice. The Soviet deal with Hitler, publicly a nonaggression pact, might be excused on the grounds that, having been treated as of no account or ignored, Russia was properly justified, when the Western powers showed no great eagerness for agreement in 1939, in making the best arrangements it could for its own security. This seemed to Stalin and his fellows to be served by neutrality.

It is futile to seek to assign guilt. Behind the diplomatic failure were stark political realities which no individual could overcome or brush aside. It is clear that the Russians, particularly in their world view of the dichotomy of socialist and capitalist, had no reason to trust Britain and France. That these powers, whose relations with the Soviet Union had recently been so poor, would risk very much to carry out an agreement with it could not be assumed. If at any time they could find a *modus vivendi* with Hitler, they would have preferred this, the Russians were aware, to arrangements with Stalinist Russia.[27]

[27] Recent Soviet histories make such accusations as that the Western powers were trying to make a deal with Germany at the expense of Poland, and that the United States was intriguing to bring about war in 1939 for the sake of profits from munitions sales F. G. Zuev *et al.* (eds.), *Mezhdunarodnye otnosheniia i vneshnaia politika SSSR 1917–1960* (Moscow, 1961), p. 167; A. A. Akhtamzian (ed.), *Istoriia mezhdunarodnykh otnoshenii i vneshnei politiki SSSR,* Vol. I, 1917–1939 (Moscow, 1967), p. 423.

Wide World Photos

Signing of German-Russian Nonaggression Pact, August, 1939. Around Molotov, affixing his signature, are three German diplomats. Nazi Foreign Minister von Ribbentrop and Stalin look on from behind, pleased with the bargain which cleared the way for the opening of World War II.

It must also be recognized that Stalinist Russia was a difficult and unpleasant political partner for the Western powers in the 1930's. If only for internal political needs, Stalin kept up the idea of a general capitalist threat. The Soviet Union and its proxies abroad, the Communist parties, continued verbally to maintain the purpose of the overthrow of the existing social order. If they had practically, although not openly, abandoned internationalism, this hardly helped. There arose a new band of embittered critics on the Left to add their voices to those of the Right; and Communism had clearly not been abandoned as a tool of Soviet power. A nation that lays its bets on social revolution must expect the hatred of the established of this world, who are those with power of decision. There was at least as much fear of revolution in the West as there was hope for it in Moscow. Even the more democratic countries were apprehensive that security arrangements with the Soviets would lend respectability to local Communist parties, and the expansion of Communist parties in France and Spain in 1936–38 frightened conservatives more than the moderation of their line—which could always be reversed—reassured them.

But if association with the Soviets was politically disturbing to the West, this was only a faint apprehension compared with the dread of East European states of having Soviet forces on their territory. For such governments as those of Rumania and Poland, first on the list to be guaranteed, it was hard to visualize defeat by Germany as much worse than assistance by Russia. What sympathies there had been for the Soviets in these largely agricultural countries had been much diminished by Soviet collectivization policies, hardly less a threat to peasants than to landlords. Nor did historical experience suggest to either Poland or Rumania the wisdom of collaboration with Russia against Germany, whose ambitions were less clear. The depth of dislike for closer association with Stalinist Russia is suggested by the fact that in industrialized, democratic Czechoslovakia, with a tradition of Slavic friendship with Russia, there were not a few who preferred surrender to fighting with Soviet support.

The Fascist powers made the most of this repugnance. An essential element of fascism was anticommunism, both domestically and externally its strongest card. The notorious Communist purpose made it possible to denounce as a tool of the world conspiracy any nation assisted by the Soviet Union; Hitler could with some effect brand even Czechoslovakia as a Soviet puppet because of its halfhearted military agreement, and conjure up horrors of Red power in the middle of Europe. British conservatives were less than eager to see the unpleasant Nazi regime overthrown because it seemed to be the most powerful counterweight in Europe to the Red menace and the growing might of industrializing Russia which stood behind it. The Nazis presented themselves as the only possible alternative to bolshevism in Germany, and the Communists did their best to make this thesis believable. Not a few thought that the proper stance, as well as the easiest one, was neutrality in the struggle of the evil ideological giants.

It was easier to make a political tool of anticommunism and to alarm with exaggerated visions of the Bolshevik plot against civilization because the Russians did so much in the 1930's to cut themselves off from the world. Stalin deeply feared collaboration with liberals, who were potential leaders of antifascism. As the dictatorship hardened, it cut down foreign contacts of all sorts and alienated foreigners by arbitrary behavior both at home and abroad, especially in the critical years 1936–38. Foreign technicians were eschewed. A symptom of the times was the refusal to enter any Soviet film in international contests from 1937 until after World War II,[28] although earlier they had reaped numerous successes. In 1938 most foreign consulates were closed, those of democratic and peace-loving as well as those of fascist-aggressive states. Even the stream of ideological pilgrims to the Fatherland of the Workers, in full spate around 1932, practically dried up by 1938. Part of this isolation was the purposeful reduction of foreign trade, which might have done much to improve the Soviet image. Soviet trade shrank to only about 1 percent of that of the world, and the Soviet authorities congratulated themselves that, in volume of exchanges, the Soviet Union stood nineteenth in the world, although allegedly second in industrial production.

Hitler did not need, however, to exaggerate the evils of a society shut off from the world. They were real enough. The most monstrous of the many wrongs, the purges, swelled to an incredible climax in 1936–38. In part, these were directed at removal of disloyal and subversive elements; the Japanese and German secret services were active in the Soviet Union as elsewhere. To a far greater extent, their purpose was the destruction of potential alternative leadership to Stalin's. Idealists in the party and those of the international revolutionary tradition were nearly all shot; to have addressed a Comintern Congress before 1935 was practically a death warrant. So far as they came to trial, the internationalist leaders were accused of conspiracy with Germany or Japan, a charge nearly as discrediting to the Soviet system as to the accused. But not only old Leninists and persons possibly capable of aspiring to replace Stalin were purged. Tens and hundreds of thousands, many loyal Stalinists, others simply apolitical and insignificant, were killed, while millions were sent to labor camps, where their exploitation became a major factor of the Soviet economy.

Stalin may have been stimulated to large-scale purging by the success of Hitler's blood purge of June, 1934. But he far outdid his teacher, and

---

[28] Frederick C. Barghoorn, *The Soviet Cultural Offensive* (Princeton, N.J.: Princeton University Press, 1960), p. 52.

the Stalinist purges lacked historical parallel until Hitler furnished one in the wartime annihilation of the Jews. Western students have sought in vain a rational explanation of their extent and ferocity. Debilitating to the Soviet state, extremely costly in terms of talent and productivity which they removed from Stalin's service, they must be considered the product of a grave abnormality. In view of them, it was difficult to say in 1938 that Hitlerism was more evil than Stalinism, unless one were so convinced of Communist goals as to view any action taken by the Communist leadership as justified. But in the democratic society, foreign friendships and enmities must be based in part, or at least rationalized, in terms of the moral qualities of the states concerned.

The purges, although their magnitude was not fully appreciated at the time, gave an impression not only of arbitrary ruthlessness but of unreliability and weakness. How, Western statemen asked, could one rely on a state so many of whose leaders had been, rightly or wrongly, accused of plotting with national enemies? Who, then, could be trusted? What could be expected of an army most of whose senior officers were shot for treason? It was a black mark, too, that political commissars were reintroduced, potentially hamstringing military direction with party interference. At best, the Red Army would require, as events showed, a considerable period of readjustment and relearning before it could become an effective force. This, together with memories of the early years when Poland had defeated Soviet Russia, led to the common judgment, ridiculous in retrospect, that Poland represented a weightier military power.

The Byzantine and fear-ridden currents of Russian politics also flowed directly into the conduct of foreign affairs. Soviet embassies were terrorized, inhibited from any sort of initiative, independent intelligence, or appearances of friendliness with foreigners, and given to clandestine operations. Their staffs were chosen not for skill or experience but for political reliability, and if ambassadors were capable they lacked competent support. The conduct of Soviet foreign policy was a mirror of the morbid Stalinist state. Even when its message may have been the most virtuous, its motives could be suspect; when the Soviets called for a stronger League of Nations, it was asked whether this was not designed to embroil the capitalist nations. Stalin's approach to the outside world was the same as that toward his domestic opposition, to weaken by division while exposing himself as little as possible until he should be ready to step in and gather the harvest of power. It was unreasonable to expect frank and fair dealings from a leader capable of not only liquidating millions but terrorizing his closest associates, even if Soviet negotiating tactics had not been unpredictable, narrow-minded, and careless of implied commitments. Capable of falsification as the Stalinist leadership was in internal affairs, there was no reason to rely on its word in external matters; no Western power felt it could count on a Soviet pledge. For his part, Stalin seems to have felt more comfortable in dealing with Hitler, a man nearer his own political character. There was certainly a less common ground for understanding between Western democratic leaders and the Stalinists than between these and the Nazis.

3. COEXISTENCE WITH HITLER

Nazi-Soviet Pact

The epitome of secret diplomacy, which the Bolsheviks had violently denounced in their first years, negotiations for an understanding between Russia and Germany were conducted in the shadows long before they were announced to the world. Stalin, having been slow to recognize Hitler as a menace, hardly ever gave up on the idea of renewing the friendly and mutually beneficial relations which had prevailed between Soviet Russia and rightist elements in Germany, especially the military, through the 1920's and into Hitler's first year in office. Stalin was less afraid of Hitler because, with his crude political realism, he thought the army, which was friendly to Russia, must be the real power in Germany. The Nazi party in its beginnings was rather close to bolshevism and had no special antipathy to it, although Hitler found anticommunism the most useful instrument for securing the support of the wealthy and powerful.

Anticommunism was much more important to the Nazis than antifascism was to the Communists; and in the oratorical battle before and after the Nazis gained power, the latter were usually the aggressors. The Soviet leaders never closed the door to improved relations, and they made it clear that repression of the German Communist party was no obstacle. Off and on from 1935 to 1937, Stalin made feelers, chiefly, it seems, behind the back of the Foreign Commissariat and through the Soviet commercial office in Berlin. It may have been a purpose of the purges to eliminate the Leninists who might have stood in principle against contracting with Hitler; at least, that was their effect.

In the first half of 1938, the Soviets delivered to the West some subtle warnings that if collective security were not promptly organized, they would feel free to look elsewhere, while Berlin received renewed hints that normalization would be welcome. As tension mounted in that summer, there was an understanding to moderate press polemics between the ideological antagonists. The Munich deal was a powerful stimulus for the Russians indeed to turn elsewhere, and Stalin again hinted his readiness to do so in a speech in January, 1939, in which he accused the Western powers of wishing to make trouble between Russia and Germany. He repeated this message, saying that Germany did not have designs on the

Ukraine and that the Soviet Union would be no one's catspaw, a few days before German troops marched into Prague.

Although since Munich Hitler had toned down his vituperation against the Soviets, he had not yet resolved to turn away from the anticommunist, anti-Soviet line which served him so well. In a curious move in January, Hitler sent out a trade delegation to the Soviet Union but recalled it on the way. He preferred to work with Poland if that were possible, giving Poland part of the Ukraine in exchange for the Polish Corridor. But at the beginning of April, the situation had radically evolved. In occupying the torso of Czechoslovakia, Hitler had liquidated the puppet state of the Carpatho-Ukraine, which would have been useful for any designs of detaching the Ukraine from Russia. And the Poles, backed by a British promise of full support, refused to consider the territorial concessions which Hitler—and probably most Germans—thought indispensable in the east. Henceforth, the stage was set for a deal between Russia and Germany at the expense of Poland, and the chief wonder is that five months were required to consummate it.

The reasons for delay seem to have been that Stalin wished to bargain with both sides to get as much as possible, and that Hitler, perhaps from old Austrian prejudices, was more deeply opposed to rapprochement with Russia than most influential Nazis. The initiative at first was the Russians', although the official Soviet history depicts Russia as the shy object of competitive courtship. In April the Soviet ambassador again made clear that ideology had no necessary relevance to state relations, as shown by Soviet-Italian relations. *Pravda* accused Britain and France of inciting Germany to seize the Ukraine. In May the Soviet government in effect gave *de facto* recognition to the German appropriation of Czechoslovakia, and the Soviet chargé in Berlin let it be known that his country preferred an understanding with Germany to a defense pact with the Western powers. Molotov suggested restarting the trade talks which had nearly begun in January, and in mid-June the German trade delegation arrived in Moscow.

In July bargaining got underway in earnest. Now, however, the eagerness was on the German side because a date had been set for the attack on Poland and the wheels were turning for war. With a deadline ahead, and the British and French evidently firm in their determination to allow Hitler no more aggrandizement, the Nazis now felt an accord with Russia was urgent. They took the realistic view that they could give more material advantages than the Western powers. They explicitly offered neutrality, whereas the Britain proposed an opportunity to participate in a European war; and they hinted Soviet control of the Baltic states which Britain could not give. And whereas the Soviet negotiator had dismissed ideology as unimportant, the German made the interesting suggestion that, whereas bolshevism had been subsumed in nationalism, Germany,

Italy, and the Soviet Union really had equivalent ideologies. The Soviet side had raised its demands from a simple entente to a nonaggression pact and then to a delineation of spheres of influence in Eastern Europe.

In the first days of August, Hitler gave instructions for rushing the negotiations to completion. On the 19th, a trade treaty was signed, and Stalin gave the desired permission for the German foreign minister, von Ribbentrop, to come to Moscow to complete the political agreement. Hitler fell into rare inarticulateness from joy. The published treaty of August 23 was only a nonaggression pact, a promise by the partners to abstain from hostile actions against each other. But it lacked the clause, usually inserted in Soviet nonaggression pacts, voiding the obligation if one party should attack a third party; and, because of Hitler's haste, it was to come into effect without delay for ratification. More sinister was the secret protocol turning over to the Russian sphere the Baltic states, eastern Poland, and Bessarabia.[29] There was also an agreement, in the spirit of alliance, for future consultations on matters of mutual interest, and a commission was to be set up to settle possible differences. With a certain insensitivity, the Russians tried to keep up their conversations with the Anglo-French military mission for a few days after the pact was signed; but the Soviet Union had turned definitely away from the West.

At the time, this seemed a major stroke for Stalin. At the minor cost of the Soviet reputation as champion of peace, independence of nations, and antifascism, he received the promise of being able to remain out of the coming conflict, at least until it should suit him to enter, plus the dividend of recovering a major part of the tsarist lands lost after the Revolution. Stalin may have believed that the Anglo-French allies would refrain from entering an unpromising war, as he would have done in comparable circumstances. But when they, somewhat relieved not to have Stalin for an ally, showed continued determination to fight for Polish independence, this was enormously promising. From at least 1925, Stalin had been looking and perhaps hoping for war between capitalist states; capitalist war should bring an extension of communism, that is, as communism and revolution were understood by Stalin, of Soviet power.

The deal was entirely in the Russian autocratic tradition. Tsarist Russia had during most of the nineteenth century held to a Prussian or German orientation; and down to the outbreak of World War I, Russian conservatives or reactionaries had longed to return to it. After World War I, too, the feeling had been strong among Russians, Bolshevik or not, that Russia had been maltreated by the West and should better associate itself with the fellow-sufferer, Germany. Even Litvinov, apostle of the pro-Western slant, in 1938 said that the Allies had held back to permit Germany to destroy Russia (a curious idea in view of their millions of dead) and that

[29] This is ignored in Soviet historiography.

in return Russia would let Germany and the West fight and would intervene only to settle the peace[30] or to pick up the pieces. It was a profound relief for the Russians to escape the necessity of treating with the British-French centers of liberal capitalism and to find their way back to a German entente ruptured for a few years by Hitler's caprice.

The Nazi-Soviet deal is also understandable in terms of the personalities of the participants. Whereas Chamberlain had an extremely poor opinion of Stalin and his state, Hitler and Stalin could not find a great deal to object to in each other's political system. The supreme law of both was the will of the leader, who ruled by force, terror, manipulation, and propaganda and received corresponding adulation. Both regimes were nationalistic, antiforeign, and hostile to capitalistic democracy. Stalin even shared more of Hitler's anti-Semitism than was apparent at the time. Hitler admired Stalin and was much afraid that he might be replaced by an inferior. Stalin, highly suspicious of honest and decent people, seems to have had some real, although naïve trust in Hitler, with whom he must have felt some community of spirit. At the signing of the pact, he toasted, "I know how much the German nation loves its Fuehrer; I should therefore like to drink to his health."[31]

Whether it was wise or not is a different question. It was obvious as *Realpolitik*, and at first it seemed entirely successful, as Germany, France, and England went to war while the Soviet Union calmly digested its spoils. As Molotov said in its defense, "Is it really difficult to understand that the USSR is pursuing and will continue to pursue its own independent policy, based on the interests of the peoples of the USSR and only their interests?"[32] Of course, the Soviet Union had been long and loudly claiming to look beyond its selfish (and short-term) interests. In seeking neutrality, Stalin was probably doing about as well as he could in view of the difficulties of understanding between Russia and the West; when the British, by their hasty guarantee of Poland, presented the opportunity, it would have required far more idealism than Stalin possessed to resist the temptation. The secret division of spheres was much more reprehensible, and it actually brought grief, as the territories acquired could not be made an asset in the short time they were held; and this greed did far more harm to the Soviet moral position than standing back from the war. But history would perhaps have forgiven Stalin this sin, if in consenting to the partition of Poland, he had not overestimated (as everyone did) the ability of the Western powers, particularly the overrated French army, to check the Nazis and had not underestimated the danger of having them as immediate neighbors.

---

[30] Josef Korbel, *The Communist Subversion of Czechoslovakia* (Princeton, N.J.: Princeton University Press, 1959), p. 33.

[31] Angelo Rossi, *The Russo-German Alliance* (Boston: Beacon Press, 1951), p. 39.

[32] Alvin Z. Rubinstein (ed.), *The Foreign Policy of the Soviet Union* (New York: Random House, Inc., 1966), p. 157.

The world did not have to wait long to see consequences of the deal, as on September 1 the Nazis slammed into Poland in the new style of blitzkrieg, smashing resistance more rapidly than anyone, including Stalin, had expected. Within a week the Polish army was practically destroyed, although strong points, such as Warsaw, held out a good deal longer. The Germans immediately invited the Soviets to enter and take their share, but they held back a little, for fear of appearances, until German armies were slicing toward the lands allotted to Russia. On September 17, the Red Army crossed the border to give the Soviet Union its first territorial increase since the times of the civil war.

This was a significant step toward joining Germany in aggression. At the very beginning of the war, on September 2, there seems to have been an inclination to observe strict neutrality; there was even a hint of selling munitions to Poland. The Comintern shifted its position only partially on August 23; Communist parties could still be anti-Nazi and support the British and French stand and the war against Germany. The French Communist party took a patriotic position, and its leader, Thorez, joined his regiment with party approval on September 6. The sharp turn came after the Soviet entry into Poland. Communist parties around the world assessed the war as a purely imperialistic struggle of predatory capitalist powers for world markets; those in Britain and France assumed the posture of "revolutionary defeatism," hoping that defeat by Hitler should bring revolution. The Soviet press swung from a neutral to a pro-German position. "Warmonger" came to mean "Anglo-French imperialist," and the old theme of Germany as victim of the exploitation of Versailles returned. When Germany proposed making peace on the basis of the new status quo, the Soviet Union vocally supported this suggestion, perhaps with fears that it might be accepted.

As Britain and France refused to acknowledge the suppression of Poland and rejected Hitler's peace, Molotov found that they had become aggressors by continuing the war. This theme was upheld in months following; as *Pravda* stated on January 26, 1940, "The war was declared by Britain and France. The peace proposals were not rejected by Germany but by Britain and France, who insist not only on continuing the war but on spreading it."[33] The world could fairly well judge during these months that Russia and Germany were allies. Von Ribbentrop was received in Moscow in late September with great pomp and cordiality. A new and much larger trade agreement was then signed, including extensive technical assistance for the Soviet Union, which in return for this and perhaps as token payment for territorial acquisitions, extended credits for German purchases of raw materials to defeat the blockade. Distrustful as he was of Western experts, Stalin received large numbers of German ones. Von Ribbentrop, most enthusiastic among the Nazis for the Russian

---

[33] Quoted by Rossi, *The Russo-German Alliance*, p. 82.

alliance, assured the Italian foreign minister that Stalin, having abandoned world revolution and become the champion of Russian nationalism was turning to a Russian version of German national socialism. In December Stalin received gushing birthday wishes from the German foreign minister, and replied, "The friendship between the peoples of the Soviet Union and Germany, cemented by blood, has every reason to be solid and lasting."[34]

Expansion

Lenin profoundly changed the outlook of Marxism by his insistence that revolution should be made by an elite leadership in the party. For Stalin, revolution, if it can be so called, was the extension of state power. Stimulated by Hitler's successful aggrandizement and favored with golden opportunities in war-divided Europe, he added some 22 million souls to the Soviet state and took his place as successor of the fifteenth-century grand princes of Muscovy, another great "gatherer of Russian lands" and non-Russian as well.

The first payoff of the compact with Hitler was the territory beyond the Curzon line, largely inhabited by White Russians and Ukrainians, lost to Poland as a result of the war of 1920. This area, in which Poles generally had superior status, was a sore point between the two countries, and as a non-Soviet Ukrainian area it caused some discomfort to the Soviet state. Hence it was with satisfaction that Stalin sent the Red Army to claim it as soon as the German blitzkrieg had broken major Polish resistance.

There was some difficulty in explaining this action to the world. Enough of earlier attitudes remained that Stalin had a little feeling for world opinion and the charge of collaboration in banditry with the Hitlerites, whom the Soviets had recently been denouncing in the name of the rights of small nations. Hence at first Molotov wished to present the action as coming to the rescue of peoples threatened by the Germans. Not unnaturally, the Germans protested against this. The communiqué was modified to speak of "kindred Ukrainians and White Russians" abandoned by the dissolution of the Polish state. As the Polish state was regarded as having ceased to exist, the Polish diplomats in Moscow were held to have lost their immunity and were jailed—an innovation of diplomatic practice—until released upon German and Italian intercession.[35]

The Soviet forces occupied the area assigned to them rapidly against

[34] *New York Times*, December 25, 1939.

[35] Adam B. Ulam, *Expansion and Coexistence* (New York: Frederick A. Praeger, Inc., 1968), p. 282.

slight and disorganized Polish resistance. It included a rather populous slice of ethnic Poland extending nearly to Warsaw. By a subsequent deal with Germany, this part of Polish Poland was traded for the part of Lithuania which had previously been assigned to Germany; the new frontier was drawn to the east, close to the ethnic frontier. This was prudent and fortunate for future Soviet handling of both Lithuania and Poland. The incorporation of the occupied lands into Soviet White Russia and Ukraine was carried out rapidly, with pointless harshness and massive arrests which made much more reprehensible an action which could have been plausibly justified as protection of conationals of Soviet peoples. Molotov on October 31 summarized the demise of the Polish state: "One swift blow to Poland, first by the German army and then by the Red Army, and nothing was left of this ugly offspring of Versailles."[36]

With a haste that suggests fear lest the opportunity be missed, Stalin turned to the Baltic states. Despite nonaggression treaties concluded in different times with all of them, they were rapidly placed under Soviet occupation. First the Estonian foreign minister, representing the weakest and most exposed of the states, was summoned to Moscow and presented with a mutual assistance treaty providing for Soviet bases in Estonia; this was signed on September 28. There was also an agreement for a fourfold increase of trade. It was promised that Estonian sovereignty and its economic system would be respected. Immediately afterwards, Latvia was given almost identical treatment. Then in methodical sequence came Lithuania's turn, with the sweetener in this case that the old Lithuanian capital of Vilnyus, held by Poland between the wars, was returned to Lithuanian sovereignty, to the rejoicing of some Lithuanian nationalists.

At first, the Soviet hand in the Baltic states was kept gloved. The military forces stayed out of sight of the population. Some persons thought that the advent of Soviet power meant that revolution was now in order, but no disturbances were permitted, and the economic and social order was at first maintained with little change. With Hitler's victory over France, however, Stalin moved to incorporate them as Soviet republics. Soviet prestige seems to have required emulation of German aggrandizement.

The take-over presented no problems. More troops were pushed in; there were protests over incidents or supposed incidents; leftist but noncommunist governments were installed by ultimatum. The press was placed under control, the local armies were put under Communist command, and there were held one-slate elections, with only Communist candidates. Although some workers' efforts to seize factories were suppressed—Stalin had no love for spontaneity—the new governments pro-

---

[36] *New York Times,* November 1, 1939.

ceeded to nationalize the economy and to petition for admission to the Soviet Union. As *Pravda* said, "The sun of the Stalinist constitution now casts its beneficent rays upon new territories, new peoples."[37]

This acquisition of territories not inhabited by Russians but of strategic importance to Russia and with a long history of Russian sovereignty boosted Stalin's prestige with Russians, non-Communist and Communist. But it in no way improved the Soviet military situation and probably complicated the defense of the area by causing many of the inhabitants to rise in anti-Soviet insurrections when the war with Germany began and then to regard the invading Germans as liberators. It greatly hurt the Soviet image in the world. The manner of it was about as disagreeable as the fact, as it involved much naked force camouflaged with hypocrisy, brutal repressions, and deportations. Unhappily for Soviet prestige, political philosophy precluded the most understandable justification, that it amounted to reclaiming the tsarist patrimony relinquished under duress in a time of weakness, although this must have figured largely in Stalinist thinking. The action caused considerable bad feeling in England and the United States, both of which refused to recognize its legality. There were various minor causes of friction, as over the legations and funds of the Baltic countries claimed by the Soviets; worse was the view of a greedy, lawless, and unreliable Soviet government. Relations with Germany were also marred, as Germans, prominent in the area for centuries, were sent to the Reich. This was done in agreement with the German authorities; but the manner of evacuation, although not commented on at the time, gave Hitler a grievance he stored for 1941.

Relations with Germany, which had been so sweet a few months earlier, were also soured by the Russian grab of Bessarabia and northern Bukovina. The Soviets had never accepted the loss of Bessarabia to Rumania in 1918, although a majority of the population was Rumanian by language and culture. They had secured German assent to its recovery by the partitioning of spheres of influence in August, 1939. After the fall of France, Stalin hurried to claim it lest the Germans, now almost lords of the continent west of Russia, should renege. Stalin dispatched a short ultimatum to Rumania, and in his anxiety to have all the Ukraine under control he included in his demand Bukovina, a formerly Austrian province inhabited largely by Ukrainians. The Germans protested, as Bukovina had not been allotted to the Soviet sphere, but they somewhat grudgingly consented and advised Rumania to yield. Again, from the point of view of security it was an error, as the Soviets acquired a small territory which could yield no strength but some disaffection when

---

[37] David J. Dallin, *Soviet Russia's Foreign Policy 1939–1942* (New Haven, Conn.: Yale University Press, 1942), p. 259.

invaded a year later. Rumania, on the other hand, became a willing partner of Nazi Germany and a valuable ally in the attack on Russia, while Stalin's appetite and violation of the agreement were factors in Hitler's determination to invade.

The Soviet Union was thus shifted a hundred or so miles westward along the whole frontier from the Black Sea to the Gulf of Finland. This is often treated in the light of subsequent events as basically defensive, the pushing of the first line of defense farther from the heartland of Russia, giving more time and space to halt the Nazi invasion. It is doubtful that this was the main motive. There is no real evidence that Soviet leaders in 1940 considered invasion probable; although rearmament and mobilization were accelerated after Hitler's easy victory over France, this may have been merely an effort to keep up with rising German power for general purposes. Certainly Molotov when conferring with Hitler in the fall did not behave as though aware of any great dangers to his country, as he set forth demands on the Straits and other areas which Hitler regarded as belonging to the German sphere. No energetic effort was made to fortify the new Soviet positions to make them useful defensively. And when the German attack was really on the way, the Soviet leaders had great difficulty in believing it despite a myriad of warnings from their own as well as other sources.

When the attack came, Soviet armies were not well installed in their new emplacements, and they had to begin the war among a more or less unfriendly population. The whole area was lost in a matter of days, and the retreating Soviet armies were perhaps in a poorer situation than if they had waited in the homeland. If defense were the chief purpose, the Soviet Union would doubtless have behaved as it did in the 1920's when it was aware of weakness and mindful of the recent intervention. Its strategy then was to reassure its neighbors and secure their engagements not to lend themselves to hostile actions against the Soviet Union. Defensively, this would have been far more promising in 1940 than depriving them of their independence, as in the case of the Baltic states, or snatching part of their territory, as in the case of Rumania.

War with Finland

After dispatching Lithuania in the fall of 1939, Stalin turned as though in logical sequence to Finland. But the case was different from that of the Baltic states to the south. Unlike them, Finland had enjoyed much autonomy under tsarist rule, being joined only by the personal link of allegiance to the tsar—Grand Duke of Finland. It was regarded as nearly an independent country, and the Bolsheviks were quite prepared in 1917 for its separation, as for that of Poland. During the latter 1920's and 1930's, likewise, Finland was considerably more distant than the other Baltic states; and when the Soviet military protectorate was forced on Estonia, Latvia, and Lithuania, the Finns were resolved not to yield.

Stalin began quietly pressing for territorial improvements in the neighborhood of Leningrad even before the outbreak of the war, and he approached the subject in earnest when the other Baltic countries had been cared for. In secret negotiations through October and November, Molotov and Stalin demanded a strip of land next to Leningrad, some small islands in the Gulf of Finland, and the port of Hanko at the mouth of the gulf; largely to salve pride, they would cede a larger piece of land to the north as compensation. At first unwilling to yield anything, the Finns began bowing to superior power and agreed to various cessions; but they refused to surrender Hanko, and the Soviets insisted upon this.

Talks having reached this impasse, at the end of November the Russians created or alleged a minor border incident, threatened reprisals, and sent an ultimatum. The Finns, now seriously concerned, offered to withdraw troops and tried to reopen negotiations. But the wheels of the Soviet war machine had started to turn and there was no stopping them; and Stalin wanted the whole cake. In any case, he thought the campaign could not last nearly so long as the Germans' overrunning Poland, a much larger and stronger nation.[38]

Four days after opening hostilities, the Soviet government committed another egregious error by setting up and recognizing the "Democratic Republic of Finland." This was composed of Finns who had taken refuge in Russia on the defeat of the Finnish Communists in 1918, who seem to have been sufficiently out of touch with reality to persuade Stalin that the Finnish people would rise at their call to welcome the liberating Red Army. Their only recorded activity was the making of a few statements and the publishing of a paper. But they requested Soviet assistance in freeing Finland from the White Guard, and the Soviet government

---

[38] A semiofficial Soviet account of the beginning of the war relates, "On November 26, 1939, in order to raise tensions Finnish forces fired on Soviet troops in the Mainil district. The Soviet Union that same day warned Finland of the danger of such provocations and demanded the withdrawal of Finnish troops in the Karelian isthmus by 20–25 km.

"To the proposal of the Soviet government there was a provocative Finnish response, denying the fact of the attack on Soviet troops. . . . The Finnish military began to repeat the acts of armed aggression on Soviet border forces. This compelled the Soviet government on November 28 to declare that in view of the provocative behavior of the Finnish side, in violation of the Soviet-Finnish non-aggression pact of 1932, it considered itself free from the obligations undertaken by virtue of that treaty. On the following day, the Soviet Union broke diplomatic relations with Finland. Since Finnish troops continued provocations, on November 30, 1939, forces of the Leningrad military district began military actions against Finland . . ." (V. B. Ushakov (ed.), *Istoriia mezhdunarodnykh otnoshenii i vneshnei politiki SSSR*, Vol. II: *1939–1945* [Moscow: Izdatel'stvo "Mezhdunarodnye otnosheniia," 1967], pp. 21–22).

generously signed a mutual assistance treaty with them, including arrangements similar to, but more favorable than, those proposed to the Helsinki government. This "government" was probably an improvisation reflecting lack of planning, as even after the beginning of the war, Molotov had spoken of the government of Finland as legitimate and as the party with whom the Soviet government would treat. It may have been that the Soviet government felt that invasion was less aggressive if someone could be found to call for it, as in the invasion of Czechoslovakia in 1968 they claimed that unnamed party leaders had begged for help. But hardly anything could have done more to stiffen the resistance of the Finns than proclaiming a puppet government and the overthrow of the social order. The defense of border territories was turned into a struggle for national survival.

Resistance was stiff indeed. Expecting a victory parade, the Red Army was prepared for little more. The war which was to last two weeks was still stalemated six weeks later. Only toward the end of January did the Red Army, which had finally taken the measure of the situation, begin a strong drive. Masses of men and artillery were too much for the Finns to cope with; early in March the Finnish line was broken and they had to seek terms.

Because of threatening international complications, the Soviet Union was willing to scrap the puppet government and settle for little more than it had demanded in November. When, in the first weeks of the war, Germany had tried to mediate, the Soviet reply was hard, as though prestige depended on complete victory and fulfillment of the commitment of the "people's government." But the war became increasingly dangerous. The Finns appealed to the League of Nations, which, in almost the last gasp of its existence, took its strongest but futile action in expelling the Soviet Union from the League and exhorting member states to help Finland. Sympathy for Finland was widespread in the world, especially among the democracies, as this was the only state between Germany and Russia to remain democratic. Feeling was high in Scandinavia, as Finland is more or less Scandinavian, with old Swedish associations and cultural influences. The German government took a formally correct attitude toward its Soviet friends and halted munitions shipments, but it regretted having to oppose the Nordic Finns. The United States had especially warm feelings for Finland as the only country to pay its war debts, added to natural admiration for a brave democratic people. The war brought U.S.—Soviet relations to their interwar nadir, and a moral embargo was laid on trade. Reinforced by the subsequent annexation of the three Baltic states, this deep chill lasted until concern over Japanese intentions began, after August, 1940, to push the Baltic into the background.

Complications with Britain and France were potentially much more explosive. These countries had gone to war against Germany in the name of the independence of small nations, and it seemed to weaken their case if they should condone aggression by the Soviet Union while fighting Germany for it. A good many leaders, moreover, especially in the higher ranks of the armed forces, were more disposed to fight Soviet Russia than Nazi Germany. There also seemed to be possibilities of halting the shipment of iron ore from northern Sweden to Germany. Hence, there being no active warfare on the western front, Britain and France set about supplying arms to Finland; and plans were made for an expeditionary force to the Finnish front. Sweden, under German pressure to block Allied entry into Scandinavia, refused permission for transit. Preparations, however, went forward, perhaps for an operation to help Finland coupled with occupation of northern Norway to cut iron ore shipments to Germany. In February, as the battle was going ill for the Finns, the Allies did their utmost to persuade them not to make peace;[39] if the war had lasted another month, the Western powers might well have found themselves at war with the Soviet Union as well as Germany. Even after the March 12 Finnish-Soviet peace, they continued to work in this direction by planning to knock out the Soviet Caucasian oil fields by bombing in cooperation with Turkey. This folly was to begin about the end of June. They were saved from it by the German blitz against the Low Countries and France on May 10.

In this urge, the idea of hurting Germany by striking its supposedly weak virtual ally and economic partner was mixed with old anti-Bolshevist sentiments. It was also a demonstration of indifference to *Realpolitik* on both sides. So far as the Soviet war on Finland had any relation to the European contest, it was directed against Germany, the only power which could possibly threaten Russia through Finland; and it made the Germans very uncomfortable. The Allies, while deploring the means, could applaud the result. The Germans, on the other hand, far from welcoming embroilment of Russia with the Allies, made every effort to keep them out of the Finnish war and to bring this to a close. It is one of the speculations of history whether Allied involvement on the side of Finland would have led to a Soviet-German alliance (as the Germans proposed a few months later), in which the former would have been definitely junior, or to a settlement of the war between German and the Western powers as the latter turned from antifascism to anticommunism.

Saved by fortune from such troubles, Russia reaped from the Finnish adventure a harvest commensurate with its political misjudgment. Bad feeling between Russia and the Allies was immensely heightened on both sides, weighing against potential for cooperation down to, and even after,

[39] Anatole G. Mazour, *Finland between East and West* (Princeton, N.J.: D. Van Nostrand Co., Inc., 1956), pp. 123–25. For this episode, see also Douglas Clark, *Three Days to Catastrophe* (London: Hammond, Hammond, and Co., 1966).

the day German armies thrust into Russia. No less important, it gravely undermined amity with Germany. This power had been much more concerned with Finland than with the three weaker Baltic states. Having consented to Finland's being in the Soviet sphere by the agreement of August, 1939, Hitler kept his peace during the war. But after it, the Germans felt free to help the Finns, with whom they had sympathized in vain; and Finland became, to Soviet distress, part of the German sphere of influence. In due time, Finland provided a large part of the moral justification, perhaps not necessary but certainly useful, for the anticommunist campaign of June, 1941. Observation of the Russian difficulties also encouraged the Germans to undertake the campaign, as they concluded that the Red Army would not be a difficult antagonist. They tended to forget that Russians, too, can learn; and the deficiencies exposed on the battlefields of Karelia provoked a thorough overhaul of the Soviet armed forces.

In another way, too, the Russians showed that they could learn. Having been burned by the Finns' unexpectedly fierce resistance, they have since treated their small neighbor with caution and respect. Alone of former tsarist lands, Finland has been spared a real drive for total Soviet control.

Interlude of Isolation

Political treaties remain in effect as long as they suit the parties. It was not to be expected that the treaty of August, 1939, would continue to govern relations between Germany and Russia when the needs of the partners had changed. Germany's purpose in the agreement was assurance against war on two fronts; Russia's was to look on from the sidelines while Germany and the West battered each other. Both of these purposes were undone when Germany became victorious in the West, faced only by England. Germany then found itself perfectly capable of fighting against Russia while holding off England. The Soviets, on the contrary, no longer could count on any other continental power to check Germany. After the fall of France, relations between the two countries were consequently fluid; they might conceivably collaborate in the division of the world or live in uneasy and distrustful peace or come to blows.

Nazi-Soviet economic collaboration was at its highest in the first part of 1940, providing Russian oil, grain, and minerals of the utmost value for the Nazi war machine. German engineers were at work in the Caucasian oil fields. The transshipment of goods through the Soviet Union, in defiance of the Allied blockade, was very helpful to Germany. There was also some cooperation between the navies of the two powers. When the German forces went into Scandinavia in April, the Soviet press found it fitting retribution for Allied efforts during the Finnish war and more or less echoed the German explanations. The rapid German success in Norway, in the face of British sea power, was something of a jolt, but the Soviet Union was not unhappy at the opening of the big western campaign, on May 10, 1940, expecting a replay of the long and exhausting conflict of World War I, which would leave it well situated to decide the fate of the world.

The Soviet leaders apparently found the speed and completeness of the Nazi victory incomprehensible, as the Soviet press took a very optimistic view of the French position even as it was crumbling. In July, when France was out of the war and the British outlook seemed desperate, it continued to play up British strength. Molotov, perhaps to console himself, gave the Soviet Union part of the credit for the German triumphs. There must have been great uncertainty, for the leading papers published no analytical articles on the war through June and very few in following months.[40]

The Nazis were happy to be relieved of the necessity of making further disagreeable concessions to the Soviets, whose neutrality no longer had to be purchased. The Russians, on the other hand, rapidly placed their economy on something close to a war footing, looking for compensation for German aggrandizement while making some moves to propitiate the Nazis. The primary area they sought to contest was the Balkans, where Russia made most obvious its concern for the age-old objective of the Straits. In May and June, Pan-Slavist themes were revived, and diplomatic and trade relations were restored between the Soviet Union and Yugoslavia. With the Vienna award of August, 1940, under German arbitration, Transylvania was awarded to Hungary; German forces occupied what remained of Rumania, and the pretense of Soviet-German understanding in the Balkans was dead. With Finland, the Soviets failed to effect a reconciliation but rather alienated the Finns by various minor demands, which grew as they saw German influence growing and which further strengthened German influence. After June, 1940, there was no effort to cultivate friendship for Germany in the Soviet press; and there was no pretense of support for the German peace offensive of July, unlike that of the previous October. By this time, German deliveries to Russia were beginning to fall behind schedule.

Hitler was giving thought to invasion of the Soviet Union soon after France was laid low, in July, 1940. The definite decision was, however, made later; and the Nazis attempted in the fall of 1940 to establish a new and stronger basis for cooperation with Stalinist Russia. In September, Germany, Italy and Japan signed a Tripartite Pact, or broad military alliance. This specifically reserved relations with Russia, and the Nazis hoped to include this country in a mighty four-power alliance to con-

---

[40] Beloff, *Foreign Policy of Soviet Russia*, Vol. II, p. 327.

vince England of the uselessness of resistance and the United States of the folly of intervention, and so to share the rule of the world. The Soviets were cool to this idea; but in October Molotov, returning von Ribbentrop's visits to Moscow, went to Berlin, where he was received with much pomp and manifestations of solidarity.

Bargaining, however, was anything but cordial. The German side wanted a general agreement delimiting spheres, with the Soviets taking the area south of Russia in exchange for keeping out of the Balkans. Persia and India were the prizes Hitler offered, much as Napoleon had once urged Alexander I to invade India. Molotov wanted to play his own game with regard to Eastern Europe. Not listening but demanding, speaking tactlessly and as an equal to Hitler, who was now less than ever inclined to recognize equals, he expressed a Soviet interest in almost all the countries of southeastern Europe, especially Bulgaria and the Straits. The implication that the Soviet Union was entitled to compensation for German victories was entirely unacceptable to the Germans and to Hitler in particular. In sum, Molotov gravely overestimated the Soviet bargaining position, with the sole result of irritating the Nazis and giving them to understand that Soviet ambitions necessarily clashed with their own.

Apart from this overconfidence, Molotov misunderstood the psychology of the Nazis, as he was later to misjudge the psychology of Western leaders. He thought, in Oriental fashion, that it was smart to ask for as much as possible in order to settle for less. But his antagonists regarded his demands as a statement of aims; as these were unreconcilable with German requirements, they felt agreement was impossible. After leaving Berlin without results, Molotov expected to continue dickering, and he sent back from Moscow a few weeks later a list of Soviet conditions for joining the proposed quadripartite pact. First was that German troops be withdrawn from Finland. This Hitler had promised earlier, but Finland was of some importance to Germany, among other considerations, as a route to supply forces in northern Norway, and there was no intention of permitting the country to fall under Soviet domination. Second was that Bulgaria and the Straits be allotted to the Soviet sphere, which in the light of past practice might be taken to mean Soviet sovereignty. This was unthinkable for Hitler, as his route southwards lay here. Third was that Soviet aspirations be recognized toward Iran and India, as the Germans suggested. Fourth was that Japan renounce its coal and oil concessions in northern Sakhalin, putting Germany under the onus of securing this from Japan without compensation.

The Nazis did not reply but used the Molotov proposal to frighten small powers with evidences of Soviet designs, which only German protection could forestall. In January, 1941, Molotov made inquiry again, apparently still in hopes of joining the Axis. In the meantime, Hitler had decided to attack. Orders for "Plan Barbarossa" went out from his headquarters on December 18, with the tentative date for beginning May 15, 1941. It is too much to say that the invasion was definitely decided, as Hitler could and often did change his mind. But thereafter it was at all times easier to let the military machine roll on.

With Japan, however, Soviet relations improved. The Japanese were taken aback by the Soviet-German deal of August, 1939, and did not react to it immediately. A few days after August 23, the biggest Soviet-Japanese border clash occurred. But probes were discontinued, and the Japanese gradually smoothed various issues with the friends of their ally, regulating sundry outstanding differences in the perennial areas of friction, border demarcation, the Soviet fisheries, and Sakhalin concessions. Basic hostility continued, however, until 1940, about the time Soviet-German cordiality was evaporating. Japan was now expecting conflict with Britain and the United States and needed Soviet neutrality just as the Nazis had needed it in 1939. In April, 1941, the Japanese foreign minister, on his way home from Berlin stopped in Moscow and signed a nonaggression pact. This freed the Japanese for their southward march and the attack on Pearl Harbor in December, but it did not represent nearly so broad an agreement as the pact with Germany. Somewhat like von Ribbentrop, Matsuoka found ideological community with the Soviets, as the Japanese enjoyed "moral communism" and stood with the Russians against Western liberalism, egoism, and individualism.[41] But the Soviet government made no concession on its policy of aid for a China fighting Japan; there was never any collaboration or pro-Japanese propaganda.

Failure to find accommodation with an extremely powerful and possibly dangerous Germany would logically indicate a serious effort to find better understanding with the powers which might be able to assist if Germany attacked Britain and the United States. The government of Winston Churchill, who took charge from the less dynamic Neville Chamberlain when the invasion of Norway brought home the seriousness of the war, was much more disposed than its predecessor toward good relations with Russia. An outstanding statesman, Sir Stafford Cripps, was sent as ambassador to Moscow; but his hosts remained very cool, either from anxiety of provoking Germany or belief that Britain wished to involve Russia in the war. Although the Soviet government wanted to encourage England to keep up the fight, there were continual minor irritations, mostly over questions of shipping and the blockade, and little friendliness until, on the morrow of the German attack, Churchill hastened to pledge full support. When, in the spring of 1941, Churchill tried to interest Stalin in cooperation to check German progress in the Balkans, the response was quite negative. Much the same occurred in respect to relations with the United States, the principal improvement being the

[41] Beloff, *Foreign Policy of Soviet Russia*, Vol. II, p. 371.

lifting of the moral embargo in January, 1941. There seems to have been no idea that the prospect of the Anglo-Saxon powers coming to the assistance of Russia might have deterred a Nazi attack. It seemed harder for the Soviet Union to view these powers as potential friends than Hitlerite Germany.

In Europe, and especially the Balkans of everlasting Russian concern, Soviet diplomacy from the fall of 1940 through the spring of 1941 played a dubious and unsuccessful role of trying to check without provoking Germany, a policy of pinpricks which were only irritating. When German troops went into Rumania and Hitler guaranteed what was left of the country in September, 1940, this amounted to notice that no more Soviet claims would be allowed in the Balkans. However, the Soviet Union in October demanded, to the annoyance of Germany, a share of the control of the Danube. The next month, it protested indirectly the Hungarian decision to join the Axis; this was done in a manner much used by the Russians during these months, by quoting and denying foreign press reports. Toward the end of 1940, the Soviet government was trying to claim Bulgaria as part of the Soviet security sphere, or at least to impede its adherence to the Axis and occupation by German troops. These entered in January, 1941, and Bulgaria, despite Soviet protests, officially joined the German alliance in March.

From the end of 1940, Communist parties in the Balkans began opposing German influence; von Ribbentrop claimed to be worried by their activities. A bolder move was the attempted rapprochement with Yugoslavia just as that country was incurring Nazi wrath for its defiance. Hitler demanded that Yugoslavia, like Bulgaria, subscribe to his New Order; despite moral support from Britain, America, and Russia, the government bowed. But a popular outburst overthrew the pro-Axis regime and repudiated the agreement with Germany. This clearly meant invasion, but eight days after the coup the Soviet government signed, over German protest, a nonaggression and friendship pact with Yugoslavia. Stalin emphasized its importance by personal presence at the signing. He seems to have supposed that the Yugoslavs could hold out for a long time in their mountains and so thought it worthwhile to encourage them. However, the German offensive, which began hours after the signing of the treaty, required only twelve days to end organized resistance.

When the invasion came, the Soviets had no official reaction; and shortly they were trying again to conciliate the Nazis. Hitler, however, was infuriated. He forbad further negotiations with the Russians; and if previously there may have been some doubt, afterwards the decision to invade was fixed. But the invasion date had to be changed after the Balkan campaign against Yugoslavia and Greece from May 15 to June 22.

On seeing Matsuoka off in April, 1941, Stalin turned to the German ambassador and said, "We must remain friends and you must now do everything to that end." To evince friendliness, he made concessions in regard to the Baltic frontier and relations with the German navy. Extra grain was delivered, although German deliveries were coming to an end. In May the representatives of the governments of Belgium, Norway, and Yugoslavia, which had been driven into exile by the Nazis, were expelled from Russia, while official recognition was given to an ephemeral pro-German regime in Iraq. There was a clear sign of danger in the flight of Rudolf Hess, the Nazi Deputy Leader, to England on May 10, for the purpose of enlisting British cooperation in the coming crusade against bolshevism. But no effort was made to encourage friendlier feelings on the part of the British, as Cripps continued to be ignored and the two sides haggled over questions soon to become trivial, such as the assets in Britain of the former Baltic states.[42] Most remarkable of all, the Soviet army was ordered not to shoot at the German planes which were beginning frequently to overfly border areas.

The massing of millions of men and many thousands of tanks and everything else required for a grand assault on Russia could not pass unperceived, and there were countless warnings. Yet when the blow fell, June 22, the Soviet Union was entirely unready. There were no orders, apparently no plans; there had been no mobilization, no rushing to completion of fortifications, no regrouping of armies for defense. For some hours, units under attack lacked authorization to shoot back. In incredible folly, Stalin and his entourage refused to believe the obvious. As Molotov somewhat plaintively said and repeated in his broadcast shortly after the invasion began, they could not believe that Hitler would attack without presenting demands of some kind, which the Soviet leaders probably assumed they could bargain over. This is the way the Russians would proceed, but it was not a realistic assumption in view of the Nazi record; nor would it preclude preparations to strengthen the Soviet bargaining position. Probably more determinant was inane confidence both in the cleverness of Soviet diplomacy and military strength, in view of which it could not be conceived that Hitler would gamble on a second front before liquidating British resistance.

In short, Soviet policy in this time of testing, far from being well planned, coherent, and cunning, was ignorant, deluded, and contradictory. As though designed to make enemies and repel friends, it brought Lenin's state to its gravest danger since the days of the civil war. Only the enormous hatred that Hitlerism brought upon itself saved the Soviet Union. Because of this hatred, the Western powers were willing to forget the past and the sins of Stalinism and lend a hand to bludgeoned Russia, and the Russian people threw themselves into the support of the Stalinist regime to escape a harsher fate.

---

[42] Ivan Maisky, *Memoirs of a Soviet Ambassador. The War: 1939–43* (New York: Charles Scribner's Sons, 1967), p. 143.

IV

Stalinism: From Alliance to Cold War

1. SOVIET ALLY

Nations which participated in World War II emerged from its strain and torment deeply and permanently changed. But if Britain came to a complete reassessment of empire and its part in keeping the peace, and the United States shifted from a high degree of political isolation to a higher degree of worldwide involvement, the Soviet Union was strongly driven toward reconsideration of its entire political philosophy. The war was the most powerful contradiction of Leninism that could be imagined. It was launched by the power on which Leninist tradition laid most hopes, a power the political system of which could hardly be called finance-capitalism—during the war the Nazis spent much more effort denouncing capitalism than did the Bolsheviks—while Soviet Russia found itself not the victim of the antisocialist coalition which Lenin expected to return to the attack but the ally of the states of the most highly developed capitalism, Britain and the United States.

No less significant and closer to the consciousness of most Russians, the war was not fought on a class or internationalist basis but as a national and primarily Russian struggle. The victory was Russian and national, not proletarian and socialist. An experience that overwhelmed all old values, the war could not fail to have a profound effect on political thinking. The nation, fighting not for a long-faded utopian ideal but for its very existence, inevitably became something quite different from the revolutionary center of early Leninist days or the isolationist and self-regarding but nominally universalist autocracy of the 1930's.

The shock was profound. There had been little sense of danger but great complacency in the face of an obviously mounting danger. The Soviet leadership attributed the speed with which the Nazis overran Poland to national and class divisions within Poland, while they laid the fall of France to treason and the fifth column, troubles from which the

Soviet Union should be exempt. They had reorganized and enlarged the army since the Finnish difficulties, and one may assume that terrorized, inexperienced and incompetent generals gave extremely optimistic reports of their preparations. They allowed themselves to indulge such ideas as that the German soldiers could not be made to fight against the workers' state. The possibility that the Red Army might be driven back in case of attack was not contemplated, and provision was not made for it, but it was assumed that Soviet forces would be quickly driving into enemy territory. Indeed, Stalin seems to have contemplated opening hostilities himself in 1942, if the Nazis did not start sooner,[1] which certainly would not have occurred to him unless he thought it safe enough.

Payment for such monumental stupidity and bureaucratic negligence in preparation was the unmitigated disaster of the first three and a half months of the war. Most of the Soviet air strength was destroyed in the first few days, most of the tank force in the first few weeks. The German forces stabbed through again and again and encircled whole Russian armies, taking hundreds of thousands of prisoners at a time. Here and there a fortress held out, bypassed by the onrushing offensive. The first heavy resistance was at Smolensk, which held up the advance from the middle of July to the middle of September. But the Germans swept on to surround Leningrad and entered the suburbs of Moscow, where there was near-panic for a few days in October. Saved partly by the weather, as the German forces overreached their transportation and were poorly prepared, in their optimism, for the Russian cold, the Soviet armies pushed the front back during the winter. But the invaders the following summer smashed still farther across the south, taking a large share of the north Caucasus. Until after the battle of Stalingrad, a year and a half after the invasion, the fate of the state hung in the balance. This was a time not for ideology but the grimmest realism, and an appeal was made to the basic emotions of the nation to fight not a class but a national enemy.

Reversion to a clearer nationalism was easier because the Nazi advance had shorn off, like the treaty of Brest Litovsk, most of the non-Russian areas of the domain—the Baltic states, the Ukraine, and Bessarabia, and part of the Caucasus as well. Russia was pushed back nearly to ethnic Russian lands. Moreover, in the testing, the internationalist ideology proved sadly wanting. Virulently nationalist Germany gathered much more of an international following, with Italy, Hungary, Slovakia, Rumania, and Finland joining the crusade. The only ally of the Soviet Union at first was Great Britain, an ally not by choice but by circumstances. The world proletariat, courted for so long, whose first duty was to protect the Fatherland of the Workers, stood passive. There was no

---

[1] Alexander Werth, *Russia at War, 1941–1945* (London: Barrie & Rockliff, Ltd., 1964), pp. 123, 134–35.

significant resistance to Hitler's war in Germany as long as the Nazis were winning, and even when they were clearly losing, internal resistance was much more Western than Soviet oriented. Not even in junior members of the Axis did the workers offer any appreciable opposition to the war, and the Communist parties, or what was left of them in German-occupied Europe, were slow to stir.

Probably more serious was the failure of internationalism within the Soviet Union. Stalin took it for granted that the Volga Germans, who had had the benefit of Soviet rule for a generation, preferred that of Hitler. He scattered them shortly after the war began and before they engaged, so far as is known, in any anti-Soviet activity. Wherever the Germans penetrated minority areas, they found considerable anti-Russian feeling; probably only their own overbearing manners and insistence on the treatment of Slavs as subhuman prevented their mobilizing these sentiments to achieve the ruin of the Soviet state. Baltic peoples and Ukrainians generally welcomed the invaders until these had demonstrated their tactlessness; the Crimean Tatars were especially helpful, as were various Moslem groups of the North Caucasus. There was some effort to recruit the latter and Cossacks for the German cause, but the signal failure of the Hitlerites was to mobilize real and potential nationalism of the most numerous of all, the Ukrainians. The Crimean Tatars and several Caucasian nationalities were deported as punishment after Soviet forces recaptured their areas and there was no longer any military reason for this action. The Crimean Tatars and Volga Germans have never been allowed to return to their homelands. According to Khrushchev, Stalin would have exiled the Ukrainians if he had had a place to send them. The Soviet government had consequently to be dubious of its peoples except for the solid mass of Great Russians, and probably the Armenians.[2]

For these reasons, internationalism was overlaid by nationalism and the communist was dissolved in the patriotic cause. Ideology and ideological restrictions were largely dropped; literature was practically free, with the sole requirement that it support the war. The doors of the Communist party were opened not to ideologues but to good soldiers. The war was called by no socialistic term, not even "World War" but the "Patriotic" or "Fatherland War," a term which had been applied long before to the fight against Napoleon. In official statements there was no mention of a purpose of social change, only of justice, patriotic defense, and liberation from fascism.

Perhaps partly in imitation of Hitler's successful whipping up of a frenzied German nationalism, there was more emphasis on historic values of Russianism; and the people responded with dedication and enthusiasm. Stalin in November, 1941, urged the army to take inspiration from "the

---

[2] Werth, *Russia at War, 1941–1945*, p. 573.

gallant examples of our great ancestors: Alexander Nevskii, Dmitri Donskoi . . ." and the like, all Russian aristocrats. A typical return to past institutions was the establishment of army and navy cadet schools, in the tsarist tradition. In the same spirit, officers' ranks and authority in the army were strengthened; gold epaulettes were brought back, as were elite guard regiments, and the title of marshal was added to that of general. Similarly, diplomats were given dress uniforms of gray with gold braid in 1943, and they were divided into eleven classes of seniority.

As Russianism, even jingoism, was amalgamated with new Soviet patriotism and the friendship of the peoples of the Soviet Union, minority nationalities were flattered, given flags, and allowed more use of native languages. Most minority peoples were Slavs, and Pan-Slavism was brought out of the tsarist closet, to make the fight—as Hitler had done much to make it—a struggle of the Slavic peoples together against the secular Germanic enemy. This later had utility for Soviet expansion in Eastern Europe, but there can have been little thought of this when Pan-Slav congresses met in Moscow in August, 1941, and April, 1942, with representatives of all the important Slavic peoples. Stalin accused Hitler of seeking to destroy all Slavic nations, and this was the theme of the Pan-Slavic movement, its committees, and its monthly publication. One purpose was to gain support for Russia in the Slav-descended groups of Western nations.

Pan-Slavism mingled with Pan-Orthodoxy, and the reconciliation of Stalinism with religion was extremely important for solidifying the state. As soon as the war began, attitudes and policies toward the Orthodox church began to be eased. Church leaders with few exceptions resisted the temptation to welcome German forces as anticommunists. There was mutual acceptance: the church found Stalinism more acceptable as it became less communist and more patriotic, while Stalin called for the unity of all in the war. It took time for wounds to heal or at least to be covered over, but a general agreement was reached in 1943. The church regained much freedom and was allowed to restore the patriarchate, and it blessed the war effort and in many ways cooperated with it. Stalin may have been partly converted himself. Skeptical as he was of international communism, he wanted Moscow to be the world center of Orthodoxy. In 1944 he told the British ambassador that he believed in God in his "own way."[3]

Marxist-Leninist ideology was even more discordant with the international situation in which the Soviet Union found itself. It had been inconceivable that the Soviet state should be ally of a bourgeois state; but it appeared that cooperation with capitalists was not only feasible but perhaps indispensable for the salvation of the Soviet system. When the

[3] Werth, *Russia at War, 1941–1945*, pp. 437–38.

Nazis struck, Russia faced the grim possibility that Britain, under the leadership of the inveterate anti-Bolshevik, Churchill, would act more or less as the Soviet world view dictated and as the Soviet Union hoped itself to do, stand back from the war with or without some sort of understanding with the Nazis. Relations previously had been very cool, as the British ambassador had no access to Stalin and little even to Molotov. But Britain, injured by German bombardments, brought to the edge of unthinkable defeat, and utterly opposed to Hitlerian hegemony, did not vacillate. Stalin waited for twelve days before speaking out, but Churchill sent strong assurances of support the day after the attack. Happy to be no longer alone, the British welcomed the previously scorned ally.

Pro-Soviet feelings grew rapidly in England in the following months. The resistance offered by Soviet arms, although seldom successful at first, seemed the most concrete promise of eventual victory; failure before Moscow was the first reverse encountered by the German march to dominion. Although on a small scale at first, the British began sending military supplies by the dangerous route around Norway. In September, 1941, Britain and Russia joined hands in the military occupation of Iran to prevent a possible pro-German turn and to secure an alternative supply route. In May, 1942, a formal twenty-year alliance was signed between the powers, a pledge for cooperation long after the war could be presumed to last.

The United States likewise left behind its coolness immediately after the German attack and moved to give maximum support. President Roosevelt's emissary, Harry Hopkins, went to Moscow in July and brought back an encouraging report. He principally helped to set to rest the first fear of the Anglo-Saxon powers, that Russia might be swiftly defeated and give up the war, hence making fruitless the furnishing of supplies. In the desperation of the first months, Stalin was ready to welcome American or British troops on Soviet soil. The United States was far better able than Britain to give material help. Emergency and small-scale supplies were sent rapidly. Large-scale shipments were pouring in from the latter part of 1942, eventually to total many billions of dollars, including all manner of equipment essential for war purposes, the more important because the United States could fill many critical deficiencies in Soviet production.

Formally friendly relations were also quickly established with all the Allied governments in exile (with the partial exception of the Polish), especially the Free French, led by de Gaulle. In December, 1941, the latter offered and Stalin accepted a French division to fight on the Russian front. The idea was dropped, partly because of British opposition,[4] but a

---

[4] Alfred J. Rieber, *Stalin and the French Communist Party, 1941–1947* (New York: Columbia University Press, 1962), p. 9.

small French air squadron did fight in Russia. Cordiality had, of course, its ebbing and swelling tides, but it tended rather to grow through the war as the two sides became accustomed to dealing with each other and mutual respect grew, especially after the Western allies found themselves, like the Russians, fighting on the European Continent. Churchill was welcomed with exceptional warmth on his visit to Moscow in October, 1944; and the high point of hopes for indefinite cooperation came at the Yalta Conference, February, 1945, when Russia's need was far less desperate.

The numerous contacts of Allied statesmen with Stalin and Molotov made a rather favorable impression, although subordinates were more apt to be wooden-headed in old habits. The American Secretary of State, Cordell Hull, found Molotov a very agreeable gentleman, shrewd and able, although quiet and reserved,[5] and Stalin was characterized in high terms as a negotiator and statesman by Hull's successor, James Byrnes, a man very far from communist sympathies.[6] Their apparent decency can hardly be dismissed as mere pose and expediency. The Soviet leaders gained by turning a pleasant face to the West in these years, but they would also have gained by smiling on many subsequent occasions. In the war, they undoubtedly saw the world differently and responded appropriately. Suspicions, if never eliminated, were mitigated; and feelings for the capitalist allies seem to have been genuinely friendly.

A token of this attitude was the dissolution of the Comintern in May, 1943, for the stated and realistic purpose of facilitating prosecution of the war. This organization had no general meeting since 1935, and many of its leaders had been transferred to the direct employ of the Soviet Communist party in subsequent years. It had little significance, in any event, in the era when it was evident that communism was to be spread, if at all, by Soviet power. In 1943 bureaucratic functions of the Comintern were simply taken over by the foreign parties' section of the Central Committee of the Soviet party. But the gesture, amounting to repudiation of Lenin's favorite child to please such men as Churchill and (especially) Roosevelt, was not pure opportunism; it came well after it was most needed to induce the Allies favor. It represented some real weakening of organizational control, although habits of obedience remained strong in foreign Communist parties until into the Khrushchev era. As Zhdanov complained at the founding of the weakling successor organ, the Cominform, in 1947, ". . . some comrades understood the elimination of the Comintern to imply the elimination of all ties, of all contacts, between the fraternal communist parties. . . ."[7] "The Internationale" was dropped as a national anthem (though retained as a party song) and was replaced

[5] Cordell Hull, *Memoirs* (New York: Macmillan Co., 1948), Vol. II, p. 1174.

[6] James Byrnes, *Speaking Frankly* (New York: Harper & Bros., 1947), p. 44.

[7] Alvin Z. Rubinstein (ed.), *The Foreign Policy of the Soviet Union* (New York: Random House, Inc., 1966), p. 238.

by a good nationalistic-Stalinist hymn to Russia and to the Soviet Union.

It seems that the Soviet leaders began to feel real doubt of ideological axioms. They were certainly disenchanted with the old concentration on Germany and German Marxism. They no longer felt sure of the irretrievable hostility of the capitalist world, and they perceived possibilities of useful cooperation with "progressive" capitalist countries.[8] A book by a Soviet economist, E. Varga, spelled out this attitude: the American government, he concluded, represented all classes; hence there was no reason that the Soviet Union should not have good relations with it. In 1943 Deputy Foreign Minister Korneichuk spoke disparagingly of the "old ideology of leftist trends," preferring the "tradition of the Russian and Ukrainian people."[9] There is no evidence that Stalin or anyone around him consciously repudiated any part of the philosophy with which they had lived for a generation, but there was diminished certainty about it, and some became more disposed to pragmatism and questioning. The Soviet ideology of the postwar period, close as it was to that of the prewar years, was not simply a carry-over but a response to the political situation and needs of the time as perceived by the Soviet leaders.

At best, however, the Stalinist system could only very partially overcome, in the short space of four years, its political primitiveness. Despite a degree of relaxation in the new national purpose and unity, the state remained bureaucratic-despotic, with little lessening of the separation of rulers and ruled. Many idealistic or naïve visitors were shocked by the feasts the elite allowed itself amid the extreme privations of ordinary Russians. What later came to be called the "cult of personality" was not toned down but, especially after the tide turned at Stalingrad, elevated to deification, as Stalin took to himself credit for much of the Russian achievement. His picture became a common icon. When Eisenstein received orders soon after the war began to remake his film of Ivan the Terrible, it was not only to romanticize the darker Russian past but to glorify extreme Oriental despotism.

Consequently, there were a thousand irritants in relations between the Soviet Union and its allies for reasons having no direct relation to Marxism. The best an American coordinator found to say was, "It was not all bad."[10] Much of it was bad, and stiffness of the system operated to the Soviet detriment. It was very difficult for Allied officials to obtain information which they deemed useful for military judgments; old habits of secrecy and xenophobia stayed strong. Having retreated from the initial

---

[8] Barrington Moore, Jr., *Soviet Politics—The Dilemma of Power* (Cambridge, Mass.: Harvard University Press, 1950), p. 387.

[9] Josef Korbel, *The Communist Subversion of Czechoslovakia* (Princeton, N.J.: Princeton University Press, 1959), p. 84.

[10] John R. Deane, *The Strange Alliance* (New York: Viking Press, Inc., 1947). Ch. XII.

willingness to welcome British or American forces, Stalin gave up an opportunity to acquire a strategic bomber force because of reluctance to permit American bases on Soviet territory. Only with great difficulty and partial success was it arranged to have bombers land on a Soviet airfield after missions over Germany. In some cases, downright stupidity intervened, as in the refusal to give visas for American officers to instruct in the use of bombsights being furnished to the Soviets.[11]

Lower echelons, more bound to the system, were less reasonable than the upper, and there was a general feeling that if one could only get to Stalin everything could be arranged.[12] Because of their frustrations in dealing with Soviet officialdom, Allied representatives in Russia were apt to be much less friendly to the Soviets than the home governments. This was a curious reversal of the situation in the first months of the Revolution, when officials stationed in Russia were frequently influenced by the ambient idealism while their governments saw no reason for friendliness with the Bolsheviks.

A good deal of the reluctance to allow the Western powers much latitude for work in Russia was probably concern for face, fear of letting the foreigners see much behind the wall where conditions were inevitably poor and far below Western standards. There was not much inclination to give credit for assistance received; in March, 1943, the American ambassador complained on this score, and was rewarded by some good articles in the Soviet press. There was a strong tendency, perhaps only natural in an ally suffering great hardships, to believe that Russia was bearing more than its share of the common burden, as the bulk of German armed forces were on the Russian front, not only before but after the establishment of the Second Front in France in June, 1944. The Western powers were well aware that the Russians were fighting only because they had been attacked and consequently failed to appreciate the suggestion that they were failing to carry their end. Churchill particularly was inclined to feel that the Russians had brought their troubles on themselves by their Machiavellian conduct in 1939. There were some acrimonious exchanges about the convoys to northern Russia, which were suspended for a time because of excessive losses; the Russians saw their own losses and needs as incomparably greater. Warmth toward the Western powers would swing according to the view of what they were doing or failing to do on their various fronts and according to the Soviet feeling of pressure on the Russian front.

The Soviets and the Western powers fought two separate and only slightly coordinated wars, and a prime source of misunderstanding was the question of the Second Front. Suspicions hovered that the Western

---

[11] Deane, *The Strange Alliance*, pp. 235–36.

[12] Walter B. Smith, *Moscow Mission, 1946–1949* (London: William Heinemann, Ltd., 1950), p. 48.

powers were not entirely unhappy to see Germany and Russia tearing at each other's throats, while British and American armies were engaged only on a small scale. Stalin in his belated reply to Churchill's assurances of support, by his letter of July 18, 1941, began the long series of Soviet proddings for a Second Front. Russian disillusionment was heightened by promises or half-promises of an early cross-Channel offensive.

The United States particularly seemed to promise a Second Front for 1942. When this failed to arrive, as the Soviet need was most dire in the Stalingrad campaign, the Russians became decidedly suspicious and bitter. In February, 1943, Stalin was much disturbed to learn that it was envisaged only for late summer 1943. The African campaign and then the invasion of Italy helped somewhat, but the Russians were hardly to be assuaged by such chipping at the periphery of Nazi power. After the failure of the German summer offensive of 1943, Soviet armies made continual progress, morale was high, and anxiety for the Second Front was diminished. Its opening raised feelings of solidarity with the West, but suspicions still lingered that the Nazis might be fighting so much less hard on the western than the eastern front by virtue of a secret understanding with the Western powers.

By the time the Second Front had ceased to be an issue, a new and much graver area of differences between the Soviet Union and the Anglo-Saxon powers was coming to the fore. This was the question of the control of Eastern Europe, the borderlands between Germany and Russia and the Balkans. Although in the background, this was an issue from the very beginning, if not from before the war, as negotiations for a collective security agreement between Russia and the Western powers in 1939 hit the snag of Soviet desires for dominion in the Baltic area. Britain and the United States took a very dim view of the occupation of these countries in 1939 and their annexation in 1940. The seizure of part of Poland, in the name of whose independence Britain and France had gone to war, was also a very touchy point. Doubtless anticipating Western objections, the Russians had, from the beginning of their part in the war, made a point of pressing for recognition of their 1941 boundaries. When Eden visited Moscow in December of that year, the greater part of the negotiations were devoted to this problem, which had little relation to the war then being desperately fought.

Agreement could not be reached. Then and later, Britain was inclined to accept the Soviet position as something which could not be altered anyway, while the United States stood on principles and declined (as it declines to this day) to recognize the incorporation of the Baltic states. The American government feared compromising ideals and raising suspicions among the nations fighting the Axis powers;[13] there were also

[13] Hull, *Memoirs,* Vol. II, pp. 1167–68.

apprehensions of potential Soviet aims in East Europe beyond the 1941 borders. Because of this American stand, the Anglo-Soviet alliance agreement could do no better than ignore the question. It is a tribute to old habits of thought that, despite this difference, the Russians usually showed more cordiality toward Americans than Britishers.

What became of Eastern Europe depended primarily on military events. At the Teheran Conference in November, 1943, the British wanted Anglo-American forces to cut into the Balkans in a way that would have forestalled Russian control of this area. The United States, with less thought of postwar spheres of influence, stood for a great blow across France, and this was, of course, the Soviet choice. Thereby the pattern of division of the Continent was set. In March, 1944, the question of the future of East Europe became acute as Soviet troops entered the first non-Soviet territory, Rumania. The West sighed with relief when Molotov assured the Rumanians and the world that there was no intention of "changing the existing social order of Rumania."

The Russians behaved, in fact, with a good deal of circumspection as their area of power expanded. Antifascist resistance was emphasized as a national, not a communist cause, and the role of Communist parties was checked in the interests of unity. When the Red Army moved in, it, not the local Communists, took charge. While a Communist party, such as that of Czechoslovakia, may have advocated joining the Soviet Union, such ideas were not encouraged. But fairly soon the area of Soviet military domination, which was made as large as possible for political purposes, began taking shape as a Soviet sphere of influence. In October, 1944, Churchill recognized this, suggesting an odd bargain: Rumania would be 90 percent Soviet "responsibility," Bulgaria 75 percent, while influence should be shared equally in Hungary, and Yugoslavia and Greece should be 90 percent British. Stalin accepted without discussion. In February, 1945, Stalin began showing what this meant, as Vyshinsky, backed by tanks, ordered the king of Rumania to oust the non-Communist but very cooperative government and to install a Communist as prime minister. Soon thereafter it was becoming evident that the Western powers were to be squeezed out, step by step, and sole control left with the Soviet command wherever the Red Army was the occupier.

The United States was unhappy with this division of the Balkan pie, although it was much more favorable to the Western side than the ultimate result. Although at first rather inclined to leave concern for Eastern Europe, as an area of no historic American concern, to the British, the United States was firmly opposed in principle to all spheres of influence except its own largely commercial one in Latin America. The United States shrank equally from taking strong measures to reduce Soviet control of the area and from recognizing a delimitation of spheres which would have minimized friction. In the American view, Soviet security should be based not on territorial control but on strong arrangements for collective security. It was conceded that the Soviet Union was entitled to have friendly states on its borders, but these should not be subject to coercion—a piece of unrealism which did not impress Stalin, who was ready to concede at the Potsdam meeting in July, 1945, that "A freely elected government in any of these countries would be anti-Soviet, and that we cannot allow."

The largest single object of contention was Poland. Of special concern because of its intrinsic importance in European affairs and strategic concern for the Soviet Union, as well as because of moral obligations to secure its independence, Poland was the subject of bitter dispute and wearisome negotiations through the entire war. This was the sole sign of a future rift at the rather harmonious Teheran Conference, and at Yalta it was the biggest topic as well as the subject of most passion on Stalin's part. For Allied unity, the Soviet Union resumed relations with the old Polish government domiciled in London, but relations never came near friendliness. The Poles adamantly refused to recognize Soviet title to the area annexed in 1939, despite British urging, and the Soviet government obviously wished a very different complexion for its postwar Polish neighbor.

In March, 1943, a Polish group in Moscow, the "Union of Polish Patriots" began publishing a Polish paper and formed what appeared to be the germ of a future Communist government. Soon afterwards, Nazi authorities announced the finding of mass graves of thousands of Polish officers allegedly murdered by the Russians in the Katyn forest near Smolensk, then still under German occupation. The London Polish government, concerned for the fate of its strongest supporters, naturally but somewhat hastily asked for an investigation by the International Red Cross. The Soviets made a counteraccusation that the murderers had been the Nazis; but most Western observers believe the evidence points to Stalin's guilt. At least, the Russians prejudiced their case, whatever it may have been, by extreme secrecy and refusal to permit any independent examination. Whatever the right, the Soviet government took the opportunity to blame the Polish government for collaborating propagandistically with the Nazis and severed relations. Thereafter, the Russians proceeded without inhibitions to build up the Union of Polish Patriots, which became the Lublin committee, and also to form a Polish military force under Soviet command.

As Soviet forces passed into ethnic Poland, preoccupations grew, and a more serious incident cast its shadow. When the Red Army approached Warsaw in August, 1944, the underground Polish organization affiliated with the London government rose against the German authorities. This uprising was remarkably successful for a time, but the Soviet army failed to move forward, and the Germans were able to crush the Polish movement in some eight weeks. Perhaps the Russians were unable to go to its rescue; they did not, in fact, take Warsaw until five months later. But there was a strong surmise that they held back, not displeased to see destroyed a movement and organization which they denigrated and which was anti-Soviet as well as anti-Nazi. That the Stalinists would be willing to let the Germans thus facilitate the formation of a pro-Soviet regime for Poland is fairly understandable, but again they proceeded without cunning in refusing to allow American planes helping the Poles to land behind Soviet lines—a minimum of cooperation which would have had little effect beyond greatly reducing the opprobrium falling to the Russians. Only as it became evident that the uprising was failing did the Russians furnish some supplies.

When the Polish premier, Mikolajczyk, had conversations with Stalin in October, Stalin assured him that communism was not suitable for Poland. But by this time, the Soviet government had officially recognized the Lublin committee as the government of Poland; the only Poles the Russians could rely on were Communists. The Allies thereafter also drew away from the unfortunate but stiff-necked London Poles, who still refused to countenance loss of the eastern lands, which were after all largely non-Polish in population. But while conceding the Curzon Line, drawn long before by a British commission, as the approximate Soviet border, with unspecified compensation for Poland from Germany, the Allies still insisted at Yalta that Poland should be democratic. This clashed head-on with the Soviet insistence that Poland be assuredly friendly or better; and Soviet armies were on the spot. Appearances were saved by agreement that some London Poles should enter the Lublin provisional government and democratic free elections should be held. But the issue of Poland was still to cause much wrangling and ill will.

In the meantime, the ideological slackening was gradually giving way to a reimposition of discipline and emphasis on doctrine and party line. By 1944 there had begun a process of purification in science, philosophy, economics, literature, and art, to reach its climax in the cultural purges of 1947–49. The Marxist interpretation of war was revived, that war arises from class and economic contradictions, with the implication that there could be no secure peace until the abolition of capitalism. Stalin interpreted nazism in Marxist terms as an outgrowth of German capitalism and began stressing the need for attention to Leninism. The recovery of occupied areas brought to the fore the question of reindoctrination; particularly in the Ukraine this meant combating infections of nationalism.[14] The subsequent Soviet penetration into formerly independent countries of Eastern Europe more strongly required education in the ideology of party and proletarian internationalism. The Soviet mission of unity

[14] Werth, *Russia at War, 1941–1945*, pp. 944–45.

U.S. Army

Yalta Conference, February, 1945. The Big Three—Churchill, Roosevelt, and Stalin—meeting here for the last time, turned their attention from the conduct of the war to the postwar settlement. Although problems which were soon to divide their countries were already looming, the leaders believed they could cooperate to assure the peace of the world.

could not permit the weary Russian people to relax in deed and thought.

Not too much should be made of frictions during the war. All alliances have their differences, the Russians were in many ways prudent and pragmatic, and the greater wonder, considering the disparities of outlook, is that there was fair harmony. The most important of the grand wartime conferences, that of Yalta, the last to assemble the three great leaders, Roosevelt, Churchill, and Stalin, went smoothly enough and laid the outlines of a settlement of the war. The American Secretary of State felt that the Soviet side made more concessions than the Western.[15] Although not much interested in the subject, the Russians accepted proposals, earlier agreed upon in principle, for an international peace-keeping organization. This they wanted to have headquarters in the United States as a check on American isolationism. The United States, on the other hand, made a concession to the appearances of Soviet federalism by agreeing that the Ukraine and Belorussia, the two Soviet republics most afflicted by the war, should have separate representation. Although Germany was divided into zones of the three powers, it was assumed that they could work together well enough to govern the conquered land as an entity. It was also taken for granted that the powers would cooperate in the delivery of reparations to the Soviet Union. The amount was not settled, but the Russians understood that they were promised $10 billion of a total of $20 billion that Germany would pay.[16] The Soviet Union had been expecting a large reconstruction loan from the United States, although the American State Department showed no warmth to the idea. About this time, when the British beat down a popular resistance movement in Greece, the American press reproached them for imperialist designs, while the Russians, faithful to the division of spheres, remained indifferent. The cold war was probably fated by the political environment and human nature, but the future participants, well aware of the importance of concord, did not know it until long afterwards.

Russia at War with Japan

Hardly anything could have been farther from Lenin's way than going to war at the behest of a capitalist power to avenge the injury inflicted on tsarist Russia by Japan in 1904. Stalin said the Soviet Union would enter the Pacific war because Japan was the "historic enemy" of Russia. After it, gloating in the recovery of everything lost in 1905 and more, Stalin spoke in a spirit of pure nationalism of how the men of his generation had

---

[15] E. R. Stettinius, *Roosevelt and the Russians* (Garden City, N.Y.: Doubleday & Co. Inc., 1949), p. 295.

[16] Byrnes, *Speaking Frankly*, p. 29.

waited forty years for vengeance—vengeance for a defeat which Lenin had once welcomed.[17]

When the Germans began to encounter serious difficulties in Russia, they tried to persuade Japan to hit the Soviet rear in Siberia. Likewise, shortly after Pearl Harbor, the United States wanted air bases in the Soviet eastern provinces, which would have brought Russia into the conflict. This was impractical, but Stalin was quite willing to settle scores with Japan as soon as victory in Europe untied his hands; and the United States, particularly the military leadership, strongly desired Soviet cooperation. Despite progress toward the atomic bomb, Japanese fanaticism and probable American casualties in an assault on the home islands were grossly overestimated. In April, 1945, the Soviet government denounced the neutrality pact. By its terms, the pact remained binding for another year, and the Japanese expected that it would be observed. However, it did not trouble the Russians, nor for that matter the Americans, and Stalin promised to go to war in Asia within ninety days after the end of the war in Europe. The Japanese had somewhat naïvely asked, as early as February, for Soviet intercession to make peace; but the Soviets did not pass this bid on to their allies. In the summer, the Japanese government again tried to get Soviet cooperation in ending the war, while also somewhat desperately trying to forestall Soviet action by concessions. The last demarche to this effect was interrupted by the Soviet declaration of war, on August 9, three days after Hiroshima.

The exhausted Soviet people had no appetite for this little adventure, which seemed more like a colonial than a national endeavor. The Soviet armed forces, however, performed well against slight resistance and in a few days swept over Japanese-held Manchuria and the northern part of Korea. At the time and thereafter, the Russians gave themselves major credit for the Allied victory over Japan. More tangibly, they regained losses, southern Sakhalin, influence in Manchuria and northern Korea, the old Russian-built railroad across Manchuria, and the Kurile islands, long ago traded to Japan in return for southern Sakhalin. They hoped to

[17] ". . . Therefore, we have a special account of our own to settle with Japan. . . . Japan began her aggression against our country as far back as 1904, during the Russo-Japanese War. As is well known, in February, 1904, while negotiations with Japan and Russia were still in progress, Japan took advantage of the weakness of the Czarist Government and unexpectedly and treacherously, without declaring war, attacked our country and assaulted the Russian squadron in the Port Arthur area to disable several Russian warships and thus to place her own navy in a position of advantage. . . . But the defeat of Russian troops in 1904 in the period of the Russo-Japanese War left grave memories in the minds of our peoples. It was as a dark stain on our country. Our people trusted and awaited the day when Japan would be routed and the stain wiped out. . . . For forty years have we, men of the older generation, waited for this generation, waited for this day. And now this day has come." (*New York Times*, September 3, 1945.)

participate in the occupation and have a share of control over Japan, but this the United States firmly denied them, and General MacArthur paid little heed to the Allied Control Commission on which a Soviet representative sat. The Soviet Union acceded to this exclusion in December. In effect, as the United States bowed out of East Europe, with only minor and rather formal concessions to American feelings, the Russians accepted the facts of power in Japan.

On neither the American nor the Russian side was policy well calculated in this phase of the war. Soviet military cooperation was unnecessary and brought many a complication, down to all the troubles born of the division of Korea. Least of all was it necessary to purchase Russian help at the expense of China, including the Port Arthur base. From the Soviet viewpoint, on the other hand, it was an unnecessary and unrewarding adventure. Russia could have reasserted its place in the Far East without incurring permanent Japanese ill will for perfidy.

2. COLD WAR

The sole reason for an alliance between Soviet Russia and Britain and the United States being the common antagonism of Hitlerite Germany, seconded by a militaristic and expansionist Japan, their friendship withered when its nourishment was removed. As soon as the war was finished, the two sides encountered opposition not in a menacing power between, but in each other. Instead of an overriding shared interest, they turned to divergent and often conflicting interests. Moreover, differences which because of wartime restraint and secrecy could be settled in the corridors or by quiet diplomatic exchanges became public political issues, and it became more politically profitable to take hard positions toward former allies than to smooth over differences by compromise. During the war, if Stalin wrote an offensive letter to Roosevelt accusing him or his advisers of duplicity in connections with negotiations for the surrender of German forces, he could express regrets afterwards and the incident had little repercussion. Afterwards, instead of minimizing differences for the sake of solidarity, leaders publicized them to mobilize support. The perennial cold war between Russia and the West was renewed as men lost the habit of thinking of former allies as friends and became accustomed to regarding them as adversaries.

Shortly after Yalta, with its warmth in the glow of approaching victory, the Soviet Union began dragging its feet on interallied cooperation, as in the unilateral and highhanded installation of a Communist government in Rumania, holding up the reorganization of the Polish government, failing to cooperate in the formation of a control commission for Germany, and the exclusion or hampering of Western observers in Easter Europe. Such frictions, mostly minor, multiplied in following months, and an attitude of ideological hostility was rapidly forming or reappearing. In August Kalinin, the formal Soviet head of state, warned that "the perils of capitalist encirclement" had not disappeared with Hitlerite Germany. Molotov amplified and emphasized this message in his speech on the anniversary of the Revolution; and shortly afterward Stalin, blaming World War II on monopoly capitalism, reaffirmed the basic hostility of the capitalist world.

There were more occasional mutterings than systematic polemics, which hardly began in form until 1947. But the evolution of policy and opinion was quite as marked on the Western, especially the American, side. Having been led or permitted by American officials to hope for large-scale help in reconstruction,[18] Stalin in January, 1945, suggested a loan of $6 billion; this meeting no sympathy, he applied for a mere $1 billion in August, but the application was lost in the State Department. Economic cooperation was made contingent on broad changes of Soviet economic policy, including opening of Soviet accounts to international inspection. Meanwhile, the United States had halted lend-lease aid to Russia on the very day of the German surrender, a bit hastily it seemed to the Russians, especially as they were pledged to go to war with Japan. Consideration for Soviet feelings became much less as possession of the atomic bomb—news of which was given to Stalin at Potsdam—reduced the need.

Immediately after the Japanese surrender, Secretary Byrnes made a statement of American purpose which, while more sophisticated than the Soviet counterparts, was no less portentous of conflict. Stressing the importance of trade, he opposed the liberal American approach to ideologies denying economic freedom.[19] The American army had already threatened force to compel the Yugoslavs, then regarded as practically Soviet agents, to withdraw from Trieste; and early in 1946, President Truman was moving toward the idea of a military alliance to contain Soviet expansion. In March, 1946, Churchill made his epoch-making speech popularizing the phrase, "Iron Curtain"; to the applause of Truman, he practically called for the Anglo-Saxon powers to roll back Soviet hegemony of Eastern Europe.

Part of the shift away from alliance was a shift of leadership. When the great need was for cooperation with the Russians, persons sympathetic to this cooperation came forward or were found more suitable for negotiations. Afterwards, they were generally replaced, perhaps less because of their sympathies than because of the turnover of governments, attritions, and the demands of a different world. The somewhat leftist entourage of President Roosevelt gave way to men of much more conservative views.

[18] Stettinius, *Roosevelt and the Russians*, p. 120.

[19] Walter Lafeber, *America, Russia and the Cold War, 1945–1966* (New York: John Wiley & Son, Inc., 1967), p. 7.

James Byrnes, President Truman's Secretary of State, had little sympathy for the social and economic claims of Leninism. Decisive for the increasingly bipolar world was the philosophy of Truman. To some extent, Roosevelt had tried to make himself a mediator between Churchill and Stalin; but England was so severely weakened that it dropped back more and more, leaving the field to the United States and Russia. If the latter was to be checked, only the United States could do it, and Truman was willing. Two days after the German invasion of Russia, Truman (as a senator) had expressed the hope that Germans and Russians would kill as many as possible on both sides, and he was from the first unabashedly hostile to the Soviets. Roosevelt had tried hard for understanding, realistically or not; Truman felt that the Russians understood only force and so must be met with force wherever they overreached themselves, that the United States should as well be tough sooner as later. Immediately after taking office, in April, 1945, he gave Molotov a scolding on Soviet behavior in Poland, which shook that steady man, although it had no apparent effect on the fate of Poland. In due course, Truman led the United States into the policy of world-girdling alliances to hem in Soviet power under the threat of nuclear attack.

If Truman did little to bridge differences with the Soviet Union, he was not markedly aggressive, and antagonisms would undoubtedly have grown regardless of the leading personality in Washington—perhaps regardless of the leader in the Kremlin as well. If there was no necessary conflict between communism and capitalism, there certainly was between the two strongest powers left in the world, each of which became *ipso facto* the principal check on the will and influence of the other; and contention over the boundaries of the respective spheres from Germany to Korea could only have been avoided by high statesmanship and mutual willingness to accept delimitation, both of which were lacking. But all differences were much intensified, and their compromise made much more difficult by great differences of psychology and political philosophy.

After the war Russia suffered all the enduring contradictions of its relations with the West. In the exhilaration of victory in the greatest of wars, bought by tremendous loss and suffering, there was great pride and confidence; yet Russia was desperately poor. Russia emerged with a much expanded realm yet was painfully aware of insecurity, as the United States held the superweapon which could destroy cities in an instant. Prior to the war, Soviet industrial production had been several times smaller than the American; while the Soviet economy was devastated, industrial production being practically cut in half, the American was greatly stimulated by unlimited wartime demand. Soviet steel production in 1945 was only one eighth that of the United States, and this indicator was and is relatively favorable for the Russians. The impoverished Soviets had immense needs for rebuilding and nothing to spare for other countries; rather they extracted what they could wherever they could. The United States, by contrast, could grant or loan billions of dollars with the satisfaction not only of aiding needy peoples but of helping to keep the economy booming. By aid, first to Britain and subsequently many other countries, the United States began soon after the end of the war the consolidation of a Western economic sphere. This appeared to the Soviets as the building of an anti-Soviet coalition which they could oppose only in ways which earned more ill will. The United States could offer wheat, coal, and machines; the Soviet Union could furnish indignation and words.

Having engaged and defeated the bulk of Nazi forces, the Russians came out of the war with enormous pride and confidence in their power. Yet they were suddenly robbed of superiority, indeed of security, by a technological fluke; the determination and sacrifices of millions were outweighed by the wizardry of the laboratory. A major purpose of using the atomic bomb to devastate Japanese cities seems to have been to impress the Russians and make the bomb more useful in diplomacy. When Stalin was told of the new weapon at Potsdam, a few days after the first test explosion, possibly having advance information, he betrayed no emotion. The news of atomic destruction of Hiroshima and Nagasaki was played down but was obviously depressing.[20] Afterwards, nuclear weapons were belittled in statements for the world and ignored in discussion at home. The Soviet state went to work behind the scenes very energetically and successfully on nuclear energy and missiles, but not until the middle 1950's could Russia feel reasonably near military security. And just ten days after Hiroshima the Soviet planning agency was instructed to draw up plans for a new and ambitious five-year development to secure the "technical and economic independence of the Soviet Union."

Material inferiority was balanced by claims and convictions of political superiority, which meant a universal righteous destiny justified by possession of the truth and by the sacrifices of Russia in the cause of victorious humanity. The result was a passionate quest for security, to be achieved only by power and control, not in cooperation with other states but in opposition to them. The staking out of an exclusive sphere, which appeared to the West as mere empire building, the Soviet leaders could regard as entirely moderate, especially in view of the gains of the United States in Germany, Italy, Western Europe, and Japan. The exclusion of the Soviet Union from the control of Italy was thus taken to justify the exclusion of Allied representatives from Eastern Europe. In the Soviet interpretation, these lands had become prey to overwhelming American monopoly-capitalism, a far greater reward for much smaller sacrifices.

---

[20] Werth, *Russia at War, 1941–1945*, p. 1037.

Having come through the war with an unchanged leadership in the person of Stalin and his Politburo, the Soviet Union not surprisingly made the same general responses to political needs as in prewar years. The Soviet Union and to a high degree the entire area of its control was isolated by the well-known Iron Curtain, the impermeability of which has been largely forgotten. Travel and exchanges of any kind between East and West were almost nonexistent except for a necessary minimum of official business, a few politically approved, that is Communist, visitors, and contacts essential to the borrowing of technology, itself feared as bearing ideological infection. A continued regime of terror, never renewed on the cataclysmic scale of 1936–38 but sharp and persistent, operated to repress divisive or dangerous currents at home. The Soviet people were denied, in the interests of unity and the building of new strength, the release and renewal they felt they had earned by loyalty through hardships; and for this it was necessary to keep to the fore the antithesis of the right and wrong, the socialist and capitalist, worlds. The supranational ideology was more than ever essential. Stalin, too, emerged as a powerful unifying symbol, and the exaltation of his person rose to new extremes after the war. His word was law, and his image was godlike not only in Russia but in the entire sphere, quite in the style of the most lordly tsar.

The United States came out of the war in an incomparably easier situation and with a very different outlook. Far from feeling desperately weak for the needs of its destiny, the United States was overwhelmingly strong but uncertain of the use for power. The main point of the American political philosophy was satisfaction with the existing order, which had worked so well for America and which should likewise for others lead to indefinite progress, if only no disturbers of peace, order, and decency like Hitler (and soon Stalin) were allowed to trouble the world. The experience of conflict with a powerful evil made it easier to turn such feelings against the new revolutionary danger from another dimly understood totalitarianism. Much less aware of Russian sufferings and more aware of its own large contribution to victory, unconscious of having asserted anything like an American empire in its protection and assistance for many lands, America saw no reason why Soviet victory should give title to domination of various small countries. If the Russians could attribute their temporary alliance with major capitalist powers to the inherent contradictions of capitalism and hence to no merit of the Allies, the Americans felt they had given generous help in the purely Russian struggle for survival. Moreover, America like Russia was distrustful of power politics, more disposed to view the world in terms of simple right and wrong than to bargain over political stakes.

Possession of the superweapon and a certain awe of the ideological potency of the Soviet system gave a slightly hysterical cast to American foreign policy thinking. There was a feeling, possibly justified, that issues had somehow to be settled properly in short order. Otherwise the world would be subjected to the military danger of a spiraling nuclear arms race threatening the destruction of civilization, and to the political danger that a break in the front or a serious setback anywhere might lead to a general collapse of morale. The revolutionary surge which the other side continually claimed to foresee might then bring about the isolation of the United States in a hostile totalitarian world. Prior to the acquisition of a nuclear stockpile by the Russians, this feeling suggested a diplomacy of ultimatum; the bomb should be used, while America had an atomic monopoly, to compel Russian acceptance of a just world order. But this was by no means official policy; rather, America counterbalanced nuclear power by rapid demobilization of the armed forces, removing the direct means of occupying territory. Although Soviet military manpower was probably reduced in more or less similar measure, it was generally believed that the Soviets retained the means to sweep rapidly across Europe. And instead of nuclear ultimatums, the United States presented the world and the Soviet Union with the Baruch Plan for the international control of nuclear power. This seemed to the United States a generous offer to share nuclear secrets which the Russians were not expected to penetrate for perhaps a decade; the Russians saw it as an attempt to make permanent the inferiority from which Soviet science and engineering were already lifting them.

Soon after the war each side saw the other exerting power, military, political, or economic, to its detriment. Soviet military power held down Eastern Europe and menaced countries around the Soviet borders from Greece to Korea and Japan; American power threatened the whole Soviet camp and inhibited pro-Soviet leftism in most of the world. American economic might helped rebuild devastated Europe and thereby threatened the stability of Soviet East Europe. The Soviet Union through Communist parties sabotaged the revival of the West; looking to the postwar breakdown of capitalism as its opportunity, the Soviets could only see American-sponsored and American-guided recovery as a profound danger; least of all could Soviet communism favor the American goal of improving and protecting opportunities of capitalistic development and the free flow of trade. Two mighty civilizations of contrary aims, premises, and interests faced and menaced each other.

Yet neither was extremely purposeful in promoting its interests. America, feeling itself suddenly responsible in all manner of situations which it had been accustomed to leave to other nations, had neither a clear idea of its aims nor great skill in promoting them. The confusion and frustration of Soviet foreign policy were worse, as the narrow and dogmatic leadership completely failed to translate the enormous prestige of victory into broad political influence but successively frittered it away. When a Soviet strategy failed, as in Germany, Iran, or Turkey, there was no alternative but withdrawal and angry words. Bad diplomatic manners and strong language gave satisfaction by showing contempt, but they won few if any advantages, just as little was gained from belittling, from the eve of victory, the Anglo-American role in the war. Negotiations carried on with the idea not of possible agreement but of presenting the Soviet case as strongly as possible meant reaching no agreement when it might well have been advantageous to the Soviet Union, as in the reparations issue. Failure to agree on settlements even where the Russians were physically unable to exert control meant keeping in Europe American forces that enormously reduced the chances of spread of Communist and Stalinist power. Broadly speaking, when weakness might have indicated the wisdom of restraint and suavity, the Soviet approach was merciless verbal attack.

Increasingly, the tendency was to turn away from the world and, neglecting the old axioms of dividing the potential antagonists, to regard all who were not unconditional friends as enemies. It was not quite clear whether Britain and the United States simply formed an anti-Soviet coalition or must be divided, as Leninism dictated, by capitalist rivalries; but little indeed was done to cultivate the British Labour government, associated as it was with moderate socialism. Even more striking was the failure to encourage France in an independent stand. Only Soviet inflexibility prevented de Gaulle from trying, as he long wished, to pursue a more or less neutral policy between East and West. In December, 1944, France had partially reverted to the historic pattern by signing a twenty-year treaty of alliance with Soviet Russia, but Stalin opposed giving France a share in the new bodies and commissions for making the peace settlement, declined to support French interests, such as for the separation of the Rhineland, and usually treated the French government with a mixture of suspicion and scorn for its military weakness.

Perhaps the strongest side of Soviet diplomacy was its appeal to the overwhelming longing for a stable peace and the playing on fears of war, so much strengthened by the nightmare of nuclear holocausts. This appeal was played up as the cold war deepened; reminiscent of the Bolshevik appeals for peace in 1917, it endeavored to bring popular pressures to bear on governments regarded as hopelessly hostile. It was by no means a failure, as it spread the idea that concessions to the Soviet viewpoint were a contribution to the reduction of tension while measures opposing it carried dangers of conflict.

Areas of Conflict

For most of the postwar years, the greatest exacerbant has been Soviet marking off a sphere of Eastern Europe and the American desire to restrict that hegemony. The quarrel has largely been in terms of political institutions, the Western insistence that the East European countries be permitted democracy in the way democracy is understood in the "bourgeois" world: full rights for competing political parties, freedom of the press, fair and contested elections, and so on. The Soviet occupation made more or less concessions to these desiderata as a gesture to appearances and Western public opinion but insisted on single-party rule and controls of communications media while it stifled opposition. The Soviet position was rather an embarrassing one. The United States could call for the lifting of curtains and broad freedoms with no risk to its own areas of predominant influence, while the Russians could be sure of retaining their sphere only by cruder and more coercive means.

Byrnes said complacently in 1945, "Our objective is a government both friendly to the Soviet Union and representative of all the democratic elements of the country."[21] Possibly he was unconscious of the contradiction. The Soviet Union was not and is not a democratic country in any Western sense of the word, but has a horror of "bourgeois democracy." It could not realistically be expected to promote a political system which it despised, and it indicated by deed and sometimes explicitly by word that it did not expect democratic governments to be friendly. This idea may have been exaggerated; the example of Finland shows that it is fully possible for a small state to remain capitalistic and democratic and yet be an acceptable neighbor of the Soviets. But Stalin felt unsure of control that was less than total. The countries on the western borders of Russia are potentially much stronger than Finland, with much larger populations and so more capable of independent, presumably anti-Soviet conduct; and their strategic position, whatever this is worth, is much more critical. Hence, in the aftermath of World War II, the Russians, not offering economic assistance but engaged in exploitation, unable to admit their own unpopularity, had practically to choose between surrendering control of Eastern Europe and holding it by force swathed in much ideological hypocrisy. To have given up would presumably have meant that the area acquired at the cost of such fearful suffering would have reverted to its anti-Sovietism of the interwar period, and the war would have been won half in vain. The choice could not be in doubt.

It was not easy for the West to accept this. There was a certain feeling that the United States, as a superpower, could not permit its influence to be arbitrarily excluded. Perhaps some countries of Eastern Europe had little potential for democracy; less was said of Rumania and Bulgaria. But such potential seemed to exist in Poland and perhaps existed in Hungary; there was no issue over the functioning democracy of Czechoslovakia until it was crushed by the Communist coup of February, 1948. There

---

[21] Byrnes, *Speaking Frankly*, p. 98.

was also some moral question, so far as moral questions do not merely ornament political stands; it was a poor outcome of a war to prevent extension of Hitlerite tyranny over Eastern Europe if the area was left to another tyranny. The permanent presence of Soviet military power near the center of Europe also seemed intolerable; at least, it demanded permanent countermeasures, that is, the presence of an American army. It was not easy, perhaps not possible, to distinguish defensive concern for the Soviet borderlands with a potential thrust over all of Europe and a bid for world hegemony. Russian dominion of such a large part of the Continent also seemed economically unbearable and a threat to the viability of what remained. This fear proved less real than it seemed in 1946 or 1947; the West could and did learn to live with little access to Eastern European markets and sources of materials.

If for these reasons the West, led by the United States, felt that Soviet dominion of the borderlands was intolerable, aside from being a violation of the Yalta agreements, the Soviet side saw Western interference there as unreasonable. They were not contesting the American position in far more valuable Western Europe, which seemed, particularly in Marxist lenses, dominant enough; and they expected to be allowed their poorer portion. The United States had long accepted that the Soviet Union was entitled to have friendly governments there; this much having been allowed, it seemed captious to quibble over details. It could only serve to encourage a subversive anti-Sovietism which the Russians saw no need to tolerate. Western opposition to the Soviet hold on Eastern Europe was unrealistic unless the West was prepared to compel or adequately reward withdrawal of Soviet armies. It probably served no useful purpose but led to intensified repression.

The West would have accepted more easily Soviet sway in the East, just as it would have resigned itself to Hitler's swallowing of Czechoslovakia, if it had not appeared that this was a springboard and encouragement to further progress. The most vital area was Germany, representing a power potential much greater than all of Eastern Europe. In line with the old hope of the Comintern and Soviet expectations, the West seriously feared that a beaten and depressed Germany, incapable of liberal democracy, would turn from nazism to communism, thus facing the West with a gigantic power bloc from the Rhine to the Pacific. But these fears were not well founded. Although Stalin attributed immense importance to Germany and expressed sympathies for its people above any other,[22] he had no real German policy and no plan for securing Germany's conversion. From 1944 there were separate and contradictory policies of punishment for war crimes and conciliation of the German people as distinct from the Nazi government. Through the war, Stalin had usually advo-

[22] David J. Dallin, *Soviet Foreign Policy after Stalin* (Philadelphia: J. B. Lippincott Co., 1961), p. 46.

cated dismemberment, but at its end he advocated a unified Germany, doubtless in the expectation that it would be communist. He also and presumably for the same reason opposed the neutralization of Germany, while in the Allied Control Council the Soviet representative called for a centralized Germany, as Marx had once done in the supposed interests of socialism. An indication of the confusion of policy toward Germany was the insistence on the transfer of a large slice of German territory to Poland, land necessarily taken from the Soviet occupation zone, an injury which made it very difficult for Russia to expect German friendship.

As the Big Three settled down to the control of their respective zones (increased to four by a zone given to France by the Western powers), the idea of a unified administration became less and less realistic. Wrangling at all levels over the future of the land became more and more acrimonious and less and less fruitful. Much of the discussion centered on reparations for the Soviets, most of which were to come from the wealthier Western zones. The end of any possible agreement on a unified Germany came when American authorities, feeling they were subsidizing an unfriendly power, ended removals of equipment to the Soviet Union in May, 1946.

In the following years, the United States and the Soviet Union were vying for German favor, a contest in which the United States held all the cards except physical control of the Soviet zone, holding over a quarter of the population. The Germans generally were much more willing to entrust their fate to Americans than to Russians, just as during the war they had preferred to surrender to the former. The United States could offer large-scale economic assistance; the Soviet Union was torn between trying to communize and extracting reparations, and the latter had priority. The Soviet zone was first largely stripped of equipment and then required to deliver from current production, a burden contributing to the extreme difference of standards of living that embarrassed Soviet Germany in following years. The Soviet zone was converted into a Stalinist-Communist state under the leadership of Walter Ulbricht in tempo with the conversion of the Western zones into a liberal-democratic-capitalist state under the leadership of Konrad Adenauer. Not many Communists had escaped both the Gestapo and the NKVD to return in 1945, but the shortage of cadres was partly compensated for by the merger of the Communist and Social-Democratic parties. In the West the Communist party was at first free to operate, but it found surprisingly few enthusiasts. Millions of heated words over Germany caused nothing but acrimony, and its cold war fate came directly out of the rather casually drawn military demarcation line.

In Germany, the Soviet Union held and profited from at least the area of military occupation; in Iran, it reaped nothing but humiliation. The country had been occupied jointly by Britain and Russia in 1941. They had at the time pledged to withdraw their forces after the war; the deadline was later set at March 2, 1946. The Soviet forces made no moves to leave but patronized the formation of a leftist-nationalist separatist regime in northern Iran, as though in a replay of the Ghilan Republic a generation earlier. The Iranian government complained to the United Nations, and for the first time the Soviet delegate walked out of the Security Council. Under diplomatic pressure and in fear of a sharp confrontation—Truman was decidedly irate—the Soviet government agreed with Iran to withdraw in return for an oil concession. This was a remarkable demand for a socialist country, particularly an oil-rich one. The separatist Azerbaidzhan regime was left to its own devices; and its fate was that of the Ghilan Republic. The Iranian army went in against minimal resistance, as hardly anyone was prepared to fight for Soviet satelliteship; and the leaders who did not escape over the border were hanged. Having secured the evacuation of the Soviet army, the Iranian government banned the Communist (Tudeh) party and dragged its feet on the ratification of the oil concession. Finally, in November, 1947, it felt strong enough with firm American support to reject the concession. The Russians could only fume and attempt subversion, which increased Iranian hostility.

Soviet behavior in Iran was far from crafty, gaining nothing and losing much. The Soviet Union found itself pilloried in the world forum, able to make only the feeblest rebuttal against the charges of a weak neighbor. More directly important, the United States was started on the road to forcible containment. America saw the case as a clear contest between totalitarian expansionism and the freedom of small nations, in which there was no room for hesitant neutrality, a feeling which was not diminished by the importance of Iranian oil fields. A program to help the Iranian gendarmerie was quickly set in motion, and by the middle of 1947, quantities of military equipment were going to Iran. America was on the way to the formation of anti-Soviet military blocs.

Cause for still more alarm in the West was the Soviet attempt to drive across Turkey and stake out a foothold on the Mediterranean. In 1945 and 1946, Molotov repeatedly asked or demanded that the Soviet Union receive trusteeship over a former Italian colony, preferably Libya, for a naval-commercial base. There seems to have been a feeling that great-power respectability required overseas possessions, not to say a colonial empire. But Soviet, like tsarist expansion, has never been successful except in contiguity, and the bid for an African colony was dropped in the face of Western inflexibility.

More stubborn was the Soviet revival of tsarist claims on Turkey and the gateway from the Black Sea. Repudiation of this aim was a strong point of the leftist parties in 1917, and a Soviet manifesto shortly after the Revolution declared that Constantinople must remain Turkish. As late as

1934, Radek proved the fundamental difference of Soviet from tsarist foreign policy by pointing to the fact that the Soviet Union had not moved to acquire the Straits (also Port Arthur, the Baltic states, and eastern Poland, all subsequently recovered).

But geography and historical precedent were stronger than idealism; from 1939 the Straits were a major issue in Nazi-Soviet relations. At the Yalta and Potsdam Conferences, Stalin raised the question, and the Western allies agreed to the revision of the Montreux Convention, which regulated transit between the two seas. The Russians could have had an improvement, but they desired more and desired it not by a multilateral convention but by dealing directly *à deux*, with Turkey.

Having denounced (March, 1945) their treaty of friendship, the Soviet government began demanding a base on the Dardanelles plus the provinces of Kars and Ardahan, taken by Russia in 1878 and retaken by Turkey in 1918. Wider territorial claims were also staked out (on grounds of possession by Georgia before this kingdom came under Russia[23]), probably only as the ordinary device of asking much to settle for less. Turkey, with its long anti-Russian tradition, would not possibly have capitulated unless pressed by the Western powers to do so; to the contrary, Britain and the United States, alerted to Soviet aims by the plea for an Italian colony, were prepared to do whatever they could to support the independence of Turkey. Soviet pressure consequently pushed Turkey into a firmly anti-Soviet position and dependence on, and in a few years military alliance with, the United States. By the beginning of 1947, the Turkish question became mixed, in the American view, with the support of the Greek government against Communist or near-Communist guerrilla rebels. This led to the Truman Doctrine, the strongest turn toward cold war.

Despite these probings toward what might have been areas of weakness, Soviet policy was, as usual, basically defensive, and offensive only where risks seemed slight. Where met by determined resistance, as in Germany, Iran, and Turkey, the Soviets backed off ungracefully. Moreover, if the Soviet Union before 1939 was a revisionist power, its historic irredenta were recovered during the war, with minor exceptions, and the large acquisitions in Eastern Europe were more than could be easily digested for a long time. Common sense dictated restraint.

Neither was Russia a revolutionary power. The common impression that the Stalinist state was dedicated to a great mission of upheaval and change was based on talk, not deeds. The Stalinist state emerged from its trials more frankly nationalistic than ever; symbolic of its evolution was the renaming in 1946 of the "Workers' and Peasants' Red Army" to the

---

[23] Dallin, *Soviet Foreign Policy after Stalin*, p. 109.

colorless "Soviet Army," while the departments dubbed "commissariats" in 1917 to deny continuity with the tsarist government were rebaptized "ministries." Uninterested in leftism, Stalin told Churchill in 1945, probably sincerely, that he hoped the Conservatives would defeat the Labour party in the elections. It seems clear that Stalin had no eagerness for Communist regimes which he did not control, and he rather sought to dampen than to inflame revolution in Yugoslavia and China, perhaps in Albania and Greece.

Little attention was paid to Communist parties outside the Soviet sphere, and they were instructed to collaborate with British and American occupation authorities and to join the broadest national fronts, including even (as in Italy) the monarchists. Least of all should they engage in violence inviting counteraction. Consequently, the Communist party, after having played a leading role in the resistance movements in most places, made little effort to secure control of the newly formed governments, although it strongly desired to participate in them. In France, for example, the Communists gained a share in General de Gaulle's administration by the end of 1943, thanks to their effectiveness in the underground, and in 1945 they worked with and not against the de Gaulle regime and on Stalin's advice dissolved their strongest arm, the Communist-led militia. They looked to gaining power by legal and parliamentary means, as their mentors urged, and called for no innovation more radical than workers' sharing in the administration of industry. Although they were expected to follow blindly the Soviet lead, they did not even receive much advice but were left to learn the correct line from reading the Soviet press.[24] In order to remain in the government, the Communists had to resist wage demands, and they sometimes in 1946 actively opposed strikes. Their un-Marxist function in practice was to restrain workers' demands during the most trying period of reconstruction.

Deepening Conflict

Through 1946, as peace treaties were laboriously agreed with Italy and minor Axis partners, it could be widely assumed that some kind of regulation of differences could restore enough of the wartime harmony between East and West to enable them jointly to keep the peace. Measures led to countermeasures, however, and from crisis to crisis such hopes were abraded. After the summer of 1947, there was no pretense of Allied unity on either side. Ideas, habits, and institutions gradually became fixed in patterns of antagonism. The cold war became an occupation or career and a national purpose of the superpowers.

The sharpest turn in this direction was the Truman Doctrine, which in

---

[24] Rieber, *Stalin and the French Communist Party*, p. 366.

March, 1947, set forth the American purpose of preventing any further gains by communism. Somewhat ironically, this far-reaching anti-Soviet policy, coming after a number of somewhat menacing unilateral Soviet actions, was elicited by a situation for which the Soviet government was not directly responsible. Greece, like other East European countries, came out of the war and German occupation in a fluid political situation which immediately developed into civil war. The British, who regarded Greece somewhat as an imperial sphere of influence, forced the disarming of the Greek partisans and assisted conservative and royalist groups to form the government. Stalin was probably opposed to the Greek guerilla war from the first. Under no illusions as to the likelihood that the United States would permit it to succeed,[25] he made no complaints about the British actions until they became tied into broader issues. But the violence continued to be unmanageable, and at the beginning of 1947 the British, hard pressed economically, decided that they could no longer afford to keep forces in Greece to support the pro-Western government.

This faced Truman with the problem of whether to permit the Communist-led movement to gain control of Greece, as it had of Albania, or to engage the United States in a program, unprecedented for this country, of political intervention in a distant land. The decision was not difficult; if Greece were to join the Soviet sphere, Turkey would be outflanked and a corner of the Mediterranean would be Soviet-ruled. The fact, also, that the United States had already undertaken to shore up the British economy with huge loans made it easier to think in terms of assuming British political responsibilities.

Consequently Truman went to the Congress for authorization for aid to the Greek government and to the Turks, pressed by Soviet demands. To justify this, which to many Americans seemed unwarranted intervention, Truman drew the lines between good and evil and stated, as never before, the broad purpose of combating communism. The key sentence of his message was, "I believe that it must be the policy of the United States to support free peoples who are resisting attempted subjugation by armed minorities." Only Communist or pro-Soviet minorities were intended, of course; and the United States was in the business which filled its foreign policy for the next twenty years and culminated in war in Vietnam, of supporting anticommunist governments, especially those around the periphery of the Soviet bloc, with economic aid, military alliance and materials, if need be with American combat forces.

Of such interventions the first was among the more successful, as the Greek government was stabilized fairly soon and without great difficulty. A large share of this success should, however, be credited to the Commu-

---

[25] Milovan Djilas, *Conversations with Stalin* (New York: Harcourt, Brace & World, Inc., 1962), p. 182.

nists. Stalin was ever skeptical of the Greek guerrilla cause, although making the most of it propagandistically, and most of its outside support came from Tito's Yugoslavia, willful in foreign policy even before the dramatic break with Stalin. In the first part of 1948, Stalin urged the Yugoslavs to avoid involvement for fear of complications with the United States. Shortly afterwards came the rift, and Stalin insisted that the Greek Communist party subscribe to the anti-Tito line of the Cominform. Tito naturally withdrew support, and the insurrection, factionally divided, died out.

The Soviet Union was less alarmed by the Truman doctrine than the subtler threat of the Marshall Plan. As European recovery languished in 1946 and the first part of 1947 and Communist parties throve, the American Secretary of State, General Marshall, and others concluded it would be to the American interest to sponsor an economic recovery program, which, unlike the piecemeal aid previously handed to various countries, should be broadly coordinated. This idea, enunciated in June, 1947, was addressed to the Soviet Union and its friends as well as to Western Europe; and it was eagerly received on both sides. In the same month an exploratory meeting was held in Paris; Molotov arrived with a large delegation, spoke in relatively reasonable terms, and probably seriously considered participation—which might have effectively stymied the whole plan, as the Congress would hardly give funds for the Soviet Union under any conditions which that country would accept. Such a ploy, which was not in the Soviet mentality, was not attempted. Perhaps because he was overruled by Stalin, Molotov walked out. Poland, Czechoslovakia, and Finland were required to cancel their hasty acceptance of a larger meeting to discuss the Marshall Plan, which now became in Soviet eyes an infamous imperialist design to stake out markets and extend American rule.

In reality the Marshall Plan became a massive program to build up and unify that part of Europe which remained noncommunist and practically by definition anti-Soviet. A well-conceived program fortunate in its bases, it was rapidly successful, and its success for the West was equal to its dangerousness for the Soviet sphere. It greatly increased American influence in Europe for a number of years, and it facilitated the developing strategy of building maximum deterrent power around the Soviet sphere. It practically extinguished the previously glowing prospects of Communist parties everywhere in Western Europe. It represented a competition that the Soviet Union could not hope to meet. The image of the United States financing rapid recovery while the Soviet Union, although progressing rapidly, was still below prewar levels and in need of assistance, could not be countered effectively by talk of sellout to monopoly capitalism and surrender to imperialism. While the American-oriented part of the Continent advanced, the eastern fell still farther backward, an economic penalty added to the political control to which it was subjected. Having rejected the material help which would have cost a large measure of control, the Soviet government had to counter by tying the realm more tightly together. As ever, a threat to the Soviet domain brought a political hardening.

A response was the Communist coup or assumption of complete power in Czechoslovakia in February, 1948. This step like many others seemed defensive to the Soviets and decidedly aggressive to the West. Czechoslovakia had had a mixed leftist government in which the Communist party, representing the largest single bloc of voters, had a prominent but not dominant position. By early 1948, it was clear that the Communists, whether because of their mistakes and Czech taste for bourgeois democracy or because of the increasing economic advantages of westward orientation, were losing ground. They sought to solidify their position in ways the other parties refused to accept, particularly in the administration of the police; in the ensuing government crisis, they mobilized forces and threatened civil war, with the blessings of a Soviet envoy standing by. President Beneš yielded; a Communist-dominated government was formed and it rapidly proceeded to clamp down full political controls. The country which had been held up as an example of compromise, a bridge between Western democracy and the Communist sphere, became as thoroughly totalitarian-communist as its neighbors.

The lesson that the West drew was that compromise with communism and the Soviet Union was impossible and that the latter would be satisfied only with absolute control. A few months later, this impression was powerfully reinforced by a rather more flagrant Russian move, the Berlin blockade, beginning in June, 1948. This was the culmination of the breakdown of four-power control of Germany, the pretense of which had remarkably lasted almost three years. If, the Russians argued, there was no all-German government, there was no need for Berlin as an all-German capital under the four powers, and it should revert to the Soviet occupation zone. More specifically, the blockade was an answer to the currency reform in the Western zones designed to lay a foundation for recovery and also to protect the currency from the economic manipulations of the Soviet zone.

The closure of transportation routes to Berlin was gradual and at first attributed to technical difficulties; alleged needs for repairs on railroads and highways grew into total stoppage. There was no clear idea how the requirements of the city of 2 million could be supplied, particularly when winter should make acute the need for fuel. Some proposed sending armored units to force entry; there arose the first clear danger of war between Russia and the West. The counsel which prevailed was to airlift supplies, but there was no great confidence in this. In August, consequently, Stalin could probably have obtained important concessions in return for lifting the blockade, perhaps a considerable degree of control over the whole city. He wanted much more, including the postponement of the formation of a West German government, opposition to which was a principal theme of Soviet foreign policy of this period. The airlift, however, was a resounding success, a great propaganda and political victory for the United States, while the blockade gradually appeared a humiliating failure. The Russians wound it up in May, 1949, for no gain at all.

It was well for the Soviet Union that the airlift was successful, as the danger of war would have been much greater had it failed. The Russians, whose first atomic explosion was more than a year away, were in no position to match American military power; it was an action rash beyond the usual Soviet style and gave evidence of poor calculation. Its results were serious enough. The Soviet Union and the Communist party were discredited in Germany. The Western powers went ahead with more determination to set up a firm government in the nearly three fourths of Germany which they controlled; and in the first elections, August, 1949, the Communists received less than 6 percent of the votes, only a small fraction of the percentage they had regularly got under the Weimar regime. The Soviet authorities reacted by forming the German Democratic Republic in their zone, but the solidity of the Federal German Republic represented a major setback to Soviet hopes and a source of strength for the West. Subsequent bargaining, in which both sides claimed to have German unification at heart, repeated over and over the Western demand that any all-German government be based on free elections. This the Russians could only reject, calling for the two German states to meet on a basis of equality.

The Berlin blockade plus the Czech coup stimulated the Western countries to look to stronger means of security. The North Atlantic Treaty, uniting most of the countries of Western Europe in a defense alliance, was signed shortly before the Berlin blockade ended. With the Marshall Plan it completed the anticommunist stabilization of Western Europe. West Germany was still excluded because of feelings left over from the war; only five years later, in the wake of the Korean war, were the other European powers prepared to accept German participation in the defense of the West.

NATO was only one aspect of hardening American policy toward the Soviet Union. As the Truman program of halting communism was getting underway, there appeared one of history's more important magazine articles, a rationale of the doctrine of containment of Soviet power. "The Sources of Soviet Conduct," anonymously published in July, 1947, by George F. Kennan, a former American ambassador to Moscow and leading State Department expert, set forth the necessity to deny stimulating victories and further expansion to the Soviet state, which, if checked, could be expected gradually to become less hostile and aggressive. Although not entirely sound in reasoning, especially in regard to expectable change in the Soviet state, this statement expressed much of the fundamentals of American policy toward the Soviet Union for many years thereafter. Others took a less detached view; for example, Senator Vandenberg, who mobilized congressional support for the Truman foreign policy, concluded that the Russians were simply Asiatic barbarians, a characterization as accurate as the common assumption that they were simply Marxists.

The American military budget, which never shrank after World War II as after World War I, reached a low of $11.7 billion for 1948 and thereafter rose substantially year by year. Three years after the Yalta Conference, hailed as a triumph at the time, its agreements were harshly berated as appeasement, even to the edge of treason.[26] In the autumn of 1948, the United States was pressing friendly nations to join in embargoing a wide range of strategic goods to the Soviet bloc, a project which became effective with the Korean war. The victory of the Chinese Communists and the explosion of the Soviet nuclear bomb in the fall of 1949 further increased American nervousness and defense expenditures. It came to seem necessary or at least justifiable to counter Soviet influence and possible Communist expansion by an indefinite program of foreign economic and military aid to scores of countries; and American bases and alliances girdled the world. Some began calling for a rollback of Soviet power in Europe, even a breakup of the Soviet Union into its component nationalities, while any reduction of American influence anywhere was seen as an intolerable danger; and in recurrent crises there were murmurs of the desirability of blitzing Russia while it could still be done cheaply.

On the Communist side of the heightened militancy, the parties in West Europe were sent into the battle against Marshall Plan, NATO, and American influence in general. Especially in Italy and France, the only countries where the Communists retained (and have never lost) real strength, there were strikes, protests, demonstrations, and riots, with threats of civil war. Their effect was, of course, rather to hasten than retard the ratification and implementation of the new alliance, as they caused the danger of Communist power to seem real and near to many who were previously doubtful. Typically tactless was the calculated statement of Thorez, the French Communist leader, in 1949 that Communists should welcome the Soviet army if it invaded France. As in 1928–32, leftist violence led to little more than repression; and it cost the Communists most of the prestige they had earned by their part in the war. It confirmed their political isolation; having left or been expelled from the French and Italian governments, the Communist parties were consigned

[26] Stettinius, *Roosevelt and the Russians*, p. 5.

to futility, to work their way back to political respectability only many years later.

Communist parties in Asia also turned to violence. The Comintern had never paid much attention to Asian parties, and before the war they were small groups of intellectuals, undisciplined and troubled by Trotskyite and other heresies. In the disturbed situation after the defeat of Japan, they could grow rapidly. Encouraged by the successes of Mao and the world confrontation of socialism and capitalism, from 1948 through 1950, they led disorders or attempted insurrections in India, Indonesia, Malaya, Indochina, Burma, and the Philippines. Their cause was successful only in Vietnam, where it merged with a genuine struggle for independence. Fighting against the French began there in 1946, but the Soviet Union took no interest as long as the French Communists remained in the government. These, drawing a parallel with the role of Russia in communizing non-Russian areas, thought they should be the ones to bring revolution to the French colony,[27] although they opposed the war. Their dilemma was solved by their expulsion from the government in 1947; thereafter they and the Soviet government were free to support Ho Chi Minh.

A supplement to Communist party militancy was the peace campaign, which fed on and in turn intensified the rising apprehensions. This was something of an extension of old United Front ideas to enlist neutrals against the antagonists of the Soviet Union. It mingled the fear of nuclear destruction with anticapitalism and the assumption that only socialism was *ipso facto* pacific. At times the Peace Movement, with its petitions, meetings, and protests, became rather belligerent; and it was undercut by the harshness of Soviet foreign policy, the intensified dictatorship in Eastern Europe, and Soviet refusal to come to settlements. For example, although the main points of the Austrian treaty were early settled and the defection of Yugoslavia removed the last major issue (Soviet support for Yugoslav territorial demands), the Russians refused agreement until Soviet policy took a new direction in 1955. Moreover, the most important target of the peace agitation, the intellectuals, were progressively alienated by extreme politicizing of the arts and persecutions of intellectuals in Russia.

Victory in China

The triumph of communism in China not only settled the form of government of the immense Chinese nation, which had been in flux since the fall of the Manchu dynasty, but also greatly raised world tensions. Communists saw the splendid results of violence and gloated in the

[27] Rieber, *Stalin and the French Communist Party*, p. 324.

immense potential accretion of strength to the Communist camp. Those fearful of communism trembled, as it seemed that the followers of Lenin were growing like a mighty avalanche; more than ever it appeared necessary to deny them further victories.

Yet the victory of Mao and his party was by no means the work of Stalin. The Chinese Communists became essentially independent after 1927, when the conventional party, following Comintern directives, was practically annihilated. The peasant-based group of Mao was contrary to Comintern ideas and owed nothing to Moscow. Yet in the years after 1935, when Mao became supreme leader, the Chinese Communists followed the lines of the Soviet Union with a faithfulness not easily understood in view of the poor treatment received—a faithfulness which reflects the need of the struggling party to identify itself with the universal cause. Even the Soviet nonaggression pact with Japan while the Chinese Communists were making headway by fighting Japan caused little cooling of relations.

Stalin doubted the possibility of a Chinese Communist victory and probably was not eager that they should make a strong independent Communist power. For that matter, he may, like many Americans, have doubted that they were in any real sense Communists; Molotov made a remark to this effect in 1945. For Stalin, it seems to have been preferable that the civil war continue after 1945 in order to engage American strength and maximize Soviet leverage. If the Communists progressed slowly or not at all, they could be kept dependent. After the defeat of Japan, the Soviet Union gave some cheap help to the Communists by letting them enter Soviet-occupied Manchuria and help themselves to Japanese munitions stores; but the Soviet posture in the civil war was not far from neutral, while the United States provided $2 billion of aid to Chiang in his fight against the Maoists. Stalin's repeated advice was that the Communists should come to some kind of arrangement with the Nationalists.

In these circumstances, Soviet policy was to deal with the Nationalists for maximum advantages. The tsarist losses of 1905 were recovered, and domination of Mongolia was intensified to the extent that it became practically a Soviet republic; its independence was recognized by Chiang. (The Chinese Communists approved of the sovietization of Mongolia at this time in the expectation that it would be rejoined to an eventual Communist China.[28]) Soviet relations with the Nationalists were good enough that in 1946 Chiang asked the Russians to delay evacuation of Manchuria to impede Communist occupation of the province. The Soviets had grandiose plans for economic cooperation with the Nationalists,

---

[28] J. W. Davidson-Houston, *Russia and China* (London: Robert Hale, Ltd., 1960), p. 144.

looking to numerous Sino-Soviet corporations and far-reaching Soviet participation in Chinese industrialization[29]—collaboration prospectively larger than that later realized with the Communist regime. Because of concern for appearances or from inertia of policy, the Soviet government was very careful of relations with the Nationalist government, even after 1947 when it was succumbing to decay and corruption and the Communists were evidently winning. As the Nationalists were routed from their capital at Nanking to Canton, the Soviet ambassador was the only foreign diplomat to go along at the time. Only in May, 1949, was he recalled.

Evidently surprised by the Communist victory, Stalin tried to make the best of it. In December, 1949, two months after the proclamation of the Chinese People's Republic, Mao led a delegation to Moscow to settle relations. Bargaining must have been hard, as he stayed two months. By the treaty of alliance which emerged, China confirmed the independence of Mongolia; the Soviet side extended a small loan ($300 million) and agreed to surrender its rights in Manchuria, including Port Arthur, Dairen, and the railroad, in two years.

In the remaining years of Stalin's power, the alliance between the two Communist giants seemed very firm. Economic cooperation was fairly substantial, and a number of Sino-Soviet joint companies were established, especially for the development of natural resources. The chief apparent ideological difference was the greater willingness of the Chinese to mitigate class warfare and collaborate with former elite and capitalists, a revisionist deviation to which Stalin made no objection. The Russians never tried to interfere in China as in Eastern Europe. The Chinese, on the other hand, went very far in accepting the Soviet way and popularizing their Russian brothers. The Korean war, also, beginning short months after the Sino-Soviet alliance was signed, seemed to bind the two together in common purpose and antagonism to the United States. This reflected a certain amount of trust; later, when trust had been dissipated, a common cause in Vietnam did little to bridge the gap.

Korean War

There is no clear evidence regarding the Soviet part in starting the war, but in view of the political relations of the parties and the dependence of the North Korean regime on Soviet material, there must have been at least Soviet approval. Probably it seemed riskless to give the Korean Communists, who had set up a Stalinist regime under Soviet occupation north of the 38th parallel, authorization to take the southern part of the country, where American occupation had fostered a rightist pro-Western regime.

---

[29] David Dallin, *Soviet Russia and the Far East* (New Haven, Conn.: Yale University Press, 1948), p. 146.

In January, 1950, while Mao and Stalin were conferring, the American Secretary of State, Dean Acheson, had excluded Korea from the American defense perimeter with a view to possibly smoothing relations with Maoist China. This would seem to the Russians practically an invitation. The North Korean military buildup began thereafter. Tensions, incidents, and Communist guerrilla activity increased. In May, Acheson made another declaration of American disinterest. On June 25, the North Korean army smashed across the demarcation line.

At first, the North Korean offensive was completely successful against the less coherent forces of the south, and victory looked easy. But if military preparation was excellent, political calculations were poor. Probably the United States would have done little to halt a guerrilla movement in South Korea, but an outright invasion was too much of a challenge to be ignored. It might seem ridiculous to Stalin that the United States, having given up in China, should make a fight over Korea; but the fact that Communist force had been successful in China made it the more necessary that the tide be halted. Moreover, the United States intervened much more willingly and effectively by virtue of United Nations sanction. Soviet planners apparently did not conceive the utility of obstructing action in this body, although it had dealt extensively with Korean problems, its main function was security and threats to peace, and it had been successfully mobilized against the Soviet Union before. Consequently, when the United States asked for condemnation of the aggression and authorization for counteraction, the Soviet delegate was still boycotting sessions of the Security Council as he had been since January, in protest against the exclusion of Communist China. Nor did he hurry to return; only on August 1 did he swallow Soviet pride and resume his place, after the enabling resolutions for the United Nations force in Korea had been passed.

By the impetus of their advance, the North Korean forces came close to taking the whole country. However, a well-equipped United Nations (practically American) army was able to halt and then rout them by an amphibious operation halfway up the peninsula. For such a war, the Communists had clearly not planned. The Russians, having equipped the invasion force, were slow to resupply it as its needs grew. In June the Chinese were still demobilizing the huge army which had come out of their civil war, and they made no move to come to the aid of the North Koreans when a small exertion might have tipped the balance. Chinese intervention came only to redress the situation after the North Korean forces had been virtually eliminated militarily. The Soviet Union, ever cautious, left the fighting to the Chinese. But it made the most of the conflict propagandistically, loudly accusing the American military of the most horrible atrocities, massacres of prisoners, and especially bacteriological warfare.

With military skill which raised their self-confidence, the Chinese Communists were able to restore the Korean People's Republic approximately to the area which it had held prior to the attack. On Soviet suggestion, armistice negotiations were started, but they were snagged on the issue of Chinese and Korean prisoners in the hands of the United Nations command. One side insisted on repatriation of all; the other, that they be allowed to choose to go elsewhere, which for the Chinese meant Nationalist Taiwan. This could not be settled while Stalin lived, and there was much useless fighting while talks dragged on with little change of the military situation.

For no gain, North Korea was bled and battered. But the outcome was much worse for Soviet foreign policy. The effectiveness of Chinese armies against American diminished the willingness of the Chinese to regard themselves as secondary to Russians, and serious resentments were stored up because much Chinese blood was shed for a cause as much Soviet as Chinese. The Russians not only limited themselves to providing munitions but demanded payment. The venture, moreover, like the Finnish war raised unforeseen dangers. If the American president had not restrained General MacArthur from bombing supply routes in China, events would have been incalculable. By good fortune, the Soviets escaped this complication, but their position was gravely injured around the world. It was not easy to sustain the image of peace-loving Communist states in the face of facts of aggression and U.N. condemnation. American military expenditures, which had been rising somewhat with growing tension, increased more than fourfold and remained at or near the new level. There was a great militarization of American policy, with renewed emphasis on foreign bases. Anticommunist alliance building, set in gear by Czechoslovakia and Berlin, gathered real momentum. The United States was able to override Soviet objections and make a peace treaty with Japan whereby American bases remained in the islands. Even the rearming of West Germany, an event most dreaded by the Russians, became acceptable, as the French withdrew their previously violent objections. If the Russians felt insecure before the Korean war, they had far more cause to do so afterwards.

3. EAST EUROPEAN DOMINION

For the Soviet Union, the most important permanent effect of World War II was the expansion of Soviet power, practically of the Soviet state, over a large area of central and eastern Europe, including all the Slavic lands (except that Yugoslavia broke away) plus Rumania, Hungary, and a slice of Germany. The spread of communism in Asia was more spectacular, as it involved a population and territory several times larger; but this was of much less significance for Russia. Because of distance from the central mass of historic Russia, as well as cultural and racial distance, Communist China was never so closely affiliated and was able to separate entirely. Now it is only an embarrassment for the Soviets that China calls itself communist. Soviet attention remained at all times concentrated on Eastern Europe; indeed, that preference was one of the reasons for Chinese determination to go their own way.

Despite this, the Russians never seem to have had any clear-cut plan for the formation of a Soviet bloc in Eastern Europe. The Soviet Union has never had a timetable for world revolution or expansion but has watched and waited, happy in the first years to greet a revolutionary outbreak wherever it might occur, subsequently to inject itself into areas of weakness or take advantage of troubles of others. Its approach to expansion has not been a grand design but improvisation, availing itself of favorable circumstances for piecemeal gains, much as tsarist Russia did.

The first apparent aim in Eastern Europe was to recover the tsarist heritage, with the partial exception of Finland. As Stalin's regime took on much of the complexion of old Muscovy, it is not surprising that he should have wished to show himself a worthy successor of the great tsars, whose achievements acquired an aura of historical virtue. He insisted strongly on all of the territories acquired in collaboration with Hitler, particularly the Baltic states, eastern Poland, and Bessarabia. This was hardly farsighted; with the assurance of military control of all of Poland, it would seem that Stalin could have not only helped relations with the allies but avoided much cause for rancor with both Poland and Germany by some territorial adjustments. Similarly, there was no inclination to turn over Bessarabia or part of it to a Soviet-controlled Rumania, although the population is mostly Rumanian by language; there was apparently more desire to incorporate Bessarabia than to communize much larger Rumania. In what had been the eastern tip of prewar Czechoslovakia, annexation followed not the boundaries of the old empire but the long-held ambition to bring together all Russians, a category including Ukrainians; the district was coveted by Nicholas II. On entering the Carpatho-Ukraine, the Soviet army proceeded rather hastily to treat it as Soviet territory and to permit the population to express its will to join the Union; it remained for the Czechoslovak government to give formal recognition to the *fait accompli*.

Thus, the task of unification of the Russias, begun by Ivan Kalita in the fifteenth century, was completed; and the western borders of the Soviet Union were drawn by nothing more revolutionary than ethnic and historic considerations. The state officially ruled by Stalin remained, however, somewhat smaller than that under Nicholas by virtue of the noninclusion of Finland and ethnic Poland, lands which had strong claims to special status under the tsars. Why Stalin did not move to incorporate more is not clear. It had long been assumed that new Communist states would become Soviet republics, as the Bolsheviks took for granted and as is strongly implied by the basic claim of the ideology to transcend nationalism and individual sovereignty. It would not have been difficult to arrange plebiscites; perhaps many persons would have willingly voted to enter the Soviet Union in hopes of alleviating their condition, as belonging to the hegemonic state may be preferable to living under its control. Fears of arousing the West excessively, when Russia was militarily much inferior, may have been the chief reason for restraint; it would have been an especially grave affront frankly to annex Poland. Even if there were no dangerous reaction, it would end hopes of any extension of control, which could be cherished until about 1947. It was prudent to remain content with the fact of practical sovereignty, sacrificing the appearances of political unification. There may also have been hesitations about trying to incorporate large non-Russian populations with strong historical traditions and their own sense of superiority into the Soviet economic and administrative apparatus; the small Baltic states caused some indigestion.[30]

At the outset there was probably not even a clear idea of communizing the occupied territories. In the summer of 1945, Stalin again denied that communism was for Poland, stating that the Soviet system was not exportable. The highest Soviet military decoration was conferred on King Michael of Rumania, a very Machiavellian move if it were intended at the time to remove him. Independent, or even Soviet-encouraged and fomented revolutionary movements were permitted nowhere in the occupied areas. Probably Stalin merely desired conformist governments; and the pressure, step by step to make them more conformist, amounted to making them at length Communist, as only Stalinist Communists were fully reliable. Eastern Europe between the wars had been anti-Soviet, and Hungary and Rumania made important contributions to the Nazi crusade. In view of the Russian inability to compete economically (and perhaps culturally) with the offerings of the West, they had to be held by force; and as force brought discontent, it was necessary to tighten the grip lest it be loosened. Having by the military facts come into possession of a large part of Eastern Europe, the security-conscious and authoritarian Soviet Union, already possessing a universalist ideology for its own multinational dominion, was bound to make the subjected area something like an extension of itself. Eastern Europe followed the course on which Mongolia was led long before, from sphere of influence to sovietized republic.

---

[30] In 1920, when the Bolsheviks thought a tide of revolution had to sweep over Europe, Stalin suggested that Soviet Germany, Soviet Poland, and the like, should at first be joined only loosely to Soviet Russia because of their traditions. (Xenia J. Eudin and Harold H. Fisher, *Soviet Russia and the West, 1920–1927, A Documentary Survey* [Stanford, Calif.: Stanford University Press, 1957], p. 151.)

Not only was there initially no drive to social change; there was no sophisticated or coordinated policy of management. What was at hand was used. Prime was the Soviet army, which was withdrawn only from Yugoslavia and Czechoslovakia. Elsewhere, Soviet military authorities had their way, officially as occupiers in Bulgaria, Rumania, and Hungary, until peace treaties were signed. Soviet police agents operated more or less freely. Propaganda flooded over the land, the press being reserved for approved material, proclaiming Soviet virtues and benevolence, the values of socialism, and even such themes as Pan-Slavism, revived at the beginning of the war. Stalin spoke of "the age-old struggle of the Slavic nations for their existence and independence [which] had ended with victory over the German invaders and German tyranny." A great Pan-Slav Congress was held in Belgrade in December, 1946, but the idea was not very exciting and was dropped on Tito's defection.

Increasingly, the Communist parties were utilized. In many places, they had gained real strength in the resistance, where firm organization was a prime requisite and democratic procedures were not appropriate. The Communists who had spent the war underground or in jail were soon joined by those who had been kept in Moscow and went home in the wake of the Soviet armies. Each East European party hence had its native and Muscovite leaders, who usually formed separate factions, to the enlivenment of the Byzantine politics of the satellite countries.

Beyond securing of basic control, the duty of Soviet forces or Communist parties was not to change or communize but to serve Soviet interest, primarily economic. The preference for immediate material results was so strong that they sometimes opposed the nationalization of industry for fear that it might delay deliveries to Russia. Soviet soldiers on first entering East European lands more affluent than their own freely liberated or expropriated a great variety of useful articles (much as Russian soldiers invading France in 1815 displayed a passion for watches).[31] The officers showed a good deal of tolerance for such human weaknesses, despite their negative effect on relations with the occupied countries. On a higher level, the occupation armies lived so far as they could off the land. It was not surprising that the Soviet leadership felt that East European countries, especially those that collaborated with Nazi Germany, should be made to contribute to the rebuilding of a Russia which had suffered much more devastation than they had. Besides unofficial and irregular removals, reparations were taken from all the junior Axis partners, including Finland and the Soviet zone of Germany, at first in equipment or machinery, then in manufactured goods. All assets that could be treated as having been German property became Soviet property

[31] Thomas A. Bailey, *America Faces Russia* (Ithaca, N.Y.: Cornell University Press, 1950), p. 23.

by right of conquest. This gave the Russians a large share of the respective economies, as German penetration had been very extensive.

The chief use made of these confiscated assets was to enter them as the Soviet contribution to joint corporations with the local government, as Soviet-Yugoslav, Soviet-Hungarian, and most prominently of all, Soviet-Rumanian. Mongolia furnished a precedent; Soviet-Mongol corporations had been established in the 1920's to handle the principal exports and means of transportation.[32] These corporations, in the best capitalist tradition, enjoyed many advantages—extraterritoriality and exemption from taxes—and direction was kept on the Soviet side despite a facade of equality. Trade treaties were also quickly signed between the Soviet Union and all countries of its East European sphere. In the political predominance of one side, it was only to be expected that terms of trade should favor that side, and in Stalin's time the Soviet Union bought cheaply and sold dearly. The Soviet Union thus benefited materially at some cost in the goodwill of the populations affected. The Russians did not behave with the systematic cruelty of the Nazis, but it was very difficult under these circumstances for Communist parties to gain much real popularity as representatives, apologists, and administrators for an exploitative occupying power.

But for this incubus, Communist parties should have achieved great popularity in postwar Eastern Europe. Democracy was hardly familiar in most places; the aristocratic-oligarchic old order was discredited; the Soviet system had the prestige of enormous victory. Much potential competitive leadership was purged for collaboration with the Germans, while some of those vulnerable sought the best refuge by shifting to the Communist fold. Leninist communism suited the fairly authoritarian societies of the region (except Czechoslovakia) just as bolshevism had proved strong in the Russian milieu. Personal liberty and dignity were not of the highest priority, while effective political organization was. The Communist parties were best prepared to attack energetically the old social injustices, to undertake land reform, to attack and expel the unpopular German minorities, to end the remaining monarchies and then undertake rapid industrialization—all politically profitable measures. The Communist parties could most advantageously deal with the occupying power, a potent asset in a frightened nation. They were also the indicated leaders in the building of a general security system, which should transcend at least part of the petty nationalistic differences which made Eastern Europe so vulnerable in the 1930's.

Despite these advantages, the Communist party nowhere within the Soviet-occupied area gained power by popularity or proletarian action.

---

[32] Marshall I. Goldman, *Soviet Foreign Aid* (New York: Frederick A. Praeger, Inc., 1967), p. 11.

The countries were not so much revolutionized as sovietized, and the agent was Soviet military and police force, except in Czechoslovakia. At first, there was a more or less genuine coalition of communist and non-communist parties except in Poland, but Communists would hold key ministries, especially that of the interior, governing the police, the basic Stalinist reliance. They then built up power gradually and behind the scenes. The situation of Poland was peculiar. Because of the great Russian security interest (in terms of the preceding war) and fairly justified mistrust of nationalist and *ipso facto* anti-Russian elements, it was the first one Stalinized; yet it was allowed to retain appearances of democracy longer than Rumania and Bulgaria, about which the West cared much less. By the Yalta agreement, the government was broadened to include several London Poles, but from March, 1945, Poles were being arrested for anti-Soviet actions, and noncommunist political activity was gradually reduced. Managed parliamentary elections in January, 1947, eliminated most of the opposition, and after the merger of the Social Democratic with the Communist party in December, the country became a full-fledged party-state or partocracy.

The consolidation of power was quicker and smoother in Bulgaria, a poorer country with a tradition of Slavic friendship for Russia. Almost immediately after declaring war and entering Bulgaria, the Russians imposed a Communist government, which became and remained the most faithful of all the satellites, the only one never to show a trace of overt opposition. In Rumania, Communist rule was much more artificial, as the party was insignificant and there was no historic or linguistic affinity but a tradition of hostility toward Russia. Communization was practically achieved by Vyshinsky's ultimatum backed by a mixture of Soviet tanks and workers' marches. The traditional parties were rapidly eliminated, but the king was kept to lend legitimacy to the Communist regime until the end of 1947.

Sovietization was much more hesitant in Hungary, a more advanced country bordering on the West. The Communist party acted circumspectly, cooperating with democratic leaders and stressing national themes, talking not of communism but of democracy and patriotism. It insisted only on full control of the police. Partly free elections in August, 1947, gave the Communist party 22 percent, allied parties 38 percent, and opposition parties 35 percent. Thereafter progress toward partocracy was rapid.

In the Soviet zone of Germany, the same theme of coalition was played, although Soviet control was at all times unqualified. Formation of a separate government was delayed in hopes of impeding the organization of the larger western part of Germany; at the Moscow conference in March, 1947, Molotov was still strongly pressing for a unified German government.

Coalition lasted longest in Czechoslovakia, and there alone it was ended by a facsimile of proletarian revolutionary action. The Czech Communists probably could have seized power in the flush of victory, in May of 1945, when the Soviet army was in most of the country and Soviet prestige was at its height. Presumably because of Soviet sensitivity for Western feelings, perhaps alloyed with convictions that the outlook was secure in any case, they refrained. Free elections were held in which the Communist party got a plurality (38 percent); and it received the premiership and key ministries, including defense and interior, while other leftist parties shared ministries according to their strength, all under the presidency of the prewar statesman, Beneš.

There followed a few years in which Czechoslovakia was a land of parliamentary democracy, although without a regular opposition in the Western style, and of democratic freedoms under a Communist-headed government. The Communist leader Gottwald himself spoke of a national road to socialism without violence or dictatorship.[33] Internationally it tilted toward the East, partly because the British and American governments did very little to assist Beneš' effort to balance. This compromise began to be strained in the rising tension of 1947. An ominous sign for Czech independence was the revocation, under Soviet pressure, of acceptance of the invitation to discuss participation in the Marshall Plan. Worried by declining popularity, the Communists tried to solidify their position. The other parties made an issue of the replacement of police chiefs by Communists, a popular issue, and resigned to force early elections. The Communists resorted to demonstrations by workers' militia and menaces of civil disorder, but the decisive factor was not control of the streets—the bourgeois parties also held meetings—but control of the levers of state power, the army, police, and ministry of information; the president could call on no official agency to oppose them in the name of public order.

A Soviet troubleshooter, Zorin, showed up in Prague; the Soviet press denounced the militant reaction in Czechoslovakia in terms much like those used twenty years later; and Czech Communists hinted that they could count on Soviet help.[34] On the other hand, there was no prospect of Western support for the pro-Western parties. Hence, when the Communists could muster sufficient defectors from the bourgeois parties and leftist Social Democrats to show a parliamentary majority, Beneš felt that he had to accept a strongly Communist-dominated government, which proceeded to Stalinize the nation and make it almost indistinguishable from the other satellites. Thus, in 1948 as in 1968, there was resort to strong-arm tactics when it seemed that otherwise Communist

[33] Korbel, *Communist Subversion of Czechoslovakia*, p. 141.

[34] H. Ripka in Roger Pethybridge (ed.), *The Development of the Communist Bloc* (Boston: D. C. Heath & Co., 1965), p. 50.

power might be lost. In both cases, the same objective could probably have been secured less heavy-handedly; as so often, Soviet actions were much more offensive for their manner of execution.

Hardening Control

The Czech coup was part of the general response of the Soviet sphere to the heightened cold war of 1947 and after. In the face of a threat of dissolution and loss of power, the Stalinist leadership set about tightening party rule, intensifying ideological commitment, and nailing down its acquisitions. Before 1947 there had been a variably relaxed atmosphere. The People's Democracies, as they were dubbed, admitted a good deal of compromise with private ownership in small industry and agriculture. Political repression was sharp enough but not yet absolute. Communist parties sought to identify themselves to some extent with national feeling, and the Soviet pattern was not yet everywhere mandatory. But if in 1944–47 the Soviet Union staked out a zone of domination, in 1947–52 it was transformed into a Stalinist empire.

Not only was the Communist party made sole power, but something like a dictatorship was established within each party. The satrapies under Stalin each had its little Stalin, Gottwald in Czechoslovakia, Rakosi in Hungary, Bierut in Poland, Dimitrov in Bulgaria, Gheorghiu-Dej in Rumania, Ulbricht in East Germany. Native revolutionary and radical traditions were cast aside in deference to the all-pervading light from Moscow. As support of the Soviet Union (not of the socialist camp) was the essence of proletarian internationalism, any opposition to it was counterrevolutionary and by definition capitalist inspired. After the defection of Tito's Yugoslavia in 1948 created a new threat to the conformity and stability of the satellites, there was a series of purges with waves of dismissals, arrests, and trials not unlike the spectaculars of Moscow in 1936 and 1937; those suspected or accused of nationalism or Titoism, generally native as against Muscovite leaders, were accused of espionage or conspiracy and imprisoned or executed. Like latter-day Stalinism, these purges were markedly anti-Semitic, especially in Czechoslovakia and Hungary. Economically, also, the satellites were brought into the Soviet pattern. Economic demands lowered the standard of living, which before the war had been generally higher than the Russian. Since the authoritarian mentality required uniformity, relatively advanced East Germany and the other satellites had to apply the economic methods found useful in Russia. The plans of the bloc nations came out alike as peas in a pod with emphasis on metallurgy and machine-building industries.

Control was exercised through the Soviet military forces, governmental relations, and the party. By April, 1948, the Soviet Union was linked with each satellite by treaties of friendship and alliance (except Albania, subsatellite of Yugoslavia until the Titoist break). These provided among other things for consultation on all important international questions, which was interpreted to mean that the satellites' foreign relations were practically handled by the Soviet Union. There were treaties between them, but they were secondary; the Soviet Union maximized its superiority by opposing amalgamation or joint action by the satellites,[35] whose isolation from one another was only less than their isolation from the West.

Cominform, the multilateral organization of the ruling Communist parties of Europe, plus the powerful parties of Italy and France, had only a symbolic importance. When it was set up as a gesture of party unity in 1947, the West regarded it as an ominous reborn Comintern, but it was never given a consequential organization, and almost its sole activity was the publication of a paper, subject to the supervision of the Central Committee of the Soviet party itself.[36] The only other function of the Cominform was the official expulsion of Tito and the coordination of Stalin's campaign against him; and after Stalin's death and partial reconciliation with Tito it was discarded entirely. A feeble afterimage of Lenin's Comintern, it showed mostly how little internationalism remained in the Communist movement.

Stalinist distaste for multilateral bodies was also shown by the emptiness of the economic coordinating body, the Council for Mutual Economic Assistance, or Comecon. A sort of answer to the disconcertingly successful Marshall Plan organization of Western Europe, this was set up in January, 1949, for economic coordination of Soviet Eastern Europe. It was emphasized at the founding that Comecon, in the Soviet concern for national independence, would in contrast to Western economic integration respect the individual sovereignty of member states. Under Stalin, it did even less than the Cominform. It had two sessions in 1949, one in 1950, and no more until after Stalin's death in 1954, when it began to acquire vitality. The Soviets preferred bilateral trade relations in order to deal more advantageously with each satellite. In these they were successful, trade turnover with Eastern Europe growing six and a half times from 1947 to 1952.

The principal apparatus of management of the satellites was the party —quite appropriately as the party was the organ of primary political decision, the bearer of ideology, and the prime supranational instrument. Control through party channels was uninhibited in a way that governmental management could hardly be in the lack of constitutional arrange-

---

[35] Michael Kaser, *Comecon* (London: Oxford University Press, 1965), p. 14.

[36] Guenther Nollau, *International Communism and World Revolution* (New York: Frederick A. Praeger, Inc., 1961), pp. 248–49.

ments. It was a plea for liberalization when Gomulka in 1948 argued for government-to-government relations between Poland and the U.S.S.R. separate from party relations. To the contrary, the Soviet ambassadors, proconsuls in the satellites, were rather party bosses than diplomats and more representatives of the party than of the foreign office. Their contacts were more with the ruling party than with the government to which they were accredited. On the Moscow end, they reported to a bureau of the Central Committee, headed until his death by the hard-liner Andrei Zhdanov. The party secretaries of the satellite countries also received commands directly from Stalin, to whom they were summoned from time to time but who never deigned to visit his domain.

Thus, Russia found a new imperial role in Europe, and Russian overlordship within the vast Soviet Union went over into overlordship of half a dozen formerly proud nations, the whole bound up in an ideology which converted dominion into a mandate of history for the building of a utopian era. Stalin, as a Georgian, was much more pro-Russian than many Russians. In celebration of victory in Europe, he toasted the Great Russians as the "leading nation" of the Union, somewhat as the Communist party was the foremost sector of the working people. Within the Soviet Union, hints of minority nationalism were condemned as despicable bourgeois deviations. As far as Soviet power extended, the same principle prevailed. Under the divine image of the all-powerful personality, in the rationalizing framework of Leninism-Stalinism, the satellites, practically provinces, were pressed into harshly conformist but not ineffective discipline.

Titoist Heresy

To the outward view, Yugoslavia was very much part of a compact community at the beginning of 1948, and readers of the Communist press were amazed to learn suddenly that the apparently faithful Tito was really a treacherous heretical reactionary. He had seemed an unconditional Stalinist, the most revolutionary-aggressive of the leaders of Eastern Europe. One of his intimates, Kardelj, at one time spoke of Yugoslavia as a prospective Soviet republic, a bit of zeal which Stalin rebuffed. Yugoslavia first pushed for the institution of the Cominform, which was to improve conformity. It collectivized agriculture ahead of other Eastern European countries; its methods were generally the most Soviet-like. During 1946 and 1947, it was most violently anti-Western; Yugoslavs shot down American planes and called for anti-imperialist militancy when the Soviet Union was still making some effort toward accommodation.

A basic cause of the split was the greater revolutionary zeal of Tito's communism than Stalinism. This caused friction from the beginning of Tito's rise as a Maoist-style guerrilla leader in the hills; at all times there were differences beneath the surface. Stalin wanted Communists in the resistance movement to work not for Communist power but for maximum military effect by cooperation with all elements in national fronts, and he reproached Tito for promoting the sovietization of Yugoslavia when the latter refused to work with the royal government-in-exile but set up his own administration. Stalin even wanted the partisans to remove the red stars from their caps lest they make a bad impression on the West.

Stalin was perhaps as reluctant as the West to see a Communist regime in Yugoslavia, if he could not control it. He sent a military mission to the Tito forces nine months after the British did, and he recognized the royalist government which Tito had repudiated long after the Western powers had transferred their recognition to Tito. When the war was over, Stalin opposed the establishment of a Communist dictatorship in Yugoslavia. The Yugoslav leaders yielded to the extent of forming a paper coalition. The Yugoslav leaders very early became aware that their understanding of events and the needs of revolution was different from that of Moscow; however, they tended to attribute this to unfamiliarity of the Russians with their situation and problems and remained deeply faithful to the Soviet Union and the leader, Stalin.

With the end of the war, frictions increased. The misbehavior of the Soviet army disillusioned the Yugoslavs, who expected more inspired conduct and perceived the incongruities of selfish actions and brotherly professions. Tito's determination to press territorial claims in and around Trieste annoyed Stalin, who saw his diplomacy complicated by an issue in which he had little interest. Much more important, Yugoslavia was complicating the Soviet ordering of Eastern Europe. Tito, alone of the local bosses, was a genuine military hero and enjoyed huge popularity; this made him a potential rival for influence and sufficed to merit Stalin's enmity. The concrete danger was that under Tito's leadership two or more countries, especially Yugoslavia and Bulgaria, perhaps also Rumania and others, might seek to confederate, thereby strengthening their position vis-à-vis the Soviet Union. When talk of such plans surfaced in the latter part of 1947 and the beginning of 1948, the Soviets reacted sharply (after having at first seemed to register approval), calling particularly Tito and Dimitrov of Bulgaria on the carpet. The Soviets were also displeased because the Yugoslavs wanted to have Albania in a special, perhaps federal relationship to themselves, whereas the Russians wished it directly subordinate.

The total despot at home could countenance no spontaneity in any part of his domain. Stalin was so sensitive to any critical judgment that in his view Djilas became a permanent enemy, despite a lifetime of dedicated service to communism, because he made in a closed meeting an unpleasant remark about the conduct of Soviet troops. Prepared to acknowledge a

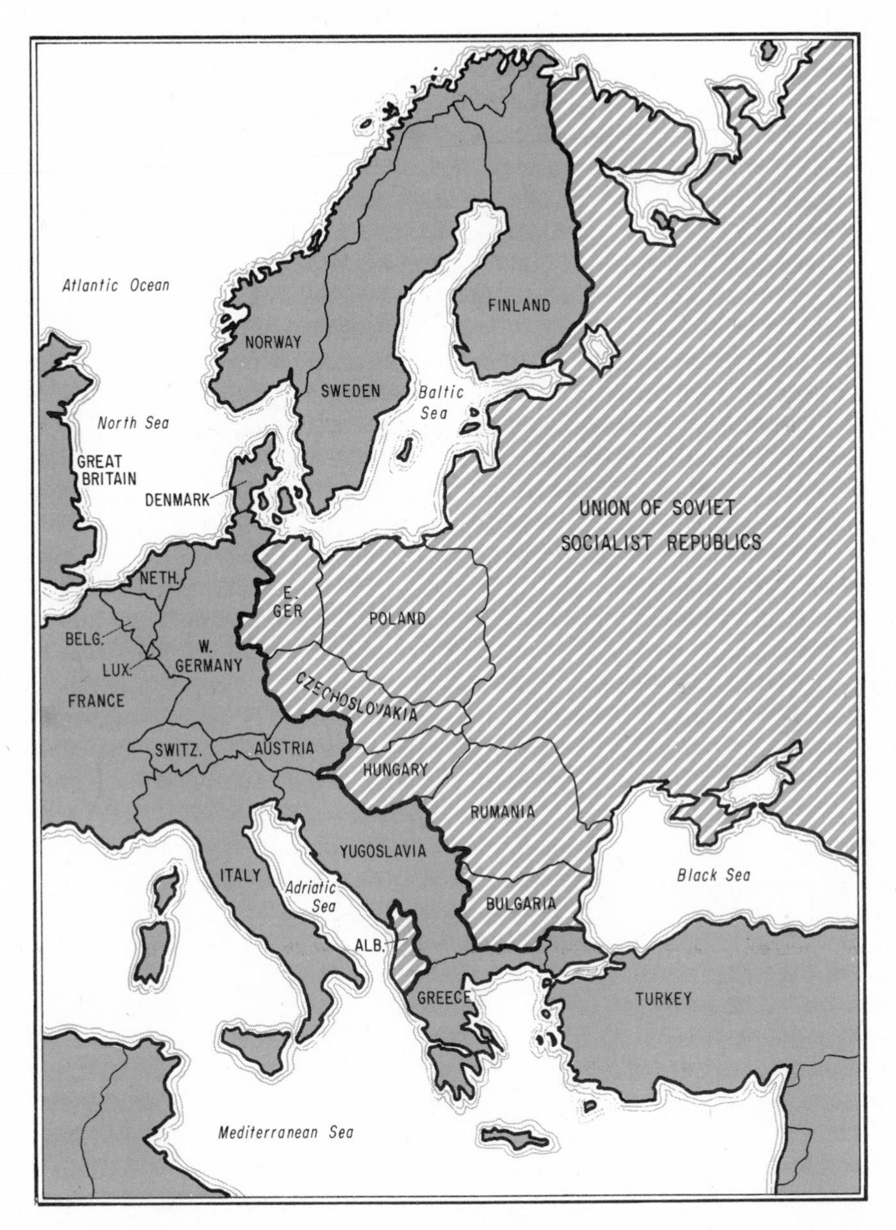

Central and Eastern Europe in 1948. The shaded area shows the Soviet sphere after the defection of Yugoslavia (Albania fell away a decade later). The population of the satellites was nearly half that of the Soviet Union.

Communist state only so far as he could control it, Stalin felt the Soviet Union should have the same suzerainty in Yugoslavia as in Rumania, Bulgaria, and so on. This meant, *inter alia*, freedom of operation for Soviet police agents, including the unhampered recruitment of Yugoslavs for its service; and when the Russians accused Yugoslav officials of being imperialist spies (i.e. anti-Soviet), prompt dismissal was expected.

The Yugoslavs rebelled over no question of doctrine but over the simple issue of independence; Stalin demanded a change not of the social or economic order but of relation to his dictatorship. Having made a revolutionary-liberation war by great sacrifices and with a good deal of heroism, they felt entitled to their own Communist state and no longer accepted the dictum that communism was merely loyalty to the Soviet state. Once the parties began to state their positions, the dispute escalated quickly. In February Stalin demanded of Tito an undertaking to consult the Soviet Union on all foreign policy questions. To support this, he began economic pressure; when Tito stood firm, he withdrew the Soviet military advisors serving in Yugoslavia. Tito made a polite but dignified inquiry as to the reasons for this unfriendly step. The Soviet reply, signed by Stalin himself, was haughty and insulting. It brought up many old sores, ranging from Yugoslav complaints about the liberating Soviet armies to accusations of the supreme sins of Trotskyism and Menshevism. Tito responded firmly but still civilly, refuting the accusations and inviting an investigation. In a reply as though designed to infuriate the Yugoslavs, Stalin insisted that the quarrel be submitted to the Cominform. When Tito rejected this, Yugoslavia was expelled by that obedient body.

There followed revealing recriminations. Correspondence was published on both sides, and the polemic grew into a propaganda war. The Yugoslavs, who repeatedly expressed "amazement" at the way they were treated, threw many charges of interference and high-handedness against the Russians, including rank economic exploitation. The Soviet accusations were of faithlessness, doctrinal deviation, and ingratitude. Zhdanov accused Tito of being an imperialist agent, and it was charged that the Yugoslav party failed to pay sufficient attention to democratic procedures. The Soviet press campaign became utterly ferocious. The respected people's democracy of Yugoslavia in a few weeks became a fascist dictatorship; no language was too strong. All means of pressure short of military force were applied. Diplomatic relations were cut; trade was ended, perhaps in the conviction that the United States could not bring itself to assist the recently abhorred Tito. Yugoslavs abroad were organized against the Tito government. Subversion within Yugoslavia was encouraged and financed, and Tito's real or presumed friends in Eastern Europe were struck down.

The only sure method of punishing the heretic would have been military force. It may have been considered; one can only speculate as to why it was not employed. One reason certainly was noncontiguity. If Yugoslavia had been an immediate neighbor, the Russians would undoubtedly have been much less inclined to permit its separation. The difficult terrain and the Yugoslavs' reputation as guerrilla fighters must have given pause. Invasion would have been risky and damaging to the Soviet position. Moreover, it probably seemed unnecessary, as the Stalinists could not imagine that Tito could stand against them. Loyal Communists in Yugoslavia would rise at the call of the supreme leader and cast down their perfidious chief. The economy could not resist being severed from markets and supplies. Tito's army needed Soviet equipment and training. When such measures had visibly proved inadequate, the heat of crisis had subsided and the West had had time to revise its attitudes toward Titoism. The Berlin blockade, too, was in full swing, distracting attention and making more dangerous another provocative action.

Tito could resist because the Yugoslavs had developed firm *esprit de corps* in their arduous and inspiring struggle, in the course of which they had emerged as the most effective exponents of the Yugoslav ideal. The fact that Tito was the only important Yugoslav Communist to escape the prewar purges had made it possible for him to form a guiding nucleus of the party wholly loyal to himself. Badly as the trade embargo hurt, the dislocation was bearable because about half of Yugoslav trade was outside the bloc—satellite countries of the 1950's and 1960's commonly conducted only 20–30 percent of their exchanges with the outside world. Most important, the Yugoslavs, like the Chinese, had won out by their own efforts and saw no reason to surrender power to anyone, even the master in Moscow. Stalin insisted in vain that they, like the regimes of other bloc countries, owed their authority to the Soviets.

Tito was reluctant to accept the fact of schism and probably hoped for reconciliation until late in 1949. Only then did the Yugoslavs really begin to assess the consequences, to shift from the defensive to a general attack on Stalinism, and to set out on their own road to socialism. There was a gradual loosening of the state and the economy, with more autonomy and rights for the component states of the federation, communities, and workers' councils. The economy was progressively freed toward a sort of market-oriented socialism, with a large measure of consultation, if not control by the proletariat who were supposedly the masters of any communist state. Western assistance was accepted, and Yugoslavia assumed a stance of principled neutrality, often siding with the Soviet bloc on international issues but decrying military alliances and great-power hegemony. In due course, the Yugoslavs decided that not they but the Stalinists were the deviants from true Marxist socialism; and they took on a mission of propagation of the non-Soviet truth.

A minor Trotskyite splinter had annoyed the Soviet-led Communist movement; now the Soviet bloc itself was riven, and dissident communism was supported by the resources of a lesser but important state. There was no longer a single communism with Moscow as its capital and Stalin as its leader. This blow to pretensions of universal truth was difficult to explain away or ignore. In the Marxist book, only capitalists should have a capitalist ideology; Tito's Yugoslavia, a partocracy like the Soviet Union, had an equal claim to proletarian truth, which could only unconvincingly be negated by alleging that Tito had sold out to American imperialism. The effect was strongest on the satellites of Eastern Europe. Russians were not apt to be much impressed by whatever Yugoslavs might do, but Tito was an East European, a prestigious self-made Communist, and he successfully defied the boss whose arrogance many East European leaders must have secretly resented. His influence and news of his effort to establish a more humanitarian communism on a national basis could not be entirely excluded; and it always served to make absolute control, especially of the intellectuals, more difficult, and to stimulate Soviet fears that other countries might be seduced.

The episode was also a monumental failure of Soviet foreign policy, due mostly to the lack of tact of an aging autocrat. Tito and his party badly wanted to remain close to the Soviet Union and could not at first imagine any other condition for themselves; to drive them away was outstanding folly. Even if it were held inadmissible that Tito be as autonomous as he wished to be, a mixture of pressure, cajolery, and rewards would probably have sufficed to bring Yugoslavia to a satisfactory degree of conformity. Leninism had always been ready to expel heresies, but the policy of offense and coercion was personal to Stalin; almost immediately on his death, the Soviet press dropped its anti-Yugoslav tirades.

4. STALINIST OUTLOOK

Lenin presided over the infancy of the Soviet system and left an imprint indelible as his image is ubiquitous. Stalin presided over its youth and maturation; and, although his image and quotations have disappeared, his imprint is perhaps stronger than that of Lenin in the style and manner of the state, whose ways he did much to shape and whose leaders rose in the warmth of his favor.

Stalin was above all a machine politician, and his outstanding contribution was in building up the Soviet bureaucratic and party apparatus. During the first years of his power, his attention was concentrated first on consolidation of his own position and then on the cataclysmic changes of Soviet society. Until the latter 1930's, it would not seem that Stalin personally had much to do with the ordinary running of Soviet foreign policy. But after 1938 and until near the end of his life, Stalin seems to have taken much more direct interest. Foreign policy centered on himself, as it had centered on the tsars, and his chosen advisers. How much of Soviet foreign policy in that period can be attributed strictly to Stalin's personality and how much flowed from the mentality and philosophy of a despotic system can hardly be guessed. The two aspects merged, as Stalin and his personality were part of the system. He was in command because there was room for such a commander, and he did what the system permitted.

One aspect of the Soviet outlook of this period which may be closely associated with the idiosyncracies of the leader was Russianism. Stalin left his Georgian past behind and became Russified with the superpatriotism of the convert; he seems to have wished to prove his worth as a Russian tsar by the recovery of the tsarist domains. He also emphasized strongly the Russian side of Soviet patriotism during the whole period of his absolutism, before, in, and after the war. Tsarist imperialism became "positive" and "progressive," and its nationalist opponents villains. It became a great theme of Soviet propaganda in the latter 1940's that Russian was the future world language, the "synonym of a new world and a new culture."[37] Other racial-national sentiments of Stalin had some reflection in Soviet foreign policy, such as his scorn for Balkan peoples, Chinese, and especially Jews. Dislike for the Comintern had an anti-Semitic flavor, as did the new Soviet-Russian nationalism.

Another prominent trait of the dictator was his exceptional suspiciousness. As his daughter testified, he was perpetually afraid—beyond even the needs of a nonlegitimate autocrat—of almost everyone around him, to the extent that he destroyed, for example, practically all his wife's relatives. In the postwar period there were no more mass purges but continual terror, and Stalin in his old age became if anything more paranoic. If he conceived or received a suspicion of a person, it was almost impossible by any material evidence to clear the suspect. In dealings with foreign powers he was likewise always ready to believe that any proposal concealed an evil intention, that any compromise was a trap. Few persons could be trusted to act abroad; and no one, even the faithful Molotov, had any latitude. Officials were sent abroad only under extreme precautions against defection, for which families at home were punishable.

Soviet embassies, mirroring the Soviet homeland, became little closed and barred fortresses. Negotiation was hence difficult and usually fruitless, and contacts with the uncontrolled outside were to be shunned so far as possible. Normal contacts which might have made friends for the Soviet

---

[37] Frederick C. Barghoorn, *Soviet Russian Nationalism* (New York: Oxford University Press, Inc., 1956), pp. 253–54.

Union were abhorred, as well as the influence which comes through trade. Even Soviet science was largely cut off from the West. By a State Secrets Act of 1947, it became espionage to disclose almost any information to foreigners. It was forbidden for Soviet citizens to marry foreigners, rare as this must have been in the lack of contacts. Barriers to travel between the Soviet Union and the People's Democracies were as high as those between the latter and the West.

Much more of Stalinist foreign relations was ordinary and normal for any first-rate despotism, as Marxist-messianic drives were replaced by chauvinist authoritarian ones. Increasingly secluded by his entourage and withdrawn into the reassuring recesses of his palace, the autocrat hardly visited the provinces of his own country, still less the satellites, while foreign travel was out of the question except to Soviet-controlled Teheran during the war. Much flattered by all around him, the ruler was less disposed to appreciate unpleasant realities thrust at him by foreign powers. In the lack of frank and open discussion, in an atmosphere of obedience and sycophancy at all levels, any myth could pass for truth. Sometimes Soviet diplomats did their homework well for purposes of argument, but the American Secretary Stettinius, for example, was continually amazed at the misinformation of his Russian counterparts regarding the United States.[38]

In the cold war, the aging Stalin raised dogmatism and isolationism to a new height. In the latter part of 1946, Andrei Zhdanov, who was one of Stalin's most trusted aides, began a campaign against ideological slackness and everything which smacked of the West in literature, art, music, and even biology and other sciences. The most intriguing aspect of this discrediting of the West was the attribution to noncommunist Russians of the invention of many basic devices, such as the radio, the incandescent light, and the steam engine. Ideology was mixed with military doctrine, as victory was made to depend primarily on morale, by which was meant loyalty, which capitalist states could not hope to match. There was enormous self-glorification, exalting both Stalinist present and tsarist past, the Stalinist image and the superior Soviet variety of mankind, entitled to leadership by its virtues.

The capitalist world was denigrated as never since the civil war. The enmity of America was projected backward, sometimes as though America had been the chief foe since 1917, organizer of the intervention to strangle the new Soviet state. The Second Front which the Russians had so passionately urged was seen as more an attempt to crush the popular resistance movements than to fight the Nazis.[39] Part of the effort to isolate the Stalinist realm was a campaign against "rootless cosmopolitans," which

---

[38] Stettinius, *Roosevelt and the Russians*, p. 113.

[39] Rieber, *Stalin and the French Communist Party*, p. 113.

usually meant Jews. The unholy outside world belonged to the class enemy. Leninist flexibility permitted dealing with practically any potential opponent of the principal enemy; but the Stalinist motto, like that of a pretentious universal monarch, was that those who were not wholeheartedly with were against.

Far from appreciating the potential utility of the United Nations, the Stalinists reduced their already slight participation in it and its specialized agencies, and hardly used it except as a forum to attack the West.[40] Neutrality was as inadmissible in the world arena as it was on the Soviet political stage. It was hardly admitted in principle, except perhaps in Finland, and the idea of a "Third Force" was regarded as a subterfuge for the defense of capitalism. Postwar Stalinism was quite truculent toward even such alleged servants of imperialism as the Arab League, anti-British revolutionaries in Egypt, and Gandhi and his associates in securing the separation of India from the British Empire. Such was the dislike for neutrals that Soviet trade with the Third World, pitifully small in 1948, shrank by a third to 1953, while Western trade was expanding vigorously. Vigilance and pressure against the outside, sharply setting off the socialist, peaceful, democratic, and progressive from the capitalist, imperialistic, and oppressive, helped consolidate the Soviet sphere. That it made more difficult or impossible further expansion was of secondary importance, as Stalin concentrated on keeping the great acquisitions made. If the rest of the world reacted by hostility, this was seen by the Stalinists as proof of virtue.

Soviet diplomacy and propaganda were accordingly often ignorant and rude, even while unscrupulous and superficially clever, in agreement with internal political methods. The dogmatic approach and fixations made even ostensibly reasonable Soviet initiatives for reduction of tension ineffective and deprived the Soviet Union of credit it may have deserved. Stalin's policy in the Greek civil war was moderate and prudent, but intransigent attitudes and language made it seem truculent. To a very large extent the image of Stalin as fiercely aggressive derived from manners and violence of language rather than deeds, the slanders against opponents more than real injuries inflicted. It was very hard for such a government as Stalin's, haughty and tolerating no dissent at home, to see that mild and indirect tactics would usually have been more effective, particularly for the security of the Soviet Union, their overriding concern.

Soviet propaganda had no subtlety nor any theoretical ideas of importance, as practically nothing was done to adapt Leninism to the postwar world. There was no new message to the many countries becoming

---

[40] Harold K. Jacobson, *The USSR and the UN's Economic and Social Activities* (Notre Dame, Ind.: University of Notre Dame Press, 1963), pp. 12–14.

independent, nor to the new brother-socialist states, nor any reconsideration of the fundamentals of conflict in the technological age. The old doctrines, having worn very thin, gained only stridency. Soviet propaganda was burdened by boastfulness, carelessness of feelings, and extremism. For example, not long after the end of the war, broadcasts to England were pouring scorn on the Allied military effort. When the Netherlands, yielding to world opinion and a difficult situation, withdrew from Indonesia, the Soviet delegate accused it of imposing "shackles of colonial slavery."[41] Not surprisingly, the prestige and credit of the Soviet Union, so high in the aftermath of the war, sank to an extreme low by 1949–50. In the United Nations it was practically a wolf in the fold;[42] aside from its satellites it was friendless in the world. So lacking in support was the second strongest power that the temporary seat on the Security Council reserved by agreement for an Eastern European state went in 1949 to anti-Stalinist Yugoslavia.

Great despotic states, such as imperial China, have often been rather passive, and Stalinist tendencies to xenophobia and isolationism reduced the will to foreign adventures. There were no ventures far afield; and the risky actions, as in Berlin and Korea, were intended to tidy up the borders of the empire. According to the creed, the correct line lay between leftist adventurism and rightist inertia; and this Stalin or the bureaucratic apparatus fairly well followed, in the postwar years, in a basically calculated response to the power position.[43] It is foolhardy indeed for a weaker power to be really aggressive, although it may sustain some bravado and try the patience of the stronger. American military power was much greater than the Soviet until well after Stalin's death, and the Soviet leadership was fairly well aware of it. Thus, the first Soviet nuclear explosion, in the fall of 1949, was treated very carefully and with uncharacteristic lack of boasting, probably to minimize chances of a dangerous American reaction.

While the United States felt some insecurity in the face of vague menaces of Communist expansion, especially after the conquest of China by the Maoists, the Soviet Union had much greater cause for fear. It was for this reason and in the awareness that modernization was indispensable to power, not love of learning, that Stalin promoted the large-scale and intensive education which ultimately made his type of dictatorship obsolete. In a typical contradiction, while the Stalinist military doctrine centered on areas of real or supposed Soviet strength, morale and mass

---

[41] Louis Fischer, *Russia, America and the World* (New York: Harper & Bros., 1961), p. 24.

[42] Alexander Dallin, *The Soviet Union at the United Nations* (New York: Frederick A. Praeger, Inc., 1962), p. 37.

[43] Marshall D. Shulman, *Stalin's Foreign Policy Reappraised* (Cambridge, Mass.: Harvard University Press, 1963), pp. 3–6.

potential of ground forces, the government devoted very large resources to the development of newer weapons, laying the basis of the technological military power of the latter 1950's.

Toward the end of Stalin's life, although he was becoming more inaccessible and less balanced, there were hints of moderation and slight perceptions of change. By 1949 the Berlin blockade had failed, the Greek insurrection had failed, pressures on Iran and Turkey had failed, and Yugoslavia, against Stalin's fury, had made good its exit from the Communist bloc, while a flourishing Western Europe had joined in NATO and the West German state was progressing firmly. The blockade fiasco cost Molotov his position as foreign minister, and he was replaced by Vyshinsky, notorious prosecutor of the purge show trials. There seems to have been some perception that the rough tactics of the French and Italian Communist parties were counterproductive and fostered Western solidarity. The storm of protest which greeted Thorez' declaration of support for the Soviet army was taken as a lesson; the Communist motto became national independence and sovereignty.

With the acquisition of the A-bomb and the steady progress of the economy, Soviet statements became rather more confident and less frantic. Perhaps the Soviet leaders believed what they said about rearmament steadying capitalism and preventing the awaited crisis and so decided that truculence was not useful. A bit more subtlety came into Soviet diplomacy after 1950, hints of efforts to divide the anti-Soviet nations and to play up to neutrals, despite the "two-camps" dogma. There was more talk of "peaceful coexistence," an old but sometimes neglected phrase in the Soviet vocabulary. Perhaps much of this change of temper and outlook, which was to remain inchoate as long as Stalin lived, was ascribable to the death in 1948 of hard-liner Zhdanov. His position next to Stalin was inherited by Georgi Malenkov, a matter-of-fact man of comparatively moderate outlook.

A sign of changing times was Stalin's modification of Lenin's theretofore still official doctrine of inevitable war. War was inevitable, Stalin propounded in September, 1952, but between capitalist nations and not between the capitalist and socialist camps. This argument, that antagonisms between capitalist states, all militarily allied against the Soviet Union, were stronger than those obviously straining relations between the Soviet Union and the West, was a wishful reversal of political logic and commonsense. But it was pacific in effect, as it implied that the Soviets were in no great danger and might, as was attempted in 1939–41, remain on the sidelines of a new great war. It was a real step away from the two-camp approach and toward that of the Khrushchev period. Russia, like other nations, can change policies which are not rewarding; and the outlines of a new era were appearing in the last years of Stalin's reign.

V

Khrushchev and Competitive Coexistence

End of an Era

When a picture was published showing Stalin with gray hairs, the Russians found it hard to believe that the immortal master was indeed growing old.[1] But on March 5, 1953, he was dead; and an era was closed.

The passing of a harsh and long-endured autocrat removes a key element of the stern political order and is inevitably followed by a relaxation. Those that followed Stalin could not rule as he had. The atmosphere of tension and terror, heavier as Stalin was seemingly moving toward a major purge at the end, was eased. The apparatus of party and bureaucratic rule showed solidity and continuity—more than the leadership evidently expected, as they warned unnecessarily against panic. But authority became somewhat more diffuse. With the strong hand removed, it was possible for many organizations and groups to stake out areas of relative autonomy. The various agencies of Soviet society began to find themselves not merely executive agents of higher orders but foci of separate collective wills capable of channeling demands and exerting influence upward onto the higher bodies.

Rulership, less able to command, had to consult more. Soviet society became less an amorphous mass under the mobilizing despotism and more of a crystallized structure suggestive of the complicated pluralistic societies of the West. Politics became less deadly. Beria, head of the Stalinist police, was the last major leader to be executed. Some disagreement became possible without charges of treason. With more discussion and flow of ideas, there could be more innovation and experiment, and Russia stirred from its stupor. There was obviously an evolution toward the

[1] Walter B. Smith, *Moscow Mission, 1946–1949* (London: William Heinemann, Ltd., 1950), p. 47.

genus of society traditional and respectable in the West, an evolution the strength and depth of which was sometimes overestimated in the years from 1953 to 1968.

The Soviet Union grew and matured under Stalin. Primarily for the sake of strength, Stalin had industrialized, educated, and modernized to such an extent as to make his dictatorship obsolete. Hence, when Khrushchev had eliminated various rivals, Beria, Malenkov, Molotov, and others, he did not find himself alone in majestic power, as Stalin had made himself after pushing aside Trotsky, Kamenev, Zinoviev, Bukharin, and others. Only for a few years, from 1957 to 1962, did Khrushchev's power approach that of a dictator; and after him a new collective leadership headed by Brezhnev and Kosygin showed remarkable ability to avoid great concentration of authority in the top individual.

The Soviet Union evolved from a revolutionary to a bureaucratized state administering a complex economy and interested in order and stability. Leadership fell away from revolutionary politicians, with their charisma of association with Lenin, to rest with educated and skilled managers. Khrushchev, who at least received his communist baptism in the civil war, was transitional between Stalin, a teammate of Lenin before the Revolution, and the wholly post-Revolutionary Brezhnev-Kosygin team. In the Khrushchev years the party Politburo changed membership entirely (except for Khrushchev himself), from a board largely composed of ex-agitators to one mostly of technicians with higher education. It is understandable that Soviet policy became more sophisticated.

The post-Stalin leadership was also able to cash in assets built up by Stalin. Escaping from the paranoiac sense of encirclement, the Soviet Union had the material means, by the time Stalin died, to act as a global power, militarily and economically. Khrushchev reaped, in the hydrogen warhead and the missile to deliver it anywhere, the fruits of Stalin's investment, giving Russia the capacity to challenge the United States as never before. With the completion of postwar reconstruction, it was possible after Stalin to give more thought to raising the Soviet standard of consumption and so to make admissible more contact and comparison. The Russia of Khrushchev, although still poor enough by Western standards, no longer felt it necessary to shut itself off in shame of conspicuous poverty. It was no longer indispensable to hold Eastern Europe in tight rein to compel it to aid the Soviet economy, but the new leadership could think in terms of using Soviet economic power to bind the bloc. It even became practicable to reach out and offer economic and technical collaboration and assistance, in competition to America itself, anywhere on earth. Finally, the technical progress of once backward Russia became itself a mighty instrument of foreign policy as Soviet sputniks pioneered the space age. New strengths opened up endless vistas.

The man who laid his stamp on the new era was a very different personality from Stalin, a thorough Stalinist who saw the need for new style and improved approaches. Probably Khrushchev deeply hated the man before whom he had groveled; his anti-Stalin outbursts of 1956 and 1961 seem utterances of a man with a personal grudge; and his changes were more extensive for that reason. He assumed that Stalin's faults were a major bar in the way of Soviet or Communist power in the world and that by avoiding them he could do much better. He looked to a relaxation and end of terror to make possible the progress necessary for the victory of communism in the Soviet Union and abroad. Whereas Stalin dwelt in the Kremlin, secluded and mysterious in the best imperial style, a symbol and exalted image, given to theoretical pronouncements and above ordinary affairs, Khrushchev exulted, far beyond the usual Communist manner, in contact with the masses for whom communism supposedly existed. He was very fond of the excursions and meetings which Stalin entirely eschewed. More human and accessible than Stalin, Khrushchev was more flamboyant and demagogic, with some of the crudity of the uneducated man arrived at the pinnacle of power; and he talked to the world in somewhat the same terms he used in berating the collective farmers of Kazakhstan.

Foreign policy was very much Khrushchev's province, and its execution bore the mark of his assertive personality. Gromyko, who became foreign minister in February, 1957, had, like Chicherin and Litvinov, no party standing. He might better have been called custodian of the Foreign Office, as Khrushchev did not hesitate to tell visitors that Gromyko's job was merely to carry out orders. Although not so free to work his will as a Stalin, Khrushchev enjoyed speaking, often extemporaneously and colorfully, in the name of historically victorious socialism. His grand tours were characteristic, as was his fondness for summitry, which was useful not only for his personal image but for possibilities of negotiation, since the deputies could decide nothing without reference to the top. He was able to attend only one summit conference, however, that of 1955. An attempt in 1959, when Macmillan visited Moscow, failed; and the grand projected summit in Paris in 1960, fruit of much preparation, blew up or was blown up by Khrushchev after the U-2 spy plane incident. He loved, however, to do the unusual, and his personal diplomacy reached its apogee that year when he attended a United Nations meeting in New York. Many other heads of state imitated him to no particular purpose. Eisenhower also came but avoided encountering Khrushchev. The latter proceeded to make his presence felt at the United Nations by removing his shoe and using it to bang loudly on his desk.

Unlike Stalin, Khrushchev made (except feebly in his latter years of power) no claim to be an ideologue, but he revised doctrine freely and expediently. He was a believer not in the letter of the creed but in the spirit of the Revolution, true Leninism as he saw it, which he wished to revive for a political renewal, to breathe new strength into the Soviet party and the world movement toward communism. He was a good deal of an idealist, and he seems really to have believed it when he told foreigners that they should become communists for their own benefit and that their children or grandchildren would certainly be. He may even have believed it when he said the Soviet Union was a true democracy. He looked to popular participation in the execution, although hardly the formulation, of political decisions and apparently thought of a society of brotherly communism, wherein education and persuasion should replace coercion in the keeping of order, as a real and proximate possibility. Similarly, he felt that the common faith should unite the Soviet bloc with minimal use of force, that the errant Yugoslavs could be lured to return, and that other nations could be enticed to adopt the Soviet way and join the socialist community with little or no use of force.

Faith in the ideological spirit meant flexibility in tenets, as the articles of Leninism had become poorly adapted to the problems of the day, and Khrushchev was pragmatic above all. He recognized that the capitalist nations were not unified by a single class purpose, that neither the line between capitalism and socialism nor the specific meaning of the latter was strictly fixed, that revolutionary violence was more or less dysfunctional for Soviet purposes, and that change depended as much on science and technology as on political action. He half acknowledged that there was not much expectation of the long-awaited revolutionary crisis of capitalism and even edged toward reconsideration of the nature of capitalism. In theory, however, he never strayed from the central article of Soviet faith, that the party exercises power as representative of the progressive proletariat compelled to struggle against backward enemies for the realization of the good society.

It is always hard to guess, in Soviet foreign policy pronouncements, how much is for the benefit of the people at home and how much for allies, neutrals, or antagonists; how much is serious statement and how much is purely for effect. This is particularly true of Khrushchev, who liked to play up to his constituency by boasting abroad and teaching socialist lessons to the heathen. Words were a main reliance in seeking at times to calm, at times to raise, Western fears in hopes of some sort of concession; and Khrushchev greatly overestimated the usefulness of bluff and bluster. Impetuous and often rude, he was not very aggressive in deeds, perhaps less so than Stalin, while possessing much superior military means. A minority of crises of the Khrushchev era arose by Soviet initiative; they were principally the multiple Berlin crises and the Cuban missile crisis. Usually, as in the Suez, Lebanon, or Congo difficulties, the Soviet Union was reacting to or trying to take advantage of a disorder of others' making.

Throughout, Khrushchev was much less successful than he seems to have anticipated. He did not manage to forward the cause of communism to any large extent nor to recruit an important number of uncommitted nations to the Soviet side. If he let some fresh air into the Soviet bloc, he could by no means end its conflicts or maintain the full force of Soviet leadership over it. He was compelled to resort to force to hold the satellites together at all, and the greatest of triumphs was lost when China turned from slavish admirer to bitter foe. There was no progress toward securing American withdrawal from Europe. It might only be claimed that Khrushchev fairly well succeeded in affirming the Soviet claim to Eastern Europe, a claim which was theoretically in dispute at the death of Stalin but which was fairly taken for granted by the time of Khrushchev's departure. More broadly, and this should be enough for most leaders, the Soviet Union, brought back by Stalin to a remarkable state of friendlessness only a few years after the magnificent victory, under Khrushchev's leadership returned to respectability. No longer oppressed by any psychology of inferiority or encirclement, it was accepted and recognized as not merely a great power but a superpower.

Unlike the relative fixity of Stalinism, the Khrushchev era was a time of uncertainty and changing policies, now harder, now more accommodating, a time of improvisation and adaptation. Steps toward relaxation were often balanced or undone by contrary measures. However, through a multitude of minor and several major crises the cold war never revived in full intensity, and there was always communication and some desire for settlement between East and West. Khrushchev's "Peaceful Coexistence" explicitly excluded the idea of any general settlement or permanent harmony between the Soviet Union and leading Western states. The possibility of such a settlement is mostly an American delusion, since the most powerful states are inevitably, within traditional international mores, antagonistic. But there was a degree of stabilization with freedom for maneuver, and ideas and impulses of revolution receded further as the Soviet Union seemed more like a state playing the game of power with other states.

1. THAW, 1953–56

Malenkov: Uncertainty

The change brought by the disappearance of the autocrat was more abrupt in spirit than in policies, because the Soviet state is a ponderous apparatus with a usually slow reaction time. A turn toward a new outlook began well before March 5, 1953.[2] Stalin's thesis of inevitable war between

[2] Cf. Marshall D. Shulman, *Stalin's Foreign Policy Reappraised* (Cambridge, Mass.: Harvard University Press, 1963).

capitalists instead of between capitalist and socialist camps was a concession to the new spirit. More important, in the Soviet association of political and commercial relations, were moves to revive badly languishing Soviet trade with the West. Malenkov, Stalin's nearest aide at the time, urged that by trade capitalist nations could be relieved of the necessity to buy prosperity by rearmament, a quite un-Stalinist idea. After some talk, at the beginning of 1953, the Soviets agreed to international discussions on trade. About this time also, the Soviet Union began joining or rejoining specialized organs of the United Nations, such as the World Health Organization and UNICEF; and some of the truculence went out of Soviet delegates' speeches.[3] Perhaps Stalin felt that his control was slipping. The principal organizational changes of the nineteenth Party Congress in 1952, the doubling in size of the highest party committee, the Politburo (Presidium), and the Secretariat, were clearly designed to reaffirm his power. Stalin showed his concern in the Doctors' Plot, wherein a number of leading, mostly Jewish, physicians were accused of conspiracy for murder and treason, with hints of developing purge. His statements in his last weeks were markedly anti-Western. Even while pointing with pride to the progress and strength of the socialist camp, magnified by the accretion of China, he insisted for domestic reasons on capitalist encirclement and the impossibility of the slightest relaxation.

In this complicated situation and under suggestively mysterious circumstances, Stalin died. The strong first impulse of the henchmen left suddenly leaderless was to keep the lid on, stress continuity, and continue on the known, and hence safest, course. Even as changes and concessions were made in following months, they were at pains to deny that policies had changed. But these concessions gradually gave substance to hopes, at times exaggerated, that Soviet policy had in reality taken a turn toward flexibility and reasonableness. With a reaction time of four weeks, charges against the allegedly plotting doctors were dropped, although the anti-Zionist campaign lasted some weeks longer in the satellite press. The territorial claims against Turkey, which Stalin had refused to retract, were explicitly renounced in May without any concessions from Turkey.

The strident abuse which had been poured on Yugoslavia since 1948 was quickly halted, and in June the Foreign Ministry proposed the restoration of diplomatic relations. The Yugoslavs were not quickly convinced of a Soviet change of heart, however; as late as August, 1954, they signed a little alliance with anti-Soviet Greece and Turkey. The Soviet Union also resumed diplomatic relations with Greece and Israel. Stalin had turned hostile to the latter as the United States became its protector and in the beginning of 1953 severed relations on the pretext of a bombing incident at the Soviet embassy.

Soon after Stalin's death, moves were made toward ending the Korean

[3] Harold K. Jacobson, *The USSR and the United Nations' Economic and Social Activities* (Notre Dame, Ind.: University of Notre Dame Press, 1963), pp. 12–14.

war, as his successors accepted the principle of voluntary repatriation of prisoners. An armistice was agreed upon in July. With the end of the Korean fighting, the spiraling arms race showed signs of slowing. The Western alliance, for which it had been a potent tonic, began to show some debility, and in time arms budgets were reduced in both the United States and the Soviet Union. This did not mean much relaxation, however, as the Soviet Union had not changed very greatly; and Dulles, who suspected that negotiation weakened a moral cause, made little effort to ascertain how much it had changed. Both sides continued to develop better weapons.

There were many other changes of tone. Two days after Stalin died, an Eisenhower speech was published without abusive comment in *Pravda*. The new Soviet leaders began showing some concern for the Soviet image in the world. Soviet diplomats became somewhat more conventional and agreeable. Pressure on the minority nationalities was reduced, and they (except the Jews) received more leeway in cultural affairs. In June a wave of riots in East Germany and disturbances in Czechoslovakia jolted Soviet control of the satellites, and the new course became perceptible in Eastern Europe. Hungary received a new premier, Nagy, famed for his role in 1956; he permitted peasants to leave collective farms and turned emphasis from heavy industry to consumer goods production. It is possible that at this juncture Beria and Malenkov were prepared to write off the German Democratic Republic entirely, although a Big Four foreign ministers' conference on Germany early in 1954 got nowhere.

At the 1954 Geneva Conference, Soviet diplomacy worked strongly for a settlement of the war in Vietnam to induce France to refrain from joining the European Defense Community, a scheme designed to facilitate German rearmament under suitable controls. This was achieved, and both the Soviet Union and China emerged from the negotiations with much enhanced prestige.

The old style, however, was persistent. Propaganda continued to hammer at the old themes of the evils and approaching crisis of capitalism, keeping alive Stalin's theory of inevitable war between capitalist states rather than against socialism, allegedly grown too strong to be attacked. Molotov, Stalin's sturdy negotiator, took back the foreign ministry on the demise of the dictator, and it was not to be expected that he would much change policies with which he had been closely associated. In his new tenure, the Foreign Ministry regained some of the authority which it had lost since the 1920's; and he worked to brake efforts at relaxation (as Khrushchev accused him later) until 1955.

Fears also limited detente. The June, 1953, disorders shook Soviet confidence, made leaders look back to the success of strong-arm methods, and caused some hardening toward the West. The posture of America seemed definitely threatening. When running for president in 1952, Eisenhower had declared, "We can never rest . . . until the enslaved nations of the world have in the fullness of freedom the right to choose their own path. . . ." The Republican administration which took office at the beginning of 1953 had made liberation, or rollback of Soviet power, one of its professed aims. This was not taken very seriously in the United States; if held desirable, it was not deemed worth major efforts or great risks. But it touched a very sensitive nerve of the Soviet Union, which in 1953 was still markedly inferior militarily, with only a very limited capacity to strike the United States,[4] which was in a position to demolish Russia from bases in Europe and Asia.

While the United States remained basically pacific, the Secretary of State, John Foster Dulles (who held this post almost to the end of the Eisenhower years) took a rather moralistic and simplified view of world affairs as a struggle of good versus evil. Like Stalin he found neutralism unacceptable; and he wished to unite the non-Soviet world in a series of alliances. Hence, American diplomacy in the first years of the new Soviet regime kept trying to extend the anti-Soviet alliance system, which seemed successful in Europe, around the whole periphery, or in the Soviet view to encircle the Soviet Union with hostile pacts and bases. America came to look more to military power as the answer to world political problems, as it had been successfully employed in Korea. According to Dulles' doctrine of "massive retaliation," the United States, in case of local Communist aggression, might not limit itself to a local response as in Korea but would feel free to retaliate against the center of Communist strength with nuclear weapons. This somewhat unrealistic doctrine, evoked by the unpopularity of the Korean war and the desire to base American superiority comfortably and cheaply on long-range bombers rather than large ground forces, raised doubts in the United States and certainly greater doubts and fears in the vulnerable Soviet Union.

A deep division in the Soviet leadership became evident. Malenkov, the premier (chairman of the Council of Ministers) and governmental chief, stressed the destructiveness of nuclear war and the desirability of settling for a minimal deterrent, and suggested that aluminum could be better utilized for pans than planes. But Bulganin and Khrushchev, the first secretary of the Communist party, talked of the need for strength and vigilance, sometimes in the most aggressive terms of the cold war. The principal argument in the latter part of the year was that Malenkov by diverting resources from heavy industry to light industry and consumer goods was deviating from sound doctrine and damaging the industrial development, and by implication the military power, of the Soviet Union. In a rare departure from the Soviet practice, invariable since Stalin

[4] Arnold L. Horelick and Myron Rush, *Strategic Power and Soviet Foreign Policy* (Chicago: University of Chicago Press, 1965), p. 17.

consolidated power, of screening major political discussions, the controversy appeared in the press. The government paper, *Izvestia,* was opposed by *Pravda,* which, as party organ, took the harder ideological position. With the support of the advocates of heavy industry and more weaponry, Khrushchev was able to force the resignation of Malenkov in February, 1955. Khrushchev was now on top, although Malenkov remained in the inner circle and Khrushchev was not able yet to take the premiership but turned it over to Bulganin, a rather inconsequential political marshal.

1955, the Good Year

Khrushchev, who took a hard line against Malenkov for internal political reasons, when confronted with the realities of the world situation led his government into the most considerable series of accommodating moves it has ever ventured. But no means always was his foreign policy flexible or conciliatory, but he seemed decided to turn his back on Stalinist rigidity until the fall of 1956, when troubles in Poland and Hungary seemed to show that if Stalin's policy was sterile it was safe, while Khrushchev's was hazardous.

In various ways the Soviet Union turned a new face to the world: in opening a bit to visitors, in speaking more seriously of disarmament and reducing Soviet armies, in withdrawals from occupied positions, in meeting in a friendly fashion with Western heads of state at Geneva, in establishing diplomatic relations with the Western-sponsored Federal German Republic, in making apologies to Yugoslavia, in showing a friendly interest in noncommunist neutrals, and in a warmer attitude toward the United Nations. Rationality seemed to be dissolving the dogmatic hostility of the past.

A surprising turn was the inauguration of tourism to Russia. In the 1920's a fair number of adventurous tourists saw the sights of Russia, but the stream dried up as the war approached, and a view of the Soviet Union during the 1940's was the privilege of a few diplomats and journalists. With the doors partially opened in 1955—touring has not to this day become nearly so free and easy as in Western countries—there were more visitors than in any prewar year. A still greater departure from Stalinist practices was the permission given in that year for a few Soviet tourists to travel in Western Europe, albeit in organized and escorted parties. Soviet cultural export, from tours of artists to Friendship Societies, which had blossomed briefly after victory but withered in the cold war, revived in the more benign atmosphere of 1955.[5] Material exchanges also revived. As the Soviet market began looking more attractive, the embargo lists of

---

[5] Frederick C. Barghoorn, *The Soviet Cultural Offensive* (Princeton, N.J.: Princeton University Press. 1960), p. 50.

Korean wartime were whittled away, and Western nations found themselves competing in the offer of credits.

Visitors had been excluded largely because of the sensitivity of poverty and weakness. By 1955 Russia had left behind a good deal of the postwar shabbiness, and there was more optimism than for many years past. The new confidence was especially important in the military aspect. Soviet nuclear capacity was raised, although it was still much inferior to that of the United States, with bases on the Soviet periphery. With the development of the hydrogen bomb, in which the Soviet Union was on a par with the United States, Soviet military doctrine was modernized away from Stalin's emphasis on politics toward emphasis on technology. This called for a new ideological approach to war, which appeared slightly later. The armed forces were reduced by about a third in 1955 and 1956.

Disarmament became a major diplomatic theme, in the tsarist and earlier Soviet tradition of its advocacy. A stimulus in this direction was the rearmament of Germany, finally sealed by the Paris agreements in the spring of 1955. The Soviet Union tried to forestall this extremely undesired event by threatening denunciation of the respective alliances with Britain and France; and this gesture, hurtful only to the Soviet Union, was carried out. A more diplomatic effort to dissuade the West was the presentation, in May, of conciliatory disarmament proposals, which permitted the first fairly promising discussion of the subject in seven years. Previously it might be fairly stated that the Soviet Union, intensely distrustful and apprehensive of a freezing of its inferiority, was primarily responsible for the deadlock, but in 1955 Soviet proposals became more realistic and the Western position more evasive.

Both sides have shifted positions more than once on disarmament, as the desire to take a publicly attractive posture has conflicted with serious negotiating purposes, and unsettled Soviet attitudes seem to have reflected differences within the leadership.[6] In 1955 the West failed really to explore the Soviet propositions but turned to the areas of inspection and control, where progress was nearly impossible because secrecy was a major Soviet asset. Publicity suited the stronger side, even more in nuclear than nonnuclear weaponry, as the primary utility of the former is psychological. The Soviet Union wished to magnify the deterrent effect of its arsenal by keeping the opponent in uncertainty. It was willing to surrender secrecy only in return for major strategic concessions, especially the liquidation of American overseas bases. Contrary political drives also made negotiations more difficult, as the Soviet Union saw disarmament as a means of halting or controlling German rearmament, while the United States was determined that no will-of-the-wisp of disarmament

---

[6] Alexander Dallin *et al., The Soviet Union and Disarmament* (New York: Frederick A. Praeger, Inc., 1964), p. 4

should prevent building of a major military power in central Europe to block possible further Soviet expansion.[7]

Although disarmament pourparlers were thus inconclusive, as they have nearly always remained, the Soviet Union was willing to make the large unilateral cuts of military manpower mentioned. It also undertook a series of withdrawals of slight military but considerable political significance even as the United States, in the momentum of the cold war, was still extending its global commitments. One of these was the relinquishment of Port Arthur to the Chinese. This had been promised for 1952 but was delayed because of the Korean war; in May, 1955, the Soviet Union finally found its longtime special position in Manchuria at an end. More important was the signing of an Austrian peace treaty (or, strictly, a state treaty, as Austria had never declared war) in the same month, and the evacuation of the Soviet zone of that country.

Soviet troops were the first of the Allies to enter Austria and occupy Vienna in 1945, and Soviet authorities set up an Austrian government on their own. Although this government was headed by a noncommunist, Stalin seems to have cherished hopes of sovietizing the country like other occupied lands. But the Soviet zone was neither politically nor economically viable apart from the rest of Austria, and the Austrian Communist party failed to gain mass support because of the concurrent presence of the Western powers, traditional Germanic-Austrian superiority to Slavs, the Russians' exploitation of their zone, and the absence of the social questions which gave Communist parties popular causes in most of Eastern Europe. It became difficult, consequently, for the Soviet leaders to contemplate satisfactory long-term control of part of the country, and the danger arose that NATO might be extended to the Western-controlled zones of the country. In spite of this, although points at issue were fairly well settled, the Soviets tried to use Austria as a lever against Germany and took the position that the Austrian settlement could not precede the German. Surrendering this hope, in the spring of 1955 Khrushchev negotiated remaining differences, agreeing to surrender the Soviet-occupied area in return for some economic concessions and, in a new approbation of nonalignment, the guarantee of permanent Austrian neutrality.[8]

Not long afterward, the Soviet Union yielded the naval base at Porkalla, near the mouth of the Gulf of Finland. The military importance of this position had become slight, although its acquisition was a point Stalin had insisted on in 1939 and for which he had gone to war. Its abandonment was a gesture to Finnish independence and neutralism. Stalin had

---

[7] Lincoln P. Bloomfield *et al.*, *Khrushchev and the Arms Race* (Cambridge, Mass.: MIT Press, 1966), p. 26.

[8] William B. Bader, *Austria between East and West, 1945–1955* (Stanford, Cal.: Stanford University Press, 1966).

hoped after the war to acquire Finland, like Austria, as a satellite but, perhaps because of bitter memories, was hesitant to do much to this end. In deference to Western feelings, the country was not occupied in 1945; but it was presented with a reparations bill which it was not expected to be able to meet and which was to tie its economy firmly to that of the Soviet Union.

In 1948 there was an attempt to emulate the Czech coup and communize the country. It should have been easy, as Communists held the vital ministries of interior and defense and others, and so were in command of the instruments of force. But Finnish Communists proved better Finns than Communists, and the coup failed before it began. Stalin, who had called for a mutual defense treaty, settled for a treaty of friendship. Communists lost ground in subsequent elections, and the Communists were removed from the government without interference by the Russians. In Finland, then, the Soviet Union accepted a not very friendly but neutral regime on its border, although its neutrality was and still is hedged by ties to the Soviet Union. One reason was appreciation of Swedish neutrality, which would probably be jeopardized by any manhandling of Finland. Again in 1954 the Soviets wanted Finland to join a common defense arrangement, but refusal was not punished. If one purpose of the evacuation of Porkalla was to exert pressure for the evacuation of American bases, this was a kind of pressure which Stalin did not see fit to apply.

By the summer of 1955, the international climate was warm enough for the first summit conference since Potsdam ten years before. The fact that Eisenhower could have a smiling meeting with Khrushchev and Bulganin in Geneva was a major accomplishment which gave rise to hopes of return to something like wartime cordiality. Not much more substantial than smiles was exchanged, however. The main problem at issue was Germany, concerning which the only feasible agreement would have been acceptance of the disagreeable status quo. Dulles went to Geneva with expectations of obtaining major concessions because of the Soviet weakness which he wished to perceive; and he pressed such questions as German unification, arms control, and freedom of information. President Eisenhower brought out his "open skies" proposal for aerial inspection, entirely advantageous to the United States. Soviet leaders yielded nothing, but did so with geniality. The issues were passed on to the foreign ministers; and in their subsequent talks Molotov declined to implement even the limited agreement implied in the spirit of the summit conference, perhaps because of disagreement with Khrushchev, perhaps because Soviet interest in the summit was mostly in the appearances of detente, not material settlements. Khrushchev, whose personal prestige was well served, made much more of the "Spirit of Geneva" than did the West.

Detente could continue despite the lack of substantive progress. Germany, the main stumbling block, became less of an obstacle, since on both sides desire for German reunification was more vocal than deep. The West refused to recognize any legitimacy in the German Democratic Republic but was unwilling to take strong measures against it. The Soviet Union for its part invited the West German chancellor, the doughty Adenauer, to Moscow, and came to an agreement for the establishment of full diplomatic relations. The price included liberation of a number of German prisoners still in Russia (publicized as a favor to the East German regime). Thereafter the Soviet policy was clearly, although not explicitly, directed toward the indefinite separation of two Germanies. The German question gradually lost interest for Western as for Soviet diplomats, Berlin remaining as the outstanding sore point.

At the same time that the Soviet Union was accepting the neutrality of Austria, it was starting energetically to cultivate other neutrals. In May Khrushchev suddenly landed in Belgrade, in a rather humble gesture of reconciliation with Tito. He placed blame for the dispute on Beria, recognized Tito as a good Communist, and acknowledged that there might be different roads to socialism. This was not a small sacrifice to make in hopes of luring Yugoslavia back to its former allegiance, as the pardoning of heresy inevitably emboldened others and made Titoism more or less respectable within the bloc. It was done over the objections of Molotov, who lost most authority (although he held the post of foreign minister until the following year) after a Central Committee plenum repudiated his approach in July.

Farther afield, the Soviet Union began in 1955 its wooing of the neutrals of Africa and Asia. Soviet influence leaped over the barrier American diplomacy sought to interpose by the Baghdad Pact of Middle East nations and, beginning with the sale of Soviet arms, built a bridgehead in Egypt, which has become stronger and broader in years since. Heads of state of India, Syria, and Iran visited Moscow, and in the latter part of the year Khrushchev and Bulganin made an unprecedented and much publicized tour of India, Burma, and Afghanistan. This developing campaign was designed to undermine the influence of the West in the areas involved and so was no great contribution to the reduction of tension. The arming of Egypt was as irritating to the West as a less legitimate act of violence might have been. The principal theme of Khrushchev's statements in Asia was the evil of Western imperialists. In India, he went so far as to state that British, French, and American interests started World War II and sent the Germans against Russia.[9] The cultivation of the uncommitted nations was, however, a further departure from Stalinism. It presupposed a climate of detente in the world and stability in Europe. It implied ideological relaxation and acceptance of

[9] David J. Dallin, *Soviet Foreign Policy after Stalin* (Philadelphia: J. B. Lippincott Co., 1961), p. 309.

diversity where Stalin had seen only unconditional friends or unredeemable enemies.

In this same spirit, the Soviet Union in 1955 found new virtues or utility in the United Nations, where it had seemed in Stalin's latter years that a Soviet presence was maintained for little more than hampering actions directly or potentially damaging to the Soviet bloc. It was a small but significant step that the Soviet government began furnishing economic and social statistics, previously refused on grounds of national sovereignty. In December the atmosphere had improved sufficiently that it was possible for the Soviets and the West to break a long deadlock and agree on a package deal whereby four Soviet satellites were admitted along with twelve Western-sponsored countries. Here as very often a degree of detente was advantageous. The Soviet bloc was nearly doubled at one stroke, and the enlargement was the beginning of the end of Western dominance of the Assembly.

Twentieth Congress and De-Stalinization

By the beginning of 1956, the evolution of the Soviet outlook on the world had proceeded far. The economy was continuing to expand rapidly, converting the Soviet Union from a country with little materially to lose from disorder to one of the more modernized and potentially satisfied powers, for which not only war but revolutionary disturbance of any kind would threaten more loss than gain. With the passing of the revolutionary generation, among the last of whose representatives were Stalin and Molotov, the passions of the Revolution ceased to be a personal commitment of the leadership. A new and technically educated generation coming to the fore called for modern interpretations of dogma.

There was a profound change of feeling since the days when Russia had emerged with overpowering exhilaration of victory only to find itself in dangerous military inferiority because of the unforeseeable atomic bomb. A decade later, the intoxication of victory had worn off through many frustrations, while the development of Soviet weaponry had given for the first time some sense of security. No longer was it felt necessary to regard the Soviet fatherland as a besieged fortress, to be guarded by all vigilance against a hostile world; but Soviet foreign policy looked out with growing confidence, claiming its share of the world stage. The potentialities of nuclear weapons were at the same time becoming far more serious. The hydrogen bomb, as much more powerful than the atomic bomb as this was more powerful than the conventional one, was being perfected; the Leninist approach to war was no longer realistic.

In Soviet practice, theory does not precede but follows actions, and the new departures of 1955 called for rationalization and incorporation in the conglomerate of Soviet ideology. The forum was the Twentieth Congress of the Soviet Communist party in February, 1956. Party Congresses, held frequently under Lenin, were at first important assemblies at which major questions were discussed and decided. Stalin used them to mobilize his supporters against his opponents. Having achieved this, he had no interest in a gathering of important people where ideas contrary to his might conceivably develop or spread; from 1934 to 1952 there was only a single Congress (1939). It was part of Khrushchev's attempt to revivify the party that Congresses were held with some frequency; and these convocations of thousands of local bosses, with notable and faithful guests from the parties of the world, were pleasing to the flamboyant and exhibitionist First Secretary. There, as the world listened and the multitude applauded, he could orate for hours, laying down what was *ipso facto* the official doctrine of the Soviet party if not of world communism.

Having attained a large measure of authority, Khrushchev by 1956 was ready to undertake his own revisions of Leninism. He practically accepted the charge of rewriting the canons by pointing out that conditions had fundamentally changed and it was dogmatism not to take them into account; Marxism-Leninism required constant development in tune with the progress of history. In particular Lenin had not contemplated nuclear weapons. For Khrushchev, in other words, doctrine had fairly frankly become descriptive of ongoing reality rather than prescriptive, an explanation or rationalization of policy rather than a guide to it. But he could not make changes freely. A large sector of the party leadership seems to have disliked the whole set of innovations at the Twentieth Congress; standing firmest was Molotov, the truest Stalinist of all, flanked by others, such as Malenkov and Kaganovich, in whose motivation rivalry with Khrushchev was mingled with conservatism. Partly because of this opposition, partly because of the dynamics of the Soviet system, amendments of doctrine were mixed with, often quite buried under, a mass of conventional verbiage about class, proletariat, international revolutionary struggle, and opposition to imperialism. If one picked at random snatches of the interminable speeches of the Twentieth Congress, he might well suppose that they were from Stalin's day, perhaps even 1919.

Withal, the Congress saw a renovation of thinking extraordinary within the Soviet framework. The whole view of the world became much more elastic and realistic. Instead of two camps, each supposedly uniform in class-dictated outlook, Khrushchev saw a more complicated world. Between the Soviet bloc and the American-allied West were the uncommitted nations of Asia and Africa, which by their at least potential opposition to imperialism and their desire for peace could be considered as forming, with the Soviet bloc, a huge "Zone of Peace." Nations could supposedly slip from the American alliance to neutralism and from this to the Soviet side; and it was the broad purpose of Soviet policy much less to forward a revolutionary change than to assist this progress toward universal socialism, stressing class conflicts within capitalist nations less than the conflicts between imperialism and nationalism. Within each group there was recognized some diversity; and as nations were expected to join the socialist sector, there had to be allowance for different ways of building socialism. By this opening it was hoped to entice Tito's Yugoslavia to closer and closer ties, and states farther afield might follow; that states already closely bound in the Soviet orbit might wish to loosen bonds was hardly contemplated.

This also implied that violent revolution was no longer necessary for the leap to socialism. There were various ways, including the parliamentary, and many states, perhaps the majority, could expect to rise peacefully to socialism with the help of the mighty Soviet Union and its allies. In this respect, Khrushchev practically went over to a Menshevik position of gradualism, that revolutionary change could be achieved without violence. This was to become a major point at issue with the Chinese Communists, who remained in this regard more faithful to Lenin's tenets. It was an essential concession, however, if neutrals were to be wooed; there was not much hope of converting governments while contending that they must be forcibly overthrown.

It was the more necessary to argue the likelihood of peaceful transition to socialism as the old Leninist link of war and revolution had to be broken. The October Revolution came out of one world war, and a dozen more communist states out of another, but a nuclear war promised to be far more destructive than the Russians (although not the Chinese) were willing to contemplate. The thesis of the inevitability of war, politically useful as it was, had to be sacrificed, while it was asserted that socialism could nonetheless triumph less dangerously. This idea, which emerged in November, 1955, soon after the Soviet hydrogen bomb had been tested, was justified on the grounds that the growing strength of the Soviet Union made violent revolution unnecessary and war improbable. This was political rhetoric rather than logic; it might as well have been said, in the Stalinist vein, that the growing desperation of declining capitalism made an attack on the socialist states more likely, or, as the Chinese were to advocate a few years later, that swelling Soviet power meant that the crusade against capitalism should be conducted more energetically. But strength is an acceptable reason for doing anything. The important matter was the basic Soviet interest in more or less detente for the sake of survival.

It was politically suitable, also, to decrease emphasis on military strength. The party apparatus, on which Khrushchev relied, was not interested in military but only in ideological tension. Military authorities were less controllable when the master's hand had been removed; and Soviet leaders have always been conscious, with the French Revolution in mind, of the dangers of Bonapartism. Heavy industry hardly represented a strong munitions lobby,[10] and in the shortage of manpower and capital for needs of rapid industrial growth, the Soviet Union had more to lose than the United States from an arms race. If nuclear capability could provide an effective deterrent to military action by the United States, then the Soviet Union should be able freely to work on the various contradictions of the capitalist world by whatever means were suitable—propaganda, pacific political and parliamentary struggle, economic penetration, or low-level warfare if necessary—advancing the Soviet cause toward ultimate and inevitable victory.

This was Khrushchev's celebrated theme: Peaceful Coexistence. The idea was as old as the Peace of Brest Litovsk, when Lenin had begged for a "breathing spell" to consolidate his state. The respite had stretched out indefinitely, but not until Khrushchev was it accepted as no mere postponement of the cataclysmic confrontation, a tactic of survival for the weak state, but as a permanent necessity wherein the strong state could carry forward its mission.[11] It took inspiration also from the "Panch Sila" or Five Principles of mutual noninterference, non-aggression, mutual respect for sovereignty, and equality, which were stated as official policy of India and China in October, 1954, and which were solemnized by the Bandung Conference of Asian and nonaligned powers of 1955. Made explicit and rounded out, the doctrine that the struggle between socialism and capitalism, in practice the competition of the Soviet Union and the United States for world leadership, should be conducted without dangerous violence, was incorporated into the official canon at the Congress. It was repeated and reemphasized that this did not mean any ideological accommodation or compromise with capitalism-imperialism, and in many subsequent crises Khrushchev tautened Western nerves with veiled or open threats of missiles and multimegaton warheads. But it was the policy of the Soviet Union not only to avoid major perceived risks (as it had been under Stalin) but to take positive steps, hesitant though they were and offset by moves which the West found aggressive, against the dangers of war. And however the party might warn against softness on the ideological front, the exclusion of violence as a suitable means of conflict inevitably affected Soviet psychology.

But the impact of all such modifications of Stalinist doctrine was slight compared to the attack on the image of Stalin himself. The peaceful transition to socialism and the noninevitability of war were comparatively academic. For a generation raised in the shadow of the great Stalin, the inspired genius-leader, to learn from the governing authority that he had

---

[10] V. V. Aspaturian, "Internal Politics and Foreign Policy in the Soviet System," in R. Barry Farrell (ed.), *Approaches to Comparative and International Politics* (Evanston, Ill.: Northwestern University Press, 1966), p. 276.

[11] Michael P. Gehlen, *The Politics of Coexistence* (Bloomington, Ind.: Indiana University Press, 1967), p. 63.

been a very fallible, egotistical, and ruthlessly bloody despot was a blow to the heart of communist faith. De-Stalinization, not Peaceful Coexistence, was Khrushchev's outstanding contribution.

The denunciation of Stalin was accomplished half furtively and without evident preparation. In the regular sessions of the Congress, there were stronger denunciations of the "cult of personality" than had yet been heard in Russia; but Khrushchev's blistering indictment—which fell far short of telling the entire truth of Stalin's misdeeds—was delivered in a closed session and later made known to party members. It has never been published in the Soviet Union; when divulged by the U.S. State Department, it was neither confirmed nor denied. There was reason enough for shame, of course, as Khrushchev and his cohorts had their share of guilt, but the compulsion was strong to speak out. Those who had trembled and groveled before the all-powerful dictator must have found it sweet to blacken his name in death, much as the Roman senators who had lived in terror of Domitian after his death expunged his name. It evidently seemed necessary to Khrushchev to let the truth, or a share of it, be known in order to facilitate the undoing of the rigors of the old system and to permit Soviet society to advance into modernization. Optimistic of revolutionary idealism, Khrushchev hoped to purge the Soviet Union of Stalinism and to find a rebirth of Leninist spirit and renewed vitality, especially in the ruling party. De-Stalinization was also politically useful to Khrushchev, whose principal rivals, such as Malenkov and Molotov, were closer to Stalin and more associated with him and his deeds. The fundamental criticism was that Stalin terrorized good party men. Stalin's basic economic policies were praised, and his foreign policy was nearly ignored except as he was blamed for the break with Tito.

If he had foreseen the consequences of his revelations, Khrushchev would doubtless have checked himself and let the breaking away from the Stalinist past proceed gradually. For the Soviet party and people, the effect was not overwhelming; trained to obedience and seldom possessed of much ideological enthusiasm, they absorbed their disillusionment or accepted their vindication and kept at work. But for foreign Communists, who had given faith and who obeyed Soviet leadership under less compulsion, the shock went deep. Not many tore up party cards, but belief in infallibility and the rationale for blind compliance were destroyed, never to be restored. Stalin had imposed himself, and Communists the world over had believed in him; that belief was the essence of being Communist, and the veneration of the great personality was a chief bond of unity for erstwhile revolutionary parties in a postrevolutionary world.

The Khrushchev policy was more rational and modern and less narrow or paranoiac than that of Stalin. But Khrushchev expected too much. He wished at the same time to have an essential relaxation of tension and a Soviet drive toward world supremacy. He wanted different roads to socialism so that various countries could take them, yet within the Soviet sphere he wanted all to be willingly obedient. He wanted the vitality of (limited) freedom, but he did not look to freedom from the firm control of the Soviet party. He could not be successful. The changes which he patronized could go only a little way before dangerous consequences began to appear. When the detente which had proceeded amiably through 1955 and the first part of 1956 led to serious rumblings in Poland in June, to a grave confrontation in Poland in October, and to an anti-Soviet revolution in Hungary at the end of that month, detente had to come to a halt.

2. THE CHALLENGE, 1956–62

With the declarations of the Twentieth Congress, the Khrushchev course was set, so far as there was any course, for the remaining years of his tenure. Shortly after the Congress, the much-traveled Khrushchev and Bulganin were off for a state visit to England. Khrushchev could not refrain from boasting of hydrogen bombs and ballistic missiles, a slightly chilling topic for the crowded island, and there were efforts to break down the embargo on strategic exports to the Soviet Union and to woo Britain from the United States. An attempted rapprochement with the Labour party came to grief on Khrushchev's anger at the Labourites' interest in socialists persecuted in Eastern Europe and Russia, which he could only see as currying favor with the reactionaries.

As frequently, the Soviet leaders found the socialists harder to deal with than the conservatives because the former were more exercised over political freedoms. However, the establishment of any sort of dialogue was a landmark. Later, when leading French socialists visited Moscow, results were similar. No positions were changed, but barriers seemed less impenetrable. More significant was the hero's welcome given Tito, received in Moscow like a lost brother. So warm were relations, as the evil past seemed to have been wiped away, that Khrushchev was earnestly seeking Tito's assistance in the late summer in coping with the burgeoning unrest of Eastern Europe. Soviet openness and cordiality reached a zenith at this time.

The ferment which reached its climax in the Hungarian rising restored much of the steel in the Soviet attitude. If liberality led to subversion and counterrevolution, it had to go, and counterrevolutionary trends had to be suppressed. Tito, the dear friend of 1956, was treated in 1957 and 1958 as something of an enemy, although never a reactionary beast as in Stalin's time. To the great fortune of Khrushchev, the Hungarian crisis coincided exactly with the Suez crisis, and he used this to distract attention as much as possible, going so far as to threaten rockets on his recent British hosts and French guests. Some of the old ideology was brought back, also, to meet the renewed demand for socialist discipline, for example, harping on the inherent aggressivity of capitalism.

The Soviet position in Eastern Europe was restored without great difficulty in 1957, and stability reduced worries, but Stalin was partially rehabilitated and Stalinist tendencies predominated in 1958. Nagy, Hungarian premier at the time of the attempted withdrawal of Hungary from the bloc, was wantonly executed, along with a number of his companions, for no other apparent reason than as an expression of vengeful defiance. However, the post-1956 tightening, brought by events in the bloc, was mostly confined to it. East-West dealings were not drastically impeded. And it did not go very far. After 1958, the course was now toward relaxation and compromise, now toward aggressiveness and confrontation, with a bit more of the former during the remainder of Khrushchev's tenure.

One reason that reversion to Stalinist ways did not go far was that Khrushchev managed to retain power. The poor results of rash de-Stalinization gravely weakened his hold, however, and in the winter of 1956–57 he was insecure and unable to speak with much authority. Having bided its time, the opposition moved to oust him in June. The party Presidium voted to remove him; only three of eleven members supported the party boss. But Khrushchev claimed that he had been elected by the Central Committee (which was only formally true) and was removable only by it. With military assistance, Khrushchev gathered his supporters, who, perhaps preferring the de-Stalinizer to the Stalinists, voted him in and his chief opponents out of office. The expulsion of the so-called "antiparty group" placed Khrushchev for the first time in a position of clear supremacy, although not until March, 1958, did he assume the premiership.

One of the charges against Molotov, Malenkov *et al.*, was opposition to reconciliation with Yugoslavia, the conclusion of the treaty with Austria, normalization of relations with Japan, disarmament negotiations, and relaxation in general. This accusation indicated Khrushchev's intention of carrying forward Peaceful Coexistence. Peaceful Coexistence, however, was not peace but a better way of advancing Soviet interests. To support the ideology which supported and justified the state and to fulfill its imperatives, doubtless no less to secure his own position, Khrushchev felt driven to seek successes, real or apparent progress toward world supremacy.

Consequently, the period from 1956 to 1962 was marked by a series of crises, as Khrushchev tried one or another expedient to fulfill his role of Soviet and Communist paladin, turning from one area and scheme to another without clear direction. But it was probably not nearly so dangerous as it seemed then, for Khrushchev was leading much more from bravado than strength and determination, hoping for the maximum return at minimum real cost. Crises usually were not of his making, but in the agitated world there were never lacking troubled situations inviting intervention. There were all manner of meetings and negotiations, the visible result of most of which was nil. When the period was over, things were in most respects much as they were when it began; in the fundamental purpose of raising the Soviet world position, Khrushchev achieved little. There were two major results of his administration: the Soviet Union made itself present potently in many countries of the noncommitted world; and the Soviet bloc lost its unity, the biggest member, China, departing wrathfully, while dominion over the European satellites was badly shaken. These two developments were complementary, as the effort to expand afield did much to weaken bonds nearer home; and a leader of Stalin's temper could not have achieved the one and would not have permitted the other. Because of their long-term importance, they merit more detailed treatment.

The Grand Contest

Khrushchev paid much more attention than his predecessors to foreign affairs. However, their priority in the Soviet system has never been very high, and resources and attention of the government and party have been primarily dedicated to the economy. The contradiction might be resolved by making economic growth a major means of world influence. It may seem odd that Khrushchev would choose the economic arena, in which the Soviet Union was still very far behind, to challenge the West. But this corresponded to the fundamental Marxist insistence on the primacy of economics, and it was encouraged by the statistics, perhaps somewhat misinterpreted, of rapidly expanding output. From 1946 to 1956 and 1961, as indicated by the accompanying table, the Soviet Union took giant steps toward catching up with American industrial production, at least in the basic commodities favored by Soviet planners.

U.S. Percent of Soviet Production

	1946	*1951*	*1956*	*1961*
Steel	457	304	214	123
Oil	1092	720	363	214
Coal (with lignite)	471	257	157	85
Electricity	560	417	357	267
Cement	1030	346	226	106

Source: Based on U.N. statistics.

It was easy to project these trends and guess that within a decade the Soviet Union would be the leading industrial power of the world. Clearly, the American position, based on material production only, would become untenable, as the world balance swung against capitalism, which would help dig its own grave by its crises and contradictions. Force would be unnecessary; national leaders, seeing the tide flowing irresistibly, would swing over to the side of socialism. Exuberance over the prospects varied with the statistics; 1958 was Khrushchev's most successful year, and in the optimism of 1958 and 1959, there was much talk of the world victory of the toilers. But through the whole period the prospect of Russia overtaking the United States industrially seemed very real. In 1961 it seemed to as sober an observer as Alfred G. Meyer that "world communism is growing in strength and is confident of victory."[12] Khrushchev hoped the ruble would replace the dollar in world finance, and he promised to overtake the United States in industrial output by 1965.

It is not clear how much was to be gained by touting this relative economic success. Many leaders of poor and would-be developing nations were impressed, seeing in the Soviet Union a model for mobilization and rapid modernization, but in no case were they disposed to become satellites. In fact, as the Soviet Union became richer, many leaders in the underdeveloped world became inclined to regard it, as the Chinese do, as bourgeois and alien, in the same class as the United States. In a sense, if the Soviet Union had a secret of rapid growth, it would have been better served by keeping it a secret. But the image was useful for broad political and propagandistic purposes. The 1961 Program of the Soviet party stated the international task mostly in harmless terms of building the Soviet economy. There was a sort of rosy vision of a world in which economic progress under Soviet leadership would erase national differences and bring all into a magnificent amalgamation—an updated version of the Communist world revolution. To stress productive capacity is a more sensible and modern approach to international relations than stressing means of destruction, and it was a suitable cornerstone for a policy of true Peaceful Coexistence. Let the system prevail which proves itself better in peaceful competition, as Khrushchev said.

His confidence in saying so was not entirely justified, however. Although the Russians were credited with producing impressive quantities of steel, the United States seemed incomparably better able to provide consumption goods, from clothes to automobiles and meat. Toward the end of Khrushchev's years, the Soviet rate of industrial growth visibly slowed down as the American sped up, so the Soviet advantage was less or sometimes nil. Nor was it always clear that the Soviet economy, in its

---

[12] Alfred G. Meyer, *Communism* (New York: Random House, Inc., 1962), p. 190.

bureaucratic fetters, was modernizing more rapidly than the American. There was a growing impression that Soviet methods were better for lower than higher stages of development. Countries of Western Europe also demonstrated the enormous possibilities still inherent in capitalist or mixed economies, while Japan recorded industrial growth much faster than that of the Soviet Union without oppressive controls and the gross waste which seemed a part of Soviet industrialization. Soviet agricultural productivity remained very low, and it availed little that Khrushchev turned to his people with a call to overtake American production of meat, eggs, and so on—a nonrevolutionary urging which propagandized American superiority quite effectively and which undercut boasts about the Soviet key to progress. Economic growth paid dividends in world prestige, but the overall superiority of the socialist camp was far over the horizon.

For economic growth and modernization, it was necessary to depart to a degree from Stalinist autarky, and the 1950's saw foreign trade rise to a new plateau. The Soviet Union by 1959 was the sixth trading nation, with 4½ percent of world trade, against rank of sixteenth and about 1 percent before World War II. Strategic controls dating from the Korean war were gradually relaxed and were unimportant by 1960. Exchanges with advanced countries were carried on for practical and commercial reasons with little political purpose, but the Marxist-trained Soviet leaders did not fail to attach political significance to them, and they involved reduction of hostility on both sides. They also implied the admission of foreign ideas; if Khrushchev wanted his state to aspire to commercial and scientific leadership he could not keep it isolated. Travel and scientific and cultural exchanges were much increased in 1956 and after. Foreign papers and magazines, almost entirely excluded in Stalin's day, became slightly available in Khrushchev's, by mail or in libraries although not for public sale. Jamming of foreign broadcasts was reduced, although not ended until 1963.

It was becoming less of an adventure to visit the Soviet Union, and tourism, purposefully although inefficiently guided, became increasingly important in impressing the world with Soviet accomplishments while gathering hard currency. In the years shortly after the Revolution, foreigners were received mostly as proletarians or potential converts, but in the latter 1950's capitalists by the thousands were shown the achievements of the Soviets. A whole gamut of means of influencing the world, radio, periodicals, book publishing in foreign languages, artistic events, student exchanges, and the like, were brought increasingly into play. Fond of the spectacular, the Soviets made a speciality of exhibitions abroad; their pavilion was the star attraction at the Brussels World Fair in 1958. It cost from $40 to $60 million, against $14 million which the U.S.

Congress allocated.[13] There was a Soviet exposition in New York the next year, balanced by an unprecedented American exposition in Moscow.

It was an assumption of Communist faith that this enlargement of contacts with the outside world, much of which inevitably escaped control, would benefit the Soviet side politically. Usually the Soviet people have been more receptive to Western culture than the reverse, and Stalin was likely right; the Soviet system had more to lose from erosion by foreign ideas than to gain by convincing the world of its virtues. But Khrushchev believed that his was the way of the future and that Marxism-Leninism, in the Soviet version of the time, should impose itself or be imposable. He did his best to assist it, also, by the adoption in 1961 of a new official statement of aims of the party to refurbish doctrine by restating its ideals and utopia.

Again, however, success largely eluded the indefatigable First Secretary. Few people were much fired by a restatement of revolutionary purposes, more modest than that of forty-two years earlier, and Soviet doctrine seemed increasingly dull in the rapidly changing world. Propaganda in its various shapes was of some import in poorer and less sophisticated parts of the world; but it had little effect, except for Soviet space exploits, in the advanced lands. It was and is a handicap of Soviet public relations that it relies on organized, official, and overt action, which lacks spontaneity and variety and is less effective in attitude formation than the less visible and direct image making of looser societies. Secrecy and exclusiveness continued to hurt. Many areas both of the land and of Soviet affairs continued to be screened, thereby inviting doubts. Not many Soviet citizens could be allowed abroad, where they might presumably spread the gospel. In 1957 there were about 1 percent as many Soviet citizens as American working abroad.[14]

More broadly, Soviet propaganda and messianism were (and are) lame because of lack of cultural creativity. Little new and exciting came from the Soviet land. To remedy this in part, Khrushchev permitted Soviet artists much more freedom to use their talents than had Stalin. He explicitly recognized that the party authorities were in no position to tell the writers what to write. But soon he encountered the recurrent Russian dilemma. Given freedom, artists and intellectuals began to deviate from accepted norms and to criticize Soviet society and by implication the party and leaders. Khrushchev became angry, but he refrained from tightening reins very much. His successors seem to have felt that he was inviting political decay, as they have undone a good deal of his relaxation of party control over the arts.

---

[13] Barghoorn, *Soviet Cultural Offensive,* p. 89.

[14] Barghoorn, *Soviet Cultural Offensive,* p. 7.

Armaments and War

The Khrushchev approach was basically nonmilitary, but he wanted to make the most of all available means, and the fear of nuclear war was a promising political weapon. However, in the face of the needs of industry, agriculture, transportation, and housing for very large investment, his regime could not afford to spend very heavily on military strength, and it did not. The armed forces ceased their rapid decline in numbers in 1956, but they were not enlarged and remained nearly stable or declined slightly until near the end of the Khrushchev period. The public military budget was nearly constant and a declining percentage of the total budget until 1961, when it rose nearly a quarter (Khrushchev announced an increase of one third) in response to the U–2 incident, abortion of the 1960 summit, and the sharp increase of defense spending of the new Kennedy administration.

The acknowledged appropriation for defense covers only direct support costs of the forces, omitting much that is included in the American defense budget. Moreover, the pay of Soviet soldiers is only a small fraction of that of American, and Soviet prices for military wares are quite artificial. However, budgetary changes reflect the intensity of Soviet military preparations, and it is clear that the Soviet Union failed to follow through its successes in the hydrogen bomb, concurrent with American development, and in long-range missiles, in which it had priority, to build in 1957 and afterwards a force which could in reality threaten American primacy. This reflected confidence that the United States, which had not attacked in a time of overwhelming superiority, would not attack when this had become dangerous, and belief in the efficacy of bluff. If the Soviet Union demonstrated the capacity to produce intercontinental weapons and kept secret the actual production, this was enough. The effort made was enough to serve as a deterrent against a direct attack on the Soviet bloc and to qualify the Soviet Union as protector of its vassals, an important element of overlordship.

Fairly moderate military budgets also reflected the Soviet political reality. There was less pressure from heavy industry for a big armaments program because its civilian products were always in heavy demand. The party apparatus, always apprehensive of military influence, was interested in ideological and not military tension. The state bureaucracy, clamoring for funds for a thousand purposes, preferred detente in general, as did light industry, agriculture, and the intellectual community. Khrushchev himself painted Soviet society[15] as inherently pacific, with no class interest in imperialism. Nor were the armed forces politically prominent. Not

[15] As in an article in *Foreign Affairs,* October, 1959.

long after Marshal Zhukov had helped save Khrushchev's position in 1957 by bringing in his supporters in air force planes, Zhukov was removed from power. Thereafter no representative of the army sat among the top leaders, although the Soviet defense minister has customarily been a soldier, and a few, perhaps 5 percent, of the Central Committee were military men. Most of these were from the technical branches, less threatened by detente. The group most inclined to resist was the ground forces, especially the officers, who encountered difficulty in finding suitable civilian relocation in Soviet society.[16]

Military resistance, however, prevented Khrushchev from going as far as he would have liked toward streamlining and reducing the forces with reliance on nuclear deterrence. The argument for a large army in the missile age, not for limited or peripheral wars as in American thinking but to help assure survival under nuclear attack and probably victory after it, was a prominent part of Soviet military thinking. In the same tendency, Soviet generals, or the more traditional among them, liked to see the world in rather Stalinist terms of uniform hostility, from which Khrushchev was trying to move. There was a remarkable dearth of thinking as modern concepts jostled uneasily with surviving Stalinist clichés and the refighting of the previous war. One reason that Soviet military thinking, unlike American, had little impact on foreign policy was that there was little of it. Soviet diplomats and disarmament negotiators were more familiar with Western than with Soviet strategic ideas.[17] In 1962 there was published the first Soviet treatise on strategy since 1926, one moderately sophisticated volume (by a group headed by V. D. Sokolovskii) against many shelves of American analyses.

Without much help from his generals, who had been thoroughly indoctrinated in letting the party think for them, Khrushchev was somewhat confused in his ideas about war, which varied to suit political circumstances. Nuclear war, being inadmissible, was held avoidable. Yet the thesis that only socialism could bring an end to wars, a prime attraction of Soviet doctrine for many and especially intellectuals, was too valuable fully to surrender. In January, 1959, the Party Congress heard the strongest declaration yet of the need to avoid nuclear war; in June, 1961, Khrushchev returned to his 1955 view that it would mean the end of capitalism but not of socialism. He was more desirous than many in the Soviet Union to reduce arms and make international contention nonviolent, and he wished to put all the eggs in the nuclear basket, despite the fact that nuclear weapons are least suited for intervention or subjection of weak countries.

---

[16] Aspaturian, in Farrell (ed.), *Approaches to Comparative and International Politics,* pp. 270–76.

[17] Dallin *et al., Soviet Union and Disarmament,* p. 61.

Sometimes Peaceful Coexistence sounded like *Pax Sovietica*, wherein only military actions approved by the Soviets were permissible. Redefined in 1960 as the "highest form of the class struggle," it included no condemnation of war as such but left the door open to "wars of liberation," which Khrushchev espoused to the grave displeasure of the West. In 1961, Khrushchev divided wars into three categories: general war, local war, and liberation struggle. The first was conceived only as a capitalist-imperialist aggression against the socialist camp, with no idea of war through accident, miscalculation, or anything less than evil design. The distinction between local and liberation wars was unclear, the latter perhaps simply representing those approved. But Soviet support for liberation wars was more theoretical and verbal than material. It was handy to threaten support in hopes of deterring counteraction by the West, i.e. the United States, but there was a healthy fear of dangerous complications in peripheral causes.

Despite marked strategic inferiority to the United States, Khrushchev did his best to create and use for political purposes the opposite impression, partly by deliberate deception, partly by secrecy mixed with tantalizing bits of information and suggestive misinformation.[18] The gap between pretense and reality was greatest from 1958 to 1962, when the missile crisis radically changed assumptions. In these conditions the Soviet Union, while unprepared to take military action outside the bloc, indulged freely in bluster; Khrushchev, making the most of space successes, loved to talk of superweapons and hundred-megaton bombs. Threats were made in a vague manner or after the crisis had passed its climax to support subsequent claims of having brought about the peaceful settlement. After promising to protect Cuba from American attack by Soviet rocketry, Khrushchev did not mind explaining that the threat was symbolic. Threats of rocket reprisals were made in the Suez crisis when it was clear that the affair would be settled otherwise, in order to take credit with the Arabs for having compelled British-French withdrawal. In this line, Soviet propaganda stressed the horrors of nuclear war to the world while making very little of this theme at home.

The campaign was not unsuccessful. The world assumed from about 1956 until after the missile crisis that the Soviet Union was roughly the military peer of the United States. But political gains were slight, except perhaps in the Arab world. Rocket rattling undid many of the gains of Peaceful Coexistence and was no way to win friends in a world terrified of the potential holocaust. Threats of violence alarm most of the world, which only desires to live in peace, and galvanizes those against whom they are directed. An exaggerated notion of Soviet rocket capacities led to an exaggerated response by the Kennedy administration in 1961 and after,

---

[18] Horelick and Rush, *Strategic Power and Soviet Foreign Policy*, p. 39.

which forced much increased spending on the Soviet side. The Chinese, taking seriously Soviet claims of strategic superiority, thought this should be used to help their cause and that of world revolution. When Khrushchev declined, they regarded this as a betrayal.

Disarmament

The contradictions of the Soviet military posture hindered progress in an area of Soviet interest, disarmament. As in the 1920's, the Soviets had much to gain from the advocacy of disarmament, an impeccable cause, and potentially much more from its realization. The Soviet economy needed all resources that could be diverted from military spending, while the Russians frequently asserted, in accord with their philosophy, that the stability of capitalism depended on armaments, and some Western opinion supported this thesis. Hence disarmament should lift the Soviet economy and expose its rival to stagnation and crises, hastening the anticipated victory. Disarmament also would give more security to the weaker power and would tend to seal the status quo in Europe, a major Soviet objective, while hindering not at all the expected spread of communism elsewhere. It fitted entirely Khrushchev's faith in the ability of the Soviet way to advance by pacific means. Finally, as China began to appear potentially more menacing after 1959, the Russians cherished hopes of checking the nuclear armament of their ally.

If there was much to be gained from disarmament, the difficulties were no less. The fears and tensions which made it urgent caused too much distrust; each side tended to assume that any proposals of the other were designed to gain a strategic advantage, if they were not mere propaganda. Khrushchev was pretty frank about the propagandistic value of being for disarmament. The ideological conflict redoubled the trouble. There is no reason to take seriously an offer of an innate class enemy or of a state dedicated to destroying the present social order. If the proposal should seem attractive, it was the surer to be deceptive. The West came back again and again to the demand that fulfillment of any agreement be subject to international or impartial inspection; but for the Soviets, inspection was practically equivalent to espionage and could be permitted only after disarmament. The Western negotiators would have received Soviet stubbornness on this score with more sympathy if they had realized how relatively naked the Soviet Union was behind its curtain of secrecy.

In 1955 and 1956, the Soviet negotiators accepted some elements of control by international teams or aerial inspection; but arms control was ordinarily linked to the status of West Germany in ways the United States would not accept. In 1959 Khrushchev made a spectacular plea before the United Nations for disarmament in stages to be completed in four years. This was naturally not taken seriously, but it is noteworthy that its final stage, wherein the peace of a disarmed world should be guaranteed by a police force from the Western-aligned, Soviet bloc, and uncommitted nations was a far cry from the traditional Marxist utopia. The West failed at times to explore in earnest the possibilities of Soviet projects during these years, and the Soviet side failed to give sufficiently sympathetic attention to Western ideas; the psychological impediments to meeting of minds were excessive.

Seen in retrospect, the proposals the neglect of which was most unfortunate for prospects of long-term detente were those for mutual withdrawal of forces. The Rapacki Plan, put forward by the Polish foreign minister in 1957 and 1958, provided for a nonnuclear zone in central Europe; but the United States considered it more important to have nuclear weapons in Federal Germany than not to have Soviet nuclear weapons in East Germany, Poland, and Czechoslovakia. There were Soviet proposals about the same time for the demilitarization of all the East European satellites, plus West Germany, Greece, Scandinavia, or other countries. The Soviet purpose was the removal of American forces from Europe, and for this reason it was not accepted. But if it had been possible to secure withdrawal of the Soviet army to Soviet territory, this would have been of tremendous significance.

Only in the area of nuclear testing, where inspection was not so critical and where the United States and Russia shared an interest in inhibiting the spread of nuclear weapons, was there a concrete achievement. A treaty to ban nuclear explosions was under discussion from 1955 onward, but the United States insisted on elaborate controls of observance, while the Soviet Union insisted on no controls but good faith. The question of controls related only to underground testing, as explosions in the atmosphere could be monitored around the world, but this was sufficient to prevent progress. The Soviet position may have been indecisive also because the Russians were unable to persuade the Chinese to go along and were reluctant to break with them.

In March, 1958, the Soviet Union, having finished a series of tests, announced a unilateral moratorium. This was denounced as propaganda, but the United States followed suit. However, in August, 1961, as a move to restore Soviet military prestige after the U–2 affair, and to develop larger warheads to counter the superior numbers of American missiles, the Russians tested a series of monster bombs in the atmosphere. Only after the Cuban crisis did discussions for a treaty make headway. Then the two sides came fairly close to agreement on a few inspections to be permitted yearly. In July, after the Sino-Soviet quarrel had flared into public name-calling, the negotiators cut the knot by agreeing to ban only atmospheric testing; and the first disarmament agreement of any kind between the superpowers was signed and ratified.

Russia and America

As other nations were more and more left behind by the rapid advances of the technology of destruction in the 1950's, nuclear and disarmament questions were almost entirely bipolar issues. Lesser nations might sit at conferences, but they could do little more than make suggestions. Other states had to adjust themselves to United States–Soviet relations, and these were, especially from the Soviet side, complicated and ambivalent.

The United States was the chief of the capitalist-imperialist camp, at the evil end of the Soviet ranking of states by virtue. In 1918–34, Britain and France had been the antagonists, and fascism was the enemy from 1934 to 1939 and in the war; but now, to liquidate imperialism meant simply to destroy American power. Stalin felt to the end that Britain and France were important, but for Khrushchev they were quite secondary. It might be said that the essence of his policies was anti-Americanism, almost from first to last.

Yet Khrushchev did not hold the United States an unequivocal antagonist, the irreconcilable class enemy. He did not even treat it consistently as an opponent in balance of power or realpolitik terms. Frankly asserting the absence of direct conflicts between the two (which implied that ideological or class conflict was unimportant), he felt (at times, at least) that Soviet-American cooperation should settle the problems of the world. It was as though the Soviet Union, a universal power, saw the necessity of recognizing as a near-equal the other universal power, with which the mission of world order might be shared in condominium. Consequently, Khrushchev seemed to be aspiring usually to general hegemony or at least influence over a larger part of the world but at times to dyarchy with the United States, and alternately menaced this country and proposed cooperation with it.

A remarkable incident in the latter direction came when the United States surprised the Soviet leaders by its vigorous opposition to the Franco-British-Israeli descent on Suez. Then the Russians with ideological elasticity proposed joint Soviet-American military operations to restore peace. One wonders whether they seriously supposed that the United States would join arms with the Soviets against its two principal allies on behalf of Egypt. The United States, of course, found military cooperation with the Russians against American allies unthinkable; and the proposal may have cost the then foreign minister, Shepilov, his job. On the other hand, the Russians noted with relief the disinclination of the United States to give more than verbal assistance to Hungarian rebels in 1956; the Eisenhower administration, having spoken of rollback, accepted the Soviet sphere. As the feelings raised by Hungary wore off, relations between the two countries improved again. In January, 1958, there was set up a cultural exchange program which has sputtered along ever since. There was a brief setback when in the aftermath of the overthrow of the pro-Western government of Iraq American marines went into Lebanon, to considerable Soviet alarm. But the situation was stabilized and the marines fairly soon departed.

In 1959 Mikoyan, who often served as a high-level Soviet ambassador, became the most elevated Soviet personage to have visited the United States. He acted as pathbreaker for Khrushchev, who secured an invitation from an American government eager to have him see with his own eyes the country his propagandists so violently denounced. Khrushchev's journey to America, in September, 1959, was a personal triumph for him and perhaps the best time of his life, as he gave Americans his views of almost anything, chiefly the virtues of socialism. It was ended and climaxed by a session with Eisenhower at his Camp David, Maryland, retreat. The two agreed on a summit meeting to be held in Paris in May, 1960, and emerged in the cordial "Spirit of Camp David," a rebirth of the "Spirit of Geneva" of four years earlier.

If the encounter with America was a propagandistic triumph for the head of world bolshevism, he was also influenced thereby. Returning home apparently convinced that the United States was opposed to war, he delivered a number of rather heretical pronouncements to his people: that most Americans supported their government, that the American economy did not rest on armaments, and that Eisenhower was a man of peace. It was a major revision of the Marxist-Leninist view of the state to recognize, as Khrushchev did up to the following May, that the American government was not merely the creature of the monopolists and Wall Street but that various forces, from unions, churches, and farmers to industrialists and the Pentagon contended in its decision making.

Hopes for a major improvement of the climate were dampened as soon as specific views on concrete problem areas, such as Germany, were brought forward, and went crashing with the U–2 incident at the beginning of May. Khrushchev craftily trapped the United States in an embarrassment which was ultimately disadvantageous to him. First, he simply announced the downing of the plane in the heart of the Soviet Union. The State Department thereupon made excuses of navigational error by the allegedly weather-research plane. Then he announced capture of the pilot, and the espionage mission had to be acknowledged. In response to Khrushchev's blustering, Eisenhower undiplomatically assumed personal responsibility for this activity. This was a blow indeed to Khrushchev, who had rested his hopes of a Berlin settlement on Eisenhower and had commended him to the Soviet people as a man of goodwill. What had seemed an opportunity to separate Eisenhower from the militarists—Khrushchev had been careful not to associate him with the U–2—turned into the opposite. Soviet air defenses were shown up as inadequate; Khrushchev, exposed to charges of having been fooled by Eisenhower's smiles, may have been weakened; and the military influence in Soviet policy was strengthened. Not surprisingly, Khrushchev's reaction was violent and well beyond good taste. He went to Paris only to demand that Eisenhower humiliate himself as the price of sitting down together in a Big Four summit meeting.

Soviet policy, however, did not really turn from detente; truculence in the following months was more show (partly for the benefit of the Chinese whom Khrushchev felt it necessary to placate by a quick visit after leaving Eisenhower) than substance. For example, the Soviets walked out of the Geneva Disarmament Conference but did not break off negotiations. In the spring of 1961, they facilitated a compromise settlement in Laos, where the CIA had undertaken to install a pro-Western government. But that year saw an intensification of the arms race and much tension over Berlin. In May Khrushchev tried to bluff and bully the young new President, Kennedy, at an encounter in Vienna. Perhaps influenced by Kennedy's restraint in the Bay of Pigs affair, he apparently believed that he could get favorable changes in the status of West Berlin, if not control of that outpost within the Soviet sphere—a bone in his throat, Khrushchev called it. After the Berlin Wall had ended what was much less cause of suffocation than of hemorrhage, as thousands departed socialist for capitalist Germany via Berlin, relations between the superpowers were again on the way to improvement until the missile crisis of October, 1962. This sobering confrontation set the tone of American-Soviet relations for the remainder of the Khrushchev tenure and beyond.

Perhaps under the impression of the *fait accompli* which the West accepted passively in Berlin, Khrushchev tried in Cuba the last of his schemes for turning the world balance in favor of the Soviet Union. Aware of special U.S. interest and sensitivity over Latin America, the Soviet government paid rather little attention to this area in the 1950's. When in 1954 a leftist Guatemalan government which tried to procure arms in Czechoslovakia was overthrown with complicity of the CIA, the Soviet Union showed little concern. When Castro came to power at the beginning of 1959, more by a general revulsion against the Batista dictatorship than by the military prowess of his guerrillas, there was no quick Soviet move to intimacy. The Russians seem to have found Castro, a revolutionary in need of an ideology, somewhat puzzling and were hesitant to become involved so close to the United States. Not until a year later, in February, 1960, were important economic relations started by a visit of Mikoyan to Cuba. Diplomatic relations were established only in the Soviet pique after the U-2 incident. The Bay of Pigs affair, of April, 1961, wherein an invasion attempt by Cuban exiles supported by the CIA failed miserably, was welcomed as a humiliation of the Kennedy administration; and Khrushchev took the occasion grossly to insult the President. Nonetheless, when Castro first proclaimed Cuba a "socialist" state, the Soviet government evinced no pleasure. But thereafter, because of American economic blockade and ostracism of Cuba within the hemisphere, Castro became something of a hero to the Soviet Union as a genuine revolutionary and bold anti-American.

It is not clear whether Khrushchev wished to use missile installations in Cuba to bargain for American concessions elsewhere, such as the prohibition of nuclear arms for Germany or possibly American withdrawal from Formosa, which might be used to return China to cooperation with the bloc. It seems that Castro was told that his duty to the socialist cause required admitting Soviet missiles although Khrushchev afterwards stated that they were installed at Cuban request only for the defense of the island. This would have been a poor calculation, for they came very near bringing on an American attack. They were, in any event, of much longer range than could be considered defensive. As the buildup was being prepared, there were many assurances that no such thing was contemplated. As the falsity of such statements was bound to become apparent, making them indicated a remarkable unconcern of the Soviet government for its reputation.

There was incredible carelessness in neglecting to camouflage the installations until well after they had been observed. Nor did the Soviets precede them with antiaircraft missiles which might have prevented the United States from obtaining accurate information until after the missiles were ready and aimed at American cities. Moreover, a gradual buildup, with weapons of successively longer ranges, might have been successful, as American intervention at any stage would have been far more difficult; haste was Khrushchev's nemesis.

The management of the affair was clumsy also in that Khrushchev obviously had no plans to deal with American counteraction. On Kennedy's declaration of a blockade, he only fumbled and hesitated, trying to save something from the debacle. His best idea was exchange of U.S. missile bases in Italy and Turkey for Soviet bases in Cuba; Kennedy allowed him to save some face by a conditional undertaking that the United States would not invade Cuba, thereby, Khrushchev said, making the missiles unnecessary.

The results were unhappy for Soviet diplomacy. The European satellites, not consulted or informed, were annoyed at having been brought to a danger of war for a fruitless adventure. The Chinese, although they loudly supported Khrushchev during the crisis, after it attacked him bitterly for adventurous entry and cowardly exit. In the tensest confrontation, the Soviet Union had appeared both weak and foolish, while the prestige of the United States soared. The Soviet backdown gave rise to possibly exaggerated ideas of Soviet weakness after years of exaggeration of Soviet strength.[19]

The cold war was action and reaction, and the policies of each side were in large part response, or overresponse, to policies of the other. When the Russians, whether for security or power and glory, sought to extend their influence or control in Iran, the Balkans, Germany, and so on, the United States responded with a series of alliances embracing some forty countries and bases for nuclear bombers around Soviet borders. These provided the Russians with one of their principal themes until the rise of long-range missiles relegated bombing planes to secondary importance; on almost any occasion and in almost any context of international discussion Soviet representatives would raise the question of American bases. The United States, for its part, with some feeling of destiny of its own, was inclined to take Soviet statements seriously and to accept that a major purpose of the Soviet state was the undoing of an economic and political order which the United States found basically satisfactory or at least far better than what the Russians seemed to offer.

If Khrushchev was less of a tyrant than Stalin, this improvement was offset by arrogance and intrusiveness, which often seemed more aggressive than it was intended. When Khrushchev said, "We will bury you," this sounded like intent to murder, whereas it was meant more as "We will outlast you." He probably really wanted a lasting detente with the West, but his approach was inappropriate. Boasting of Soviet successes, military might, and future superiority achieved little more than a tautening of American nerves. Specifically including class warfare (understood as Communist subversion) in Peaceful Coexistence, often discrediting a reasonable case by violent language, Khrushchev did much to confirm the considerable body of American opinion which regarded communism as

---

[19] The account of the missile crisis in a recent semiofficial Soviet history is of interest: "Becoming convinced of the impossibility of choking Cuba with the assistance of the Latin American countries, the United States government began to prepare its forces for an attack on Cuba. In October, 1961, the president gave the corresponding orders, and preparations were completed by the autumn of 1962. As a pretext for the assault of American troops on Cuba it was proposed to use the receipt by Cuba of military assistance from the Soviet Union.

"On October 22, 1962, President Kennedy spoke on radio and television. He declared that Cuba had been turned into 'an important strategic base' of the Soviet Union and 'presents a danger to the peace and security of all the countries of America.' The president needed these inventions to justify the establishment of a military-naval blockade of Cuba. . . ." Naval, marine, and armored units were readied for the attack. However, "As a result of diplomatic measures undertaken by the Soviet Union, and also the decisive condemnation of American aggression by world public opinion, the threat of a world war was forestalled and the attack on Cuba was halted. With the cooperation of the Secretary General of the United Nations, U Thant, messages were exchanged between the U.S.S.R. and the U.S.A. to overcome the crisis. . . ." (I. A. Kirilin [ed.], *Istoriia mezdunarodnykh otnoshenii*, Vol. III: 1945–1967 [Moscow, 1967], pp. 410–11.)

the only major political evil, a world conspiracy unswervingly dedicated to the destruction of the United States.

This was by no means the position of the American government, but it seemed at times that of John Foster Dulles. Before and after him, the United States has regularly taken a more anti-Soviet position than European countries much more directly threatened by Soviet power. It is characteristic that American trade with the Soviet Union and other Communist countries has been much restricted and remained insignificant, although practically all European countries have been willing to deal with the Russians since shortly after the Revolution on strictly business principles. The first major break came with wheat sales authorized by Kennedy in 1963. Disinclination to trade was interpreted by the Russians, in Marxist vein, as indicative of basic hostility.

If Khrushchev challenged to all-around competition, the American reaction emphasized military buildup. This was partly because the American government, unlike the Soviet, did not run the economy. It responded primarily in the areas of its competence, diplomacy, the enlistment of allies, and the building of military strength. A little baffled by the unconventional menace, with less confidence in its own amorphous doctrine and less organized propaganda, America was prone to seek simple military answers to the complex political problems. Military superiority should offset Soviet doctrinal aggressiveness; the Kennedy defense program was evoked by Soviet boast and bluster. Detente in this contest was not desirable; many saw it, just as Khrushchev did, as offering better chances for the spread of Soviet influence.

Thus, the American position was often more militaristic and at times seemed more aggressive than that of the Soviet Union. The latter, if the control of Eastern Europe were accepted as legitimate, was basically defensive, aimed at making secure the status quo. In many questions, the Russian position was reasonable. For example, they regularly advocated, and the United States regularly opposed, the seating on international bodies of the government of some 97 percent of the Chinese. Secretary Dulles practically boycotted the 1954 Geneva Conference because Chou En-lai was there. The United States, on the other hand, seemed to be pressing for changes highly adverse to the Soviet Union: a unified Germany allied with the West, Soviet withdrawal from Eastern Europe, even, as in the Captive Nations Resolution of the American Congress, for the breakup of the Soviet Union by separation of all minority areas. Hence there were fears, which Russians nourished, that nuclear war might be unleashed by American action; and not only Russians could believe that there were imperialistic strains in American as well as Soviet policy. Such feelings were a major asset of Soviet diplomacy and would have been much more important if the Russians had known how to present their case more suavely.

Western policy, although more sophisticated than Soviet, frequently neglected opportunities, suffered its own although less opaque ideological blinders, and was less successful than it seemingly might have been. If the West wanted to secure a Soviet retreat, this might have been achievable either by actual force or threat of force, or else by negotiation and mutual concessions, buying the freedom of the satellites. Neither means was chosen; the pressures unsystematically exerted confirmed the Soviet determination to hold fast to what they had. In this line, Adenauer's policy of seeking German reunification by building up strength which the West was not prepared to apply forcefully was perhaps good internal politics but obviously no means to its avowed object. The vague and wholly unwarranted feeling in the West that the Russians could somehow be painlessly pressed or persuaded to return to their homeland evaporated only with the triumph of sputniks in 1957. In terms of his objectives, Khrushchev achieved little. But American and Western policy, despite great material superiority, could count even less positive gains.

German Question

The central issue in Soviet-American relations from shortly after the end of the war until late in 1961 was the German question. It became apparent fairly soon that not much could or would be done about Poland, Hungary, and other satellites. In Japan there was no room for discussion. But Germany stood divided by a demarcation line which could not be regarded as permanent, and arrangements supposedly should be worked out for a reunification and a peace treaty with the reunited Germany.

The West felt obliged to support the reunification of Germany as the major national aspiration of that country. To a less degree, the Russians also felt they had to seem to support reunification, although there were no hypothetical circumstances in which they would gain thereby, and they had much to lose. East Germany was very profitable, with substantial and growing export capacities integrated into Soviet plans. It became the largest trading partner of the Soviets and principal supplier of machinery. Strategically, allowing reunification would mean turning over to potential enemies a position near the center of Europe. Politically, it would mean renouncing a government to which the Soviet Union was increasingly committed, the dissolution of a Communist regime and backing out of the Germany to which Communist tradition paid so much attention since the days of Karl Marx. It would also mean permitting the reemergence of a power which might well dominate Western Europe and which would indubitably be hostile to the Soviet-ruled East because of the German lands incorporated in 1945 into Poland and the Soviet Union.

The West, too, might contemplate some difficulties in the incorporation of a united Germany into NATO and subsequently the European

Economic Community. But the West was free to demand, on many occasions through the 1950's, that Germans be allowed to decide their future and set up an all-German government by free elections, which would certainly repudiate the German Democratic Republic and humiliate its Soviet sponsors. The latter could only respond, somewhat uncomfortably, that the sovereignty of their Germany must be respected and its socialist achievements preserved, hence that reunification should come by agreement between the two Germanies. This would involve as a first step the recognition of the East German regime, a major Soviet aim quite unacceptable to the West.

Such recognition, the acceptance by the West and the Federal German Republic of the German Democratic Republic and of the title of Poland to its formerly German territories, became a prime Soviet demand from the time when the Russians could no longer hope to undo the rearmament of West Germany and its incorporation into NATO. Only on condition of neutralization of all of Germany, somewhat in the Austrian manner, was the Soviet Union prepared to consider relinquishment of its Germany; and interest in such a bargain decreased steadily as the Ulbricht regime was more and more incorporated into the Soviet system. It may be that the ability to hold up a specter of German revanchism was highly useful to the Russians and that they would have been inwardly displeased if the West Germans had recognized the territorial losses of Germany, renounced the pretension to speak, as the only freely elected German government, for all Germans, and accepted the legitimacy of the Ulbricht regime. The dependence of the governments of Poland and East Germany on Soviet support, along with fears of a German resurgence elsewhere in Eastern Europe, would have been correspondingly reduced. In the latter 1950's another theme was added, alarm lest West Germany obtain nuclear arms. Again, it is impossible to guess how much was genuine fear, understandable in view of Russia's wartime experiences, and how much was the exploitation of a sensitive issue. However, the Russians made explicit what was long implied, that they would tolerate reunification only if all Germany were "socialized."

The question which remained open was the status of Berlin, the Western enclave which served as a window in the wall shutting off the Soviet sphere from the West. Because of the remnant of four-power control and the difficulty of splitting a large city, traffic went freely, or nearly so, between the eastern and western sectors. East Germany was the only Communist land whose citizens could emigrate fairly easily, and about a tenth of them did so, up to August, 1961. The open gate was damaging to the East German economy in permitting a drain of skilled personnel, who were lured not only by freedom but by the prosperity of the West. This was probably the chief reason for Soviet pressure on Berlin in 1958 and afterwards, although they could hardly admit it but spoke of many other things, from territorial rights of the German Democratic Republic to the alleged use of West Berlin for espionage.

The chief gambit was the threat to make a separate peace with the Ulbricht government, whereupon, in the Soviet interpretation, wartime occupation rights would cease. This threat was made in November, 1958, with a time limit of six months. It was repeated with more or less urgency in following months and years, giving rise to crises and tensions whenever Khrushchev desired to press the button; and ultimatums were several times delivered and withdrawn. At one time the Western powers were prepared to yield a good deal of their control, but the Russians demanded more and got nothing.

After the failure of the 1960 summit, Khrushchev saw no more prospect for dealings with the Eisenhower administration. He hoped to squeeze more from the inexperienced Kennedy. In March, 1961, the threat and demands were repeated, and Berlin was the most important and disagreeable subject of the Kennedy-Khrushchev meeting in Vienna. Kennedy reacted by measures of military preparedness, including a call-up of reserves. Meanwhile, the tension and Soviet deadline much damaged the Eastern position by speeding up the exodus of refugees, which became a torrent of thousands daily in midsummer. In the veritable emergency, the Soviets and their East Germans took the obvious countermeasure, on August 13, of closing the border with the well-known Berlin Wall. This brought them considerable opprobrium, but it achieved their urgent and principal aim without major complications.

The United States took it very calmly at first; after hearing the news, Kennedy went sailing and Secretary Rusk watched a baseball game. It was almost a relief; the flow of refugees had created a good deal of tension, and it was feared the Russians might do something more drastic. The limit of American involvement was clearly drawn at the border. Popular indignation in West Germany and West Berlin required a firmer stance; protests were made and for a time U.S. and Soviet tanks glared at each other. But the Soviets, having fixed the status quo, slackened pressure, although only gradually, as foreign policies have a momentum of their own even when they have lost their reason. Now able to govern its people much more firmly, the East German regime found political stability and began an impressive economic ascent.

Friction continued over details, especially of conditions of Western access, and it was feared that the Russians might try to cut down Allied rights bit by bit to make West Berlin untenable. However, they may have had little desire to force the Western powers out and turn all Berlin over to the Ulbricht regime, thereby increasing the potential independence of their vassal. Berlin is useful as an issue and point at which pressure can be exerted at any time. Soviet policy toward West Germany also was, and remains, ambivalent. Good relations serve practical purposes, while a clamor over alleged German militarism and revanchism is politically and propagandistically useful. Khrushchev seems to have been inclined to favor the former at the end of his tenure, as he was planning a visit to West Germany when he was discharged.

Declining Khrushchevism

After the missile crisis, Soviet policy went into a time of quiescence, preoccupied by domestic concerns, troubles within the bloc, and the now violent dispute with Communist China. But a year or so earlier, the exuberance of the good Khrushchev years had been fading as various drives seemed to bring little or no return; far from rising quickly to supremacy, the Soviet Union faced a long, perhaps indefinite period of standing second.

In 1960 and 1961, the rate of growth of the Soviet economy was declining, creating greater pressure on resources and undercutting confidence in a rapid overtaking of America. New approaches were evidently called for, and questions of the management of the economy became urgent. Agriculture, despite Khrushchev's crash programs, continued to stagnate—there was a disastrous crop failure in 1963. The allocation of resources was no less a problem in the more modern and more pluralized society. Khrushchev several times, during 1962–64, blamed military costs for the failure of the standard of living to improve much. Soviet artists and intellectuals were taking advantage of their new liberties to transgress the limits of Soviet propriety. Problems were mushrooming in Eastern Europe, where economic growth slowed much more sharply than in the Soviet Union; and the quarrel with China was becoming burdensome, although it was as yet mostly submerged and in fact denied in public statements.

The Twenty-Second Congress of the Soviet party, in October, 1961, proved rather inglorious, although it approved Khrushchev's Program for the building of communism. It was marked by intemperate denunciation of Albania, premature departure of the Chinese, and further incriminations of Stalin and the "Antiparty Group." Its tone in foreign affairs was moderate, as Gromyko called for Soviet-American cooperation in keeping peace. The tasks of the Soviet Union were stated in terms which, Marxist jargon being deleted, were entirely normal for a great power: strengthening of alliances, checking aggression, keeping the peace, developing commercial relations, and businesslike dealings with all states.

If Khrushchev hoped that missiles in Cuba would restore momentum to Soviet foreign policy, the failure was the more dispiriting. Generally, in the months up to October, 1964, Soviet foreign policy was confused, variably friendly and hostile to the United States, and much preoccupied with China, looming as a greater problem than capitalist America. One

Berlin Wall, August, 1961. The need for a concrete and barbed wire barrier to prevent people from escaping a Communist country was a discredit to the Soviet system. But it stemmed the drain of manpower from Ulbricht's realm and removed the urgency of the Berlin question.

lesson taken from the crisis was the necessity of managing the nuclear dangers. As stated in a letter to the Chinese, "The atomic bomb does not adhere to the class principle; it destroys everybody within range of its devastating force." Direct emergency communications (the "hot line") were set up between Moscow and Washington to reduce possibilities of war by misunderstanding. The Test Ban Treaty was finally negotiated and signed, reportedly against some opposition of Soviet military figures; possibly the illness in May of hard-liner Kozlov made this possible. Another lesson of Cuba was the folly of distant adventures without adequate covering force. On the one hand, interest in penetration of the uncommitted world decreased. On the other, the armed forces were modernized. Military manpower was cut down by another million men from 1963 to 1965, and the Soviet defense budget was reduced in 1964, as was also the American. But there was begun a nuclear missile buildup which was to carry the Soviet Union near parity with the United States by 1969.

These were years of improvisation and experiment after the rigidity of Stalinism. The major changes of outlook for which Khrushchev was responsible, the admission of peaceful transition and different roads to socialism, the recognition that war was not doctrinally inevitable and that capitalism was not wholly decadent, and the call for nonviolent competition of socialism and capitalism, were all in the direction of rationality and departures from revolutionary tradition. Although Khrushchev was unable to find a suitable balance between Peaceful Coexistence and the universal mission, he moved still farther from identification with world revolution into which the Soviet regime was born. It continued to be the basic thesis, as under Stalin, that what was good for the Soviet Union was good for the cause, and that the chief contribution of the Soviet state, beyond avoiding nuclear war, was to build itself up. But Soviet interest might be best served by detente, which would reduce Western unity, permit access to Western technology and credits, and permit diversion of resources from military to constructive purposes.

Although Khrushchev tried to revive Leninist purpose and made much more effort than Stalin to spread Soviet ideas and patterns through the world, his emphasis was still less revolutionary. "Revolutionary change" began to take the place of simple "revolution," and the idea of a single world Soviet state in the utopia was dropped in the 1961 Program. It was recognized that proletariats were not growing larger or more radical in the advanced countries, and more of the Soviet appeal was directed to middle-class and nationalist sentiments. Communist parties lost importance as the Soviets began using more effectively other means of influence, military, economic, cultural, and scientific. They were valued mostly as a reassurance of the truth and universal validity of the principles on which the Soviet state based itself. Although it could not be admitted, the Soviet

Union was becoming a stable hierarchic-bureaucratic society and hence basically conservative. As an increasingly prosperous country in a very poor world, it was identified less and less with the truly deprived and had no desire to share its relative wealth. The divergence of the reality of Soviet diplomacy and the vague but ritualistically repeated ideological purposes was becoming ever greater.

3. WORLDS TO CONQUER

Renewed Expansionism

Stalin sat isolated in the Kremlin, never mingling with the people or visiting the provinces; the ebullient Khrushchev gloried in showing himself everywhere. Stalin was concerned with what he ruled and neighboring territories which might come under his control and largely indifferent to the world without, which was better kept distant. Khrushchev thought much of Soviet prestige and standing, turned away from Stalin's narrow territorial approach, believed foreign contacts should be helpful, and reasserted the Soviet duty, abandoned by "Socialism in One Country," to forward change in the whole world toward communism or the Soviet pattern.

This was in accord with his effort to revive Leninist ideals. To revivify the party meant to restore its universal mission and its vision of itself as a world-shaping force. More specifically, Khrushchev followed Lenin's idea, alien to Marxism, of conquering the West via the East, undercutting capitalism by depriving it of colonial (or "neocolonial," as the word came to be) sustenance and breaking "weak links" of the chains of world capitalism, according to the Leninist interpretation of imperialism. Khrushchev, however, extended his vision to the whole world, whereas Lenin, like the tsars, had hardly looked beyond neighboring countries. He also went much farther in accepting neutralist, even anticommunist regimes. Lenin wished Communist parties to cooperate with bourgeois nationalists against imperialism, as did Stalin until failure in China in 1927; Khrushchev wished the Soviet Union to cooperate with nationalists, regardless of what local Communist parties did. He moved from the traditional Bolshevik denial of the possibility of neutrality to optimistic overestimation of the extent to which interests of the Third World coincided with those of the Soviet Union and of the likelihood of their being drawn into the Soviet sphere without revolution.

Just what was to be achieved in faraway lands of Asia, Africa, and perhaps Latin America, with which Russia had few relations of any kind, was not clearly articulated and probably not precisely thought out.

Vaguely, they were to be guided toward the Soviet model, not by a disciplined Leninist party but by Soviet influence. There was some logic to this, as their situation was in important ways similar to that of Russia before 1917, with antiwesternism, Western economic domination, backward social structures, and need for economic development. They might well be expected to admire and follow the anti-Western westernization which was the essence of the Russian Revolution; for them, the prime achievement of the Soviet Union was not a more just political order but industrialization. Seeing this, and leaning on Soviet support, nationalist leaders might be persuaded to take their lands down the Soviet path with no need for revolution—a concession that was indispensable if the Soviet Union were to compete for their favor at all.

It was not clear, however, why those who had fought for independence from Britain or France should care to subordinate themselves to Russia, even if they wished to copy its success. Ideological hopes were, however, less important than fairly conventional power politics. If Western, especially American influence could be weakened or removed, that was gain enough. As Khrushchev said in 1959, ideological differences should not be allowed to get in the way of the struggle against imperialism; and the Soviet attitude toward a country depended almost entirely on its policies toward the cold war, minimally on its internal policies or any theoretical expectation of advance to a socialist structure. Practically any country was a potential recipient of Soviet aid, unless it were, like the Dominican Republic in the 1950's, notoriously discredited.

For this there was no theoretical justification and only limited rationalization. The approved leadership became "national bourgeoisie" by virtue of no economic standing or relation but merely in tribute to its foreign policy. Class relationships were analyzed mostly in terms of attitudes toward foreign economic interests. But this was only an extension of Lenin's politicizing of Marxism; the Communist parties, after all, in these lands represented not a nonexistent proletariat but the unhappy intelligentsia. Somewhat more original was the invention of "National Democracy" as a new stage of history between capitalism and socialism to cover noncommunist countries willing to align themselves fairly closely with the Soviet Union.

The idea of working with governments of weak nations of Asia was almost as old as the Soviet state. In the 1920's, Kemal Atatürk's Turkey was given military and economic assistance, and help for Afghanistan was extensive in terms of the very meager resources of the Soviets. For some years, a subsidy of $500,000, mostly in goods, was paid to the Afghan king. Soviet engineers and other specialists worked there on sundry projects, such as a cotton gin,[20] and in 1928 a military force was sent to

---

[20] Marshall I. Goldman, *Soviet Foreign Aid* (New York: Frederick A. Praeger, Inc., 1967), p. 115.

the king's aid. But to the colonial and semicolonial world beyond the neighborhood of Russia neither the Comintern nor the Soviet government paid much attention. In most places Communist parties were small or lacking. In India, for example, there were only a few hundred Communists in the 1930's after a decade and more of organizing the huge potentially revolutionary masses.[21]

World War II greatly raised the prestige of the Soviet Union and of Communist parties everywhere, but Stalin, preoccupied with the borderlands, less sophisticated in his approach than Lenin, and holding to the 1928 Comintern thesis that the national bourgeoisie was bound to betray the liberation struggle, had little notion of extending Soviet influence beyond the area of his military power. He preferred to avoid contaminating foreign contacts, underestimated the force of nationalism, and was doctrinally unprepared for the end of colonial empires, which the capitalist countries should have clung to as to life itself. Nationalist leaders, as Gandhi, Nehru, and Sukarno, were treated as traitors to the people, lackeys of imperialism, in various cases accused of being in the pay of British or American undercover organizations.[22] The facade of Indian independence was regarded as result of a deal between the bourgeoisie of the two lands for dealing with popular unrest, and diplomatic recognition of independent India was delayed for three years. "Liberation" of colonial territories, it was held (this doctrine not applying to contiguous territories), could come only through proletarian or Communist-led action; and the countries of the Third World were alienated by being treated as puppets of imperialism. The very idea of neutralism was derided as an "imperialist device."

From 1949, however, there began a gradual reevaluation. In the rising confrontation with the West, especially with the founding of NATO, the Stalinists began to conceive a little appreciation of those who declined to join the enemy. The Peace Movement suggested courting the uncommitted. After Truman in 1949 began a program of economic assistance to less developed countries, Soviet delegates spoke of willingness to do the same, although there were no deeds to match until much later. Communist parties were turned primarily against the United States, not local capitalists. After the failure of risings attempted in 1948–50 in various Asian countries, Communist parties dropped the violent line and began claiming to speak for the nation as a whole. The Soviet Union began taking note of the independence of some countries of Asia, especially India, in their coolness toward the United Nations' commitment in Korea and their opposition to the American project for a peace treaty with Japan. In 1952 there were some friendly gestures toward India, and an Asian Communist

---

[21] John H. Kautsky, *Moscow and the Communist Party of India* (Cambridge, Mass.: MIT Press, 1956), p. 73.

[22] Dallin, *Soviet Foreign Policy after Stalin*, p. 292.

conference omitted the previously obligatory references to the need for armed struggle. Stalin a little later called on Communist parties to take up the banner of national independence.

This evolving attitude received concrete expression after Stalin's death. Economic aid to Afghanistan, after a lapse of many years, was resumed with a small loan for industrial projects. Assistance was offered to underdeveloped countries through the United Nations program in the middle of 1953, although the general distrust was such that for a year and a half there were no takers of Soviet gifts. A trade treaty was signed with India, followed in 1954 by an agreement to build a steel mill. In 1954, also, the Geneva agreements wrote finis to the period of militancy in Asia, the Russians began talking of the "Zone of Peace" as *de facto* ally of the Soviet Union, and "nationalism," a bad word at home, became laudable in Asia and Africa.

In 1955 Khrushchev led the Soviet Union to a broadening of outlook comparable to the abandonment of isolation by the United States. The prosperity of the West meant that Soviet prospects there were almost nil; on the other hand, the growing economic strength of the Soviet Union made available some, albeit still modest, resources for an expansionist policy; and the Russians, feeling more secure in Europe, could optimistically aspire to forward pro-Soviet change elsewhere. The Bandung Conference of April, 1955, with its outpouring of neutralist sentiments by representatives of a majority of the world's population, suggested fertile fields.

The most spectacular step was the visit of Khrushchev and Bulganin to India in the fall of 1955. This was in return for a visit of Nehru to Russia in June, on which occasion this statesman, who had been denigrated while he was playing a truly revolutionary role, was shown exceptional honors, including the privilege of being the first noncommunist foreigner to address a large public gathering. In India Khrushchev received a tumultous welcome which must have warmed his heart to greater generosity toward the peoples of Asia. From India, the Soviet travelers went to extend the blessing to Burma, although the government was actively fighting two Communist movements. After this tour, Soviet writers undertook somewhat belatedly to rewrite history to raise Gandhi and others from creatures of colonialism to liberation heroes. Khrushchev also accounted for the peaceful emancipation of colonies, which was so hard to square with the Leninist view, by crediting it to the strength and example of the Soviet Union. Peaceful Coexistence, with its call for trade and disarmament, harmonized with this new drive for influence.

The Soviet image in the Third World was not greatly injured by the suppression of the Hungarian revolution because Asians and Africans were not much troubled by what befell Europeans and because of the coincidence with the Suez crisis, which further weakened British and

French influence. The post-Hungarian hardening of the Soviet outlook and the difficulties of Khrushchev's position brought something of a pause; but after he ousted his principal opponents in June, 1957, and the Soviet Union acquired new assurance with intercontinental missiles and sputniks in the latter part of the year, the program became more active. Its best years were 1958 to 1961 or 1962, when discouragement overtook it and attention was shifted back to domestic needs. Around 1960 conditions were especially favorable. Many new nations, particularly of Africa, offered opportunities, and the expanded United Nations offered a handy ground on which to meet them. Conversion of Castro's Cuba from a "National Democracy" to a socialist state offered hopes that others, such as Egypt's Nasser, Ghana's Nkrumah, and Algeria's Ben Bella would find similar enlightenment, perhaps inspired by the 1961 Party Program pointing the way to the Soviet utopia.

Soviet Foreign Aid

The Soviet struggle for influence in the less advanced nations and against imperialism and neocolonialism (translatable as American political and economic bonds) was waged in many ways—propaganda, trade, economic aid, and military assistance. A State Committee for Cultural Relations with Foreign Countries was established in 1957 for exchanges in arts, culture, and science. Foreign students were brought to the Soviet Union, and a special institution (Lumumba University of the Friendship of Peoples) was founded for them. More was spent on books, magazines, and radio programs for the Third World than for the much more important but less appreciative advanced countries. Soviet diplomats were given new tasks of winning friends. But perhaps most important and alarming to the West was the Soviet trade-and-aid program.

The Soviet program was somewhat imitative of the American and organized in much the same way. One predictable difference was that the Soviet expenditures were only a modest fraction of the American. Actual amounts are somewhat uncertain, but it would appear that the total of Soviet credits and grants to Africa, the Middle East, Asia, and Latin America from 1954 to 1962 was about $3.2 billion.[23] Almost all of these were repayable credits; outright grants were quite exceptional. The purpose of this practice was partly psychological, to spare sensitivities, and partly to get maximum return and to tie the economy to that of the Soviet Union. But the deals were made more attractive by very low interest rates, contrasted with the commercial rates of capitalist countries, and by provision for repayment in goods.

Soviet aid differed from the American also in paying less attention to

---

[23] Kurt London, *The Permanent Crisis* (New York: Walker & Co., 1962), p. 119.

economic development and more to propagandistic and political effect. Visible and lasting projects were favored, from paving the streets of Kabul to a splendid stadium for Djakarta. On the basis that only nationally owned enterprises contributed to true independence, Soviet aid was designed to promote the public sector; this was calculated to impede American penetration, facilitate dealings with Soviet state organizations, and foster a Soviet-like political structure. It also aimed at forwarding industrialization, especially in the Soviet specialty of heavy industry, on the grounds that this would form a proletariat, presumed likely to be communist-inclined, at the same time that it hurt the Western monopoly-capitalists.

In this program, the Soviet Union was aided by the Chinese and much more by the Eastern European satellites, who provided between a third and a quarter as much as the Russians. As the industrial and technical resources of the more developed East European nations were considerable, their share in technical missions was much larger than in capital investments. Aid from Czechoslovakia or East Germany also helped the prestige of the bloc and moderated fears of Soviet domination. For this reason, Soviet aid was even channeled through satellites at times.

Another specialty of Soviet foreign economic aid was that it was inextricably mingled with trade, since Soviet foreign exchanges were as much subject to political management as the aid program. An incentive for buying Soviet goods, as for accepting Soviet credits, was that they could be repaid in goods. Contrariwise, under the barter agreements, the underdeveloped country often became creditor of the Soviet Union for lack of desired Soviet products. One form of aid was the bulk purchase of surpluses difficult to place, from Icelandic fish to Burmese rice or Egyptian cotton. Sometimes such deals turned sour, as the Soviet Union resold on the world market and depressed prices; but at times they were convenient for raw materials-producing countries.

A prime effort was to increase the volume of exchanges, thus making the neutralist country less dependent on the West and more on the Soviet Union. From the low point in 1953 up to 1960, the volume of Soviet trade with the Third World increased nearly seventeenfold, in current dollars, and that of the East European grew sevenfold.[24] But this impressive multiplication was possible only because it started from an extremely low level; the total volume was still rather slight. The Soviet Union accounted for only about 2 percent of the trade of the less developed countries, and few countries carried on more than 10 percent of their foreign trade with it. In 1956–59, the figure was regularly 20 percent or more for only Iceland, Finland, Afghanistan, Yugoslavia, and Egypt, of nonbloc nations;

---

[24] Frederick L. Pryor, *The Communist Foreign Trade Systems* (Cambridge, Mass.: MIT Press, 1963), p. 162.

and commercial ties did not seem to make even these countries very dependent on the Soviet Union.

Close kin to economic aid was military; indeed, this variety of sale may have had more importance than the more constructive type. Because of its relations to foreign policy and the orientation of wielders of power, it has had more direct political effect; and it has suffered less from Western competition. The Soviet Union is relatively more efficient in the manufacture of armaments than in that of civilian goods generally, and the Soviet world standing as an armaments producer is higher than its general economic standing. The continual modernization of Soviet equipment also permits disposing of large quantities of outdated material to countries which find it satisfactory. Arms, like other forms of aid, have normally not been given but sold and made payable in merchandise, frequently at very favorable prices. Despite frowns from the West, it has been hard for many countries to resist the temptation to buy; and it is the more pleasing for the Soviets to sell because the West disapproves. Then training is involved, officers of the recipient country being sent to Russia and Soviet instructors serving with the neutralist armed forces. Dependency, once established, is not easy to cast off, as Soviet parts, accessories, and ammunition are required. In fairly short order, armed forces of over a dozen countries were taking a usually increasing part of their armaments from the Soviet Union, and the number has not ceased to grow.

Still another feature of Soviet trade and economic and military aid is that they have been concentrated on a few, mostly the same, countries. They have included, in the Khrushchev years, India, the leftist Arab countries of Egypt and Syria, (for a time joined as the United Arab Republic), Afghanistan, and Indonesia. Some sub-Saharan African countries merited special favor for a time, particularly Guinea and Ghana; but amounts involved were smaller. Others, such as Uruguay and Argentina, Burma, Ceylon, Ethiopia, and Algeria, received a scattering.

Program in Action

The whole program was an improvisation, so its execution in any area was naturally flexible and designed to fit local needs and opportunities. In India, where the Soviet program had rather more political impact than a much more expensive American program, the opportunity was to assist badly needed and deeply desired industrialization. Outstanding was the Bhilai steel mill. Steel is a Soviet specialty; Soviet steel production, unlike many industrial branches, is at a high technical level. The Soviet builders used relatively few foreigners, quickly trained Indians and placed them in charge, and got the plant to full production and profitability sooner than competing West German and British projects. A large number of other Soviet industrial undertakings followed. Trade also prospered after the pathbreaking trade and cultural agreement of September, 1953; and Soviet-Indian relations have been increasingly close from 1955 onward.

More bothersome to the West and strategically more rewarding to the Soviets was the rapprochement with Egypt, or including Syria, the United Arab Republic. Here the opportunity rested mostly on anti-Western feelings and resentment of Israel, regarded as a Western intrusion into the Arab area. To play upon this theme came easily to the Soviet government. Prior to the independence of Israel, the Russians supported and helped arm the Zionist-liberation drive as anti-British. But enthusiasm of Soviet Jews for Israel was shocking; it struck a very sensitive nerve that a Soviet minority had a foreign point of attachment. Despite this and Stalin's anti-Semitic tendencies, however, very little was done to cultivate the Arabs until 1954, when there were several Egyptian–East European trade agreements and Arab Communists were told not to attack their governments.

The immediate event opening the doors to Soviet penetration was the American effort to prevent it by forming in the spring of 1955 a military alliance of Mideastern countries, the Baghdad Pact (later, CENTO). This exacerbated the rivalry between Iraq, which joined, and Egypt, which declined. Nasser was opposed to the Western connection of Iraq because of friction with the formerly occupying power, England. Moreover, he was having difficulties disposing of the cotton crop, and he was able to get little credit for arms purchases in the West. He therefore accepted a Soviet offer, by no means to identify with the Soviet bloc but to assert independence of the West. In September there was made an arms deal which reverberated around the world. Formally, it was with Czechoslovakia, but this was only a concession to appearances. Syria also accepted Soviet arms; and arms were followed by numerous missions, advisors, and cultural and commercial exchanges.

By their reaction to this new competition the United States and Britain pushed Egypt much closer to the Soviet embrace. They unceremoniously retracted the offer to help finance Egypt's dream project, the Aswan high dam, which Dulles confidently considered beyond Soviet resources. To the glee of the Communist world, Nasser responded by nationalizing the Suez Canal. Then Britain and France stumbled into their effort to restore by force the slipping Western predominance in the area. The Suez crisis was a bonanza for Soviet influence in a large part of the world and would have been more so but for the concurrent Hungarian repression. Making vague threats of missiles and offering to send volunteers when there was no chance of their being called for, the Soviets claimed maximum credit for saving Egypt and received a good deal. In reality, however, Soviet policy was cautious; Egypt was not permitted to use its Soviet bombers.

Mixing ideology still with straight politics, the Soviet Union made some effort, while helping the Egyptian and Syrian governments, to convert them to communism. This was more successful in Syria; fears rose in 1957 that this country was becoming a complete Soviet satellite. The Soviets claimed that Syria was threatened with invasion, and a little propaganda crisis ensued and passed, slightly enhancing the Soviet reputation as defender of the Arabs. However, Egyptian and Syrian leaders were also concerned with the progress of communism in Syria; to forestall this, the two countries were merged in the United Arab Republic.

Despite this setback, the Russians in 1958 agreed to help construct the Aswan dam. This project was slow in getting started, and there were failures of equipment and planning, but the Russians determined to make an impressive success of it and did so. The Russians also seemed finally, at the end of 1959, to lay aside ideological considerations. They had criticized Nasser for jailing Communists, but Khrushchev saw the futility of thus irritating his protégé. In May, 1964, Khrushchev seems to have let his enthusiasm carry him away, as he announced, apparently without the agreement of his colleagues, a large loan to Nasser. This contributed to Khrushchev's downfall five months later. But the Russians could take satisfaction in having, in Egypt, their most solid bridgehead in the Third World.

The good results of the Egyptian program stimulated the Soviets to go offering the same menu wherever feasible in that part of the world after 1955. After the pro-Western Iraqi government was overthrown in the summer of 1958, British forces were rushed to Jordan and American to Lebanon, in fears of a collapse of Western positions through the Arab lands with their invaluable oil resources. Soviet diplomacy fluttered in the crisis from one proposal or vague threat to another. As the situation calmed, the Western forces were withdrawn; and the Soviet Union conceived hopes for an ally, if not a satellite, in Iraq. Arms and aid were rushed in, but the generals had little inclination to surrender their freedom of action. More doors were opening in sub-Saharan Africa, where colonies were rapidly graduating to nationhood. The Comintern never did much about Africa except to deplore the absence of Communist parties; there were hardly any there when Soviet influence entered in the later 1950's and early 1960's. But there was a great deal of anti-Westernism, general discontent, and urge to a faith which promised rapid modernization. With no colonial record in Africa and a record of opposition to Western colonialism, holding itself up as the model of rapid rise to economic and political power and carrying a simple, universalist official faith of equality and brotherhood, the Soviet Union was admirably placed to capitalize on prevalent African sentiments.

The Russians tried their hand in one way of another in many countries, including Algeria, Somalia, Ethiopia, Sudan, the (formerly Belgian) Congo, Mali, Guinea, and Ghana. When the Congo received hasty independence in 1960, military support was offered the embattled Congolese premier, Lumumba. The American reaction was firmly negative, and Soviet support for Lumumba and his successors after he was murdered was mostly verbal. Mali, Ghana, and Guinea, with one-party, semi-Marxist, anti-Western governments were all given the title of "National Democracy" and for a time seemed on the fringe of, if not caught up in, the Soviet orbit. Most promising of all was Guinea, which separated with bad feeling from France in 1958. The resentful French pulled out brusquely. Russians and their allies moved quickly to the support of the otherwise friendless and needy land. There was so much Communist economic aid and technical assistance, without Western competition, that Western governments inclined to view Guinea as a permanent captive of Soviet power.

The Russians probably had such illusions, but to the general surprise, the Guinean ruler, Sekou Touré, at the end of 1961 expelled the Soviet ambassador for political interference. Touré, while appreciating Soviet anti-Westernism and wishing to rule through a Soviet-style party, always rejected atheism, historical materialism, and the class struggle, as did nearly all African leaders; and he needed economic cooperation with the West. Swallowing pride, the Soviets continued the program with diminished enthusiasm and intensity. The title of "National Democracy," instead of leading as expected to "People's Democracy" fell out of use (Cuba, the other "National Democracy," having promoted itself). The Soviet Union began to dissociate itself from the extremists, who turned to Peking. The Soviet role became rather that of a balancer offsetting Western influence, making political points here and there but doing very little for any revolutionary transformation.

Because of U.S. commitments and feelings, Latin America was much less inviting to the Soviets than Africa. Before 1954 the Soviet Union prudently paid very little attention to the area. There were Communist parties in various countries prior to World War II, but they lacked Soviet support while suffering from their connection with a foreign power and an alien doctrine. So feeble were they as a threat to the established order that in several cases military dictatorships used them to check native radicalism.[25] They became pro-American in the War and then reached a zenith of popularity. They declined in the cold war, and Soviet influence was consequently minimal by the time Khrushchev began his effort to raise the Soviet standing everywhere. There were anti-American, more or less neutralist tendencies in various countries, and Communist parties turned from revolutionism to anti-Yanqui nationalism, but the Soviet Union made no real progress.

The picture was altered and complicated by the advent of Castro. More

---

[25] Robert J. Alexander, *Communism in Latin America* (New Brunswick, N.J.: Rutgers University Press, 1957), pp. 12–13.

of a youthful rebel than a Leninist, he was by no means prepared to be docile; but he annoyed the United States, gave a bridgehead in the New World, and added to the prestige of the Communist movement. As noted, the Russians had some difficulty in making up their minds about Castro's revolution, but after the middle of 1960, they gave him the extensive material support needed to keep his regime afloat. When he announced that his regime was truly socialist—it was certainly collectivist—the Russians felt they had to admit this slightly heretical claim. However, they were faced with a dilemma of supporting Castro's ideas of guerrilla warfare throughout Latin America at considerable expense and risks or foregoing this opportunity of expansion to the disillusionment of true revolutionaries. The decision was for a somewhat equivocal caution, whereby chances of any Communist victory were made slight (Communist parties often giving little cooperation to Castroite movements), while the Soviet Union received a share of the blame for whatever troubles Castro was able to cause.

A very different sort of complication arose in Indonesia, at one time near the head of the list of receivers of Soviet aid. This was mostly military, as the ambitious Sukarno strengthened the army supposedly to overcome British-backed Malaysia. Some industrial projects were undertaken, but they were all failures. The Indonesian Communist party, with a platform of extreme nationalism, built up mass strength to become numerically the largest of nonruling parties and gained much influence within the government. However, the Soviet investment was wasted, as Indonesian communism gravitated from Soviet to Chinese orientation and possession of Soviet arms failed to convert to communism or pro-Sovietism the Indonesian generals who drowned in blood a Communist bid for power in 1965.

Soviet aid to Afghanistan, by contrast, has been markedly successful, rather more so than American, perhaps because conditions were much like those of Soviet Central Asia. The Soviets also gained favor by championing Afghan irredentism against Pakistan. Yet there was no Communist party and apparently no Soviet effort to build one up. There was actually very little Communist propaganda,[26] although the country's independence was, like that of Finland, qualified by the proximity of Soviet and the distance of Western power.

With another bordering country, Iran, Soviet relations were less felicitous. In 1952 a leftist nationalist, Mossadegh, came to the premiership; although he nationalized foreign (mostly British) oil properties, Stalin and his successors in 1953 and the Tudeh (Communist) party refused, because of narrow distrust, to support him. At one time the shah had to

---

[26] Günther Nollau and Hans Jürgen Wehe, *Russia's South Flank* (New York: Frederick A. Praeger, Inc., 1963), p. 112.

flee the country, and it seemed likely that Iran might come into the Soviet sphere. But Mossadegh was defeated, and a rightist government installed itself. In 1954 and 1955, Iran aligned itself with the West in the Baghdad Pact; but the Soviet government, having treated a leftist regime coolly, courted the rightist one with small-scale economic aid. Some friction continued, as the Soviet government refused to renounce a 1921 treaty giving them a right of military intervention if Iran should be used as a base against them, and Iran's ties with the United States remained strong. In 1962, however, Iran calmed Soviet fears by promising to allow no American nuclear bases; and relations became good-neighborly although still shadowed by Iranian doubts.

Appeals and Difficulties

Marxism-Leninism had a real appeal to many leaders and intellectuals of the poorer nations. It gave fairly simple and appealing answers to the complex questions of a frustrating existence, where more conventional Western philosophies left doubt and unclarity. It relieved them of any blame for poverty and backwardness, for which it gave the fairly plausible and very pleasing explanation of exploitation by the powerful capitalist nations. They were the world's proletariat, and they might identify with those who claimed to represent the working classes. It was satisfying to assure oneself that the Western powers acted only on selfish motives. Anticapitalism was pleasing to nations wherein much industry and commerce was foreign-owned, and they had limited understanding of Western political ideals and institutions; of the West they wished chiefly industry and technology, which the Soviet Union also promised. In the Marxist view, the last shall be first; Marxism gave significance to the insignificant, and underemployed and partly educated intellectuals could lay claim to the future in the name of the proletariat.

Khrushchev turned toward many nations troubled by accumulated bitterness toward the Western powers. Taking up the banner of emancipation once carried by the United States, the Russians found themselves encouraging extreme nationalism, remote as this was from the ideals of Marx. Nationalist leaders, such as Nkrumah, Castro, and Touré, became more or less like Communists, while Communists became like nationalists. The weaker nations might welcome a Soviet presence if for no other reason than to improve their bargaining power against the West and especially the United States, economically as well as politically. There may have been some basis for the Soviet charge that the West was not much interested in building basic industrial capacity in the less developed countries.

The Soviet example was a demonstration of the possibility of a nation's tearing itself away from the Western system. It appealed less for the Marxist economic and social justice proclaimed by the Revolution than as the prime example of rapid industrialization. It was certainly the most publicized, although the Japanese performance has actually been better; and modern industry promises riches and power. Itself formerly a relatively underdeveloped nation, unstained by overseas colonialism, Soviet Russia turned the tables by offering technological and economic assistance. It also offered ideology and institutions suitable for mobilization of resources, for ending the unemployment which burdened most of the Third World, and for the forcing of modernization against backward structures. If Russian industrialization was costly in terms of lives and suffering, this concerned African or Asian leaders much less than it did the West; there was ample suffering in their countries from poverty and disease even as they stood still. The Soviet system offered a recipe whereby the educated elite might whip ignorant and impoverished masses into an instrument of progress.

The Soviet political example has been less convincing, however, because of the insistence that it be taken uncritically despite arbitrary and irrational institutions. Much is shrouded in secrecy, and Soviet spokesmen cannot discuss political questions with individual intelligence, as they must hew to the party line.[27] As literal doctrine, Marxism had little relevance to the African or Asian context, with societies less capitalistic than pre-Revolutionary Russia. Atheism was unacceptable for most Asians, unthinkable for Africans. Proletarianism meant nothing to them, and no governing party could even pretend to base itself on a proletariat. Marxism practically ignored racial questions, which exercised minds especially in Africa. Russia could regard itself as more or less part of the advanced world to which Marxism promised the future, but the Soviets could promise backward countries nothing better than a place in the Soviet orbit. With more political sophistication and national pride than the Russians were apt to credit them, Third World leaders had no desire to join the ranks of Soviet satellites.

The Soviet attempt to overcome these handicaps and lure less advanced nations by economic means was rather feeble. The capacity of the Soviet Union to supply goods was not comparable to that of the Untied States or West Germany, or in most lines perhaps even France or Italy. To do without Western goods was a hardship, and it was difficult for the Russians to tie up so much of any country's trade as to jeopardize its independence. Soviet exports outside the bloc were in the range of a tenth of those of the United States, while the assortment was vastly less, service

---

[27] P. Wiles in Arnold J. Toynbee *et al.*, *The Impact of the Russian Revolution 1917–1967* (New York: Oxford University Press, Inc., 1968), p. 263.

deficient, and deliveries slow. With an anticommercial philosophy the Russians could not expect to be very efficient traders, although they have usually been hard bargainers.

Until Khrushchev's time, the Soviet Union quite lacked a theory of international trade, and only in the 1960's was there an attack on the principle of autarky, which is natural to the planned economy. Imports, the utility of which it is difficult to measure in the Soviet pricing system, are incidental, improvised into the system; this means that they are not only relatively small but somewhat erratic. Availability of goods for export has also been quite variable and quality very uneven. While the Russians have claimed, in superiority to the business cycle, to offer reliable markets, their trade has in fact shown wider fluctuations than that of the West. The non-consumer-oriented Soviet economy had very limited capacity to absorb the kinds of products which most underdeveloped countries could export; and without buying much the Russians could not sell them much. The red tape plaguing the economy at home was an equal hindrance to foreign transactions. Trade was conducted mostly by barter; this might sometimes be convenient for a nation eager to be rid of a surplus, but it was clumsy and inefficient. Similarly, the advantages of bulk buying by Soviet trading agencies were offset or more than offset by inflexibility and cumbersomeness.

It was soon perceived also that Soviet trade-and-aid was somewhat less selfless than advertised. The Russians would offer favorable deals at times to enter a market but, like any other profit seeker, raise prices if there were no competition. On the higher level, there were many promises and effusive declarations; in actual execution, the low-level officials were out to get the best possible deal. Although they touted aid without strings, the Russians were unable, especially in the first years of their program, to avoid the temptation to exert pressure on recipients. Thus, purchases of fish from Iceland depended on the inclusion of a Communist in the cabinet,[28] and loans to Yugoslavia were twice suspended when the Yugoslavs were out of favor. Usually, however, the Russians have been careful to eschew overt wielding of an economic club, and in practice the guiding principles of Soviet foreign trade have been ordinarily quite commercial.

The Soviet aid program has had many troubles, like those which the American has suffered, but rather greater. Aside from the expectable bureaucratic mixups, Soviet equipment was rarely manufactured especially for export and was often badly suited to exotic conditions; spare parts, a big problem in the Soviet Union, were harder to provide abroad. Soviet attempts to raise agricultural production were generally unsuccessful, as might be expected from the troubles of Soviet agriculture. Soviet personnel was usually handicapped by language, as officials of the Third

---

[28] Pryor, *Communist Foreign Trade Systems,* p. 171.

World often knew English or French but rarely Russian. By training and philosophy Russians were ill prepared to deal with people of different outlooks. For this reason or because of convictions of superiority, distrust, or simple habit, they would limit contacts with the people they were serving, causing suspicions of pride or racism and losing their advantage of living more modestly than Americans. East European technicians were likely to be more sophisticated in dealing with foreigners, but they were often lacking in enthusiasm for working for the Soviet cause. Many difficulties were a matter of inexperience, and as years passed the program went more smoothly. Others, however, were inherent in the Soviet system, as were many troubles of Soviet foreign trade, and could hardly be overcome without basic changes. It is a measure of the Russians' difficulties in peddling their wares that up to the end of 1967 only about 40 percent of the aid pledged since 1955 had actually been drawn.[29a]

Soviet cultural efforts labored under similar handicaps. Soviet expenditures for propaganda have been several times as great as those of the United States, and the Soviet message has often been a pleasing one for the ears of the underprivileged of the world. Yet the effect has been rather limited because of shortage of able personnel, misperception of alien psychology, and lack of variety, sophistication, and imagination. The image of the West, coming through a hundred different channels, was often ugly, whereas that of the Soviet Union was synthetically haloed; but the former was more interesting and credible. An example of the frustration of the Soviets was the indoctrination, or failure of indoctrination, of African students. Many brought to Moscow at considerable expense and treated with official favor were alienated by political controls and popular racial discrimination; hundreds gave up Soviet bounty to pursue their studies in the West.

Purposes and Results

A broader difficulty of the Khrushchev campaign in the Third World was uncertainty over its purpose and its relation to Soviet ideological commitments. Neither the Russians at work there nor the local Communists nor the governments understood clearly what the ultimate intention might be, and it was very difficult to square Marxism-Leninism with support for governments which, if not actually suppressing Communist parties, inevitably blocked their path. The priority Soviet objective was directly to serve the Soviet state, building up friendly relations with various states, helping and encouraging them to oppose the designs of the main antagonist, the United States, and secondarily its allies, especially

[29a] F. Holzman in J. C. Hurewitz (ed.), *Soviet-American Rivalry in the Middle East* (New York: American Academy of Political Science, 1969), p. 110.

Britain. For this it was necessary to deal with holders of power, governments in being. To wait for Communists to take over was to renounce diplomacy indefinitely; and if a Communist party interfered with good relations with the government, it was a nuisance. For a state to be a "National Democracy" it was not necessary that it carry out any social change or even grant freedom to leftists but merely that it be friendly to Soviet purposes.

The problem was not so simply resolved, however, because the Soviet Union had to justify its actions somehow in ideological terms of building socialism. It could never admit to acting simply as a state pursuing ordinary political ends but had to carry the banner of a universal cause. As protagonist of a cause, it could feel sure of the faithfulness only of allies identified with its ideals and basic values (and not even of them unless directly controlled, as schism within the bloc showed). It had to fear that any power led to the Soviet side by circumstance or bribed by aid would turn away as soon as convenient to more congenial company in the less ideological and wealthier West, which always had more to offer culturally and economically. It was also very repugnant to have to accept as virtuous varieties of socialism and pseudosocialism which were all anathema within the Soviet Union. It was difficult to renounce Communist parties in some countries without weakening the allegiance of the Communist movement as a whole. Faced with the question as to whether there should be revolution in Asian or African states, the Russians could only equivocate, claim vaguely to be for both nationalism and international socialism, and hope that Communist parties, as the best anti-imperialists, should be given freedom of operation and preferably a share in the government. It was contended, as a compromise, that the nationalist government could come peacefully to socialism, thanks to Soviet support substituting for proletarian action, without destruction of the present elite. But there was no precedent anywhere for such a development, and it has nowhere occurred.

The compromise was unsatisfactory for local Communists. Khrushchev argued that Soviet aid to their governments helped them by increasing the prestige of the Soviet Union and forwarding socialist ideals. But it was impossible for a Communist party to operate effectively against a regime patronized by the Fatherland of Socialism. The Communist party was likely, then, to be deradicalized, lose its special character and become merely another anti-Western movement. Or it might become a mere futile sect, like the Egyptian party under Nasser. Or it might lose touch with Soviet and internationalist purposes, like the Indian party, feeding largely on discontents of caste and nationality. Or if it cooperated with the government it might expect to be compromised, used, and discarded.

From the Soviet point of view, the effect on nationalist leaders was worse. They were aware that they were regarded as temporary instruments to be replaced, if possible, by more reliable adherents of the Soviet Union. From the point of view of the nationalist leaders, a Communist party in the land is only a reminder of the equivocalness of Soviet friendship. Seldom did they really give the Russians their confidence but saw them as useful in giving certain benefits and most frequently as leverage against the West, with which they would deal according to their own interests.

In the 1920's, Kemal Atatürk and Chiang Kai-shek used Soviet and Communist help in their struggle against Western powers or a pro-Western regime but eventually came to terms with the West and repressed their Communists as dangerous or inconvenient. In recent years many important recipients of Soviet aid, whose posture had alarmed the West at one time, such as Ghana, Guinea, Ceylon, Somalia, and Indonesia, have more or less turned away from the U.S.S.R. or at least manifested a high degree of independence. Seemingly, the only fairly reliable friends Russia has are some Arab states, whose loyalty would probably disappear quickly if the question of Israel were settled, and Afghanistan, under the weight of Soviet power.

It is easy to conclude that the whole Soviet program of winning friends in the Third World would have prospered much more without the baggage of the Communist movement and parties and all the complicating encumbrance of ideological commitment. But Khrushchev, striving to revive Leninist purpose, was in no position to discard ideology.

The greatest positive effect of the Khrushchev program was to alter the world image of the Soviet Union from that of an economically backward and narrowly selfish—imperialistic or conversely revolutionary—ideological power to that of a great power able generously to assist the less fortunate. At times, the Soviet advance into areas formerly regarded as pertaining only to the West gave an impression of the tide of history, the triumphant progress of one and the disarrayed retreat of the other. It had the impact of the unexpected, causing dismay and confusion in some Western circles and hopeful admiration in many of the Third World. The American State Department was inclined to see any leftist revolutionary action as opening the gates to communism and any degree of Soviet influence as a dangerous contagion likely to develop into a fatal sickness, like the Soviet dominion of Eastern Europe. Khrushchev saw the Soviet Union, especially in 1958–60, as a sort of Pied Piper seducing the masses of mankind.

In retrospect, the fears and hopes of those years, that economic conquest or subversion of the underdeveloped world might lead to global victory of communism, seem somewhat ridiculous. Nationalist leaders were not prepared to admit that they were copying a foreign system, much less to subject themselves to it. Nor were they disposed to subordinate nationalism to internationalism. In 1964 Khrushchev suggested in

Cairo that Arab unity should be a step toward broader socialist unity, but Nasser replied that Arab unity was a sufficient goal in itself. Neutralists, even while they admired its achievements, usually found enough to criticize in the Soviet system, for example its dogmatism and neglect of agriculture and the peasants. Soviet leaders watched eagerly the percentage of the economy nationalized in various countries, but the trend was only to a mixed economy; there was seldom an ideological compulsion, as in Russia and China, to dogmatic completeness of control.

If nationalization strengthened the national economy vis-à-vis Western corporations, it also increased bargaining power against the Russians. So far as Soviet influence and example led to a highly organized, centralized, and thoroughly controlled structure, the state was considerably less vulnerable to subversion or pressure of any sort from the outside. It is doubtful that Soviet aid appreciably helped any Communist party; very likely it contributed not to revolutionary possibilities but to social stability. It is in any case difficult to control people by giving them gifts which they are not likely to consider quite selfless; America also has discovered this. Even the idea of a bloc of neutrals, the supposedly pro-Soviet "Zone of Peace," faded as it became apparent, after the oratory of Bandung, that uncommitted nations also have diverse and contradictory interests.

The Western fear that the huge coordinated Soviet economy would be able to outmatch its loose Western rivals and bind weak nations to itself proved particularly empty. Some of the reasons for the awkwardness of the Soviet economic offensive have been noted. Taking them all into account, it remains truly remarkable that the trade monopolies proved so inefficacious. The Soviet Union has the world's second largest economy, but it has been turned to very slight use in the creation of dependence on either the Soviet market or Soviet supplies, except in Eastern Europe. Incomparably larger than any Western corporation, able to take losses for political purposes, it has only exceptionally and marginally used its enormous monopolistic powers. This inability is in marked contrast with the success of Nazi Germany in subjecting southeastern Europe to itself economically before World War II by bulk purchase, blocked accounts, and so on.

Soviet influence was thus able to progress markedly outside the Soviet sphere only where circumstances placed governments strongly in opposition to the West or the United States, especially in the Arab countries and Cuba. Its principal attainment was to promote neutralism and to make it easier for countries to remain aloof from American alliances, a reasonable objective which Khrushchev could have more fully achieved if he had been able to limit himself to this. Secondarily, it afforded some satisfactions to the Soviet government and people. Khrushchev obviously enjoyed bestowing Soviet bounty and harvesting tributes of gratitude, and the regime could depict itself as advancing socialism and helping the exploited. It served national pride and gave a sense of noble mission, which may have been widely shared by the people, although some wondered, as of Soviet space exploits, whether the funds might not better have been spent nearer home.

The Khrushchev program of spreading Soviet influence had other effects on Soviet society. The friendly approach to quite miscellaneous governments was conducive to tolerance and erosive of dogmatism, as was the idea that it was more useful to try to keep countries out of the opposing camp than to try to subvert or revolutionize them. The Russians had to admit that Marxism-Leninism had no answer for many problems of Asia and Africa; least of all could they imagine that the immense difficulties they encountered could be solved simply by putting a Communist government in charge. A large number of Soviet citizens were exposed to foreign contagions, a testimony to Khrushchev's greater confidence. It was educational for Soviet suppliers to work abroad under foreign and critical eyes, if not the gaze of the world, as in the big prestige projects. The Soviet Union acquired a new and nonrevolutionary appreciation of neutralism and the prosperity of noncommunist countries. Even a Communist revolution would endanger repayment of Soviet credits. Ideologically, a broadening of the Soviet view was at the expense of tightness at home. This applied, equally, to the bloc. It was harder to enforce strict conformity within a camp which admitted a variety of nonconformists on its periphery. Contrary to the theory of containment, this kind of expansion served to moderate and loosen the Soviet system instead of the opposite.

4. SPLIT WITH CHINA

Deepening Differences

From about 1959 the world watched and listened as hints of differences between the Communist giants began to pile up. Polemics became less subtle and more injurious, turning from hints of private differences to public denunciations. Finally the two sides were abusing each other with totalitarian violence and came to seem as much enemies as either was of the American archenemy. By the resulting cleavage, the once seemingly monolithic Moscow-led movement lost its biggest member and two thirds of its population, being cut down from a truly world domain—a third of the world's people—to merely Russia with satellites. This was one of the most momentous of alterations in the world's political configurations, with effects still to appear.

At times, hostility seemed to recede a little, and there would be new declarations of friendship. It could always be supposed, at least as long as the parties so assured the world, that the differences were between like-minded states which shared allegiance to Marxism-Leninism, the purpose of revolutionary transformation, and opposition to the United States. It was often noted that their quarrel was mostly about means, not ends, and it was feared that competition might make them only the more zealous in the propagation of communism. But in retrospect it seems inevitable that two great imperial states, Russia and China, should come to hate and despise each other. They differ in race, traditions and background, culture and philosophy (despite a glaze, superficial in the Chinese case, of Marxism), political style, and economic and political interests. Before the Chinese Communists gained power, many Western observers regarded them not as true communists but as "agrarian reformers," that is, peasant revolutionaries. These analysts seemed foolish when Russia and China were proclaiming indissoluble brotherly alliance, but they were basically correct. It was rather an exceptional incident of history that the governments of Russia and China were associated—more closely in appearance than reality—for a decade after the Communists overran all mainland China in 1949. The two could have been kept in close harmony only by wise and tolerant leadership on both sides, truly dedicated to the same utopian dream.

Although during the 1950's disputes were so drowned out by anti-Western propaganda that it usually seemed that the Chinese Communists automatically followed the lead of Moscow, nearly at all times there have been strong dissent and conflict of interest below the surface. The inception of the quarrel can be dated about as far back as one wishes, perhaps best to 1927 when the Chinese party came to grief following the dictates of Stalin and the Comintern. The surviving remnant took the un-Marxist but traditional Chinese road of peasant insurrection; and its means of achieving power, guerrilla warfare and fusion of revolution with nationalism, was entirely different from that of the Bolsheviks, who followed the antinational strategy of campaigning for peace in 1917 and then accepting the harsh peace of Brest Litovsk.

Despite this difference, the Maoists in the hills closely copied Bolshevik political vocabulary and party and military organization, applauded Comintern policy changes without question, and even carried out a purge in imitation of the Stalinist purges in 1937–38.[29] This identification raised them from a mere jacquerie to a part of a universal movement inaugurating the new era of history, but it did not imply much obedience. Mao became party chairman in 1935 without advice or consultation from Moscow, and it could not have escaped the Chinese that Stalin was more

---

[29] David J. Dallin, *Soviet Russia and the Far East* (New Haven, Conn.: Yale University Press, 1948), p. 136.

Khrushchev in Communist China, 1959. Seated at the head table with Mao Tse-tung, the Soviet premier was an honored guest at the tenth anniversary celebrations of the Chinese People's Republic. On the surface, all was friendship; but cooperation between the Communist giants was already almost at an end.

interested in a potentially anti-imperialist than in a communized China. Soviet help went to Chiang, who was fighting Communists as well as Japanese; in 1940 the Chinese Communists claimed or complained that they had received no assistance from the Soviet Union.

When Mao and his followers crowned their thousand battles and countless hardships with victory and found themselves rulers of a tremendous state, they had little need to feel gratitude. Practically down to the hour of victory, Stalin seemed indifferent to them. Mao, like Tito, was a successful independent strategist. From 1949 Mao claimed, although for a time in a very subdued fashion, to be an original prophet who had adapted Marxism to Asia and the underdeveloped world, as Lenin had adapted Marxism to Russia. As wielders of state power, the Communists found their interests conflicting with those of the Soviet Union. Mao went to Moscow to settle the relations which should prevail in the new conditions; that he remained there for two months while a hundred problems demanded attention at home indicated very difficult bargaining. China emerged with a mutual defense pact (which has not been denounced to date), but economic aid was not abundant and there was probably never close coordination of policies. The Korean war put the two powers on the same side, but its long-term effect was to give the Chinese a greater sense of independence.

In 1956 Khrushchev said that Stalin had brought the Soviet Union and China close to a rupture like that with Yugoslavia. For a time, the disappearance of the tyrant seemed to have removed a cause of discord, and his less masterful successors put improvement of relations high on the agenda. In October, 1954, Khrushchev went to Peking and made a number of concessions; Soviet bases in Manchuria were to be evacuated, the Sino-Soviet joint companies were liquidated, and China received another loan. There was a hint of future discord, as Mao raised the question of Soviet domination of Mongolia, and China in 1955 began looming as a potential if not actual competitor in the underdeveloped countries. But for a few years, Sino-Soviet relations seemed good, as the Soviet Union granted formal equality and made no effort to dictate Chinese internal policies. Khrushchev was the only Soviet leader with whom the Chinese Communists ever enjoyed really cordial relations.

Khrushchev's new departures, however, brought him sharply into conflict with Chinese feelings and interests. The denigration of Stalin in 1956 loosened bonds with China as it did with Eastern Europe. The Chinese party, which had cooperated in the building up of the Stalin image and was not consulted when Khrushchev tore it down, was less indignant over Stalin's cruelties, while any assault on the cult of personality and one-man rule plainly applied to Maoism. Told that the old god was something of a monster, called upon by Soviet leaders for whom they had no great respect to reverse their view of the past, they could agree only with reservations, while exonerating Mao of Stalin's faults. In Chinese eyes, Mao became as qualified to lead the world movement as anyone, certainly more so than the bumbling Khrushchev.

This meant that the Chinese were entitled to speak on the affairs of the world movement, including those of Eastern Europe; and they made themselves heard, to their rising self-esteem, in the Polish and Hungarian crises of 1956. In the latter, they stood strongly for Communist unity and supported Soviet intervention. Probably as a reward they received in 1957 a better economic agreement and promise of assistance in producing nuclear weapons, a kindness the Russians were soon to regret. But the Russians could welcome the Chinese in their garden only in case of emergency. Chinese influence took on anti-Soviet connotations, as they supported Poland's separate road to socialism, opposed the effort to entice Yugoslavia back, had ideas of extending Maoist theoretical innovations to Eastern Europe, and a little later encouraged Rumania to autonomy and Albania to complete independence.

Rivalry for leadership within the bloc was potentially disruptive, but it had less to do with the break than frictions arising from Khrushchev's campaign in the Third World. As an ambitious power, China pioneered the policy of helping economically ex-colonial Asian nations, including countries more prosperous than itself; but when the Russians did so on a large scale there arose a fierce conflict of interest. The Chinese, needy and dedicated Communists, saw themselves receiving hardly more than, in time much less than, such small and undeserving powers as Egypt and Indonesia. The Chinese soon began quietly telling Asians that the Russians were imperialists[30] and seeking to counter their superior economic capacity with revolutionary dynamism and the attractions of a poor and non-white nation for the poor and non-white masses. Rivalry grew in the various organizations of world Communism; eventually the Chinese were trying to exclude the Russians as outsiders and enemies of the Afro-Asian peoples. By the end of the Khrushchev years, Soviet and Chinese efforts in the underdeveloped countries seemed directed at least as much against each other as against the American position.

The most critical area was India, contender with China for leadership in Asia. That the Russians should invest a great deal in this power was a grave provocation to China. In the Lebanon crisis of 1958, Khrushchev indelicately proposed a summit meeting including India but not China. Worse, when the Chinese made an issue over their border with India in 1959, the Soviet government took a neutral position and tried to restrain the Chinese, as it did in 1962 when Chinese forces drove far into India. In 1961 the Soviets began supplying to India military equipment, while

---

[30] Leopold Labedz and G. R. Urban (eds.), *The Sino-Soviet Conflict* (Chester Springs, Pa.: Dufour Editions, Inc., 1965), p. 38.

holding back on furnishing arms to China. This indifference, as it seemed to China, to the rights of a communist as against a noncommunist power was unbearable.

For a time, Soviet economic assistance was of importance for China, especially as it supplied goods which were embargoed by the West during and after the Korean war and provided the only source of credits. A large part of the industrial plant which China built during the years of rapid progress, 1949–58, was constructed with Soviet designs and under the guidance of Soviet engineers. From 1950 through 1955, about half of China's foreign trade was with the Soviet Union. But as friction developed between Chinese and their Russian advisors and repayments began exceeding loan installments, the Chinese ceased to view Soviet aid as generous. They began to shift their trade to the West and in 1958 undertook to advance rapidly on their own, mobilizing peasant labor on a huge scale in the ambitious Great Leap Forward. This meant turning away not only from reliance on Soviet help but also from Soviet methods, previously accepted as obligatory, and so amounted to a declaration of independence in an effort to build quickly an independent base of economic and military power. The failure of the Leap did not increase Chinese fondness of their Soviet critics; and it was an additional wound when, in the face of the plight of China in 1959, the Russians stepped up aid to other Asian nations. In 1960 the Russians stated as doctrine that socialism could be built only in cooperation with the Soviet Union. They also withdrew their technicians from China; these carried their blueprints away and left Chinese industry in parlous condition. Soon China was almost isolated economically from Russia.

No more important but subject of much more Western commentary was the difference of approach of the two powers to the question of militancy, the pushing of communism by violent action and at possible risk of war. Khrushchev's Russia, a fairly satisfied power, with everything to lose by a nuclear war and not much to gain, looked to expansion only if feasible with minimal risks. Mao's China, having recently fought a civil war and facing a still unbeaten remnant of the enemy in Taiwan, felt much more belligerent. The specter of nuclear war was much less frightening to the Chinese, who had few objectives worth a hydrogen bomb, for whom human life was less precious, and who could figure that a nuclear war might raise China relatively in the world. As Mao calmly put it in 1957, if half the world's population were destroyed by a nuclear war, capitalism would be liquidated and the population would soon enough be restored. The stronger the Soviet line against the United States, the more the Chinese stood to benefit; any hint of understanding between the Russians and the American protectors of Nationalist China was a threat of a deal at the expense of Communist China.

The Soviet triumphs of 1957, priority in development of intercontinental missiles and the lofting of sputniks, meant to the Chinese that, as they expressed it, "The east wind prevails over the west wind." Isolated as they were from the world, it is not surprising that they should have taken Soviet propaganda more seriously than the Russians did. As they saw it, if the Soviets failed to use their superiority of weapons to push the cause and promote revolution (by which the Chinese meant attacking outlying American positions), it was lack of will, cowardice, or treason. Soon after Sputnik, a grand meeting of Communist party leaders was held in Moscow to celebrate the fortieth anniversary of the Revolution and probably to set up a new international organization. Mao then insisted on the leading role of the Soviet Union. If the Russians accepted this with more than their usual modesty, it was because the gift amounted to Chinese insistence that the Russians lead into combat.

In the course of the next year, the controversy moved from theory to practical measures, as the Chinese called upon the Soviet Union to use their strength to fulfill their responsibility. In the Lebanon crisis, the Chinese demanded that the Russians take a firmer stand. Soviet diplomacy, however, looked here and there for a face-saving device and offended the Chinese by suggesting summit conferences without them. A few weeks later the Chinese began bombarding the offshore islands still held by the Nationalists and threatening invasion. Against a firm stand by Eisenhower, Khrushchev gave some support, but both sides were probably irritated, the Chinese because support was lukewarm and the Russians because they were called upon to commit themselves for something of little interest. The Chinese response was to downgrade in propaganda the importance of nuclear weapons and insist on the superiority of Maoist morale and political mobilization, in the same manner as Stalin when Russia had not yet armed itself atomically. At the same time, like Stalin, Mao pushed the development of a Chinese nuclear arsenal.

The Russians, then, perceived the dangerousness of involvement in Chinese quarrels and had second thoughts about helping their Communist brothers to produce nuclear weapons, just when the Chinese were impressed with the necessity of procuring them. Hence it was a major, practically fatal blow to Sino-Soviet cooperation that in June, 1959, the Russians backed out of their 1957 agreement to help China to the development of nuclear weapons. A few months earlier, the Soviet Union had expressed at the Twenty-First Congress of the party more strongly than ever the inadmissibility of war in the nuclear age; at the same time, Khrushchev had expressed hopes of negotiating a nuclear-free zone of the Pacific including China. Little attention was paid to this, but from then on it became a Soviet goal to secure, by some means, that China should be restrained from making nuclear bombs. China like East European countries was expected to be satisfied with the Soviet deterrent umbrella. This coincided with the policy of detente in the West and understanding with

Eisenhower, reassessed as "man of peace." After visiting Eisenhower, Khrushchev went briefly to Peking, but the Chinese, enraged by the whole course of Soviet policy, insisted on the unchanging evil of American imperialism (which they viewed as confirmed by the U–2 incident and breakup of the Paris summit), stressed the likelihood of war, opposed Soviet moves toward disarmament, and assumed a duty to take the leadership toward revolution and wars of liberation in the Third World.

Until 1961–62 it hardly seemed that China could afford to do without Soviet support in foreign policy, but the will to independence was stronger than could be predicted. After the Cuban crisis it was clear that the two powers were unequivocally divorced. If Khrushchev had succeeded, he might have used missiles in Cuba to prove the soundness of Soviet policy and assert his basic leadership; his failure and humiliation exposed him to Chinese scorn, the more bitter because of his conduct in the concurrent border clash with India. The Russians, too, were bitter; to have been proved wrong does not make for tender sentiments. Thereafter there were negotiations for reconciliation, and in the summer of 1963, the Russians were apparently still trying to argue the Chinese out of producing nuclear arms. But the conclusion of the Test Ban Treaty with the United States, designed to exert pressure against the acquisition of nuclear weapons by new states, brought a furious outburst from the Chinese and made the split, so far as can be foreseen, unbridgeable.[31] A series of polemic articles in the strongest ideological language laid the bitterness of differences before the world for the first time. Old and new issues were fanned; each regime denounced the falsity and oppressiveness of the other in terms like those used by bitter anticommunists in the West. Russians compared their Chinese counterparts to Hitler's gang,[32] supposedly a product of capitalism, and the Chinese made the Russians servants of American imperialism. The Russians began moving for a world Communist conference to expel the heretics, while the Chinese refused to yield an iota of their position.

Previously much of the antagonism had curiously been expressed as the quarrel of China with Yugoslavia, harsh since 1958, and of the Soviet Union with Albania, loud since 1961. The Chinese resented that deviant Yugoslavia should claim Soviet assistance denied to China, and refused to admit as socialist a neutralist and nonrevolutionary power, which was friendly to the West and to India. In 1958 the Chinese fiercely attacked the Yugoslavs as revisionists in order to push the Soviet Union into a stronger position. Subsequently, they addressed diatribes against Yugosla-

---

[31] The importance of questions of nuclear armaments is stressed by Walter C. Clemens, Jr., "The Nuclear Test Ban and Sino-Soviet Relations," *Orbis*, Vol. X, No. 1 (Spring, 1966), pp. 152–83.

[32] *Pravda*, August 23, 1963.

via as a surrogate for the Soviet Union. Being anti-Yugoslav meant, however, being pro-Albanian, as this country's principal terror was of being swallowed by its larger neighbor. Hence, when Khrushchev lashed Albania at the 1961 Congress, the Chinese were much offended and redoubled their support for what was becoming their tiny and distant satellite. For a time, name-calling was carried on in the curious fashion of the Soviet Union berating Albania and China denouncing Yugoslavia while really aiming at each other. After inhibitions against direct attacks were laid aside in 1962–63, Yugoslavia and Albania received much less publicity, although China made the most of its only friend in Europe.

The public and intemperate denunciation of 1963 opened the door to other forms of dispute. The Chinese began freely and openly patronizing splits in Communist parties to build up factions or new parties favorable to their revolutionary truth, appealing to the activist spirits bored with Soviet sobriety. They also opposed the Soviet Union in international meetings wherever and however they could. Despite the shared label of "Communist," Soviet diplomats seemed to have more in common with their American than their Chinese colleagues. There was still some reluctance, however, to admit that they were hopelessly at odds.

Early in 1964, the Chinese proposed that each side publish statements of the other (they had regularly given full publicity to Soviet declarations, a courtesy which the Soviet leaders, apparently with less confidence in the loyalty of their people, declined to reciprocate). The Russians delayed publication of a long and authoritative report on the split by Suslov, the leading ideologue of the Presidium (Politburo). By March it appeared that the Chinese price of agreement was virtual surrender and complete reversal of Soviet policy. They branded the Soviet Union as capitalist and demanded the ouster of Khrushchev. The Russians replied that China had abandoned Marxism for militant nationalism. In rising fury, China soon after was looking toward entente with Japan and Western Europe against Russia.

The Maoists also began challenging the Soviet title to a large part of Siberia, and especially the Maritime Provinces. These lands had been ceded by the weak China of 1858. Although they were primitively inhabited by neither Chinese nor Russians and had been settled by Russians, they were an old Chinese irredenta; Sun Yat-sen in 1924 had questioned all Russian acquisitions east of Baikal. The Chinese privately reopened the border question in 1954, when they brought up the status of Mongolia; and they raised it again in 1957. But they refrained from making a public issue of it as long as they had any hopes of Soviet cooperation. By the time they were ready to explode their own atomic bomb (October, 1964), they no longer restrained themselves. At the end of his rule, Khrushchev, instead of looking happily to the world supremacy of his socialist camp, faced along the world's longest boundary as bitterly antagonistic a power as America had ever been, a Communist country calling his "imperialist" and threatening its dismemberment.

Ideological Split

The Sino-Soviet dispute first appeared in public as an ideological quarrel. In long and tedious articles each side expounded the deviation of the other from the letter and spirit of true Marxism-Leninism, first indirectly and fairly calmly, later directly and poisonously. The quarrel was stated mostly in terms that might be summed up as "dogmatism," narrow and sectarian application of the theory, attributed to the Chinese, and "revisionism," Soviet backsliding from revolutionary to capitalist ways. The Chinese abused the Russians in terms suggestively like those long used by Communists against the alleged social democratic traitors to the cause. Subsequently, as the enmity grew fiercer, it was expressed more frankly in terms of interest—Chinese accusations of Soviet economic exploitation, Soviet accusations that the Chinese wished to embroil the Soviet Union with the United States for the benefit of Chinese power, and the like. It is easy to conclude, then, that the basis of the quarrel was material conflict and that the phrasing in often somewhat esoteric language was simply a piece of the indirectness normal to authoritarian states, habituated to the shrouding of political reality in ideological clothes.

As outlined above, the giant states while calling themselves Communist clashed on important issues; as geographic neighbors and rivals for leadership within a supposedly integrated movement, they had many points of friction. But if they had really shared a single philosophy with one overriding goal, each should have been glad of any strengthening of the other and so of the common cause. The Russians might have seen a great duty to help the Chinese economy, while the Chinese would not have begrudged Soviet expenditures on raising the neutrals' esteem for the Communist bloc by dispensing aid to them. The Chinese Communists might have been fairly satisfied to rely on Soviet nuclear power, while the Soviets would have felt that nuclear weapons were safely to be entrusted to their Chinese coreligionists. Not only was there no such harmony; the two parties seemed actually to exaggerate their differences. The bargaining position of both, at a time when they had a common enemy in the United States, was weakened by the quarrel. Sheer power politics would have seemed to dictate putting into the background their differences in the greater interest of standing together against a power stronger than either.

Ideology evidently intensified the dissensions. It should have been possible to compromise or bargain over material interests; the numerous conversations, exchanges of opinion, and conclaves which dealt with the Sino-Soviet dispute usually inflamed antagonism, as each side was determined not so much to get the best possible deal as to score doctrinal points. As would-be leaders of the movement, they sharpened their points of dispute the better to attract adherents and exert pressure on the other side; the fact of being together in the socialist camp increased bad feeling. Moreover, in the Communist way, strategy must be justified by theory, and ideology serves state interests. Hence differing state interests and consequent strategies became ideological differences and so the more difficult to adjust in a practical spirit. In the lack of any agreed upon head or other body to make and interpret doctrine, it is probably inevitable that two independent ideologically-minded groups should come to conflicting interpretations of holy writ, the more bitter as they take seriously the creed.

In order to adapt Leninism to China, Mao had to transform it profoundly. From urban, allegedly proletarian-based socialism, which tried to bring poor peasants into the scheme as a variety of exploited workers, it became a peasant insurrection. The proletariat was no longer relevant; in Mao's movement anyone, as a party member, could act as a proletarian; and political rightness was simply made by the party. Although the Bolsheviks, while upholding theoretical proletarianism, had accepted the collaboration of many persons of nonproletarian origin, from tsarist officers to Foreign Commissar Chicherin, this was only a concession to practical necessity; and there were enough workers around to make it plausible that the party represented the working class. Chinese Communist theory accepted as revolutionary classes not only workers but peasants and youth, the latter not a Marxist class at all.[33] Mao in 1939 claimed that his party represented all nationalist classes; in other words, relation to the ideal of Chinese independence and power took precedence over relation to economic class and socialism. After victory, the Chinese Communists took the position that capitalists were not to be liquidated but so far as possible reeducated; they could remain and even enjoy benefits from their property if they were only willing to cooperate and become managers for the state. Landlords were apt to be more harshly treated by the peasant-oriented government.

Mao was not averse to taking credit for innovation, and he claimed to have put Marx into Asiatic form years before coming to power in China. But Stalin was a prestigious leader of world communism, fellow of Lenin, shaper of Soviet society, architect of the historical transformations of collectivization and the Five-Year Plans, and commander in the greatest of wars. Thus, world communism had a pope, and the Maoists were willing to defer to him.

They saw no reason, however, to defer to Khrushchev. If Khrushchev could have stayed entirely within the worn ideological ruts, friction

---

[33] Dallin, *Soviet Russia and the Far East*, p. 118.

might have been minimized; when he set out on new departures, revisions of Stalinist Leninism in ways adverse to the interests of the Chinese, these declined to follow. Peaceful Coexistence and the revocation of the inevitability of war were unpalatable to those who had a civil war still to finish and who aspired to the expulsion of Western (American) power from their quarter of the world. The downgrading of revolution was disagreeable for the revolutionary generation still in power in China. The courtship of bourgeois neutralist countries meant a low priority for China's interests and an attempt of the Russians to lead peoples who might naturally look to China for inspiration and guidance. The denigration of Stalin had unacceptable implications for a party leadership very much imbued with a cult of personality. The common ideological ground was much narrowed as Khrushchev proceeded in these ways with little or no consideration of the feelings of a proud ally whom he had no means of coercing.

If Khrushchev could reshape Communist doctrine, Mao could equally well, speaking as an older, more prestigious leader of a much larger population, claim to develop Marxism-Leninism. He asserted this prerogative overtly in 1957, with his theory of "Contradictions," a departure from Marxism which partly divorced "contradictions" within society from an economic base and recognized "nonantagonistic contradictions" in socialist society. An implication was the permanence of contradictions in Soviet society as well, with the possibility of degradation if they were not correctly handled. To allow scope for working out of such socialist contradictions Mao inaugurated a remarkable experiment in freedom of expression, the "Hundred Flowers" period. This backfired and led to a reassertion of control and a leftist turn, which culminated in 1958 in a far more serious ideological challenge to the Russians, the People's Communes and the Great Leap Forward.

It was not assumed at first that different policies signified a great schism in the socialist camp. Khrushchev had acknowledged in 1955, for the benefit of Tito, the permissibility of differing roads to socialism; and China was surely more entitled, with its different situation and problems, to find its own way, while adhering to basic socialist unity. But a doctrine worthy of the name should be universally true and valid, and there was in reality little scope for different roads within the Soviet sphere. Doctrine was supposed to guide policy. If policies differed substantially, then doctrinal infallibility was dead. The commune movement of the summer of 1958, whereby the Chinese peasantry was organized into large collectivist units with communization (including communal eating and child rearing) and equalitarianism much beyond any acceptable in Soviet practice, presented serious difficulties for the Soviet leadership. The Chinese claimed to be leaping not only over capitalism but over socialism to reach the perfect order of communism, "to each according to his need." This in the Soviet scheme was still for the distant future and was attainable, as Marx theorized, only in conditions of great material abundance, utterly opposite from the poverty of rural China.

In effect, the Chinese claimed a great moral and political superiority more than compensating material backwardness, overleaping the Russians as these claimed to overleap the West. One aspect of the People's Communes was that they looked to the peasantry, not the urban proletariat, to inaugurate the utopian order, much as it had been the peasants who had made the revolution. In the years of collectivization, the Soviet party sent city workers out to guide and organize the peasant collectives; the Chinese approach was the reverse, sending those in danger of ideological backsliding to the countryside for reeducation.

The Soviet response was rather discreet, if superior. The communes were reported fairly objectively although scantily. It was noted that the Soviet Union had once tried communes, although on a small scale, and found they did not work. Equality of economic rewards was wrong at the present historical stage; material incentives, which the Chinese held to be a revival of capitalism, were an integral part of the Soviet system. The Chinese efforts to generalize their ways in the bloc were rebuffed, as Bulgaria was pulled back from a brief experiment with communes. The Chinese were persuaded toward the end of the year to withdraw their extremer claims, and soon afterward Khrushchev made a counterconcession by averring that all the socialist countries would enter communism together, i.e., that the more advanced countries did not claim special political virtue.

The concurrent Great Leap Forward, however, added to differences. Extreme claims of doubling and redoubling production of steel and other basic commodities within a brief time made Soviet propaganda about production increases seem very tame. The Soviet press praised the Chinese mobilization until the boasting became outrageous, but the leadership may have given too much credence to it, accepting the widespread view that China was rapidly becoming a first-rate industrial power and so potential leader of the bloc. By implication, there was no further need of Soviet assistance. It seemed, moreover, that China had gone over to the Trotskyite theory of Permanent Revolution internally as well as externally. That the People's Communes were less than successful and the Great Leap Forward fell flat did not help. Chinese pride was more embittered than humbled and was ready to lay on the Russians more than their share of blame for withdrawing aid and technicians in 1960. In Khrushchev's last years of rule, Chinese communism continued to develop its doctrines of inevitable dialectic splits (in contrast to the Marxist vision of harmony, to account for the rift in the movement), of bureaucratic-careerist degradation (to account for the lapse of the Soviet Union from orthodoxy and the need for special vigilance at home), and of the primacy of peasant-guerrilla revolution (to compensate for the failure of the proletariat of more advanced countries). Maoism became practically a new creed, in which not much remained of Marxism except terminology; and revolutionary aggressiveness was the Chinese title to leadership.

Ideology serves needs, and much of the Sino-Soviet divergence is easily seen as response to different conditions. The values of a poor country with surplus population are certain to be different from those of a relatively wealthy one with a labor shortage. Politics has different meanings for a largely illiterate country and one with a Western level of education. Lacking military and economic means of influence, the Chinese understandably stressed their revolutionary ideology and the stirring of popular movements. In their view, man, not technology, should be politically decisive. Isolation also affected the Chinese mentality, as the Communist regime was cut off—largely by its own choice—from the volume and variety of outside influences impinging on Russia.

A primary cause of discrepancy from the Soviet pattern was that Chinese communism represented a markedly different polity. The Maoists were sons of a more lofty and thoroughly authoritarian-imperial society than were the Bolsheviks. Resigned only in times of weakness to recognizing other powers as even formal equals, the Chinese were accustomed as no other people to regarding their empire, which was of indefinite extent, as the center of the universe. Nowhere was the veneration of rulership deeper than in imperial China or better reasoned than in the philosophy of Confucianism; Russian tsars were comparatively humble and the tsarist bureaucratic system loose and unorganized by comparison.

For the Maoists stress was placed strongly on obedience; more fully and frankly than even in Stalinist Russia, this was the sole virtue. Class and economic relations correspondingly receded in importance. Lenin shifted emphasis from the economic bias of Marxism to organization, the party, and political action; Mao went much further. China could claim a more rapid way to communism, because it was a more authoritarian society than the Russian, more determined to overcome obstacles by political will. The three great themes of the Chinese ideological revolution of 1958, the People's Communes, the Great Leap Forward, and the General Line of the Party, reflects this: all was to be achieved by correct command and radical political mobilization. Leadership and right thinking were all-important. In this way, also, political considerations were given precedence over economic: equality in the commune was better than incentive pay to raise productivity; even in the factory, it was proclaimed, "better Red than expert." Particularly in the post-Khrushchev Great Proletarian Cultural Revolution of 1966–67, the Maoists gave free rein to the precedence of the political and allowed the drive for utter subordination to the thoughts of Mao severely to cut back production and to bring even technical education to a halt. The Russians have never felt able to give themselves such a luxury; at the height of the purges of the 1930's, every effort was made to sustain the economic progress essential to the security of the country.

In another way also, the ideological needs of Maoist China are different from those of Soviet Russia. In a polity where only about half the population belongs to the dominant nationality, or much less if the East European domain is included, it is vital to have a supranational ideology of unity. This need is handsomely filled by Marxism, elevating class (and by extension the building of socialism) to a universal principle, duty to which must override national loyalties. In China, with minorities making up only 6 percent of the population, it was not essential to appeal to class principles beyond the revolutionary desideratum of removing the former elite. Devotion to the leader was and is enough. The Chinese could also feel freer to look down, as their imperial ancestors had done, on everyone who refused to accept their authority. Hence, particularly as they began to feel entirely independent after 1964, with a beginning nuclear force, emancipated from economic bonds to Russia, the Chinese Communists quarreled violently with practically every one with whom they came into contact, not only the major rivals, the U.S.S.R., the United States, and India, but Japan, Burma, Indonesia, and so on.

In view of their fundamental outlooks, as well as their conflicting interests, it would seem that Russia and China had to quarrel. Neither state is capable of a real alliance with an independent power in peacetime. For the Soviet Union to work in harmony with China, it would have been necessary for the latter to permit itself, like an East European satellite or Outer Mongolia, to come under the Soviet ideological blanket, or for the former to bow to the Chinese Communist principle of order, the authority of Chairman Mao. The real question is not why they quarreled but why the Maoists long seemed so faithful before the break and were so utterly bitter after it.

Flawed Utopia

The separation of China from the Russian leadership practically put an end to dreams of a unified world Communist movement, a universal socialist community under Soviet leadership. As the dispute was boiling up, it was the main object of attention in several general Communist conclaves, the last in 1961. Thereafter, Khrushchev tried repeatedly to gather a new meeting of Communist parties, in which a majority, because of dependency or conviction, would certainly favor the Soviet view, either bringing the Chinese to heel or to expelling them. But most parties were undesirous of such a meeting for the same reason that the Russians wanted it, that it would increase the authority of the Soviet party and reduce the bargaining position of the lesser ones, who had gained much since

1959 by the dissidence of the two leaders. Expulsion of the Chinese would imply ideological lines drawn tighter after a period of relative slackness. The Chinese, of course, would hear to no meeting in which they might be outvoted. What the Soviets saw as coping with factionalism they saw as unfair coercion. The Soviets preferred to have the Chinese formally out in order to reconstitute some kind of international unity; Khrushchev's last victory was the announcement (retracted after his fall) of a preparatory conference for December, 1964, to be followed by a full-scale assembly in 1965. Whatever might remain of a world movement, it must inevitably be very different from the Comintern of the 1920's or the looser but still universalist agglomeration of ruling and nonruling parties which recognized the primacy of the Soviet Union in 1957.

Basic assumptions of the movement have also been shaken. A fundamental of the Communist appeal has been its promise of earthly concord, the peace and brotherhood which should reign on earth once exploiting classes have been abolished; the end of the exploitation of people should be the end of the oppression of nations and so of their enmities. This dream has ever been the inspiration of Marxists and Leninists and a large part of the rationale for the sacrifices demanded of the present. But the Sino-Soviet dispute showed that contradictions between socialist states could be stronger than those between capitalist states. To continue to assume, as Soviet propaganda did, that communism would mean "peace and friendship of peoples,"[34] was obvious fantasy. The Russians could find no better explanation than that Maoism was a deviation of immaturity, like but worse than Stalin's, and faintly hoped that good Marxist and Leninist party sense would return. Ironically, this blow to the Communist image of the future fell shortly after Khrushchev had, by his 1961 Party Program, painted a prospectus of worldwide triumph in which national boundaries should gradually fade to insignificance. The facts of antagonism between Communist states also cast doubt on the whole Marxist insistence on the primacy of the economic. Conflicts could arise, it appeared, from political, perhaps even racial causes. This was implicit in earlier splits, as that of Tito, but these could be glossed over or ignored as that with China could not be.

For Soviet foreign policy, it meant the end of the illusion, already battered, that there was no conflict of interest between the Soviet state and world communism, and that the extension of communism necessarily was beneficial to the Soviet Union. Certainly, the propagation of communism could not be considered worth appreciable sacrifices if the converts turned out as ungrateful and self-willed as the Maoists, the less rewarding as the Chinese might be the beneficiaries. Perhaps this lesson was taken, for Soviet foreign aid ebbed and the slight revolutionary impulse of Soviet

---

[34] *Izvestiia,* August 11, 1968.

foreign policy practically disappeared in Khrushchev's last year and under the succeeding collective leadership. Russia became in reality a fairly conservative power in the world, in many or most ways closer to the United States than to the fellow Communists of Peking. But political faiths are nourished by emotional and political needs, and ideologies die not because they conflict with facts but because they cease to be useful.

5. TROUBLED DOMAIN: EAST EUROPE

Loosening, 1953–56

It is the essence of the Soviet system to cover maximum central control with maximum apparent respect for rights. Thus, the Soviet government combines a verbally very democratic constitution with the firm rule of a small elite. In Eastern Europe, formal sovereignty is dovetailed into a high degree of domination by the Soviet government. Under Stalin this was managed fairly smoothly, or at least without overt mass protest or disorder. It was possible to control proud, formerly independent and highly nationalistic peoples thanks to the prestige of Stalin, his firm purpose and known readiness to employ whatever coercion was necessary. The psychological shock of the war, occupation and (for Hungary, Rumania, and Bulgaria) defeat at the hands of the occupiers also reduced resistance to Soviet domination.

Before Stalin's death there were signs of the breaking down of the system. As the war and its hardships receded, there was some recovery of morale and decrease of willingness to accept Russian tutelage. The example of Tito's independence could not be entirely excluded, and the purges of Titoists weakened Communist parties and discredited them toward the end of the Stalinist period. There was a spreading demoralization; and Stalinism was worn out economically, with excessive concentration on heavy industry and industrial autarky to the neglect of agriculture and consumer goods. The system was ready to crack when the dictator died in March, 1953.

The news set East Europe alive with wishful rumors of an end to the cold war and the Iron Curtain, of more and better consumer goods, and the relaxation of party dictatorship. Such hopes were quickly deflated, but from the spring of 1953 to the Hungarian revolt of October–November, 1956, was a time of improvement in the European satellites. It was also a time of thawing in Soviet attitudes toward the world in general, movement from the rigid authoritarianism of Stalin's day to a degree of consultation and local autonomy and initiative—"polycentrism" as it came to be called. The weakening of central authority by the disappearance of the autocrat and transfer of power first to a collective leadership and then to a less than omnipotent Khrushchev made it difficult to rule with the old firmness. Seeing unpopularity as a burden, if not a danger, to Soviet hegemony, Khrushchev adopted the same basic remedies that he sought for the Soviet Union: an effort to revive the ideological legitimation of Communist authority, improvement of morale with promises of world victory, and limited relaxation to ease strains and raise productivity. Seeing the necessity of some liberalization, he sought to channel and guide it safely.

Because of habits of rule and the fears of the little Stalins that opening the gates of reform would let loose a flood to sweep them away, not much happened quickly. But instructions went out from Moscow for a "New Course," curtailment of collectivization campaigns and relaxation of pressures on religion and of police controls, much as pressure on minority nationalities within the Soviet Union was eased soon after Stalin's death. Emphasis was shifted slightly from producer to consumer goods, and wages here and there were raised. It was in an atmosphere of political and economic improvement that there came the first important popular outbreaks against Soviet rule in Pilsen, Czechoslovakia, and Berlin and other cities of East Germany in June, 1953, the first of a series of proletarian risings against the Communist regimes.

The Czech disturbances, incited by economic grievances, had strongly pro-Western overtones, perhaps influenced by the fact that the area had been liberated by the American army, and American forces were not far away in West Germany. Some may have hoped for a new "liberation" which Eisenhower seemed to have promised. The Prague government, however, was not badly shaken, and the most important result was possibly encouragement to the much more serious East German riots two weeks later. The Ulbricht regime treated workers' grievances with great arrogance. The workers, having been often told that the government was theirs, expected that it might at least listen to them, now that Stalin was gone. Protests grew into a little rebellion which the police were unwilling or unable to put down; Soviet army units had to intervene.

The protesters at least earned the German Democratic Republic concessions. Reparations were ended, Soviet enterprises were transferred to German control, and some credits were extended. In 1955 the German Democratic Republic received from the Soviet Union full nominal sovereignty to act internally and externally as an independent state, while Ulbricht remained the most faithful and skillfully elastic of viceroys. Apparently the Russians had no very clear ideas of economic integration of Eastern Europe at this time, or saw the advisability of limited retreat in order to advance better, as the Soviet-dominated companies which weighed heavily on Rumania and Hungary were also wound up in 1954.

Rioting in East Berlin, June, 1953. Expectations of improvement after Stalin's death made an explosive atmosphere. Disorders quickly flared out of control in Berlin and other cities of East Germany; the Soviet army had to be called upon to repress them.

The arrest of Soviet police boss Beria shortly after the German riots was also welcome news for the satellites; the subsequent reduction of secret police power in Russia considerably decreased its potential for coercion in Eastern Europe.

A dramatic turn came with Khrushchev's surprise visit to Belgrade in May, 1955, to express regrets to Tito and his errant Communists in hopes of enticing them back to the union of all Communists around the Soviet Union. Diplomatic relations were resumed shortly after Stalin's death, and a barter agreement was signed in September, 1954. This would have been enough with a noncommunist state, but it was and is impossible for the Soviet Union to treat a fellow Marxist-Leninist state detachedly as a "bourgeois" state, and conciliation of Tito was essential for the developing campaign of wooing uncommitted nations.

The visit to the unrepentant Tito was a humiliating gesture which would have been unthinkable for Stalin, who hardly showed himself even to his faithful servants. Khrushchev sought to speak over Tito's head to the faithful, as though he still had some of the old Stalinist illusions that the party masses must be loyal to the Soviet faith while the leadership had gone astray. He argued that only with Soviet help could Yugoslav independence be really assured, somewhat as the Russians contended they had to protect Czech sovereignty in 1968. He particularly wanted the restoration of party-to-party relations, and doubtless assumed that party lines to Yugoslavia would assure, in the absence of Stalinist unreasonableness, a good deal of the conformity which they facilitated with the satellites. He laid most of the blame for the maltreatment of Yugoslavia in 1948 on Beria, already branded a capitalist agent. But when he returned to Moscow, where a section of the party led by Molotov opposed the whole idea of softness to Tito, Khrushchev defended the Cominform revolution expelling Tito in 1948 as "basically correct."[35]

Tito was not easily convinced. The Yugoslavs had developed rather far since 1948 toward a looser and more humane socialism than the Stalinism which had rejected them. To rationalize the split, the Yugoslavs had developed something of a theory of bureaucratic degeneration; in accord with this, they went on to workers' councils possessing real authority, decentralization of planning, a semi-market economy, and a somewhat reduced role of the party. They substantially revised their vision of world affairs, noting the dissolution of Western empires, the growth of progressive elements in capitalistic society, the changed character of war, and the need for cooperation much beyond Khrushchev's concept of coexistence.

Unwilling at first even to enter party relations with the Russians, Tito might affiliate with the bloc only if this were a means of propagating

---

[35] Richard Lowenthal, *World Communism* (New York: Oxford University Press, Inc., 1966), p. 74.

Yugoslav ideals of equality and independence of Communist parties. Even while hoping that Soviet repentance would bring reparations for some of the damage caused to the Yugoslav economy by the breaking of agreements in 1948, Tito set a price for peace, including the repudiation of Stalin's policies toward Eastern Europe, the rehabilitation of executed and jailed "Titoists," the ouster of leading Stalinists in the satellites and of Molotov in the U.S.S.R., the end of the Cominform, and the acceptance of the right of different nations to build socialism in their own way. Khrushchev was reluctant to acknowledge "separate roads to socialism" except for those who could not be bound, China and Yugoslavia. But much of Tito's price was paid. Soviet-Yugoslav relations developed promisingly through most of 1956, and it seemed at one time that the whole bloc might be guided as an ideological community on bases somewhat like relations between Yugoslavia and the U.S.S.R.

The event which most encouraged Tito and all the forces of independence in East Europe was Khrushchev's attack on Stalin in February, 1956. Shortly afterwards, the Cominform, lifeless for years, was dissolved. De-Stalinization and rehabilitation of victims spread irregularly through the satellites. The Yugoslav Communists, some of whom welcomed the Soviet connection as a check on solvent tendencies at home, acceded to the Soviet plea for interparty relations. Khrushchev went so far as to agree with Tito, in June, that "The multiplicity of forms of socialist development tends to strengthen socialism."[36] It was agreed, moreover, that Tito might have some influence with the southern satellites, Hungary, Rumania, and Bulgaria, although he would not interfere with the northern tier, Poland, Czechoslovakia, and East Germany. Khrushchev sought Tito's aid and advice, and relations were notably warm up to the crisis in the fall.

De-Stalinization, however, was not well calculated for foreign purposes. Khrushchev must have hoped that the casting off of evils of the past would make Communist regimes more secure abroad as well as in the U.S.S.R., restoring spirit and revitalizing parties; he wanted liberalization and "national communism" to mean only healthier relations, not an opening for "reactionary forces" or real loosening of bonds. But the satellites were not so disciplined as Russia, and hints of relaxation led to serious crises. The national parties, given little guidance and unaccustomed to thinking for themselves, suffered a crisis of nerves. Old leaders stood more or less discredited, yet it was difficult to find new ones both flexible and surely loyal to Soviet leadership. Terror became less useful, and there was nothing quickly to put in its place to check dissent, which rose as the people learned of the admitted faults of the former master.

---

[36] Ghita Ionescu, *Breakup of the Soviet Empire* (Baltimore, Md.: Penguin Books, Inc., 1965), p. 54.

Scandalous blackening of the previously deified leader put an end to the infallibility indispensable for ideological unity. Not wishing to be duped again, foreign parties wanted to judge better for themselves. The best expression to the new attitudes was given by Togliatti, longtime leader of the Italian Communist party. He contended that Stalin's misdeeds could not be laid merely to an accident of personality, as Khrushchev would have it, but were a result of the Soviet system. Hence he would recognize no primacy for the Soviet Union but called for free development of various countries, his "polycentrism." These views were widely publicized in the bloc and even the Russians seemed half to concur.

Polish October

Stalin may have been right in feeling that it was better for Soviet rule of East Europe to cut off entirely the part, Yugoslavia, which could not be closely controlled. It was easy for Poland and Hungary to believe that if Tito and company were to be rewarded with honors and influence for heresy and insubordination, they deserved no less. By the fall of 1956, the two countries of strongest nationalist and anti-Russian tradition, Poland and Hungary, were prepared to test the limits of Soviet tolerance.

Although Poland was under a harsh Stalinist rule, it had a sufficient shade of independence not to execute but only imprison the leaders purged in the last Stalin years for nationalist deviation. De-Stalinization was particularly welcome to the Polish Communists because they had been especially poorly treated by Stalin. He had dissolved the Polish party in 1938 and executed most of its leadership; a report on this subject to the Soviet Party Congress in February, 1956, was an important part of de-Stalinization for the Poles. With Stalinist charisma removed, with the remaining Stalinists more or less discredited, the Polish party was ready to accept the popular demand for change.

The demand came primarily from the favored class, the workers who were supposedly the rulers. The Poznan riots came in June, less than a month after the publication of Khrushchev's anti-Stalin speech and a few days after Tito had been feted in Moscow. They were much like the disorders three years earlier in Czechoslovakia and East Germany, a spontaneous outburst of economic discontent with political overtones. Again the local police was too weak or demoralized to cope with the trouble, and the Polish army had to be called in. Bulganin gave a warning in words almost exactly the same as those used against the Czechs twelve years later: "Every country can go a different way to socialism but Soviet Russia cannot permit this to be used to break up the solidarity of the peace camp."[37] But the disorders led to the first public manifestation of

---

[37] Ionescu, *Breakup of the Soviet Empire,* p. 62.

discord between Soviets and satellite; the former insisted there was an imperialist conspiracy, while the Poles recognized that bad conditions were responsible. When persons implicated in the riots were brought to trial, it was very different from the trials of a few years before. No evidence of foreign agitation was presented; defendants were fairly treated and mostly found not guilty.

Having made good this independent action, the Poles were gripped by a little euphoria of freedom. By October 15, it was decided to convene the Central Committee within four days to elect a new Politburo, which would exclude Rokossovsky, the Soviet marshal who had long been commander of the Polish armed forces, and return to power Gomulka, an independently minded and formerly imprisoned leader. Khrushchev, in the old style, summoned the Polish leadership to Moscow; they counter-invited the Russians to Warsaw, whither Khrushchev went with Mikoyan, Molotov, and Kaganovich on the 19th. There ensued a stormy confrontation, wherein Khrushchev shouted and threatened to intervene with Soviet troops, which were set marching toward Warsaw. The Poles almost incredibly promised to fight, however hopelessly. Khrushchev, fonder of bluster than fight, allowed himself to be convinced that Gomulka and the Polish party were basically loyal Communists and that judicious retreat was the best way to save both Communist authority in Poland and its collaboration with the Soviet Union. Faced by a united Polish party in which the reform elements had come to the fore and were backed by strong popular feeling, Khrushchev compromised. He felt able to do so because, unlike Hungary of a few days later and Czechoslovakia in 1968, Poland, with no open border to the West and deeply apprehensive of Germany, was in no position to break away from the Soviet alliance. Polish Communists could hope to remain in power only by leaning on Soviet power, and there was no threat of a noncommunist regime.

By the settlement, the Poles were allowed substantial autonomy to build, within Leninist framework, their own kind of socialism, including noncollectivization of agriculture, while they remained faithful in international and security matters under Soviet tutelage. Soviet military advisors, including Rokossovsky, went home; amnesty and rehabilitation of political offenders were extended, and police repression was much mitigated. Planning was somewhat decentralized, there was recognized a right to strike, and small private enterprises were allowed to operate. Contacts with the West were somewhat opened, and there was limited freedom of opinion. A *modus vivendi* was reached with the church, which had stood by the regime; religious education was reintroduced in the schools. Parliamentary institutions were given a little reality, and voters had some choice of candidates. But Gomulka carried out his part of the understanding, as he framed his program in terms of strengthening socialism by moderation and flexibility while excluding anything anti-Soviet. Poland remained a valuable and loyal ally, of whose conduct the Russians had little cause to complain.

They had cause to congratulate themselves for more wisdom than they had in reality possessed when bowing to apparent necessity. Poland was kept in the Soviet fold without odium or violence, and Polish autonomy proved harmless. For some years, as the freest regime of the Soviet bloc, it was able to secure much more popular loyalty than before; and looser control was more satisfactory to both sides. Meanwhile, Communist rule was consolidated, and after 1957 a countertrend set in with gradual reduction of liberties and of the privileges of the church, the closing of deviant newspapers, and restrictions on intellectuals. Gomulka, whom Khrushchev roundly berated in 1956, became his great friend and effective servant. By 1968 Poland had become one of the most faithful of satellites, willing accomplice of the invasion of Czechoslovakia, and Gomulka was dependent on Soviet support against his opponents in the Polish party. The happy experience has encouraged the Russians to temporize with other dissident movements as long as they retain ultimate control.

Hungarian Frustration

As discontent rose in Hungary, the Russians tried to proceed as they had just done in Poland, slackening control sufficiently to ease pressure while maintaining basic control. When it seemed that the land was straining to escape their grip entirely, they played their ultimate card, military force, and brought it back into line. For the Hungarians were considerably more anti-Russian and anti-Soviet than the Poles. The latter had some reason to stick with fellow Slavs against Germany, which had given good cause for lasting resentment during the war and which declined formally to renounce claims to large historically German areas incorporated into Poland. The Hungarians were perhaps the best allies of Germany in the Russian campaign, had no grievances against Germany or particular reason to fear its revival, and had very little reason in history, traditions, or culture for fondness for the Russians. Worst of all, whereas the Polish party remained thoroughly in control in October, the Hungarian party quite fell apart and opened the door to a noncommunist, conceivably an anticommunist regime. The Russian reaction, although hesitant, was sure to be more violent.

After a harsh experience of Stalinism, Hungary enjoyed some relief in 1953. In May Hungarian leaders were summoned to Moscow to make changes in the government; Nagy was appointed premier over the opposition of the Stalinist party boss, Rakosi. Nagy, although previously considered a good Stalinist himself, carried through the most significant liberalization of Eastern Europe in this period, in parallel to the Malenkov "New Course" in the U.S.S.R., emphasizing legality and an end of terror. However, in the spring of 1955, Rakosi secured Nagy's dismissal by intrigue, assumed full power, and reasserted controls. The Hungarian party was weakened and divided while trying to rule harshly. By June, 1956, when Rakosi tried to crack down on the opposition in the old style, he was no longer strong enough; and he was ousted on direct Soviet orders (and in accordance with the demand of Tito). His replacement, Gerö, was hardly more tactful; although some 11,000 political prisoners were released and the government promised legality and improvement of the standard of living, the ferment grew among intellectuals, students, and workers, the latter two the classes most indoctrinated and pampered by the regime.

In October the pot suddenly and unexpectedly boiled over. Nagy, restored to party membership, became the center of hopes. On the 14th, Gerö went to Belgrade, thereby calling attention to the Yugoslav advantages. Gomulka's triumph stirred enthusiasm; and liberal Communists, who had been gaining control of the press and radio, raised the cry to emulate it. On the 22nd, university students began meeting to put forward political demands. The next day, excited crowds were milling around government buildings. Gerö, back from meeting Tito, dashed hopes that he, like Gomulka, might stand for the national cause against the Russians. Police fired on demonstrators and then partly went over to them as fighting spread and arms were given out from the military barracks.

On the 24th, Gerö yielded and Nagy was named premier. Soviet troops, which had remained in the country without official, at least public, agreement entered Budapest, thereby exacerbating feelings. In the following days, Mikoyan and Suslov, members of the Soviet party Presidium, were on the scene in Budapest. Kadar, who had been incarcerated and tortured by the Stalinists, was made party secretary. Gerö fled to Moscow, and Nagy put together a cabinet including several non-Communists and announced abolition of the secret police and freedom of political parties. On the 28th, Soviet forces were pulled back from Budapest, a gesture of weakness, although more forces were entering the country.

By October 30, the Hungarian revolution seemed entirely successful. A spontaneous rising, as Marx had envisioned but the possibility of which Lenin had denied for Russia, had overwhelmed an unpopular government. The new coalition government was backed by workers' and soldiers' councils, the best soviets to arise since the Russian Revolution, even as the Communist party fell apart. It is possible that the Soviet government expected to live with this regime, as it had just resigned itself to living with the Gomulka regime, as the Soviet press up to November treated it as acceptable and played down the troubles. If so, the Khrushchev government was more inclined to reconcile itself to a system of free press and contending political parties than the Brezhnev-Kosygin government in the case of Czechoslovakia. In this spirit, or to disarm the opposition, the Russians issued the most conciliatory declaration they have ever made on Soviet-satellite relations. Admitting past mistakes, they offered respect for "Leninist principles of equality of nations" and suggested revision of economic and other relations with full respect for national sovereignty and equal standing of Communist parties.

But the Russians were not prepared to tolerate loss of Hungary from the Soviet military sphere. The Nagy government overplayed its hand, on November 1 asking for withdrawal of the Soviet army from the country and release from the alliance. The United Nations was called upon to support Hungarian neutrality, and Communist ministers left the cabinet. The decision to crush this neutrality by force was made easier by the simultaneous Israeli–Anglo–French attack on Egypt, which served to distract attention, reduced the cost in prestige and the dangers of a Western response, and made an atmosphere of tension in which it was less acceptable for a vassal to desert. If Khrushchev reportedly hesitated, it may be guessed that the reason was mostly awareness that Hungary had been sorely misused under the Stalinist regime and had genuine grievances. He believed ideas should prevail; and force, with its possible dangers, should be unnecessary if the causes of discontent were removed. He was probably disappointed that the reaction to the rather glowing Soviet declaration of principles of October 30 was a demand for full independence two days later. When Soviet officers met a delegation of top Hungarian generals to discuss the evacuation of Soviet troops, the Hungarians were arrested. Janos Kadar, the party secretary, proclaimed a new government, and early on November 4, Soviet forces reentered Budapest. Resistance was sharp but was mostly broken by nightfall. The greatest loss to Hungary was the departure of some 180,000 persons across the unguarded border with Austria.

The consequences for the Soviet Union included general discrediting of the myth of Communist solidarity and the love of the masses, especially the workers, for their Communist government. The absolute power of totalitarianism was exposed as a myth, and a decade of intense propagandizing seemed to have had remarkably little effect. A Communist party had shown itself to be no tight band of fanatics but a bunch of opportunists, ready to desert in trouble. In the United Nations, the Soviet Union stood condemned, but there was no real effort to give force to the condemnation; the Hungarians learned, by the failure of the U.N., NATO, or the United States to act that they could expect only sympathy from the West. They received some sympathy in the Communist world also, as droves abandoned the party in Western Europe, especially the ever unhappy intellectuals. Many also in Russia were disturbed by the thought that Soviet troops killed thousands in a country which had left capitalism behind long before; there were murmurs against the intervention in leading Soviet universities. Khrushchev lost standing, and the influence of Molotov was enhanced.

In Hungary, however, Kadar managed rather skillfully to put back together the shattered Communist order. A largely new party was built up, mostly of state employees. The army was purged and reduced in size; officers were increasingly drawn from Soviet training schools, and arms supplies were placed under close control. Soviet forces, although inconspicuous and isolated from the population, were stationed near the cities. Many Soviet advisers were placed in the sensitive departments, the army, security police, and Ministry of Foreign Affairs; Soviet citizens of Hungarian origin were also favored for these organizations.[38] To reduce tensions, there was little ideological pressure, and controls were relaxed in unessential matters. An effort was made, with Soviet help, to restore the economy. Concessions were made to the dominant Catholic Church, and as many as possible of the priesthood were drawn into collaboration with the regime.[39] Farmers were conciliated, collectivization having been nearly undone; when they were recollectivized a few years later, it was made less painful by many incentive payments.

Nagy, whom the Hungarian government had granted a safe-conduct to lure him from the Yugoslav embassy, was executed by the Russians in 1958; and this embittered feelings and set back the reconciliation. But after 1960, Kadar, having fairly well eliminated opposition, proceeded to further liberalization, under the motto, "He who is not against us is with us." Relations with the West, which had been cold to Kadar's regime as a puppet government, were improved; travel and censorship regulations were eased; party membership was held less important than doing a good job. Hungary, while totally conformist in foreign policy, became relatively liberal internally. Kadar, regarded as a traitor in 1956, rose to some real popularity.

There was no doubt, however, where residual sovereignty lay. Hungary was assured that it was truly independent because it was not under the influence of any imperialist power, and Khrushchev in the same breath boasted of shattering counterrevolution in Hungary and strict noninterference in the affairs of equal socialist states. The presence of Soviet forces, although occasionally discussed, came to be part of the permanent political landscape. The economy, too, was increasingly bound. Large reparations payments had originally made it dependent on Soviet markets, and the neglect of agriculture, accompanied by uneco-

[38] Ferenc Vali, *Rift and Revolt in Hungary* (Cambridge, Mass.: Harvard University Press, 1961), pp. 430–36.

[39] G. Urban, in *Hungary Today*, by the editors of *Survey* (New York: Frederick A. Praeger, Inc., 1962), pp. 14–15.

nomic industrialization, much increased its dependence, by design or not. Lacking the former agricultural surpluses for sale in the West, requiring Soviet industrial raw materials and able to sell only in the U.S.S.R. or bloc countries most of its products, Hungary was less and less able to imagine pulling away. It was legally forbidden, in any case, to propose such treason. Hungarian law forbade criticism of other socialist countries or agitation against treaty commitments of the state.[40] Thus Kadar, Khrushchev's great friend, blended "proletarian internationalism" and local self-rule.

Reconsolidation, 1957–61

Taking the dual lesson from Hungary that the satellites should be better treated and more effectively controlled, Khrushchev set about putting Soviet dominion on a more stable basis. Some autonomy had to be permitted to make the area governable, but there was to be no "counter-revolution" or serious departure from Soviet principles; Peaceful Coexistence could not be taken to condone neutrality. "Different roads to socialism" could not be excluded in view of the Chinese independence, but they had to go clearly in the same direction. Domestic autonomy was subject to Soviet foreign policy and ideological leadership based so far as necessary on force but preferably on consent. Loans, economic pressure, propaganda, personal diplomacy, and political intrigue were all used; and considerable effort was made to make policy making for the bloc multilateral, at least in appearance, with more formal and informal consultations.

The reassertion of Soviet authority was successful; by the end of 1957, leadership of the bloc was more solid than it had been since the death of Stalin. The first sputnik in October did a great deal to restore Soviet prestige, and Khrushchev made as much of it as possible. At the fortieth anniversary celebrations of the Russian Revolution in November, sixty-four top Communists from around the world met for the first general Communist assembly since 1935; leaders of all the Communist countries and parties were there except Tito, who sent a high-level delegation. They joined (except the Yugoslavs) in a policy statement accepting the leadership of the Soviet party and supporting its aims. Compromising on the issue of diversity versus conformity, they agreed that the "basic laws" should be applied according to the "great variety of national peculiarities" and respect for the equality of states. These basic laws were broad. They included "dictatorship of the proletariat" under the aegis of the party, a planned noncapitalist economy, and "proletarian internationalism," which was synonymous with loyalty to the Soviet Union, perhaps the key point. But the Soviet Union even at this high point was not able to establish a

---

[40] Urban, in *Hungary Today*, p. 11.

new international organization to check divisive tendencies. Such an organization was mooted since the Hungarian troubles, but many parties, the Polish, Chinese, Italian, and others, felt more comfortable with only loose and informal gatherings; and the best that could be agreed was the founding of a journal, *Problems of Peace and Socialism* (later *World Marxist Review*), published in Prague with an editorial board of many countries headed by a Russian, the feebleness of which showed how true internationalism had withered from the days of Lenin and the Comintern.

The Titoists declined to join the family. Yugoslavia, like the satellites, had been consulted regarding the Hungarian intervention, and Tito had with misgivings approved. But Khrushchev saw that Titoism was at least partly to blame for his troubles. In any case Tito lost credit by his public condoning of the intervention and was never again so influential among the satellites. In frustration he turned more critical of Soviet policy. The breach of the safe-conduct of Nagy was also quite irritating. In the following summer, an effort was made to smooth over differences, but the Soviet leaders pressed for too much—military ties, coordination of general policies, and in November for adherence to the declaration recognizing Soviet bloc leadership. Tito and his associates probably always wanted to return to the international fold, but they were unwilling to surrender hard-earned autonomy. Their obduracy brought a campaign of invective on them. In 1958 the line was still harder, as Soviet spokesmen took violent exception to the new Yugoslav party program, although this contained nothing which the Russians had not accepted in 1956. In a reversion to Stalinist ways, they even attempted to coerce by economic sanctions. As Soviet relations with China deteriorated in 1959 and after, those with Yugoslavia correspondingly thawed, but there was never a return to the friendship of 1956.

One means of hegemony of which the Yugoslavs were especially wary was military collaboration under the Warsaw Treaty. This pact, labeled a response to NATO and particularly the inclusion of West Germany in it, provided a basis for keeping Soviet forces in Hungary and Rumania, where they had previously had the excuse of guarding communications with Soviet forces in Austria. At first, not much flesh was put on the bones of the treaty; consultations provided by it were not held, and no unified staff was set up, perhaps because of the satellites' unreliability. But the organization was gradually strengthened. In 1960 Khrushchev, wishing to save money by reducing the Soviet army and yet keep his marshals happy with the level of forces, decided to square the circle by giving more responsibilities to improved and reequipped satellite armies integrated into the Warsaw Treaty Organization.[41] Joint exercises were held

[41] T. Wolfe in Kurt London (ed.): *Eastern Europe in Transition* (Baltimore, Md.: Johns Hopkins Press, 1966), p. 214.

in 1961 and yearly since; placing non-Soviet officers in command of the maneuvers gave them a sense of participation, although the supreme WTO commander was always a Soviet marshal. Held by the Soviets to be an instrument of proletarian internationalism, WTO became, as the Czech crisis was to demonstrate, a powerful means of assuring the integration of the bloc.[42]

Khrushchev also strove after 1956 to tie the satellites together by such means as coordination of scientific research, cultural and social policies, assistance in development of nuclear energy, improvement of transportation, and so on. But, as a Marxist, he placed most reliance on economic integration. After 1956 there was a large increase of credits to the vassal states, and many debts were written off in exchange for proclamations of loyalty. Unfair terms of trade were modified. Although when prices are politically determined it is always likely that the stronger side will get the better deal, the situation changed greatly from Stalinist days, when control of East Europe enabled the U.S.S.R. to draw large advantages from it. In some ways at least, it may have been that after 1956 political influence in East Europe, as in Castro's Cuba, was purchased at an economic price.

It was sought to organize economically through the agency of the Council for Mutual Economic assistance (CMA or Comecon). This body was set up in 1949 mostly as a symbolic response to the Marshall Plan and to isolate Yugoslavia, but Stalin made very little of it; he always disliked consultative bodies and had adequate direct control. Khrushchev breathed some life into Comecon, but it only belatedly, in 1959, received a charter and a council, with equal representation for members, formal equality contrasting refreshingly with actual domination. From merely seeking to expedite trade, Khrushchev advanced toward coordination of production. The five-year plans of the satellites were synchronized with that of the Soviet Union beginning in 1956. At first, this was only a symbolic marching in step, but in a few years Khrushchev was proposing overall centralized planning that was hardly compatible with national sovereignty.

The political pendulum thus swung back from the modest slackening which had ensued after the physical and ideological deaths of Stalin. The consolidation was general. Within the Soviet Union, authors and writers found their new freedoms curtailed. The constituent republics of the Soviet Union, which had been scenting prospects of genuine autonomy, lost many of their gains after the middle of 1957. Through the satellite domain, the supremacy of Soviet will was again recognized. Even Finnish independence was reduced. In 1958 economic and political pressure was

[42] Cf. U.S. Senate Government Operations Committee, *The Warsaw Pact* (Washington, D.C.: U.S. Government Printing Office, 1966).

used to force changes in the Finnish government, and it was fairly well established that the Finns could have no one in office or undertake any action seriously opposed by the Russians.

Fissures and Albanian Defiance

Khrushchev's world and the solidity of his domain was at its best from the fall of 1957 until the failure of his envisioned summit conference in May of 1960. Thereafter, success eluded and power decayed, perhaps basically because of economic troubles. Eastern Europe was even worse visited by economic woes and a sense of failure than the Soviet Union. If the rate of industrial growth in the latter diminished from 10 percent in 1960 to 8 percent in 1963 (a figure low only in terms of high hopes), in East European countries (except Rumania) it sank to about half; in Czechoslovakia, it became negative, a novel disgrace for a planned economy. Pressure rose for devolution of planning authority, more reasonable economic goals, and rationalization of prices and distribution, all contrary to the spirit of total authority of the party. As talk grew in the Soviet Union itself of profit and economic liberalization, in 1963–64 East Germany and Czechoslovakia were even able to inaugurate rather extensive reforms without waiting for Soviet word.

Meanwhile, the European Economic Community was riding ever higher, making the dream of early Soviet bloc preponderance seem very empty. Khrushchev responded by trying to strengthen Comecon, at once to reinforce political with economic ties and to revive the growth rate; he called for full specialization of production among Comecon members. But this proposal met objections, principally from Rumania, convinced that it would perpetuate the backwardness of the less developed economies. There had been adopted a unanimity rule, and Khrushchev's plan, after stormy discussions, failed of adoption. The U.S.S.R. had to go over to bilateral or partial arrangements, and the best Comecon could do was to sponsor particular projects, such as a large pipeline to distribute Soviet oil to the northern satellites, an electric power grid, and finally, near the end of Khrushchev's rule, a bank to reduce the difficulty of multilateral exchanges.

The Soviet Twenty-Second Party Congress, in 1961, like the Twentieth in 1956, contributed to the loosening of Eastern Europe, as the demolition of the Stalin image was carried yet further and recriminations and charges against more of Khrushchev's one-time rivals further dissipated what little air of infallibility there could be generated around the post-Stalin party. The Chinese rejection of Soviet leadership also made control more difficult; Khrushchev felt the need to solicit the support of the East European parties, while these saw a source of support in standing against Soviet wishes. In 1962 the missile crisis was a devastating blow to the notion of matchless Soviet strength and an encouragement to nationalistic feelings of the vassal states. Intellectual pressures, the voices of writers whom parties no longer felt capable of so thoroughly muzzling, challenged conformity in Czechoslovakia, Hungary, to some extent even in East Germany. Old issues, buried under the blanket of general control, resurfaced, such as the question of Transylvania and the rights of national minorities.

As barriers between the satellites and the West fell more than those between the former and the Soviet Union, tourism was more encouraged for the sake of foreign exchange; and Western visitors multiplied. They were accompanied by more and more Western publications; and the greater the exposure to Western influences, the more people in Eastern Europe complained of their condition. Western Communists, too, contributed to heretical ideas. The testament of Togliatti, strangely enough published in the Soviet Union as well as in other Communist countries in 1964, postulated that, contrary to Lenin's dictatorship of the proletariat, opposition parties should continue to exist under socialism, and that Communist states should form a free commonwealth with no center. Far from leading a grand march toward the Soviet-dominated world socialist system, Khrushchev was hard pressed, by 1964, to hold together the Soviet domain in Europe.

A corner which was lost completely was Albania. The most backward land of Europe, virtually an ex-colonial territory, Albania was until 1948 a Yugoslav, not a Soviet satellite, not directly represented in the Cominform. The Yugoslav break with Stalin enabled Albania to free itself of this bondage by coming directly under the Soviet wing, but Albania was dependent on the Soviet Union in much the same way as Cuba, without being closely controllable like contiguous satellites. After 1948 it was not exploited by the U.S.S.R. but was given substantial economic aid. Ties began to weaken after the death of Stalin, as Khrushchev sought reconciliation with Tito; the Albanian leaders feared that their independence would be sacrificed to secure his return to the bloc. This fear was the stronger as the pro-Yugoslav clique had been blood-purged.

No longer interested in helping Albania to hurt Tito, the Russians much reduced their assistance. To compensate, the Albanians began looking to China, whence growing amounts of aid began to flow in 1955 and after, as the Chinese sought allies in their bid for leadership within the bloc. Seeing Albania siding with China in the warming dispute, the Soviet Union practically ended economic assistance in 1960, supposing, as with Yugoslavia before and China afterwards, that the weaker power could thus be taught a lesson. The Albanians reacted, like the other victims of such treatment, not submissively but angrily, and the quarrel escalated. Contacts were reduced; one side snubbed the other. To please the Greeks,

Khrushchev hinted they should have a stretch of Albanian territory. Albania refused to attend some meetings and was no longer invited to Comecon discussions. The Russians withdrew from their submarine base, a strategic loss which they have doubtless much regretted.

Khrushchev, unlike Stalin, had no machinery to excommunicate his enemies, but the denunciation of Albania was a prominent feature of the October, 1961, Soviet Party Congress. Khrushchev was so angry with the Albanians, who by now were using even more insolent language than his, that diplomatic relations were severed in December. Other bloc nations followed, but they did not entirely copy the Soviets in cutting off trade. Subsidized by the Chinese, in whose propaganda Albania figured as one of the most important countries of the globe, Albania continued to spout fury against Khrushchev and his successors, additional evidence that possession of Marxism-Leninism is no surety of harmony without preponderant power and that it was not necessarily beneficial to the Soviet Union (as Stalin realized) that a country become communist if it could not be governed.

Rumanian Dissidence

Yugoslavia, Albania, and China showed that a country which had come to communism not by grace of the Soviet army but by a local struggle might be refractory to Soviet control. The Communist government of Rumania, however, showed a comparable self-will, as far as geography and facts of power permitted, although no regime was more imposed by Soviet arms. The Rumanian party was insignificant when the war ended, and the Russians did not bother with niceties and quiet pressure but brusquely installed a government of their choice by force. Having been strongly at odds with the prewar Rumanian government, and having seen Rumanian forces fighting against them and attempting to annex much of the Ukraine, the Soviets were determined to treat the land as they pleased. But the Rumanians were proud to regard themselves as non-Slavs and superior to their Slavic neighbors, and they wished the benefit of their own resources, principally oil. Having learned through a long history of subjection to preserve their national identity while bowing to superior force, somewhat like the Czechs, they gradually asserted their wishes, pushing to the edge of the permissible and thereby gradually extending its boundaries, disarming the Russians by orthodoxy while carving out what independence could be fitted into the Soviet order.

There was no hint of deviation in Rumanian policies until after the death of Stalin; than Gheorghiu-Dej there was no better Stalinist or firmer opponent of "bourgeois nationalism." In the slackening of Soviet guidance under the post-Stalin leadership, however, he began reaching out for broader support. In 1954–55 he made trade and cultural agreements with Yugoslavia, China, and France, to which the Latin-inclined Rumanians traditionally looked; more effort was also made to popularize the regime at home. When Khrushchev called for de-Stalinization, Gheorghiu-Dej declined to heed the call for, in effect, the undoing of his own power. In 1952 he had already been able to eliminate the principal Moscow-trained leaders in the name of loyalty to Stalin; afterwards he only tightened control. Having removed a pro-Khrushchev group in 1957, he obtained the firm control of the Rumanian party which enabled it to withstand Soviet pressure. Meanwhile, the Rumanians had been making the most of all Soviet statements about equality and sovereign rights of Communist states to strengthen their demand for internal autonomy, even while insisting on their loyalty to Soviet leadership.[43]

Because of nationalistic antipathy and strictness of Communist rule, there was little echo in Rumania of the Hungarian revolution, but the leadership took the lesson that it was necessary to identify with popular aspirations. While admitting no pluralism, the party was opened to anyone willing to support Rumanian "socialist patriotism." Having shown loyalty in 1956, Gheorgiu-Dej was able in the summer of 1958 to secure the withdrawal of nearly all Soviet troops, a concession which perhaps indicates that Khrushchev had no long-term plan for amalgamation of the bloc. Thus strengthened, the Rumanians were almost sure to come into more or less conflict of interest with the Russians, the severity of which depended on the freedom of action of Rumania and the inclination of both sides to compose differences.

The area of conflict was economic. Their ambitions stimulated by a higher rate of growth than that of the Soviet Union or other satellites, the Rumanians were disinclined to subject themselves to centralized Comecon planning, which would be dominated by the Russians, and they forced abandonment of Khrushchev's plans. Probably without plan but proceeding from one careful improvisation to another, the Rumanian leaders did whatever they could to stress equality and independence within the bloc, developing contacts with the West, Maoist China, and Titoist Yugoslavia at the same time, all while pointing to Soviet policies and statements and reiterating fealty, at no stage giving sufficient provocation for forceful intervention.

Specifically, the Russians declined to approve a major steel mill at Galati, although they found a similar project suitable for the more congenial Bulgaria. For the Rumanians, this project, which was sounder than many satellite steel plants, was symbolic of independent progress. Emboldened by the Soviet setback in Cuba, they proceeded to secure Anglo-French assistance in building it, and they looked to India instead of Russia

[43] Stephen Fischer-Galati, *The New Rumania* (Cambridge, Mass.: MIT Press, 1967), pp. 52–55.

for iron ore. Percentage of trade with the West was slowly increased; Rumania had oil and grains for sale, and Western tourism became big business. Rumania took a neutral position between China and the Soviets, taking pleasure in the praise the Chinese lavished on them; and as long as China was counted in the bloc, this inhibited Soviet measures against Rumania. Rumania also ventured some praise for Albania and renewed diplomatic relations in 1963.

In 1963 Rumania began occasionally voting against the Soviets on minor questions in the United Nations. Russification was reversed, as Soviet cultural institutions were shut. Russian was reduced to the status of other foreign languages, and Russian names were erased. Jamming of foreign broadcasts ceased, and Western publications were admitted more freely. The Communist party began insisting that it and the Rumanian people deserved most credit for the liberation of Rumania, thereby seeking to legitimize independence as Yugoslavia had done. There were allusions from 1963 onward to Rumania's "historic frontiers"; to counter this, Khrushchev had to threaten to reopen the status of Transylvania, Hungary's historic irredenta in Rumania.

By the end of the Khrushchev period, the West became aware of what had seemed impossible, that a thoroughly dominated Soviet satellite had raised itself a considerable way, within the Soviet bloc, toward real independence, so far that by 1964 Rumania was trying to mediate between China and the Soviet Union and Tito was seeking rather to smooth Rumanian-Soviet relations than to encourage further separation. This was mostly the result of skillful maneuvering by Gheorghiu-Dej and the solidarity of the Rumanian party and nation. But it was permitted by the Russians only because it represented little threat. Although doors were opened slightly to Western influences, Rumania became no dangerous example of liberalization. Moreover, Rumania did not and could not escape the Soviet sphere but was always careful to pay obeisance to communism and friendship for Russia. Khrushchev in 1963 apparently tried to overthrow Gheorghiu-Dej by suborning other leaders;[44] having failed, he and his successors showed restraint. They praised the Rumanians as good Communists and let them be a little wayward, apparently in the conviction that Rumanian willfulness would be eroded by time; force could always be applied if indispensable.

Problems of Unity

Under Khrushchev Eastern Europe changed from the apparently uniform gray of Stalinism to a slightly variegated patchwork of different

---

[44] J. F. Brown, *The New Eastern Europe—The Khrushchev Era and After* (New York: Frederick A. Praeger, Inc., 1966), pp. 67–68.

shades, although still far from the violent clashes of political color of prewar times. The Soviet Union was still in a sense suzerain of the area, but its word no longer caused the vassals to jump in unison. For example, all obediently boycotted Yugoslavia in 1948, but in 1963 they declined to cut trade ties with Albania. Changes came much more readily in domestic affairs than in foreign and military security policy, wherein the Russians were more determined to make their will prevail; but nearly everywhere there were stirrings. Since the disturbances of 1956, the Soviet government struggled, to some extent to the detriment of its attention to the world without, with an insoluble problem of assuring permanency of control while keeping good order within the sphere, with maximizing Soviet preponderance with minimum violence and repression, with finding the right way between accepting separate roads and insisting on uniformity under Soviet primacy. There was no ideological answer to the questions of a "Socialist World System," and no new theory or system of control was evolved, only an intellectual and political patchwork.

The departure of Stalin meant not only the loss of the keystone of rulership, at once a symbol and revered leader and a powerful personality, but also a change of Soviet political ways, as he had no real replacement. Divisions and compromise within the ruling group in Moscow made it much harder to make satellites hew the line exactly and encouraged them to discussion and questioning instead of prompt obedience. Khrushchev achieved a strong personal position and began cultivating a little personality cult of his own, but he remained far from a regal figure suitable for the focus of an empire. He was also torn much more than Stalin by the contradiction between policies suitable for ruling the Soviet sphere and those indicated for enlarging it. It was necessary to treat satellites as gently as possible and make them seem quite independent if any outside state were to be enticed to approach their condition. Stalin, expecting no additions to the Soviet domain unless by Soviet force, was little troubled in this regard, although he also made some effort to keep up appearances; he preferred to expel the indocile member of the bloc. Khrushchev tried to bring Tito back, doubtless hoping that it could be done without appreciably affecting Soviet hegemony in the bloc; but he could not have his cake and eat it. Another misfortune was the Sino-Soviet rift, which destroyed many illusions and left Marxism-Leninism morally weaker than as though China had never been welcomed to the brotherhood.

The recovery and prosperity of Western Europe, which became striking during the Khrushchev years, contributed to the difficulty of Soviet rule. As the West grew shinier, the eyes of Eastern Europe turned more toward it. To endeavor to exclude Western currents was costly in economic terms, in trade, tourism, and modernization, difficult to enforce, hard to justify, and exasperating; to let in a little could not satsify but stimulated appetites. Glimpses of a half-forbidden world led people of the satellite lands rather to idealize the West beyond its merits. The rulers of satellite nations were under compulsions to improve standards of living so far below those of Western neighbors, to put a better political face on their regimes, and to show their peoples that they were independent.

Contacts with the West contributed to the revival of nationalism, reminding Hungarians, Czechs, and others, that they were not merely citizens of the socialist camp headed by the Soviet Union but heirs of historic nations with their own tradition and perhaps destiny. The passing of the war-scarred and demoralized generation, the healing of wounds and the washing out of the humiliation of defeat, meant a recovery of morale, self-assurance, and national awareness. This resurgence of nationalism has been a surprise for Americans as well as for Russians, both ready to suppose after World War II that ideology was relegating it to insignificance; but it is part of the modern trend toward self-awareness. In the Soviet Union, there was increasing use of nationalistic themes, as patriotism became central in an ideology for which Marxism was becoming steadily less relevant. Satellite regimes also were tempted to appeal to nationalism for popularity, but there it was necessarily in some conflict with "proletarian internationalism." National communism, on the Russian model, was no recipe for unity. The Soviets saw the bright side; at times national variations were praised as strengthening the peoples' democracies in building socialism. But nationalism also gave the governments more reason to stand up to the Russians and better means of so doing.

Although the world was slow to realize it, handling Communist parties in power thus became a very different matter from dealing with struggling parties in opposition, usually isolated from national mainstreams, in awe of the Soviet patron, and often in need of subsidies. The ruling party came into a very different set of activities and problems and soon discovered that its interests clashed in many ways with those of the Soviet Union. The thesis that first loyalty was to the latter was sustainable only so long as the party had no country of its own; afterwards, loyalty was really owing to Russia only so far as it supported other Communist states; and as the formal equality of Communist states was conceded, the parties also were invited to demand equality, granting the Soviet party only the respect due seniority. A good deal of the willingness of East European leaders to follow Soviet leads and see their lands more or less subject to Soviet dictates was due to fear that without Soviet forces behind them they could not maintain themselves in office. But again and again East European peoples showed willingness to back Communist leaders if these would only take the national part against the Russians; and there was a temptation to win popular favor by pushing, as Gheorghiu-Dej did, to the limits of the permissible. If, on the other hand, Communist regimes were able to fortify themselves by good organization and effective indoctrination, they were in a much better position than a looser liberal state to resist pressures from anywhere.

Khrushchev seems to have been fundamentally uncertain how to handle this problem. He had no clear concept of what to make of the bloc, whether it was to be enlarged or tightened, only a general conviction that amalgamation was the order of the new age. The simplest answer to disobedience was force, but the disadvantages of this were obvious from the point of view of Soviet foreign relations. It was also undesirable from the Soviet internal point of view, as Khrushchev wished to govern his own country as modernly as possible with minimal force and terror. It was necessary both in Russia and in the bloc to keep increasingly advanced economies functioning efficiently; this required that obedience be so far as possible voluntary. The Russians could not themselves administer the People's Democracies; Czechs, Poles, and others could not be merely whipped into being good managers, but had to be given sufficient freedom and incentives to work well. It was particularly important to keep up some spirit and ethics in the governing parties to keep East Europe an asset to the Soviet Union and not merely a costly prisonhouse of peoples. The problem became more acute as the obvious tasks of rebuilding the economy were completed. Demands increased, the systems became more complex, and new directions and inspiration had to be found.

The chief answer was the formula which had served the Bolsheviks so well in making the Revolution, winning the civil war, and reshaping the former Russian empire into the Soviet Union: reliance on ideology and party. The basic Soviet ideal has always been unity, and Khrushchev had great faith in the unifying power of Marxism-Leninism and socialist cooperation. Nationalism he believed to be dying; with the victory of communism, state borders would disappear, leaving only insignificant ethnic frontiers. By 1958 he was speaking of the "coming together" or "fusion" of nationalities, and frontiers of socialist nations were expected to become like those of Soviet republics. This theme became more insistent in 1960–61 as trends within the bloc made it less realistic. It was part of Khrushchev's grand vision, coupled with the promise of entering the condition of communism by 1980; he apparently really believed that free and independent Communist countries could find their way to harmony and political fusion.

This faith was not entirely naïve. Western observers have been inclined at times to overestimate, at times to underestimate the effectiveness of opinion controls, censorship, propaganda, and purposeful education. Ruling parties were certainly unable to bring their peoples generally to love their Russian big brothers or to believe fully in the evils of the capitalist world. But, as years stretched to decades and Communist governments became the accepted order of things in satellite states, patterns of thought, especially of the urban middle class and elites, were profoundly altered. Rumanian resistance was all in the name of Communist principles and phrased in Marxist-Leninist language; this became the only language of politics. An article by the Rumanian foreign minister in November, 1963, asserting Rumanian independent rights, was entitled "The Unshakable Foundation of the Unity of the International Communist Movement."[45]

This acceptance of basic formulas of the system did not prevent Rumanians and others from making their case, but it circumscribed their thinking and was a handicap in argument against the centralist wielders of a basically centralist doctrine. While rejecting many aspects of the regime, people soaked up its forms of discourse, values and attitudes, and the will to rebel was half smothered. Even as people admired Western styles or literature, they gradually came more or less to accept that "imperialism" was bad and "socialism" was good; if things went ill, it was the fault of men, not the basic system. Thus, with passing years East European nationalism became no less anti-Soviet but less anticommunist, suggesting that with tact and generosity the Soviet Union might be able indeed to weld the various nations into a solid mass.

Ideology became effective through the party, at once keeper of truth and guide of society, whose mission was legitimated and given by the social-political theory of which it was the incorporation. The main channel of Soviet authority to the satellites was through their ruling parties; like Stalin, Khrushchev spoke not to premiers and governments but to first secretaries and Leninist parties. For Khrushchev much more than for Stalin, it was not a personal but a party empire; and the restoration of the role of the party within the Soviet Union went with increased use of the party to keep the bloc together. There was a special section of the Soviet party Central Committee for relations with the parties of other socialist states. Even formally intergovernmental diplomatic relations were handled by party men, as party officials were named ambassadors in satellite capitals. Soviet diplomatic relations were of two kinds, those outside the bloc, handled by professionals for the most part, and those within, handled by men whose career was within the party apparatus.

Another fundamental means, equally sanctioned by Leninism, of securing the coherence of the domain was economic integration. This, however, was more difficult than at first appeared; and it required institutions which could only gradually be developed. Contrary to what ordinary reason might lead one to expect, it is more difficult to integrate planned than unplanned economies; Comecon was much less successful than the European Common Market in developing trade among members. Planners wanted supplies under their control to be sure of their requirements, in the same way that Soviet machinery factories made their own screws

---

[45] Fischer-Galati, *The New Rumania*, p. 98.

(and anything else which they could) at high cost to be sure of having what they needed. Neither did they like to plan exports to markets where other planners were likely to prefer to develop their own production. For a free economy, national and export sales are about equally attractive, with the government perhaps favoring the latter; the planned economy gives priority to its own, as Khrushchev found even within the Soviet Union when some authority was devolved to regional councils.

Pricing causes much difficulty in the non-market economy; there was no real way to compare costs of production in Russia, Bulgaria, or Hungary, as input prices were artificial. The parties are always ready to suspect that a price is unfair when it is political, and for every complaint within Comecon there was a countercomplaint. As planning deals with commodities, not money, bilateralism was built into the system, greatly restricting advantageousness of trade. In the authoritarian states, the free flow of labor which greatly helped the European community was practically excluded. The drive to heavy industry at any price meant many poorly productive investments had to be protected. Hence, urgings by Khrushchev and many agreements in the years after 1956 had quite limited effect, and the percentage of trade of Comecon members among themselves declined from 77 percent under Stalin to 69 percent by 1960.[46] The East European countries, having developed economic nationalism with Stalinist autarky, felt that it was an infringement of their sovereignty when they were asked or ordered to specialize. It was; the economic integration of planned economies seems to require a central planning agency, which implies an overall political authority.

The interrelations of states within the Soviet bloc were thus somewhere between the political dickering of factions or provinces within an empire and the diplomatic relations of independent states. Khrushchev, although willing to admit discussion, expected basic conformity. But he lacked a proper organization of authority. It was feasible within the Soviet Union to proclaim equality and freedom of nationalities, even their right to secede from the Union, because the united party and state were at hand to impose the higher duty. But in Eastern Europe there was no overall organization, only the shadow of Soviet material superiority and the presence of Soviet armed forces. There was no regular way of resolving the disputes bound to arise from conflicts of interest, no satisfactory court or supreme judge for the resolution of quarrels. There was no acceptable supranational planning authority. There was hardly an overall military authority, except as the satellites simply surrendered their armed forces to Soviet command. There was no infallible doctrinal authority, in the lack of which different interpretations were sure to arise and divide the bloc. Doctrinal disputes are the more likely, of course, as societies are

---

[46] Pryor, *Communist Foreign Trade Systems*, pp. 38, 165.

committed to doctrinal formulation of political issues. But diversity makes a mockery of claims to absolute truth; even the admission of different roads to a supposedly identical goal reduces the attractiveness of Marxism-Leninism as pure truth and its usefulness as a guide. Revision could slide into neutralism, and the Soviets were always afraid that deviations in fellow socialist states could lead to questioning at home.

Despite the obvious need, it seemed very difficult to set up any sort of organizational authority for the Soviet bloc. The Eastern European ruling parties, even those thoroughly faithful to the Soviet leadership, were not prepared formally to accept Soviet sovereignty, legally to become dependents of the Soviet Union; if they had been willing, their authority with their own people would have suffered unbearably. Their great contention was that they were guarding independence from the demons of Western imperialism. On the other hand, it was not feasible to set up anything like a bloc assembly or parliament with guaranteed rights and powers of equal members. Stalin abhorred consultative bodies of any sort as detrimental to his authority, and his successors disliked tying their hands by fixed procedure. A congress with real powers would be hard to manage; a true congress or parliament, indeed any effective constitutional ordering of power, is not part of the Communist, Marxist-Leninist way of governing society. If there are binding legal relationships between Communist parties or within the parties, the dictatorship of the proletariat is qualified and diluted. If one really must run things, the recipe is tyranny.

This was, in effect, the ultimate Soviet answer. Satellite leaders were well aware that overstepping some ill-defined limit—at the most, seeking to separate from the alliance—would bring Soviet force upon them. This does not mean that there were no relations of stability and mutual advantage between the Soviet Union and its East European vassal states; lord and vassal almost always both profit somehow from their connection. Economically it was potentially advantageous for Eastern European countries to be tied to a huge and not very highly developed country. Forced-draft industrialization had created dependence on the U.S.S.R. for both materials and markets. Whereas for the West they were more or less backward hinterland, they, at least the more advanced of them, were ahead of Russia in many ways and could furnish it manufactures in return for raw materials, a usually advantageous relationship. East Germany in particular, as leading supplier of machinery to the bloc, doubtless was more intensively industrialized than it would have been as part of the Western sphere. Reunification was a faint prospect by the end of the 1950's, even if there had been no great political obstacles, as only a tenth of the foreign trade of East Germany was with Federal Germany, only a quarter with all nonbloc countries. Similarly, the bulk of Poland prospered fairly well before World War I as supplier of manufactures, especially textiles, to the protected market of the Russian empire. After many years of Eastern orientation, it was very hard to contemplate the costs and difficulties of switching back.

Another appreciated aspect of Soviet hegemony of Eastern Europe was the classic imperial role of bringer of peace and order. The Balkans and the lands between Germany and Russia in their brief time of maximum freedom were riven by all manner of essentially petty and destructive quarrels, senseless nationalistic antagonisms and stifling economic barriers raised by rivalries and hatred. By virtue of this dividedness, the area was easy for Nazi Germany to penetrate; in nearly all countries, the Nazis could find a party which preferred them to its own government or was willing to accept their help against a neighbor. It was fortunate for Soviet influence, also, that their occupation was preceded by that of the Nazis, who erased traditional Western influence before the Russians appeared. After the war, many persons hoped for political unification of the weak and exposed countries to avoid troubles as beset them after 1918. The Russians would countenance no unification but their own, but the region has indeed enjoyed a long tranquility which is not less tranquil for being based on common subordination. No country of the Soviet bloc needs to fear an attack from another, as all are under one protector. The Russians repeat that their power is the only safeguard against imperialism; they could better say that they have ended the internecine quarrels of Eastern Europe so far as their sway extends.

Finally, to understand the relationship of vassal countries to the Soviet Union, it must be borne in mind that political relations in the course of years create interests favorable to their maintenance. Elites among the minorities of the Russian empire before the Revolution were favorable to the imperial power which sustained them. Likewise, elites which have grown up under the patronage of the Soviet Union and have become accustomed to it and to enjoyment of their place in the power structure do not look to radical change. They may seek more dignity and autonomy but they enjoy leaning on a higher power in this age of the dissolution of authority. Least of all do they desire to shift to alignment with the West. Thus the Rumanian Communist leadership in the early 1960's and the Czech in 1968 were probably perfectly sincere in insisting that they had no desire for divorce from the Soviet connection, only to find more freedom within it. As long as there is a real East-West antagonism, or as long as people are convinced that there is, switching sides would seem almost surely to mean overthrow of the ruling groups; and even neutralism is dubious. During much of the Khrushchev period, the United States cooperated with Soviet purposes in this regard by treating satellite regimes as comparable in evil to the Soviet Union itself; it is much more threatening to the Russians if the United States or West Germany, as in the post-Khrushchev era, accepts the satellite regimes as legitimate.

VI

Collective Leadership; Conservative Communism

1. THE SUCCESSOR REGIME

Reign of the Establishment

Revolution turns into bureaucracy, Lenin observed to his dismay as he saw the new regime being consolidated on old foundations. Stalin kept fairly well atop the system by crafty politics and ruthless terror, but under him the apparatus acquired a power and momentum of its own. The aging Stalin seems to have felt its pressure in his last years, and it must have been to reassert a control which he felt was slipping that he reshuffled offices and moved toward broad purge in his last months. Khrushchev lacked the time, prestige, and temperament to dominate as his master had. He particularly lacked the ability to remove those who were inconvenient to him, much less to terrorize; in 1961 he was still seeking to expel associates of the "Anti-Party Group" of 1957 from office. Unable to balance powers as Stalin had done, he relied on a single base, the party. When the top layer of the party convinced itself that he was no longer necessary, he was ousted by the very men whom he had raised up.

Khrushchev's subordinates took advantage of his absence on vacation to organize a palace coup. Summoned back to Moscow on October 13, 1964, Khrushchev was dismissed by vote of the Politburo. He appealed to the Central Committee, as he had successfully done in 1957. He was rejected by a large majority, probably because his opponents now were not so feared as Molotov and company had been and were not less in tune with the times than Khrushchev but more so. It was announced that Comrade Khrushchev had, in view of his age and poor health, been released from his duties. Two men took his place: Leonid Brezhnev as First Secretary of the party, and Alexei Kosygin as Chairman of the Council of Ministers. Thus, by the nearest to a constitutional procedure in the history of Russia, a ruler had been removed from office.

To all outward appearances, the change was smooth and quiet. Not only was there no public controversy; there was practically no explanation. The name of Nikita Khrushchev simply disappeared from the press and statements, as though it were intended rather to erase than blacken his memory. He was referred to only seldom and indirectly. The principal charge was of light-headedness and unpredictability, "harebrained schemes," probably reflecting mostly bureaucratic ire at his reorganizations and the hope to achieve order and stability by removing him. Foreign policy being usually secondary to domestic in the Soviet scheme, his conduct of external affairs was apparently secondary in the dissatisfaction against him. There were, however, important complaints in the area of foreign policy. His move toward rapprochement with West Germany, whither he planned a tour, seems to have aroused fears for the faithful Ulbricht regime; the policy was quickly reversed. He was blamed for taking foreign policy decisions without consulting his colleagues, as in the loan for Egypt. He was held responsible for some of the friction with Rumania and for the heat of the Sino-Soviet dispute. Polemics with Peking ceased, and the conference of parties scheduled for December was postponed. The debacle of the Cuban crisis had been a heavy burden for his prestige, and he was apparently blamed for doing more boasting than building of Soviet strength. Ever since then, the section of the party more interested in arms than butter had been causing him trouble. Khrushchev's cuts in military spending were revoked, and his successors were as quiet, while improving Soviet capabilities, as Khrushchev had been vocal.

Probably much more important for Khrushchev's fortunes, however, was the unhappiness of tens of thousands of party bosses over his division of the party into agricultural and industrial sections. The keynote in external affairs was continuity, as the world was assured, with the accent on Peaceful Coexistence. There was no question of principle involved. After Lenin's passing, his successors fought over ideological and theoretical matters, or at least expressed their political rivalry in such terms. After Stalin, there were some questions of principle in the expulsion of Beria, Malenkov, and others; with the departure of Khrushchev, none at all appeared publicly. Apparently there was no longer felt any need to justify changes in doctrinal terms. There was no ideological attack on Khrushchevism, and no purge of a Khrushchev party; only a handful of his immediate associates, headed by his rapidly risen son-in-law, lost their positions.

The world assumed, in view of Soviet precedent and the ordinary association of dictatorship with a dictator, that there would soon be political battles, shakeups, and removals of some or many from leadership until a single figure emerged as the new strong man. This did not occur, and the years since Khrushchev have brought only minor changes in the directorate. It seemed that members of the Politburo were almost irremovable since Khrushchev's last years, and four fifths of the Central Committee were reelected in 1966. In no other great power do leading political figures enjoy such tenure.

One of the chief reasons for ousting Khrushchev having been his propensity for shakeups, his successors settled down to enjoyment of stability. Something like a principle of civil service tenure seems to run through the new Soviet political system, with little or no provision for timely retirement. The result is that the Soviet government has become one of the upper-middle-aged, run by a directorate of men in their fifties and sixties. The top men of the Politburo, Brezhnev, Kosygin, and Podgorny, are in their middle sixties, and the average age is over 60; very few of even the junior members of the top circle are under 50. The average age of the Central Committee, which was 49 in 1952, in 1969 was 60. This is widely the situation; directors of Soviet institutes, even of scientific establishments, and the military leadership, are regularly in their sixties or seventies. Men rise slowly on bureaucratic ladders in patterns of seniority of an increasingly stable society.

It is almost a truism that this government, run by men for whom the Revolution is history and who earned their spurs not by contributing to it but by dutifully following orders under Stalin, is profoundly conservative. Its leaders have a vested interest in tranquillity and avoidance of risks, and they prefer to act in accustomed ways. From revolutionary bravado, Soviet Russia evolved to an isolationist but socially mobilizing and transforming autocracy under Stalin; after Khrushchev it appeared as a settled and massively immobile structure. It appears even less prepared to think about new departures than societies with no revolutionary pretenses.

Khrushchev was able to try some reorganizations, although they did not go deep and were not very successful; the Brezhnev-Kosygin leadership seems to have little capacity for reform. For years a new constitution has been promised, in substitution of the Stalinist document, and there is a commission to draft it, but nothing appears. An economic reform, first steps toward which were taken under Khrushchev, was so denatured as to leave power practically unchanged. There have been only negative innovations of doctrine, as some of Khrushchev's touches have been dropped. The nearest to a theoretical development has been the "Brezhnev doctrine," the assertion of a right of intervention throughout the "Socialist Commonwealth," itself only a reaffirmation of declarations of 1956. Initiatives in foreign relations have been either defensive, as in Czechoslovakia; or cautious self-assertion, as venturing into the Mediterranean and building up the Soviet position in the Arab world; or efforts to avoid disturbance, as in the Tashkent mediation of the India-Pakistan war.

It is not clear to what extent conservatism finds its expression in committee rule and to what extent immobility is part of the collegial decision making which dominates all areas of Soviet government. But an essential feature of the *sui generis* authoritarian system is dampening of contest and avoidance of widespread controversy through secrecy and anonymity. Oddly enough, in little more than a decade, the Soviet system has evolved from one of maximum adulation of an all-powerful autocrat to the most collective and impersonal of the major powers, whose leaders are gray shadows operating behind a curtain in the name of party or government. The rulership is invisible as nowhere outside the Communist world, and nothing has come of Khrushchev's efforts to expand discussion of some issues beyond the narrow circle of leadership. If debates are published in the Soviet press, this is evidence enough that they have no importance.

In this situation, the outsider can only guess who or what groups are most influential in the setting of policy. Brezhnev, as General Secretary of the party, has ranked first ever since the fall of his patron, Khrushchev, and is presumably the most influential individual. Kosygin and Podgorny have regularly followed in official seniority, and they have often spoken for the Soviet government, the one as Chairman of the Council of Ministers, the other as President of the Presidium of the Supreme Soviet, or formal head of state. But it is not clear that they really wield more influence than other members of the hierarchy. Reportedly, the Politburo acts as a committee of equals, but outsiders have no idea how freely junior members can outvote their seniors.

Pronouncements on major issues are usually made anonymously in the press, by articles in *Pravda* or *Izvestiia*, and foreign diplomats are left to guess whether some group or other, the military, party ideologists, or whatever, is behind them. This was most noticeable in regard to Czechoslovakia in the late summer of 1968; no personality discussed the issue beyond echoing the official line laid down in the press. It may be ventured that policy making is based on something like majorities of interests represented in the top circles, with increased consultation and respect for technical competence in the declining force of ideology. With no strong will at the helm, the Soviet government may be regarded as a conglomeration of pressure groups.

This, however, tells little, as the pressures within the Soviet system are obscure. Neither the party as a whole nor the government bureaucracy nor the technocratic-managerial elite represent any sort of coherent grouping capable of formulating a collective policy and pushing for its acceptance, although many smaller sectors represent fairly well-defined interests. The security forces, like large and well-financed agencies for similar purposes elsewhere, undoubtedly have a strong voice in politics and foreign policy; they seem to have ventured at some times even crudely to sabotage detente with the West. There was a strong effort after Stalin to put the secret services under party control, but efforts in recent years to glamorize them suggest that they have recovered much importance.

Much more attention has been given to the role of the military, or the military-industrial groups, the manufacturers and wielders of arms being probably closer together in the Soviet Union, where industry is state owned and operated, than in the United States. It is obvious that the makers of munitions have foreign policy interests, but their influence can be estimated only in the most general fashion. The Soviet military has been credited with some part in the removal of Khrushchev, but there is no clear evidence. The military certainly did not play a role comparable to the assistance they rendered to Khrushchev in his hour of need in 1956. The inference that they contributed to his downfall is based mostly on the fact that they had reason to be dissatisfied and their dissatisfactions were removed by the new rulers.

There have been many reports, however, that the Soviet marshals, who were on a tight rein under Stalin and were fairly closely controlled by Khrushchev, have secured a good deal more latitude under the less decisive successor regime. The Soviet defense minister, unlike the American, is a professional soldier. The present holder of the office, Marshal Grechko, is said to have been foisted on the civilian political leaders by the military establishment; and he may enjoy some power in his own right. He has clearly taken on political prerogatives. In April, 1969, he went to Prague to reorganize the Czech government; previously he had gone on apparently important missions to various countries of Eastern Europe and India. It is also indicative of the importance of the military that so far as Stalin's merits have been reweighed recently, discussion has been not of his economic, political, or ideological role but of his wartime leadership as seen by the generals. Especially in the last few years there has been an enormous amount of glorification, in the press and on television, of the soldiers and military life and virtues, the discipline, fidelity, and sacrifice of the guardians of the motherland. Less has been made of disarmament in foreign propaganda. The press campaign after the armed clash with the Chinese in March, 1969, had more to do with the valor of the Soviet border guards than with the politics of the case.

One should not make too much of contradictions between the party and the military, as the two are very close together. There is a large and elaborate party apparatus for the penetration and control of the armed forces, while a good party record is essential for an officer's career. The party indoctrinates the army, and the army is a very important agency for the moral, political, and ideological indoctrination of the population. Army and party are not dissimilar organizations, both emphasizing conformity, discipline, and dedication. In the past as today, the party has placed at the top of its priorities the strength of the Soviet Union, to be secured by firm political direction and the development of means of force through heavy industry. Army and party share an overriding interest in the preservation of the integrated political system. Even if the military forces should become clearly preponderant, they would undoubtedly find most of the present ideological ethos useful for the same reasons which make it useful for the party. One could expect only changes of tone, perhaps toward still greater pragmatism in practice, along with franker reliance on force.

Contradictions and Repression

The Soviet elite may be broadly divided into two categories, those who govern and profit by it, and those who produce. The former include especially the party apparatus, the ideologists and propagandists, the security forces, and to some extent the military. On the other side are those who have standing by virtue of nonpolitical capacity, such as intellectuals, industrial and business managers so far as concerned strictly with production, artists, writers, scientists, perhaps jurists, economists, and other specialists. The two categories intermingle a good deal, but by and large the first stands for the tightly controlled political-ideological state, preferably more or less isolated and at odds with an evil and hostile outside. The second favors a looser, more rationally oriented—one might say more modern—system, open and friendly to the external world, in which they see not so much a moral-political evil as a source of trade, technology, and ideas. They hardly participate as political pressure groups, although they may be consulted and heard with respect in matters of their specialty. They are rather sources of pressure from outside the regime or from its fringes, against which the political elite use their means of control, psychological and physical.

Another and more diffuse force for change is the mass of Soviet consumers. Totally unorganized and lacking even the rather meager channels consumers have in most Western countries for bringing wants to the attention of the authorities, the Soviet consumers have seen ample proof of their ineffectiveness in the exiguous attention paid to consumer as against producer and military wares. However, they represent a potential force for detente.

Nonpolitical interests, thoroughly suffocated or harnessed during the Stalin regime, were able to come somewhat to the fore under Khrushchev because there was a greater sense of necessity for modernization if Russia were to hope to overtake the leading capitalist countries. The successor regime being less coherent and purposive, it was to be expected that nonpolitical groups would gain more latitude and influence and that the whole outlook of Soviet society would become more fragmented and looser. In hopes of restoring vigor to the economy, growing too complex for centralized planning, concessions were made to profit criteria and managerial responsibility in industry, although overall control was recentralized. Collective farms were given a little more freedom to operate independently and were promised better returns for production. For the first time in Soviet history, the production of consumer goods, only a minor fraction of Soviet industrial output, was planned to grow slightly faster than that of producers' goods. The basic commitment to heavy industry was not really modified, but standards of Soviet consumption, housing, appliances, and the like began to rise perceptibly faster.

Tourism was encouraged, and contacts with the West became more pervasive. The regime largely gave up the battle against Western musical styles and allowed "socialist realism" to be diluted in art and literature by nonpolitical entertainment and human emotions. It was potentially an opening wedge that a few noncommunist foreign papers were, in the spring of 1968, put on sale in Moscow hotels for the benefit of tourists. There was growing awareness of the conflict of generations, a topic which came to the fore in Khrushchev's last years, as educated and alert young people questioned old stereotypes.

The utopianism which Khrushchev had sought strenuously to revivify waned further. The somewhat anemic and revisionist promise of full communism made by the Party Program of 1961 was allowed to fall out of sight; even his reinterpretation of dictatorship of the proletariat into the "whole people's state" fell by the wayside. Comparisons with the West became fewer and predictions of early surpassing America ceased in view of the evident stability and vitality of American and West European economies and the failure of the Soviet economy to rebound vigorously from the dullness of Khrushchev's last years. There was no basis for a conviction of early victory of communism by economic growth; having rather steadily advanced relative to American industrial output, Soviet industrial indices made only slight progress in the years after 1961. Aside from the rather modest and fairly realistic targets of the Five-Year Plan, Soviet leaders made hardly any effort to depict the future state of society; and the old Marxist goals of the assimilation of mental to physical labor, the end of inequality, and the withering of the state were ever less appropriate. The vision of the future communist world held little more exciting than the expectation of mechanized affluence, hardly more related to current politics than the American dream of prosperity.

In the growing sophistication and awareness of the true complexity of the world, ideology became emptier and less inspiring, and the utopian mission of the party seemed more than ever hollow. In a highly geared society dominated by bureaucrats and the party "intelligentsia," the Marxist view of the man at the forge or the factory bench worker as the bearer of political order, in whose name the party rules, became quite irrelevant. There remained no revolutionary temper either in the Soviet masses or political institutions; the concept of revolution was practically to be swept into a dark corner. Equalitarianism, a social demand much broader than Marxism, also retreated, as Khrushchev's effort to check or reverse the stratification of Soviet society was largely given up. Even under Khrushchev, Soviet officers, more than those of any other major power, were devoted to insignia and distinctions of rank,[1] and Soviet diplomats were more protocol conscious.

Both Brezhnev and Kosygin made less use of doctrinal stereotypes than Khrushchev;[2] and the tendency to justify policies on the basis of principles, already weak under Khrushchev, diminished further under their more technocratic-engineering-minded government. With greater fragmentation of decision making and different interests pulling their several ways, ideology at best had to be more generalized and bloodless, its language increasingly divorced from reality and behavior. The statements of intelligent men with access to the foreign press were probably more than previously at variance with their awareness of the world. For example, after a conference of Communist parties in Budapest, which agreed to postpone consideration of a world Communist assembly and so represented a setback for the Soviet party, a *Pravda* editorial[3] lauded the meeting at great length as showing the unbreakable unity of the world socialist movement. More than ever before Soviet ideology found itself on the defensive, turning from confidence in victory in open competition with bourgeois ideology to bitter complaints of subversion of Eastern Europe and Soviet intellectuals by the West.

Up to the Czech crisis in the summer of 1968, intellectual dissent, noticeably stirring in Khrushchev's time, became bolder. There were public demonstrations, on a very small scale to be sure, of opposition to some policies of the regime, particularly to sanctions against dissident intellectuals. A retired general could make many protests against arbitrary actions, including a funeral address to denounce political repression, without being arrested until he ventured away from the limelight of Moscow to plead for Crimean Tatars in Tashkent.[4] More writers were circulating unpublishable manuscripts, or at least many more of these reached the West.[5] A remarkable statement by a Soviet nuclear physicist published in the United States[6] may indicate views of part, at least, of the upper ranks

---

[1] Raymond L. Garthoff, *Soviet Military Policy* (New York: Frederick A. Praeger, Inc., 1963), p. 37.

[2] Jan F. Triska and David D. Finley, *Soviet Foreign Policy* (New York: Macmillan Co., 1968), p. 126.

[3] October 7, 1968.

[4] *New York Times,* November 16, 1968, and May 8, 1969.

[5] Many are published in *Problems of Communism,* Vol. XVII (July-August and September-October, 1968).

[6] *New York Times,* July 22, 1968.

of the scientific community: de-Stalinization must be completed and freedoms guaranteed; for the future of humanity it is necessary that the United States and the Soviet Union come together to end the danger of nuclear war and grapple with the worldwide problems of hunger, overpopulation, and environmental pollution.

The critics seem to have thought of themselves not as heretics but as purifiers, seeking not to overthrow Marxism-Leninism but to improve its application. But their free-ranging ideas, particularly the demand for freedom of criticism, represented a real threat to the prevalent order, and they evoked a multiform backlash by the political elite who saw their world threatened. This has meant partial re-Stalinization. At the Twenty-third Congress of the party, in March, 1966, Stalin's title of General Secretary was revived for the benefit of Brezhnev; and the guiding Presidium recovered its old name of Politburo. The image of Stalin was restored in various publications and movies, especially in his role as war leader, in the interest of a more "balanced" evaluation, giving him credit for unflinching will and firm authority. Khrushchev had made a special effort to deflate the exaltation of Stalin as forger of victory, his best claim to the gratitude of the Soviet people. After the invasion of Czechoslovakia, the refurbishing of Stalin's image became more emphatic.

Re-Stalinization was not merely symbolic. In 1966 the police services decentralized by Khrushchev were recentralized and given more powers of arrest and imprisonment; in November, 1968, they were returned to the Ministry of Interior, the MVD of sinister memory from the days of Beria. Sundry repressive measures were sharpened against dissenters. Penalties for disorderly conduct were made stiff enough that any sort of protest demonstration, even the telling of anti-Soviet jokes, was theoretically punishable by three years' imprisonment. Khrushchev exploded at deviant intellectuals; Brezhnev and Kosygin said very little but put some of them to forced labor. In and after 1966, there were several trials of writers and intellectuals, theoretically not for ideological deviation but for anti-Soviet, that is, antipatriotic behavior; and minor dissidents were subjected to all manner of pressures.

Repressive measures, however, have been only selectively and rather carefully applied; the prime effort has been toward persuasion and the guidance of minds. In an effort at ideological revival, terms such as "imperialist reaction," "solidarity of the world revolutionary workers' movement," the "social-political crisis of monopoly capitalism," and the like dotted the Soviet press, especially after the Czech intervention, as hardly seen since Stalin. Countless articles warned against the evils of "revisionism." Considerable attention has also been given to the old evil of Trotskyism. As an authoritative journal put it, reversing Khrushchev's interpretation that the strength of socialism permitted some relaxation, "We as patriots and internationalists do not forget that the deepening of the world revolutionary process is accompanied in our time by the activization in all areas of the forces of the imperialist reaction."[7] There was a new campaign of vigilance against Western ideas and "bourgeois morality." Most indoctrination was in terms of patriotism and general moral duty to socialism and Soviet society. On any given date, the majority of dramatic and cinema performances would be likely to glorify in some way the Soviet Union compared to its enemies. Education should be "in the spirit of dedication to communist ideas, of Soviet patriotism and internationalism" for the inculcation of a "communist relation to work and social property,"[8] as is repeated with ponderous insistence. To stimulate socialist patriotism, the Lenin cult has advanced apace; his features have become almost inescapable in Russia, and the preparations for such a transcendent occasion as his 100th birthday, in April, 1970, began two years in advance.

Soviet society thus seems to be increasingly divided between its authoritarian-ideological and its modern and rationalistic sectors; a nationalistic, dogmatic, somewhat anti-intellectual and coercively minded elite presides over an increasingly advanced and restive intelligentsia. Striving to improve standards of living and culture even while governing arbitrarily, the rulership is in some ways suggestive of the "Enlightened Absolutisms" of the nineteenth century. It is still more suggestive of a strong tsarist Russia, with no living but only a dead tsar, with a self-perpetuating bureaucratic elite ruling theoretically for the benefit of the people in the name of sacred principles.

New Style in Foreign Policy

In its conduct of foreign policy the post-Khrushchev regime, while in some ways reverting to Stalinist themes, has shown itself to be bureaucratic and careful. The Foreign Ministry has been strengthened and for the first time has gone far toward developing a career diplomatic service, staffed by graduates of a training school, the Institute of International Relations. In this, there reportedly was considerable effort to develop objective information and political discernment.[9] The Foreign Ministry, divided along both geographic and functional lines, would seem to be in structure much like that of other powers and the American State Department. A notable difference is that policy research staffs seem to be much weaker. Soviet embassies, becoming steadily more conventional since Stalin's departure, have come to resemble their noncommunist counterparts, particularly the American, fairly closely, except that, in addition to

---

[7] *Kommunist*, January, 1969, No. 1, p. 9.

[8] *Pravda*, June 12, 1968.

[9] Aleksandr Kaznacheev, *Inside a Soviet Embassy* (Philadelphia: J. B. Lippincott Co., 1962), p. 30.

sections corresponding to those normal in an American embassy (reporting to military departments, the Ministry of Foreign Trade, the security services, and so on), they have sections for party affairs.

The head of the Foreign Ministry remains Andrei Gromyko, the first career diplomat to hold the post. Deputy foreign minister from 1947, foreign minister since 1957, he has far outlasted his counterparts of other lands. A member of the Central Committee only, his position is more like that of Litvinov than that of Molotov; real decisions are still made in top party circles. However, as the rulership is collegial, Gromyko seems to have more authority than when Khrushchev disparaged him as a messenger boy. More diplomatic business also falls to the formal head of state, the president of the Supreme Soviet. This position, hardly used under Stalin, became of some importance under Khrushchev when it was occupied by Brezhnev. The recent head of state, Podgorny, ranking next to Brezhnev and Kosygin, has figured prominently in negotiations. At the top, Brezhnev and Kosygin have divided responsibilities in the usual Soviet dichotomy: the former, as party chief, has dealt with bloc nations; the latter, mostly with nonsocialist countries. Concomitantly, the execution of Soviet foreign policy has become smoother and more professional; the gaffes and crudities seem consigned to the past.

The interest of the new Russia in stability extends to the outside world as well. Although satisfaction is drawn from all manner of afflictions of the Western countries, especially protest movements and strikes that can be applauded as signs of the decay of capitalism, ideology has been largely disengaged from foreign policy. Beyond some lingering appeal to the discontented, there is little pretense of doing more than forwarding the interests of peace, the Soviet Union, and the "socialist camp," the latter two being equivalent. Proletarian revolution being most unlikely and perhaps undesirable, Communist parties are encouraged to do as the Soviet government does, to work pragmatically for advantages within bourgeois society. As there is not much vision of a radically different future for the Soviet Union, neither does there seem to be for the world. Although there is vague discussion of necessary "revolutionary transformation," the chief concern is not to transform but to retain. Soviet policy hardly drives forward but responds to events. The task of the Soviet "builders of a new age" seems as much technological as political. Khrushchev's expectations of greatly rising Soviet economic power guiding underdeveloped nations to socialism having been shown to be empty, his extravagances have been laid aside in favor of careful and quiet diplomacy, seeking concrete results. The grand schemes have been given up, in diplomacy as in agriculture. Whereas he looked to the whole globe, attention is again strongly concentrated, as in Stalin's day, upon areas adjacent, or nearly so, to Russia, from India and the Mediterranean region to Eastern Europe, and upon building strength at home.

2. TOWARD THE WEST: AMBIVALENCE

Positions of Strength

If the removal of Khrushchev was in part a delayed reaction to his clumsy failure in Cuba two years earlier, his successors seemed determined to avoid any such future humiliation. Instead of pushing afield without solid backing of military power, the new leadership refrained from aggressive initiatives and from the boasting which stimulated American armament, while setting to work to build up strategic strength, much as Stalin did. The public military budget (very dubious as an indicator of the amount of military spending because of the noninclusion of important items and the manipulation of prices of military goods but probably significant in showing year-to-year changes) turned upward in the year following Khrushchev's dismissal; and thereafter it rose gradually but steadily through 1969, the increase amounting to 38 percent.[10] Actual spending for 1968, announced at 16.7 billion rubles, was assessed by the London Institute for Strategic Studies at the equivalent of $50 billion, as much as the United States spent aside from the Vietnam war.[11] It appears further that economic planners have given defense industry firm priority. This may have been a major reason for the inability of the Brezhnev-Kosygin management to restore high rates of growth despite efforts to introduce more rational economic policies.

To what extent the military buildup (and ideological hardening at home) was the result of the war in Vietnam and American bombing of North Vietnam, a distant but recognized member of the "socialist camp," cannot yet be guessed. The first American bombings of North Vietnam were made in August, 1964, in connection with the Tonkin Gulf incident; the aerial attack on North Vietnam became a regular part of the American war effort in February, 1965—begun while Kosygin was visiting that country. Between these dates, in October, 1964, the Brezhnev-Kosygin team took charge. Whether or not Soviet strategists felt that American policy in Vietnam indicated a greater danger, it actually helped them, as American strategic capabilities were neglected in the concentration on Southeast Asia. As a result, by the beginning of 1967 the U.S.S.R. had gone a good way toward reducing the disproportion of missiles in its disfavor and by the end of 1968 had achieved approximate numerical parity in land-based intercontinental missiles, the Soviet missiles report-

---

[10] *New York Times,* December 11, 1968.

[11] *Ibid.*

edly averaging considerably higher in megatonnage. Only in Polaris-type submarines did the United States retain marked superiority.

In conventional weaponry, the Russians have also worked well, and Americans have expressed admiration for the quality of their arms. The efficiency with which they moved large forces into Czechoslovakia in a few hours was decidedly disconcerting to NATO planners, as was the realization that the Russians had acquired a substantial airlift capacity. They also have felt it their duty as a superpower to build up a navy which, although not yet comparable to the American and lacking particularly in aircraft carriers, has become the world's second biggest by a large margin and has caused some anxiety in the West. Stalin would have liked to have a real navy, and one was slowly built after World War II. But Khrushchev called navies outmoded, and Soviet naval power became a real factor only after 1966.

In 1968 the Soviet navy moved in force into the Indian Ocean and particularly the Mediterranean, previously nearly an American preserve. The Soviets acquired bases in Egypt and Syria and were working closely with Algeria, and Americans became much more concerned with the implications of fifty Soviet vessels in the Mediterranean than with the possible attractions of Soviet doctrines for radicals of that region. The Russians stated clearly their purpose, namely, to make a "sea of peace" in the struggle to liquidate "American imperialism's political and military systems in the Mediterranean." The American fleet should have the grace to depart.[12]

The Soviet nuclear posture has been characterized by American observers as basically deterrent, a response to the American overbuilding of missiles after 1961, which was itself based on erroneous assumptions of Soviet strength. The Bolsheviks have usually given priority to economic factors in history and to political action and economic construction as means to change its course. Until recently, it seems fairly clear that the Soviet government did not overestimate military force as an instrument, being perhaps less disposed to seek a military solution to political problems than the United States. After Khrushchev, however, it may be that, as the Marxist part of ideology weakens, the military ethos takes its place as a unifying force. The glamorizing of soldiering and patriotic struggle have been remarkable, and pacifism has been much decried. The Brezhnev-Kosygin leadership seemingly accepted the view, held more or less firmly by the superpowers since 1955, that nuclear war was unthinkable; but Kosygin has been the only member of the hierarchy publicly stressing the destructiveness of nuclear war. Since 1965, there have been suggestions that nuclear war might indeed be winnable and that it would mean the end not of civilization but of capitalism. There have even been hints

---

[12] *Izvestiia,* November 11, 1968.

of the inevitability of war; a Soviet general wrote in the army paper,[13] "So long as imperialism survives, these most important problems [of disarmament] cannot be fully solved."

It is an illiberal aspect of the modern state that weapons production becomes a major industry and hence represents a very large interest, the political potency of which is hardly lessened by its incorporation into the apparatus of the state. The Soviet state, moreover, seems to be considerably more effective in the production of military than civilian goods, in the creation of strength than of material welfare. It would be natural that the Russians should stress the area in which they excel. Unable to spread their system and so their power by proselytizing or example, they might seek in earnest, as Stalin partially did, to expand by military means. That they have refrained thus far from resort to force except in what they viewed as defensive needs may be laid to Russian and Bolshevik tradition, memories of great sufferings in war, perception of the dangers of a nuclear cataclysm, and the Marxist component of the ideology.

In 1969, as the Soviet deployment of strategic weapons continued, American military planners began asking themselves what its ultimate goal might be. The nuclear capabilities of the superpowers were already ample to destroy them many times over as a new escalation of the arms race seemed in prospect. However, the Russians had already achieved palpable results. In any future crisis, the Soviet Union will obviously find itself in a different situation, militarily and psychologically, from that of October, 1962. The postwar era of American supremacy and guardianship of order throughout the noncommunist world appeared to be at an end.

Trade and Diplomacy

While the Soviet Union was arming itself as never before in peacetime and was reasserting the evil and imperialistic nature of capitalism, it saw no reason to refrain from taking maximum advantage of trade with the capitalists. Although Soviet exchanges outside the bloc remained very modest in proportion to the dimensions of the Soviet economy, in the post-Khrushchev years the Soviet Union became a major participant in the trade of the West, especially Western Europe. Foreign corporations were freely called upon, in the new pragmatic way, to help the Soviet economy to a greater extent than ever since the First Five-Year Plan. Western eagerness to trade with the U.S.S.R. has grown, too; countless large installations have been made or contracted by foreign firms, and Western credits have grown ever more generous. A notable example was the 1966 agreement with Fiat to build a plant nearly tripling Soviet output of passenger cars—itself a significant concession to modern demands

---

[13] *Krasnaya Zvezda,* February 10, 1969.

which Khrushchev, more convinced of the value of communal than individual means of transportation, was unwilling to make. Italian firms and state trading organizations have been especially favored, to the extent that Italy has become the leading Soviet commercial partner outside the bloc.

There has come about a much greater willingness to participate in the international life of business. Soviet banking has become more active in the West, and there have been many deals for marketing Soviet oil. A Russian-owned company has service stations in Britain and in 1968 projected a refinery in Belgium. Participating in more and more trade fairs and commercial promotions, the Soviets added many lines of machinery, from hydrofoils to small cars, to their exports of mostly raw materials. The Soviet airline, Aeroflot, flies to some fifty countries. It secured a major breakthrough when direct Moscow–New York flights were begun in July, 1968, after ten years of diplomacy. Reaching out to world commerce, the Soviet Union has quadrupled its merchant fleet in the last eight years. Now sixth largest in the world, it may be first, projecting its rate of growth, by the middle 1970's. It has secured admission to several very capitalistic shipping conferences for rate fixing. Instead of proceeding with its own communications satellite network, the Soviet Union evinced interest in joining the American-sponsored Intelsat consortium.

This turn to business for business' sake has altered attitudes on both sides. Western Europe has come to take trade with the Soviet sphere for granted; as late as 1963 the United States could inconvenience Russian planners by opposing the sale of large-diameter pipe, but anything like this has become impossible. The Russians, on the other hand, have become readier to leave ideology entirely out of consideration. In July, 1968, when a *Pravda* correspondent wrote up a large Swedish engineering firm, nothing was said about exploitation of the workers, much about its good relations with Soviet trading organizations since the 1920's.

The Russians were generally ready to treat with any country according to the advantages expected, including the regime of Franco, still belabored frequently as a bloody murderer. Soviet ships regularly call at Spanish ports. If the Soviet Union dealt only very hesitantly with South Africa, it was seemingly much less for any ideological compunctions than through fear of losing influence with native African states.

If the Soviet Union was prepared to traffic with practically any regime, it was also willing to let political utility override ideology, as in its flirtation with Gaullist France. Although de Gaulle's grand design for restoring the independence and grandeur of France implied a more or less neutral stance between superpowers, with the Soviet Union brought back into Europe to balance the United States, Khrushchev was not very appreciative of its utility. Striving rather toward duopoly with the United States, he was much opposed to the French nuclear force and, at least in regard to the banning of atmospheric nuclear tests, wanted France more amenable to the desires of Washington. As the Franco-American chill deepened, however, warmth grew between Paris and Moscow, particularly as de Gaulle withdrew from the NATO military organization (although not from the political alliance) and became bitterly critical of the American role in Vietnam.

In June, 1966, de Gaulle received a very royal welcome in Moscow. Although solid results were not great, there was talk of a possible renewal of the historic Franco-Russian alliance, and doors were opened to a wide range of improvements in relations, from scientific and space cooperation to expanded trade. In the following December, Kosygin made a less spectacular return visit to France. The main obstacle to intimacy was disagreement over Germany. A principal aim of rapprochement, from the Soviet point of view, was to weaken the Bonn-Paris axis and to secure French recognition of the German Democratic Republic. But relations with Federal Germany were too important for de Gaulle to sacrifice; he would not go beyond his earlier recognition of the Polish title to the Oder-Neisse lands. The Soviet policy, then, was to encourage Gaullist France for the sake of weakening NATO and strengthening Europeanism and nationalism but not to lean exclusively on it. The French were somewhat displeased that the bulk of the Soviet automotive business went to Fiat instead of Renault. But trade grew rather rapidly, and in 1967 the French government took the step toward complete neutralism of ordering that defense planning should ostensibly look to a potential attack from any direction. By the spring of 1968, French concepts for Pan-European security arrangements, nearly or entirely excluding the United States, were fairly close to ideas which the Soviet Union had been intermittently promoting for many years; and a powerful realignment of world forces seemed possible.

In the following months, Franco-Soviet friendship was severely tested. In May student riots in Paris and clashes with the police blew up into something like a revolution. Such an upsurge of protest against the status quo would surely please a Leninist; but, as it was not Communist-led, the French Communist party and the Soviet press at first denounced it as adventurous, Trotskyite, and anarchistic. When the movement spread to the factories, however, and became the largest and most solid general strike ever known, the French party felt compelled to assume leadership over it so far as possible and to try to topple the de Gaulle government. The general then declared that "totalitarian communism" threatened France with dictatorship, and this was made the government's theme in the following electoral campaign. Although anticommunism was carefully separated from foreign relations, its implications were inescapable. The Soviet response was cautious criticism of de Gaulle, mostly borrowed from foreign sources, while apparently urging French Communists to moderate their attacks on him. When the Communists lost severely in the elections, the setback was received very calmly by the Russians. But France and the world were reminded of a basic antagonism standing in the way of real cordiality with a power determined to regard itself as communist.

The invasion of Czechoslovakia in August wounded Franco-Soviet amity more deeply. This move, of which even the French Communists disapproved, smashed Gaullist illusions that Soviet attitudes toward the outside world had been liberalized sufficiently to permit rapprochement with both the Soviet Union and an independent Eastern Europe. The French reaction was bitter; further detente, it was declared, required the withdrawal of Soviet forces, an unlikely prospect; and there was renewed friendliness for America. The Russians, however, ignored criticism and continued to court France in hopes of erasing the evil impression as quickly as possible. They were not unsuccessful. In January, 1969, the Franco-Soviet commission on trade and technical matters resumed its labors, proposed doubling trade between the two countries within five years to $1.4 billion, and discussed ongoing cooperation in space research, scientific interchanges, atomic energy, color television, civil aviation, and other areas. This was, as *Pravda* put it,[14] "an important step on the road to further strengthening of traditional links between France and the USSR." At the same time, French policy in regard to the Israeli conflict seemed close to that of the Soviet Union, as France took a strongly pro-Arab position and supported the Soviet peace plan. The Bolsheviks were somewhat incongruously sympathetic with the plight of the French franc in money markets; and when the Soviet supersonic airline was tested, it was charitably called the "Soviet brother of the 'Concorde.'" The United States, however, could offer the French more solid support in the monetary crisis; and when the North Atlantic alliance came to the end of its statutory period in 1969, the French government made clear that it would remain a member.

The resignation of de Gaulle, after the loss of a referendum in May, 1969, represented a setback for Soviet diplomacy, as no other French leader seemed likely to create so much difficulty for the West. Although the election of Poher, the centrist candidate, would have been very advantageous to the French Communist party, the Soviet leadership was pleased to see him defeated by Pompidou, a Gaullist—rightist and internally the firmest anticommunist. The broad policy of detente with the East had become generally accepted in France, and Pompidou seemed unlikely to abandon it, although he evinced more friendliness toward the United States and European integration than his former chief.

Toward Britain, there have been waves of cordiality at times, but this country is seen as too tied to the United States to be worth cultivating

[14] January 4, 1969.

very seriously. British criticism of the invasion of Czechoslovakia, unlike the French, was returned by Moscow with scornful wrath. In the latter part of 1968, there was an exaggerated propaganda campaign against the British, *inter alia* accusing the BBC of serving British espionage in Russia. Trade was not allowed to suffer, however. Toward Japan, the Soviet attitude has been similarly ambivalent. There has been an effort to promote trade, especially for the needs of East Siberia, and the Russians would like to see the rapidly growing influence of Japan as a valuable counter to China. But they regard close political contacts as impossible as long as Japan is bound by its security treaty with the United States and shelters American bases, and with a certain niggardliness they refuse to consider return to Japan of some tiny islands off the Japanese coast. Yet the Japanese was the first foreign airline to be allowed to fly across Siberia.

German Problem

The ambiguity of Soviet foreign policy is deepest of all in Soviet relations with West Germany, hostility to which is virtually a point of dogma bearing little relation to actions of the Bonn government, yet which was until recently the most important Western supplier. For numerous reasons, it would be advantageous for the Russians to have friendly relations with their important neighbor, and a dialogue has long been carried on (interrupted for some months by the invasion of Czechoslovakia) between Moscow and Bonn. But the West Germans regarded improved relations with the Soviet Union as a means toward closer contact with Eastern Europe and especially East Germany, hoping to forward liberalization in that area and perhaps eventually to make possible the reunification of Germany. Any such course of events is the last thing the Russians want. Much as they would like advantages of working with the prime industrial power of Western Europe, it is more important to minimize West German economic and cultural penetration of Eastern Europe. It is also essential to keep up a fearsome image of the German danger. Anti-Germanism, supported by memories of the war and assisted by the circumstance that Germany is the only major Western country bordering on the Soviet sphere and so presumably capable of launching an invasion, is useful if not vital for the coherence of the bloc. It enables governments of Poland and Czechoslovakia to proclaim the necessity of reliance on Soviet protection against German territorial interests, and it is an actual or potential excuse for military intervention from Finland to Rumania. Above all, antagonism against capitalist-revanchist and neo-Nazi West Germany is the chief title of the Ulbricht government to legitimacy.

By 1966, Soviet-German relations had eased; the atmosphere had warmed sufficiently that former Chancellor Adenauer, one of the staunchest of anticommunists, called the Soviet Union a peace-loving power. But when the Kiesinger-Brandt coalition government took office in December, 1966, with a program of relaxing tensions with the East, the Soviet line began to harden. Proposals for dissolution of alliances on both sides were dropped. There was discussion of a treaty for the mutual renunciation of force, but the Russians raised new conditions and eventually broke off conversations. They had denounced the Hallstein doctrine of nonrecognition of states which had diplomatic relations with the Ulbricht government, but they were much more alarmed when the Kiesinger government sought to establish formal relations with satellite countries. After Rumania opened relations with Bonn, heavy pressure was put on Hungary, Czechoslovakia and Bulgaria to decline. The Russians saw their fears confirmed in the first half of 1968, as economic relations between Federal Germany and Czechoslovakia grew with the latter country's slipping away from Soviet-style communism. Vituperation rose to exceptional intensity as the Russians sought to justify military intervention in subsequent months. Most Soviet citizens seem to have been fairly well convinced and to have accepted the invasion as necessary to forestall German occupation of Czechoslovakia.

Characteristic of the Soviet regime was the empty furore raised in March, 1969, over the election in Berlin of a new president of the Federal German Republic. This was called an illegal and dangerous provocation, and a crisis seemed building as the world wondered what drastic measures might be taken to support violent and threatening language. There were military movements. The Soviet ambassador proposed a compromise settlement, but the price was raised before negotiations could proceed far. Traffic was interrupted from time to time on the highways to Berlin. Yet when the election was held, nothing at all was done; Soviet planes did not even bother, as they had occasionally done in previous years, to jar the delegates with sonic booms. A few days later, East Germans were treating West German businessmen with exceptional cordiality at the Leipzig trade fair while negotiating for an increase of trade, and the Soviet ambassador in Bonn was indicating readiness to discuss a wide variety of issues. The Soviet tactics were not unsuccessful. They harvested some propaganda points, and they were able to cause sufficient uneasiness in the West that it seemed doubtful that the Bonn government would ever again elect its first magistrate in Berlin. Yet they had not perceptibly injured their diplomatic position in Bonn nor their standing with the Nixon administration.

It is not clear to the outside observer, and possibly is not fully clear to the rulers of the Kremlin, how far they are really afraid of the revival of German power and how far they feel the need to cultivate fear of Germany. Corresponding questions are whether they really desire the dissolution of NATO, the real harmlessness of which can hardly escape them despite ferocious caricatures and diatribes, and the withdrawal of American troops, which would free the German army; and whether they would be happy to see Bonn recognize the Oder-Neisse frontier and the German Democratic Republic. Hostility is practically dictated by political geography. Soviet relations with West Germany are determined more by the needs internal to the system—by relations with Eastern Europe and particularly with Soviet Germany—than by considerations having strictly to do with West Germany. Only if the Russians should either renounce East European domain or should feel much more secure in it would relaxed relations with the bulk of Germany seem possible. Soviet policy toward Germany thus suffers, in a slightly different way, the fundamental contradictions of Soviet foreign policy arising from the clash of internal and external needs.

Detente with the United States

For Soviet Russia today, Communist powers have to be counted enemies, and capitalist powers are neutral to friendly. China is an ideological relative with whom no business can be done; France is an ideological alien and friend. The Soviet government has in practice come to a rather material concept of interest in the behavior of nations, wherein class relations hardly enter. This means that it is largely conservative in world affairs and in favor of the status quo. The Khrushchev experience and various failures showed that no grand breakthrough was in sight without excessive risk, and the successor regime has seemed neither to expect any great victories nor willing to do much to seek them, whether in principle or pending better and safer opportunities. Desirous of avoiding disorders, the Soviet Union has usually supported international law, treaties, and security. Particularly in relation to the United States, the only real danger, the Russians have sought to avoid crises since 1962.

It is inadmissible from the ideologists' point of view that the Soviet Union and the United States have a great deal in common, but this is increasingly a fundamental reality of the world picture. They share various political interests, from checking the spread of nuclear weapons to shoring up India against China. In a world where problems and opportunities created by technology loom ever larger, it is incumbent upon the two strongest powers to cooperate for their solution. They have done so in some small ways, as in agreements to limit whale catches, to neutralize Antarctica, to ban nuclear weapons in space, and to rescue astronauts. Much more may be necessary in the future, as at least some Soviet intellectuals are aware, to meet rising needs quite outside the framework of conventional political doctrines; from exchanging weather information they may go on to weather control.

One of the world's mounting issues is the contrast and conflict between the more advanced industrial nations and the impoverished majority of mankind, which sees itself falling farther behind year by year. In this regard, the United States and the Soviet Union are squarely in the same camp, and they have seen themselves subjected to the same complaints and demands of the less fortunate. Applying Leninism somewhat loosely, Afro-Asian nations can, as the Chinese emphatically do, see the two superpowers as potential if not actual exploiters of the weaker and poorer. There is decreasing concern, moreover, on the part of both the United States and the Soviet Union for bringing to their side the underdeveloped world, which is more a burden than an asset except in terms of prestige. In 1968 the United States and the Soviet Union together opposed a majority of the United Nations which wished to exclude South Africa from a specialized agency; the principle of international order was more important to them than the favor of the black African nations. Both have had the lesson of spending considerable sums in the Third World without reaping corresponding political advantages or even gratitude. Alliances with secondary powers have lost much of their charm, as the United States and the U.S.S.R. have seen that allies, in the modern age, easily become restive and demanding, while their military utility is slight when any target can readily be obliterated from anywhere on earth. Missiles soar over allies, who promise more complication than advantages.

The United States has in recent years made practically no effort to shake the Soviet grip on Eastern Europe, as in fact it has never done except in a rather theoretical manner. As Rumania was seeking to loosen its ties with the bloc, the United States gave virtually no moral or economic support. In the first half of 1968, the American State Department almost ostentatiously kept hands off Czechoslovakia's striving toward liberalization, refraining even from such harmless measures as releasing impounded Czech gold or removing trade discriminations. This detachment was designed to avoid giving the Soviet Union provocation to intervene, but it amounted to assurances that the United States would not seriously oppose intervention. When this came, the American official reaction was unexpectedly mild, showing only the indignation required by world opinion and less than Western Europe hoped to see. The attitude of Washington, as that of Paris, was that a few months' decent interval sufficed to permit business to be resumed practically as before.

The Soviet Union on the other hand has not done very much to wean nations from the American alliance and has not seemed very unhappy to have American forces in West Germany. It has shown considerable respect for the American sphere in Latin America. It was nearly a year and a half after Castro's revolution that diplomatic relations were established with his regime, and the Soviets have never been enthusiastic to join his campaign to open guerrilla warfare fronts in the Americas. While the

Soviet Union has made some effort to build relations with whatever Latin American countries were amenable, it has carried on no great diplomatic or economic offensive toward that area; and its interest has hardly seemed to grow in recent years. Probably the Soviet leadership has much the same hesitation about meddling in Latin America—the socialist country established there being no great asset—that the United States has for Eastern Europe.

Having a superior position, the present superpowers have a strong interest in maintaining it. They have no desire to see their very exclusive club enlarged; another superpower, they fear, would raise all manner of problems and a real break in their nuclear duopoly would require all manner of new calculations. The rivalry of power and urge to supreme leadership, to maintain or achieve top place if not to secure something like hegemony, is very strong and sets the champion and challenger perpetually at odds. But the world is still big, and within its own sphere of relative domination each superpower has cares enough demanding attention. When it is so hard to keep order in part of the world, the superpowers are inclined to work together for world order rather than strive very hard to enlarge their respective areas of predominance.

The Soviet-American community of interests was overshadowed, however, by the Vietnam war, the effects of which on Soviet thinking, although perhaps not determinant, cannot be overlooked. It is possible that the intensification of the conflict in the summer of 1964 undercut Khrushchev's policies of adjustment and his prestige. In 1965 and after, the Soviet Union had to assist North Vietnam to sustain the claim to leadership of the socialist camp, for leadership implies the ability to protect; and the Soviet Union found itself contributing directly on an increasing scale to the fight against American forces and talking tough to deter expansion of the war. It was still galling to the Russians that they could, in fact, do little to prevent American planes from operating rather freely over North Vietnam. At home, there was more talk of dangers of attack, and this was either a reason or pretext for a reinjection of ideological militancy. Peaceful Coexistence acquired more belligerent tones; and the economic reforms, with their liberal or capitalistic overtones, were watered down.

In 1964 Soviet writers had departed farther than ever from Marxist stereotypes in judging the American government to represent a variety of forces and to respond to public opinion and in conceding that it might not be seeking world dominion. But in 1965 the official picture turned back, viewing President Johnson as a tool of sinister interests and America as bent on universal empire.[15] It should not, however, be inferred that the

[15] W. Zimmerman in Alexander Dallin and Thomas B. Larsen (eds.), *Soviet Politics since Khrushchev* (Englewood Cliffs, N.J.: Prentice-Hall, Inc., 1968), pp. 171–74.

Soviet view was as fixed on Southeast Asia as that of many Americans. The Russians did not make so much of the Vietnam theme as they might have, despite its obvious utility for stilling youthful and intellectual protest. In 1968 Soviet propagandists habitually bracketed American policy in Vietnam with Israeli aggression and West German revanchism, as though these three were quite comparable evils in the world.

Hostility did not prevent calm contacts. In July, 1967, Kosygin went to the United Nations for the condemnation of Israel in connection with its brief and victorious war with the Arab states, and he used the occasion to meet Johnson at Glassboro, New Jersey. They could solve no problems, but their disagreement was civilized to the point of cordiality, and Kosygin showed himself tactful and dignified. The Vietnam war did not prevent an American-Soviet treaty for consular relations. Possibly it was negotiated just for the purpose of reducing its impact.

With the restriction of bombing of North Vietnam after March, 1968, and the beginning of talks about peace discussions, the Russians moved toward placing relations with the United States on a better footing. A treaty to check the spread of nuclear weapons was finally agreed upon, after years of negotiation. In July, Gromyko expressed approval of a long-standing American proposal for negotiations to restrict the missile arms race. Agreement for a meeting of Johnson and Kosygin was to be announced at the very time when Soviet forces went into Czechoslovakia.

After the election of President Nixon, the Russians, who had manifested considerable misgivings of his anticommunist attitudes in the past, maintained an attitude of correctness, as though inviting him to forget the past on a basis of live and let live. They greeted his inauguration with a stronger call for ratification of the nuclear nonproliferation treaty and discussion of strategic arms control. Not long afterwards, they proposed the opening of some consulates in cities other than the capitals of the respective countries, for the first time since 1948. It was also a gesture toward the West and the United States in particular that May Day was celebrated without a military parade for the first time since 1917. The basic Soviet desire remained, as under Khrushchev, to come to an accommodation with the United States so far as possible without sacrificing Soviet interests.

The major common interest of the United States and the Soviet Union is the negative one of avoiding nuclear destruction, an area of shared concern in which they negotiate practically alone, over the heads of all other powers. As principal nuclear powers, they are the principal targets, and nuclear war would be much more threatening to them than to China or most of the smaller powers. The wealthy and politically sated nations have such an interest in the avoidance of conflict that it should logically override their differences and bring them to a fair degree of harmony. Consequently, it seemed of great significance that the Soviet

Union appeared ready, in 1969, to talk about a wide range of disarmament measures, from restrictions on the military use of the seabed to the old proposal for complete and general disarmament. Perhaps the moment was suitable, now that the two powers had reached approximate parity and neither had much to fear from the freezing of the status quo.

The Soviet Union was also pressing another familiar pacific objective, the calling of a European security conference to be followed by a European security pact. It was not clear whether this was intended as a general measure for the relaxation of tensions and the reduction of the military confrontation between NATO and WTO blocs, or whether it aimed to create pressure for the exclusion of the United States from a new, inevitably Soviet-dominated European system.[16] It was also unclear, as in connection with disarmament proposals, how much was seriously intended and how much was designed to repair the damage caused to the Soviet image by intervention in Czechoslovakia.

If the aim was primarily propagandistic, it was at least partly successful. The world has always been ready to listen hopefully to Soviet proposals for lifting the burden of fear of nuclear devastation. Many Europeans felt that any proposals for general security discussions should be tested, although the American government was more skeptical. Perhaps the Kremlin, too, was a bit uncertain of its objectives, as its alternately speaking softly and stridently may have reflected not so much a desire to confuse the world as differences between "hawks," eager to act from strength, and "doves," hopeful of gains from a policy of smiles if not actual detente.

Limits of Detente

The Soviet desire for settlement or negotiation of a dyarchy of some sort with the United States has usually receded behind power competition and ideological differences. Soviet-American cooperation—conspiracy as the Maoists see it—may be expected to come to the fore in situations of special danger, but it has usually been much less conspicuous than nagging friction and hostility. Publicly, the Russians have almost always made far more of their differences than their common interests with the United States. As the two strongest nations, each tends to see its achievements as relative to those of the other. In this spirit, the chief aim in the space race has at times seemed to be to surpass the contender. Soviet firsts were hailed as triumphs for socialism, if not simply for the Soviet people; as Sholokhov, a vocal supporter of the establishment, put it, "We heard on the radio about the new victory of our science, the soft landing on the

---

[16] As suggested in *Pravda,* March 18, 1968.

moon, and our heart leaped up; a wonderful job, boys! But there is another reason for joy: we've gotten ahead of the Americans again. Those conceited fellows on the other side of the ocean, who haven't learned not to put their feet on the table. . . ."[17] The American manned orbiting of the moon in December, 1968, was given limited publicity, perhaps a fiftieth of the space devoted in leading papers to the previous Soviet recovery of a vehicle after a voyage around the moon. Shortly afterward, the Russians restored their self-esteem a little by being the first to test-fly a supersonic transport, and when they transferred cosmonauts between vehicles in space, the American moon voyage seemed totally overshadowed. Later, stories on Russian probes of Venus filled the Soviet press while scanty reporting of the American Apollo program contained a sour note, stressing that U.S. astronauts had been subjected to excessive risks and hardships. Soviet scientists, however, were complimentary. Subsequently, astronaut Borman and his family received a warm welcome from both the Soviet public and officialdom during their tour of the U.S.S.R.[18]

As by far the two strongest powers, the United States and the Soviet Union are rivals not only in space but everywhere. So far as there is an urge to extend and use political influence, they inevitably clash; each is the chief limitation on the effective will of the other. The Russians back the Arabs more strongly because they see Israel as close to the United States; the United States is firmer in support of Israel because the Russians are with the Arabs. Both are also well aware that the Near East contains the world's largest oil deposits. Both like to tally adherents, and it is counted a great evil or a great good if a nation should become "communist," much beyond any actual or potential accrual of material strength to the "socialist camp."

The rivals for world leadership see their own power and security as something achievable at the expense of the other. Security is still viewed as deriving from power, although this has become questionable; and power is relative. The discomfiture of the other side is, then, to be welcomed. This feeling is mild and covert as the United States observes Soviet failures in agriculture or the slowing rate of industrial growth. But the Soviet Union dwells with unabashed gloating on the many woes which beset American society, from strikes and race riots to the crime rate and monetary speculation. Even stock market declines are fondly reported, for reasons which may be as much nationalistic as ideological.

Ideology is a tool in the political contest, frankly and openly on the Soviet side, less clearly and explicitly on the Western or American.

---

[17] *Pravda*, February 5, 1966.

[18] *New York Times*, July 10, 1969.

National or state differences are framed in ideological terms. The United States does not often admit acting simply for a national interest, and the Soviet Union never does so but always speaks in moral-ethical terms. The national cause is put in terms of generally recognized virtue against evil, socialism and justice against capitalist exploitation and imperialism, or communist totalitarianism against freedom and democracy. Each side hopes by propagating its message to the peoples of the other to weaken its opposition.

Being in opposition, the two superpowers tend to stress their points of difference, although this is more emphatic from the Soviet than the American side, where it has become acceptable to seek to "build bridges." Each side has a large apparatus of propaganda for the promotion of its image and philosophy, that of the Soviet Union being larger and more expensive, that of the United States profiting by better channels in most of the world and much more private and unorganized cooperation.

But the ideological battle would be much less earnest if it were only an adjunct or outcome of the contest for leadership. All contentions, indeed, would be much more negotiable, and the outlook of the world would be brighter, if there were not deep differences of society and political philosophy between the two strongest powers. It is part of the difference that ideology is a pillar of the Soviet way. It is something which cannot be surrendered, no matter what other powers do short of subordinating themselves to the Soviet system; and central to it is the dichotomy of our good and their evil, the light within against the dark without.

The Soviet leadership is always afraid that a real detente might break down the barriers to Western influence, bringing loosening of economic controls (as they observe to have occurred in Yugoslavia), more demands for legalism, restriction of party rule and of governmental authority, and the possibility of a whole range of (as they see it) political and social disorders.

They find it reassuring to view the present era as that of the overthrow of the competitive and threatening system, the "struggle against imperialism, for social and national liberation, for the socialist remaking of society."[19] Such essentially self-congratulatory statements, intended to bolster the Soviet system and increase acceptance of it, have been endlessly repeated in countless variants in recent years as in the 1920's: with the continual "strengthening of the socialist system" and the "deepening of the general crisis of capitalism," world politics are interpreted as little more than the contest of socialism and capitalism or imperialism.

Such ideas are always in the background to be brought forward on ritual occasions, as May 1 and November 7, and otherwise as circum-

---

[19] A. A. Akhtamzian (ed.), *Istoriia mezhdunarodykh otnoshenii i vneshnei politiki SSSR*, Vol. I, 1917–1939 (Moscow, 1967), p. 5.

stances dictate. Since 1967, they have again become more prominent, probably because of feelings of insecurity. The policy of doing business with the West has been balanced by neo-Stalinist emphasis on the crisis of capitalism and the sharpening of the struggle between the two worlds. "Building bridges is essentially a means of ideological attack on the U.S.S.R.";[20] and, "The imperialists, not daring to attack the forces of socialism head-on, resort to their underhanded tactics of seeking weak links in the socialist commonwealth, trying to organize subversive activities within the socialist countries . . ."[21] A loosening of blocs would be only dangerous, and the call for general European security arrangements was offset, in the spring of 1969, by a ferocious blast against NATO.

Thus, the Soviet Union, while behaving mostly like a state, speaks mostly and feels partly like a movement, as the Brezhnev-Kosygin government continues the Khrushchev policy of external Peaceful Coexistence with no compromise of ideology at home. Its relations with the United States, so crucial for the world's future, hover uncertainly between cooperation for the security of both and political and ideological warfare, swinging according to issues and circumstances but usually nearer the latter than the former. This uncertainty is somewhat confusing for the world and may be rather unproductive for Soviet diplomacy, but it may represent an endurable compromise.

3. TOWARD THE THIRD WORLD: LIMITED OBJECTIVES

The diplomacy of the Brezhnev-Kosygin government toward the uncommitted nations was in harmony with its general style. Khrushchev's flamboyance and hopes of rapid and spectacular victories were left behind. If it was impossible to control Communist countries at a distance, there was little point in trying to convert non-Communist governments into satellites. The new government endeavored to secure such diplomatic, commercial, and strategic advantages as were achievable, to extend Soviet influence gradually and without great cost. They withdrew from a number of foreign quarrels—territorial disputes between India and Pakistan and between Afghanistan and Pakistan. They paid most attention to improving or solidifying the Soviet position in adjacent countries potentially to be brought into a Soviet zone of influence, perhaps without conversion to communism. The failure of the Khrushchev approach was evidenced in the fragility of regimes on which he had laid

[20] *Pravda*, August 31, 1968.
[21] *Pravda*, April 20, 1969.

stakes, several of which fell in 1965. Nkrumah in Ghana was succeeded by an anticommunist military government. Sukarno, having received over a billion dollars of Soviet aid, turned toward the Chinese as more expressive of Asian aspirations, and then lost power. The Soviet government observed with equanimity the massacre of hundreds of thousands of Indonesian Communists or supposed Communists and continued relations with the generals' regime.

The Brezhnev-Kosygin government somewhat reduced, especially in its first years, the attention which Khrushchev had generously given to the uncommitted world, as it concentrated energies on complicated internal affairs. Economic aid was somewhat cut down, placed on a more commercial basis and put to better calculated effect. Military aid was emphasized, and Soviet arms exports became as large as those of the United States or larger and a very important factor in the politics of the Third World. Naval expansion and the quest for facilities were interwoven into the program.

The competition in the Third World was more confused than it had been in the days of Khrushchev. The Russians directed much of their activity against the Chinese, until these largely withdrew from or were expelled from most contested areas, because of the disorderly truculence of the Cultural Revolution, after the summer of 1966. The politics of the Third World became more tangled as the antagonisms to former colonial powers wore off and countries found themselves more at odds with their neighbors than with leading Western states. Under its unexciting new leadership, the Soviet Union lost a good deal of its emotional-ideological appeal to radical elements, for whose favor the Chinese could bid higher, while more sober nationalist leaders became more willing to look to advantages of dealing with the Soviet Union, whether to offset Western influence or for the material benefits expected. The Russians continued, of course, to make many small gaffes and blunders, mostly because of inexperience; but in the basic endeavor of improving the Soviet standing in the world they were considerably more successful than in earlier years.

With all the lands along the Soviet border from Europe to China, the Soviet position was improved. The Turkish premier was an honored guest in Moscow in 1965, and Turkey began receiving credits the next year. In 1968, the Soviet government was engaged in many industrial projects. The Western affiliation of Turkey did not quickly change, but anti-American feeling in that once very faithful ally, nourished both by Soviet blandishments and American support of the Greeks in the Cyprus issue, became very strong. In December, 1968, Turkey was anxious that the passage of American destroyers into the Black Sea should not injure its comfortable relations with the Soviet Union, while this power fumed entirely at the United States, not at Turkey for allowing the vessels to pass.

With Iran, the Russians were able to develop some cordiality, as they agreed to build a steel mill, a smelter, many silos, a railroad, and so on, in exchange for Iranian raw materials. Probably a positive factor was the subsidence of Iranian communism under an energetic conservative-reformist shah. Soviet aid going to Afghanistan was somewhat reduced. It remained, however, much larger than the American, while here as nowhere else the American and Soviet aid programs cooperated to the benefit of the recipient country. The Soviet Union displayed no interest in building up an Afghan Communist movement where it could make a satellite at any time. Perhaps the country is simply too poor, with one of the world's lowest income figures, or it is held better to avoid frightening noncommunist Asians. There is no danger of Afghanistan escaping Soviet influence.

More remarkable has been the Soviet ability to cultivate at the same time both India and Pakistan, the latter until recently a Western ally although supported by Communist China against India. In the war between India and Pakistan over Kashmir in September, 1965, the Chinese urged Pakistan into battle, but the Russians wished neither government badly injured or overthrown. Both parties accepted Kosygin's offer of mediation, and the Indian and Pakistani heads of state met with him in Tashkent in January, 1966. This exercise of purely conventional diplomacy was very successful. The outstanding issues could not, of course, be settled, but the antagonists agreed upon a truce which has proved stable; and the Soviet Union gained much prestige from its first peacemaking between noncommunist powers, where neither Britain, the United States, nor the United Nations had been able to achieve much. Subsequently the Russians promised economic assistance to Pakistan, including the inevitable steel mill, and even some arms, at the risk of offending India. Pakistan responded with warmth; a concrete return to the Soviets was the ending of the American lease on the base from which the U–2 flew over Russia in 1960.

The Soviet government continued, however, to lay much more emphasis on its friend of longer standing, India. There was some contradiction, since the Russians tried to play up to both sides. They found, as the United States had, that each was nearly as much offended by military assistance to the other as pleased by assistance to itself. When the Indian government protested in 1967 against pro-Pakistani and anti-Indian broadcasts from Tashkent, the Soviet government lamely disavowed them on the grounds that the station was privately owned and represented individual views.[22] Later, Radio Peace and Progress began supporting the Indian Communist movement and attacking the government and non-Communist parties, while Radio Moscow maintained a correct and friendly attitude,

[22] *London Times*, August 5, 1967.

reflecting the official view. However, having acquired a good reputation from the Bhilai steel plant, the Russians moved deeply into the Indian economy, being engaged at the end of 1968 in some forty industrial projects, mostly basic. Trade grew rapidly, and they were able to create some dependence, as by a huge order for railroad cars. Soviet-Indian trade tripled from 1961 to 1966–67 and continued to grow rapidly. In India the Soviet government has mounted one of its largest cultural-propagandistic efforts encompassing activities ranging from book publishing to scientific and artistic exchanges, all designed to promote not so much communism but the image of the Soviet Union as an admirable friend. Politically more significant, the Soviets became furnishers of large amounts of military equipment. Cooperation of the Soviet Union with the Indian navy has been particularly close, with Soviet advisers serving with Indian crews. Reportedly, the Russians became so confident of their standing in India as to conduct themselves in a rather lordly manner in negotiations.[23]

More menacing for the West has been Soviet penetration of the Arab world, where complicated tensions around the rise of Israel gave the Soviet Union a splendid opportunity to gain a strong foothold. The pro-Arab policy of the Soviet Union, upheld steadily from shortly after the birth of Israel, resulted to some extent from the anti-Semitism traditional with Russians and other peoples, especially Moslems of the Soviet Union (in reversion to old associations of Jews with capitalism, Uncle Sam has been caricatured with Jewish features, and in the post-Czechoslovakia hard line, it sometimes seemed that every Jew was seen as a potential spy for Israel) and anti-Zionism fearful of a foreign loyalty for Soviet Jews. These were mixed with straight power politics seeking advantages from association with the anti-Western cause, and quite possibly interest in the world's best oil fields.

For Soviet purposes it has been necessary to sustain the Arabs but not to intervene decisively to make them victorious; if that were possible, it would probably be disastrous for Soviet influence with the strongly nationalistic, even xenophobic Arabs. The chief Soviet reliance in the area was Nasser's Egypt or the United Arab Republic as it was hopefully called. Relations warmed and cooled from time to time from the beginning of Soviet arms deliveries in 1955, but they generally became closer as Nasser became more dependent on assistance from Moscow in his difficult battle at once to industrialize and modernize and to combat Israel. A point of friction was Nasser's intolerance of the local Communist party, but this was removed when the party dissolved itself in 1965, with the explanation that Nasser's ruling party was adequate to carry on the Egyptian revolution. When a number of Communists were jailed, *Pravda* dismissed them

---

[23] *New York Times,* September 28, 1968.

as a "group of provocateurs calling themselves the 'Arab Communist Party.'" In due course, *Pravda* was writing of Nasser's "revolution" as though this were a proper revolution in the Leninist sense and part of the world socialist transformation.[24]

The June war, when Israeli forces rapidly defeated the Arabs in 1967, was at first a setback but in the longer run a boost for Soviet standing among the Arabs. Apparently feeling that they had been encouraged to positions and actions which led to war, the Arabs expressed some bitterness that the Russians did not intervene militarily to prevent their defeat. It was also a discredit for the Soviets that those whom they had abundantly armed and to some extent advised were so rapidly and thoroughly beaten. But the experience made the Arabs more hostile still to Israel and to the Western powers, especially the United States, which supported Israel, and more dependent on the Soviet Union for reequipment and the support which might make possible their recovery. Soviet technical and economic aid was enlarged, and a large number of advisors went to manage the Egyptian armed forces and other departments to help restore the battered nation. Nearly two thirds of Egyptian trade, almost as much as that of a bloc nation, was with the Soviet bloc. The economic and political system was tightened and made more socialistic, in line with the Soviet insistence that "bourgeois elements" were responsible for defeat. Nasser had apparently given up the idea of maneuvering between East and West to cast his lot entirely with the Soviets.

Elsewhere among the Arab nations the Soviets made themselves strongly felt. Their new naval presence in the Mediterranean was based in Syria and Egypt. Soviet arms were the reliance of Iraq, Sudan, Algeria, and Yemen. In Algeria, Soviet influence was assisted by a running quarrel with the former colonial power, France, and made spectacular progress in 1967 and 1968. The Algerian regime, while banning the Communist party, showed strong overtones of Marxist socialism and inclined to anti-Western nationalism. It may have intended only to improve its bargaining position by bringing in the Russians; however, the presence of several thousand Soviet military advisors and increasing economic dependence suggests that Algeria may present the Russians major strategic advantages in the western Mediterranean.[25] Southern Yemen (formerly British Aden) was somewhat closer to the Soviet Union than its neighbor, Yemen, strongly Marxist and Soviet-armed. Its title of "People's Republic" suggests that the Soviet Union had something like a satellite in the strategic former British colony, potential base for operating in the Indian Ocean.[26]

The Soviet Union has succeeded in making itself thoroughly at home

---

[24] *Pravda*, July 6, 1967; July 25, 1968.

[25] *New York Times*, July 16, 1968; December 26, 1968.

[26] *New York Times*, March 3, 1969.

in an important region, while no populous Arab nation remains friendly to the West. Thus progressing comfortably, it seems desirous of working through client states instead of Communist parties and of avoiding the dangerous violence which might lead to revolutionary situations. As in the Indian subcontinent, the Russians oppose renewal of fighting and have presented some peace proposals reasonable enough to gain them some credit as peacemakers and to irritate Arab extremists, whom the Chinese would cultivate. Ever wary, the Russians have refused to support the Arab guerrilla movement. But they continue arming the Arabs and encouraging them to military and economic reliance on Moscow, with some confidence that political guidance follows. As long as the basic tensions continue, no other part of the world is so promising of an extension of the Soviet sphere of influence.

It has been characteristic of tsarist, Stalinist, and post-Khrushchev foreign policy to concern itself primarily with the borderlands where political drives are supported by the proximity of power. If Turkey can, as the Soviet press has urged, be brought to leave NATO, there might be formed a solid area of Soviet dominance to the south, somewhat like the sphere dominated by the United States in Latin America. Farther afield lies Negro Africa, more difficult of access, more alien, and much less promising of lasting gains. The Khrushchev policy of dashing into the tumult of disintegrating empires caused a good deal of expense for no real return, and where a Soviet foothold seemed established, in Guinea, Somalia, Ghana and Mali, or where one was in prospect at one time, as in both Congos, it turned infirm. Consequently, attention to sub-Saharan Africa was reduced, although spread more widely, even as more was given to North Africa; and the Negro countries turned back toward reliance on Western help.

In the middle of 1967, however, a new opportunity arose with the outbreak of civil war in Nigeria. This country had been among those least Marxist-socialistic and best disposed to the West, which had regarded it as exceptionally promising for orderly development. Perhaps partly in chagrin at the setbacks suffered in neighboring countries or to efface their reputation of favoring insurgencies against established governments, the Russians hastened to the aid of a regime for which they had no ideological affinity. While Western powers were more or less reluctant, the Soviets sent fighter and bomber planes and other military equipment; technical and economic aid followed. The Soviet embassy mushroomed, and Soviet influence in Nigerian intellectual circles and unions grew rapidly, to some discomfiture of Western businesses. It would be very difficult, however, for Soviet penetration to rival the large British investment in Nigeria, and the end of the civil war would remove the major lever of Soviet entry. Characteristically, the Chinese Communists supported the Biafran cause because it was a revolution, while the anticommunist Portuguese did so because it weakened a Black government.

Still farther afield in Latin America, where risks are great and calculable rewards less, the Soviet role has been decidedly cautious. Their main problem has been to live with a would-be activist and revolutionary Cuba, welcomed by Khrushchev to full membership in the socialist camp but indocile to Communist discipline and expensive to maintain. At times Castro has seemed much irritated with Soviet actions or inaction and has seemed to wish to break away, but he has found the Chinese domineering and unwilling to assist without a large measure of control, while his economy subsists on Soviet support in the face of the American embargo. The Russians feel compelled to continue this support despite occasional slaps from Castro. A Communist Cuba may be no great asset, but its loss would be a severe blow to the image of socialism marching in the direction of victory.

In June, 1966, at a Tri-Continental Congress of assorted Communists and revolutionaries from Africa, Asia, and Latin America, the Soviet delegate (significantly Sharif Rashidov, highest-ranking Central Asian in the Soviet hierarchy) commended guerrilla movements. However, the general Soviet policy in Latin America has been quite the contrary, to build a reputation for respectability, dealing with practically any government willing to establish diplomatic and commercial relations. It has made advances in this regard, as Colombia, Ecuador, and Peru agreed to the opening of Soviet embassies; the U.S.S.R. finally has established relations with the bulk of Latin America. It made only modest efforts, however, to take advantage of the quarrel between the United States and Peru over the latter's expropriation of oil interests.

Soviet ambassadors usually avoided much contact with local Communist parties (which were generally shy of guerrilla movements in the backwoods) and spoke more to the upper than the lower classes. They extended credits and cooperation to a rightist military government in Brazil as to a left-center government of Chile. For this approach, association with Castroism was quite detrimental. In the aftermath of Czechoslovakia, however, Castro began to move closer to his Soviet protectors, probably easing their problems in this hemisphere. Soviet interest in Latin America has remained relatively feeble; but the potentialities of the area are great, as shown by the hostile reception given to President Nixon's envoy, Nelson Rockefeller, nearly everywhere.

In sum, the Brezhnev-Kosygin leadership could chalk up real, although unspectacular, gains. The Soviet Union was at once able to extend its influence in the conventional ways of a great power and to identify itself with the revolutionary and nationalistic sentiments of the Third World, no small achievement for a basically conservative antinationalistic regime.

4. MAOISM, THE NEW ENEMY

Perhaps because it was antithetical to the Maoist style, the one area in which the quiet, calculating approach of the Brezhnev-Kosygin regime failed entirely was China. A principal purpose of the new government was to moderate the Sino-Soviet dispute, but it exploded to violent enmity little short of actual war.

The Brezhnev-Kosygin leadership seems to have felt that the split with China was at least partly the result of Khrushchev's tactlessness and irascibility in somewhat the same way that Khrushchev blamed Stalin for alienating Yugoslavia. This was an understandable interpretation in view of the difficulty of accounting ideologically for disharmony among socialist states and the Marxist lack of appreciation for strictly political causes. The Chinese Communists had a similar misperception, and they were optimistically persuaded that Khrushchev had been ousted primarily in protest against his anti-China policies. Hence both sides looked to an improvement, and shortly after Khrushchev's dismissal, Chou En-lai headed a delegation to Moscow. The Russians were willing to drop Khrushchev's plan for a conclave to excommunicate the Chinese fraternal party and to drop polemics, but they were unwilling to contemplate any larger concessions of policy. So far as they considered change, it was in the direction of disengagement from distant and revolutionary entanglements. The Chinese demanded a complete reversal of Soviet course. Hence, there could be only a slight temporary moderation of the dispute. The Chinese were invited to the November anniversary celebration, but so were the Yugoslavs; for a few months, until March, polemics were muted and there were a few expressions of friendship.

Antagonism continued below the surface, as the Chinese would abate none of their rigidity and continued to try to convert other parties. It burst out in disagreement over the response to be made to American bombing of North Vietnam, beginning in February, 1965. The Soviet policy was to do no more than furnish some material assistance to North Vietnam. The Chinese did not welcome this, which involved a Soviet intrusion into what they considered their sphere. The duty of the strongest socialist power, as they saw it, was to attack American positions elsewhere. For the Russians, Vietnam represented an opportunity to restrain Chinese influence; for the Chinese, it meant that the U.S.S.R. and the United States should come to political if not military blows. From 1963 the Soviet leaders had been increasingly apprehensive that the Maoists intended them to risk or fight a nuclear war. The Chinese burst again into invective, denouncing "Khrushchevism without Khrushchev" as more hypocritical than Khrushchev had been, and sought to impose their policy by impeding Soviet arms deliveries across China.

It was not easy for the Maoists to explain this uncooperativeness and their refusal to join the Soviet Union in aid to North Vietnam (the Chinese did a good deal independently) except in the most doctrinaire terms. Most parties, especially in Europe, approved the Soviet middle course in Vietnam and also the relative patience and moderation of the Soviet leadership in the quarrel. In March, 1965, the Soviet party had enjoyed little support; only eighteen of twenty-six invited parties came to a Soviet-sponsored conference, Rumania and North Vietnam not responding; and they could agree on nothing except further consultation. Thereafter, the Soviets recovered much ground and succeeded in largely isolating the Maoists, who were driven to working with radical factions within parties or setting up splinter groups. Mounting Chinese charges of Soviet-American conspiracy, although not absolutely without foundation in view of the community of interests of the two, appealed to few of the old-line Communists, especially in the Western world, and the accusation of selling out Vietnam was less convincing coming from those who rejected proposals for united aid. The Chinese set themselves further apart by growing emphasis on guerrilla warfare, an approach understandable in view of the fact that this and propaganda were the only Chinese means of action, but one quite alien to the Leninist mentality.

In September, 1965, Lin Piao, the anointed successor of Mao, enunciated the non-Marxist interpretation of the global contest as the villages against the cities, the latter including Russia and America; the struggle was not even nominally to be of Marxist classes but of peasants. "The countryside, and the countryside alone, can provide the revolutionary bases from which the revolutionaries can go forward to final victory. . . . Taking the entire globe, if North America and Western Europe can be called 'the cities of the world,' then Asia, Africa and Latin America constitute 'the rural areas of the world.' "[27] In Chinese ideology, Marx and Lenin tended to disappear behind the swelling figure of Mao Tse-tung, for whom they became precursors and adulation of whose word was raised to incredible heights.

In 1966 the feud was intensified. The Chinese for the first time boycotted the (Twenty-Third) Soviet Party Congress. This, while piously expressing hopes for improvement of relations with the Albanian and Chinese parties, called for unity of action against them. Earlier, the Soviet leadership had told other parties that there was danger of an attack on the Soviet Union by Chinese communism, not American capitalism. In the summer, China went amuck in the so-called Great Proletarian Cultural Revolution. The causes were presumably mainly internal political;

---

[27] *Peking Review,* September 5, 1965.

but the Chinese were embittered by insecurity, isolation, and a sense of betrayal by the Soviet Union and the less radical majority of the world Communist movement; and their nerves were strained by the American military presence in Vietnam. As disorder swept China, all its latent xenophobia burst out, and the fury was directed most of all at the Russians to whom the Chinese had recently deferred. Soviet personnel were derided and manhandled. The Soviet embassy was for weeks besieged by a screaming mob of Red Guards, as though to provoke a break of relations. Trade between the two countries shrank to insignificance, only a twentieth of its value at the high point, 1959—by fault of the Chinese, the Russians claimed. The Chinese are more inclined than the Russians to let ideology and politics prevail over practical benefits.

In March, 1967, disputes over the transportation of Soviet war materials to Vietnam were settled by an agreement whereby Vietnamese officials took charge at the Chinese border. But nothing else could be resolved in the deep hostility of the giants. Even a common cause in Vietnam seemingly could not moderate it, as each accused the other of using the war for its own purposes at the expense of the Vietnamese. However, as attention turned from the war with the beginning of peace talks in 1968, antagonism became even fiercer. The language on both sides left little to be added. The Chinese condemned the Soviet invasion of Czechoslovakia more violently than the Western powers, although it was directed against the liberal-revisionist trends against which they had been thundering so furiously; and they were even moved to some friendly gestures toward Yugoslavia. They were so eager to fault the Russians that they accused them of such sins as encouraging religion. According to the Peking news agency: "To paralyze the revolutionary will of the Soviet people, the Soviet revisionist renegade clique brazenly prettifies religion and makes wide publicity about religious activities through its press and news agency. . . . *Komsomolskaya Pravda* has even published proposals for the reinstitution of religious education in schools. . . ."[28] Long having called the "Soviet revisionists" collaborators of "American imperialism," the Maoists raised the Soviet Union to the position of greatest enemy.

Soviet writers characterized Maoism as tyranny having nothing to do with communism. Thus *Pravda* spoke of it as a "great-power adventurous policy, based on a petty-bourgeois-nationalistic ideology hostile to Marxism-Leninism and proletarian internationalism . . . a prolonged reactionary campaign only disguised by 'leftist-revolutionary' phraseology, in reality directed to the establishment of a military-bureaucratic regime having nothing in common with the dictatorship of the proletariat, with the true ideals of socialism and democracy, with the real interests of the

[28] *Christian Science Monitor*, March 1, 1969.

Chinese people."[29] Rivaling the Maoists in irrationality, Russian spokesmen associate Maoism with American "ruling circles" and their anti-Soviet plotting and regard any hint of contact between Peking and Washington as proof of conspiracy.[30]

This verbal warfare was accompanied by friction along the Sino-Soviet frontier from the Pacific to Central Asia, and there were numerous incidents in 1968–69. There had been many exchanges of gunfire in earlier years, but they had been kept from the light of publicity. In March, 1969, however, the Russians chose to make an issue of a clash over a worthless island in the Ussuri river, between Manchuria and Siberia. Thirty-one Soviet border guards were reportedly killed, but the affair was clearly publicized beyond its intrinsic importance, if it was not (as each side accused the other) created for political purposes. It became subject of a massive propaganda campaign, with glory heaped on the heroic defenders of the motherland, who refused to abandon their posts even when sorely wounded, and abuse piled on the barbarous Chinese soldiers and the Maoist clique of traitors, helpers of the imperialists. The Chinese were treated not as ideological deviants but as a military danger and called "treacherous" (*verolomnyi*), an exceptionally strong word in the Soviet lexicon. The popular poet Yevtushenko compared the Chinese to the Mongol invaders of Russia. Brezhnev, speaking to the Communist leaders gathered in Moscow in June, 1969, made the condemnation of the "Maoist clique" official at the highest level. The Chinese regime, he said, was anti-Soviet and helpful to "imperialism"; and he warned of the danger of war.

In this propagandistic assault against Maoist China, the Soviet regime declined to mitigate its verbal hostility toward the West but continued to warn against its dire evils. The two fronts were used to reinforce each other, as Maoism was linked to Bonn and German revanchism or to American capitalism. The Chinese allegedly acted in concert with Bonn to distract attention from the provocatory holding of the presidential election in West Berlin.[31] The diplomatic reaction was entirely different. Soviet diplomats politely presented the Soviet case in all major capitals, and there was a perceptible warming toward both of the major Western antagonists.

It seemed that the Soviet Union and Communist China were propagandistically as useful to each other as America was to each of them. The rulers of Peking, who found the Soviet leaders "worse than tsars," called on their people to turn anti-Soviet sentiments to the raising of production. The incident also provided a suitable backdrop for the Chinese Party

---

[29] *Pravda*, January 11, 1969.

[30] *Pravda*, December 15, 1968.

[31] *Pravda*, March 14 and 18, 1969; *Sel'skaia Zhizn'*, March 19, 1969.

Congress, convened shortly thereafter. The Russians turned patriotic feelings and the defense of the sacred frontiers of the Soviet Union against an alien people into a stimulus of patriotism probably much more effective than outpourings against the iniquities of America. Anti-Chinese feeling was incidentally used to discredit nationalism by ascribing the Maoist evil to lapse from "proletarian internationalism." The Russians also seem to have taken it as a means of gathering more support among world Communist parties for the long-awaited conclave in June.

Neither side, however, had anything to gain from pushing the issue toward all-out war. The Chinese allowed the area to calm down and did not even press their broad claims to Soviet territory. The Russians refrained from using aircraft, supposedly from fear of complications. They made proposals for negotiations to demonstrate their reasonableness, although the harsh language used hardly seemed designed for reconciliation. After a good deal of hesitation, the Chinese agreed to hold discussions. Probably both sides desired neither war nor a real peace.

From the point of view of propaganda, the Russians seem to have had the better of it, mostly because the Chinese have done so much to isolate themselves by their immoderate statements and actions. They have even broken most of their links with the world Communist movement; the Russians have no need to seek formally to expel them. Such was the Chinese distrust of alien Communists that the foreigners who had gone to China to give themselves to the service of the revolutionary cause had by 1968 been nearly all expelled or jailed. At their anniversary celebrations in October, 1968, the Chinese could boast the support of only the Albanians and some trifling splinters. The Chinese Party Congress of April, 1969, had no foreign guests, in contrast to the Soviet practice of making party congresses as much as possible into international gatherings. The only foreign support which Lin Piao cited then was that of Albania.

In spite of this, the Russians had not quite given up the habit of regarding the Chinese as basically Communist, however deviant. In ideology, the two powers do not have a great deal in common, beyond some loosely used Marxist terminology, a commitment, weak on the Soviet side, to radical change in most of the world, and respect for Lenin, whom the Chinese still regard as a great leader betrayed by the successors who outwardly idolize him. To salvage something of Communist hopes, however, the Russians would still like to regard the Chinese as errant faithful who may yet return. The official position seemed to remain that stated by Kosygin in an interview for a Japanese paper at the beginning of 1969:

We consider that difficulties in Soviet-Chinese relations were created artificially and not by our fault. No matter how difficult the adjustment of our relations may seem, we view this process optimistically. The true interests of our peoples demand that the Chinese people should take its place in the united front of socialist peoples and all anti-imperialistic forces. . . . We are convinced that sooner or later the cause of Soviet-Chinese friendship will triumph."[32]

This bland and seemingly idle hope reflects the difficulty for the Russians of analyzing Maoism. Marxist categories do not apply; really to recognize the reality is to recognize the unrealism of the entire Marxist approach. It is far enough from Marx's scheme of history that a backward Asian country could come to socialism. It is still worse that after having done so, and now possessing a fair amount of industry and hence a proletariat, it should leave socialism for some nameless political condition or, remaining socialist, behave in a nationalist-chauvinist manner. It is also a serious reflection on the principles of Leninism to admit that a Communist party, a party long hailed as a great brother to the Soviet party, could lose its character of vanguard of the workers.

A difficulty hardly less severe for the Soviet analysts of Maoism is that nearly all the evils they perceive in it, from national selfishness to failure to hold democratic elections within the governing party, have their counterparts in Soviet practice. Soviet citizens do not have to be very perceptive to observe that such sins as suppression of the opposition, manipulation of public opinion, repression of intellectuals, and stirring of feeling against foreigners for political purposes are to be found in their homeland.

Probably for these reasons, there has been remarkably little theory in Soviet writing about China. It is simply treated as an unfortunate case of Mao and his coterie having gotten the better of and perverted the essentially virtuous Chinese Communist party. Translated into Marxist language, "The present situation in China is characterized by the open appearance of a contradiction between the social-economic basis, which rests on the social ownership of the means of production, and the political superstructure . . . military-bureaucratic dictatorship. . . ."[33] There is no explanation of how and why this contradiction of Marxist fundamentals should have occurred, although it has been recently discovered that the Maoist regime was never properly Marxist-Leninist but was always infected with alien reactionary or petit bourgeois ideology.[34] The obvious parallel with the Stalinist "cult of personality" is neglected. Nor is it made clear why the Maoists should be considered antisocialists, beyond the fact that they are, for reasons hard to penetrate, anti-Soviet. This seems to suffice, in conformity with the long-standing definition of a communist as one who supports the Soviet Union. In this regard, the Chinese have the advantage, as they cite evidence that the Russians have

---

[32] *Pravda,* January 5, 1969.

[33] E. Honecker, *Pravda,* May 16, 1969.

[34] L. P. Deliusin, *Voprosy filosofii,* January, 1969, pp. 87–98.

slipped back toward capitalism—unsocialistic inequality, ruble chasing, and bureaucratic degenerative tendencies.

The ultimate significance of the quarrel for the Soviet Union may lie in the fact that it cannot be accounted for in ideological terms and does not have to be. The more acute it becomes, the more ideology is pushed into the background. It has led the Russians to making quite unideological responses. Not only have they made the approaches previously mentioned to their favorite enemies but they have apparently made moves toward a *modus vivendi* with the fiercely anticommunist Chinese Nationalist government on Taiwan.

China represents a more visible and stirring danger for Russia than any capitalist power. The Soviet people are well aware that Siberia remains largely empty and has not been filling up in recent years, while China grows ever more crowded and supposedly land-hungry. The Chinese nuclear arm is potentially much more of a threat to Russia than to America, and in case of war the distant regions of Siberia might be difficult to defend. In response, the Russians seem to have shifted large military forces to the East-Siberian–Mongolian area, much as they did in the latter 1930's. The power of Communist China, more menacing to Communist Russia than to America, has brought about a qualitatively new and flexible world condition.

5. THE DECAYING MOVEMENT

The Soviet leaders are not so much champions of the underprivileged as successful administrators who wish maximum advantages for their state and maximum privileges for their children while themselves enjoying a good life. They have nothing to gain from radical change at home and little from disorders abroad except as these embarrass their rivals. They can expect less obvious benefit from the achievement of world communism than the United States might look forward to from the universal rule of liberal-capitalistic systems. An independent communist India or Germany would promise much trouble for the Russians, whereas making the whole world a free field for business would be most advantageous to the power which best excels in production. It is unrealistic, despite Marxist-Leninist phraseology, to expect the Soviet rulership to take any great interest in the promotion of change which they cannot control; and it is evident that they cannot control a state because it is communist unless there are forces of the Soviet state present, while they may come to exert a large degree of influence over a noncommunist state, such as the U.A.R.

The fading of optimism contributes to decline of interest; if Khrushchev may have been convinced in 1959 that the next generation of

Americans would live under communism, it was difficult for his successors a decade later to feel the same imperative of marching with history. Soviet statements looking to world communism as a goal have not had much more operative significance than American hopes, subdued in recent years, that freedom might triumph throughout the world. At the Twenty-Third Party Congress in 1966, the Cubans, with some of the same reasons as the Chinese for looking to advancement by violence, called on the Russians to support revolutionary movements. They received no encouragement; Brezhnev made it clear that the Soviet contribution to the world movement remained, as it had been since 1923 if not since 1918, the upbuilding of the Soviet Union.

Soviet diplomacy is very little concerned whether its actions are good or ill for a foreign Communist party. There has, moreover, been a substantial move toward gradualism. The Russians have credited their Revolution with helping the working classes of the West to electoral rights, education, and social welfare;[35] according to Suslov's analysis in May, 1968, the advanced industrial societies have taken a leaf from the Communist book in adopting direct and indirect state regulation and controls and thereby making real progress. Clearly, violent revolutionary action is dispensable. In token, the ritual formula was altered in 1967 from world revolution to world revolutionary transformation, an amorphous concept into which many ideas, as of change by economic or technical means, could easily be fitted.

Communist parties, at least where they can operate freely, have generally come around to seeking power within the system instead of trying to overthrow it entirely. But efforts to gain within the system have a further moderating influence, as any measure of success gives the party a stake in the political machinery, local offices, and the established order. Parties seeking to advance by peaceful or parliamentary ways must eschew extremism and violence and seek the favor of more or less of the middle classes by broad national appeals. Competition for votes of itself leads toward moderation, as appeals to be successful should be fairly broadly framed. Particularly in Western Europe, where unexampled prosperity has narrowed the appeal of economic radicalism, the Communist parties have for years invested much in qualifying to become part of the establishment. Rowdyism and disturbances are only a threat to their investment in a good image.

With the lack of international organizational unity it became somewhat unclear what constituted a Communist party. Communists could be distinguished from other socialists, Marxists, or sundry radicals not by greater revolutionary zeal but by loyalty to the Soviet Union. However, loyalty to the basically conservative Soviet state became inconsistent with

[35] Akhtamzian (ed.), *Istoriia mezhdunarodykh otnoshenii,* Vol. I, p. 17.

true radicalism. Like the Soviet regime, the parties found themselves growing older and stiffer, while tied to an ostensibly radical but outmoded doctrine. Hence, after decades during which it had been the firm principle of Communist parties to stand always on the extreme left, they found themselves outflanked by a New Left, somewhat as once radical Social Democratic parties fifty years ago found themselves outflanked (and pushed toward the center) by Leninist movements.

Those looking for a more exciting politics and desirous (they claimed) of destroying the old society root and branch, turned for inspiration to Mao, Ho Chi Minh, Che Guevara, and such militants. The rapidly growing non-Marxist but influential class of students played a large part in this radicalism. For them, although they usually paid some lip service to Marxism, the Soviet Union represented a bourgeois degradation, and Soviet ideology was staid and uninteresting, far from the new intellectual currents. The Soviet-affiliated Communists, for their part, had little understanding of this violent unrest and romantic revolutionism, which was contrary to their preconceptions. Anti-intellectual in temper since the rise of Stalin, they gave it little sympathy. Presumably the bourgeoisie were to blame. As a writer in *Pravda* put it, "Bourgeois ideologists" looking for new anticommunist arms "brought into play ultra-leftist, anarchist ideas, often echoing those of Mao Tse-tung, in an effort to cause confusion and disorient ardent but politically inexperienced young people, divide them and turn those who fall under their influence into blind tools of provocation."[36]

No Communist party was more taken aback by this development than the French. Gradually working its way out of the political wilderness into which it had been thrust in 1947 and approaching in 1968 a broad alliance with other leftist forces which might well return it to the government, the party strongly disapproved of the student riots in May of that year. When the student disorders grew into a general strike, the Communists had to try to place themselves in charge lest they forfeit entirely their claim to represent the working classes. Even so, they were wary of joining the hue and cry for de Gaulle to resign. According to a generally pro-Communist writer, Jean-Paul Sartre, the party "was not revolutionary. It was not even reformist."

In the ensuing electoral campaign, the Communist party received more than its share of the blame for riots and strikes because it, not the organizations of the ultraleft, was running for office. But it stood for order and sought to represent political responsibility. Its proposals for nationalization of industry were moderate; in agriculture, it advocated the protection of peasant private property against the inroads of large-scale enterprises. After severe electoral losses, the party seemed still more

[36] May 30, 1968.

opposed to leftism. Its leader, Waldeck-Rochet, took the very non-Leninist position that the workers did not want political revolution but material improvement. He denounced "the old anarchist theories of the so-called decisive role of active minorities," that is, Lenin's notion of the party. Such a party deserved to be Communist in the traditional sense only by virtue of continued affiliation with the Soviet Union.

The other Western Communist party of importance in the politics of its country, the Italian, has gone even farther down the road to social democracy. With no exciting or radical ideas, left behind by the extreme left, it enjoys a good deal of local and trade-union patronage. It has compromised both with the Catholic Church and with constitutional democracy. Asserting its complete autonomy within the world Communist movement, it recognizes the legitimate diversity of other parts of the socialist movement in Italy. It calls for no monopoly of political power but promises respect for freedom of ideas in a pluralist socialism. Intentions might change, of course, if the party actually attained power; but the image is very different from that which communism used to present as a matter of principle.

Another significant departure is that of the German party. Reconstituted in October, 1968, after years of prohibition, the German Communist party had nothing to say of dictatorship of the proletariat or overthrow of the social order but offered the ordinary fare of the established parties, reduction of working hours, Christmas bonuses, and rights of workers and students. The Finnish Communist party remarkably freed itself from Soviet domination as its Stalinist minority walked out of a congress. The reform leadership called not for "dictatorship of the proletariat" but "peace, democracy, and socialism," and sought to qualify itself for a larger share in a leftist government.[37]

In the underdeveloped world likewise, the Communist parties, at least those harkening to the voice of the Soviets, have gone far toward shedding the old revolutionary features which frightened the respectable world. In Asia, the Russians have reason to fear that a Communist thrust for power would benefit only the Chinese. It would be particularly distasteful for communism to arrive via a guerrilla movement, which is the only promising mode in Asian conditions. True communism in the old sense has there become Maoist rather than Leninist. The Russians have turned away from the "national liberation movements" of which Khrushchev was fond despite their noncommunist motives, to favor "revolutionary trends" in capitalism, which may be interpreted as moderate political evolution. This has become a serious issue between the Soviet Union and Castro, for whom revolution is to be made by violence in the underdeveloped world and who has denounced the indifference of Communist

---

[37] *New York Times,* April 23, 1969.

parties in countries where his guerrillas were struggling. Latin-American Communist parties, while somewhat embarrassed by the choice, have stayed fairly close to the Soviet plan, while extremists have spun off into Maoist or splinter groups. The situation in Chile is striking: the socialists are far to the left of the Communists and much closer to Castro. Many Chileans regard the Communist party as supercautious and unimaginative; idealistic young Marxists go elsewhere. The strength of the Communists lies in the financial support of Moscow, established positions in unions, and strong organization for winning elections.[38]

Unity has decayed along with radicalism. But, whereas the latter degeneration has corresponded to Soviet wishes, the former has occurred despite great emphasis on "coordination and unity of action of all sections of the Communist movement," as Suslov stated it in his May, 1968, speech commemorating the 150th birthday of Marx.[39] The utility of the Soviet ideology lies largely in universalism, the appeal of a philosophic certainty and the sweep of a great historical movement in the name of which power is justified over different nationalities and cultures. Division and controversy hopelessly batter the image of infallibility and perfection in the name of which the party governs the Russian domain and holds sway over Eastern Europe. Lenin insisted on conformity in the making of the Comintern; only those were admitted who were willing to subscribe completely. Stalin subjected the movement to truly military discipline, permitting no slightest deviation. But after Stalin, it became more and more difficult to keep the parties marching in straight formation and close step.

Although the inability to manage Yugoslavia caused political and ideological trouble, the disappearance of the awe-inspiring leader represented the first major weakening of bonds; and the ideological assassination of Stalin in 1956 was worse than his physical death. Khrushchev, not so imposing a figure and lacking the revolutionary and military aura of Stalin, could not fill his boots. Even as he sought to keep Communist parties synchronized, both ruling and nonruling parties began looking more to their own interests. Worst of all, the Chinese became a hostile alternative pole of attraction. Albania followed into the anti-Soviet camp, as did several Asian parties to some degree. Khrushchev was reluctant to try to dominate in the Stalinist manner but had some faith in the unifying virtues of ideology; consequently he several times organized world conferences. These, however, led to as much disharmony as concord; and his later purpose in proposing a general conclave was schismatic, the exclusion of the Chinese as heretics.

Khrushchev was not very tactful, and his changes of front were

[38] *New York Times,* September 2, 1968.
[39] *New York Times,* May 6, 1968.

sometimes hard for other parties to follow. His ouster, consequently, and the fact that his successors made practically no doctrinal innovations might have facilitated some restoration of unity. However, most parties were more or less displeased at his abrupt removal, concerning which they were not consulted and which seemed a bit arbitrary. He had built up good working relations with many foreign heads of parties. A number ventured, to the detriment of Soviet prestige, to criticize the move. They demanded explanations but received little satisfaction. The Italians even refrained from sending a delegation to the November celebrations shortly after his removal. For the second time in a little over a decade, also, the bloc had lost its leader. Khrushchev could not wear Stalin's mantle, but he was more impressive than the gray collective leadership which succeeded him and better able to claim doctrinal authority.

As a result, when the Soviets tried to gather representatives of world communism in March, 1965, the lack of support for the Soviet party was practically humiliating. A year later, at the Soviet Party Congress, the foreign delegations could agree on little but Vietnam, which rather fortuitously made a fine subject for emotional oratory and permitted some show of agreement. The Soviet party seemed to have little claim to leadership or special authority, as though ready to shed the responsibility of being more than the first among near-equals. In the cooling of evangelical fervor, the failure of revolutionary hopes, and the lack of a respected doctrinal authority, there seemed to be little left of the common faith except the negative view of capitalism as predatory, decadent, and responsible for the world's woes; some residual equalitarianism; and commitment to control of the economy and society by a Marxist party. On many matters, such as the need for violence, the role of the proletariat, or the assessment of Stalin, there was only disagreement.

There was lacking also an essential of a churchlike conglomerate of groups, an overall organization. Multilateral gatherings, so far as they included the extremists, were more loss than gain, as they served to air and perhaps accentuate dissidence. It became, of course, impossible to agree on any ground rules for a general conference acceptable to both the Chinese and Soviet parties. The front organizations of world communism, such as the World Federation of Trade Unions and the World Federation of Democratic Youth were also rent and made the stage of passionate denunciations and political infighting, which went far to discredit them and make them useless as means of gathering noncommunists behind Communist causes.

The successors of Khrushchev were willing to postpone if not give up entirely his plan of assembling an authoritative world gathering to tackle the divergence with China, presumably to expel the schismatics. They lacked adequate support; even parties which strongly disagreed with the Maoists did not wish to see the movement narrowed and discipline tightened; any excommunication would inevitably narrow their freedom. The Brezhnev-Kosygin regime also hoped by patience perhaps to win a moderation of the Chinese position or at least a larger degree of support from other parties. After the renewal of polemics, however, they were driven by the same logic that drove Khrushchev to seek exclusion of the Chinese. These continued their effort to split parties, an effort which could best be countered by revoking their license to speak as Communists. It seemed better to reassert some sort of control or at least uncontested leadership of a reduced group of parties than to see the broader movement threatened with complete disintegration in the face of the total hostility of the two leading parties.

It became an important Soviet objective to hold a meeting, which could not anathematize the Maoist heretics but from which they would angrily exclude themselves. In 1966 the Russians were able to muster the support of most nonruling parties, but only of half of the ruling parties; consultations followed consultations until it was agreed to set a date of November 25, 1968, for the conference. There were rising apprehensions, however, among the Western European parties as Soviet pressure on Czechoslovakia grew in the spring and summer. The action taken in Hungary in 1956 had caused misgivings, but it was patently to preserve the Communist system. In 1968 the Soviet Union was moving against a Communist party which was doing no more than what most parties wished for themselves. The French and Italian parties sought to restrain the Russians. A separate meeting of Western European parties was suggested to press for moderation; the French leader, Waldeck-Rochet, went to Moscow to offer mediation. Surprised by the invasion, nearly all the parties of Western Europe condemned it, some, as the Swedish and Italian, very energetically, others, as the French, with more reserve. It seemed for a time that the West European Communist movement might, as the Chinese had done, split quite away from Moscow.

In the face of this rebellion of the weak against the strong, the much-planned world conference had again to be put off lest it turn into an anti-Soviet demonstration. However, the Communist parties, having recovered from the shock of the Czech affair, did not wish to break bonds with the Russians. The latter, at another consultation at Budapest in November, secured the assent of nearly all for their long-planned conference; the only important holdouts were the British and Swiss parties. Only two delegates, it is said, raised the question of Czechoslovakia. After more than five years' gestation, the grand conclave was set for May, subsequently postponed to June.

There was nothing, however, except the struggle against imperialism which the parties could agree to place on the agenda, while many things divided them. A number wished to be reassured that the meeting would not be used to excommunicate the Chinese; parties fearful of coercion wanted only a broad and hence innocuous anti-imperialist conclave. Intervention in Czechoslovakia was not quickly to be forgotten. Many European parties, such as the Austrian, continued to condemn the occupation months afterwards, when the Czechs themselves no longer ventured to do so, and they were further discomfited in April, when the Russians forced Dubček from leadership in Prague. Worst from the Soviet point of view was the willfulness of the Italian party, largest outside the bloc and the one with best apparent chances of securing a share of power in an important country. The Italians, unlike their French comrades, were unwilling to drop the Czech issue but continued to accuse the Soviet Union of "violation of the fundamental principles on which the labor movement is based."[40] At their February, 1969, party congress, they went so far as to contrast their democratic socialism with the questionable Soviet system of rule over the bloc, and questioned the essence of Leninism by calling it "mystical" to assert that the party speaks for the people. On this occasion, the Soviet delegate ventured no condemnation. But when the Italian Communist organ, *Unità*, criticized the ouster of Dubček and pointed to the contradiction between intervention in Czechoslovakia and efforts to secure European detente, *Pravda* replied sharply, accusing the Italians of violating "proletarian internationalism."[41]

The outlook was consequently stormy when the world gathering finally assembled after still more preparatory meetings in March and May. But from the Soviet viewpoint, the poor state of the movement made remedial action the more necessary, and by skillful management they were able to achieve a good deal. Seventy-five parties were represented, a quite respectable number, although a little under the number at the 1960 conclave. The Chinese and their Albanian friends were absent, of course, as were the North Koreans and the North Vietnamese (who could not afford to offend Peking), and most nonruling Asian parties from Japan to Burma. The apprehensive Yugoslavs were also missing, but the Cubans sent an observer and Rumania participated fully. The sessions, which were closed but were reported in some detail in the Soviet press, were agitated only by Soviet standards of unanimity. Brezhnev proceeded, contrary to previous agreement, bitterly to attack the Maoists as splitters and enemies of the world socialist movement headed by the Soviet Union; he was compelled to do this, he said, by the anti-Leninist positions of the Congress of the Chinese Communist Party. Rumania's Ceausescu deplored, in the name of Communist unity, the attack on the Chinese. The Italian representative, Berlinguer, did likewise, but he softened his rebuke to the Russians by blaming the Chinese for equating Soviet policies with American imperialism and substituting Maoism for Marxism-Leninism. But a long string of

---

[40] *Le Monde*, November 5, 1968.

[41] April 17, 1969.

speakers supported the Soviet position, and a Soviet reader interested and patient enough to plow through the verbose declarations would easily conclude that the few critical remarks were out of step with the masses.

Perhaps the real purpose of raising the Chinese issue—concerning which no action was suggested—was to distract from the much more embarrassing question of Czechoslovakia. If so, it was reasonably successful. Such criticism as was expressed was cautious and mostly indirect. The Rumanians, in the most sensitive position, ventured only to stress that "independence and national sovereignty, equal rights and noninterference in internal affairs" are principles of equal validity with proletarian internationalism.[42] Berlinguer criticized the occupation in general terms and called for unforced unity on the basis of the "autonomy of individual parties." Only the Australians took a rather sharp position on the issue; the large majority either ignored Czechoslovakia (as the Czech leader, Husak, urged) or stood faithfully behind the Russians.

No party was evidently inclined to break away, but only to protect a degree of autonomy. In the end, nearly everyone signed the long declaration drafted in advance, a document of some forty pages of denunciation of the "imperialism" of the United States and its friends, and exhortations to proletarian solidarity. The Dominican party held out entirely, on the grounds that it was too mild, and fourteen parties for various reasons withheld assent to part or parts of it, among them the Rumanian, Spanish, Swedish, Swiss, British, Norwegian, Sudanese, and Cuban. The Australians and the Italians, who at one time indicated unwillingness to sign anything, accepted only the section attacking "imperialism." There was no attempt in the declaration to give the Soviet party a special place, and it paid the usual tribute to sovereignty and equality. But it also upheld the claims of "proletarian internationalism," to which all parties were held responsible.

This may have been the key element and reason enough for the Soviets to hail the conference as a glorious triumph. As understood by the Russians, loyalty to proletarian internationalism is practically equivalent to obeisance to themselves, especially as the majority of Communist parties are controlled by or dependent upon them, the many small and weak—usually illegal—parties as well as those of the satellite nations. Hence "proletarian internationalism" could be the potential cornerstone of a new Comintern. Something like this is clearly felt necessary; Stalin could make his puppets dance but the present regime, lacking charisma or ideological appeal, needs organization. Nostalgia for the Comintern was evident in the celebrations, in March, 1969, of the fiftieth anniversary of its founding. There were many eulogies of that futile organization; hitherto unpublished Comintern documents were brought out, amid indi-

[42] *New York Times,* June 10, 1969.

Tass-Sovfoto

Communist World Conference, 1969. Self-appointed representatives of the world's proletariats gathered in Moscow in June as the Soviet leaders sought to put the Communist movement back together. The setting was St. George's Hall at the Kremlin, replete with the glories of tsarist imperialism.

cations that something like it was required for the world struggle against "opportunism" and the coordination of the international contest.[43]

Perhaps the holding of conferences could gradually restore some organizational unity to the movement, or at least to a part of it; and a committee was set up, as the 1969 gathering dissolved, to prepare its successor. The Soviet rulership needs the world movement to uphold its legitimacy as master of a multinational realm, and it is prepared to do much to sustain the appearance of leadership of a universal working-class mission. The task, however, is complicated. Well over half the approximately ninety Communist parties of the world have less than 5,000 members, many of them less than 1,000, and have only propagandistic importance as a Soviet claque. Legal and important parties hopeful of electoral gains remain mostly wary of the Soviet embrace; the Italians particularly can hope to qualify themselves for office by independence. The Cuban party is faithful only so far as it needs Soviet economic and political support. The Chinese are increasingly divorced from Soviet-style Communism, but they are close enough to exert substantial influence on many, especially Asian, Communist parties; pro-Peking groups exist, according to Brezhnev's speech before the Moscow conference, in some thirty countries. The solid nucleus of the movement is only the Soviet bloc. Without the strong political interest of a superpower, there would be no Communist movement, and the movement's future depends on the ability of the superpower to give it cohesion and strength.

6. INTERVENTION IN CZECHOSLOVAKIA

Threats of Dissolution

In the first years of the Brezhnev-Kosygin period, the disintegration of world communism seemed a historical trend, gradual and irregular but irreversible; and it probably would have been irreversible but for the Soviet determination, in the summer of 1968, to halt it by force. Hopes that ideology and economic ties to the Soviet Union could counter permanently the influence of the West proved false. The strategy of proclaiming the free sovereignty of the satellites while the party enforced the class will for unity was inadequate without unified organization of force. As independence budded from 1965 to 1968, it seemed that the myth of national sovereignty might turn into reality, and this raised unknown dangers. Sudden release from a long period of unequal relations

---

[43] For example, Gus Hall in *Pravda,* March 6, 1969.

might bring a sharp reaction. Withdrawal, whether forced or voluntary, of Soviet power from Eastern Europe would be a body blow to the Soviet political system. To have allowed the satellite lands to develop independent socialism would have been to call the rationale of the Soviet Union itself into question.

The international situation was propitious for the stirrings of the satellites. The feud with China distracted attention and weakened Soviet moral authority, although after the split became definitive the Russians began thinking more of reaffirming their control where still possible. The Vietnam war brought a reduction of American interest in Europe and reduced the sense of insecurity of Eastern European governments and so their need to lean on the Soviet Union. In giving something of a common cause and in discrediting the leading Western power, it seemed to reduce the danger of any Eastern European country being drawn into an anti-Soviet alignment. If it was more difficult to improve relations with the United States, it was easier to move closer to Western Europe. American leadership in the West being questioned more than ever since the beginning of the cold war, the world seemed to be swinging away from bipolarity and opposing blocs.

The defection of France from NATO was an alluring example, and it offered the possibility of an opening to the West without going over to an adversary power. Britain seemed weakened, and West Germany, under a coalition government including the Social Democrats from 1966, adopted more conciliatory policies. To improve cultural, economic, and political relations with its natural hinterland, the Federal Republic offered diplomatic relations to the Soviet satellites—something attractive to most of them but correspondingly unattractive to Moscow. The idea of a strongly united, perhaps federalist Western Europe retreated before newly resurgent forces of nationalism. Indeed, as the United States engrossed itself in Southeast Asia and the Soviet Union turned cautiously inward, it was a time of released national feeling and decay of blocs; even the Afro-Asian world became more fragmented and incoherent as each country looked more to its own interests.

East Europeans seemed to feel themselves less members of a socialist camp and more Europeans and Rumanians or Czechs. Sentiments of nationality, shattered by the war and occupation, stifled by Stalinism, and partly released by Khrushchev, continued to grow at the expense of "proletarian internationalism" and in refutation of Marxist tenets. Old urges returned to the political foreground. Bulgaria, for example, began celebrating the Bulgarianism of Macedonia, a national aspiration since 1878. Russification was reduced, especially in Rumania and Hungary, but also to some extent in Czechoslovakia and Poland. Cultural exchange programs were less pressed. Countries shaped their Communist systems to meet their own tastes and needs.

To meet a popular demand and to facilitate modernization and economic improvement, governments opened doors to the West a little; but this taste only made the West seem more enchanting and belied official propaganda. Politically, most satellite regimes edged farther from the Soviet Union as they moved faster toward a degree of liberalization. They, unlike the Soviet elite, welcomed many formerly imprisoned leaders, now respected as defenders of a national interest, back to positions of authority; and stronger libertarian views were thus brought into the leadership. There were timid concessions to democracy in several countries, such as allowing voters to choose between party-approved candidates in some cases. There was some talk of making elections a real reflection of popular feeling. An example of the political divergence was that Hungary, with only 80,000 Jews, had a whole network of Jewish cultural institutions, while the Soviet Union, with some 2 million, permitted only a handful of synagogues.

The most compelling pressure was probably economic. Obviously, if trade were guided only by economic considerations, the East European countries would prefer to reorient much of their trade toward the West. As controls slackened, they looked more hungrily in that direction and resented that they were not able to deal more freely wherever they could find needed goods and technology. The influence of Western patterns also grew. From 1964, all Eastern European governments, taking a cue from the needs for change recognized in Moscow itself, began turning away from the Soviet model toward capitalist techniques, toward pragmatism and rationalization of their distorted economies. They began experimenting with use of profits, new accounting techniques, more autonomy for enterprises, and loosening of planning. Concepts ranged far ahead of realizations, which were hamstrung by bureaucratic conservatism and fears of loss of control. But the various countries were as never since World War II feeling their own way toward their own realizations instead of blindly following. They also conceived an urge to bargain more energetically for their own interests against those of the Soviet Union and to compare Soviet-bloc goods unfavorably to those available in the West. In a turnaround from the previous situation, the Russians began complaining that they were being underpaid for raw materials.

Only Yugoslavia was willing or able substantially to dismantle the planning structure, allow the market to determine most prices, and permit real freedom to producers to manage as dictated by economic considerations. There, small-scale private businesses were allowed, as in restaurants and artisan shops. Western publications were admitted with little hindrance, and Western investments were encouraged. Political freedoms were extensive. Although it was not permitted to start an opposition party, it was possible to criticize the heart of Leninism, the monopolistic party. Yet it was impossible to exclude from the bloc the example of a country being wooed. In 1964 Yugoslavia was given observer status in Comecon, and it became a member of some Comecon commissions. In 1966, at the Twenty-Third Congress, the Yugoslav delegates were treated as representatives of a full-fledged socialist country for the first time since 1948. Thereafter, the Yugoslavs have been considered a fraternal party, even when, as after the Czech intervention, they did not desire this honor. But it is very difficult to admit a deviant to the company without admitting deviations.

Still more serious was the willfulness of a country not on the edge of the bloc but in the middle of it, Rumania. Having carved out a large measure of independence under the somewhat irascible Khrushchev, Rumania seems to have been encouraged to grasp still more from his less dynamic successors, the more so as one of the charges leveled against Khrushchev was that he had tried to press Comecon specialization improperly on that country. Still playing Chinese against Russians, Rumania in December, 1964, expressed "understanding" for Chinese nuclear ambitions and was counted as leaning to the Chinese side of the dispute. In March, 1965, the architect of Rumanian independence, Gheorghiu-Dej, died, but his successor, Ceausescu, was at least equally nationalistic. Rumania stayed away from the party meeting in 1965, began hinting of the need for loosening the Warsaw Treaty Organization, made some moves toward liberalizing the economy, and developed better relations than ever with the West. At the 1965 Party Congress, Ceausescu spoke of industrialization insuring national sovereignty and called resolutely for the abolition of all military blocs. At the anniversary celebrations, the Soviet delegates were galled to see delegates from China and Albania, which had abated no whit of their hostility, given courtesies equal to those shown themselves.[44] If there were few hard words between Rumania and the Soviet Union it was only because the latter seemed to accept Rumanian terms for cooperation.

Rumania did not resist the temptation to raise occasionally, although tactfully, the Bessarabian question. A more serious act of defiance was the establishment of diplomatic relations with West Germany, contrary to Soviet policy. Rumania also tried Soviet patience by rejecting the Soviet line of total condemnation of Israel for the June, 1967 war; Rumania alone retained normal relations with that nation. In July West German and Rumanian companies were planning a pioneer capitalist-communist project to build a petrochemical plant in Pakistan. Rumania was critical of the nuclear nonproliferation treaty, on which the Soviet Union laid considerable stress. Although the Rumanians continued to pledge loyalty to the Soviet connection, their actions had become such that, reportedly,

---

[44] David Floyd, *Rumania, Russia's Dissident Ally* (New York: Frederick A. Praeger, Inc., 1965), p. 120.

Rumanian diplomats in Moscow were subject to the same surveillance as those of Western countries.

Confronted with this troublesome situation, unaccountable as it was in the ideological framework, the Brezhnev-Kosygin government seemingly had little idea of doing more than avoiding trouble and, as Khrushchev before, trying to patch a bit their political edifice in Eastern Europe. They hoped, not entirely without reason, that relaxation of demands for conformity make possible the preservation of fraternal bonds. Perhaps because of the slowdown of economic growth in the Soviet Union and throughout the bloc, they were less inclined than Khrushchev to rely on economic integration to bring political unity as Marx had postulated. They wished to activate and overhaul Comecon to overcome the difficulties of separate national planning, but this prospered no better than before. It was not even possible to bring about mutual convertibility of currencies through a Comecon bank. For a socialist economy, economic planning is the largest aspect of sovereignty; and the satellites were loath to surrender it.

The new Soviet leadership, in a reversion to Stalinist spirit, laid more stress on military integration through the Warsaw Treaty Organization. They moved more firmly than Khrushchev had done to modernization and standardization of weaponry throughout the bloc and training the satellite armies in joint maneuvers.[45] Plans may have been drawn for the wartime incorporation of East European armies into Soviet army groups. But there was no sharing of nuclear weapons, and Soviet officers kept all important command posts.[46] Increasingly restive satellites were restive allies; Rumania held back, as in Comecon, refusing to participate in some meetings and all maneuvers. The WTO seemed, as in fact it was, a threat to liberalization and a token of Soviet power to countries which mostly wanted more of the one and less of the other.

It should not be inferred that, as of the middle of 1968, all the satellite countries were feverish to break bonds with Russia. None of the governments desired to move away from alignment with Moscow; they only wished, to varying degrees, for more latitude for themselves. Bulgaria, highly dependent economically on Moscow, aware of traditional kinship with Russia, innocent of democratic experience, and little exposed to the liberal advanced West, seemed satisfied to do the Soviet will. A slight nationalist stirring in 1965 was easily repressed. The Rumanians seemed pleased with their substantial freedom and good relations with both the West and the Soviet Union, to which they paid the homage owing to

---

[45] T. Wolfe in A. Dallin and T. Larsen (eds.), *Soviet Politics since Khrushchev* (Englewood Cliffs, N.J.: Prentice-Hall, Inc., 1968), p. 124.

[46] Andrew Gyorgy, "Diversity in Eastern Europe: Cohesion and Disunity," *Canadian Slavic Studies,* Vol. I, No. 1 (Spring, 1967), p. 34.

power. The Kadar government in Hungary had fairly well settled down to its compromise of accepting the Soviet protectorate in defense and foreign affairs in return for a degree of autonomy. In a relaxed atmosphere, wherein almost anything not overtly hostile to the regime was permitted, most people were thankful that the situation was so much better than it had been before 1956.[47]

Polish Communists allowed themselves to be persuaded, as a sector of Polish political leadership had come to feel before 1914, that their future inevitably lay with Russia against Germany. The nationalistic sector of the party, the Partisans, were not more but less liberally inclined than the Muscovites led by Gomulka. The Ulbricht regime most of all rested on Soviet support and was consequently determined to uphold ideological conformity and keep its distance from everything that smacked of liberalism. The Czechs, if they had begun to dream of a democratic, free, and humanitarian communism, did not conceive that this should be injurious to the Soviet bloc; perhaps, rather, it would enable them to take the leadership in improving it.

But the trends were disquieting. The kind of liberalization which seemed on the way in parts of Eastern Europe was incompatible with the Soviet political system, as was real national independence or a consultative-cooperative system of equal powers. Yet it was impossible at once to bind Eastern Europe to the Soviet Union and exclude its influence. More bonds meant many more areas of contact between Soviet and satellite citizens and opportunities for infection or at least erosion of ideology. To counter nationalist-divisive tendencies, it was necessary to reinforce an ideology of "proletarian internationalism" which was losing ground in the Soviet Union and becoming increasingly empty and lifeless in Eastern Europe. Consequently, a new note appeared in the first half of 1968. The cardinal ideological sins had long been dogmatism and revisionism, emphasis swinging from one to the other according to the needs of the day. Now nationalism was placed ahead of these as the main enemy.

Democratic Communism

It is possible that if change in Eastern Europe had come gradually and smoothly in an atmosphere of general detente, the Russians would never have perceived the occasion nor the need to intervene forcibly to bring it to a halt. If this had been the case, the Soviet empire might have been slowly dissolved, like the British and French empires. But if the British could feel fairly safe in releasing control of alien overseas peoples, there was no place where the Russians could easily draw a line. If Czechoslova-

---

[47] H. Klocke, in D. S. Collier and Kurt Glaser (eds.), *Elements of Change in Eastern Europe* (Chicago: Henry Regnery Co., 1968), p. 167.

kia moved away, this menaced the Soviet position in Hungary and elsewhere. Broad retreat would threaten loss of East Germany, Poland, and the entire Soviet strategic position won in World War II. If these Communist countries could go their own way, the demand of the Ukraine and other parts of the Soviet Union for an indefinite degree of autonomy might be difficult to resist. Moreover, in the first half of 1968, change did not creep over Czechoslovakia with unalarming slowness but swept up like a conflagration, frightening those who saw their kind of political system suddenly questioned and shaken in its foundations. There was no pausing for digestion, but appetites for reforms grew as they were fed; and those who observed with amazement, either from East or West, could only guess where it would end.

Perhaps the Czech spring of 1968 would have been less like the breaking of an ice pack if there had been an earlier thaw. But after the riots of 1953, the Czechs were quiet under an exceptionally conformist and Stalinist government. Purges continued a year after the death of Stalin. The rumblings of 1956 in neighboring Poland and Hungary did not echo in Prague. Stalin's statue overlooked the city until late in 1961. The rehabilitation of purge victims began only in 1963; and de-Stalinization left untouched the hard core of the party around Novotny. In the second half of 1964, Czech writers and movie makers acquired a good measure of freedom, the result of which was the appearance of many works and films of bold conception and artistic excellence. By 1966 Czech literature and art were fairly free as long as they did not positively challenge the regime. The ouster of Khrushchev was a blow to the standing of the colorless Novotny, his personal friend; and discontent of the Slovaks, an old theme in Czechoslovak politics, was building up into a political opposition.

The intellectuals' call for fuller reforms and the demands of the Slovaks caused a growing ferment in 1966 and 1967. The party took punitive measures against writers and students but without sufficient determination to cow them. The prestige of Novotny sank until by November his ouster was rumored. Concerned by the agitation, Brezhnev went to Prague to help the harassed leader. Apparently perceiving the discontent as only an internal political squabble, he washed his hands of it and told the Czech comrades it was their affair. There followed a battle between hard-liners and reformers in the party directorate, in the course of which Novotny tried to mobilize the army and police forces to save himself. The ground was slipping from beneath him, however; on January 5, 1968, he was replaced as party secretary by Alexander Dubček.

By 1968 there had come forward a generation for whom Munich and the claim that the Soviet Union had been prepared to defend Czechoslovakia while the Western powers betrayed it was only history. Memory of the German occupation and of the expulsion of the Sudentenlanders faded, and with them fears of German aggression; memories of the repressions of 1949–54 were closer and keener. Those educated under communism largely accepted the values it proclaimed, but they were ready to ask why the regime did not conform to them, why noble aims should be incompatible with freedom, and whether the national sovereignty and equality of which much was said should not be real. The national aspiration to change was so broad that only a few of the police and old-line party men seem to have remained untouched by it and so deep that any concession made more reforms in order. The best way, it seemed the only way, for the Communist party to govern was by going with the tide.

Movement toward reform was rapid following the installation of Dubček as party leader. Adherents of Novotny lost their positions, and the upper party leadership was renovated and rejuvenated. Censorship was relaxed, then made inoperative by the censors themselves, and finally abolished by law. The Czech press and television rapidly cast aside their conformity and dullness to enjoy an emotional outburst of freedom, questioning and commenting with much skill and interest. Some reputations were dashed and others restored. The case of Jan Masaryk, who had died mysteriously not long after the take-over of 1948, was brought up, and the official party newspaper found evidence of Soviet guilt in his death and in the victimizations of the purges. Liberalization of the economy came to the fore, and radical innovations were mooted. There was a questioning of ideological tenets; some ventured to suggest that Leninism was not of universal validity but especially suited to Russian conditions.

Although leaders underlined continued adherence to the Soviet alliance, Czechs began hoping for closer relations with the West to help revive the sluggish economy. There were demands to reduce politically dictated commitments under Comecon, and talk of loans from the West. Bonn offered to negotiate a declaration of absolute nullity of the Munich agreement. Czechoslovakia desisted from the Soviet program of military aid to Nigeria and began instead to furnish civilian relief to Biafra. The churches were released from restrictions, and Czechs were given full freedom to travel to the West. Democratic elections, freedom of association, and real parliamentary government were all on the agenda. In the general exhilaration, May Day became a genuine popular festival, and the Dubček regime enjoyed the fullest and most unforced popularity any Communist government has ever held. Toward the end of June a group of intellectuals called for true and rapid democratization, with removal of all the leftovers of repression.

The Czech government dissociated itself from the radicals and urged calm and patience. But the ferment awakened deep misgivings in Moscow, and the Russians began to build, as though instinctively and without plan, counterpressures. *Pravda* began answering Czech critics with invective, although the Soviet public was told practically nothing of the Czech reforms; and denunciation of nationalism became the ideological theme of the day. Much was made of alleged dangers of West Germany taking over Czechoslovakia. In May, there were Soviet troop movements near the Czech borders; but the Soviets disavowed any intention of intervening. Kosygin went to consult with the Czech leaders and secured their consent to Warsaw pact maneuvers in Czechoslovakia. These were supposed to be only "communication exercises" beginning June 22 and ending June 30, but more troops than expected entered Czechoslovakia and they did not leave the country when their time was up. Sometimes crossing and recrossing the border, they seem to have been intended to intimidate but probably served more to irritate and increase Czech determination to be masters of their own house. The Soviets and their most faithful allies, the East Germans and Poles, protested the course of affairs and more insistently demanded that Czech "reactionaries" be curbed lest Czech independence be endangered. The Czechs were strongly supported by Rumania and Yugoslavia, forming a curious revival of the Little Entente of forty years earlier. West European Communist parties, seeing the Czech experiment as evidence of the compatibility of communism and democratic freedoms, expressed solidarity and tried to dissuade the Russians from choking it. When the Soviet press cited the "world press" in support of its position, it was limited to East Germany, Poland, Bulgaria, Hungary—which was least enthusiastic—and Mongolia; so far had Soviet sway diminished.

In the middle of July, the leaders of the Soviet Union and its four supporters in Europe met in Warsaw to discuss the case. The Czechs were invited but declined to appear as defendants before the self-appointed judges. These sent to the Czech party a remarkable letter full of a pained sense that communism is incompatible with freedom even after twenty years of indoctrination and energetic suppression of capitalism. Warning that the Soviet Union could not permit the socialist camp to be breached "peacefully or forcefully, from without or from within" and that in Czechoslovakia "the counterrevolution takes one position after another," it flatly demanded the restoration of dictatorship—the suppression of "antisocialist organizations," control of the press, and firm rule by the party—all while proclaiming noninterference in Czech affairs.[48]

The letter called for "healthy forces" in the Czech party to take action. Possibly, the Russians contemplated intervening on behalf of a loyal section of the party. But Soviet attempts to generate support were remarkably unsuccessful, and the Czech leadership could rightly respond that any return to the old ways would be opposed by "an overwhelming majority of party militants, workers, farmers, and intellectuals." Far from

[48] *Pravda*, July 18, 1968.

wishing to destroy their own authority, the Czech leaders walked a tightrope in trying to reassure the Russians that communism was not in danger, while meeting the demands of the people who were clamoring for ever more freedom and cheering resistance to Soviet pressures.

On July 23, the Soviet government announced large-scale maneuvers to be held in proximity to Czechoslovakia. A few days later, after the Czechs had refused an invitation to Moscow, Czech and Soviet leaders met at a town on the border. This was a unique encounter of practically the entire Soviet Politburo with the Czech party Presidium, an indication of the importance the Russians attached to the matter and a novelty in diplomatic practice corresponding to the unconventional nature of relations between Czechoslovakia and the Soviet Union, relations more of parties than governments. Speeches were made like those of a debating society, it was reported, and tempers were lost during three dramatic days. Then the Soviet party seemed to have retreated from its exigencies, admitting the right of the Czechs to continue democratization. The last Soviet troops left Czechoslovakia, and the Soviets hailed the meeting as strengthening proletarian solidarity and ceased polemics. A joint declaration of the party leaders of the WTO (except Rumania) at Bratislava reaffirmed the right of each country to manage its own affairs.

Czechoslovakia was thus recognized as a member of the community, and its critics were silenced. Although the agreement was somewhat ambiguous, it seemed as though the Russians, having met a unanimous rebuff and perceiving the firm Czech will to independence, unwilling to offend world opinion and the strong feelings of most foreign parties, bowed to opposition. The Czechs continued developing Western contacts and preparing for democratic renewal of party bodies, which would sweep out the remaining hard-liners under new party rules. Tito was received in Prague with great public enthusiasm, as was Ceausescu shortly afterwards. The crisis was apparently ended, and one might guess that Czechoslovakia would become fully democratic and consequently cease in all probability to remain in any way subordinate to the Soviet Union, or that the Soviets would by political and economic means pull it back to a fair degree of conformity as freedom lost charms of novelty and practical politics returned to command.

Invasion

It may be that the Soviet rulers decided, at their confrontation, not to come to terms with the stubborn Czechs but to remove the incorrigibles by surprise. If so, subsequent declarations and appearances of normalization were only intended to make surer that no resistance would be organized. Whenever the decision was taken, intervention came totally without warning. About the middle of August, there were a few critical articles in the Soviet press but nothing suggestive of an ultimatum. *Pravda* of the day before the invasion contained not a word to prepare the Soviet people for such a step. Dubček received a letter from Brezhnev at the very time Soviet troops were landing at the Prague airport and tanks were smashing across the borders; it accused the Czechs of permitting persecutions of pro-Soviet workers but held no hint of invasion.

Thrusting from all directions, in the night of August 20–21 some 200,000 soldiers entered Czechoslovakia with exceptional speed and efficiency, as though in continuation of the maneuvers on which they had long been engaged—their ability to take a country by surprise was a jolt to the West. The bulk of them Russian, they were joined by a few divisions of East Germans, Poles, some reluctant Hungarians, and a symbolic contingent from Bulgaria. This idea was possibly borrowed from the American intervention in the disorders of the Dominican Republic in 1965, when United States forces were joined by those of five Latin-American nations. It helped to internationalize the undertaking and give it a flavor of cooperative enterprise, and it deflected some of the Czech bitterness. The powers assisting the Russians had all been against Czechoslovakia in the Munich crisis thirty years earlier (except for the incidental participation of Bulgaria). The Soviet Union was perhaps using national antagonisms to reinforce proletarian internationalism. Throughout the crisis the East German regime had been strongest for intervention; not only did it have the most to fear from liberalization, but Germans under a Russian protectorate were most likely to take pleasure in the frustration of Czech dreams of independent development.

Czech forces offered no resistance. Very likely, many or most officers would have found it hard to fight forces with which they had been closely associated for twenty years. Soviet forces quickly swarmed over airports and cities and most strategic buildings, with only sporadic clashes with civilians and only a few score fatalities. There was some collaboration of members of the Czech security forces, which had long worked closely with the Russians and which the Dubček government had been unable to purge; and sundry officials, such as former censors, and some of the conservatives still in high places may have had advance information of the action. But contrary to the Russians' expectations, no respected figures came forward to form a new government after Dubček and his fellows were led away from their offices at gunpoint.

In the next few days, popular repugnance for the invaders seems to have been as total as could be aroused when a foreign army floods over a proud country. Crowds swarmed over tanks. Street and road signs were removed, and no one would give the occupiers directions. Clandestine radio stations took over the task of directing resistance. More than twelve hundred of fifteen hundred delegates elected to the party congress scheduled to convene in September met secretly in a factory, in a better than

Wide World Photos

Soviet troops occupy Prague—August, 1968. When the Russians moved to repress Czechoslovakia's attempt to liberalize communism, they met passionate and nearly unanimous repugnance from the citizenry.

Leninist manner, and elected a new and liberal central committee. Spat on and reviled, the occupiers could find no one to sell them a glass of beer.

For a few days the country lay paralyzed. The president, the aged General Svoboda, flew to Moscow (where he was humorlessly received with full state honors) and demanded restoration of the government of Dubček. To this the Russians agreed, apparently reluctantly and after a good deal of bullying. Dubček, whom the Soviet press had hastily branded as a traitor, was released. With his government the Russians made an outwardly rather mild agreement: the legal government would be retained; Soviet forces would be withdrawn in step with the "normalization" of the country; the Czech leadership would take suitable measures to strengthen socialism. The Soviets expressed approval of the Czech liberalization program, and they pledged noninterference in the internal affairs of Czechoslovakia. These phrases, however, were entirely subject to Soviet interpretation, while the liberal and popular Czech leaders were given the task of satisfying the Soviet masters. "Normalization," which meant strong evidence of fidelity to the Soviet Union and its political style, was to be the prerequisite for relief from the occupying armies. This relief, in any case, was to be only relative. The Czechs were given to understand only vaguely that they might have their freedom back in return for good behavior. But a few weeks later the seal was placed on the Czech condition by a treaty permitting the indefinite presence of Soviet troops, free to enter or leave the country at Soviet discretion. The majority were withdrawn, and all those of the lesser occupying powers, but enough remained to exert continual pressure, and behind them always lay the threat of a new and worse occupation of the cities.

The Soviet Decision

The course of Soviet foreign policy up to the middle of 1968 was mostly what would be expected of bureaucratic committee government: few initiatives, none spectacular; a cautious and temporizing approach. On this basis in May of that year most observers felt fairly sure that the Soviets would not resort to force to bring the Czechs to heel but would avoid the opprobrium which came from the Hungarian invasion. It seemed clear that the Czech development, led by the Communist party, was not an effort to reject communism and the Soviet alliance. The Czechs made every effort to avoid the fatal mistake of the Hungarians in seeking to abandon WTO; and even the radicals asked that the renovation come through, not against, the ruling party. Moreover, it seemed that the Russians had ample means, economic and probably political, of exerting quiet pressure on Czechoslovakia and in due course braking the reforms or reversing them. Czechoslovakia was economically completely dependent on Soviet supplies, as well as markets for a great deal of production unsalable in the West. It would have been fully in character for the Brezhnev-Kosygin government to take the smoother and less risky approach.

The Soviet leaders may, however, have reflected that economic boycotts and similar measures were ineffective against Yugoslavia, China, and Albania. These countries were much less dependent on the Soviet Union than Czechoslovakia, but the latter had better relations with the West and could expect much more assistance if it chose to break away. Moreover, the Soviet leaders felt pressed for time. In the first days of September, a new Czech Party Congress was to meet, and this would remove most of the remaining friends of the Soviet system from the upper echelons. The Ministry of the Interior would be purged of friends of the Soviet Union. There seemed a likelihood that pro-Soviet generals might be removed from command. The Soviet forces could no longer count on even a few well-placed collaborators; and invasion would be more difficult, perhaps openly resisted by Czech armed forces. It must have seemed more dangerous to wait. The Brezhnev-Kosygin team was more prudent than Khrushchev, but it had less faith in economic modes of action and the unifying power of the Communist ideal. If they had felt, as Khrushchev did, that theirs was really the wave of the future, they would hardly have stooped so to sully the Soviet record.

No doubt they recognized the gravity of the situation. The economic importance of Czechoslovakia to Soviet Europe was enormous, as was its military importance, since it lies in the very center of Europe between Russia and Germany. This may have been decisive; it is said that Suslov, the ideologist concerned with the world movement, was opposed to the use of force, while the marshals, more aware of strategic than political realities, insisted that it was necessary to assure the integrity of WTO. It was an absurdity to accuse the Czechs of wishing to subject themselves to the Germans, but it was unpalatable that they might normalize relations. Letting Czechoslovakia go implied a loosely bound Eastern Europe, wherein German might compete with Soviet influence, and the signs of an entente among Yugoslavia, Rumania, and Czechoslovakia seemed sinister to the Russians. The collective leadership seems to have been less able to resist pressure of the military interest, and with decreased confidence in peaceful means, had less will to do so. Shortly before the invasion, the conservative high command showed its temper by the replacement of the commander of WTO exercises in Czechoslovakia by General Shtemenko, an outright neo-Stalinist.

The Soviet leaders were less prepared to witness a deviant evolution of Czechoslovakia because they had already suffered the Chinese schism. There being a second world center of communism, a third, with Czechoslovak communism showing its affinity for West European, would be intolerable; that the French and Italians interceded on behalf of the

Czechs may have only raised Soviet suspicions. These were certainly heightened by the popularity of Dubček and his government. A government that did not have to rely on monopoly control of information and constant vigilance of the security forces simply was not a Communist government in their understanding. Its popularity was also dangerous because it gave a basis for true independence of the Soviet Union; and if the people of a democratic Czechoslovakia should demand an independent foreign policy, no given promises could hold the government.

As Marxists, moreover, the Soviet leaders could not grant any depth and sincerity to the Czech movement. They could visualize it, on the basis of doubtless distorted information, only as the result of evil machinations of some kind of class and imperialist enemy, whose success was a measure of the weakness and lack of vigilance, perhaps corruption, of the Czech party. The entire affair was the more disconcerting as Czechoslovakia had been something of a model in the Communist world, an advanced country where Communist power had come most nearly by democratic process. The Russians had reasons enough to fear fundamental changes in the nature of communism in Czechoslovakia. If Prague could prove that communism was really compatible with democracy, this might be as ominous for Soviet bureaucratic authoritarianism as though it rejected communism entirely. The Brezhnev-Kosygin directorate represents above all the apparatus, and the apparatus saw its title to power called into question. There is a certain brittleness in the Soviet order, which, however powerful and imposing, might collapse if the linchpin of faith were lost, as when the party suddenly lost control in East Germany in 1953 and in Hungary in 1956.

Not only was the Czech deviation threatening to the East European heritage but to the order of the Soviet state itself. The Russians betrayed their worry over "creeping subversion" and the insidious infiltration of noncommunist ideas, a fear which was once largely that of the West toward bolshevism, and it was feared that the contagion might infect millions of Soviet citizens and make ever so much more difficult the task of government. Scientists and intellectuals, already unruly, would be tremendously moved by the example of full freedom in a Communist country, and Marxist indoctrination could raise no bars to dialogue with it, as it could and does against Western intellectual influences. How strong the potential urges of Soviet masses for more political participation may be, no one in the West (and perhaps no one in the East) can really tell, but it is undoubtedly enough to worry the holders of power, and they could be sure that a democratic Czechoslovakia would give it the richest nourishment. The sclerosis of doctrine is such that attractive new ideas, such as a democratic and humane communism, the realization of Lenin's dream, might gather the force of a storm; and the bureaucratic reaction is to halt the infiltration instead of searching for reinvigoration at home.

The Czech example was more infectious because of cultural proximity. The Rumanians could be viewed more tolerantly because they did little to make their system more attractive; they expressed mostly a nationalist self-will which spoke seducingly only to a relatively small number of Rumanian-speaking Bessarabians. The Czechs are Slavs, and their language is fairly easily understood, at least by Ukrainians. Hence, on July 26, Soviet tourists were stopped from traveling to Czechoslovakia. There were attacks on the old danger of "bourgeois nationalism" in the Ukraine, and Czech papers were excluded—not long after some Western noncommunist newspapers had been admitted in small quantities.

Apparently the most crucial point was that Czech success would have fired aspirations of the Soviet minorities, especially the Ukrainians. Contrary to the practice of Khrushchev's day, few speeches, even expurgated, were published which might indicate at least some of the issues; however, the list of speakers at a Central Committee plenum called specifically to discuss the Czech question[49] gives a strong hint. Of fifteen party bosses named, three represented the Ukraine or parts of it, and three represented other minority areas known to harbor discontent, Latvia, Lithuania, and Kazakhstan. Two, the representatives of the Writers' Union and the Academy of Sciences, were concerned with problems of the intelligentsia. One, the head of Tass, might be expected to have spoken of foreign reaction, while four represented Russian regions. Shelest, the Ukrainian proconsul, was said to have been most determined to bridle the Czechs bordering on his province.

The Czech example might abet subversive influence among any nationalities, and more among those facing west; according to reports of travelers, the people of Lithuania became much more self-assertive at the time of the Czech ferment. But the problem of the Ukraine was the gravest. The Ukrainians are by far the most numerous of the Soviet nationalities, and they have long been inclined to believe that their powerful industrial plant contributed more to the general economy than it received in return and to resent that their future is largely decided by Russians in Moscow. In 1967 and 1968, there were many protests, on subjects varying from religion and the muzzling of thought to the prohibition of Western musical styles; and scores of intellectuals seem to have been arrested. Although the Ukraine has not had much independent history since prior to the Mongol invasions and has been joined to Muscovite Russia since the middle of the seventeenth century, it has a far sounder basis for nationalistic aspirations than, for example, Scotland or Wales, where the modern

---

[49] *Pravda,* July 18, 1968.

mood has fired substantial urges to autonomy. Yet, if concessions were made to the Ukraine, it would be hard to deny similar ones to other Soviet minorities, and the entire structure of the Soviet state might be deeply altered or broken entirely.

In this situation, the Czechs were so bold as to attempt to speak directly to the Ukrainians across the border, with broadcasts not only in Czech and Slovak (nearer than Czech to Ukrainian) but also in Ukrainian itself, invitations to Ukrainians to visit Czechoslovakia, and playing up to Ukrainian pride.[50] It is understandable that Shelest in July warned "certain fraternal parties" that "proletarian internationalism cannot be equated with the independence and equality of nations."[51] This must be taken to mean that in the bloc there could be no independence beyond what the Soviet Union might see fit to allow, which is what Brezhnev said in justification of the invasion.

The Soviet leadership thus had very compelling motives to intervene. It was probably also encouraged to do so by an optimistic assessment of the prospects. If the Czechs, with a fairly large and well-equipped army, had been determined to go down fighting, this very likely would have deterred the Soviet leaders, as the consequences in and outside the bloc would have been incalculable and the action would have been very difficult to explain to the Soviet soldiers and people. But they seem to have had good reason to expect no military opposition. It was reassuring that the United States almost ostentatiously disinterested itself from the fate of Czechoslovakia; unless the American position should change radically, the Russians knew they need fear little more than verbal slaps from the West. Moreover, the Soviet military buildup had proceeded sufficiently that the Russians could act with more confidence within the generally recognized Soviet sphere than in 1956. Less accurately, the Soviet leaders seem to have been badly misled about the temper of the Czech people. It was not easy for them to admit even to themselves that many years of propaganda should not have brought the Czech masses basically to their side. The agitation must be the work of a few malcontents if not imperialist agents. The Soviet ambassador in Prague seems particularly to have led the Russians to expect a warm welcome. The lack of political preparation for a pro-Soviet government may have been due to this optimism; if numerous Czechs would rally to the Soviet standard as soon as it appeared, there was no reason to try to organize a replacement regime in advance.

Although there must have been some wishful thinking, it is difficult to say that the Russians made a mistake, from their imperial point of view, in

[50] *Christian Science Monitor,* November 5, 1968.

[51] *Le Monde,* September 12–18, 1968.

deciding to use force. They lost a good deal in prestige around the world, but prestige is a somewhat vaporous possession. They assured themselves of permanent control of Czechoslovakia; if the people were unhappy, the Russians have dealt with discontented minorities before and with patience could expect to master the situation. The examples of Poland and Hungary were highly encouraging. In the permanent presence of Soviet power, people might be left sufficient local autonomy to assuage feelings while the Soviets slowly solidified political control and brought the one-time dissident countries closer to the common pattern. To have admitted the Czech deviation would have been to have sanctioned all manner of deviationist tendencies; in crushing it, the Soviet regime immediately and firmly dampened the agitation which was becoming troublesome. The Czech intervention was basically defensive, aimed not at changing the power balance, as the Russians reassured the West, but at preserving it. It was in the secular tradition of the Russian empire to use force where it was useful and no strong resistance was to be expected and not to yield to rebellion but to consolidate authority.

The Soviet View

There has not been a reasoned theoretical defense of the decision to override treaties and countless statements of respect for independence and sovereignty of bloc nations by intervening in Czechoslovakia. However, press articles and, long after the event, speeches by major leaders attempted to rationalize the action, and in so doing they developed a substantial modification and hardening of the Soviet ideology in regard to foreign relations. This amounted to a nullification of Khrushchev's approval of separate roads to socialism.[52] Not long after the invasion, *Pravda* denounced "liberalization" of socialism as nothing but concessions to antisocialist forces, and "democratic socialism" as an impossibility where antisocialist elements were allowed to prevail.[53] Further, "There can be no 'other' socialism after the development of scientific socialism," and Lenin was quoted as saying ". . . bourgeois or socialist ideology, there is no middle way . . . *every* departure from socialist ideology signifies of itself a strengthening of bourgeois ideology." Soviet ideology, it explained, is not applicable only to the Soviet Union but "contains general laws, without which the construction of socialism is impossible."

---

[52] It was closely in accord with the literal doctrine, although not the spirit, of Leninism. In arguing for peace with Germany in January, 1918, Lenin wrote: "But no Marxist, without flying in the face of principles of Marxism and socialism generally, can deny that the interests of socialism are higher than the right of nations to self-determination."

[53] *Pravda*, September 22, 1968.

On this premise, any deviation from the socialist truth must be laid to enemy-class actions. Ordinarily one thought of the capitalist-imperialist counterattack as military, as a *Pravda* writer, Kovalev, explained,[54] but in the new era of socialist strength the enemy was becoming slyer and resorting to subterfuge, as in Czechoslovakia. Not daring to attack openly, the enemy seeks to distort and undermine in the pretense of "improving" socialism, pretending to oppose "bureaucratism," "dictatorship," and so on, while really aiming at the overthrow of the entirety of socialism. Therefore, freedom of speech and press are inadmissible until the final victory of communism. Many in Czechoslovakia were deceived; but, as the bourgeois many times have acted to suppress the working class of other countries, it is perfectly licit for socialist countries to help the toilers of another land to defend socialism.

The *Pravda* statement went on to revive something of Stalin's thesis that the class struggle grows sharper as the bourgeoisie nears final defeat: "Experience shows that the liquidation of the exploitative classes does not automatically end the class struggle, that remnants of the exploitative classes . . . continue to nourish fierce hatred for the socialist system. Imperialism counts on them in its subversive actions against socialism. . . ."[55] Thus the Soviet representative in the United Nations derided the interest of the West, particularly the United States, in the freedom of Czech communism; by his book, such an interest could not be disinterested but only proved the guilt of Western imperialism and its anger at the frustration of its evil designs.

Shortly afterward a *Pravda* article, a speech at the United Nations by Gromyko, and still more authoritatively, one by Brezhnev, spelled out the logical consequences of this reasoning in what was termed the Brezhnev doctrine, of the right of intervention in "socialist" countries, equivalent to Soviet sovereignty over an inviolable sphere. In effect, this asserted the right of the Soviet Union to determine whether socialism was in danger in any country of the "socialist commonwealth" and take whatever action deemed proper to set things right. It is not necessary for any authority to request help; the contention, raised on the morrow of the Czech invasion, that unnamed Czech comrades had called on the fraternal help of the WTO countries was dropped. In Gromyko's statement, the countries of the "socialist commonwealth" constitute an "inseparable entity cemented by unbreakable ties,"[56] in effect a Soviet-ruled political unit. The Eastern European countries to which the Brezhnev doctrine applied were left with more freedom than Uzbekistan or Latvia only so far as the Soviet Union saw fit to allow. This accords with basic Soviet concepts that the

[54] September 11, 1968.

[55] Zionism was sometimes mentioned by the Russians as a danger in this connection, often by the Poles.

[56] *New York Times,* October 4, 1968.

nation has of itself no legitimacy but that of its ruling party, the legitimacy of which depends on its loyalty to the Leninist (Soviet) state.[57]

The Brezhnev doctrine was more alarming than a less self-righteous statement of strategic or other necessity in the Czech case would have been, as it was capable of expansion. Soviet statements have declined to draw the boundaries of the "socialist commonwealth." Rumania is clearly included, and Yugoslavia probably, despite its reluctance to be counted for this purpose. Albania is a possible candidate, and Arab socialist states might come into question. Russian universalism cannot set itself limits. The Soviet assertion of the right to export counterrevolution to socialist states was a humiliating turnaround from Khrushchev's repeated denunciation, in days when he thought the Soviet sphere was expanding, of what he saw as American export of counterrevolution to states freeing themselves from the capitalist camp.

But the Soviets would have the superior right of proletarian internationalism apply still more broadly. Kovalev, a Soviet jurist, writing in *Pravda* of September 26, 1968, also indicated that the world's "progressive forces" should not be inhibited from intervention in the Federal German Republic, or against such regimes as those of Franco and Salazar or the Greek colonels because of considerations of "sovereignty." More immediately to the point, it was the duty of Communists to support the people of Vietnam in their struggle. "True revolutionaries, being interna-

---

[57] As Brezhnev put it in a speech to the Polish Party Congress: "It is common knowledge that the Soviet Union has really done a good deal to strengthen the sovereignty and autonomy of the socialist countries. The C.P.S.U. has always advocated that each socialist country determine the concrete forms of its development along the path of socialism by taking into account the specific nature of its national conditions. But it is well known, comrades, that there are common natural laws of socialist construction, deviation from which could lead to deviation from socialism as such. And when external and internal forces hostile to socialism try to turn the development of a given socialist country in the direction of restoration of the capitalist system, when a threat arises to the cause of socialism in that country—a threat to the security of the socialist commonwealth as a whole—this is no longer merely a problem for that country's people, but a common problem, the concern of all socialist countries.

"It is quite clear that an action such as military assistance to a fraternal country to end a threat to the socialist system is an extraordinary measure, dictated by necessity; it can be called forth only by the overt actions of enemies of socialism within the country and beyond its boundaries, actions that create a threat to the common interests of the socialist camp.

"Experience bears witness that in present conditions the triumph of the socialist system in a country can be regarded as final, but the restoration of capitalism can be considered ruled out only if the Communist Party, as the leading force in society, steadfastly pursues a Marxist-Leninist policy in the development of all spheres of society's life; only if the party indefatigably strengthens the country's defense and the protection of its revolutionary gains, and if it itself is vigilant and instills in the people vigilance with respect to the class enemy and implacability toward bourgeois ideology; only if the principle of socialist internationalism is held sacred and unity and fraternal solidarity with the other socialist countries are strengthened." (*Pravda*, November 13, 1968.)

tionalists, cannot refrain from supporting progressive forces in their just struggle for national and social liberation." According to Kosygin, the hand of Moscow is "the hand of a friend and brother always ready to go to the aid of those who struggle for their freedom and independence."[58]

There was a strong tendency to proclaim the pro-Soviet forces as inherently superior and *ipso facto* in the right. Thus, the Kovalev article in *Pravda* also explains, "Those who speak of the 'illegality' of the actions of the allied socialist countries in Czechoslovakia forget that in the class society there can be no nonclass law. Rules and norms of law are subject to the laws of the class struggle, the laws of social development. . . . It is wrong to give up the class approach for formal-juridical considerations." Since the Soviet way is right in a class sense, no more need be asked.

This view was not entirely new. The Soviet Union had long claimed that a special international law applied to the socialist system of states.[59] As another writer in *Pravda*[60] had it, "Socialist armies can have no other task than the defense and strengthening of socialism. . . . The Soviet army cannot be used for seizing territory, acquiring colonies, nor for aggression against peoples. The Soviet army is only a liberating army." *Pravda*[61] reacted indignantly to the charge made by Czechs that some were "collaborationists." Impossible, the author exclaims, because the dictionary defines "collaborationists" as "persons working with *fascist aggressors*." Collaborationists can be only class enemies of the toilers, now as in the days of Hitler. In this chauvinistic view, Soviet and allied forces could be conceived as going into Czechoslovakia only to preserve the independence of that country, which was jeopardized by the supposed effort to break away from the socialist camp. The imperial protection being inherently benevolent, rejection of it can come only from inherently evil, that is, class-enemy forces. Those forces can have nothing to do with such acceptable concepts as independence, sovereignty, and democracy.

Probably the Soviet soldiers who went into Czechoslovakia generally shared this sentiment and believed they were coming as friends to help threatened brothers, although some were certainly shaken by the failure of so many Czechs to appreciate their good intentions. The opposition to them was seen as not representative of the "broad masses" but of people who might act on behalf of the German revanchists. In a sense, the Czechs were beaten either way: if they welcomed the Russians, this confirmed the rightness of the invasion; if they resisted, this proved its necessity to deal with hostile forces which had crept in. The Russian soldiers and

---

[58] *Kommunist,* January, 1961, No. 1, p. 12.

[59] Alexander Dallin, *The Soviet Union at the United Nations* (New York: Frederick A. Praeger, Inc., 1962), p. 8.

[60] October 9, 1968.

[61] In an article of Iurii Zhukov, September 13, 1968.

people seem particularly to have taken to heart the sinister threat from West Germany, the utter evil of which has been relentlessly expounded by the press for many years, keeping wartime memories green. A common sentiment seems to have been, "How do those people who owe their liberty to us dare insult our soldiers?"[62] Many meetings and acts of solidarity were organized to express support of the invasion, as customary in such crises, and countless resolutions were passed. It seems probable that most citizens were prepared to accept the virtuousness of their country's intentions and to credit reports of manifestations of friendship by the true Czech working people. The barriers between Soviet citizens and foreigners, whether of fear, distrust, or hostility, were visibly raised.

Lest patriotic sentiments be undermined, American and British broadcasts were again jammed after five years of freedom of the airwaves. There were a few small-scale protests by intellectuals, and letters were circulated. But the reaction of an elderly Russian at the time of the trial of five who tried to demonstrate in Red Square seems more typical: "Why did they attack our tanks? I would have run them over." Or, "If our tanks weren't in Prague, the German tanks would be there. . . . Which do you prefer?" One of the defendants spoke of the loneliness of the political dissenter in the face of general apathy.[63] An American pacifist who tried to hand out leaflets denouncing the occupation seems to have encountered more hostility than sympathy in the few minutes before she was taken into custody. The volume of protest seems generally to have been small and rather less than there was in 1956, perhaps largely because few people were killed and the previous government remained in authority, ostensibly accepting the Soviet presence. The chief Russian reaction was indifference.

Foreign Reaction

The absence of much bloodshed made the feelings of outrage and indignation with which most governments and informed persons outside the Soviet bloc reacted to the overrunning of an inoffensive small country less deep and lasting than they might otherwise have been. As U Thant pointed out, the Russians were not bombing Czechoslovakia as the Americans were bombing North Vietnam. However, reactions were at first severe, and the Soviet Union found itself the subject of general reprobation as never since the war against Finland thirty years earlier. It had even to deplore the incomprehension of foreign Communist parties.

Real support came from East Berlin, Warsaw, Budapest, Sophia, and Mongolia. North Vietnam, grateful for Soviet arms, joined. Castro some-

[62] *Le Monde*, February 13–19, 1969.

[63] *New York Times*, October 10, October, 15, 1968.

what hesitantly added his voice, apparently anxious lest Soviet freedom of intervention in Eastern Europe might imply similar freedom for the United States in the Caribbean area. Rumania denounced the invasion, at least for a short time. The Yugoslavs did so more harshly and firmly; it showed, they said, that the Soviet Union was going from the word to the sword. As they proclaimed readiness to fight if attacked, relations with the Soviets fell to the lowest point since 1953. Although the Russians claimed that Yugoslavia owed its independence only to the "socialist commonwealth," the Titoist government moved further toward liberalization and a neutral stance.

It might be supposed that the Maoists would look on with approval as the Soviets stamped out liberalization and took a hard anti-Western line; instead they roundly berated aggression, called on the Czechs and others to fight for freedom and socialism, and promised to come to the assistance of Albania if attacked. Albania shouted its loathing and gave thought to improving relations with its neighbors. It called upon the Czechs to fight the invaders, and then to overthrow the Dubček government as this collaborated with them. In an odd turn, the World Federation of Trade Unions, long nourished by Moscow, ungratefully condemned, although somewhat mildly, the military intervention.[64]

For the most important nonruling Communist parties, those of Western Europe, the action was wholly lamentable and difficult to justify. They wanted a maximum of the freedom, which was denied to the Czechs and by extension to all Communists, to go beyond narrow limits set by the Soviet Union. For years they had been at pains to build the image of respectable, orderly, law-abiding and democratic communism; and if the Dubček experiment had succeeded, it would have been their best advertisement. Such hopes were battered if not smashed. Soviet-style communism seemed incompatible with national sovereignty and freedom of expression, and its claim to being a genuine faith was made to seem emptier than ever. What little of the ideals of freedom and equality had survived Stalinism was too obviously submerged by selfish and unscrupulous great-power interests. It was hardly comprehensible to parties struggling for power to say that a party which had come to power and ruled for twenty years could not protect itself without Soviet intervention. It was bitter for them to imply that if they should come to power, their countries would, like Czechoslovakia, be subject to occupation at Soviet will. Not only did this make much more difficult the acquisition of power, but the prospect was not agreeable to the Communists themselves, increasingly inclined to patriotism of their own.

Different parties reacted with different degrees of energy. The Communist parties of such countries as Britain, Switzerland, and Sweden

---

[64] *New York Times,* October 2, 1968.

blasted the Soviet action with particular violence. The Italians were much more emphatic than the French, as both were under great pressure from their supporters to repudiate the Soviet line. Only a few minor parties, such as those of Luxembourg and the hard-pressed Greek Communists, stood by Moscow. Many criticisms went far beyond the single act of invading Czechoslovakia. Numerous Communists in Europe, especially among the youth, denounced the Soviet Union as a bureaucratic, not a workers', state. Latin-American and most Asian Communist parties also broke with Moscow although with less vehemence. In the Third World, only the Arabs, fearful of possible reconciliation of the Dubček government with Israel, abstained from condemnation. For almost all, it was a strange new experience.

If Communist parties were driven to protest the Soviet action, governments and ordinary people around the world did so with much more vehemence. Student marchers turned from attacking U.S. to Soviet embassies. The few exceptions were a return for Soviet aid. Egypt, Iraq, and Syria accepted the Soviet explanation, despite some disquieting parallels between their situation and that of Czechoslovakia, Arab socialism being more deviant than Czech and Soviet power being visible. Nigeria was silent. Algeria and India abstained from a condemnatory resolution in the United Nations, although Mrs. Gandhi was sharply critical. Other recipients of Soviet largesse, however, such as Tanzania and Ethiopia, were bitter. De Gaulle, whose cordiality with the Russians had been growing steadily, damned the act roundly, although he coupled it with denunciation of power blocs in general.

Western Europeans, disillusioned in aspirations to detente and seeing themselves next in line, were most disturbed. The image which they had allowed themselves to cultivate of an increasingly sensible and moderate Russia seemingly had to be discarded. The sudden, well-concealed, and militarily overwhelming blow showed up their insecurity before a huge power capable of ruthless and, as it seemed to most, irrational action. The invasion of Czechoslovakia, with the vast loss of prestige and of world stature in order to bring a small, friendly nation to conformity, seemed quite contrary to national interests as ordinarily conceived. It was not easily understood that the act answered needs internal to the Soviet system, and the Soviet Union seemed to have shown itself dangerous and unpredictable.

To Europeans, the rather calm reaction of the United States was upsetting. The United States seemed, more than most European countries, to accept the Soviet sphere of influence as a fact of international existence and Soviet freedom of action in an area which, to Europeans, was part of one continent. It was something of a relief that fingers of shame should be pointed not at American but at Soviet actions; and the United States, with troops in dozens of countries, could not easily contend that the mere presence of Soviet forces was incompatible with Czech sovereignty as long as the same government was in charge. When a condemnatory resolution in the Security Council of the United Nations was vetoed by the Russians, neither the American delegation nor any other saw fit to carry the question to the one-time respected world forum of the Assembly. NATO received a psychological boost, and voices on both sides of the Atlantic calling for the withdrawal of American forces from Europe were stilled, but not much was done to spruce up the alliance militarily. There was no attempt to impose any real diplomatic or economic penalty, and even cultural exchanges were shortly proceeding about as before.

Making as much as possible over the alleged threat of German revanchism, talk of a NATO buildup, war in Vietnam, and the sundry disorders of the West, the Russians sought to give the impression that nothing much had been changed and waited calmly for the storm to pass. Within half a year, the world was showing the shortness of its memory. In June, the French electorate showed its unconcern by giving the Communist candidate, Duclos, over 21 percent, nearly four times the Socialist vote. Aside from the shattering of countless hopes, not a great deal was visibly changed on the diplomatic front. Czechoslovakia was, as before, in the Soviet sphere of influence. As the Russians had said, it was a move to conserve, not change the balance of power. Yet a great deal had been changed in the aspect and outlook of world relations. The Russians were not likely to be much trusted for a long time.

7. THE NEW EASTERN EUROPE

Occupied Czechoslovakia

Most Eastern European societies, like the Russian, are deeply divided; almost anywhere, as in Hungary after the fiercely anti-Soviet rising of 1956, the Russians could find a fairly large section of the population prepared to do their bidding. But the more democratic and better integrated Czech society proved remarkably refractory. The Russians demanded "normalization," by which was meant that the Czechs should seem to love and approve them. It was only normal, in the Russian view, that a party would come forward to protest loyalty and obedience while the masses should submit passively. The Russians came claiming to be friends and probably believing that they were, acted without vindictiveness, killed few, left alone for the most part those who did not trouble them, and here and there offered comradely assistance. That a people should hate them because of the abstract principle of national independence was beyond comprehension.

In the first days of the occupation, the Czechs declined offers of economic aid and rejected such pleasantries as cultural visits. Villagers refused sporting contests with Soviet soldiers; factory workers declined offers of advice and assistance; intellectuals turned down invitations to travel in the Soviet Union. The government, desirous of avoiding trouble and lightening the occupation, tried to placate the Russians without too much offending their own people. Thus, they reinstituted censorship but enforced it lightly and allowed the truth to appear in thin disguise. Czech journalists practically made a sport for a time of speaking with tongue in cheek. There were few changes in personnel at the top. If a liberal was dropped because offensive to the Russians, he was replaced by another liberal. The reputed conservatives, too, usually proved better Czechs than Soviet-style Communists. For weeks, or even a few months, it seemed that the occupation had achieved very little. The Soviet press underlined this by harping on the continuing battle with the reactionaries.

Much, however, was achieved. The Russians were masters of the land and used their power as they saw necessary. If they wished a hotel or a barracks for their use, they took it. They placed their advisors in the Ministries of Defense and Interior to be sure of control of the agencies of force. But most of all, they held a sword perennially dangling over the government, which had to plead with the population to avoid provocation and possible bloodier tragedy. Concessions were demanded as the price of pulling Soviet troops out of the cities, and the threat remained that they might return at any moment. To obtain removal of most Soviet troops, it was necessary to agree to the permanent presence of part of them. The government promised to retain as much as possible of the reforms, but they were little by little whittled down. Travel was once more restricted. Economic liberalization was checked, and plans for worker participation in management, somewhat on the Yugoslav model, were dropped. A good many of the dissident intellectuals left the country and so simplified the problems of the Soviet occupiers. Those who remained, aware that they could be deported to Siberia any day the Russians chose, were increasingly intimidated and fearful of contacts with the West.

Popular sentiment wearied as months passed and nothing was achieved even by students' self-immolation. The trade unions, perhaps the most powerful force for liberalization, were persuaded largely to desist from demands for early elections. Hardliners were placed in strategic positions. Soviet advisors saw to the advancement in the army of "realist" officers. To the distress of the Czech in the street, more and more of the old-time secrecy enveloped the councils of government, and the government was gradually separated from the people. The police became effective guardians of the Soviet-imposed order, breaking up protest demonstrations. The militia was strengthened as an antiliberal force. The censorship was tightened step by step. Czech journalists were purged, and there was much pressure against foreign correspondents. Reorientation of trade to the West was vetoed, and the economy was still more closely linked with the Soviet; it became hard to hope for prosperity except by collaborating. Josef Smrkovsky, perhaps the most determined of the liberals, pleading against plans for strikes to oppose his demotion, told his supporters, "Please all understand, from the left to the right and the right to the left, that our socialist republic simply cannot live in this divided world" without leaning on the Soviet Union.[65] A rebel who acknowledges his dependence on the master has more than half surrendered. After a few months Czechs ceased to ask aloud, except in vague terms or indirectly, for complete independence, that is, withdrawal of Soviet forces, but only for a decent amount of freedom and autonomy under the Russian aegis.

Until April, 1969, the Russians allowed Dubček to remain nominal leader, although his authority was chipped away. But Czech sentiments, increasingly repressed in preceding months, erupted suddenly. Elated by a victory over the Soviet team in an ice hockey tournament, Czech mobs went on an anti-Soviet rampage, attacking Soviet offices in many cities. The Russians, who had previously expressed dissatisfaction with the slowness of "normalization," saw this outburst as a reason and excuse for a crackdown. Soviet Defense Minister Grechko and a deputy foreign minister, Semyonov, rushed without invitation to Prague. They threatened to take charge and reoccupy the cities, and the Czech government bowed. Dubček was replaced by the Slovak leader, Husak, who, if not an unconditional adherent of the Russians, was a rather hard-line Communist without much sympathy for liberalization.

Heroics do not last forever, and the Czechs seemed to recognize that their status was that of a protectorate of a power which they could not physically oppose, much as thirty years earlier they had seen their country reduced to the status of a German protectorate. There were some efforts to organize protests and sit-ins against the ouster of Dubček, but they rapidly withered. In May there were anti-Soviet disturbances in Pilsen, liberated by Americans a generation earlier. But these and occasional manifestations of discontent were only isolated incidents in a largely demoralized country, of little more moment than the mutterings of the citizenry. The trade unions were tamed and made again into fairly docile instruments of Communist power, as in other lands of the Soviet sphere. The press was more and more subjected; it reverted to the gray uniformity of the party line, and the liberal journalists who had caused so much concern to the Russians were removed. The party was slowly but effectively purged under the direction of such unconditional adherents of the Soviet Union as Lubomir Strougal. It became a mortal sin to have opposed the treaty providing for the presence of Soviet troops in the country.

---

[65] *New York Times*, January 6, 1969.

In foreign affairs, Czechoslovakia was entirely submissive. Husak, visiting Moscow and other bloc capitals, made all the declarations expected of a Communist boss. Propagandistic blasts blamed the United States for Czechoslovakia's troubles. Czech units participated in WTO maneuvers, which were so frequent as to constitute not so much exercises of allied national armies as joint training of bloc forces. Husak affirmed that the only important boundary was that between two class worlds,[66] and the Czechoslovak government officially subscribed to the Brezhnev Doctrine. At the Moscow conference in June, Husak begged the leaders of the world's Communist parties not to discuss the invasion of his country, which he held entirely justified.

Under Husak, the Czechs could cherish little hope for anything better than a regime like that of Kadar in Hungary, whereby the nation earned a degree of internal freedom by complete subordination to the Russians in defense and foreign policy. The alternative was the rule of such men as Strougal, the second-ranking leader, compared to whom Husak was a liberal nationalist.

The Russians have for centuries had experience in dealing with refractory subjects, and they have never failed to bend them to their will. They divide weaker peoples while appearing as bearers of order. They make it clear that they have overwhelming power and are willing to use it; yet they are skilled in wearing down opposition by judicious use of compulsion and incentives, with force ordinarily inconspicuous. They are patient and prepared to make minor concessions, mostly formal or verbal, as long as their basic aim is secured. They have usually not been racist nor so haughty as most imperial peoples, and they have shown capacity for assimilation, generously rewarding those who cooperate. They are bearers of a supranational ideology which relegates nationalism to the category of outworn nonsense and morally disarms the nationalists. Most of the Czech students who so desperately fought for freedoms were convinced of the basic rightness of socialism and Marxism, creeds more or less inconsistent with nationalism.

It was consequently difficult for Czechs consistently to oppose the Soviet system. They might easily find themselves in the position of the Soviet intellectuals who fundamentally accept the Soviet state but demand that it measure up to the ideals which it proclaims. If the Soviet Union can convince the Czechs that there is no future in resistance, that by causing disorders they hurt chiefly themselves, that the way to power, privileges, and material welfare is by service to the system, there would seem to be no reason that they might not be gradually brought to the same degree of acceptance as that of other peoples of the Russian domain and in the long run to the degree of integration into the Soviet system that the Russians may desire for them.

---

[66] *Pravda,* May 9, 1969.

Reconsolidation

The Soviet rulers, although probably a little disconcerted by the general reprobation of their deed, could congratulate themselves that the occupation of Czechoslovakia achieved its primary objective, the reversal of the process of diffusion of authority in Soviet East Europe; and they could survey their domain with some satisfaction. Poland, East Germany, Hungary, and Bulgaria, by participating in the enforcement of the limitation of sovereignty in Czechoslovakia, clearly accepted it for themselves. Bulgaria, its economy closely geared to the Russian, gave unstinted and unquestioning fealty. Nothing was done in any way contrary to Soviet wishes, and Soviet power seemed free to operate in Bulgaria so far as it chose. The two most important members of the bloc, Poland and East Germany, although not quite so humble as Bulgaria, were even more sternly loyal to Soviet-led communism than before. Liberal ideas seemed to have faded out, and the Polish party congress in November, supervised by Brezhnev, was wholly in the Soviet image. The chief opposition, that of the "Partisans," was nationalist in tone but authoritarian, anti-Semitic, and at least as anti-Western as Gomulka. Those suspected of revisionism were eliminated, and "sausage socialism" seemed to have vanquished socialist humanism.

The East German regime, unloved and insecure in the face of a stronger and more prosperous West Germany, was most devoted of all to Prussian-flavored communism and Soviet overlordship and firmest in rejection of "bourgeois" ideology. Erich Honecker, heir-apparent to the top post, declared that the most important criterion of fidelity to Marxism-Leninism was love for the Soviet state.[67] Having marked up considerable economic success, and having become a very important supplier for the Soviet Union, East Germany regarded itself as a subleader in the bloc and proposed tighter political integration, within which East Germans could hope to exert disproportionate influence as the best Leninists.

Maverick Rumania, after sharp protest against the invasion, turned circumspect. Tentative moves toward democratization and freedom of expression previously underway were halted; and Rumania seemed again firmly within the fold. It was difficult for Rumania to resist Soviet domination in the same way as Czechoslovakia because the people had never had much inspiration of freedom. There was no Rumanian student movement to be suppressed, Western contacts were always quite limited, and there was only slight abatement of party control.

After a few months during which it seemed that Ceausescu had been cowed, he began speaking again somewhat as before August, appealing to

---

[67] *New York Times*, October 8, 1968.

national sentiments and rights of sovereignty in contradiction to the Brezhnev doctrine. Rumania was again standing against strengthening of WTO and Comecon and withholding support from the Russians in their dispute with China. The Rumanian party sent warm greetings to the Chinese party congress which the Soviets condemned as a farce. But Rumanian forces joined Soviet and Bulgarian in WTO maneuvers in Bulgaria. The very day the Rumanian foreign minister arrived on a visit to Moscow, *Pravda* saw fit to reassert the Brezhnev doctrine.[68]

Economic integration took on a new look. In the months following the Czech crisis, sundry trade treaties tied satellite economies closer to that of the Soviet Union. *Pravda*[69] denounced autarky as alien to socialism. A Soviet economist expressed the new or renewed approach of integration: "International duty requires the socialist countries to . . . subordinate profitability of foreign trade to the political tasks of leveling economic standards and increasing cohesion."[70] Little was to be bought in the West if it could be procured within the bloc, as planners in Moscow, in consultation with Comecon members, set trade targets. Talk of economic reforms subsided, and the market element and experiments toward the Yugoslav model were pushed only carefully, perhaps farthest in Hungary. Anything suggestive of a "free play of market forces" was, according to the leading Polish paper, merely "peaceful counterrevolution in disguise." The drive for efficiency went on, but it was not allowed to conflict with ubiquitous party authority. The Russians made little effort, however, to force Comecon specialization; so far as there was progress in this direction, it was made by special bilateral or multilateral agreements. Shortly after Dubček was removed from power, there was held in Moscow the Comecon summit conference for which the Russians had been pressing for many months, but it seems to have served mostly prestige.

Military integration was apparently of more political importance. Joint maneuvers of WTO pact forces were held frequently after August, 1968, and one may assume that their purpose was less to practice tactics than to accustom national armies to operating as part of a supranational force. In March, 1969, a WTO summit meeting was held in Budapest, Dubček being somewhat ironically called upon to preside. Chiefly a demonstration of harmony, the meeting announced formation of a joint staff.

Dwarfed economically, politically, and militarily by the Soviet Union, with no hope of assistance from abroad, the Eastern European countries could enjoy the latitude and consideration it suited the Russians to allow them. This might be more if the Russians were preoccupied with China or desirous of improving their appearances with Western Europe or Amer-

---

[68] April 7, 1969.

[69] September 30, 1968.

[70] A. Vaks in *Voprosy ekonomiki,* October, 1968, No. 10, pp. 113–118.

ica, or it might be less if a tough-minded Kremlin leadership desired to consolidate its dominion. But developments in Eastern Europe could only follow, not precede or force developments in Russia. Disorders within the bloc would probably lead only to a tightening of controls. If there were to be liberalization, it had to come from Moscow.

There was not much in the Soviet scene after Czechoslovakia to encourage the liberals. This tendency to reaffirmation of party control and Leninist fundamentalism, evident in a small way from the trials of dissenting writers early in 1966, became much more marked after the invasion, as though the use of force to rectify communism abroad called for similar use at home. Well aware that pluralistic, loosening tendencies within the Soviet Union encouraged all manner of willfulness in the bloc, and that liberalism makes more difficult a rule based fundamentally on force, the Kremlin stepped up communist-patriotic propaganda. Glorification of the military became an even more regular theme of the Soviet press. A speech in celebration of the fifty-first anniversary of the Revolution laid out practically a neo-Stalinist program. It insisted on the necessity of Communist parties hewing to a single revolutionary line, the values of which were exalted more as heroic than utilitarian. The party monopoly of power, in the words of Politburo member Mazurov, could not be shadowed: "There can be no social group in the Soviet Union which views its activities differently from those of the party."

The drive of Soviet foreign policy usually has been defensive, designed primarily to retain acquired positions. But this may demand extension of control. When tsarist Russia had difficulties with restive Poland or disorders in Central Asia, it strengthened administrative powers over the Poles or reached out to subdue troublesome areas along the borders. The Soviet state seems similarly motivated: to erosion of control in Eastern Europe, culminating in the dramatic Czech reforms, the reaction was reassertion of authority by force. There is no evidence that Stalin or his successors planned or desired to incorporate Eastern Europe into the Soviet Union, although this thought must have occurred to them; and there has been little appearance of any systematic design. It remains unclear how strongly the Soviet leaders desire to integrate Eastern Europe in the Soviet administrative system. At all times, however, they have wished to make secure the position acquired, and affirming security of the hegemonic power means reducing the independence of those under it. Both Stalin and the successor regimes have wished to assure a safe margin of control; and experience taught, in Yugoslavia, Albania, Czechoslovakia, and elsewhere, that without strong military-political bonds a country is likely to fall into dissident ways.

The West bespeaks economic and cultural progress to Eastern Europe; what the Russians offer is primarily political: a nuclear shield, decisive power, and a principle of interstate and internal harmony. The Russian interest, moreover, is primarily political, although there are economic and even in the nuclear age some strategic advantages in overlordship. The bureaucratic apparatus of party and state relations will never voluntarily break itself up. The long-term trend and probably the short-term response to pressures from the economic and cultural attractiveness of the West and threats of dissolution arising therefrom is hence increased political control and integration, just as the tsarist state assimilated more or less to itself all the lands it was able to call its own: Baltic regions, Central Asia, Poland, and to some extent Finland.

There are strong trends in modern civilization toward self-awareness, demands for autonomy, and hence breakup of the empires put together by European states since the early Renaissance voyages of discovery. But Russia is not a state like Britain or France; and the Russian empire, a continental mass under a single sacrosanct authority, cannot untie itself as the British and French empires have done. It must assert itself as sacred, and this admits neither compromise nor retreat. As customs of rule grow, the appropriate habits and institutions become fixed, and surrender of control could come only through weakness or decadence of the sovereign power. There comes to be less reason to tolerate political deviations of any kind, which may be dangerous to the whole fabric; bourgeois nationalism is dangerous in Tadjikistan, or perhaps in Rumania, not because the small people could possibly represent a threat to the Soviet Union but because the example is evil. The closer the satellites to the Soviet Union and the more persons involved in relations with them, the more necessary is it to bring all into the same mould and the more reason that all should be under the same law and form part of one great political body.

The loosening or liberalizing forces within the Soviet domain are powerful, but they cannot prosper without hope. Especially after the glow of Czechoslovakia, many turned to the "inner emigration" which is a long step on the road to apathy. As instruments of control, Communist parties are very useful. All are nominally based on the same creed, the interpretation of which is the prerogative of the Soviet Union; in promoting this creed for the sake of their own power they at the same time undermine their ability to resist the hegemonic authority. The way to advancement in any area of political importance is through standing with the party, dedication and loyalty. The prime qualification for leadership of national parties within the Soviet Union is approval of the central apparatus, which is given for usefulness to it. So far as Soviet domination is affirmed in eastern Europe, political ambition requires acceptability to the ultimately sovereign power and at least ability to serve its purposes while gaining the support and cooperation of as many as possible of the local population, in the manner of Ceausescu. The ultimate responsibility of the national leaders is more to the hegemonic power, which can expel them, than to their people, who cannot. Even so far as they claim a limited freedom, it is to be earned by zeal in adherence to fundamentals and assurances of basic loyalty to the system which imprisons them. The psychological and political drive to identify with the supreme power is very strong; yet so far as an elite does so, it becomes separated from its people and the more dependent on Soviet power and legitimation.

Whether the domination of Eastern Europe is really rewarding is a question the Russian leadership probably does not ask itself; to remain there is a political compulsion. Perhaps they do not ask themselves, either, how popular Soviet domination may be; it suffices that it is effective. But there would seem to be hardly any organization to mobilize rebellious feelings. The people are reduced to looking to improvement of the fundamental system instead of its replacement and to hoping for liberalization through a Marxist-Leninist party. Communists are called upon to lead them away from the Russian grasp. This is like expecting apples from an oak tree. The parties are basically authoritarian and interested in the preservation of order; where Soviet force predominates, this means a Soviet order, to oppose which is to risk the gravest troubles. As Western Europe is swept by strikes, student protests, and riots, Eastern Europe goes quietly about its business. Even in Czechoslovakia order was sufficiently maintained through 1968 that industrial production, it was claimed, actually rose slightly. There is little sign on the surface that the Soviet empire is not effective and viable.

This does not imply that the nations of Eastern Europe must soon be converted into Soviet republics. As long as the Soviet Union has strong hopes of extending its sway or is even greatly concerned with the regard of the outside world, there is probably much more to be lost than gained by formally extinguishing the independence of nations which have formed part only of the new, not the old Russian empire. But the Soviet Union may be impelled to more or less aggressive positions for the security of its holdings. Thus, it has never felt able to remain indifferent to the Titoist heresy but has striven, ever since 1948, either to overthrow it or to entice it back to the community. Stalin spent a great deal of effort, and Khrushchev was willing to sacrifice dignity to this end. This anxiety has been much beyond the intrinsic importance of the country. It is evidently due to the fact that Tito's Yugoslavia is a kindred country, both socialist and Slavic, and as such the worst possible influence, much more dangerous than Austria or Finland. After the Czech affair, the Russians were assailing Yugoslavia as the chief remaining channel for bourgeois influences flowing into the socialist camp, the stalking-horse for imperialism. According to a Soviet political journal,[71] Yugoslavia was to blame for the economic heresies which had seduced Czechoslovakia; there was an implication that socialism in Yugoslavia might have to be saved as it was in Czechoslovakia.

---

[71] *International Life*, December 1968.

VII

Ideology, the Soviet State, and Foreign Policy

1. THE PERSISTENT MODE

Soviet papers still carry at their masthead the motto, "Proletarians of all lands, unite," an unyielding assertion of the universalist revolutionary imperative. According to a slogan for the fiftieth anniversary of the Revolution, Marxism-Leninism remains "the ideological banner of the Great October Socialist Revolution, the lodestar of the working people of all countries in the struggle against the class and national yoke, for the victory of socialism and communism!"[1] Other states, especially very strong ones, have been at pains to give more or less ideal coloration to their dealings with the world. Rome expanded, as it was asseverated, not for the sake of Roman power but to bring peace, order, and law to the world. Sixteenth-century Spain fought, in the Old World and the New, for the True Faith. Revolutionary France conquered in the name of freedom. The British Empire upheld itself as bearer of civilization and justice to backward peoples. The United States has long had a penchant for moralizing foreign policy even when this was clearly in the material interests of this country, viewing itself as bearer of some sort of world mission, speaking in terms of universal validity. But such idealizations of foreign policy have been unsystematic and usually marginal; there is hardly a parallel in history to the insistence of Soviet Russia on setting itself apart as exponent of an elaborate political-religious doctrine which allegedly furnishes the entire motivation and justification for a fundamental challenge to most existing institutions.

Most remarkable is the continuity of Soviet ideology. Ideology, like Lenin's corpse, seems a permanent part of the scene. The advanced

[1] *Pravda,* October 15, 1967.

industrial society of today, substantially urbanized, with a level of education comparable to that of any state, ruled by an essentially conservative bureaucracy and pleased with its status in the world, nominally maintains the same doctrinal core that was suitable for making a social revolution in a poor, illiterate agricultural country in the throes of military defeat. The Revolution, as an emotional storm, felt itself to be an expression of universal truth and justice. Over half a century later, Russian leaders talk of revolutionary struggle throughout the world and speak in terms of global confrontation of their and the evil opposing forces. Although less clear as to how it may come about, they have not outwardly abandoned the idea of a general victory of their social-political order. They swore by the word of Lenin forty-five years after his death perhaps more assiduously than ever. The Soviet state still encourages the belief that one of its prime aims, if not its chief motive, in world affairs is support for "socialism" and "class" interests, however strategies change.

At times, notably in 1939–45, this idea has been allowed to recede, but it again recurs. For over half a century, the Russians have been pointing with pleasure to strikes in the capitalist countries, even those most friendly to themselves, as signs of the coming crisis of capitalism, while claiming that the working classes are increasingly oppressed, as Marx predicted. Khrushchev, after making efforts to bring doctrine more into conformity with contemporary reality, was determined to repeat that the nature of imperialism had not changed from that seen by Lenin. In the 1960's, learned Soviet writers were explaining war as due to class antagonisms and financial expansionism. In Khruschev's day, socialism was defined as including the main tenets of Leninism: dictatorship of the proletariat under the guidance of a Communist party, planned economy, and proletarian internationalism. In 1968, the definition was strengthened to include control of the press and the duty to help wherever socialism might be in trouble.

The predictions and expectations of world communism have corresponded very poorly with reality over half a century, and the successes have been those of the Soviet state, seemingly more despite than because of its Marxist definitions and approach. Yet the litany is so persistent as to suggest a compulsion, as that of chiliastic sects which reiterate more fervently the sacred teachings and seek more eagerly to convert others to them when the prophecy fails, as though to prevent themselves from falling into doubt.[2] It is difficult to surmise when Soviet exponents of ideology literally believe what they say, when they are uttering verbiage without significance, and when they are speaking more or less cynically. It is hard for them to perceive conflict between the interests of the Soviet state and the world movement, as these should coincide. However, it is

---

[2] Jerome D. Frank, *Sanity and Survival* (New York: Vintage Books, 1968), p. 179.

clear that they are not confident of the popular loyalty which the ideology implies. Stalin had a manipulative approach; the war scares of the 1920's were plainly designed for political effect, and he was apparently surprised that the people actually supported his government in the war. At different times, words like *communism*, *internationalism*, and *revolution*, have had different meanings so far as they have had any operative significance. Even while using the same language, Soviet doctrine has shifted between more and less authoritarian-dogmatic and activist-revolutionary positions—using Lenin's words as authority for both. When there was a call to leftism, his writings of 1917 and 1918 were useful; when moderation was in order, works of later date, as *Left-Wing Communism: An Infantile Disorder*, could be brought out.

Marxism-Leninism has been and is entirely the servant of the Soviet state and not its master. The Soviet Union has not been interested in making revolution for its own sake, as a religion might be interested in saving souls. In Afghanistan, for example, where little was to be gained, it has refrained from any real effort to promote social change. It has been capable of rapid evolution, as when the outlook changed from the Popular Front of 1936 to the outrightly nationalistic dealings with Hitler in 1939, or when it changed so much in temper in the brief years from the death of Stalin to the Twentieth Congress. If it has remained stable to a degree, this must be because the needs of the Soviet state, as perceived by the ruler-priests, have remained basically the same.

No fixed canon, Soviet ideology is a mass of politically applied convictions, continually subject to interpretation and application according to circumstances and the outlook of the leadership. Dealing less with facts than with justice, the ideology represents the current orthodoxy of the system, the set of approved themes of education and propaganda, the explicit nonrational or at least nonprovable beliefs on which the structure rests. It includes, at least on the level of higher refinement, Marxist philosophy, economics, and historical interpretation, so far as still suitable. Unsuitable parts, such as Marx's attachment to political democracy and his strong feeling for freedom of the press, are forgotten. Lenin's revisions regarding imperialism, the character and role of the party, and the tactics and strategy of revolution, are essential. Emotional equalitarianism was strong in and shortly after the Revolution and has had varying strength since. Flexibility became the watchword as the Soviet state matured and dreams of radical improvement faded, and the frequently repeated "Marxism-Leninism is not a dogma but a guide to action" meant that it was elastic enough to cover whatever the situation required.

Many other ideas have been wrapped around or woven into the Marxist-Leninist core and have so taken on ideological character. The theme of peace, and in Khrushchev's time the idea of Peaceful Coexistence as the description of the struggle between capitalism and socialism in the nuclear age, have seemed at times central.[3] Rather specific matters of foreign policy, such as the threat to peace from one or another capitalist power, have seemed unquestionable dogma. The Stalinist priority for heavy industry was and with modifications continues to be an article of faith; it was extended to Eastern Europe when this came under Soviet control. The interpretation of Soviet history is also part of dogma, perhaps fixed, as in the rightness of Lenin's judgment on the peace of Brest Litovsk, perhaps varying, as in the assessment of Stalin's role in World War II. In part, ideology is a penchant for a certain jargon and form of discourse corresponding to a simplified way of viewing the world. In the early years, "world proletarian revolution" and its variants were repeated *ad nauseam; class*, *internationalism*, *socialism* and such words continue to make easier the tasks of Soviet political writers. Ideology might also be understood to include unacknowledged anti-Semitism, which has long been used to reinforce anticapitalism as well as for sundry political purposes.

One might perhaps better speak of Soviet mentality than ideology, since doctrine, ways, and attitudes of the authoritarian state, and Russian traits are entirely intermingled. The fondness for secrecy may be attributed to ideologically dictated distrust of the capitalist world, *ipso facto* inimical, but has probably had more to do with the Byzantine nature of the state; the Russians have at times shown little more confidence toward socialist allies. The habit of secrecy extends far beyond questions of political significance to such matters as space launchings and production and stocks of gold. Messianism, suspiciousness, exclusivism, stubbornness, self-righteousness, and tactics of delay and indirection, may appear as characteristic of the Communist approach to the capitalist world; they are, perhaps in heightened measure, traditional Russian.[4] If such traits have waned in recent years, this may be simply a sign of leaving behind more primitive conditions; secrecy is less today than in Stalin's day because there are more improvements to show and less backwardness to hide, without really implying ideological change.

Ideological-political style inclines to pay great attention to words. Not only are Soviet speeches, declarations, and diplomatic notes typically verbose; there is also a propensity for legalism and attention to manner of phrasing somewhat out of keeping with the Marxist interpretation of law as an essentially hollow part of the superstructure determined by the economic base of society. There has been tremendous emphasis on propaganda (a word which has no bad connotation in Russian, just as it had none for the Christian missionaries who coined it) and public opinion, despite frequent complete lack of appreciation of foreign psychology.

---

[3] Michael P. Gehlen, *The Politics of Coexistence* (Bloomington, Ind.: Indiana University Press, 1967), p. 59.

[4] Victor S. Mamatey, *Soviet Russian Imperialism* (Princeton, N.J.: D. Van Nostrand Co., Inc., 1964), p. 91.

This arises partly from a conviction of rightness; our truth surely will prevail if it can be brought to the ears of the masses. This faith was strongest in the first years, when Trotsky thought the message would keep the German troops from advancing into Russia. It was still evident in 1969, as the occupiers of Czechoslovakia made a great point of distributing their newssheet, although it seems to have been much more irritating than convincing. Confidence in propaganda may have deterred Stalin from more forceful measures against Yugoslavia in 1948.

Ironically, Soviet propaganda, often crude and ineffective, has done as much as Soviet actions to alienate the West. Along with faith in the word has gone a certain nonchalance about material reality; the permanently correct statement should override accidental contradictory facts. Communist diplomats blandly insisted that all was well with relations toward Communist China long after the split had become public knowledge. Manipulation of terms is considerably more brazen than usual in Western practice, as in Stalin's assertion that the best way for a nation to preserve its independent sovereignty was to join the Soviet Union.[5] It has seemed that Soviet leaders hardly expect their language to be taken seriously; often they have wrathfully denounced people in the most offensive terms and shortly afterwards expected to deal with them with complete equanimity, seeming surprised if the proffered hand of friendship was not clasped. Relevance may be neglected; there is an anecdote that a visitor in the 1930's asked the Soviet guide why there were no trains in the palatial Moscow subway. "What about the lynchings in your southern states?" the guide retorted. During part of the cold war, almost any American political proposal or statement was likely to be answered by denunciation of American bases around the Soviet Union.

Arguments must be stated so far as possible in doctrinal terms. Something bad cannot be attributed simply to human backwardness or weakness; it must be "bourgeois," "feudal" or "fascist." Antagonisms between states cannot be treated in simple political terms but must be analyzed in more or less Marxist jargon and attributed to corresponding motives. Instead of simply speaking of the inadmissibility of nuclear war, it was necessary to develop a doctrine of Peaceful Coexistence as a revision of an earlier doctrine of the inevitability of war. At least up to the ouster of Khrushchev, the clashes of Soviet politics were not so much of men over policies as of men using ideologically posited policies as weapons against their rivals, as Stalin hammered and destroyed Trotsky with Socialism in One Country, and Khrushchev ousted Malenkov over the priority of heavy industry.

A foreign policy issue may be expressed very indirectly. In February, 1955, Molotov denied that socialism had been built in the U.S.S.R.; the

---

[5] Elliot R. Goodman, *The Soviet Design for a World State* (New York: Columbia University Press, 1960), p. 124.

implication was that the country should devote itself to its own problems and refrain from trying to spread its influence beyond the bloc, as Khrushchev desired. The latter countered that socialism had irrevocably triumphed, that is, it was time to look outside. In negotiation, the Soviet representatives ~~have~~ preferred to argue from general principles and to characterize positions as "correct" or "incorrect," whereas the American would ask about practical effects and characterize proposals as "acceptable" or "unacceptable." In regard to disarmament, Westerners have also been much readier to proceed by small steps, whereas the Russians would demand a complete scheme agreed upon as a whole.[6]

The doctrinal approach serves to simplify complicated issues, as justification for almost anything can be pulled out of the Marxist bag and everything is reduced to a phase of the grand issue of good and evil. Soviet discourse is sprinkled with stereotypes and simple formulations; there has been a great fondness for slogans since the days when the Bolsheviks were concentrating on brief statements to be written on the banners of parading workers in 1917, and the party line of the hour was given by the slogan currently being pressed. The Russian language itself is prone to absolutist formulation; *authority*, for example, means total power, while *compromise* has negative overtones of corruption.[7] Bargaining hence implies a sacrifice of principles.

The ideological set is more perceptive of evil than good. Hatred is much more prominent than love or the search for any positive good, and there is little commendation except for unconditional adherents. Every setback or annoyance is attributable to some malevolence, which, when not directly attributable to class position, is the result of treason. The failure of Social Democratic leaders to join Communist movements was laid to their having been bribed, literally or in effect, by the bourgeoisie; if Communist parties fell flat, the reason, through Stalin's day, was usually held to be the betrayal of the leaders, just as Stalin attributed economic shortcomings to sabotage. As authoritarians, the Russians have had a good deal of difficulty in dealing with friendly equals, being inclined to treat them either as subordinates or enemies and often regarding their favorable disposition as hypocrisy. It has often seemed that they would rather bargain with an American capitalist than a European socialist.

2. IDEOLOGICAL PERCEPTION

The priorities of the Soviet Union seem to be much like those of other states, with first consideration for preservation of the state and political

[6] Frank, *Sanity and Survival*, p. 204.

[7] P. Mosely in R. Dennett and J. E. Johnson (eds.), *Negotiating with the Russians* (Boston: World Peace Foundation, 1951), p. 293.

system, next for close associates, and far below, the fostering of the Communist system in the world at large. The Russians are prepared to give or risk little for any distant or hypothetical cause.

Engrossed as Soviet leaders are in the problems of managing their huge state, it would require exceptional idealism for them to be much concerned with the vision of political transformation elsewhere, except as this might contribute to the security or greatness of the polity which they control; and revolutionary idealism has not been an outstanding characteristic of Soviet politics since Stalin's rise. The chief importance of ideology is in the way the world and the affairs of nations are perceived, as it affects the ordering of facts, the assignment of significance, and the choices seen available. It determines to some extent what kind of information is believed and defines channels of thought which lead to decisions. It gives categories and values in terms of which decision makers justify conduct to the world and to themselves. It lends interest to events everywhere. It is more applicable to viewing the foreign than the domestic scene, as facts far away are less obtrusive and Marxism treats not the socialist but the capitalist world. The Russians claim, in effect, that their perception is ideologically oriented, as they say that Marxism-Leninism gives true understanding of (capitalist) politics.

In the first flush of power, the Bolsheviks sometimes seem to have been practically hypnotized by ideology. Their fixations on the German revolution were a mild compulsion. Because Leninism stressed the urban proletariat and the Russian Revolution was made in the cities, it was believed that a Chinese revolution could come only in the same way. Only after many massacres and the decimation of the party in urban "proletarian" uprisings and after years of success of Mao in rural areas was it half-conceded that the revolutionary force in China could be the peasantry.

The importance of ideology in guiding Soviet foreign policy, however, has never been so great as would appear from the contention that its practitioners believe in and follow it. Much of it has no direct or obvious relevance for political action, and much can easily be used on either side of an argument. The basic assumption of progress through class conflict can be taken to promise spontaneous development, for which activity may be unnecessary or premature, or to encourage helping and taking advantage of historical trends; it dictates nothing. Belief in inevitable victory justifies either caution or boldness; "rightism" says to be careful, "leftism" to press forward, in the great dichotomy within the Communist outlook. Almost anything can be accounted for within the general framework; the bourgeoisie act in conformity with class interest or the personal profit motive. Theory for Lenin, and his successors in varying degrees, was always something to be modified according to the needs of the day. Theory has derived from strategy as much as vice versa; and as the Soviets envisioned different ways of approaching a goal, such as world revolution, the goal itself was changed. Expedients, found acceptable, are made doctrine, as Socialism in One Country or Peaceful Coexistence.

The significance of ideology is much greater for long-range expectations than for day-to-day operations, in which (although not in statements) Soviet diplomacy is often hardly distinguishable from traditional great-power politics. It is observable in speeches that premises are more doctrinal in relation to general and distant trends than to immediate problems; Marxism-Leninism claims to tell about the climate, not the weather.[8] When there is no pressure of crisis, the Soviet leaders seem more prone to indulge in ideological pronouncement, as though to occupy minds. In crises, it is pushed into the background by the needs of the state. Doctrinal considerations then probably do not seriously impede communication, as they did not, for example, in the missile crisis. The Soviet Union has, moreover, developed since Stalin a corps of diplomats accustomed to dealing with foreigners and capable of reasonable, even cordial, relations on a personal level.

The Soviet government has been capable of considering or doing almost anything as an expedient. Lenin suggested turning Kamchatka over to American firms as a concession, and Litvinov, in justification of friendly relations with Hitler in 1933, said, "But we as Marxists are the last who could be reproached with allowing sentiment to prevail over politics."[9] In the 1939–41 period of dealing with the Nazis, ideology seemed to carry little weight alongside ordinary considerations of power, and there is little reason to guess that it has become more important as motivation since. In postwar Eastern Europe, nationalization of industry was disapproved if it seemed harmful to Soviet trade. In 1961 Khrushchev is said to have criticized Gheorghiu-Dej for pushing collectivization of the peasantry lest it interfere with deliveries to Russia;[10] it was possible to be skeptical of the merits of collectivization abroad although not at home. If, after years of growing cordiality, French trade with the Soviet Union in 1969 had forged ahead of that of the much denigrated Bonn republic, this was apparently much more the result of the favor of the French than the preference of the Soviet government. In 1969 the latter was offering to the Neo-Nazi revanchists a favor denied the friendly French, an air route across Siberia.[11] Not only is doctrine freely ignored; the fact that it was and is at the service of the state means it is more manipulable than more detached idealism. In the time of the formation of the Popular Front in

[8] Jan F. Triska and David D. Finley, *Soviet Foreign Policy* (New York: Macmillan Co., 1968), pp. 119, 147.

[9] Julius Braunthal, *History of the International*, Vol. II, 1914–1943 (New York: Frederick A. Praeger, Inc., 1967), p. 398.

[10] David Floyd, *Rumania, Russia's Dissident Ally* (New York: Frederick A. Praeger, Inc., 1965), p. 68.

[11] *New York Times*, January 18, 1969.

France, it was easier for Communists than socialists to lay aside their principles of antimilitarism for political purposes.

Ideology has never weighed against security, and the rationality of Soviet foreign policy has been served by the fact that the U.S.S.R. has largely been on the defensive in reality, although verbally offensive. Unlike the Hitlerites, Soviet leaders have been very much bent on survival. The Russians have been accustomed to overlooking principles for urgent practical reasons; it was America, not Russia, which kept diplomatic relations suspended for sixteen years for ideological reasons. America felt able to give itself this small luxury. Faith in history in any case justifies postponing conflicts as long as possible, and postponement is avoidance. Even Lenin's idea of inevitable war was not nearly so belligerent in Soviet understanding as it was to Western ears. Marxism suggests no time limits, and the Russians have set none. An ideological statement of foreign policy aims, then, can be a mixed bag of mostly rather ordinary objectives, as in an authoritative statement of 1967:

> Soviet foreign policy is designed to secure peaceful conditions for the building of socialism and communism, to cement the unity and cohesion of the socialist countries, to support the liberation and revolutionary movements, to promote solidarity and cooperation with the independent African, Asian and Latin American countries, and to further the principles of the peaceful coexistence of states with different social systems.[12]

Marxist-Leninist glasses, even when kept close to the eyes, have not always impeded clarity of vision. If they have led to underestimation of political factors, they have given acuity in perception of economic determinants and their relations to the political, sometimes slighted by Western statesmen. The determination to oppose "capitalist imperialism" corresponds entirely with sound balance-of-power considerations, although more idealistic in appearance. To help the weaker against the stronger is a principle at least as old as Demosthenes; to help Latin America free itself from the alleged control of U.S. monopolies is rational power politics, as Stalin's effort to let Britain and France fight Germany alone would have been but for his overestimation of the strength of the Western powers. Even where ideology leads to an apparent irrationality, this may serve a deeper cause. For example, the Stalinist drive for a heavy industrial base in the Eastern European satellites may have been economic nonsense, but it served to divorce them from the West and bind them to the Soviet Union.

It must be conceded, however, that to an indeterminable but real degree the prisms of ideology have distorted the Soviet view of the world and hence reduced freedom of maneuver and made more difficult initiatives and responses suitable to the interests of the Soviet state, whether as

[12] V. Israelian *et al.*, *Soviet Foreign Policy, a Brief Review* (Moscow, 1967), p. 21.

viewed by outsiders or by Soviet leaders, and so have frustrated Soviet designs. Men cannot divorce their own thinking from ideas which they propagate, and ideology by definition is more or less myth and illusion, certain to deviate widely at some points from reality; its purpose is to get men to believe things beyond factual evidence.

There has been distortion of some degree in Soviet foreign policy for a number of reasons not directly ideological. The separation of rulership from reality, the atmosphere of conformism if not bootlicking, and the lack of objectivity of a highly authoritarian state could not fail to influence decisions, especially under Stalin. The state capable of the madness of the purges could not be expected to be entirely sensible in external dealings. In some ways, the Soviet government has seemed simply bureaucratic, as in the pettifogging quarrel over the assets of the Baltic states which worsened relations with England in 1940–41. Molotov's bargaining with Hitler in 1940 bespeaks no questions of principle but a very narrow view of the Soviet interest. Some of Khrushchev's outbursts and rocket rattlings may be seen as simply the emotional reactions of a man accustomed to being treated with great deference at home and annoyed not to receive similar respect everywhere.

Other nations, too, have suffered delusions of ideology. For France and England to rush to the defense of Finland in the Winter War would have been inconceivable but for the misperceptions of antibolshevism, and the United States would hardly have become involved in Vietnam if the situation had not been viewed in terms of ideological values. But a political philosophy which claims to hold the keys to understanding of past, present, and future is a serious burden to the intellect. If consideration of policy is fitted into an artificial scheme of any kind, advantages not covered by that scheme are more or less neglected.

As motives in foreign policy are very difficult to disentangle, it is hard to point to particular actions as ideologically predicated. An example might be the Soviet insistence on a centralized German government in the first postwar years. The most obvious reason for this policy was Marx's argument of nearly a century earlier in favor of centralization on grounds that local authorities would be an obstacle to proletarian revolutionary activity; in the conditions of the 1940's, it would seem clear that a weak German government was much more in the interests of the Soviet state and of communism in Germany. In a different vein, when the Bolsheviks were handing out the leftover gold of the tsarist regime in the first years after the revolution, they were undoubtedly confident that it was soon to lose monetary value, considering themselves clever to unload an obsolescent asset.

For the most part, however, ideology has made itself felt more subtly and broadly, as in the impeding of understandings and agreements with the heathen, although such understandings may well be in the Soviet interest. Superior virtue, which the Russians do not hesitate to claim, makes dialogue less fruitful, and the Soviet leaders and diplomats remained largely excluded from alien cultures and impervious to them when exposed. They have been markedly suspicious, frequently inclined to regard concessions of the other side as evidence of insincerity or possible traps. Ideology makes into issues of principle and emotion many questions which could otherwise perhaps be disposed of simply as practical matters; this has been most notable in the Sino-Soviet rift. Differences with Tito in the latter 1950's could not be treated as a clash of interests but had to be brought into the framework of revisionism. The Soviet estimate of the concrete situation has been much less distorted than the analysis of motives, which is always unflattering to the other side. Capitalists and their hirelings can have only attitudes of narrow self-interest and must be deeply antisocialist and anti-Soviet. Exasperating and fundamentally undiplomatic attacks on the motives of those with whom the Russians may be bargaining sorely tried the patience of Western diplomats in Stalin's time, and such an approach has by no means been given up.

As motives are supposed to be given by economic situation, by and large, there is little room in the Soviet scheme for human caprice and irrationality. There is inadequate appreciation of all the diversity and complexity of the world; it is a basic function of ideology to make the unintelligible universe simple, hiding confusion behind the myth. Since Social Democrats and Nazis were alike agents of the bourgeoisie, there was little to choose between them, and prior to Hitler's taking power it was held tactically more advantageous to concentrate fire upon the rivals for leadership of the working classes. In the Marxist-Leninist framework, Maoism is quite unanalyzable and hence unintelligible. From the premises that socialism overcomes all troubles and that the capitalist nations wish only to keep the less developed countries in subjection, it follows that efforts to promote birth control in the latter are disguised imperialism. Schematic Marxist philosophy encourages the belief that development should follow, with minor local variation, the same course everywhere, hence that the Russian model is universally valid. This led, when revolutionary enthusiasm was raw, to some naïve comparisons. The November, 1918, semirevolution in Germany was the counterpart of the overthrow of the tsar; Ebert was Germany's Kerensky; the Kapp putsch was equivalent to the Kornilov putsch. Hence, in disregard of enormous differences of circumstances, Germany's October Revolution had most certainly to follow in prescribed order; and Soviet Russia laid heavy stakes upon it. This approach also justified the centralization of control of the world Communist movement in the Soviet center of Marxist practice and theory. It subsequently clouded Soviet understanding of failures of the movement, making at least theoretically incomprehensible many a conflict, down to the split with China and the Czech heresy.

Nationalism has been particularly underestimated by the Russians. Americans, seeing the spread of their influence in the postwar period, have been subject to the same failing; but it is much more severe when reinforced by the requirement that all be interpreted in terms of class. It is simply unrealistic to regard the fundamental unit of international conflict as class instead of nation, and this has brought much unnecessary isolation on the Soviet Union. In the Leninist revision of Marxism, Soviet leaders have been inclined to exaggerate the likelihood of conflict between capitalistic powers; but they find it difficult to regard conflicts of national interest as normal, and they have regularly attributed national opposition to class motives. If they have realistically doubted the likelihood of impartiality in international affairs, they have wrongly attributed this to class instead of national prejudices and thereby have often repelled potential friends.

The assumption that the working classes are fundamentally internationalist, coupled with wishful estimates of the strength of pro-Soviet forces, has led to many grave misjudgments: Trotsky's assumption in 1918 that German soldiers would refuse to shoot at their Russian brothers; Lenin's hopes for a rising of Polish workers in 1920; Stalin's bets on a Finnish welcome for the Red Army in 1939; probably a conviction in 1968 that the Czech masses were much more pro-Soviet than the vocal minority. Overestimating the role and potentialities of Communist parties, it has been very hard for Soviet leaders to perceive the grave disutility of supporting them even verbally. Such illusions have much receded in the last few years, but even in 1968, despite the enormous advantages of friendship with de Gaulle, the Soviet Union was not prepared fully to dissociate itself from the French Communist party. Even if nothing were actively done about it, it has been a handicap for Soviet diplomacy to speak and to a degree to think in terms of a future bound up with the success of a particular movement or set of radical but largely impotent and much disliked parties.

Ideology deals with means as well as goals. In the Leninist assumption, the transformation of quantitative change into qualitative requires violence, and Lenin considered it desirable as well as necessary to inaugurate the Soviet state by use of the Red Guards instead of by political pressure. Czech Communists thought it admirable and fitting to bring their followers into the streets in 1948 to make their takeover more gloriously like Lenin's. Similarly, there has been an emphasis on mass or mob demonstrations and strikes beyond their probable efficacity; such actions against, for example, the Marshall Plan, served not to decrease but to increase its acceptance in Western Europe.

Preference for sometimes rather crude tactics, along with dogmatic narrowness and insistence on all-or-nothing conformity, has alienated many who might be promising allies of communism. With amazing arrogance, the Leninists slammed the doors of the Comintern in the face of those who eagerly wanted to be good friends of the first socialist state. The secrecy with which so much in the Soviet system is enveloped greatly reduced its persuasiveness for the uncommitted, the noncommunist left of the West and the Third World.[13] The Russians find foreign individualism hard to deal with, and they have consequently fallen short in appealing to the large sector of disenchanted intellectuals of the West. In view of the Soviet denial or artistic freedom, it is remarkable that such artists as Picasso and Sartre have been willing to identify themselves so far as they have with communism. The rigidity and unimaginativeness of Communist doctrine have largely deprived it of influence over the contemporary effervescence of youth and racial and national minorities. A doctrine supposedly oriented to basic change has seemed impotent in situations of so much apparent promise.

When the answers are already given and thinking may be uncomfortable or dangerous, mental inertia is the rule. Soviet diplomacy has usually been rather wooden and uninventive. In the first years, under Chicherin, who had a prerevolutionary education, there was some originality, as in the approach to peace, nonaggression pacts, and disarmament. Since then, imitation has been more evident. Stalin aped Hitler. The organizations of Soviet Europe, Comecon and WTO, followed and were copied after the corresponding Western organizations. Khrushchev's Peaceful Coexistence was based on the Chinese and Indian example. His program of foreign aid was clearly inspired by the American; he was not even ashamed to start a Soviet Peace Corps. In putting rockets in Cuba, he was taking a leaf from the American book.

Any firm ideology easily becomes conservative, as it looks back to the world in which it originated and speaks for an increasingly settled and conservative political order. It stands squarely in the way of rethinking of assumptions. One goes on saying the old things until they are blatantly unsuitable, and frank innovation is avoided; changes perforce accepted must be bolstered with quotations from the classics to prove that they are not really changes. New situations are squeezed into old categories; if amendments are accepted, they are laid on like patches without an effort to rethink fundamentals or even much attempt at sound reconciliation. Since Marxism-Leninism should confirm the answers given by Soviet practice, there can be little or no analysis of institutions, Soviet or foreign. The given is sacred; it cannot be objectively compared with existing or possible alternatives. Political science is impossible in the Soviet scheme, and sociology was nonexistent until recently and remains rudimentary and strictly utilitarian.

---

[13] P. Wiles in Arnold Toynbee *et al.*, *The Impact of the Russian Revolution, 1917–1967* (New York: Oxford University Press, Inc., 1968), pp. 363 ff.

The Soviet mental set thus limits flexibility and inventiveness in dealing with a wide range of problems of modernity, from urbanization and automation to nuclear control. Particularly in the last area, Soviet doctrine is much less developed than American; Soviet strategic doctrine is not subject to the same kind of public discussion and is very much less sophisticated. The problem of accidental war is hardly touched; there are supposed to be no accidents nor miscalculations, only evil intentions. Because of weakness of political thinking, together with fear and dislike for organizations they cannot control, the Russians have contributed nothing to thinking regarding an improved international order. The many postwar Western schemes for peace-keeping and security met from the Soviets mostly derision.[14] Cosmopolitanism, anathema in Stalin's day, has always been hated; it is an antinational strategem of imperialism.[15] While accepting the United Nations as fairly useful, the Russians are in principle opposed to any supranational organization which is not theirs. Marxism-Leninism, looking to no stable world, encourages no norms for a stable order, and international law figures poorly in the Soviet canon as a temporary expedient between capitalism and socialism.

A by-product of Soviet universalism is hostility to any suggestion of a competing universalism, even though it might suit Soviet interests; no other than the Soviet answer to the problem of international order can be considered. Pan-Islam and Pan-African schemes, Arab unity, and the like have all been very poorly regarded, although they would seem to be anti-Western in effect. Federations of neighboring states are very unwelcome also. For example, ideas put forward after World War II for Polish-Czech federation or Balkan union were opposed; but here straight power-political motives reinforce the ideological perception.

3. BURDENS OF THE CAUSE

If ideology affects thinking about the world, this is by no means all or even the larger part of the burden it lays on Soviet foreign policy. Worse is the identification of the Soviet Union with a radical cause. The Russian regime which came out of the Revolution at first regarded itself more as a movement than a state in the conventional sense, and to this day it has not fully shed this feeling. Thus, Soviet foreign policy has been basically schizophrenic, torn by contradictory drives: for the undoing of foreign states or normal relations with them in the first years; for seeking collective security or advancing communism in the 1930's; for checking Ger-

---

[14] Goodman, *Soviet Design for a World State*, pp. 396–97.

[15] *Kommunist*, January, 1969, No. 1, p. 6.

many or collaborating with it in 1939–41; for cooperating with or at least reaching a settlement with the United States versus expansion of the Soviet sphere in postwar years; for Peaceful Coexistence or ideological warfare in the time of Khrushchev; for normalizing relations with the West or securing the Communist sphere in the last years, for revolutionary dynamism or preservation of the status quo. To strive for contradictory goals, however, is to invite frustration. Both the practical-minded Russian ambassador and the idealistic Communist have been much disappointed, and the story of Soviet diplomacy has been one of achievements eked out despite contradictions.

The task which Russia gratuitously undertook in claiming to inaugurate the new, socialist era was an unrewarding one unless it should have proved rapidly victorious. Even in the first years, the idea of seeking to save the regime by fomenting the overthrow of foreign governments was, if understandable, highly misguided as practical policy. The apparent chances of further widespread revolution were practically nil after 1923, but the Soviet state could never dissociate itself from it. To put oneself on the side of social revolution is to raise the hackles of most of the world, which is almost always nonrevolutionary. The poor and oppressed whose cause the Soviet Union has supposedly espoused are also the weak. The slavish loyalty of the Communist party of a country was poor compensation for the fear and hatred of most of its middle and upper classes and the government. The foreign proletariats have never done anything of importance for the Soviet state since the end of the civil war. The whole idea of sponsoring the demolition of all existing governments can be characterized as a preposterous effrontery, which, to the good fortune of Soviet Russia, the West never took quite seriously. As time passed, there was less and less obviously to be gained, even if it were successful; worst of all, when independent Communist states came out of World War II, it appeared that they might be anything but subservient to the Soviet Union and even, as China, hostile.

The Soviet Union has caused itself endless difficulties in the world by making so much of something so essentially negative as revolution, and it has laid much more emphasis, as seen from abroad, on the tearing down than on the building of a better new society, which in the Russian exemplar was not outstandingly attractive. The Soviet approach seemed, to most of those not already filled with hatred for their own social order, to be destructive if not hateful. The fundamental Marxist concept of class warfare is repugnant to most accepted values of settled civilization (including the Soviet, if applied to it). Thoroughly antipatriotic, it threatens to rend the social fabric and make violent schisms among the people, the worse as Leninism insisted on the taking of power by force. Not content thus to affront the world and especially the respectable and powerful, the Bolsheviks proceeded to challenge—at first to spit upon—the most cherished values. In the early years, all the bourgeois virtues, from thrift to chastity, were held up to scorn as selfish and hypocritical; accusations that the Bolsheviks were even bent on destroying the family had just enough truth to give them force. The nation-state, the foundation of international affairs, was denounced as a fraud.

Worst of all, religion was blackened and persecuted, and this has been a permanent drag on Soviet diplomacy. That the Bolsheviks were militant atheists seemed to many to range them with the devil, and anticommunist propaganda has found no stronger point. There is not much room for trust between real believers and aggressive nonbelievers. Roosevelt pointed to Soviet antireligion as the greatest obstacle to American support in 1941, and Stalin's reconciliation with the Orthodox Church was much more significant for the outside world than his dissolution of the Comintern. But the Soviet regime reverted to the promotion of atheism, albeit less forcefully than in prewar years, and this has remained a major bar to Soviet influence. If Europe has come to take the religious question more lightly, nations of Africa and the Near East still have difficulty in squaring close relations with the Soviet Union with their religious consciences.

If much of the ideological fixation has thus made it more difficult for the Soviet state to win friends in the world, their ways and manners have also detracted from their popularity and success. Insistence on a right of intervention everywhere by the sponsorship and more or less control of Communist parties has been injurious even where ineffective. The Soviet-style organization of Communist parties presents a hateful challenge to their more inhibited competitors, and their narrowness and harshness have almost intentionally created enemies. Insistence on the whole cake of revolution has hurt both the Soviet cause and that of revolution, which is more expeditiously made not by terrifying the elite of its prospects but by bringing forward reasonably acceptable demands in the name of traditional values and moving forward as the ground is prepared. Even when the Bolsheviks were actually doing very little, by talk they made themselves as threatening as possible; not surprisingly, many in the West have credited them with irredeemable hostility and seriously believed that their main purpose was the destruction of Western society. Talk of spreading communism is as damaging to the Soviet image as material efforts to this end; proclamation of any sort of a crusade invites a real countercrusade. The posture of the Soviet Union has made it and the "world Communist conspiracy" an appropriate whipping boy for not only sincere conservatives but any reactionaries in need of an excuse for repression.

The Soviet Union has also made many actions more abhorrent by the manner of their execution or the gestures accompanying them. For example, the most reprobated step it has ever taken, the war against Finland, would have seemed much more understandable if not pardonable to the world had it been presented merely in terms of strategic necessity, not the overthrow of the Finnish government (which was, of course, not achieved). The Finns could never have fought with such desperate courage just to keep a small strip of territory. Likewise the crudities of the appropriation of Eastern Europe made it far less acceptable to the West. Even the Brezhnev-Kosygin government, relatively sophisticated as it is, made the occupation of Czechoslovakia less acceptable by associating it with a broad interventionist doctrine. The West is more inclined to forgive the sins of national interest of which it admits its own guilt; and it finds more offensive the seemingly hypocritical justifications and assertions of universal-imperial authority. Communists and anticommunists have cooperated to make the Soviet Union look purposefully dangerous.

From one point of view, it has been advantageous for the Western powers that the Soviet state has made a generally repellent image of itself, as it has thereby been far less successful in terms of power than it might have been. The separation of the borderlands after World War I would have been unlikely had there been no question of social revolution, giving Western powers strong reasons to support national movements. Whereas the tsarist government was looking forward to rule of the Straits and a large part of Persia, the Soviet government had to swallow, temporarily, the loss of Bessarabia. The great difficulties Russia experienced in regaining, through the 1920's and 1930's, much of the influence once wielded by the tsarist government must also be laid as a debit to ideology. Collective security failed, the Spanish Republic was sacrificed, and understanding with the West against Hitler was impossible primarily for the same reason. Hitler made his war against Russia a crusade against Bolshevism, and he received the support of a fair part of Europe in the name of extirpating this alleged evil. Soviet expansion after the war was far more feared and opposed because of fear that the spread of communism was indefinite and any aggrandizement enlarged the base for the world mission.

Communist parties have been most successful when least bound by dogma and Soviet direction, as in the Popular Front and wartime alliance periods. It may even be surmised that Soviet subversive activities have been markedly handicapped by ideological cast. The Nazis were rather successful in the subverting of weaker governments, and the American CIA has several coups to its credit; the Russians despite great exertions have none. In short, thanks in part to a backward political tradition, a good deal of crudity, internal political needs, and a compulsion to associate itself with radical change in the world without, Soviet foreign policy has suffered many unnecessary difficulties, and Soviet prestige has been much inferior to the importance of the Soviet Union in the world.

The successes of the Soviet system and its ideology, on the other hand, have been basically internal. The faith helped knit together Lenin's party and enabled it first to capture the government and then to win the civil war. It made possible a complete renewal of the political system, permitted rapid recovery from terrible losses, and in due course facilitated the collectivization of agriculture and the rapid construction of a powerful industrial plant. With the party structure which it promoted, it held the country firmly together through the trials of World War II, in contrast to the breakdown in World War I, and assured rapid growth of military and economic strength afterwards. The Russians have cause to congratulate themselves, but not for successes in foreign policy or for the promotion of communism through the world.

4. NEED FOR IDEOLOGY

Some of the benefits of ideology for Soviet foreign policy are quite obvious. It lends some credibility to claims, such as a less doctrinaire state would hesitate to put forward, of social justice and joyous progress toward a golden utopia. It promises equality, or more than equality, to the multitude who feel themselves discriminated against and abased. It gives an apparently reasoned optimism for those who despair of the unsatisfactory present order, which is seen as doomed as well as wrong, while the future is as inevitable as it is right. A sophisticated doctrine, it seems, like Platonism, to raise the role of the thinker and has correspondingly appealed to many unhappy intellectuals, for whom it offers a philosophic alternative with the respectability of great-power backing. It provides certainty in a fluid and uncertain world; to join the Communist movement has meant in the past and to some extent still means to escape the responsibilities of freedom and individual decision. The party gives a firm direction to the individual and answers his deeper questions in terms of general truth.

Communism also promises peace; only by abolishing self-seeking capitalism can the nations be brought to harmony and concord, Lenin proclaimed and the Soviet Union maintains to this day. The appeal to war-weariness more than anything else brought the Bolsheviks to power. Advocacy of disarmament and appeals for peace have always served the Russians well. It was also useful from time to time to raise alarms of war, from talk of capitalist intervention in the 1920's to stress on the destructiveness of nuclear weapons under Khrushchev. The appeal of communism as promising an end of war has been much diminished by dissidence within what used to be the Sino-Soviet bloc. But this appeal may come yet more to the fore as the social-economic utopia of communism recedes: to avoid strife let the nations accept the protection of the mighty Soviet Union. There have consequently been in almost every country a number, sometimes a rather large number, of persons prepared to lay hopes on the Soviet Union and so to favor what it favored and oppose whatever seemed injurious to it. Ideology has effectively served Soviet foreign policy by dividing and confusing the potential opposition.

Ideology would thus seem to have direct political utility. The Soviet leadership, pleased to have foreign admirers, would tend to overestimate their importance and utility as the Communists did of themselves. Communist parties were clearly annoying to governments unfriendly to the Soviet Union, hence desirable for the latter (and in circular fashion, the more the parties caused foreign governments to be hostile, the more virtuous and useful they appeared to be). The Communist movement offered a lever for subversion of foreign states, not a good one in reality but one which was attractively present, had little direct cost, and the importance of which was inflated by ideology. It seemed an excellent tool, at least in certain areas like Iran, for acquiring strategic advantages; elsewhere, it served to divide and demoralize the hostile or potentially hostile outside world, while wishful and ideological thinking prevented perception of its true cost to the Soviet state.

A more important reason, however, for the firmness with which the Soviet leadership has held to the Marxist-Leninist world view is its enormous psychological utility. During the decades when Russia was relatively weak and poor, it was especially comforting to have an excuse for feeling morally superior, just as today the abysmal poverty of China makes the doctrinal exaggeration of Maoism a pleasing reassurance for a proud nation and culture. It is no small satisfaction to regard oneself, with the support of a well-worked-out body of supposedly scientific teachings, as riding in the vanguard of history ahead of other nations, destined for ultimate glory, engaged not in protecting banal national interests but in promoting a crusade of universal justice. In self-idealization, Soviet leaders could consider all their actions meritorious contributions to a cause, and extension of their power became noble. Opposition to them and their purposes they could regard as inherently evil, produced by class bias and bourgeois selfishness. There has consequently been total self-righteousness in Soviet foreign policy, as it has claimed absolute purity of motives on a higher plane; very seldom has even a slight error of judgment been admitted in Soviet chronicles.

Self-righteousness has weighed on many peoples who have felt the intoxication of great power, as it has upon Germans, Japanese, British, and Americans in modern times and many others in history; but for the Russians it has been peculiarly supported by an elaborate framework of dogma. If it has not detracted more from the sobriety of Soviet foreign policy, this may be because of the primacy of internal affairs in the attention of the regime, amply occupied by cares at home, and because of the sufferings of the land. The woes of 1914–21 were enough to dictate caution for a long time, and so were the losses and devastation of 1941–45;

but the self-confidence and pride given by ideology are very strong, and they are beneficial to morale and political resolve. The Russians have usually been on the offensive in the arguments. They have been bolstered by their certitude of right, and they have usually defined the issues in their terms.

If the capitalist powers hate the Soviet Union, this is taken as evidence of its virtue. Ideology also serves the legitimacy and self-image of the Soviet Union through the foreign Communist parties. This has been the most important function of the world Communist movement ever since the Bolsheviks claimed power in 1917, not as mere malcontents seeking to displace a disliked government but as the vanguard of world revolution and renovation. It is wholly understandable that loyalty to the Soviet Union soon became explicitly the chief criterion of communism; and this is a permanent thesis, restated for the benefit of the Czechs in 1968. "Socialist" in Soviet parlance refers to nothing more nor less than the Soviet system or what is approved by it, and a country has long been approved or disapproved by virtue of its relation to the Soviet Union with little reference to its class structure.

One must look mostly, however, to internal needs for understanding the force and persistence of ideology in foreign policy. For Marx, ideology was a set of ideas helping to justify bourgeois domination, but it is really a reflection much more of political than economic interests, and authoritarian-imperial states make much greater use of ideology than liberal-bourgeois. An authoritarian regime, especially if it controls a very large country, is in a position to impose ideology as no liberal government could dream of doing, and there is no reason for it to refrain from doing so. Being a regime in which rulers feel free to defy the wishes of most of the people indefinitely, it is not likely to admit that it holds power by force for the benefit of those in charge but practically requires a higher reason, some doctrine authorizing a few to assume rights over the many. This is necessary partly to make more understandable the need for submission. It is also very important for the moralization of the regime, to give standards of virtue by which the leadership can demand loyalty and probity from the bureaucrats and hold themselves to reasonable standards of virtue. It is much easier to command, too, if one first believes. Unless there is a convincing faith and some willingness to look beyond self-interest, an authoritarian system must quickly degenerate in complete corruption and gangsterism. The view of historical progress and a role in which they find it agreeable to believe has served the Soviet elite well to this end.

There is no conflict between ideology and political interests, because ideology, perhaps always and certainly in the Soviet case, exists to serve the interests of those who make, guard, and propagate it, the political elite. It can be adequately defined as the set of beliefs which support the authority of the Soviet state. Abstract idealism hardly enters. Elements of the teachings of Marx, Engels, or even Lenin, which are not useful for this purpose are irrelevant. Ideology is not very constricting, since components are dropped or added in conformity with ongoing needs. The canon, however solid in fundamentals, is quite elastic in application. Communists can stress will or determinism, initiative or discipline, freedom or centralization, democracy or leadership, while denouncing both dogmatism and opportunism. The so-called laws of dialectic have no predictive use but can be applied to the justification of any policy. Ideological virtue is synonymous with political conformism. If one can point to little in Soviet foreign policy evidently done mostly for reasons of ideology, still less is to be found in domestic; the imperative is never or practically never ideology or even the need for consistency but (aside from practical necessity) political will or the advantage of the holders of power expressed as general principle.

The Soviet is an elitist, authoritarian government rationalized and strengthened by a relatively humane ideology. It is no contradiction that an arbitrary government should wear an attractive garment; in a sense, the more dictatorial the more useful for it to have a good facade. That Marxism-Leninism encourages education and social security for the masses is to the good of rulers and ruled alike. Equalitarianism, a very appealing doctrine, helped rather than hindered the real (as against the ostensible) concentration of power. Most great despotisms have been outwardly equalitarian in some degree.[16] It is desired to remove potential alternative foci of power; not infrequently, Moguls or Sultans have relied on slaves to govern the realm rather than aristocrats, who were likely to show much more independence of mind. In the proletariat, the Soviet creed exalted the class most subject to political manipulation and most effectively usable against peasants and aristocrats alike. The abolition of large-scale private property also satisfied socialistic urges and at the same time removed a potential challenge to political power and ideology and integration of society. Soviet emphasis on mass participation in the lower levels of administration is also highly suitable, making concessions to the modern ethos and giving some sense of participation without denting the power of decision of those on top. The Soviet system is a remarkable combination of popular appearances and hierarchic reality, of authoritarianism and progressivism.

The heart of Marxism-Leninism is the justification of the rule of the Communist party,[17] and ideology and party are two aspects of a single whole, like creed and church, the word and the flesh. It is the modern equivalent of a caesaropapism. When the making of the Revolution, the

[16] Robert G. Wesson, *The Imperial Order* (Berkeley, Calif.: University of California Press, 1967), pp. 145–53.

[17] Alfred G. Meyer, "The Functions of Ideology in the Soviet System," *Soviet Studies,* Vol. XVII, No. 3 (January, 1966), pp. 229 ff.

overthrow of the semisacred tsardom and the catharsis of the state required a claim to a new sacredness, the Bolsheviks declared themselves bearers of a universal mission sanctified by historical destiny. As self-anointed representatives of the proletariat, the class of future, they were entitled to replace the former ruling classes, and they had more need of ideology as they were outsiders pushing aside traditional and accepted holders of power. They had to portray the old order as categorically and absolutely bad, the new as absolutely good.

Having grasped power, Lenin found in the Marxist world view (as modified by himself) excuses for consolidating it, a suitable explanation for opposition and reasons for crushing it. The object of Lenin's devotion, the party, stood forward as representative of the embattled workers in a backward and hostile world, carrying a mission of supreme justice; and with the legitimacy, principles of order, and morale based on this vision it went on to win the civil war. Victory went far toward making Bolshevik rule acceptably legitimate, but it remained and remains important to have Leninist rationalizations for rule. Ideology is a major means of keeping supremacy against the military, the administrative apparatus, the police, or the economic managers. Stalin, ruling more by arbitration among groups, somewhat cut down the role of the party. To restore it, Khrushchev looked to a revival of Leninism.

The preservation of the wholeness of the realm is perhaps the greatest permanent excuse for authoritarianism, and the Russian empire badly needed a substitute for the nationalism which gives coherence to Western states. The Bolshevik ideology gave a common and glorious destiny to the whole Soviet conglomerate, as it did to the party more particularly. It brought together rulers and ruled, raising everything Soviet and socialist morally above the rest of the world, which it should lead into utopia. It set off the noble Soviet from the base and irreconcilable alien world. Western ideas of democracy and nationalism, dangerous in Soviet as in tsarist times not only to the rule of the party but to the integrity of the state, were excluded as products of the enemy. The uncontrolled was branded as evil externally as internally; and ideological instruction served not only to form correct attitudes but to exclude alternative world views.

5. SOVIET PRUSSIANISM

Most purposes of Soviet ideology could be served by a simple collectivist-authoritarian ethos. Any very strong government might by all means at its command inculcate patriotism and obedience without the involved and schematic ideas of a nineteenth-century German philosopher-economist. Revolution and class struggle are irrelevant to the modern Soviet state, and Marx's generally democratic and libertarian sentiments are inconvenient to its elite. The communist utopia of complete equality and the withering of the coercive state is neither credible nor politically very desirable. As a relatively wealthy power, the Soviet Union finds it more difficult to identify, even in an abstract way, with the world's poor. The Soviet state, which rejects workers' control while it increases managerial authority, is much like a gigantic corporation,[18] and the pretense that it is a working-class organization has worn very thin.

The idealization of Lenin also has some drawbacks, as the picture of the rebel standing nobly against the corrupt but mighty state may well inspire communist idealists who see in the Soviet regime a failure to achieve the promises of the Revolution. But the Soviet faith is much more Leninist than Marxist. For Lenin, politics took priority over economics, and he set about establishing in Russia a rulership nominally proletarian but really elitist. His lack of faith in spontaneity and his sanctioning of the dictatorship of a few in the name of the many are quite in accord with the imperial power structure. For him, as for the present leaders, morality consisted much more in loyalty than in any doctrinal correctness. Still, the Soviet Union has moved far from Lenin. He had a good deal of faith in a proletariat, although as followers only, and distrusted the bureaucratism which he saw reasserting itself shortly after the revolutionary purification. But his semiproletarian party has become a quite nonclass power-political apparatus. His teachings, moreover, referred mostly to prerevolutionary political struggles and the making of the revolution; less and less are they reasonably applicable to any modern problems except as quotations are arbitrarily brought out to make particular points.

Hence, the Soviet ideology is much more apotheosis of Lenin, whose glory is that of an earthbound Christ without recognized disciples, whose image glowers over every event of importance, than Leninism, as embodied in scores of volumes of his writings. He is the great of the great, the towering figure of modern history. Countless tales and reminiscences are brought out regarding the all-wise, brave, humane, and utterly selfless leader. Lenin dominates the kindergarten as much as the university, as children swear to conduct themselves as he taught. Lenin lived, the Soviet people are told, Lenin lives and will live forever. As *Pravda* editorialized:[19]

> All our lives, all that we have won and built and are building in the beloved Soviet land is inseparably bound with the name and teachings of Lenin, with the activity of the Communist Party he founded. . . . Forty-five years have passed from the day when Il'ich's [Lenin's] heart stopped beating. . . . Time

---

[18] Cf. Alfred G. Meyer, *The Soviet Political System* (New York: Random House, Inc., 1965).

[19] January 21, 1969.

has no power over the bright image and life-affirming spiritual heritage of our leader and teacher. His ideas are immortal, like the cause to which he gave his life. . . .

There is a mystic relationship:

When the picture of Lenin appears on the giant screen and seems to come close to us, when it seems that Il'ich is looking into each of us in a fatherly, questioning manner, ever more intently, there comes a striking feeling of *your personal* meeting Il'ich, the same feeling which inspired Maiakovskii when he wrote, "There are two of us in the room, I and Lenin, the photograph on the white wall." Yes, each of us in the two-thousand-seated auditorium is at this moment alone with Il'ich.[20]

The principal mission of probes to Venus in May, 1969, it seemed from newspaper headlines, was to place the image of Lenin on that sister planet. In Eastern Europe, also, Lenin-worship is promoted as a supplement to more academic ideology: to be anti-Soviet is to oppose the work of the great Lenin.

Similarly, socialism has come to be equivalent simply to Sovietism, or practically to patriotism. The social order is in fact the state; having started out to shift loyalties from state to class, the Russians found themselves by political realities building new and perhaps stronger loyalties to a new state, even as against others recognized as having the proper "class" leadership. Central planning and controls, the direction of the arts, and foreign policy objectives are all justified by the needs of building socialism, but this can have no other definition than the main outlines of the Soviet system. The state, somewhat as in Hegel's conception, is an end in itself. It was once conceived as the base of the world movement, but if it now looks to the world movement at all it is as a means of raising Soviet glory and prestige.

Since the 1930's, when Stalin, perhaps paying Hitler the tribute of imitation, strongly revived traditional Russian values and the theme of Russia's services to civilization, a somewhat vague but intense nationalism has been central (alongside the apotheosis of Stalin while he lasted) if not dominant in Soviet ideology.[21] This is a varying mixture of traditional Great Russianism, Sovietism, pride in the Revolution and its achievements, messianism and antiforeignism, a sense of belonging to a historical destiny incorporated in the Soviet state. The modern Soviet mentality has become suggestive of that of tsarist Russia, with its mingling of Russianism, imperial pride, and concern for legitimacy and order colored by universalist themes from the Third Rome and Orthodoxy to Pan-Slavism. The Soviet state is more modern, purposeful, science- and future-ori-

---

[20] *Pravda,* January 31, 1969.

[21] Frederick C. Barghoorn, *Soviet Russian Nationalism* (New York: Oxford University Press, Inc., 1956), p. vii.

ented, but it is equally engrossed in its special virtue and pride. Communist successes since the Russian Revolution, in Yugoslavia, Albania, China, Vietnam, and Cuba, have owed more to nationalism than to class appeal.

The most important part of ideology is simple loyalty to the holy, party-ruled state, in the tradition of Prussianism. It seeks to impose order, purpose, and dedication and despises the West for its license and frivolity. The anarchic selfishness of capitalism is hated for these qualities more than because of identification with a supposedly backward order. Prussianism is puritanical, and Soviet ideologues regard encouragement of sex, gambling, and other vices as an attempt to draw people away from communism. Writers are attacked less for ideological deviation than for lack of patriotism and for allowing themselves to be used by Western interests. There is more than Marxist stress on collectivism; the individual is continually reminded that he belongs to collectives of various orders, to which he owes complete fidelity. There has been developed a mystique of duty; even collective farmers swear an oath of allegiance, in one case as follows: "Entering upon the honorable ranks of tillers of land of the Union of Soviet Socialist Republics, I solemnly promise: to love labor, which is the source of abundance and happiness; to cherish the honor of my collective farm; to live and work the Communist way; to remember always that land is the greatest national resource."[22]

Although the idea of world power by military means is neither Marxist nor Leninist, a crusading party almost inevitably finds itself taking up the sword if it can find one, and a good deal of military thinking was implanted in bolshevism by the civil war, which contributed much more than the relatively painless revolutionary seizure to the lore and traditions of the Soviets. Then the grandeur and heroism, the losses and deep wounds of World War II made an indelible imprint. The memories have been kept fresh by innumerable books, movies, dedications, and memorials. A great value of military training is the elevation of moral qualities,[23] which in the Soviet system are practically equivalent to political qualities. Recently, military motifs seem to have become still more frequent; any newspaper is likely to have one or more little pieces exalting the deeds and life of the armed forces, a note of what is owed the guardians of the land or a reminder of past heroism. As *Pravda* stated, for example:

" 'By his death he defended the life of you who live today. And may the holy blood of Young Communist Tipanov fertilize and make fruitful your labors for the welfare of the Fatherland, for the happiness of which his young heart ceased to beat.' These valiant words, firm as a military oath, are carved in gold on a marble plaque attached to a concrete bunker not far from Krasnoe Selo. On January 18, 1944, a nineteen-year-old youth from Riazan,

---

[22] *New York Times,* January 15, 1969.

[23] For example, *Krasnaia Zvezda,* July 4, 1964.

Sasha Tipanov, took his last steps in life in order to stop with his breast a stream of lead. . . ."[24]

A Soviet folk-hero is Danko, a character in a tale of Maxim Gorky, who saved the people (whom he called a flock of sheep) by tearing out his heart.[25]

Spacemen are likewise "positive heroes" for Soviet youth to emulate. Always military officers, they are perfectly trained, disciplined, and given to the party and the state, the beloved land which they see with joy from on high and which they embrace with love on their return. The significance attributed to space exploits is indicated by the tremendous amount of newsprint devoted to them—for example, about half of the (slender) leading newspapers for nearly a week at the time of docking manned spacecraft in January, 1969. Cosmonauts stand for Soviet progressiveness and technical leadership; they are given the immense publicity which the political leaders deny themselves. They, not the men of the Politburo, are to be envied and emulated. The conquest of space gives a unifying pride, demonstrates the competence of the regime, and inspires young minds with fitting ambitions. Perhaps it does much of the work of ideology.

6. VIRTUES OF MARXISM

Despite the fact that it is in important ways unsuitable, Marxism and the class struggle have not been abandoned but are kept always in mind and from time to time are brought forward and reemphasized. The Marxist approach meets basic needs and has many uses. Some of these are marginal or might be otherwise met; some are quite vital.

The direct utility of Marxism for the sustenance of party supremacy is difficult to estimate. Its virtue is that it gives a special role and mission to one sector of humanity, the ill-defined working class. The idea of the intrinsic historical and moral superiority of one class over another is favorable for authoritarian rule. This makes it possible to discredit opponents on class grounds. It permits an elastic, more or less extralegal but politically convenient class justice; law is only superstructure. Marxism generally fudges questions of freedom; only workers' class freedom is real.

However, the class approach may be inconvenient if it is taken seriously. Not infrequently, workers in Eastern European countries have demanded some of the authority grandly promised them. In Poland in

---

[24] *Pravda*, January 18, 1969.

[25] The world mission of the Soviet Union is compared to his. *Kommunist*, January, 1969, No. 1, p. 3.

1956 they are said to have cried, "We do not want to be better paid workers, we want to rule."[26] The notion that a small group, in which nonproletarians are prominent, gives itself the authority to speak for all is hardly harmonious with the general Marxist outlook. It is an addition made by Lenin, with the practical but undialectic excuse that in tsarist Russia a mass workers' party was impossible; the kind of leadership which he proposed was essential for the making of the revolution. The class will he assumed to be indivisible and knowable, hence expressible by the small group steeped in the proper philosophy.

The intellectual excuse for a continued party monopoly of political power after the Revolution remains foggy. It would be more logical to call the party representative of the whole people, a position toward which Khrushchev moved. But it was a special value of Marxism that it bespoke westernization and progress to a Russia lagging several generations behind the West. It was agreeable for Russian Marxists to feel that they had for a teacher a man enjoying real prestige in Western intellectual circles, whose "scientific socialism" was taken as the acme of science. It stood for a material-scientific approach, a therapy for a Russia steeped in mysticism and backward resignation. Marxism hence was a westernizing influence, in borrowing which the Bolsheviks thought that they were overleaping the politically still backward West.

That Marxism sanctifies change and struggle to this end was very useful for remaking the government, society, and economy. Collectivization was not mandatory by Marxist canons, which could well be squared with an independent peasantry or small cooperatives, but it could be justified by them. Modernization and industrialization, essential for power and prestige as well as welfare, were particularly favored by the Marxist outlook. For Marx, industry was everything; if his Russian followers looked upon economic progress as the result instead of the mainspring of political change, this was not serious. Marxism made easier borrowing from the Western economies which were acknowledged as more advanced; it glorified labor in an environment where physical labor had been scorned and work generally regarded somewhat dimly. It also encouraged the idea that people should be happy to toil, not for their own selfish purposes but for the collectivity, a happy idea for the governors of society.

Marxism has consequently seemed closely associated with the industrialization of Russia and has reaped credit for its success. But in some ways Marxism has been decidedly unfavorable to industrial progress. For example, by stating that only labor has value, it has encouraged careless and wasteful attitudes toward capital, the charging of interest for the use of which was long ideologically unacceptable. It has seemed to some

[26] J. M. Mackintosh, *Strategy and Tactics of Soviet Foreign Policy* (New York: Oxford University Press, Inc., 1963), p. 161.

people that, for ideological or political reasons, the success of Soviet industrialization has been short of the immense sacrifices demanded. Japanese modernization has been just as successful or more so, without benefit of Marxism or any coherent Western dogma but under the aegis of Shinto and emperor-worship; purposeful organization and nationalism seem to have been the key. But the entire Marxist bias against markets and profits favors public, i.e. political, control of the economy.

A clearer political value of Marxism lies in its contribution to the discrediting of political alternatives and isolation from Western, i.e. bourgeois influence. There is no other weapon of comparable psychological potency to protect the claim to exclusive authority. Tsarist Russia had no such shield against individualistic and libertarian ideas from the West and no comparable basis for asserting the moral superiority and necessity of unity against the world outside. A simple attempt to close the frontiers, as under Nicholas I, was dubiously effective. It is essential, moreover, to borrow what might be necessary for technological progress while excluding politically harmful influences. But Marxism decrees not only that the bourgeois West is politically decadent but that it is inherently bad and of necessity maliciously hostile to the virtuous socialist order. Outside critics are by class nature evil-intentioned, even if they may pretend to be disinterested. The intensity of their hatred is, in fact, a tribute to the success of socialism in the Soviet Union.

The falsity of the bourgeois world is a major theme; a favorite expression has always been to "unmask" the enemy. Apart from the hostile interest of the capitalist nations, their people are morally crippled. "The petty bourgeois, being by his social nature a convinced and deep egotist . . . inclined to nationalism and oblivious of the class consciousness of the proletariat. . . ."[27] Capitalism is morally degrading, it could be urged, while in the Soviet realm people were dedicated to building a bright future of justice and true freedom. The basic immorality of bourgeois society, the urge for profits or the greed of the hated rich, gave a ready and acceptable explanation of opposition both at home and abroad. The dislike of the bourgeois states for the socialist state has nothing to do with any faults or selfishness of the latter; indeed, the Soviet Union could only be unselfish: "In contrast to all classes which have ruled at different stages of history, the proletariat is the only class in the actions of which there is no self-seeking and narrowness of interests."[28]

Trotsky's phrase, "Neither war nor peace," uttered near the beginning of Soviet history, expressed a basic position. The Soviet state has remained mostly on the defensive and has never wished major war, but it has always preferred if not required tension against the outside. The contest should

---

[27] *Pravda*, February 7, 1969.

[28] *Pravda*, February 14, 1969.

be ideological, not military, and between worlds, not nations; but it was suitable for Lenin and his successors to contend that communism or capitalism, struggling like the forces of light and dark, must eventually succumb; and if the inevitability of war has been set aside, the inevitability of contest has not. There can be no "coexistence of ideology" in Peaceful Coexistence.

The theme of two worlds with their antithetical ways and outlooks has been perennial. Everything Soviet should be qualitatively different; "socialist" industrialization, competition, law, and international relations are held to be different in kind from their "bourgeois" counterparts and incomparably superior. Bridge building between the worlds is disguised imperialist subversion, and the thesis of convergence of the two worlds, popular in the West, is rejected indignantly. For this reason, too, the Soviet state has at times displayed remarkable indifference to world opinion, even, as under Stalin, appearing to welcome enmity when no danger was in sight. It has also seemed to feel that duplicity toward the unscrupulous bourgeois world was quite justifiable.

Soviet media have devoted corresponding attention to the discrediting of the West, particularly those parts of it more capable of exerting a subversive influence. Marxism is most applicable where class struggle can be perceived, in the advanced industrialized countries of the West; and there, since the inception of the Soviet state, the Russians have been looking eagerly to disorders and conflicts. Readers of the Soviet press are probably the world's best informed concerning the outbreak of strikes (although not of their settlement). All manner of disorders are given revolutionary meaning; and if governments may be unfriendly, the true people, it is taken for granted, are friends of socialism and the Soviet Union. With waves of intensity according to political exigencies, life in the United States is portrayed as a hellish stew of riotous disorder, unemployment, poverty, hippyism, police beating Negroes and workers, and so on; rarely is approbation expressed for anything that happens in the United States unless it reflects discredit on the American way of life. West Germany receives similar treatment, with added thrusts at sinister neonazism and the longing for a new war; other American allies receive an appropriate share of abuse.[29]

---

[29] There seems to be a fondness for accusing Western societies and governments of faults at least equally evident on the Soviet side. For example, they are blamed for censorship, for using education to indoctrinate, for failing to consult public opinion, for ignoring civil rights, and the like. As the Russians write history, in 1939 Britain wanted to sacrifice Poland, the United States was looking to a European war, and Finland coveted its neighbor's territory; in 1968, it was the West which intervened in Czechoslovakia. This probably has not only a political purpose, but a psychological one of relieving guilt feelings. It need not be quite hypocritical, as it is easy for Soviet leaders to assume that Western powers must have had motivations like their own.

It is easier to regard something as utterly bad if there is a theoretical reason that it should be, and Marxism is more cogent in its critique of capitalist society than in its schemes for a better replacement. It is possible for any power to excuse its own faults and call for unity on the grounds that others are very much worse and unreasonably hostile. By pounding Marxist dogmas into their consciousness, the regime makes it difficult for its citizens to reject the view of the West as evil unless they reject the whole social order.

Philosophically, too, Marxism is of great utility. The intellectuals are ordinarily troublesome for authoritarian regimes. Some, like Chinese emperors of recent dynasties, have contained their discontent in a rather sophisticated fashion by busying them with classical studies. The problem has always been difficult for Russia because of the proximity of a stronger culture and the need to borrow from it; and tsarist Russia had little means of checking the permeation of the intelligentsia by such attractive Western notions as freedom and constitutionalism, often its alienation from Russian values. Dialectical materialism is a plausible structure capable of indefinite scholastic development and sufficiently protean to reconcile practically any facts with Marxism-Leninism. The mind trained to it, as the highly educated of the Soviet Union have to be, is placed in a cocoon of intellectual isolation from Western-individualist ways of thought and deprived of its chief psychological weapons against the party-state. It is difficult indeed for a single mind to overturn the elaborate supposedly scientific and demonstrable doctrine, concerning which there is no public doubt. For many, it becomes difficult to approach any social or political question without reference to Marxism-Leninism and the party's teachings. Even the discontented vent their feelings in Marxist-Leninist terms and hobble their discontent by accepting the language and basic concepts of the system. To argue for improvements they must use the texts of the fathers of the creed and acknowledge the authority of these texts when used against them. Not only in the Soviet Union but with much less reason in Eastern Europe, scholars seem generally to accept Marxism as a faith and a value system essential for society; and their critique is not a rejection of the system but an effort to improve it.[30] If they should flee to the West, they are likely to have difficulty in adjusting to it.

The Marxist *Weltanschauung* also serves as a substitute for religion and so as a unifying force over the inherited differences of creed of the peoples of the Soviet Union. The tsars relied heavily on orthodoxy, but this excluded or antagonized too many: Moslems of Central Asia and the Caucasus, Catholics in the western and Baltic areas, Lutherans of the Baltic, a few Buddhists, and a good many million Russian schismatics. The materialist creed of Marxism, although lacking in emotional fervor, serves

---

[30] Richard T. de George, *The New Marxism* (New York: Pegasus, 1968), *passim.*

as a nationally neutral philosophic meeting ground for all creeds and cultures. Probably for this reason, as well as because of the belief that religion was a hindrance to modernization, Lenin added militant atheism to Marxism. Marx himself regarded religion as a foolish part of the capitalist superstructure but saw no great need to combat it. The relation of atheism to the effort to assure unity is most clearly visible in the harsh attitude toward Judaism, the Jews being more than any other religious or national group suspect of divided loyalties. The Orthodox Church, still as before the Revolution practically a national force, has been treated more mildly and has at times enjoyed fairly friendly relations with the government. Powerful motivation has been necessary to keep atheism in the forefront of Soviet policy, despite the cost in foreign antagonism and the much greater cost in popular, especially peasant, resentment at home.

Despite some negative points, Marxism-Leninism offers a remarkably apt justification for Soviet power. As the only admissible conflicts are those of class, there must be complete unity within the system: differences of religion, race, nationality, or social group (as between workers, peasants, and bureaucrats) can be dismissed as unreal, and any play on them is bourgeois inspired and counterrevolutionary. Even the old antithesis of fathers and sons or the generational conflict is attacked as a false confrontation, to be met by the "class education of the new shift of builders of communism."[31] So neat is the system that it does not even allow for differences of interest between rich and poor, groups obviously present in Soviet society, but only between owners and workers—and in the Soviet scheme everyone is co-owner and worker. The only real conflict is that between the socialist world led by the Communist party and the capitalist world of the greedy bourgeoisie. The party, representative of the intrinsically unitary working class, has the indispensable and unimpeachable right to maintain the unity of the socialist realm against all weakening divisions. In the name of class solidarity the party stands over the united people and the central core stands over the united party.

7. MARXISM AND THE NATIONALITIES PROBLEM

Marxism serves the unity of the domain and the right and unity of the party as its guardian. But the gravest threat apparent is that of nationalism. Half of the population of the U.S.S.R., nearly two thirds of that of the entire empire, is ethnically non-Russian and potentially discontented with a Russian-dominated system. Hence, probably the greatest utility of Marxism lies in the furnishing of a transnational cause, a banner of unity

---

[31] *Pravda,* March 17, 1969.

of "socialist" nations which at the same time divides them from potentially attractive societies beyond the pale. This has brought about a remarkable coupling of Soviet-nationalist and internationalist themes, whereby nationalities can be allowed appearances of freedom and yet be held firmly together, as "class" conflict overrides national separatism.

For Marx, the workers had no country and the alleged national interest was only the interest of the bourgeoisie. Concerned with economic causes, he and Engels had no sympathy for nationalism in any manifestation; national differences rather interfered with class conflict. They were much impressed with the economic integration of the world; hence, when revolutionary action destroyed the bourgeois class state and ended exploitation of individuals and nations, there would be no more national conflict. The idea that while French, German, and other sections of the bourgeoisie are apt to be mortal enemies, while the French, German, Russian, and other proletariats would live in perfect harmony is unrealistic and not borne out by the sentiments of flesh and blood workers, who are apt to be much more parochial in interests than aristocrats or owners. But the thesis that only private property interests stand in the way of peace has a deep appeal. It rests on the supposed moral superiority of the poor and exploited, in whose name the Communist party claims the right to rule.

The Bolsheviks made the Revolution with these two ideas, fairly logical in theory but contradictory in practice, that the nationalities should be released from the exploiting state by the socialist revolution, but that nationalism was the result of capitalism. After the revolution they should, with no real conflict of interest, be in full concord and agreement. The nations were ostentatiously to be set free so that their masses, led by the proletariat and its party, would remain united. If they did not, it was the fault of capitalism only. As Stalin said in 1918,

> . . . bourgeois nationalist governments, hastily formed in the border regions and composed of representatives of the upper sections of the propertied classes, endeavoured, under the guise of settling their national problems, to carry on a definite struggle against the Soviet and other revolutionary organizations. . . . And if the bourgeois elements of this or that region sought to lend a national colouring to these conflicts, it was only because it was advantageous to them to do so, since it was convenient for them to conceal behind a national cloak the fight against the power of the labouring masses within their region. . . .[32]

By virtue of ideology, the Bolsheviks could thus be internationalists without permitting division. In fact, they centralized far more effectively than the tsarist government while speaking grandly of independence. Willing to gild reality, they guaranteed a right of secession while forming

[32] J. Stalin, *Works,* Vol. IV (Moscow, 1953), p. 32.

a unified government. According to Stalin (in 1923), "We are not creating a confederation but a federation of republics, a single union state, a state that in no way diminishes the sovereignty of the individual republics:"[33] As Lenin remarked, "Federation is a transitional form to the complete unity of the workers of the various nations."[34]

Loyalty to the working class, its mission, and its political form of socialism, requires loyalty to the historical expression of all these, the Soviet party and state. *Pravda's* "Proletarians of All Lands, Unite," means in essence, "Peoples of the Soviet domain, unite." As in the tsarist empire, divisive nationalism for the Soviet Union is of primarily Western and bourgeois inspiration, and it can be denounced as due to foreign influences and domestic reactionaries. In the judgment of *Pravda*,[35] "The poison of bourgeois nationalism, by their reckoning, should assist in the division of the proletariat by nationality." It was and is the duty of the international party and the workers to unite the Soviet peoples.

Sovietization, including some russification, was called socialization and the new dawn of history. Stalin made this retroactive to the tsarist era; the expansion of the old empire was "progressive" as it brought backward peoples to a higher culture and made possible their transition from feudalism to capitalism and socialism. Soviet minorities are still happier; they are by definition free because the Soviet Union, being socialistic, cannot be imperialistic.

Like the Soviet national minorities, the satellite countries are free. In days of high Stalinism, Malenkov described relations among socialist states as "based on the principles of equality, economic cooperation, and respect for national independence. . . ." But it is inconceivable that they should use—or be allowed to use—their freedom against the interests of socialism and the working classes; and the Soviet state, serving the toilers of the world, must protect their unity. Duties are reciprocal. Soviet citizens, as "internationalists," are duty-bound to risk their lives for communism;[36] and "Awareness that this great task [the building of a communist society in the U.S.S.R.] is in the interests of the entire world socialist system, in the interests of the international working class and the toilers of the whole world, multiplies the strength and energy of the Soviet people in the struggle for new victories of communism."[37] Since the interests of all proletarians are the same, they are those of the Soviet Union, and true proletarians cannot but be loyal to the Soviet leadership.

The nationalism of the bourgeois state is held to be only a cover for

---

[33] Goodman, *Soviet Design for a World State*, p. 245.

[34] Alvin Z. Rubinstein (ed.), *The Foreign Policy of the Soviet Union* (New York: Random House, Inc., 1966), p. 361.

[35] September 22, 1968.

[36] *Krasnaia Zvezda*, July 19, 1968.

[37] *Pravda*, December 26, 1968.

exploitation; nationalism may be encouraged in the West, but it has no place in the Soviet sphere. The same approach is used there as within the Soviet Union: class and socialism override nationality and sovereignty. The nation is at best a survival of backward class relations, not a real basis for political action. No quarrels or conflicts are accepted as having a real national significance, and national issues are fudged or erased. A Czech Communist advocating trust and friendship for the Russians stressed, "We must consistently apply a class approach, not forget that there is a relentless struggle between socialism and capitalism. . . ."[38] The peoples should be happy in freedom while conforming to the pattern, and Soviet dominance means "socialist principles of proletarian internationalism." Only "enemies of communism . . . strive to convince the peoples . . . that socialism and proletarian internationalism are enemies of national sovereignty."[39] As a Soviet jurist wrote,[40] sovereignty is "based on a nonclass approach." Among the socialist countries, "norms of mutual relations . . . cannot be interpreted . . . in isolation from the general class struggle of the modern world." Socialism is "indivisible, and its defense is the common cause of all communists and progressives in the world." Self-determination must hence yield to a "higher" principle.

Brezhnev discussed this idea in a slightly different aspect.[41] Class warfare in capitalist countries, he declared, bespeaks the continued progress of the working class and its revolutionary vanguard; and the ranks of their allies are growing. But this has brought into the struggle people of nonproletarian ideology, who indulge in rightist opportunism or "leftist" adventurism.[42] Both of these tendencies distort Leninism and "degrade the role of the working class and its vanguard, the Marxist-Leninist party . . . depart from the principles of proletarian internationalism thereby weakening the struggle against imperialism . . . characteristic for both is national narrowness in the grasp of many important questions of the revolutionary struggle, sometimes going over into real chauvinism." Brezhnev thus attributed the Chinese and Czech deviations to the same thing, departure from the class-party approach, ascribable in the latter case at least to Western imperialist machinations.

Those who keep the proper internationalist faith have a broader view. As stated by a *Pravda* editorial:

> Our relations with the brotherly countries of socialism are permeated with the spirit of socialist internationalism. As stressed in the Program of the CPSU, the party, while developing the love of the Soviet people to its homeland,

---

[38] *Pravda*, January 31, 1969.

[39] *Kommunist*, January 1969, No. 1, p. 6.

[40] *Pravda*, September 26, 1968.

[41] *Pravda*, November 13, 1968.

[42] In Soviet writing, "leftist" is always used in quotation marks in such a context.

takes the view that with the formation of a world system of socialism the patriotism of citizens of socialist society is manifested in dedication and loyalty to their Fatherland, the whole commonwealth of socialist countries. . . . We rejoice in every piece of good news about the glorious deeds of our friends [from Poland and Bulgaria to Mongolia]. . . . International education is an organic component of the communist education of the toilers. . . .[43]

Thus, the proletarian ideology, politically incarnated in the Communist parties, should make a single Fatherland of all the lands that may be called socialist as it unites the peoples of the Soviet Union.

How successful the internationalist ideology may have been in practice we cannot measure. The Soviet Union holds itself a model family of nations and congratulates itself on the harmonizing of many peoples and cultures as one of its outstanding achievements; making the best of a necessity, it claims multinationalism as a special virtue of Soviet patriotism. Yet it cannot be doubted that the problem of nationalities is acute. Russia is so easily taken as equivalent to the U.S.S.R., and the culture of Moscow and Leningrad stands so fully for the whole, as usually seen by the outside world, that it is easy to forget that ethnic Russians by census data are only a little more than half of the population. This may be somewhat inflated over reality, as it is more desirable to be a Russian than anything else, and a good many persons may take on Russianism for official purposes. Ukrainians are slightly under a fifth, and non-Slavs a quarter, of the population. The latter are largely quite alien in culture, racially rather different from the Slavic majority, and hence not readily assimilable. They are also increasing in numbers much more rapidly than the majority, so that by the end of this century they may comprise a third of the total.

The Soviet Union thus faces a problem potentially much more explosive than racial unrest in the United States, a source of weakness if not a threat of dissolution in some crisis. It would be quite extraordinary if, as modernization progresses, the U.S.S.R. should remain entirely unaffected by the growing self-awareness of peoples around the world and Soviet minorities should fail, especially as the Communist utopia fades and economic growth slows down, to strive for more expression of the national personality and more control over their own lands and futures. It is unlikely that solid minorities numbering in millions or tens of millions —the Ukrainians are about 40 million—can be quite reconciled to rule not only by an elite party but from an alien capital unless Marxist indoctrination is very successful. The problem is held no problem in the Soviet Union; the most forbidden of all subjects is that of the real relation between nationalities.[44]

---

[43] December 26, 1968.

[44] Leonid Vladimirov, *The Russians* (New York: Frederick A. Praeger, Inc., 1968), p. 229.

The minorities were formally granted freedom and some inevitably asked why the freedom was not real. The great expansion of education has brought about a new self-consciousness and has made possible some access of Western ideas to areas formerly almost entirely isolated. The considerable spread of Russian settlers, often occupying superior positions, has created frictions. Before the Revolution, various less advanced peoples were dependent on the Russians because of their lack of technical and administratively-trained personnel; now they have cadres of their own. There is a local apparatus in minority areas, and it has an interest in what local autonomy it can protect.

The strength of national dissidence in the 1940's was indicated by Stalin's deportations of various nationalities; if the wartime foe had been less unattractive or had made a serious effort to recruit disaffected non-Russians, perhaps not many would have remained loyal. Khrushchev looked to a melting together of all nationalities in the future fully communist state; but extensive discussion, usually rather theoretical, of the course of fusion or bringing together of the Soviet peoples also justifies the deduction that the problem is real, and the failure of the leadership to come to new decisions may indicate its difficulty.[45] Since his day, national tensions have increased or at least minority leaders have spoken out a bit more boldly for protection of their language and equality of status, and denunciations and hints of nationalistic tendencies have become more frequent. Periodically the central authorities denounce "bourgeois nationalism" in the Asian republics, where Moslem customs have proved remarkably persistent, and there is little mixing of Russian and native in the countryside.[46] Frictions may have had something to do with the fact that in recent years Central Asian republics have usually failed to meet their economic goals. Somewhat alarmingly for the Soviet leadership, Moscow intellectuals took up the cause of Turkic dissidents as they did that of Czechoslovakia.[47]

The Ukraine, briefly independent after the Revolution, probably is the greatest headache. In the Stalinist purge trials, defendants were regularly accused of plotting to separate it from Russia. According to Khrushchev, Stalin would have liked to deport all its inhabitants for disloyalty in the war; anti-Soviet guerrillas were fighting there into 1949. There were many arrests of Ukrainian intellectuals from the summer of 1966, and various Ukrainian writers were quietly imprisoned. Ukrainians may particularly feel that their republic contributes more than its share to the Soviet economy. Elsewhere, party leaders in Baltic states have indulged

---

[45] Grey Hodnett, "What's in a Nation," *Problems of Communism,* Vol. XVI, No. 5 (September–October, 1967), p. 14.

[46] Alexandre Bennigsen and Chantal Lemercier-Quelquejay, *Islam in the Soviet Union* (New York: Frederick A. Praeger, Inc., 1967), pp. 197–198.

[47] *New York Times,* March 7, 1969.

in complaints against russianizing tendencies in education and against Soviet economic policies; it is not surprising that their peoples, generally of a higher cultural level than the Russians and more exposed to Western influence, should be restive. There have been stirrings even among the White Russians, nearest of all to the Russians proper in language and background.[48] How serious the discontent is one can only guess. But a *Pravda* warning points to high concern: "The national question is one of the most complicated and acute questions of social development. It has taken on special acuteness in the contemporary era, the era of struggle of socialism and capitalism. . . ."[49] Much potential separatism may lie beneath the surface. One is reminded that when the Bolsheviks offered freedom of secession after the Revolution, many groups which had never had any independent history and who had been regarded as integral components of the empire came forward to claim it.[50]

This does not mean that the Bolsheviks have not handled the broad problem intelligently. Lenin was a real internationalist who genuinely wanted justice for the minorities; and since Stalin Soviet nationality policy has been relatively sophisticated and benign, basing russianization much more on incentives than compulsion.[51] Centralization has been forwarded ostensibly on economic, not political grounds. Ideology softens the vise of sovietization. Ideology elevated the workers, who were mostly Russians, over the more purely peasant minority peoples; but it demanded complete equality and nondiscrimination and so reduced or camouflaged the advantages of Russian nationality. It is much more politic to try to persuade Ukrainians and others that they share a common destiny as workers than that they should become Russians. There are many concessions to appearances, such as the flags of the constituent Soviet republics and their nominal power to conduct their own foreign relations. For example, the first secretary of republic parties is regularly a native, although real power usually rests with a Russian second secretary.

The claim that the nationalities are really free and united only by shared class interest is a rationale for making concessions of form, and it doubtless increases their psychological effectiveness. There are more or less quotas to assure minority representation not only in the impotent Supreme Soviet but also in the Central Committee and other bodies. The entirely integrated armed forces are a probably effective agent of assimila-

[48] V. Stanley Vardys, "Altes und neues in der sowjetischen Nationalitätenpolitik seit Chruschtschows Sturz," *Osteuropa*, Vol. 18, no. 2 (February, 1968), pp. 84–85.

[49] November 26, 1968.

[50] For a treatment of some aspects of this complicated question, see Erich Goldhagen (ed.), *Ethnic Minorities in the Soviet Union* (New York: Frederick A. Praeger, Inc., 1967).

[51] V. Aspaturian in Allen Kassof (ed.), *Prospects for Soviet Society* (New York: Frederick A. Praeger, Inc., 1968), p. 163.

tion, as minority youths are dispersed among Russians and have perforce to learn their language and ways. Migration and posting of cadres away from home areas have brought about a good deal of mixing. Native languages have been treated tenderly, and there has often been a greater effort to denature them by introducing Russian words than to displace them. Nationalities have been played against one another, in the traditional imperial strategy of dividing the opposition. There may be as much friction between Georgians and Armenians, for example, as between either of these and Russians.[52] Minorities have been threatened with Russian nationalism so that they should look to the communist party to protect them.[53]

In a very difficult situation, Marxism-Leninism has achieved a great deal and has been much more effective than russification policies of the tsars, which more antagonized than conciliated. To lead nationalist opposition, there are only intellectuals educated in an antinational philosophy. Those who accept the illegitimacy of nations can with difficulty oppose Soviet domination in principle, however they may take a stand on narrower issues. Minority nationalism seems to be lacking in leadership in the Soviet Union and to some extent in Eastern Europe also. It is a measure of success, too, that many even well-informed observers in the West take it for granted that the Soviet Union, in contrast to Britain, France or even the United States, is untainted by imperialism.

The only visible alternative to the present approach of exalting loyalty to the proletariat over loyalty to the nation is pure repression, which is difficult and often unproductive. The proportion of Russians is too large for a workable confederation of equal partners while not large enough to be overwhelming. It is not easy to conceive of a democratic solution; probably the Russians are correct in regarding capitalist-bourgeois influences as a mortal danger to the integrity of the realm. So far as it is successful—and it may have built up an important group of antinationalists—it deserves to be kept; so far as it has not been successful, it needs to be applied more energetically.

It is instructive to compare the Soviet Union with Communist China. The latter, with a rather homogeneous population, does not need a Marxist class emphasis. For it (cf. p. 283 above), the working class has had little special virtue since Mao took to the hills to raise a peasant revolution, and Chinese policy has been much less considerate of minorities than that of the Soviets. The Chinese have practically discarded the emphasis on class; they stress only revolution, which is to be made by anyone against their enemies, Soviet "revisionist renegades" and American "imperialists." Having completed its emancipation from the Soviet model in the

---

[52] Similarly, Czechs were as bitter against Polish and East German accomplices in the invasion as against the Russian masters.

[53] Vardys, *op. cit.*, p. 95.

"Cultural Revolution," Maoism radically downgraded the Communist party and relied primarily on the army as instrument of unity and control. Cuban communism likewise, despite its dependence on Soviet assistance, finds little necessity to attribute a special role to the proletariat.

Yugoslavia, on the other hand, has a nationality problem like that of the Soviet Union, since the population is split into often uncongenial groups—Serbs, Croats, Slovenes, Macedonians, and Montenegrins, plus a few Albanians and others. Tito triumphed somewhat as Lenin as a unifier; his Communist partisans took a remarkably farsighted view of nationalism and handled the problems it raised with great skill. They won out as the only all-Yugoslav movement.[54] The Yugoslav answer has been like the Russian, a federal system and cultural autonomy with real power kept in the united Communist party. Hence despite long separation from the Soviet bloc and many quarrels, Titoism desires to remain ideologically linked with world communism. In the aftermath of the Czech affair, for example, Tito spoke of the French Communists as the true spokesmen of France. Despite relative impotence, Yugoslavia has some messianic spirit, the urge to see its kind of socialism spread both in Soviet Eastern Europe and in the Third World, linking rights and equality of nations to the promotion of rights of nationalities within Yugoslavia.[55]

Russian communism is primarily a phenomenon of the multinational empire. What goes by the name of communism in China, Korea, or Cuba, has borrowed some of the language, ethos, and organizational patterns of Leninism; and it may reach out for Soviet support against a common antagonist, the United States. But it has no interest in what is for the Soviet Union a central point of doctrine, the priority of class, incorporated in the party, over nationality.

8. EROSION OF IDEOLOGY

The West found it hard to believe that a band of international revolutionists had taken power in Russia and much harder to believe that they could remain masters of the great empire. From the point of view of the West, bolshevism was contrary to nature. From 1917 onward, Western observers have cherished the expectation that the Bolsheviks would be overthrown, or, what seemed more likely as the tenacity of their grip became evident, would become civilized, that is, leave behind utopianism

[54] V. Meier in William E. Griffith (ed.), *Communism in Europe* (Cambridge, Mass.: MIT Press, 1965), Vol. I, p. 66.

[55] Alvin Z. Rubinstein, "Tito's Acentric Communism and the Sino-Soviet Rivalry in the Third World." *Orbis,* Vol. XII, No. 3 (Fall, 1968), p. 690.

and messianism and take on political habits intelligible in traditional Western terms.

Hopes in this direction were strongest in the years after 1921. Leaving the Revolution behind and demobilizing after the civil war, Lenin's government restored a large amount of free economic enterprise at home and began looking to the practice of normal diplomacy abroad. It seemed that practical necessity was normalizing bolshevism and that the process would naturally continue. Stalin, of course, reversed it, but World War II showed that it was possible for the Soviet Union and capitalist powers to fight and work together fairly well. As the war came to a close, nearly everyone thought it was essential that the chief powers continue to cooperate. Most thought that they should be able to do so, as the Soviet Union had ceased to be a revolutionary power, internally or externally, and shared the Western interest in stability for reconstruction. Even as the cold war was settling down, George Kennan reasoned that the failure of the capitalist West to collapse and of the Soviet Union to expand would compel fundamental reappraisal. After Stalin's death, such expectations were felt with varying intensity as foreign and domestic policies evolved, sometimes toward revival of Leninist-Stalinist revolutionism or totalitarianism but a larger share of the time toward a more conservative, looser, and less ideological system; and hopes again seemed illusory as doctrine was reasserted in uncompromising terms to justify the squelching of Czech independence.

There have been many good reasons for the optimistic Western appraisal. It is amazing that a major state should remain faithful to the creed of a revolution more than half a century old, the major premises of which are increasingly unrealistic and irrelevant. A religion, not to speak of a social philosophy, should appear factually true to its believers; but Marxism belongs to a world increasingly antique. The study of history and economics have progressed and deepened enormously since the day of the prophets, and the character of so-called capitalist economics has changed profoundly. It may have seemed fairly realistic in the nineteenth century to speak of society as fundamentally divided into workers and owners; this is no longer the case (nor has it ordinarily been true historically, as society is much more pyramidal than layered).

Fundamental Marxist expectations have been disappointed. It became very evident, as the Bolsheviks summoned the workers to rise together, that they do have fatherlands and often more common with their middle classes than with foreign workers. The idea of class based on relation to means of production became confused; it was contended that enterprise managers in Russia remained part of the working class, while in the West corporate management became increasingly separated from ownership and much of the economy became publicly owned or controlled. Nationalization, it appeared, did not end differences but only changed their basis in an un-Marxian way. The Western workers failed to become more and more impoverished. Their standards of living rose as rapidly as those under socialism; and as workers improved themselves, they moved in manners and attitudes toward the bourgeoisie. Communism has nowhere come as Marx expected, by a workers' rising against overripe capitalism, but by war and in less developed countries.

High prophets of Leninism turned out to have been poor creatures. Trotsky was found to be, and is still regarded as, a traitor; Stalin was acknowledged to have been paranoiac; Khrushchev was dismissed as hare-brained. The dream of abundance with communal sharing has proved a mirage, and as the country moves toward material prosperity, it becomes evident that this brings neither brotherly harmony nor a high degree of happiness. The international utopia of socialist concord has also been shattered by the enmity with China and the failure of unity, except as enforced by bayonet, within the socialist bloc. Successful proselytizing is vital for keeping up faith in an ideology which largely rests upon a vision of transformation of history; yet the past decade has seen only division. Even when a new socialist state, Cuba, has remained friendly, its adherence has been unrewarding. No creed could fail to be somewhat battered by such blows.

Many a revolutionary movement has become staid, and the Soviet Union meanwhile has evolved from a revolutionary to a quite conservative society; the fundamentals of Leninism, the urgency of revolution and the leadership of the proletariat, have become wholly incongruous where there is no revolutionary program and society is ruled by clerks and bosses. A generation ago, Molotov viewed cultured persons and ordinary workers as opposites,[56] and Soviet society has become very status-conscious. Ideals and explanations designed primarily to justify change lose appeal for a stable system, the legitimacy of which comes to rest increasingly on habit and tradition; the idea of class struggle becomes ever less attractive. Younger members of the elite use fewer ideological stereotypes than those tempered by the Revolution.[57] The character of the government has changed; one should not expect a regime headed by a faceless committee to behave like Lenin's revolutionary-charismatic leadership, Stalin's boss-dictatorship, or Khrushchev's personal ascendancy. Lack of a single authoritative spokesman to interpret and apply ideology implies more pragmatism. The bureaucracy has met all manner of problems for which the Marxist-Leninist framework was wholly unsuited, both internal and external; and the government has seemed to be turning into something more like the jumble of interests and pressures familiar to the West. It has learned to deal with countries outside its sphere in a nonrevo-

[56] Walter B. Smith, *Moscow Mission, 1946–1949* (London: William Heinemann, Ltd., 1950), p. 175.

[57] Triska and Finley, *Soviet Foreign Policy*, p. 122.

lutionary and thoroughly conventional manner. Idealism has succumbed to politics.

Soviet society has become increasingly oriented to material benefits. It inevitably changes its outlook as it raises itself from relative poverty to relative affluence. Subsistence is no longer a problem and life is no longer cheap. The emotional drive of communism, to share what goods are available in a situation of penury, no longer appeals as either necessary or desirable to masses increasingly bourgeoisified like prosperous Western workers. The Soviet Union of fashion shows and low birthrate becomes akin in tastes and in many of its problems to the advanced nations of the West, not to the world's proletariat. Continued material progress conflicts with ideology today as it did in the middle of the nineteenth century when a crusty emperor was trying to shut out westernization for the stability of autocracy. Both foreign contacts and scientific education are essential, perhaps more than ever, if the Soviet Union is to maintain its standing in the world; and both are corrosive of antiquated and unrealistic dogma.

Marx thought that material progress should bring communism, but reality has been the reverse. The economy has grown too complex to be managed in the old style and badly needs further loosening, as the growth rate declines to modest levels. It is an indication of this need that the Soviet economy is most backward in the most advanced sectors of industry, particularly the application of computers, for which the system would seem to offer the greatest opportunities. Usually in the West modernization has eroded official myth and made people more difficult to manage politically, and it is not easy to see that it should be different in Russia. The general course of tsarist Russia under the impact of westernization was away from absolutism and toward a more moderate and open system, until overtaken by a disastrous war; it would be reasonable to expect Soviet Russia to follow a similar course if peace is extended. Most Western observers find it a little difficult to believe that a great and advanced state like the Soviet Union, strong by virtue of science and technology, could not manage better without an intellectually cramping official dogmatism.

Thus far, however, the currents of modernity seem to erode mostly below the surface of a superficially unyielding official ideology. The longing for freedom apparently grows on the part of a small minority, which forms an intellectual underground, with its own poetry and literature of protest in rumpled manuscript. The official voices proclaim the same well-worn truths and cite Lenin, but they ring a little hollow; as never before, cynicism has crept in. Ideology represents less an ideal aspiration and more a highly self-congratulatory excuse for rule, which is perhaps increasingly felt as heavy-handed and arbitrary. On the other hand, modernization, the dissolution of social bonds, and the rising expectations of groups and nationalities increase the need for ideology. Soviet propaganda makes so much of the disorders and depravity of modern Western society that one can assume that the Soviet leadership is determined to use every means of maintaining the relative purity of the Soviet people, especially the youth. Hard work, plenty of indoctrination and political education, and attention to technology should continue to spare Soviet universities the strife rampant in Western Europe and the United States.

One should not underestimate the ability of a well-entrenched and united elite with well-organized and disciplined police and military forces to keep itself in power even without a strong ideology to ease its task. The Franco government of Spain, with hardly a shred of theoretical justification, has gripped the land for thirty years with little relaxation; when there have arisen threats to its stability, it has met them by sheer repression. Yet the liberalizing currents which beat against authoritarian Spain are far stronger than those buffeting authoritarian Russia. Millions of foreigners swarm freely over the land, millions of Spaniards travel abroad, all manner of foreign art and literature comes in, and so on. Moreover, Spain, unlike Russia, does not have an empire to guard. There is no reason to assume that liberalization in the Soviet system must soon proceed much beyond whatever is felt necessary to keep the state abreast of modernity and correspondingly strong enough to fulfill its role in the world, even if ideology becomes, as in tsarist times, little more than an incrustation of power.

9. GRIP OF DOMINION

It is probable that liberalization of the Soviet state would have progressed far and that its social and political order would by now be fully as open as that of tsarist Russia in its last decade had not dominion over Eastern Europe enlarged the empire and multiplied its problems of control. If there are difficulties with the management of peoples who are close to Russians and have had little independence for many centuries, such as the Ukrainians, or are numerically rather few and previously fairly accustomed to Russian overlordship, such as the Balts, or were rather backward and lacking in national consciousness until recently, such as Turkic peoples of Central Asia, the problem of ruling proud and once strong nations as Poland, Hungary, part of Germany, and others, is a task of another order. The frictions, difficulties of understanding, and conflicts of aspirations dwarf those within the Soviet Union. If the whole domain be considered a single polity, Russians make up only a little over a third of the population, and hardly the most advanced and productive part. The

Soviet bloc forms a truly international empire, and for it an international faith is an essential supplement for compulsion. Repeatedly, an upsurge in Soviet stress on ideology became necessary: in 1944–45, when the satellites were being acquired; in 1947, as the Soviet domain seemed threatened by the onset of the cold war and American involvement in European recovery; in 1956, with the repression of the Hungarian revolution; in 1968, when the Russians reacted to the threat of dissolution through liberalization. Then internationalism became the cry as it had hardly been since the first years after the Revolution; Communist parties, like Soviet soldiers, were urged to fulfill their internationalist duty.

Commitment to a unifying faith is almost indispensable if the realm is to be held together. It hence becomes fairly easy for Russians, or perhaps Ukrainians as junior big brothers in the empire, to convince themselves of the truth of socialist doctrines which are almost the *raison d'être* of the state and its greatness. It is characteristic of the modern age that it idealizes politics and simplifies the unbearably complex, and ideas of great political utility have remarkable resistance to facts. One may recall the fervor with which many educated and intelligent Germans subscribed to nazism, a more absurd and less humane ideology than Marxism-Leninism, because it suited the collective egotism and was sanctified by amazing victories. Nazism appeared to serve Germany by ending unemployment, restoring German strength and prestige, reunifying Germans, and then leading on toward European or possibly world dominion. If Marxism-Leninism, already credited with great accomplishments, seems necessary for the integrity of the empire, it will be equally invulnerable. Moreover, it answers a permanent need. Modernization may undercut authoritarianism, weaken its pretenses, and gradually bring the rulership to bend with the popular current and accept limitations on power. But the need for ideology to hold the state together does not admit such gradual loosening unless other means are found to take its place. Soviet experience indicates that as ideology weakens somewhat and threats to the coherence of the empire appear, the reaction is not to retreat but to reassert the fullness of dogma. Modernization hardly lessens but perhaps increases the need for an overriding principle of loyalty.

No alternative seems a near prospect. Retreat is unthinkable not only because of resistance of organized power to surrendering part of its being but because of commitment to success; to go backward would be to surrender hopes of world leadership. Withdrawal from contiguous territories, unlike relinquishment of overseas possessions, seems strategically dangerous, the more so as it would be open-ended. Possibly in time there can be developed an overall patriotic attachment, as to some extent there is already a degree of all-Soviet patriotism. In *Pravda*'s somewhat optimistic view, "Every representative of any nation of the U.S.S.R. considers himself first of all a Soviet citizen."[58] A nearer likelihood is a degree of economic integration relieving the leadership of fears that national separatism might be dangerous. By the beginning of 1969, there were being put forward proposals for a single economic plan for the entire bloc. This might permit a mixing of economic unification with political decentralization in a true federalism for which Marxism-Leninism would be superfluous. Unhappily, however, the political system has thus far damaged the economic and cultural attractiveness of the empire, thereby perpetuating the necessity of controls.

The development of a more militantly nationalistic-militaristic state is possible, also. The armed forces and military ideals are already powerful instruments of integration in the Soviet Union, and thorough military integration of the bloc could considerably reduce anxieties and ideological tension. The Soviet establishment can more rationally claim allegiance as bringer of order, security, and economic growth than as the incarnation of any Marxist values, and the former appeal might be retained if the latter were dropped. It is not clear, however, how much such a development might contribute to improvement of relations with the West. Soviet nationalism, like that of other great states, is rather narrow and aggressive; and a military regime might look quite as much as the present one to external antagonisms to unify the state. A really democratic development would seem much more remote. Genuine popular participation in government has never seemed practical for the Russian state or for any great empire. With some justice, Soviet propagandists consider proposals for freedom of parties and the like as an effort to poison socialist unity.[59] Any attack on absolutist dogmas is an attack on the integrity of the Soviet state.

Hence, as the Soviet Union and its vassals form a supranational polity, Soviet foreign policy is frozen to an international frame and posture. The supranational ideology gives a basis for concern with world order, and the rulership derives great satisfaction from viewing itself as the pivot, inspiration, and center of a universal movement. In the ideological justification of empire the domain becomes sacred; no part can be surrendered, and new acquisitions are fully justified. To be prepared to rule the many Soviet nations means to be prepared ideologically and institutionally to rule an indefinite territory. The empire has no real boundaries, only limits beyond which it is too difficult or inconvenient to expand.

It is hardly less compelling that the Soviet Union is burdened by the responsibilities and ambitions of a very great power engaged in competition for world leadership. A small, multinational power like Yugoslavia is

---

[58] November 26, 1968.

[59] *Pravda*, December 4, 1968.

little troubled by needs of expansion, while the United States, only slightly possessed by universalism, has been drawn into the broadest engagements. The inescapable power contest sharpens ideology, as relaxations are attributable to enemy influence; and ideological unity seems a prerequisite for the necessary strength of the state. Rivals stress their differences, and warriors on both sides regard signs of reasonableness as weakness. If some in the West prefer to see world politics as a confrontation of contrary philosophies representing good and evil, one should hardly expect an early end of such an outlook in the Soviet Union.

This does not indicate, however, that the Soviet leaders are prepared to risk or sacrifice anything of importance for the sake of spreading communism. Soviet support for socialism or "progressive" causes outside the sphere is almost entirely symbolic or verbal. It is useful to apply ideology to foreign affairs—its Marxist component can hardly be applied at all except abroad, as only there can propagandists point to oppressive capitalists, suffering workers, and class conflicts; and it is easier to schematize the distant than the present reality. It is possible, moreover, continually to draw evidence of the rightness and success of the movement by pointing to some aspects of the turbulent external world. Especially when there are troubles at home, it is a consolation to speak of the great battles shaping up on the world arena, whereby prophecies are coming to fulfillment.

But this implies no drive to take action; history can be left to realize itself. The utter desirability or necessity of the inevitable victory is the aspect of ideology which has shriveled most, and Soviet internationalism has little application beyond the boundaries of the Soviet domain. Old formulas are repeated as though mechanically, expatiated and elaborated as the occasion warrants; but they demand no action, like the credo of an apocalyptic religion that has ceased to look forward to proximate salvation although it may continue to support a hierarchy. An intelligent person could hardly see world politics of our age merely as a reflection of class interests and class struggle unless the word "class" is emptied of nearly all meaning, as is indeed the Soviet practice. How purely verbal the ideological commitment has become was well shown when, in the crescendo of reaffirmation of Communist solidarity after the invasion of Czechoslovakia, the Soviet Union made every effort to continue or expand businesslike dealings with those whose foul and underhanded aggressive designs against Czech socialism had supposedly been uncovered and thwarted.

The Bolshevik approach, while verbally very offensive, has been essentially bureaucratic and nonviolent. The party *apparatchiki* desire not conflict but a politically controllable world. In the rigidities and perhaps creeping indolence of their state, they would prefer simply to avoid complications; and if the world outside is evil, the more reason to ignore it. Their first task is to keep what they have. Their authoritarianism conduces to hostility and xenophobia but not a desire to become much involved in the outside world. Abroad, they are likely to use situations of disorder but not to create them. Where they see no security question, as in relations with Afghanistan or Finland, their foreign policy can be very moderate. Much of their appeal to the world is in terms of peace, which is a major appeal within their empire: the Soviet Union is the bringer of harmony to the many peoples.

Soviet foreign policy is and has always been, like tsarist foreign policy before it, one of offensive defense or defensive aggressivity. While basically preferring peace and tranquillity, the Soviet Union makes indefinite claims to universal leadership, as the tsarist state once did; patient and averse to war, it is usually probing the weaknesses of the hostile universe without. Its approach, when stripped of verbiage, is generally fairly rational, although there have been gross errors in application. It has been successful in the long term of the past and may be successful in the future.

Conclusion: Soviet Russia and the World

Prior to the Mongol conquest, Russia was culturally and politically fairly well at one with medieval Europe. But the Oriental subjection set the land back by centuries and cast Russia in a mold of despotism. Emerging from subjection, Russia saw expansion, first the ingathering of the vast Russian lands never before united and then the occupation of territories loosely held by the former ruling peoples, as the way to freedom, security, and power. Standing between rising Europe and decaying Asia, Russia shared sufficiently in the European technical superiority to march as though irresistibly forward. Thus, while some Western powers were forming overseas empires, Russia became a continental empire. Great in mass and military power although poor and relatively backward, Russia necessarily adopted an imperial political system and became imbued with an imperial mystique, an ideological outlook. A multinational world, it was a denial incarnate of the principles of the European state system to which it owed its ascendancy. Yet it was fundamentally kindred to the Western world from which it had to learn in order to defend itself; had it not been close enough to the West in culture and religion to do this, it would doubtless, like Turkey, have lost its empire and perhaps been overcome.

Russia has lived accordingly for many generations in a tense relation with the West, requiring contacts yet fearful of them, with admiration mingled with resentment, economic and technical inferiority balanced by political greatness and confidence of destiny. Since Peter's great drive to strengthen the state by westernization, two principles have contended for the Russian soul: that of reform, looking to improvement through intellectual freedom, accepting or idealizing Western culture; and that of absolutism and unquestionable imperial power. Greatness means two somewhat contradictory things for Russia: scientific-technical progress and the subordination of the lands and peoples to a single will. Neither could be victorious, as each was necessary for the strength of the empire; there has never been a resolution of the degree to which authority and ideology had to defer to liberalization for the sake of progress, or liberalization to be restrained lest the state be weakened.

In the nineteenth century, this spiritual disjunction became more painful as Europe surged ahead more rapidly in technology than Russia could follow, while this state continued its long-term growth of territory and numbers in relative backwardness. Moreover, the steadily increasing vigor of nationalism made Western ideas more dangerous for the empire than for a more homogeneous recipient such as Japan. Efforts to resolve the problem by partial exclusion of western influences, by a slight modernization of the political system, or by the attempt to apply nationalism, in the form of russification, could not succeed. The empire had to belong to the West yet keep apart. Foreign policy fell into a corresponding contradiction, as Russia tried to sustain autocracy in alliance with liberal-nationalistic forces of Europe. The regime stumbled into a fatal war, ironically in defense of the national against the imperial principle.

Out of the calamity of war, the Revolution came to give the empire a more modern and coherent ideology and a stronger political system in the form of the Communist party. These two, the verbal and the political aspects of Lenin's imaginative adaptation of an outdated Western creed to the rulership of a semioriental empire, were phenomenally successful. But the Revolution, far from resolving the conflict of contrary principles, intensified it by making the rulership stronger and more effective while basing itself on a Western philosophy of radical social change. Bolshevism is a mixture *sui generis* of modernism, internationalism and autocracy. Under it, Russia became more authoritarian and far more messianic, absurdly promising the greatest happiness in the worst situation; yet it claimed to turn its back entirely on political traditions to overleap the West to a Western-dreamed utopia of freedom and abundance by maximum application of Western ideas and technology.

For a time the Bolsheviks could imagine that they had solved Russia's dilemma by taking the leadership of an inevitable general revolutionary transformation; they thought that the Western proletariat would rescue their movement from what they recognized was a paradoxical crisis. But the grand Revolution turned out to be Russian, not universal. And if it may have seemed at first that the principle of social transformation was dominant in bolshevism, it fairly soon turned out that the new Russia could use a basically intellectual and humanitarian doctrine to exclude Western individualism more effectively than ever while borrowing Western techniques on a larger scale than ever. Unattainable world revolution necessarily declined from a strongly felt need to a verbal commitment and instrument of state interests; yet it could not be surrendered entirely.

Russia saw the West with a mixture of admiration and hatred; feelings of the Western world toward revolutionary Russia were no less confused.

Interest in its ideals and sympathy for its effort to build a new social order were balanced or outweighed by fears of the effects of Russian influence on Western society and of the extension of Russian power through a real or pseudomessianic movement. Some saw it as essentially idea and promise of renovation, to be tolerated or welcomed; some as a passing aberration of a disturbed state which must sooner or later return to normal order; some as essentially aggressive power, to be checked or overcome for safety. The leaders of the West have not yet come to any clear decision how far it is their purpose to reach an accommodation with the Russians and how far to oppose them.

The effects of the flamboyant Russian effort to lead the world were even more mixed. In part, they have been in the overtly intended direction of liberation and renovation of society. The new idealism proclaimed from Moscow had some part in canalizing discontent and furnishing it with slogans and vocabulary in many lands at many times; the Russians have given themselves much credit for inspiring social welfare and humanitarian refinement of capitalism. The example of a state claiming to overcome exploitation and successfully industrializing without benefit of private ownership has caused a reexamination of Western assumptions, and Soviet propaganda has pricked the conscience of the West regarding many ills, such as unemployment, racial and social discrimination, and colonialism. Particularly in recent years, as the Soviet Union has come to greater power and respectability, its competition has been a stimulus, as in education and the promotion of economic growth.

But to a larger extent, so far as can readily be judged, Soviet promotion of leftist causes has been hurtful to them. An unsuitable Soviet-supported dogmatism muddied the waters of social controversy and made reform by consensus more difficult. The injection of Russian authoritarianism divided and diverted the liberating-revolutionary tendencies of the West, as groups which were organizationally powerful but associated with a relatively backward and more or less dictatorial state demanded the control of labor and radical movements. Issues of social and economic justice were tied to foreign-directed conspiratorial parties and thereby discredited. Bolshevik Russia was for decades a very poor advertisement for socialism or revolution. Zinoviev once chided the German comrades for shrinking from leading Germany toward the hunger which gripped Soviet Russia.[1]

Soviet meddling, because of unsuitable tactics and intolerance, probably much reduced the social and political renewal which potentially might have come out of the crises of the West, the wars, and economic troubles of the 1930's. Russian communism, representing a modernizing

[1] Edward H. Carr, *The Bolshevik Revolution* (London: Macmillan & Co., Ltd., 1953), Vol. III, p. 220.

dictatorship of a backward empire, has had little impact on the more successful socialist parties of mature industrial nations. The Communists who wanted to organize the working classes and use them to bring a new system were necessarily at odds with the socialists who wished to liberate them and improve them within the system. Not having much to offer, Communist parties have seldom been able to make themselves representatives of much of the proletariat. Fifty years after the Comintern set to work, there is less of a socialistic labor movement in the West than when it began. The historical role of the Russian Revolution was not to end exploitation but to modernize autocracy,[2] and it oddly reversed the thrust of tsardom, which espoused conservative causes and tended to discredit them.

Far from being the prototype of revolution in this century, Lenin's Revolution could be copied nowhere. It has not even shown a great capacity to influence the development of that large share of the globe which gained independence since World War II. The parallels with Russia are strong: the need for reordering of antiquated social structures, antagonism for the West and the need for borrowing from disliked powers, the humiliation of poverty and consequent appeal of Marxism, and the frequent unhappiness of the intelligentsia. But communism and Communist parties had very little to do with decolonization. Entirely contrary to Lenin's expectations, this came mostly because of the growth of social conscience in the West together with a realization of the unprofitability, under Western political institutions, of colonial dominion. Although Soviet messianism was always universal in pretensions and in the last decades became so in interests, only small parts of the Third World have seen fit to associate themselves with the Soviet model, and they have done so much more because of Soviet economic and military aid than because of the attractiveness of the Soviet model. Where communism has spread by indigenous action, it has owed its success not to proletarian revolution but to guerrilla warfare, strengthened not so much by Marxist-Leninist social theories as Bolshevik Russian patterns of unity, organization, and authority.

The great political influence of Russian communism has been to provide an example, excuses, and rationalizations for ruthless exercise of power. Soviet writers have claimed that the October Revolution influenced the establishment of democratic governments after World War I;[3] if this be true, it contributed more to their downfall. Everywhere, from South Asia to Latin America, conservative to reactionary regimes, espe-

---

[2] Richard Lowenthal, *World Communism* (New York: Oxford University Press, Inc., 1966), p. 26.

[3] A. A. Akhtamzian (ed.), *Istoriia mezhdunarodykh otnoshenii i vneshnei politiki SSSR*, Vol. I, 1917–1939 (Moscow, 1967), p. 7.

cially those which were more of a failure in their own right, relied on opposition to the usually exaggerated evil intentions of communism to justify arbitrary rule. The pretext of Franco's insurrection and a hundred others has been a usually inexistent or hopelessly feeble Communist conspiracy. The front of anticommunism greatly reduced resistance to aggression, as in Japan's thrust into Manchuria and China and Hitler's march across Europe. Curiously, some Latin-American military dictatorships, such as those in Peru and Venezuela, have checked movements of social reform by supporting a tame Communist party to divide and immobilize the Left.[4]

Communism contributed to the rise of fascism, which showed a far greater capacity than the Leninists to profit from economic disorder and despair. The Communist parties divided the Left, gravely undermined its ability to resist reactionary movements, and by violence in word and deed set precedents for fascist violence and made it more acceptable. Fascism copied much of the organization and some of the symbolism of the Communist movement and used it more effectively to propagandize, mobilize, and subvert, while antibolshevism was more useful for fascists than anticapitalism for the Communists. Fear of a fundamental threat to Western values, a fire that had to be fought with fire, was by no means the only card of the black- or brown-shirted legions, but it was their strongest one. As fascism lacked the revolutionary urge of communism, it is ironic that the old order in Europe and Asia was destroyed not by Communists but by German and Japanese fascists and near-fascists.

Bolshevik ideas of organization proved useful for fascists, Chinese Nationalists, and Maoists alike. Fascism, although standing at the opposite end of the conventional political spectrum from communism, is closer to it in spirit than is liberal democracy. Soviet relations have been much more profitable with the Right than the Left in Germany, as they have been much better with de Gaulle than French Socialists. The Soviet success has been in organization and control; economic growth has owed much more to austerity than to socialism or inspiration. The preponderant influence of a powerful authoritarian state is understandably on the side of authority and organization; it is incidental and unusual if it should be much concerned with social betterment. Conversely, it is of limited effect that countries organized on the Soviet model call themselves alike "Communist." Tightly integrated and centralized, with nationalized economy, control of opinion, and unified party direction, they are likely to be willful unless firmly under the Soviet shadow; factionalism has been as much the story of communism as monolithicism. Hence the dream of a natural unity of Communist powers has proved as empty as the dream of proletarian revolution.

Representing at the same time principles of violent change and stern

---

[4] Robert J. Alexander, *Communism in Latin America* (New Brunswick, N.J.: Rutgers University Press, 1957), pp. 12–13.

order, unwilling to be either fully a member or a world quite apart, Soviet Russia has weighed heavily on the Western state system and the balance of power, alien as these are to Soviet and Russian political philosophy. The effect of the injection of its political ideals and motifs has been to divide, set at odds, perhaps to cause political demoralization. This is no fault of the Russians, who have suffered as much as any nation from the conflicts of the age, or of most Bolsheviks, who doubtless felt sincere dedication to a just cause. A noncommunist Russia, insofar as it was strong, would probably have weighed heavily upon Europe and the world; it did so during much of the nineteenth century. There is an inherent incompatibility of the nation-state and the multinational authoritarian empire, and the outlook of the Soviet state, with its preference for seeing conflict in terms of ideology, must be different because the Soviet Union is a different kind of state. The U.S.S.R. cannot really have a national policy because it is not a nation. The basic split of the world into "communist" and "capitalist" is likely to be as permanent as this situation.

As a multinational polity with an ideological charter, the Soviet Union cannot behave simply as a state among states but must have, at least in form and pretense, an internationalist policy. The myth which the state holds sacred must be good for the world; and there must be some compulsion to spread the creed and to push heresy farther away. It is always desirable, although perhaps never urgent, to enlarge the sphere for moral reassurance, increase of power, and the security of a system which, in its artificiality, is never very sure of the loyalty of the peoples and so of its stability. To react to the international situation purely in terms of the gains which the Soviet state might obtain without reference to internal political needs would be like managing the economy for efficiency and welfare without reference to political demands.

Soviet relations with other states are inseparable from questions of the structure of the Soviet system. This is itself an international aggregate without completely sharp boundaries. Its center is ethnic Russia, practically the Russian republic of the Soviet Union. Attached to it are the various Soviet republics with their fictitious sovereignty, some of which, such as Georgia, may have a little more autonomy than others. Beyond the Soviet Union, satellites range from Mongolia, practically a part of the Russian state, to Rumania, enjoying considerable freedom. Outside the bloc, Finland is subject to Russian hegemony in defense, while Yugoslavia is claimed as part of the socialist commonwealth; and Soviet authority may extend diffusely to some Arab lands. More broadly, foreign Communist parties are something between truly independent political organizations and Russian tentacles in the alien world. Soviet domestic politics and foreign policy cannot be sharply separated, just as the Soviet polity has no clear and recognized borders. Gromyko refused to define "Socialist Commonwealth" to which the Brezhnev Doctrine applies.

The Soviet Union cannot admit the validity of strictly national quarrels. All issues must be placed in a broader framework related to the structure of society and government, and so far as national issues arise, they are confused or blurred. It becomes the more difficult for a nation to stand against Soviet purposes on merely national grounds, as universal issues are injected to divide the nation. Form of government and social philosophy are variously mingled in international questions by the Russians, for whom these are major issues running through their relations with other states.

Not surprisingly, the foreign policy of this universalist polity is filled with contradictions. The state is conservative yet espouses revolutionary transformation. It is cautious yet expansionist. It feels itself the keeper of order in the Soviet sphere and by extension in the world, and hence welcomes cooperation with the United States looking to joint protection of the peace. Yet it regards with glee the disturbances of the outside world and stands to profit from them, and it dislikes the United States as not only rival for world leadership but upholder of the capitalist order. Its most profound appeal is the stand for peace, yet it claims the allegiance of its peoples and adherents on grounds of the irreconcilable hostility of the two worlds. It seeks at once the advantages of working with foreign nations and being at odds with them, and its tactics seem again and again to clash with its goals. It likes, for example, to have Germany a threat but not an enemy, to moderate the arms race without stopping it, to regard the West as weak and decadent yet powerfully menacing.

Despite such apparent confusion, one cannot say that Soviet foreign policy has been unsuccessful. It has made many blunders, as recounted in preceding pages. But if the ideology has inclined to pieces of stupidity, it has given compensating political strength. Few states are so well endowed with purpose, and the Soviet Union is the only state which has an international, indefinitely unifying faith to justify and make workable indefinite extension of its sphere. It is the only great power which shows a real appetite for expansion. But through history the Russians have learned a saving patience.

It is because of grave shortcomings of the Western political, social, and economic order that a crude, relatively backward, and oppressive order could gain large numbers of adherents abroad. The Soviet Union promises security and peace in an age of turbulence and uncertainty when war is unthinkable, while it regards itself as bringer not so much of social transformation as of peace and discipline. Within, it is hardly troubled, despite whatever discontent beneath the surface, by the strikes, riots, and protest movements that roil the West. Without, it looks not to class upheaval and revolution, proletarian or not, but to any disorder to advance its cause in the world; as in the past, war is likely to provide the best conditions for its expansion. The Soviet state is likely to continue to look for and use, however it can, divisions and weaknesses in the world around, about as much influenced by ideology as a Christian churchgoer who is first of all a shrewd businessman.

Soviet foreign policy is guided by Soviet interest, but this is something different from what is ordinarily understood as national interest because it includes a political form and philosophy felt essential for a multinational existence. There is consequently a real and probably unbridgeable difference of outlooks between East and West, in view of which concessions are evidence not of good will but of weakness. In its ambiguity of form and substance, Soviet policy has harsh and conciliatory aspects; but it holds fast to the fundamental, the maintenance, possibly the enlargement, of its area of rule.

Some of the ways and purposes of the Soviet state being those of the world of independent nations and others being incompatible with it, Western statesmen have seldom known how to deal with Soviet demands. It is necessary to seek an accommodation where real understanding seems excluded. The problems have become not easier but more difficult as Soviet foreign policy has come into new sophistication and diplomatic skill while the growth of Soviet power has raised the need of cooperating with it for safety. Much wisdom will be required if the world is to be spared the realization of the old Russian-imperial-Communist dream of the end of nations without incurring dangers of inordinate destruction.

Selected Readings

Collections of Documents and Readings

Daniels, Robert V. *A Documentary History of Communism.* New York: Random House, Inc., 1960.

Degras, Jane (ed.). *Soviet Documents on Foreign Policy.* London and New York: Oxford University Press, 1951, 1953.

Eudin, Xenia J., and Fisher, Harold H. *Soviet Russia and the West, 1920–1927.* Stanford, Calif.: Stanford University Press, 1957.

———, and North, Robert C. *Soviet Russia and the East, 1920–1927.* Stanford, Calif.: Stanford University Press, 1957.

———, and Slusser, Robert M. *Soviet Foreign Policy, 1928–1934.* University Park, Pa.: Pennsylvania State University Press, 1966 and 1967.

Rubinstein, Alvin Z. (ed.). *The Foreign Policy of the Soviet Union.* New York: Random House, Inc., 1966.

Senn, Alfred E. (ed.). *Readings in Russian Political and Diplomatic History.* Vol. II. Homewood, Ill.: Dorsey Press, 1966.

General Works

Alexander, Robert J. *Communism in Latin America.* New Brunswick, N.J.: Rutgers University Press, 1957.

Baade, Hans W. (ed.). *The Soviet Impact on International Law.* Dobbs Ferry, N.Y.: Oceana Publications, Inc., 1965.

Bailey, Thomas A. *America Faces Russia.* Ithaca, N.Y.: Cornell University Press, 1950.

Borkenau, Franz. *European Communism.* London: Faber & Faber, Ltd., 1953.

Braunthal, Julius. *History of the International.* Vol. II: 1914–1943. New York: Frederick A. Praeger, Inc., 1967.

Dennett, R., and Johnson, J. E. (eds.). *Negotiating with the Russians.* Boston: World Peace Foundation, 1951.

Kennan, George F. *Russia and the West under Lenin and Stalin.* Boston: Little, Brown & Co., 1960.

———. *Soviet Foreign Policy, 1917–1941.* Princeton, N.J.: D. Van Nostrand Co., Inc., 1960.

Mackintosh, J. M. *Strategy and Tactics of Soviet Foreign Policy.* New York: Oxford University Press, Inc., 1963.

Pentoni, DeVere E. (ed.). *Soviet Behavior in World Affairs.* San Francisco, Calif.: Chandler Publishing Co., 1962.

Reshetar, John S. *Problems of Analyzing and Predicting Soviet Behavior.* Garden City, N.Y.: Doubleday & Co., Inc., 1955.

Seton-Watson, Hugh. *From Lenin to Khrushchev.* New York: Frederick A. Praeger, Inc., 1960.

Triska, Jan F., and Finley, David D. *Soviet Foreign Policy.* New York: Macmillan Co., 1968.

Ulam, Adam B. *Expansion and Coexistence.* New York: Frederick A. Praeger, Inc., 1968.

Warth, Robert D. *Soviet Russia in World Politics.* New York: Twayne Publishers, Inc., 1963.

Chapter I

Jelavich, Barbara. *A Century of Russian Foreign Policy.* Philadelphia: J. B. Lippincott Co., 1964.

Kohn, Hans. *Panslavism, Its History and Ideology.* Notre Dame, Ind.: University of Notre Dame Press, 1953.

Lederer, Ivo J. (ed.). *Russian Foreign Policy.* New Haven: Yale University Press, 1962.

Pushkarev, Sergei. *The Emergence of Modern Russia.* New York: Holt, Rinehart & Winston, Inc., 1963.

Seton-Watson, Hugh. *The Russian Empire, 1801–1917.* Oxford: Clarendon Press, 1967.

Chapter II

Almond, Gabriel. *Appeals of Communism.* Princeton, N.J.: Princeton University Press, 1954.

Bennigsen, Alexandre, and Lemercier-Quelquejay, Chantal. *Islam in the Soviet Union.* New York: Frederick A. Praeger, Inc., 1967.

Caroe, O. K. *Soviet Empire.* New York: St. Martin's Press, Inc., 1967.

Carr, Edward H. *The Bolshevik Revolution.* Vol. III: Soviet Russia and the World. London: Macmillan & Co., Ltd., 1953.

Fischer, Louis. *The Soviets in World Affairs.* Vol. I: 1917–1929. Princeton, N.J.: Princeton University Press, 1951.

Kennan, George F. *The Decision to Intervene.* Princeton, N.J.: Princeton University Press, 1958.

Meyer, Alfred G. *Leninism.* Cambridge, Mass.: Harvard University Press, 1957.

Page, Stanley W. *Lenin and World Revolution.* New York: New York University Press, 1959.

Pipes, Richard. *The Formation of the Soviet Union.* 2d. ed. Cambridge, Mass.: Harvard University Press, 1964.

Plamenatz, John P. *German Marxism and Russian Communism.* London: Longmans, Green & Co., Ltd., 1954.

Williams, William A. *American-Russian Relations, 1781–1947*. New York: Rinehart & Co., Inc., 1952.

Chapter III

Beloff, Max. *The Foreign Policy of Soviet Russia*. 2 vols. London: Oxford University Press, 1947, 1949.

Bennett, Thomas H. *The Soviets and Europe, 1938–1941*. Geneva: Imprimeries Populaires, 1951.

Carr, Edward H. *The Interregnum, 1923–1924*. New York: Macmillan Co., 1954.

Davidson-Houston, J. W. *Russia and China*. London: Robert Hale, Ltd., 1960.

Fischer, Louis. *The Soviets in World Affairs, 1917–1929*. Vol. II. Princeton, N.J.: Princeton University Press, 1951.

———. *Russia's Road from Peace to War*. New York: Harper & Row, 1969.

Fischer, Ruth. *Stalin and German Communism*. Cambridge, Mass.: Harvard University Press, 1948.

Rossi, Angelo. *The Russo-German Alliance*. Boston: Beacon Press, 1951.

Whiting, Allen S. *Soviet Policies in China, 1917–1924*. New York: Columbia University Press, 1954.

Chapter IV

Barghoorn, Frederick C. *Soviet Russian Nationalism*. New York: Oxford University Press, Inc., 1956.

Beloff, Max. *Soviet Policy in the Far East, 1944–1951*. London: Oxford University Press, 1953.

Boorman, Howard L., *et al. Moscow-Peking Axis*. New York: Harper & Bros., 1957.

Browder, Robert P. *The Origins of Soviet-American Diplomacy*. Princeton, N.J.: Princeton University Press, 1953.

Byrnes, James. *Speaking Frankly*. New York: Harper & Bros., 1947.

Dallin, David J. *Soviet Russia's Foreign Policy, 1939–1942*. New Haven, Conn.: Yale University Press, 1942.

Deane, John R. *The Strange Alliance*. New York: Viking Press, Inc., 1947.

Djilas, Milovan. *Conversations with Stalin*. New York: Harcourt, Brace & World, Inc., 1962.

Korbel, Josef. *The Communist Subversion of Czechoslovakia*. Princeton, N.J.: Princeton University Press, 1959.

North, Robert C. *Moscow and the Chinese Communists*. Stanford, Calif.: Stanford University Press, 1953.

Rieber, Alfred J. *Stalin and the French Communist Party, 1941–1947*. New York: Columbia University Press, 1962.

Shulman, Marshall D. *Stalin's Foreign Policy Reappraised.* Cambridge, Mass.: Harvard University Press, 1963.

Smith, Walter B. *Moscow Mission, 1946–1949.* London: William Heinemann, Ltd., 1950.

Werth, Alexander. *Russia at War, 1941–1945.* London: Barrie & Rockliff, Ltd., 1964.

Chapter V

Allen, Robert L. *Soviet Economic Warfare.* Washington, D.C.: Public Affairs Press, 1960.

Aubrey, Henry G. *Coexistence, Economic Challenge and Response.* Washington, D.C.: National Planning Association, 1961.

Barghoorn, Frederick C. *The Soviet Cultural Offensive.* Princeton, N.J.: Princeton University Press, 1960.

Berliner, Joseph S. *Soviet Economic Aid.* New York: Council on Foreign Relations, 1958.

Black, Cyril E., and Thornton, Thomas P. (eds.). *Communism and Revolution.* Princeton, N.J.: Princeton University Press, 1964.

Bloomfield, Lincoln P., *et al. Khrushchev and the Arms Race.* Cambridge, Mass.: MIT Press, 1966.

Brzezinski, Zbigniew K. *The Soviet Bloc, Unity and Conflict.* 2d. ed. Cambridge, Mass.: Harvard University Press, 1967.

Burks, R. V. *The Dynamics of Communism in Eastern Europe.* Princeton, N.J.: Princeton University Press, 1961.

Dallin, Alexander, *et al. The Soviet Union and Disarmament.* New York: Frederick A. Praeger, Inc., 1964.

Dallin, David J. *Soviet Foreign Policy after Stalin.* Philadelphia: J. B. Lippincott Co., 1961.

Fischer-Galati, Stephen. *The New Rumania.* Cambridge, Mass.: MIT Press, 1967.

Garthoff, Raymond L. *Soviet Strategy in the Nuclear Age.* New York: Frederick A. Praeger, Inc., 1962.

Gehlen, Michael P. *The Politics of Coexistence.* Bloomington, Ind.: Indiana University Press, 1967.

Gibney, Frank. *The Khrushchev Pattern.* New York: Duell, Sloan & Pearce, 1960.

Griffith, William E. *Albania and the Sino-Soviet Rift.* Cambridge, Mass.: MIT Press, 1963.

Horelick, Arnold L., and Rush, Myron. *Strategic Power and Soviet Foreign Policy.* Chicago: University of Chicago Press, 1965.

Jacobson, Harold K. *The USSR and the UN's Economic and Social Activities.* Notre Dame, Ind.: University of Notre Dame Press, 1963.

Kaser, Michael. *Comecon.* London: Oxford University Press, 1965.

Kautsky, John H. *Communism and the Politics of Development.* New York: John Wiley & Sons, Inc., 1968.

Kovner, Milton. *The Challenge of Coexistence.* Washington, D.C.: Public Affairs Press, 1961.

Kulski, Wladyslaw W. *Peaceful Co-Existence.* Chicago: Henry Regnery Co., 1959.

Labedz, Leopold, and Urban, G. R. (eds.). *The Sino-Soviet Conflict.* Chester Springs, Pa.: Dufour Editions, 1965.

Lowenthal, Richard. *World Communism.* New York: Oxford University Press, Inc., 1966.

Rubinstein, Alvin Z. *The Soviets in International Organizations.* Princeton, N.J.: Princeton University Press, 1964.

Zagoria, Donald S. *The Sino-Soviet Conflict 1956–1961.* Princeton, N.J.: Princeton University Press, 1962.

Chapter VI

Brown, J. F. *The New Eastern Europe: The Khrushchev Era and After.* New York: Frederick A. Praeger, Inc., 1966.

Clemens, Walter C., Jr. *The Arms Race and Sino-Soviet Relations.* Stanford, Calif.: The Hoover Institution, 1968.

Collier, David S., and Glaser, Kurt (eds.). *Elements of Change in Eastern Europe.* Chicago: Henry Regnery Co., 1968.

Dallin, Alexander, and Larsen, Thomas B. (eds.). *Soviet Politics since Khrushchev.* Englewood Cliffs, N.J.: Prentice-Hall, Inc., 1968.

Goldman, Marshall I. *Soviet Foreign Aid.* New York: Frederick A. Praeger, Inc., 1967.

Griffith, William E. *Sino-Soviet Relations 1964–1965.* Cambridge, Mass.: MIT Press, 1967.

Hurewitz, J. C. (ed.). *Soviet-American Rivalry in the Middle East.* New York: Academy of Political Science, 1969.

Jamgotch, Nish, Jr. *Soviet–East European Dialogue.* Stanford, Calif.: The Hoover Institution, 1968.

Kassof, Allen (ed.). *Prospects for Soviet Society.* New York: Frederick A. Praeger, Inc., 1968.

Chapter VII

Aspaturian, Vernon V. "Internal Politics and Foreign Policy in the Soviet System," in *Approaches to Comparative and International Politics* (ed. R. Barry Farrell), pp. 212–301. Evanston, Ill.: Northwestern University Press, 1966.

Daniels, Robert V. *The Nature of Communism.* New York: Random House, Inc., 1962.

de George, Richard T. *The New Marxism.* New York: Pegasus, 1968.

Goodman, Elliot R. *The Soviet Design for a World State.* New York: Columbia University Press, 1960.

Meyer, Alfred G. *Leninism.* Cambridge, Mass.: Harvard University Press, 1957.

Reshetar, John S. *Problems of Analyzing and Predicting Soviet Behavior.* Garden City, N.Y.: Doubleday & Co., Inc., 1955.

Seton-Watson, Hugh. *Nationalism and Communism.* London: Methuen & Co., Ltd., 1964.

Wesson, Robert G. *The Imperial Order.* Berkeley: University of California Press, 1967.

Index

C

This book has been set in 10 point and 9 point Janson, leaded 2 points. Chapter numbers are in 36 point Memphis Bold and chapter titles are in 18 point Memphis medium. The size of the type page is 27 by 45½ picas.

DATE DUE

12/6			
NO 8 '76			
DE 13 '76			
28 '77			

GAYLORD PRINTED IN U.S.A.